DATE DUE

SOME THEORIES OF ORGANIZATION

SOME THEORIES

of

ORGANIZATION

EDITED BY

ALBERT H. RUBENSTEIN, PH.D.
*Professor of Industrial Engineering
The Technological Institute
Northwestern University*

AND

CHADWICK J. HABERSTROH, PH.D.
*Assistant Professor of Industrial Management
School of Industrial Management
Massachusetts Institute of Technology*

1960

THE DORSEY PRESS, INC., AND

RICHARD D. IRWIN, INC. · HOMEWOOD, ILLINOIS

Library of Congress Catalogue Card No. 60–14052

PRINTED IN THE UNITED STATES OF AMERICA

Preface

THIS TEXTBOOK is intended to integrate scientific studies of organization from many of the traditional scholarly disciplines. Its basic premise is that the behavior of organizations and of the individuals who take part in them forms a unified whole worthy of independent study. Although the dominant emphasis is on commercial and industrial organizations, the reader will appreciate that the principles discussed apply to any type of organization, including governmental, philanthropic, military, educational, voluntary, or political. As a discussion of scientific work, its unifying thread is not the *practice of management* in organizations, but rather the *process of research* on organizations. The various theories of organization are presented as results of research or as the impetus to research. As far as possible, the research process is presented whole, with enough discussion of the methods used by the researchers and of the development of ideas in this field to make the reader aware of the potential for new knowledge as well as of the results already achieved.

It has been our intention to deal with the same general subject matter as the book *Organizations* by J. G. March and H. A. Simon. To facilitate cross-referencing, we have, where applicable, included in our index all theoretical terms included in their index. Although the field covered is the same, the objectives of the two books are different. March and Simon present a comprehensive and systematic inventory of the present state of organization theory; we offer an introduction to the research process itself, with the object of showing where it has been, where it is going, and what use can be made of it. These approaches are complementary and we hope that our readers will carry their inquiry into organization theory on through the March-Simon volume and into research reports that are still a-borning.

The idea of preparing a book such as this was generated in the series of graduate seminars on organization theory in the Department of Industrial Engineering at Columbia University, under the leadership of Robert T. Livingston and David B. Hertz. The book itself was developed out of our courses in organization theory given to advanced undergraduate and graduate students of the School of Industrial Management at the Massachusetts Institute of Technology. These courses, and the resulting book, make no assumption as to specific prior preparation of the student, but do assume the degree of intellectual maturity developed from several years of university attendance. The most directly utilizable preparation is in the areas of social science, mathematics, statistics, and accounting.

v

As the book is intended to be a general presentation of a particular field of knowledge, it is not constrained to any one place in any one curriculum. However, the principal purpose envisioned for it is in a one-semester course in the senior or graduate years of a business administration, industrial management, or industrial engineering program. Such a course might serve as an alternate or supplement to conventional courses in the principles of management. Broadly speaking, it would include the areas of "organization theory" and "human relations" in the business curriculum suggested by R. A. Gordon and J. E. Howell.[1] In our own courses this material has been covered in one semester, although this requires some compression or omission. This way of using it could be broadened, in either of two directions, into a two-semester sequence by preceding it with a semester of managerial psychology or by appending a semester on principles of management or case studies. The creative teacher will undoubtedly find other alternatives as well.

We wish to express our gratitude for the cooperation of the authors and publishers whose works are reprinted herein.

ALBERT H. RUBENSTEIN
CHADWICK J. HABERSTROH

June, 1960

---

[1] Robert A. Gordon and James E. Howell, *Higher Education for Business* (New York: Columbia University Press, 1959), pp. 178 ff., 264-65.

Table of Contents

vii

List of Contributors

CONRAD M. ARENSBERG, Department of Sociology, Columbia University
CHRIS ARGYRIS, Department of Industrial Administration, Yale University
SOLOMON E. ASCH, Department of Psychology, Swarthmore College
CHESTER I. BARNARD, formerly President of the Rockefeller Foundation and the New Jersey Bell Telephone Company
DAVID H. BLACKWELL, Statistical Laboratory, University of California, Berkeley
PETER M. BLAU, Department of Sociology, University of Chicago
FRANKLIN C. BROOKS, Technical Operations, Inc., Burlington, Massachusetts
THEODORE CAPLOW, Department of Sociology, University of Minnesota
ROBERT L. CHAPMAN, Ramo-Woolridge Corporation
A. M. J. CHORUS, Ryksuniversiteit Te Leiden, The Netherlands
KAMLA CHOWDHRY, Ahmedabad Textile Industry's Research Association, Ahmedabad, India
WALTER A. CLEVEN, System Development Corporation
ANDREW L. COMREY, Department of Psychology, University of California, Los Angeles
RICHARD M. CYERT, Graduate School of Industrial Administration, Carnegie Institute of Technology
MELVILLE DALTON, Department of Anthropology and Sociology, and Institute of Industrial Relations, University of California, Los Angeles
KEITH DAVIS, Department of Management, College of Business Administration, Arizona State University
JOEL DEAN, Graduate School of Business, Columbia University
WARD EDWARDS, Operation Research Department, and Department of Psychology, University of Michigan
FRED E. FIEDLER, Department of Psychology, University of Illinois
DAVID JOSEPH FOX, Teachers College, Columbia University
FREDERICK C. FRICK, Lincoln Laboratory, Massachusetts Institute of Technology
HAROLD GUETZKOW, Department of Political Science, Department of Psychology, and Department of Sociology, Northwestern University
JOHN K. HEMPHILL, Educational Testing Service, Princeton, N.J.
KENNETH F. HERROLD, Teachers College, Columbia University
ALEXANDER B. HORSFALL, Department of Business, Worcester Junior College

ABRAHAM KAPLAN, Department of Philosophy, University of California, Los Angeles

JOHN L. KENNEDY, Department of Psychology, Princeton University

KURT LEWIN (Deceased)

IRVING LORGE, Institute of Psychological Research, Teachers College, Columbia University

DOUGLAS M. McGREGOR, School of Industrial Management, Massachusetts Institute of Technology

OSKAR MORGENSTERN, Department of Economics, Princeton University

A. K. PAL, Ahmedabad Textile Industry's Research Association, Ahmedabad, India

DONALD C. PELZ, Institute of Social Research, University of Michigan

NICHOLAS RASHEVSKY, Committee on Mathematical Biology, University of Chicago

V. F. RIDGWAY, Department of Business Administration, Kansas State University

LEE B. SECHREST, Department of Psychology, College of Liberal Arts, Northwestern University

PHILIP SELZNICK, Department of Sociology, University of California, Berkeley

HERBERT A. SIMON, Graduate School of Industrial Administration, Carnegie Institute of Technology

NICHOLAS M. SMITH, Operations Research Office, Bethesda, Maryland

W. H. SUMBY, Air Force Coordination and Controls Development Division, Hanscombe Field, Bedford, Massachusetts

E. PAUL TORRANCE, Bureau of Educational Research, University of Minnesota

DONALD B. TROW, Department of Sociology, Harpur College, State University of New York

STANLEY S. WALTERS, Operations Analysis, Hughes Aircraft Company

MAX WEBER (Deceased)

MILTON G. WEINER, The RAND Corporation

ROBERT S. WEISS, Department of Sociology, Brandeis University

PAULA WELTZ, Institute of Psychological Research, Teachers College, Columbia University

The Nature of Organization Theory

INDUSTRIAL and business management in the United States has been extremely successful despite the lack of rigorous theories of organization or a "unified organizational theory" from which principles of management may be deduced. Success in this field, as in other fields such as engineering and medicine, is often the result of brilliant insight or guesswork on the part of outstanding individuals whose intuition provides them with a much better than average score in the performance of their arts. Nevertheless, in all these practical fields, there is always the search for more knowledge, for rules and laws, for theories which will improve general practice and, indeed, complement the insight of those who are already successful.

The field of management is no exception. For thousands of years, interested individuals have observed the practice of management (or administration) and attempted to formulate systematic descriptions of what they observed or prescriptions of how they thought this art should be practiced. Some of these observers were active participants in management of organizations—public or private. Others were merely disinterested but curious observers of this very important social activity. It is only within the past few decades, however, that the study of organizations and the way in which people behave in organizations has become a subject of systematic research.

It is the purpose of this book to explore the results of research on organizations in order to make this work accessible to students of management and others interested in the development and application of knowledge in this field. The emphasis will be on organization as a *scientific* field. Many of the contributors to this field are not primarily concerned with the way the results of their research might be used. Even though they would be delighted to have their work result in some important contribu-

1

tion to society, this is not the main motivation for their work. There is a traditional distinction between sciences and applied fields of knowledge. Consequently, this book will say very little about how organizations (or their managements) *should* behave. It is concerned primarily with contributing to an understanding of how people *do* behave in organizations and how management can improve its understanding of these phenomena.

Science, as distinguished from a particular scientific theory, is not merely an expression of empirical truths in nature. It is a human enterprise, with knowledge (in the form of scientific theories) as its product. Especially in the case of immature and rapidly developing sciences, the results existing at one point of time are often of less importance than the potential for future results that exists in the scientific community. Since this applies to the study of organization as to all social science, a major objective of the book is to acquaint the reader with the major schools of thought that are contributing to the field, as well as to present some of their results to date. The fantastic increase in the speed and scope of diffusion of information in this field has led to the publication and dissemination *to management and the public* of a large amount of fragmentary and unintegrated ideas about how organizations do or should behave. Hopefully, some systematic preparation will help the student keep track of and interpret this material.

There is not a single, well-defined community of scholars with responsibility for research in organization theory, as there is for physics, psychology, or economics. Thus, we find many people working in fields as diverse as neurology, mathematics, animal sociology, and philosophy who may be contributing indirectly, but importantly, to an ultimate theory of organizational behavior. Other contributions come from fields that are obviously directly concerned with improving the art of management: human relations, operations research, management science, occupational psychology, and management itself. Some workers in sociology, social psychology, political science, and anthropology are directly concerned with the development of organization theory for its own sake. The contributions of all three groups are subject to the same processes of criticism, empirical testing, and reformulation as in any other scientific field. The objective of this process—and one of the chief distinctions between scientific and unscientific work—is that of making the contributions *communicable, systematic,* and *cumulative.* The hallmarks of a scientific community are (1) the shared understandings among the researchers as to the state of knowledge that arise from communication among them; (2) the existence of logical (i.e., theoretical) structure in the formulations of that knowledge; and (3) the result that each individual's work relates to that of his predecessors so that the existence of a body of knowledge may be affirmed—and not merely the existence of wise men. Organization theory is only moving toward this state; it cannot yet be considered a discipline.

How it is progressing must be left to the reader to judge. Hopefully, he will judge by the "rules of the game" propounded in this chapter.

Lest this presentation be accused of "underselling" the practical advantages of studying organization theory, a brief consideration of the question of application is in order. Scientific theory is *positive* in formulation, i.e., it describes. Applications require ideas put in *normative* form, which recommend. Normative statements may either *endorse* certain goals or values (e.g., "The country needs peace and prosperity"); or they may merely *refer* to goals or values (e.g., "If you want to relieve a headache, take an aspirin"). Obviously, positive theory can contribute much to the latter type of normative formulations.

In considering the role that theories of organization might play in improving the practice of management, it is tempting to turn to the successful relationships that have developed over the past three or four decades between the physical sciences and industry, or between the life sciences and medicine or agriculture. The industrial researcher, attempting to improve his company's products, processes, or market position, has had spectacular success in finding or adapting the discoveries of physical science to his task. In many cases this has cost millions of dollars and taken many years, but it has been done successfully. Similar experiences have occurred in medical and agricultural research programs.

By analogy, then, management or students of management—the applied *social* scientists—look to the social sciences for similar results and theories that can be adapted or used directly in the practice of management. Like many other applied scientists, we should have no trouble in finding in the vast current literature on management and organizations numerous results, theories and empirical studies, which would appear relevant to the task of improving the art of management. In the role of applied researcher or student of management, however, we are not generally in a position to evaluate many of these theories or results as such. Nor need we necessarily do so. This is the task of the scientific community in each field from which this information derives. It is their burden to evaluate the theories *as* theories and the empirical results as to reliability.

On the other hand, as in the case of the industrial laboratory worker, our major criterion for considering the merit of any of these theories is a pragmatic one: Is a given theory, hypothesis, or conceptual scheme potentially *useful* to the practitioner of management? *How* useful is it potentially, and how much time and effort will be required to make the potentiality pay off? If it is useful, then we may call it "good" theory.

Of what value will theory be in the field of organizational behavior or in practicing the art of management? Traditionally, three roles have been assigned to theory. Some sciences have been able to produce theories which can perform all three. Others are limited to one or two. Useful theories of organization should help us to:

(1) *Explain* observed organizational behavior. This may not lead to any direct benefits to the practitioner except the satisfaction of knowing why the observed events occurred. It may also make him aware of aspects of the events he would otherwise not have considered.

(2) *Predict* future organizational behavior. This can be of extremely high value to both researcher and practitioner. It can provide an opportunity for the researcher to test his ideas about organization and so further improve his theories; and it can help guide the future actions of the practitioner.

(3) *Influence* future organizational behavior. While this is of least interest to the researcher, it is the essence of the practitioner's interest in learning about organizational behavior. The ability to successfully influence the behavior of people in organizations and the consequences of that behavior is of obvious importance to the success of the manager's job.

It remains now to indicate the kinds of organizational behavior that theories of organization can help to explain, predict, and influence.

Categories of Organizational Behavior

Most serious writers in the broad field of organization have presented one or more sets of categories to describe the content of the field. Often these categories are proposed as descriptions of:

The elements of organization.
The functions of management.
The principal administrative processes.

Here is a sample of these category sets:

Livingston (1)—The Sequence of Action includes:
          Deciding
          Planning
          Preparing
          Operating
          Reviewing
Fayol (2)—Management must:
          Plan
          Organize
          Control
Brown (3)—The Three Sciences of Industry:
          Purpose
          Administration
          Organization
Newman (4)—Basic Administrative Processes:
          Planning
          Organizing
          Assembly of Resources
          Direction
          Controlling

General Electric Corporation (5)—The Principal Aspects of Management:
        Planning
        Organizing
        Measuring
        Integrating

This book also employs a set of categories, to describe the aspects of organization in which theories might provide some help in explaining, predicting, and influencing organizational behavior. The categories are merely labels which perform two functions: (1) they indicate areas where practitioners encounter sufficient difficulty to warrant calling them "problem areas," and (2) they provide a focus for examining the research results of various fields that might ultimately help resolve organizational problems through the development of useful theories. These categories or problem areas are:

Organizational Structure and Process
Leadership and Morale
Communication
Control and Evaluation
Decision Making

It is clear, from a knowledge of the practice of management and the nature of organizational behavior, that more systematic knowledge and, eventually, theories in these areas will help shift the balance between intuitive art and applied science in management, with attendant gains in organizational effectiveness.

In one respect, the selection of material for this book, and for the courses in organization theory for which it is intended, presented a dilemma. Most students of organization and practitioners of management are already acquainted to some extent with traditional literature in the field of organization and management. This work is usually focused on the question of "How to Manage." Unfortunately, most of it has not contributed to an ultimate applied science of management through the development, testing, and revision of theories and empirical generalizations. A large segment even helps to perpetuate the belief that management is *by nature* an intuitive art and that the possibility of a science of organizational behavior is not great, if there is a possibility at all.

The dilemma was this: Should a portion of this book (and the courses) be devoted to examining this vast and growing literature? Should a major portion of the reader's (and students') time be given over to discovering at first hand the inadequacies of much of this material for the purposes of systematic explanation, useful and accurate prediction, and an effective basis for influencing? The essence of this dilemma is that this material is very attractive and very appealing to the intuition. Much of it is written by people who have had many years of experience in or contact with organizations, and it is a distillation of their views of and prescriptions for organizational behavior. It is frequently consistent and reasonable, and many readers find it inspiring.

The difficulty is that it is seldom in a form that is subject to empirical testing or communicable in operational form to others. Therefore, not only does it fail to help in developing general propositions or theories about organizational behavior, it is often difficult to teach in a systematic fashion. The dilemma has been resolved, therefore, in this book, by omitting this class of literature and leaving it to collateral or future reading.

A brief summary of traditional views of organization is presented in Table 1. This table provides a juxtaposition of three sets of notions about organizational behavior, contrasting some of the basic beliefs expressed in much of the traditional literature with some of the tentative conclusions stemming from the work of the behavioral scientists who have been studying organizational behavior, and with the organizational traditions of scientists in all fields. As an indication of the profound changes in managerial know-how that may result from the systematic development of knowledge about organizations, the first comparison deserves careful attention. The latter is included as a reminder of the type of social system that has produced our scientific progress to date and as an empirical example of a major social function that does not conform at all in its organization to the preconceptions of traditional theory.

Some Requirements for Theories of Organization

In many of the papers in this and succeeding sections of the book, the nature of theory is treated in different ways. Some authors begin a description of their research by describing their "theory" or their "working hypotheses" or a statistical hypothesis which is to be tested by the experiment or empirical study they describe in their article. In the next sections, for example, *Selznick* speaks of: ". . . a reconstruction, which is to say, a theory, of the conditions and forces which appear to have shaped the behavior of key participants"; *Argyris* says: ". . . we may hypothesize that agents (organizational members) ought to require functions which are so defined that they may fulfill some combination of . . . the broad trends of personality development . . . for individuals in our culture . . ."; *Barnard* speaks of: "A Theory of Cooperation and Organization"; and *Horsfall and Arensberg* discuss: ". . . some of the current theories about group structure. . . ."

To the student or reader trained in the physical sciences or, indeed, to the one without a scientific background, the use in these articles of the term "theory" and what it implies may be very confusing. To one accustomed to the simplicity and relative lack of ambiguity in physical science theory, the complex formulations and conceptual schemes, the alternative formulations offered for the same set of phenomena, and the preoccupation with definition and redefinition may be disconcerting. To the nonscientist, whose expectations for theory may be based on a few well-known "laws of nature," the uncertainty and tentative nature of theories in this field may be inexplicable, or at best puzzling.

No simple definition of the concept "theory," which is lifted directly from a given physical science, is adequate to cover the kinds of notions, propositions, hypotheses, empirical generalizations, and deductive schemes which may ultimately contribute to theories that can help to explain, predict, and influence organizational behavior. Webster's six alternative definitions spread a definitional blanket over all kinds of intellectual activity from ". . . speculation" and ". . . a guess" to ". . . A body of theorems presenting a clear, rounded and systematic view of a subject. . . ." (This latter taken from mathematics.)

Philosophical analysts have devoted much attention in recent years to the methodology of scientific theorizing. Their discussions of this question fill volumes (6), but it is possible here to say somewhat more about theories than that they must be useful to explain, predict, or influence. The earmarks of a theory seem to be that it (1) has empirical reference; (2) contains logical interconnections with other theories; and (3) admits the possibility of rejection. The first point is that some of the terms used in the theory should be directly observable, that is, placed in correspondence with empirical data. The second point is that the theory should be part of a logical structure explaining as many and as different empirical phenomena as possible. The third point is that the theory must somehow select from the number of conceivable observations in its domain of explanation, must say that some will happen and some will not, so that observation of the excluded possibilities would discredit the theory.

Reverting to our more fundamental requirement that theories in organization must be useful, we can point out a number of situations in which concepts or formulations that are not theories according to the above, may nevertheless help to explain, predict, and/or influence organizational behavior.

Is a Model a Theory? A recent upsurge of excellent work in the new fields of operations research, statistical decision making, and similar fields has focused management attention on the use of mathematical models. These models are often very useful in influencing organizational behavior and may frequently be adapted to questions of explanation or prediction. Nevertheless, many of them cannot properly be considered theory, in the sense that we have used the term in the preceding paragraph.

Although the use of mathematical models in management is a relatively new development, simpler and more obvious types of models have been a characteristic part of the manager's equipment for a long time; and mathematical models have been commonplace in many other fields. A discussion of this question is somewhat confused by variations in usage

TABLE 1 *

TRADITIONAL THEORY OF INDUSTRIAL ORGANIZATION	NEW DIRECTION OF INDUSTRIAL ORGANIZATION THEORY	ORGANIZATIONAL TRADITIONS IN SCIENCE
1. Wide Participation in Decision-making Rather than Centralized Decision-making		
If the organization has been properly designed, with rational delegation of authority and responsibility and clear and correct specification of tasks and goals at each level, the only important decision-making to be done concerns major changes in the organization's course; these are clearly the responsibility of top management; in fact, the whole point of organization design is to reduce the necessity for decision-making at lower levels in the organization	People resist tasks, goals, and changes which are imposed upon them and show a good deal of creativity in developing methods of resistance; *they* want to perform tasks, set goals, and make changes for ends to which they are committed; they are committed only to the ends of organizations which belong to them—"belong," in the sense that the members have some power of decision in areas that affect them; under these conditions creativity is used for achieving organizational goals rather than for self-defense against organizational rules	Several traditions in science insure that each scientist has an opportunity to express and argue for his opinion with respect to the usefulness or validity of proposed or generally accepted theory or with respect to other matters, in the forum provided by journals and meetings; he is taught to value independence of thought and creativity, to respect the authority of fact rather than of social power, to set his own goals and tasks, and to change them autonomously; any decisions affecting all scientists are the consequence of the "weight of scientific opinion" rather than of an individual authority
2. The Face-to-Face Group Rather than the Individual as the Basic Unit of Organization		
The organization is a pyramid of superior-subordinate relations; responsibility and authority are delegated to individuals; no two individuals should have overlapping responsibility; the term "span of control" refers to the number of individuals supervised, not the size of "group" supervised; groups in any other sense of the term have no place in traditional theory	The organization is a large group composed of numerous interlocking subgroups; the interdependence of jobs must be matched by an interdependence of the organizational members; the supervisor's main responsibility is maintaining communication between the managerial group of which he is a member and the work group of which he is a member; other overlapping memberships carry similar responsibilities; within each group all problems affecting the group's work must be shared openly; "private" superior-subordinate relations are destructive of collaboration and productive of intrigue	All messages must be broadcast to the entire scientific community to insure the growth of knowledge and proper attribution of credit; secrecy is anathema and destructive of the scientific group; power resides in the group, not in any individual; it is expressed in the "weight of scientific opinion" and in professional standards democratically determined; informally, importance is placed on small-group discussion as a source of stimulation and criticism

3. Mutual Confidence Rather than Authority as the Integrative Force in Organization

The organization proceeds on the basis of systematic order-giving and checking from top to bottom of the hierarchy of superior-subordinate relations; the orders are designed to produce behavior which will contribute to the attainment of the organization's goals; hence obedience to authority is the integrative force in the organization

Mutual confidence refers to a supportive atmosphere and a set of procedures which insure, on the one hand, that individual merit is recognized and, on the other, an absence of intrigue; standards of performance and responsible membership must be group-shared and group-supported; however, this degree of group responsibility can be maintained only if the same degree of confidence and support exists in inter group relations; that is, the supervisor must be an effective member of both groups

Several scientific traditions are concerned with the prevention of intrigue and the maintenance of confidence and trust; one is the requirement that all messages be broadcast to insure the proper allocation of credit; another is implicit in the technology of science: controlled, repeatable observation and experiment; honesty, objectivity, respect for facts, and rigorous workmanship are stressed as personal attributes in scientific training; authority does not reside in socially powerful individuals but in observed fact

4. The Supervisor as the Agent for Maintaining Intragroup and Intergroup Communication Rather than the Agent of Higher Authority

In essence, the supervisor's job is to secure obedience to orders received from his superior; he sees that his subordinates use the proper methods, stick to their jobs, and get the work done

The supervisor's main jobs are (1) to build a group with a strong sense of responsibility for getting the job done and improving their effectiveness and (2) to be an effective member of management in representing the group he supervises and in representing general organizational needs to the group he supervises

The scientific community is concerned primarily with intracommunity communication, and the sense of community is maintained by commitment of scientists to the common goal of advancing knowledge; there are community standards which define responsible behavior in science; there is no tradition for maintaining communication between the scientific community and other parts of society; the concept of "management" or "supervision" is absent from and alien to the organizational traditions of science

5. Growth of Members of the Organization to Greater Responsibility Rather than External Control of the Members' Performance of Their Tasks

Supervision should be production-centered rather than person-centered; the task is central and permanent; people are replaceable; the supervisor's job is to see that people do the job as it should be done

If the employee accepts responsibility for getting the job done, the supervisor's task is one of giving training and help rather than of policing; hence the supervisor's main responsibilities are to provide a setting in which employees are to accept responsibility and to aid them in developing their capacities to the fullest extent possible

Master-apprentice, teacher-student, senior colleague–junior colleague relations in science all stress the development of the junior member of the pair rather than getting him to perform a particular set of operations

* Reprinted from Herbert A. Shepard, "Superiors and Subordinates in Research," *Journal of Business*, Vol. XXIX, No. 4, 4, October, 1956.

of the words *model* and *theory* in many fields, but especially in social science and its applications. It is our intention to follow current usage in the philosophy of science, the field to which questions of this nature belong (7).

To begin with, let us make clear in what sense we are using the term *model*. A model is a system or object that stands in place of another, usually more complicated system or object. Simple examples are an architect's scale model for a building, or the company telephone directory as a model of the organization. A mathematical model is similar. The difficulty that arises is that the mathematical model is likely to be confused with a mathematical theory. The reason for this confusion is the similarity in appearance: both use premises and deduce conclusions in a mathematical manner. To the philosophically unsophisticated, one page full of symbolism looks about the same as another. The differences in the two systems, however, partly determine the uses to which they can be put.

The logical structure of a theory is such that the *conclusions* derived from it can be placed into correspondence with (interpreted as) empirical hypotheses and confirmed or refuted by experiments. The logical structure of a model is such that its *premises* are interpreted (i.e., empirical statements) and its conclusions are logical consequences of these. A theory can be refuted by a single contrary empirical finding; a model is not exposed to refutation, but is used as long as any benefit can be derived from it. A model can continue to be useful even though it yields many conclusions which are clearly wrong, provided only that it yields *some* conclusions that are correct (i.e., useful). A theory is expected to yield *only* true conclusions.

In general a model gives intuitive understanding of the object or system modeled. The mathematical model, therefore, serves the same function as the architect's model; it enables its user to grasp the important structure of a problem in a simple and efficient way.

Some of the models in use in a field may contain very useful suggestions for inclusion in theoretical systems. When models have proved successful in a variety of circumstances, that is, when they do not depend completely on the particular circumstances of one case, it may be possible to reformulate key parts in a genuinely theoretical system. Organization charts and job descriptions are examples of models in organization that have provided some concepts of theoretical usefulness. Thus, although models are not theories, they may contribute to theory building.

Is Taxonomy a Theory? Some natural sciences depend heavily on description as their principal tool. Descriptive botany, zoology, and geology are examples of research fields where major contributions so far have been in the taxonomic (classification) area. Where a taxonomic system begins to produce insights into relationships between classes in the system and to provide a basis for explanation and prediction, it approaches theory. When a set of propositions about, for example, the evolution of species is achieved, the stage of theory has been definitely reached. A taxonomic system in organization which merely labels phenomena, activities, and events may be very useful; but few such systems have approached the level of theory as yet.

Is Measurement Theory? By itself, measurement does not constitute theory. Without it, however, there has been little theorizing in the sciences. It is considered in many fields as a necessary condition for theoretical work, but far from a sufficient one. The basic operations of measuring can be performed on many objects and events without these "measurements" contributing to a theory-building enterprise. Absenteeism, lateness, and output per worker can be measured, but until these measurements are made to contribute to a basis for explaining why they occur in the quantity and time pattern that they do, or until accurate predictions of their future occurrence can be made, they should not be considered a part of a theoretical structure.

Is a Notational System a Theory? It has always been fashionable in many fields to construct elaborate notational schemes which are semantically useful for designating objects, events, and concepts. The use of such schemes for deducing consequences is less common. Here the reader must take care to see whether he is dealing with a completely closed system of definition and meta-definition or whether the scheme has sufficient points of contact with the real phenomena being described to lead to useful results.

The possibility of a scientific, theoretical approach to organizational problems has often been denied on the grounds that the techniques of controlled experiments are not applicable. The opportunity for adequate experimentation with organizations is very rare, and in some cases there is no proper experiment feasible. Some very successful natural sciences, however, have not been able to carry out the classical "controlled" experiment, where all factors but the one under study are "held constant" or otherwise accounted for. Despite this, substantial progress has been made in nonexperimental sciences such as astronomy, meteorology, and human genetics. It is true that the experimental sciences have proceeded more rapidly than others in which experimentation is difficult or infeasible. This has not prevented the advance of these latter fields, however, despite the lack of this means of testing their hypotheses and theories.

In spite of this handicap, there are opportunities for testing theories of organization. Experimental techniques have been developed in psychology for the study of individuals and small groups. As we shall see, the findings are relevant to problems of organization and help to establish the correctness of parts of the broader theory needed to cope with these problems. The closest approach to an experimental study involving a whole organization is the work of the RAND Systems Research Laboratory discussed in Section Two. This was made possible by advances in the technique of simulation of organizational behavior, in this case involving the use of extensive computational facilities for generating environmental inputs. Other uses of simulation are discussed in Section Six.

The development of new kinds of mathematical and statistical models also facilitates theory testing by means of a comparison of numerical results derived from the modeled theoretical hypotheses with statistics derived from the actual data. Recent years have also seen rapid developments in survey techniques for collection of data by means of questionnaires and interviews. Their uses will be illustrated in Section Three. The most important technique for organization theory, however, is the field study conducted in natural organizations, combining observation, interviewing, analysis of organization records, and the use of informants. Examples of this are found in each of the following sections. Some of the important characteristics and difficulties of field studies are discussed in Section Seven, as they represent an art of potential advantage to managers as well as to researchers.

The readings in this first section are devoted to a general exploration of methods and criteria for discerning or developing useful theories of organization. Nicholas Rashevsky presents a brief, but persuasive, argument for the possibilities of developing a hierarchy of theories—from neurobiology to sociology. This is a major open question of the philosophy of science, in that it has not been done, but not proved impossible either. Abraham Kaplan, in "Sociology Learns the Language of Mathematics," looks at a fairly representative sample of the literature on various aspects of human behavior. Much of it has implications for organization theory. His concentration on research presented mathematically gives us an opportunity to appraise this method, since relatively few mathematical studies are included in this book. Kurt Lewin discusses one of the major methodological positions developed in the behavioral sciences; it has provided the impetus for a large portion of the active research on human behavior in the past fifteen years.

These readings are included not so much to acquaint you with the specific issues involved as to illustrate the *kind* of very general, philosophical issues that scientists have to resolve, explicitly or implicitly, before they can conduct, criticize or appraise empirical research. The time will be well spent on them if it sharpens the distinction between a methodological issue and an empirical one. The essence of scientific progress and the development of useful knowledge is the gradually widening consensus of agreement on empirical issues, such as are dealt with in the rest of the book. Consensus on methodological issues is not likely (and to that extent unimportant) because the criterion by which they can be judged is indirect: the usefulness of the resulting empirical research.

The selections in this book are not intended to provide an inventory or a survey of all the work potentially related to organization theory. They emphasize the great variation in method and concept which is characteristic of research in this field, and attempt to introduce the reader and student to the vast possibilities for improved management through better theories of organization.

REFERENCES

1. LIVINGSTON, ROBERT T. *The Engineering of Organization and Management.* McGraw-Hill, 1949.
2. FAYOL, HENRI. *General and Industrial Management.* Pitman Publishing Co., 1949.
3. BROWN, ALVIN. *Organization of Industry.* Prentice-Hall, 1947.
4. NEWMAN, WILLIAM H. *Administrative Action.* Prentice-Hall, 1950.
5. CORDINER, RALPH J. "Problems of Management in a Large Decentralized Organization," *A.M.A. General Management Series* No. 159, 1952.
6. FEIGL, H. AND BRODBECK, M. (Eds.). *Readings in the Philosophy of Science.* Appleton-Century-Crofts, 1953; *International Encyclopedia of Unified Science.* University of Chicago Press.
7. E.g., BRAITHWAITE, R. B. *Scientific Explanation.* Cambridge, 1953.

1. FROM MATHEMATICAL BIOLOGY TO MATHEMATICAL SOCIOLOGY*

Nicolas Rashevsky

We are assembled here today to discuss the question: "What is scientific method?" Representatives of the physical, the biological and the social sciences will discuss the question from their respective points of view. The three fields of knowledge are not independent and not entirely separate from each other. I think, however, that it will be generally agreed that there is a closer relationship between biology and the physical sciences on the one hand, and biology and the social sciences on the other, than between the physical sciences and the social sciences. Biology takes a great deal from physics and chemistry. The highly important researches in the borderline fields, biophysics and biochemistry, prove this assertion. On the other hand, biology gives a great deal to the social sciences. Problems of behavior, the study of which is one of the objectives of biological sciences, are of primordial importance in social sciences. Social psychology deals with both psychobiological and social problems.

The answer to the question: "What is scientific method?" is clearly a definition. There are several ways of defining an object. Either we describe it in terms of other known concepts, or we merely point out the object to be defined and say: "This is what we mean by such and such a word," or, finally, we may give what is known as an operational definition, by prescribing the set of operations necessary to obtain the object under definition. In the present case the last two ways of defining become practically identical. It must be, however, emphasized that no matter what kind of definition we use, it remains always, like any definition, quite arbitrary. You may propose one definition, I may propose an entirely different one. The problem before us may then be either to agree on one definition or to propose as many definitions as possible, and then to discuss the various merits and shortcomings of the methods thus defined. While agreement is, in general, a very good thing, I am not sure at all that in the present instance a friendly disagreement may not be a better thing. It may be that if each one tries out his own method we will have in the long run more progress than if we blindly follow only one path which has been generally agreed upon.

In order not to lose ourselves in too much abstract philosophical discussion, I propose to limit myself to a much more modest task. I shall dis-

---

* Reproduced from *ETC., A Review of General Semantics*, Winter, 1951.

cuss the following, rather restricted, question: "What methods have been used in what is generally accepted as science, by men accepted as scientists, and have led to unquestionably important results?" I am fully aware that by formulating the question in this way I am actually *avoiding* some difficult problems. Perhaps I am just paying a tribute to my natural laziness!

Of the three fields represented at this symposium, the physical sciences have preoccupied mankind for by far the longest time. Compared to them, biology, all its recent progress notwithstanding, is a child. One of the reasons for this lies undoubtedly in the circumstance that no essential progress in biology could have been made before certain developments in physics had taken place. It requires a microscope to establish the existence of cells, to discover and study microorganisms, to investigate the structure of tissues. And it requires not merely *a* microscope, but *a good* microscope. But a good microscope is the product of years of development of geometrical and physical optics, of mechanics, and of the chemistry and technology of optical glass. Similarly, present-day studies in electrophysiology could not have taken place without the electronic tube, which is the product of years of research in electromagnetism. Even the purely descriptive systematic microbiologist or histologist depends in his work on the development of physics just as much as a physiologist or biophysicist does. In *this* sense we may say that Robert Koch and Fritz Schaudinn were no less biophysicists than are George Bishop or Kenneth Cole. It is not impossible that social sciences occupy with respect to biological sciences the same position as the latter occupies with respect to physical sciences. Perhaps a certain amount of development in biology is necessary before real progress in the social sciences can be made. We shall touch on that point later.

What method then did the scientists use through the ages of development of the oldest of scientific disciplines?

The word *science* comes from the Latin *scio*, which means *I know*. Essentially, science means the same as knowledge. If we accept the French dictum: "*Savoir c'est prévoir*," "To know is to foresee," or, "To know is to predict," then the test of whether we know something is determined by whether we can predict. In natural sciences predictions have been numerous. How is a scientist able to make a prediction?

Schiller has answered this question as a poet, in a highly poetical way:

> *Mit dem Genius steht die Natur im ewigen Bunde:*
> *Wass der Eine verspricht, leistet die Andre gewiss.*[1]

Beautiful and inspiring as these lines are, they do not give an answer which can satisfy a scientist. To find a more satisfactory answer we must inquire into the course of development of a natural science.

---

[1] An eternal pact binds Genius and Nature: What the one promises, the other is sure to bring about.

Every science, except pure mathematics, in its early stages begins by an accumulation of factual knowledge through observation. From observation we pass to experiment, which is sometimes described as observation under controlled conditions. Though this description is essentially correct, it does not tell the whole story. The number of conditions which may be controlled in a given situation is frequently rather large. In attempting to keep some of the factors constant, the scientist usually bases the choice of those factors on some explicit or implicit assumptions, sometimes on simple, sometimes on very complex reasoning. In the simplest experiment the investigator merely asks the question: "What is going to happen under certain conditions?" An experiment of that type was performed by Galileo when he dropped a bullet and a cannon ball from the leaning tower of Pisa, and found that they fell with the same speed, in spite of the differences in their weights. Since the bullet probably was made of lead, while the cannon ball was made of iron, the experiment showed also that the material of which the falling body was made did not affect its speed of falling. A similar experiment performed with a bullet and a feather would, however, clearly show that the bullet falls faster. Since the previous experiment indicated that the material is of no importance, the scientist looks for some other factor which may explain the different outcomes of the two experiments. He may *think* of air resistance as a possibility. But if we assume that air resistance is the factor which causes the feather to fall less rapidly than the bullet, then *it follows* that in vacuum both will fall with the same velocity. Here is a very elementary *theory*, consisting of an assumption and of a consequence derived from this assumption. To test it we perform the now well-known classroom experiment of having the feather and the bullet fall in vacuum. The result confirms the expectation of the theory.

This example is highly oversimplified, but it illustrates the point. The design and planning of almost every experiment are the results of reasoning, based on implicit or explicit assumptions. The more complex the set of phenomena which we study, the more involved is the design of the experiment and the more complex also is the necessary reasoning. Beyond a certain degree of complexity ordinary logic becomes insufficient. The elaboration of the theory, the derivation of the consequences from the assumptions or hypotheses, requires the powerful tool of mathematical analysis. But in a rudimentary form the theoretical reasoning and an element of hypothesis are present in every experiment. Even in an experiment in which we merely ask: "What is going to happen under such conditions?" there is a hypothesis involved, though this hypothesis becomes, in a sense, an accessory after the fact. When we find an outcome of an experiment we conclude that the same outcome will be found again and again under similar conditions. This is essentially a hypothesis which is justified actually by its predictive value. We assume a certain uniformity in nature.

The law of induction is essentially an expression of this assumption, which turned out to be a very useful one. When we observe an outcome of an experiment and then say that this same outcome will be found if the experiment is repeated in the same way, we essentially make a prediction, based on our assumption of the uniformity of nature.

It is true that this concept of uniformity has recently undergone a fundamental revision. From a strictly deterministic uniformity, we passed to a probabilistic, or statistical, uniformity. There is, however, a continuous graded transition between the two. In the physical sciences the former prevails. That is why frequently only one or a few repetitions of an experiment are sufficient to establish some regularity or "law." In biology, and especially in the social sciences, statistical uniformity prevails. As Professor Wolfgang Köhler once said, we may pick up a leaf from the ground, determine very exactly its mass, its area, its color, its chemical composition, etc. We shall thus make a number of highly precise measurements. Yet the scientific value of such an "experiment" would be nil. Why? Because there are no two leaves exactly alike, and we cannot therefore predict anything from our "experiment." But if we take one hundred leaves of the same species, and perform similar experiments on them, then not only can we predict that if we take another hundred such leaves the average results will be the same, but we can even predict the probability that a given leaf, picked up at random, will have given properties.

From what has been said it follows that any arguments as to whether the experiment or the theory plays a more important part has no meaning. No valuable experiment can be designed and performed without at least a rudimentary theory, but no theory has any value *per se* unless it can, at least in principle, be verified experimentally. Experiment and theory are two inseparable and interdependent parts of the same tool which the scientist uses in his work. True enough, the requirements of division of labor usually result in some scientists specializing in experimental work, others in theoretical. True also that in the design of experimental apparatus the experimenter may be temporarily involved in purely manual techniques which have nothing to do with a scientific theory. Similarly, in order to develop experimentally verifiable consequences of a theory a theoretician may have to indulge, as a necessary intermediate step, in some very abstruse speculations, which may have no relation whatsoever to any experiment. But in both these cases we have, as said above, temporary intermediate work. The close relationship between theory and experiment is not altered by this.

For some time the view was held by many scientists that the experimental verification of the conclusions drawn from a set of hypotheses constituted a proof of those hypotheses. The hypotheses were considered in such a case as actually describing *the* reality; they were considered as being "true." Since Henry Poincaré we know that this is not the case.

There is no such thing as *the* hypothesis or *the* theory. There is rather an infinite number of hypotheses and theories which can explain a given set of phenomena. We do not speak any more of "true" or "false" theories, but of "good" or "bad" ones, or of "convenient" or "inconvenient" ones. A "good" or "convenient" theory is one which enables us to make the greatest number of predictions in the easiest way. The success and importance of the Relativity Theory are not due to the fact that the new concepts of space and time are more "true" than the old ones. There is no physical phenomenon that could not be explained on the basis of absolute space and time. But such explanations would, in most cases, be very cumbersome and artificial, while they become simple and natural on the basis of the Relativity Theory. That is what makes the theory a good one.

In developing a theory a scientist tries to construct a conceptual abstract system which is isomorphic to the world which he observes. A system completely isomorphic to the observable world would enable us to predict everything. So far the systems proposed have been only in part isomorphic to the observable world. Extension of this isomorphic region constitutes progress in science.

The situation may be illustrated by the following example. Imagine a geometric plane inhabited by two-dimensional intelligent beings who can move freely in that plane. As they move around they discover points in that plane. Their world is made up of those points. They find that with great approximation the first three points lie on a straight line. They then make the assumption that all points in their plane lie on this straight line. To test this assumption they perform an experiment by moving along the line, and they actually find a few new points. Having thus established a "good" hypothesis they predict the existence of other points along that straight line, and their prediction is confirmed. Then someone discovers at a great distance a point which is decidedly not on the straight line, and then another such point. It is then found that all the points, including the newly discovered ones, actually lie on a parabola, and that the original hypothesis holds good only for a region of limited size, since any sufficiently small segment of a continuous curve is well approximated by a straight line. The old hypothesis is revised. A new theory is established, according to which the world consists of points lying on a parabola. This theory proves "good" within a certain domain. Outside of this domain deviations are, however, found and the theory is revised again, on the assumption that all points lie on a higher order curve. But though an old theory is discarded, yet it remains valid within a limited region of the universe, or within a limited array of phenomena. Gradually the theory becomes extremely complex, as more and more points are discovered. In rectangular coordinates, which our imaginary beings are "naturally" using, the equation of their "world line" becomes quite unmanageable. Then along comes a "mathematical genius" and he points out that everything becomes much simpler if we introduce appropriate curvilinear coordinates.

In fact, in these coordinates the "world curve" is represented by a linear equation, just as was the original straight line in the rectangular coordinates. The Relativity revolution in physics may be considered as just a change of the system of coordinates.

Thus we see that in formulating his hypotheses the scientist is not too much concerned with their correspondence to some ultimate reality. All he cares is that the theory developed on the basis of those hypotheses be isomorphic with the observed world. Even though a hypothesis is sometimes suggested by an observation, it is *never* formulated so as to correspond exactly to the phenomenon which suggests it. Even the simplest phenomena are too complex to be grasped by the human mind in their entirety. The scientist picks out only a few salient features of the observed phenomenon, features in which he is interested at the moment. In other words, he abstracts from the phenomenon as a whole the features which are interesting to him. The whole dynamics of rigid bodies is based on the abstraction of a perfectly rigid body, which is nonexistent in nature. Yet, *within limits*, the equations derived on the basis of this abstract, utterly unrealistic, concept find practical applications in engineering!

As we have said above, the study of the more complex phenomena of necessity leads to the use of mathematical analysis. One of the many advantages of the mathematical method is that it enables us to make *quantitative* predictions. We shall illustrate with three examples, one taken from physics and two from biology, why a quantitative prediction is of considerably greater value than a qualitative one.

The development of classical electrodynamics was closely linked to the concept of the universal ether, the carrier of electromagnetic phenomena. From various considerations of a quantitative nature, such as the theory of astronomical aberration, it was concluded that the ether could not be carried along by bodies moving through it. From this one could conclude, *without any knowledge of mathematics*, that there should exist an "ether wind" at the surface of the earth. Michelson would have devised an experiment to prove the existence of such an ether wind. Finding a negative result, what would his conclusion have been? Either that there is no "ether wind," or that if it exists it is too small to be detected by his experimental set up. The experiment with a negative result would have gone into oblivion with many other similar ones. Actually the situation was different. The *mathematically* elaborated classical electrodynamics did not merely require the existence of an "ether wind," but it required it to be of a definite magnitude. From the outset Michelson had to design his apparatus so as to be able to measure an effect of a *prescribed magnitude*. When he found no such effect, then there was no alibi that the effect might be too small to be detected. There was clearly a contradiction with the requirement of the theory, a contradiction which made a revision of the theory mandatory. The revision eventually led to the Theory of Relativity.

With a qualitative theory we may have "negative" experimental results.

With a quantitative theory the result of even a "negative" experiment is positive.

Biologists for a long time have been speculating on the possible causes of cell division. A rather appealing assumption was that it is due to electric charges. Cells were known to carry an electric charge. Charges of the same sign were known to repel one another. What was more natural than to assume that electrically charged parts of the cell repel one another, causing the cell to divide. The very superficial resemblance of the spindle fiber figure to a drawing of "lines of force" between electric charges of the same sign, as found in any physics textbook, further advanced the above-

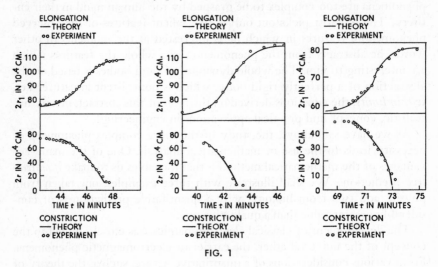

FIG. 1

mentioned hypothesis. A great deal of rather elaborate *qualitative* speculation was made in this connection.

Only relatively recently, with the advent of mathematical biology, has mathematical analysis been applied to that problem. The magnitude of the electric charges in cells is approximately known. Hence we can *compute* the forces they will exert and the effects of those forces on the cell. The mechanical strength of cells has also been measured approximately. Hence it was possible to figure out mathematically whether the known electric charges in the cell could result in the division of the latter. The result was, in general, an emphatic *no*. With some exceptions the electric forces are considerably too small to produce cell division, though in some instances they might affect the course of the division.

But the further development of the mathematical theory of cell division did much more than merely yield the above result. In reviewing possible causes of cell division, it was found that one possibility is present always in any cell which manifests signs of life. That possibility is given by the forces produced by the diffusion of various metabolites into and out of the cell. A great deal of elaborate mathematical work had to be done to develop the theory based on this possibility. When it was done it was not only possible to show quantitatively that the diffusion forces are sufficient to produce cell division. It was also possible to calculate the average size of cells, and the result was found to be in quantitative agreement with actual observation. It was shown that cells with a higher glycolytic coefficient should divide more readily, which is generally the case. Finally, equations were derived which described quantitatively the process of division of an isolated spherical cell. The equation described the process of initial elongation, followed by a constriction at the equator. At the time the equations

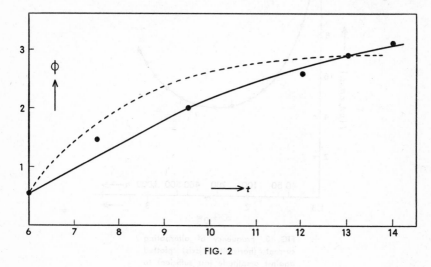

FIG. 2

were developed by H. D. Landahl, no quantitative experimental data were available to verify them. Subsequently Dr. Ralph Buchsbaum, assisted by Robert Williamson, made numerous carefully controlled experiments on demembrenated Arbacia eggs. A typical result of comparison of the theory with their experimental findings is shown on the graph (Figure 1). The theory not only explained already known facts, it predicted quantitatively the results of a quantitative experiment.

A further development of the theory of metabolic diffusion forces led to applications to some embryological phenomena. In particular, a theory of gastrulation was developed. In developing this theory, two possibilities appeared particularly interesting. One was that the cells of the blastula just before gastrulation were subject only to forces resulting from the metabolism of the other cells. The other was that each cell exhibits a certain inner diffusion polarity which makes for additional forces. The two possibilities lead to different equations for the rate of gastrulation. The second graph (Figure 2) shows the two curves, represented by the two equations in their comparison with some observations. There is no question but that the assumption of polarized cells leads to a better agreement with observations. If we had merely a qualitative theory, a discrimination between the two cases would have been impossible.

Individual instances of application of mathematical methods to biological problems date as far back as the end of the last century and the beginning of this century. Mention should be made of the work of J. L. Hoorweg, Weiss and W. Nernst on the theory of nervous excitation and of the very important work of O. Fischer on the dynamics of human extremities. The systematic development of mathematical biology is only

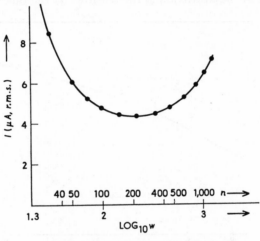

FIG. 3. Frequency of alternating current (horizontal axis) plotted against amplitude just sufficient to cause excitation.

about a quarter of a century old, but it has yielded important results. We have mentioned already two examples, chosen from a large number of cases. Important contributions have been made by the pioneering work of Alfred Lotka and of Vito Volterra. They have developed a mathematical theory of the struggle for existence, a theory which leads to definite quantitative predictions: Volterra has shown that the interaction of two species, one of which preys on the other, results, under certain conditions, in periodical fluctuations in the number of individuals comprising the two species. Periodic fluctuations of the populations of some animal species, such as fishes and insects, have long been observed. A quantitative experiment to check Volterra's theory was first performed by F. Gause, who used two species of microorganisms. Periodical fluctuations were actually found. A quantitative comparison of the observed curves with those predicted by Volterra showed, however, that Volterra's equations must be modified, to bring them into agreement with observations. Now we may say "better" equations were thus established.

In the field of nervous excitation considerable progress has been made by the University of Chicago group on the one hand, and by A. V. Hill and his school on the other. Figures 3 and 4 illustrate the agreement between the predictions of the theory, based on a set of assumptions, and the experimental findings. The two graphs are taken from the work of A. V. Hill and his collaborators.

In genetics notable progress has been achieved through the cooperation of mathematical theory and experiment. We may mention the work of Sewall Wright, J. B. S. Haldane, Hilda Geiringer, and others.

Because of the connection with the social sciences, we shall discuss somewhat more in detail the mathematical biology of the central nervous system and of behavior. The development of this field is associated with the names of H. D. Landahl, A. S. Householder, Anatol Rapoport, Alfonso Shimbel, and others. The development of the theory proceeded according to what we may call the "standard" patterns discussed above. A set of fundamental hypotheses, of a rather simple nature, was made concerning the dynamics of interaction of any two neural elements, of which our central nervous system is made up. Then hypothetic structural arrangements of different degrees of complexity were investigated mathematically. The properties of some of those

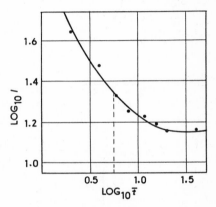

FIG. 4. Pulse duration of a constant current (horizontal axis) plotted against current thresholds.

structures have shown amazing similarity to the properties of parts of our central nervous system. Thus gradually an elaborate theory was developed, which not only accounts for a number of observed quantitative relations but which in two cases led to predictions of new relations. . . . [In] (Figure 5) we have a comparison of the theoretically derived relation between intensity of a stimulus and the reaction time to that stimulus, and the known experimental results. On the next graph (Figure 6) we have a comparison of theory and experiment in the study of the response of an individual to two stimuli which are sufficiently close to one another to cause the individual to occasionally confuse them. The percentage of confusion or errors can be theoretically calculated from the difference of intensities of the two stimuli.

The next graph (Figure 7) illustrates an application of the theory to learning. The mechanism of learning varies undoubtedly with varying types of tasks to be learned. A theory was developed by H. D. Landahl for a particular task, and a rather complex equation which determines the

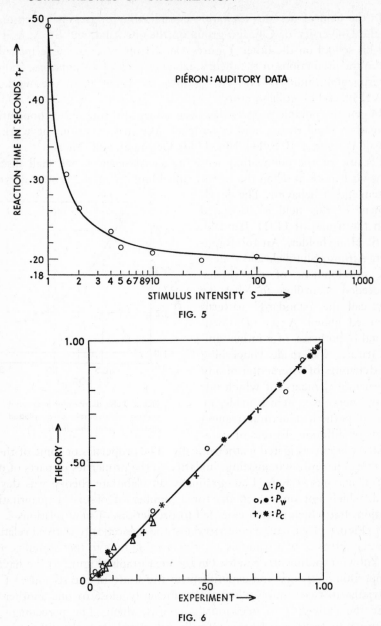

FIG. 5

FIG. 6

learning curve for different degrees of difficulty was derived. No data for this type of task were available. Therefore experiments were performed to verify the theory, with the results shown on the graph.

A mathematical theory of various emotional processes has also been developed. The results may be illustrated in Figure 8 which show a compari-

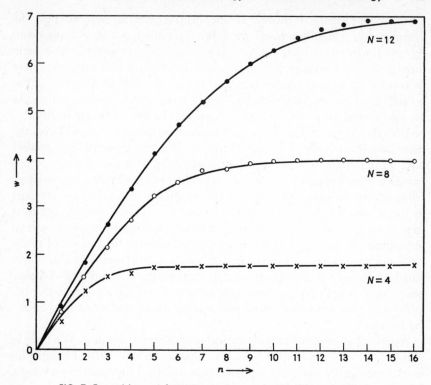

FIG. 7. Errors (n) vs. trials (w) in a memory task. N indicates complexity.

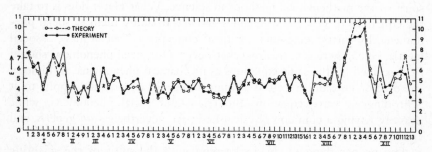

FIG. 8. A mathematical theory of various emotional processes has been developed. The results are illustrated by the above graph which shows a comparison of theoretically predicted and experimentally determined (by standard psychometric methods) relative aesthetic values of 77 different polygonal geometric figures. The theoretical prediction in this case was a real prediction, having been made more than a year before the experiments were started.

son of theoretically predicted and experimentally determined (by standard psychometric methods) relative aesthetic values of 77 different polygonal geometric figures. The theoretical prediction in this case was a real prediction, having been made more than a year before the experiments were started.

It may be objected, and it actually has been objected against the above-outlined mathematical theory of the central nervous system, that the postulates on which it is based are definitely known not to correspond to reality. But on that basis we may just as well object against the kinetic theory of gases because its fundamental assumption that molecules may be considered as rigid spheres is at least just as removed from reality as the postulates of the mathematical biology of the central nervous system. As we said above, no postulate ever corresponds to any "ultimate reality."

We thus have a fairly well-developed mathematical theory of the neurobiological basis of human behavior. We can describe and predict how an individual will behave when confronted with certain more or less complex stimulus patterns. But no individual is ever completely isolated from others. In human society the actions of any one individual are part of the stimulus pattern perceived by the others. Thus, logically, the next step is to generalize the theory to interaction between two or several individuals. In this way we are naturally led into the field of social problems, perhaps into what may be called "mathematical sociology." If mathematical biology is possible, why not mathematical sociology? A ready objection is the allegedly greater complexity of social phenomena. But the same objection was raised in the past against the possibility of mathematical biology.

Attempts at creating a mathematical sociology are not new. We have in mind Haret's *Mécanique Sociale*, which dates back to 1910. Though this work superficially looks like a physicomathematical approach to sociology, in our opinion it exhibits a complete lack of understanding of the true spirit of the mathematical methods in science. What Haret does is to take the equations of classical mechanics and try to apply them to social phenomena, by introducing such artificial concepts as "social mass," "social inertia," etc. There is no reason whatsoever why social phenomena should be described by the same equations as mechanical phenomena. In biology we do not consider a cell as a huge molecule and do not apply to it Schrödinger's wave equation. Biological and social phenomena, while possibly having a common physical basis, are nevertheless *sui generis*, and are described by mathematical laws of their own.

The proper thing to do, in keeping with the spirit of the scientific method, is to derive from the theory of the nervous system the equations which govern the interaction of several individuals, and proceed to the development of a mathematical sociology. As this task is rather difficult, we may, *as a temporary expedient*, build a mathematical sociology on a set of special postulates which deal with directly observable social concepts or with abstractions thereof, but which do not blindly mimic the postulates of physics. An attempt in this last direction was made in our *Mathematical Theory of Human Relations*. A number of interesting consequences has thus been developed, and even a comparison with some quantitative sociological data has been made. Subsequently it was found to be possible to derive the special postulates from the mathematical theory of the central nervous system, and thus to follow the direct way. The results are summarized in our book *Mathematical Biology of Social Behavior.*

The theory thus developed deals with quantities that are probabilistic or statistical in their nature. We already have seen that uniformities of such a nature are characteristic of the social sciences. It is impossible to predict with any exactitude the life history and behavior of a king, dictator, or other individual. But it is equally impossible to predict the exact course of an individual electron or atom. This latter circumstance does not worry the physicist. Similarily the sociologist need not be worried about the former. He can observe regularities between a large number of social quantities, such as, for example, divorce rates, crime incidence, church attendance, scientific output of a nation, etc. Mathematical sociology derives equations which relate to precisely this kind of quantities. Whenever enough data are available, they can be checked. If, as is at present preponderately the case, sufficient statistical observations are not at hand, the theory, even in its present very incomplete form, suggests definite quantitative sociological observation.

But, the sociologist may say, there are plenty of purely qualitative observations in sociology which are not amenable to quantitative analysis. For example, we may study the spread of ideas, beliefs, mores, etc., for which there is no quantitative measure. Well, isn't there really? We can measure, in principle at least, the relative number of individuals who accept given ideas or beliefs at any given time. The increase or decrease of this relative number gives us the increase or decrease of the spread or "popularity" of the idea. And, what is most important, the mathematical biology of the central nervous system shows that the above-mentioned relative numbers of individuals are closely related to the *average* values of certain neurobiophysical quantities characteristic of the individuals in the society, quantities which determine the psychophysiological "drives" or "preferences" of individuals toward one or another idea or belief.

Such concepts as "social rank," which can in principle be measured by appropriate psychometric methods, are given a neurobiophysical interpretation.

Of course, the value of qualitative observations cannot be denied. But the same may be said about their limitations as has been said about the limitations of qualitative relations in physics and biology.

Mathematical sociology seems to be well on its way as the youngest among the exact sciences. Like the older two systems, mathematical physics and mathematical biology, it will, if properly developed, lead to further improvement and extensions of the already existing quantitative methods of observation in sociology.

Now for a few concluding words. As we have seen, the scientist is engaged in constructing a conceptual framework which is isomorphic with the observable world, and thus enables him to predict observable phenomena. To construct this framework, the scientist takes hints from observed phenomena. We may now, perhaps, indulge in a little wild speculation and ask whether it is possible that our own thought patterns are isomorphic with the observable world. Is there perhaps a set of equivalent conceptual frameworks which is the only one completely compatible with our laws of thought? If so, it might some time be possible to derive all observable phenomena from purely *a priori* postulates. Something akin to this idea seems to underlie the work of the late Sir Arthur Eddington, summarized in his posthumous book *Fundamental Theory*. The book has caused a great deal of controversy. Personally we prefer to preserve a noncommittal attitude. Should, however, the possibility envisaged by Eddington materialize, then the words of the great German poet, which we quoted before, may really turn out to be prophetic.

2. SOCIOLOGY LEARNS THE LANGUAGE OF MATHEMATICS*

ABRAHAM KAPLAN

A TROUBLING question for those of us committed to the widest application of intelligence in the study and solution of the problems of men is whether a general understanding of the social sciences will be possible much longer. Many significant areas of these disciplines have already been removed by the advances of the past two decades beyond the reach of anyone who does not know mathematics; and the man of letters is increasingly finding, to his dismay, that the study of mankind proper is passing from his hands to those of technicians and specialists. The aesthetic effect is admittedly bad: we have given up the belletristic "essay on man" for the barbarisms of a technical vocabulary, or at best the forbidding elegance of mathematical syntax. What have we gained in exchange?

To answer this question we must be able to get at the content of the new science. But when it is conveyed in mathematical formulas, most of us are in the position of the medieval layman confronted by clerical Latin —with this difference: mathematical language cannot be forced to give way to a vernacular. Mathematics, if it has a function at all in the sciences, has an indispensable one; and now that so much of man's relation to man has come to be treated in mathematical terms, it is impossible to ignore or escape the new language any longer. There is no completely satisfactory way out of this dilemma. All this article can do is to grasp either horn, sometimes oversimplifying, sometimes taking the reader out of his depth; but hoping in the end to suggest to him the significance of the growing use of mathematical language in social science.

To complicate matters even further, the language has several dialects. "Mathematics" is a plural noun in substance as well as form. Geometry, algebra, statistics, and topology use distinct concepts and methods, and are applicable to characteristically different sorts of problems. The role of mathematics in the new social science cannot be discussed in a general way: as we shall see, everything depends on the kind of mathematics being used.

I

The earliest and historically most influential of the mathematical sciences is geometry. Euclid's systematization of the results of Babylonian

* Reproduced from *Commentary*, 1951, by permission of the editors.

astronomy and Egyptian surveying set up a model for scientific theory that remained effective for two thousand years. Plato found in Euclid's geometry the guide to the logical analysis of all knowledge, and it was the Renaissance "rediscovery" of Plato's insistence on the fundamentally geometric structure of reality that insured the triumph of the modern world view inaugurated by Copernicus. Scientists like Kepler accepted the Copernican hypothesis because it made the cosmos more mathematically elegant than Ptolemy's cumbersome epicycles had been able to do.

The study of man—to say nothing of God!—enthusiastically availed itself of mathematical method: witness Spinoza's *Ethics*, which claimed that it "demonstrated according to the geometrical manner." But Spinoza's *Ethics* failed, as demonstrative science, because the 17th century did not clearly understand the geometry it was applying with such enthusiasm. The discovery of non–Euclidean geometries two hundred years later revealed that the so-called axioms of geometry are not *necessary* truths, as Spinoza and his fellow rationalists had always supposed, but merely postulates: propositions put forward for the sake of subsequent inquiry. It is only by deducing their consequences and comparing these with the perceived facts that we can decide whether or not the postulates are true. Geometry is a fully developed example of a set of undefined terms, prescribed operations, and the resulting postulates and theorems which make up a *postulational system;* it is in this form that it is influential in some of the recent developments in the social sciences.

Perhaps the most elaborate postulational system for dealing with the data of social and psychological science was constructed in 1940 by Clark Hull and associates of the Yale Institute of Human Relations (C. L. Hull, *et al., Mathematico-Deductive Theory of Rote Learning*, Yale University Press, 1940). "Rote learning" is a very specialized branch of psychology that studies the learning of series of nonsense syllables; presumably, this tells us something about the act of learning in its "purest" form, with no admixture of influence from the thing learned.

The problems of the field revolve around ways of explaining the patterns of learning that are in fact discovered; why the first syllables in any series are learned first, the last soon after, and why the syllables a little past the middle of the given series take longest to memorize, and so on. There is a vast number of observations of this sort to be made, and Hull's ideal was to set up a postulational system which would allow observed patterns of learning to be logically deduced from relatively few postulates.

The system consists of 16 undefined terms, 86 definitions, and 18 postulates. From these, 54 theorems are deduced. The deductions can, in principle, be checked against the results of direct observation, in experimental situations or elsewhere. In many cases, as the book points out, existing evidence is as yet inadequate to determine whether the theorems hold true; in the great majority of cases, experimental evidence is in agreement with logically deduced theorems; in others, there is undoubted disagreement between deduced expectation and observed fact. Such disagreements point to basic defects in the postulate system, which, however, can be progressively improved.

The authors consider their book to be principally important as an example of the proper scientific method to be used in the study of behavior. And certainly, as a formal demonstration of the handling of definitions, postulates, and theorems, the book is unexceptionable. However, science prides itself on its proper method because of the fruitfulness of its results; and it is to the fruitfulness of this effort that we must address ourselves.

One example of the method may suggest better than general criticism the problem raised. Hull proves in one of his theorems that the greater the "inhibitory potential" at a given point in the learning of a rote series, the greater will be the time elapsing between the stimulus (the presentation of one nonsense syllable in the list) and the reaction (the pronouncing of the next memorized nonsense syllable). "Inhibitory potential" is one of the undefined terms of the system; it denotes the inability of the subject, before his involvement in the learning process, to pronounce the appropriate syllable on the presentation of the appropriate stimulus. (It may be pictured as a force that wanes as the stimuli are repeated and the syllable to be uttered is learned.)

Now this theorem certainly follows logically from three postulates of the system (they involve too many special terms to be enlightening if quoted). However, on examining these postulates, the theorem is seen to be so directly implied by them that one wonders what additional knowledge has been added by formally deducing it. A certain amount must have been known about rote learning to justify the selection of those postulates in the first place. To deduce this theorem from them has added very little —if anything—to what was already known. In short: the geometric method used by Hull, correct as it is formally, does not, for this reader, extend significantly what we already knew about rote learning from his and others' work.

In the course of Hull's book "qualitative postulates," by which is meant the "unquantified" ideas of thinkers like Freud and Darwin, are condemned because they have "so little deductive fertility"—because so few theorems may be deduced from them. In the narrowest logical sense of the phrase, this may be true. But fertility in the sense of yielding precisely determinable logical consequences is one thing; in the sense of yielding further insights into the subject matter—whether or not these can be presented as strict consequences of a system of postulates—it is quite another. The ideas of Darwin and Freud can hardly be condemned as lacking in fertility, even though they leave much to be desired from the standpoint of logical systematization.

This is not to deny that the postulational method can play a valuable role in science. But it is a question of the scientific context in which the method is applied. Newton and Euclid both had available to them a considerable body of fairly well-established knowledge which they could systematize, and in the process derive other results not apparent in the disconnected materials. Hull recognizes this condition, but supposes it to be already fulfilled in the area of learning theory. The results of the particular system he has constructed raise serious doubts that his supposition is true.

Science, basically, does not proceed by the trial-and-error method to which Hull, as a student of animal learning, is so much attached. It employs insight, itself subject to logical analysis, but too subtle to be caught in the coarse net of any present-day system of postulates. The geometric method in the new social science can be expected to increase in value as knowledge derived from other methods grows. But for the present, it is an elegantly written check drawn against insufficient funds.

II

If the 17th century was the age of geometry, the 18th was that of algebra. The essential idea of algebra is to provide a symbolism in which relations between quantities can be expressed *without a specification of the magnitudes of the quantities*. An equation simply formulates the equality between two quantities in a way that shows how the magnitude of one depends on the magnitude of certain constituents of the other.

The characterization of mathematics as a language is nowhere more appropriate than in algebra; the notation is everything. The power of algebra consists in that it allows the symbolism to think for us. Thought enters into the formulation of the equations and the establishing of the rules of manipulation by which they are to be solved, but the rest is mechanical —so much so that more and more the manipulation is being done, literally, by machines. The postulational method characteristic of classical geometry no longer plays as important a part here. Derivation is replaced by calculation; we proceed, not from postulates of uncertain truth, but from arithmetical propositions whose truth is a matter of logic following necessarily from the definitions of the symbols occurring in them. The equations that express relations between real quantities are, of course, empirical hypotheses; but *if* the equations correctly formulate the function relating two quantities, then certain numerical values for one necessarily imply certain numerical values for the other. Again, as in geometry, the facts are the final test.

In this spirit, the mathematicians of the 18th century replaced Newton's geometrizing by the methods of algebra, and the culmination was Laplace's system of celestial mechanics. Laplace's famous superman, given the position and momentum of every particle in the universe, could compute, it was thought, the entire course of world history, past and future. The development of quantum mechanics made the program unrealizable even in principle, just as the non–Euclidean geometries were fatal to the aspirations of the 17th-century rationalists. Nevertheless, this scientific ideal, so nearly realized in physics, has exerted enormous influence on the study of man, and much of the new social science is motivated by the attempt to take advantage of the powerful resources of algebra.

Among the most ambitious, but also most misguided, of such attempts is a 900-page treatise by the sociologist Stuart C. Dodd, *Dimensions of Society* (Macmillan, 1942). The author's ambition, declared in the subtitle, is to provide "a quantitative systematics for the social sciences." What is misguided is the failure to realize that a system is not provided by a symbolism alone: it is necessary also to have something to say in the symbolism that is rich enough to give point to the symbolic manipulation. Dodd presents a dozen symbols of what he regards as basic sociological concepts, together with four others for arithmetical operations. They stand for such ideas as space, time, population, and characteristics (the abstract idea "characteristics," and not the specific characteristics to be employed in sociological theory). In addition to these sixteen basic symbols, there are sixteen auxiliary symbols, compounds or special cases of the basic symbols, or supplements to them—for instance, the question mark, described as one of four "new operators," used to denote a hypothesis, or a questioned assertion. With this notation, every situation studied by sociologists is to be defined by an expression of the form:

$$S = {}_{s}^{s} (T; I; L; P) {}_{s}^{s}$$

The capital *S* stands for the *situation*, and the letters within the parentheses for *time*, indicators of the *characteristics* specified, *length* or *spatial regions*, and *populations*, *persons*, or *groups*. The semicolon stands for an unstated form of mathematical combination, and the small *s* for various ways of particularizing the four major kinds of characterizations. Thus T^0 stands for a *date*, T^1 for a *rate of change*, both of these being different sorts of time specifications. Instructions for the use of the notation require one hundred distinct rules for their formulation.

But this whole notational apparatus is, as Dodd recognizes, "a systematic way of expressing societal data, and not, directly, a system of the functionings of societal phenomena." "Facts," however, are data only *for* hypotheses; without the latter, they are of no scientific significance. Certainly a notational system can hardly be called a "theory," as Dodd constantly designates it, unless it contains some statements *about* the facts. But *Dimensions of Society* contains only one social generalization: "This theory . . . generalizes societal phenomena in the statement: 'People, Environments, and Their Characteristics May Change.' This obvious generalization becomes even more obvious if the time period in which the change is observed is prolonged." The last sentence may save Dodd, but not his "theory," from hopeless naïvety.

Dodd's hope that his system of "quantic classification" will "come to play a role for the social sciences comparable to the classification of the chemical atoms in Mendelyeev's periodic table" is groundless. The periodic table, after all, told us something about the elements; more, it suggested that new elements that we knew nothing of existed, and told us what their characteristics would be when discovered. The fundamental point is that we have, in the case of Dodd, only a *notation;* when he speaks of the "verification" of his "theory," he means only that it is possible to formulate societal data with his notation.

Dodd's basic error is his failure to realize that after "Let *x* equal such-and-such," the important statement is still to come. The question is how to put *that* statement into mathematical form.

An answer to this question is provided in two books of a very different sort from Dodd's, both by the biophysicist N. Rashevsky: *Mathematical Theory of Human Relations* (The Principia Press, 1947) and *Mathematical Biology of Social Behavior* (University of Chicago Press, 1951). In these two books the author does not merely talk *about* mathematics; he actually *uses* it. In the earlier one, the methods of mathematical biology are applied to certain social phenomena on the basis of formal postulates —more simply, assumptions—about these phenomena. In the later book, these assumptions are interpreted in terms of neurobiophysical theory, and are derived as first approximations from that theory. The results, according to Rashevsky, are "numerous suggestions as to how biological measurements, made on large groups of individuals, may lead to the prediction of some social phenomena."

As a natural scientist, Rashevsky is not seduced, like so many aspirants to a social science, by the blandishments of physics. Scientific method is the same everywhere: it is the method of logical inference from data provided and tested by experience. But the specific techniques of science are different everywhere, not only as between science and science but even as between problem and problem in the same field. The confusion of method and technique, and the resultant identification of scientific method with the techniques of physics (and primarily 19th-century physics at that) has hindered the advance of the social sciences not a little. For the problems of sociology *are* different from those of physics. There are no concepts in social phenomena comparable in simplicity and fruitfulness to the space, time, and mass of classical mechanics; experiments are difficult to perform, and even harder to control; measurement in sociological situations presents special problems from which physics is relatively free. Yet none of these differences, as Rashevsky points out, prevents a scientific study of man. That social phenomena are complex means only that techniques must be developed of corresponding complexity: today's schoolboy can solve mathematical problems beyond the reach of Euclid or Archimedes. Difficulties in the way of experimentation have not prevented astronomy from attaining full maturity as a science. And the allegedly "qualitative" character of social facts is, after all, only an allegation; such facts have their quantitative aspects too. And what is perhaps more to the point, mathematics can also deal with qualitative characteristics, as we shall see.

Rashevsky addresses himself to specific social subject matters: the formation of closed social classes, the interaction of military and economic factors in international relations, "individualistic" and "collectivistic" tendencies, patterns of social influence, and many others. But though the problems are concrete and complex, he deals with them in a deliberately abstract and oversimplified way. The problems are real enough, but their formulation is idealized, and the equations solved on the basis of quite imaginary cases. Both books constantly repeat that the treatment is intended to "illustrate" how mathematics is applicable "in principle" to social science: for actual solutions, the theory is admitted to be for the most part too crude and the data too scarce.

What this means is that Rashevsky's results cannot be interpreted as actual accounts of social phenomena. They are, rather, ingenious elaborations of what *would* be the case if certain unrealistic assumptions were granted. Yet this is not in itself objectionable. As he points out in his own defense, physics made great strides by considering molecules as rigid spheres, in complete neglect of the complexity of their electronic and nuclear internal structures. But the critical question is whether Rashevsky's simplifications are, as he claims, "a temporary expedient." An idealization is useful only if an assumption that is approximately true yields a solution that is approximately correct; or at any rate, if we can point out the ways in which the solution must be modified to compensate for the errors in the assumptions.

It is in this respect that Rashevsky's work is most questionable. Whatever the merits of his idealizations from the standpoint of "illustrating," as he says, the potentialities of mathematics, from the standpoint of the study of man they are so idealized as almost to lack all purchase on reality.

Rashevsky's treatment of individual freedom, for example, considers it in two aspects: economic freedom and freedom of choice. The former is defined mathematically as the fraction obtained when the amount of work a man must actually do is subtracted from the maximum amount of work of which he is capable, and this sum is divided by the original maximum. A person's economic freedom is 0 when he is engaged in hard labor to the point of daily exhaustion; it is 1 when he does not need to work at all. This definition equates increase in economic freedom with shortening of the hours of work; and an unemployed worker, provided he is kept alive on a dole, enjoys complete economic freedom. Such critical elements of economic freedom as real wages, choice of job, and differences in level of aspiration are all ignored.

Freedom of choice, the other aspect of individual freedom, is analyzed as the proportion borne by the amount of time an individual is not in contact with others who might interfere with his choices, to the time he spends alone plus time that is spent in the company of others with the same preferences. This makes freedom of choice decrease with increasing population, so that by this definition one is freer in a small village than a large city. Nothing is said about prying neighbors, or the presence or absence of a secret police, a most important determinant of "freedom of choice." The whole matter of the "introjection" of other persons' standards, as discussed for instance in Erich Fromm's *Escape from Freedom*, is ignored, as are such fundamental considerations as knowledge of the choices available, or the opportunity to cultivate skills and tastes.

On current social issues Rashevsky betrays that he suffers from the same confusions and rationalizations as afflict students without the advantages of a mathematical training. To explain the Lysenko case, for example, he suggests that it is possible that the facts of genetics "may be *interpreted* from two different points of view," thus naïvely substituting a scientific question (if there be one) for the real issue, which is the political control of science. His assumptions encourage him to attempt the conclusion, "even at the present state of our knowledge," that after World War II peace will be most strongly desired by the Soviet Union, least by the United States, with England and Germany in between. And he confesses that he finds it "difficult to understand why the Soviet Union insists on repatriating individuals who left the Soviet Union during World War II and do not desire to return." Mathematics is not yet capable of coping with the naïvety of the mathematician himself.

III

The 19th century saw the rise of mathematical statistics. From its origins in the treatment of games of chance, it was expanded to cope with the new problems posed by the development of insurance, and finally came to be recognized as fundamental to every science dealing with repetitive phenomena. This means the whole of science, for knowledge everywhere rests on the cumulation of data drawn from sequences of situations on whose basis predictions can be made as to the recurrence of similar situations. Mathematical statistics is the theory of the treatment of repeated—or multiple—observations in order to obtain all and only those conclusions for which such observations are evidence. This, and not merely the handling of facts stated in numerical terms, is what distinguishes statistics from other branches of quantitative mathematics.

The application of statistics to social phenomena far exceeds, in fruitfulness as well as extent, the use of mathematics of a fundamentally geometrical—i.e. postulational—or algebraic character in the social sciences. Social scientists themselves have made important contributions to mathematical statistics—which is a good indication of its usefulness to them in their work. Only two of the most recent contributions in the application of statistics to social phenomena can be dealt with here.

The first is a rather remarkable book by a Harvard linguist, G. K. Zipf, *Human Behavior and the Principle of Least Effort* (Addison-Wesley Press, 1949). Its basic conception is that man is fundamentally a user of tools confronted with a variety of jobs to do. Culture can be regarded as constituting a set of tools, and human behavior can be analyzed as the use of such tools in accord with the principle of minimizing the probable rate of work which must be done to perform the jobs that arise. It is this principle that Zipf calls "the law of least effort." As a consequence of it, he claims, an enormous variety of social phenomena exhibit certain regularities of distribution, in accordance with the principle that the tools nearest to hand, easiest to manipulate, and adapted to the widest variety of purposes are those which tend to be used most frequently. These regularities often take the form, according to Zipf, of a constant rank-frequency relationship, according to which the tenth most frequently used word, for instance, is used one-tenth as often as the most frequently used one of all. This is the case, for example, with James Joyce's *Ulysses* as well as with clippings from American newspapers.

A large part of Zipf's book deals with linguistic phenomena, since he is most at home in this field, and it is there that his results seem most fully established. But an enormous range of other subjects is also treated: evolution, sex, schizophrenia, dreams, art, population, war, income, fads, and many others. Many of these topics are dealt with statistically, as likewise conforming to the law of least effort; and all are discussed with originality and insight. For example, the cities in any country, according to Zipf, tend to show the same regularity—the tenth most populous city will have one-tenth as many people as the most populous, the one-hundredth most populous city will have one-hundredth as many. Where this pattern does not prevail, we have an indication of serious potential conflict. It seems that starting about 1820 the growing divisions between Northern and Southern economies in the United States could be seen by a break in this pattern, which reached a peak of severity around 1840, and disappeared after the Civil War!

But while this breadth of topic endows the book with a distinctive fascination, it also makes the reader skeptical of the validity of the theory it puts forward. In the human sciences, the scope of a generalization is usually inversely proportional to its precision and usefulness—at any rate, in the present state of our knowledge. Zipf's law, or something like it, is well known in physics as Maupertuis' principle of least action. But Zipf applies it to a much wider field of phenomena than physical flows of energy. It is understandable that action will follow some sort of least-action pattern if economy enters into its motivation and if the action is sufficiently rational. But that the law of least effort should be manifested everywhere in human conduct, as Zipf holds—indeed, "in all living process"—is difficult to believe.

That a theory is incredible is, of course, no logical objection whatever. And Zipf does not merely speculate; he presents an enormous mass of empirical evidence. The question is what it proves. It does not show, as he claims, the existence of "natural social laws," but, at best, only certain regularities. Brute empiricism is not yet science. Unless observed regularities can be brought into logical relation with other regularities previously observed, we remain at the level of description rather than explanation; and without explanation we cannot attach much predictive weight to description. As a collection of data that deserve the careful attention of the social scientist, Zipf's work will have interest for some time to come. But something more precise and less universal than his principle of least effort will be required to transform that data into a body of scientific knowledge.

The importance of clear conceptualization in giving scientific significance to observed fact is admirably expounded in the recently published fourth volume of the monumental *American Soldier* series (S. A. Stouffer, L. Guttman, et al., *Measurement and Prediction: Studies in Social Psychology in World War II*, Vol. IV, (Princeton University Press, 1950). *Measurement and Prediction* deals with the study of attitudes. It is concerned with the development of methodological rather than substantive theory. It deals with the way in which attitudes—any attitudes—should be studied and understood, but says little about attitudes themselves. However, methodology here is not an excuse for irresponsibility in substantive assumptions, or for confusion as to the ultimate importance of a substantive theory of attitudes.

The major problem taken up is this: how can we tell whether a given set of characteristics is to be regarded as variations of some single underlying quality? Concretely, when do the responses to a questionnaire constitute expressions of a single attitude, and when do they express a number of attitudes? If there is such a single quality, how can we measure how much of it is embodied in each of the characteristics? If all the items on a questionnaire *do* deal with only one attitude, can we measure, in any meaningful sense, how favorable or unfavorable that attitude is, and how intensely it is held by the particular respondent?

This problem arises directly out of the practical—as well as the theoretical—side of opinion study. Consider the case of a poll designed to test the extent and intensity of anti–Semitism. Various questions are included: "Do you think the Jews have too much power?" "Do you think we should allow Jews to come into the country?" "Do you approve of what Hitler did to the Jews?" Some people give anti–Semitic answers to all the questions, some to a few, some to none. Is this because they possess varying amounts of a single quality that we may call "anti–Semitism"? Or is there really a mixture of two or more very different attitudes in the individual, present in varying proportions? If a person is against Jewish immigration, is this because he is against immigration or against Jews, and to what extent? And if there is a single quality such as anti–Semitism, what questions will best bring it out for study? It is problems such as these that the research reported on in *Measurement and Prediction* permits us to solve.

The approach taken stems from the work done in the past few decades by L. L. Thurstone and C. Spearman. Their problems were similar, but arose in a different field, the study of intelligence and other psychological characteristics. Their question was: do our intelligence tests determine a single quality called intelligence? Or do they actually tap a variety of factors, which though combining to produce the total intelligence score, are really quite different from each other? Thurstone and Spearman developed mathematical methods that in effect determined which items in a questionnaire were interdependent—that is, if a person answered *a*, he would tend to answer *b*, but not *c*. On the basis of such patterns, various factors of intelligence were discovered.

In opinion study, one inquires whether items of a questionnaire "hang together"—or, to use the technical term, whether they *scale*. A complex of attitudes is said to be *scalable* if it is possible to arrange the items in it in such a way that every person who answers "yes" to any item also answers "yes" to every item coming after it in the arrangement. In the case of anti–Semitism, we would consider the complex of anti–Semitism scalable—and therefore referring to a single factor in a person's attitudes, rather than including a few distinct attitudes—if we could order the questions in such a way that if someone answered any question in the list "anti–Semitically," he would answer all those following it "anti–Semitically." Attitudes on anti–Semitism would then have the same cumulative character as a series of questions on height—if a person answers "yes" to "Are you more than six feet tall?" we know he will answer "yes" to the question "Are you more than five and a half feet tall?" and all others down the list. This type of reduction of an apparently complex field of attitudes to the simple scheme of a series of cumulative questions is of great value. In *Measurement and Prediction* Louis Guttman describes how to determine whether a group of attitudes does "scale"—that is, does measure a single underlying reality.

Guttman developed, for example, such a scale for manifestations of fear in battle—vomiting, trembling, etc.: soldiers who vomit when faced with combat also report trembling, and so on down the scale; while those who report trembling do not necessarily report vomiting too. On the other hand, it turned out, when he studied paratroopers, various *kinds* of fear of very different types had to be distinguished, for the paratroopers' symptoms were not scalable in terms of a single variable.

One of the most direct applications of scaling methods is in the detection of spurious "causal" connections. We may find, for instance, that the attitude to the continuation of OPS by the government correlates closely with the attitude to farm subsidies. Scale analysis now makes it possible for us to provide an explanation for this fact by testing whether these two items do not in fact express a single attitude—say, the attitude to governmental controls.

Scale analysis permits us to handle another important problem. Suppose we find that 80 per cent of a group of soldiers tested agreed that "the British are doing as good a job as possible of fighting the war, everything considered," while only 48 per cent disagree with the statement that "the British always try to get other countries to do their fighting for them." How many soldiers are "favorable" toward the British? It is clear that we can get different percentages in answer to this question, depending on how we word our question. Scale analysis provides a method which yields what is called an "objective zero point": a division between the numbers of those "favorable" and those "unfavorable" that remains constant no matter what questions we ask about the British. The method demands that, besides asking a few questions testing the attitude, we also get a measure of the "intensity" with which the respondent holds his opinion—we ask for example, whether the respondent feels strongly, not so strongly, or is relatively indifferent about the matter. With this method, it turns out that if we asked a group of entirely different questions about the British, the application of the procedure for measuring the "objective zero point" would show the same result. This limited area of attitude comes to have the same objectivity as the temperature scale, which shows the same result whether we use an alcohol or a mercury thermometer.

Measurement and Prediction also presents, for the first time, a full description of Lazarsfeld's "latent structure" analysis. This is in effect a mathematical generalization of the scaling method of Guttman, which permits us to extend the type of inquiry that scale analysis makes possible into other areas. Scale analysis and latent structure analysis together form an important contribution to the development of more reliable methods of subjecting attitudes—and similar "qualities"—to precise and meaningful measurement.

The prediction part of *Measurement and Prediction* does not contain any comparable theoretical developments. For the most part, prediction in the social sciences today is not above the level of "enlightened common sense," as the authors recognize.

IV

The distinctive development in mathematics in the last one hundred years is the rise of a discipline whose central concept is neither number nor quantity, but *structure*. The mathematics of structure might be said to focus on qualitative differences. *Topology*, as the new discipline is called, is occupied with those properties of figures—conceived as sets of points—that are independent of mere differences of quantity. Squares, circles, and rectangles, of whatever size, are topologically indistinguishable from one another, or from any simple closed figure, however irregular. On the other hand, if a "hole" is inscribed in any of these figures, it thereby becomes qualitatively different from the rest.

Topology, more than most sectors of higher mathematics, deals with questions that have direct intuitive meaning. But intuition often misleads us as to the answers, when it does not fail us altogether. For instance, how many different colors are required to color *any* map so that no two adjoining countries have the same color? It is known, from topological analyses, that five colors are quite enough; but no one has been able to produce a map that needs more than four, or even to prove whether there could or could not be such a map.

It is paradoxical that the field of mathematics which deals with the most familiar subject matter is the least familiar to the non-mathematician. A smattering of geometry, algebra, and statistics is very widespread; topology is virtually unknown, even among social scientists sympathetic to mathematics. To be sure, the late Kurt Lewin's "topological psychology" has given the name much currency. But topology, for Lewin, provided only a notation. The rich content of his work bears no *logical* relation to the topological framework in which it is presented, as is clear from the posthumously published collection of his more important papers, *Field Theory in Social Science* (Harper, 1951). In these papers, talk about the "life space," and "paths," "barriers," and "regions" in it, are elaborately sustained metaphors. Such figures of speech are extraordinarily suggestive, but do not in themselves constitute a strict mathematical treatment of the "life space" in a topological geometry. The actual application of topology to psychology remained for Lewin a program and a hope.

One further development must be mentioned as playing an important role in the new approaches: the rise of symbolic logic. As in the case of topology, this discipline can be traced back to the 17th century, to Leibnitz's ideas for a universal language; but not till the late 19th century did it undergo any extensive and precise development. Boolean algebra provided a mechanical method for the determination of the consequences of a given set of propositions (in another form, this is called the "calculus of propositions"). A few years later, De Morgan, Schroeder, and the founder of Pragmatism, Charles Peirce, investigated the formal properties of relations, leading to an elaborately abstract theory of relations. These results, together with work on the foundations of mathematics (like Peano's formulation of five postulates sufficing for the whole of arithmetic), were extended and systematized shortly after the turn of the century in Russell and Whitehead's monumental *Principia Mathematica*.

Among the recent applications to the study of man of this whole general body of ideas, one is especially celebrated; the theory of games presented by J. von Neumann and O. Morgenstern in *Theory of Games and Economic Behavior* (Princeton University Press, 1947). Here the focus is confined to problems of economics, but it is hoped that it will be extended to the whole range of man's social relations.

It may seem, superficially, that von Neumann and Morgenstern, in selecting games as a way of approaching the study of social organization, fall into the trap of oversimplification. But unlike Rashevsky, von Neumann and Morgenstern do not so much introduce simplifying assumptions in order to deal artificially with the whole complex social order as *select* relatively simple aspects of that order for analysis. Only after a theory adequate to the simple problems has been developed can the more complicated problems be attacked fruitfully. To be sure, the decision-maker cannot suspend action to satisfy the scruples of a scientific conscience; but neither can the scientist pretend to an advisory competence that he does not have, in order to satisfy practical demands.

While the theory of games does not deal with the social process in its full complexity, it is not merely a peripheral aspect of that process which it studies, but its very core. The aim is "to find the mathematically complete principles which define 'rational behavior' for the participants in a social economy, and to derive from them the general characteristics of that behavior." Games are analyzed because the pattern of rational behavior that they exhibit is the same as that manifested in social action, insofar as the latter does in fact involve rationality.

The theory is concerned with the question of what choice of strategy is rational when all the relevant probabilities are known and the outcome is not determined by one's choice alone. It is in the answer to this question that the new mathematics enters. And with this kind of mathematics, the social sciences finally abandon the imitation of natural science that has dogged so much of their history.

The authors first present a method of applying a numerical scale other than the price system to a set of human preferences. A man might prefer a concert to the theater, and either to staying at home. If we assign a utility of "1" to the last alternative, we know that going to the theater must be assigned a higher number, and the concert a higher one still. But how much higher? Suppose the decision were to be made by tossing two coins, the first to settle whether to go to the theater or not, the second (if necessary) to decide between the remaining alternatives. If the utility of the theater were very little different from that of staying at home, most of the time (three-fourths, to be exact) the outcome would be an unhappy one; similarly, if the theater and concert had comparable utilities, the outcome would be usually favorable. Just how the utilities compare, therefore, could be measured by allowing the second coin to be a loaded one. When it is a matter of indifference to the individual whether he goes to the theater or else tosses the loaded coin to decide whether he hears the concert or stays home, the loading of the coin provides a numerical measure of the utilities involved.

Once utility can be measured in a way that does not necessarily correspond to monetary units, a theory of rational behavior can be developed which takes account of other values than monetary ones. A game can be regarded as being played, not move by move, but on the basis of an overall *strategy* that specifies beforehand what move is to be made in every situation that could possibly arise in the game. Then, for every pair of strategies selected—one by each player in the game—the rules of the game determine a *value* for the game: namely, what utility it would then have for each player. An optimal strategy is one guaranteeing a certain value for the game even with best possible play on the part of the opponent. Rational behavior, that is to say, is characterized as the selection of the strategy which minimizes the maximum loss each player can sustain.

If a game has only two players and is "zero-sum"—whatever is won by one player being lost by the other, and vice versa—then, if each player has "perfect information" about all the previous moves in the game, there always exists such an optimal strategy for each player. The outcome of a rationally played game can therefore be computed in advance; in principle, chess is as predictable as ticktacktoe.

Not every game, however, is as completely open as chess. In bridge and poker, for example, we do not know what cards are in the other players' hands; and this is ordinarily the situation in the strategic interplay of management and labor, or in the relations among sovereign states. In such cases rationality consists in playing several strategies, each with a mathematically determined probability. Consider a type of matching pennies in which each player is permitted to place his coin as he chooses. If we were to select heads always, we should be quickly found out; even if we favored heads somewhat, our opponent (assuming it is he who wins when the coins match) could always select heads and thereby win more than half the time. But if we select heads half the time—not in strict alternation, to be sure, but at random—then, no matter what our opponent does, we cannot lose more than half the time. Rational play consists in what is actually done in the game: we toss the coin each time to determine, as it were, whether we select heads or tails. Of course, in more complex games our strategies are not always to be "mixed" in equal proportions. The fundamental theorem of the theory of games is that for every two-person zero-sum game, no matter how complex the rules or how great the range of possible strategies open to each player, there always exists some specific pattern of probabilities of strategies which constitutes rational play. It minimizes the maximum loss that each player can sustain, not in every play of the game, but in the long run. And there is a mathematical solution that tells us what this strategy is.

Unfortunately, many games are not "zero-sum": in the game between management and labor, utilities are created in the process of play; in war they are destroyed. It is simply not true in such cases that what one side loses the other gains, or vice versa. In such cases, the mathematics of the "zero-sum" game will not apply. Moreover, many games have more than two players: a number of manufacturers may be competing for a single market. Here the mathematics of a two-person game will not hold. The first difficulty, however, can be absorbed into the second. A non-"zero-sum" two-person game can be regarded as a three-person game, where the third person wins or loses whatever is lost or won by the other two together.

But how are we to solve games of more than two persons? Only if coalitions are formed, in effect making the game a two-person one. This is not an unrealistic assumption, since, obviously, if two players can coordinate their strategies against a third, they will enjoy a special advantage: odd-man-out is the simple but fundamental principle in such situations. For such games, however, the theory does not provide a detailed solution, for it cannot determine what is a rational division of the spoils between the members of a coalition in the way it can determine what is a rational strategy for the coalition as a whole. And here, of course, is the great difficulty in politics. The United States and Russia may be conceived of, in this theory, as playing a two-person non-"zero-sum" game with nature as the third player: only nature wins from atomic destruction, only nature loses if resources need not be diverted to military purposes. But the coalition of men against nature still leaves open how the utilities acquired in the game are to be divided between the participants. And here conflicting interests stand in the way of the joint interests that would make rational a coalition strategy.

From our present standpoint, the important outcome of the theory is to show that there exists a rigorously mathematical approach to precisely those aspects of the study of man that have seemed in the past to be least amenable to mathematical treatment—questions of conflicting or parallel interest, perfect or imperfect information, rational decision or chance effect. Mathematics is of importance for the social sciences not merely in the study of those aspects in which man is assimilable to inanimate nature, but precisely in his most human ones. On this question the theory of games leaves no room for doubt.

But a mathematical theory of games is one thing, and a mathematical theory of society another. Von Neumann and Morgenstern, it must be said, never confuse the two. Many fundamental difficulties remain, even within the limitations of the games framework. The theory of games involving many players is in a very unsatisfactory state; there is no way at present of comparing the utilities of different persons; and the whole theory is so far a static one, unable to take account of the essential learning process which (it may be hoped) takes place in the course of the selection of real-life strategies. Yet the theory has already provided enormous stimulation to mathematical and substantive research, and much more can be expected from it. Above all, it has shown that the resources of the human mind for the exact understanding of man himself are by no means already catalogued in the existing techniques of the natural sciences.

Thus the application of mathematics to the study of man is no longer a programmatic hope, but an accomplished fact. The books we have surveyed are by no means the only mathematical approaches to problems of social science published even within the past few years. For instance, K. Arrow's *Social Choice and Individual Values* (Wiley, 1951) is a penetrating application of postulational method and the logical theory of relations to the problem of combining, in accord with democratic principles, individual preferences into a representative set of preferences for the group as a whole. Harold Lasswell and his associates report in *The Language of Politics* (G. W. Stewart, 1949) on the procedures and results of the application of the now widely familiar content-analysis techniques to political discourse, in order to objectify and quantify the role of ideologies and utopias in politics. Shannon and Weaver's *Mathematical Theory of Communication* (University of Illinois Press, 1950) reprints the classic papers in which Claude Shannon first developed the precise theory of information now being applied in cybernetics, linguistics, and elsewhere. There are a number of other books; and dozens of papers have appeared in the professional journals of a wide variety of disciplines, including such preeminently "qualitative" fields as social organization, psychiatry, and even literary history.

But if the new language (mathematics) is widely spoken, there are also wide local differences in dialects, and many individual peculiarities of usage. Yet on the scientific scene, this is in itself scarcely objectionable. New problems call for new methods, and if for a time these remain *ad hoc*, it is only from such a rich variety of approaches that systematic and general theories can emerge. No such theories of society or even of part of the social process have yet been developed, though, as we have seen, there have been some premature attempts. But the situation is promising. If the mathematics employed is not merely notational, if it is not merely an "illustration" of an abstract methodology, if it does not outstrip the availability of data and especially of ideas, there is reason to hope that it will eventually contribute as much to the study of man as it already has to the understanding of the rest of nature.

3. DEFINING THE "FIELD AT A GIVEN TIME"*[1]

KURT LEWIN

I. FIELD THEORY AND THE PHASE SPACE

THE HISTORY of acceptance of new theories frequently shows the following steps: At first the new idea is treated as pure nonsense, not worth looking at. Then comes a time when a multitude of contradictory objections are raised, such as: the new theory is too fancy, or merely a new terminology; it is not fruitful, or simply wrong. Finally a state is reached when everyone seems to claim that he had always followed this theory. This usually marks the last state before general acceptance.

The increasing trend toward field theory in psychology is apparent in recent variations of psychoanalysis (Kardiner, Horney) and also within the theory of the conditioned reflex. This trend makes the clarification of the meaning of field theory only the more important, because, I am afraid, those psychologists who, like myself, have been in favor of field theory for many years have not been very successful in making the essence of this theory clear. The only excuse I know of is that this matter is not very simple. Physics and philosophy do not seem to have done much analytical work about the meaning of field theory that could be helpful to the psychologist. In addition, methods like field theory can really be understood and mastered only in the same way as methods in a handcraft, namely, by learning them through practice.

Hilgard and Marquis (7), in a recent publication, quote from a letter of Clark Hull the following sentence: "As I see it, the moment one expresses in any very general manner the various potentialities of behavior as dependent upon the stimultaneous status of one or more variables, he has the substance of what is currently called field theory."

It is correct that field theory emphasizes the importance of the fact that any event is a resultant of a multitude of factors. The recognition of the necessity of a fair representation of this multitude of interdependent factors is a step in the direction toward field theory. However, this does not suffice. Field theory is something more specific.

To use an illustration: Success in a certain sport may depend upon a combination of muscular strength, velocity of movement, ability to make

---

* Reprinted from *Psychological Review*, 50, 1943, p. 292–310.

[1] This is the third paper given at a Symposium on Psychology and Scientific Method held as part of the Sixth International Congress for the Unity of Science, University of Chicago, September, 1941. The first paper is by Egon Brunswik and the second by C. L. Hull.

quick decisions, and precise perception of direction and distance. A change in any one of these five variables might alter the result to a certain degree. One can represent these variables as five dimensions of a diagram. The resultant of any possible constellation of these factors for the amount of success can be marked as a point in the diagram. The totality of these points then is a diagrammatic representation of this dependence, in other words, of an empirical law.

Physics frequently makes use of such representation of a multitude of factors influencing an event. To each of certain properties, such as temperature, pressure, time, spatial position, one dimension is coordinated. Such a representation in physics is called "phase space." Such a phase space may have twenty dimensions if twenty factors have to be considered. A phase space is something definitely different from that three-dimensional "physical space" within which physical objects are moving. In the same way the psychological space, the life space or psychological field, in which psychological locomotion or structural changes take place, is something different from those diagrams where dimensions mean merely gradations of properties.

In discussing these questions with a leading theoretical physicist, we agreed that the recognition of a multitude of factors as determining an event, and even their representation as a phase space, does not presuppose field theory. In psychology, Thurstone's factor analysis deals with such relations of various factors. Any character profile recognizes the multitude of factors. Field theorists and non-field theorists can both avail themselves of these useful devices, but not everybody who uses them is therefore a field theorist.

What is field theory? Is it a kind of very general theory? If one proceeds in physics from a special law or theory (such as the law of the free-falling body) to more general theories (such as the Newtonian laws) or still more general theories (such as the equations of Maxwell), one does *not* finally come to field theory. In other words, field theory can hardly be called a theory in the usual sense.

This fact becomes still more apparent when we consider the relation between the correctness or incorrectness of a theory and its character as a field theory. A special theory in physics or psychology may be a field theory, but nevertheless wrong. On the other hand, a description of what Hans Feigl calls an "empirical theory on the lowest level" may be correct without being field theory (although I do not believe that a theory on the higher levels of constructs can be correct in psychology without being field theory).

Field theory, therefore, can hardly be called correct or incorrect in the same way as a theory in the usual sense of the term. *Field theory is probably best characterized as a method: namely, a method of analyzing causal relations and of building scientific constructs.* This method of analyzing causal relations can be expressed in the form of certain general statements about the "nature" of the conditions of change. To what degree such a statement has an "analytical" (logical, *a priori*) and to what degree it has an "empirical" character do not need to be discussed here.

II. THE PRINCIPLE OF CONTEMPORANEITY AND THE EFFECT OF PAST AND FUTURE

One of the basic statements of psychological field theory can be formulated as follows: Any behavior or any other change in a psychological field depends only upon the psychological field *at that time*.

This principle has been stressed by the field theorists from the beginning. It has been frequently misunderstood and interpreted to mean that field theorists are not interested in historical problems or in the effect of previous experiences. Nothing can be more mistaken. In fact, field theorists are most interested in developmental and historical problems and have certainly done their share to enlarge the temporal scope of the psychological experiment from that of the classical reaction-time experiment, which lasts only a few seconds, to experimental situations, which contain a systematically created history through hours or weeks.

If a clarification of the field thoretical principle of contemporaneity could be achieved, it would, I feel, be most helpful for an understanding among the various schools in psychology.

The meaning of this far-reaching principle can be expressed rather easily by referring to its application in classical physics.

A change at the point x in the physical world is customarily characterized as $\dfrac{dx}{dt}$; that is to say, as a differential change in the position of x during a differential time-period dt. Field theory states that the change $\dfrac{dx}{dt}$ at the time t depends only on the situation S^t at that time t (Figure 1).

$$(1) \qquad\qquad \frac{dx}{dt} = F(S^t)$$

It does not depend, in addition, on past or future situations. In other words, the formula (1) is correct, but not the formula (1a).

$$(1a) \qquad dx = F(S^t) + F^1(S^{t-1}) + \cdots + F^2(S^{t+1}) + \cdots$$

Of course, there are cases in physics where one can state the relation between a change and a past situation S^{t-n} (where $t - n$ is a time not immediately preceding t; $|t - n| > dt$). In other words, there are occasions where it is technically possible to write:

$$(2) \qquad\qquad \frac{dx}{dt} = F(S^{t-n})$$

However, that is possible only if it is known how the later situation S^t depends on the previous situation S^{t-n}; in other words, if the function F in the equation

(3) $S^t = F(S^{t-n})$

is known. Such knowledge presupposes usually (a) that both situations are "closed systems" which are genidentic (11); (b) that the laws are known which deal with the change of all points of the previous situation S^{t-n} and also the laws dealing with the changes in the situations between the previous situation S^{t-n} and the later situation S.

The meaning of linking a change to a past situation by formula (2) might be clarified best by pointing out that it is possible in a similar way to link a present change to a future situation S^{t+n} and to write:

(2a) $\dfrac{dx}{dt} = F(S^{t+n})$

This is possible whenever we have to deal with a "closed system" during the time-period t until $t + n$, and if the laws of the on-going changes during this period are known.

The possibility of writing this functional equation does not mean that the future situation S^{t+1} is conceived of as a "condition" of the present change $\dfrac{dx}{dt}$. In fact, the same $\dfrac{dx}{dt}$ would occur if the closed system would be destroyed before the time $(t + n)$. In other words, the change $\dfrac{dx}{dt}$ depends on the situation (S^t) at that time only (in line with formula [1]). The technical possibility of expressing this change mathematically as a function of a future or a past time does not change this fact.[2]

The equivalent to $\dfrac{dx}{dt}$ in physics is the concept "behavior" in psychology, if we understand the term behavior to cover any change in the psychological field. The field theoretical principle of contemporaneity in psychology then means that the behavior b at the time t is a function of the situation S at the time t only (S is meant to include both the person and his psychological environment),

(4) $b^t = F(S^t)$

and not, in addition, a function of past or future situations S^{t-n} or S^{t+n} (Figure 2). Again, it is possible to relate the behavior b indirectly to either a past situation (S^{t-n}) or a future situation (S^{t+n}); but again, this can be done only if these situations are closed systems, and if the changes in the intermediate periods can be accounted for by known laws. It seems

---

[2] Frequently an occurrence is said to be caused by the "preceding conditions." This term seems to have been misunderstood by psychologists to refer to a distant past situation (S^{t-n}), although it should refer to the present situation, or at least to the "immediately preceding situation" (S^{t-dt}). We will come back to this question.

that psychologists are increasingly aware of the importance of this formula.

III. HOW TO DETERMINE THE PROPERTIES OF A FIELD AT A GIVEN TIME

If one has to derive behavior from the situation at that time, a way has to be found to *determine* the character of the "situation at a given time." This determination implies a number of questions which are, I think, interesting both psychologically and philosophically.

To determine the properties of a present situation or—to use a medical terminology—to make a diagnosis, one can follow two different procedures: One may base one's statement on conclusions from history (*anamneses*), or one may use diagnostic *tests of the present.*

To use a simple example: I wish to know whether the floor of the attic is sufficiently strong to carry a certain weight. I might try to gain this knowledge by finding out what material was used when the house was built ten years ago. As I get reliable reports that good material has been used, and that the architect was a dependable man, I might conclude that the load probably would be safe. If I can find the original blueprints, I might be able to do some exact figuring and feel still more safe.

Of course, there is always a chance that the workmen have actually not followed the blueprints, or that insects have weakened the woodwork, or that some rebuilding has been done during the last ten years. Therefore, I might decide to avoid these uncertain conclusions from past data and to determine the present strength of the floor by testing its strength now. Such a diagnostic test will not yield data which are absolutely certain; how reliable they are depends upon the quality of the available test and the carefulness of testing. However, the value of a present test is, from the point of view of methodology, superior to that of an *anamnesis.* An *anamnesis* includes logically two steps: namely, the testing of certain properties in the past (of the quality, size, and structure of the woodwork) and the proof that nothing unknown has interfered in the meantime; in other words that we have to deal with a "closed system." Even if a system is left untouched by the outside, inner changes occur. Therefore, in addition, the laws governing these inner changes have to be known (see above) if the properties of a situation are to be determined through an *anamnesis.*

Medicine, engineering, physics, biology are accustomed to use both methods, an inquiry into the past and a test of the present. But they prefer the latter whenever possible.[3]

---

[3] There are cases where a historical procedure is preferable. For instance, the hunger of a rat can probably be better determined by the duration of starvation than by a physiological or psychological test of the hunger at time *t.* This conclusion from the past to the present can be made, however, only during periods and in settings

Psychology has used diagnosis by *anamnesis* rather excessively, particularly in classical psychoanalysis and other clinical approaches to problems of personality. Psychology of perception and psychology of memory have been relatively free from the historical type of diagnosis. Experimental psychology, on the whole, has shown a progressive trend toward testing the present situation.

The method of determining the properties of a situation (S') by testing them at that time t avoids the uncertainties of historical conclusions. It does not follow, however, that this method eliminates considerations of time-periods altogether. A "situation at a given time" actually does not refer to a moment without time extension, but to a certain time-period. This fact is of great theoretical and methodological importance for psychology.

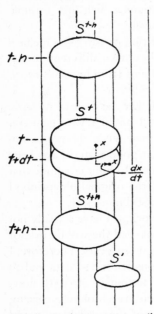

FIG. 1. S during $t - n$ until $t + n$ is a "closed system"; but S is not genidentic with S'.
$\frac{dx}{dt}$ indicates the velocity of x.

It may be helpful to go back for a moment to the procedure in physics. If the vertical lines in Figure 1 represent the so-called physical "worldlines," a "situation" means a cut through these lines at a given time t. A description of such a situation has to include (1) the relative position of the parts of the field at that time; (2) the direction and the velocity of the changes going on at that time. The first task is fulfilled by ascribing certain scalar values to the different entities; the second, by ascribing certain vectors to them. The second task contains a difficulty which I would like to discuss.

To describe the direction and velocity of a change going on at a given moment, it is necessary to refer to a certain period of events. Ideally, a time-differential should suffice for such determination. Actually, one has to observe a macroscopic time-interval or at least the position at the beginning and at the end of such interval to determine that time-differential. In the simplest case the velocity at a given time is assumed to equal the average velocity during that macroscopic time-interval. I will not attempt to follow up the details of this procedure in physics. If sufficient laws are known, certain indirect methods like those based on the Doppler effect permit different procedures.

---

where a "closed system" (no interference from outside) can be enforced; e.g., for animals which during this period do the same amount of work, which have been on a known diet, etc. The difficulties of this type of control have led Skinner (19) to link the problem of drive strength to properties of present consumption.

However, it remains a basic fact that the adequate description of a situation at a moment is impossible without observation of a certain time-period. This observation has to be interpreted (according to the "most plausible" assumption and our knowledge of the physical laws) in a way which permits its transformation into a statement of the "state of affairs at the time t."

In psychology a similar problem exists. The person at a given time may be in the midst of saying "a." Actually such a statement implies already that a certain time-interval is observed. Otherwise, only a certain position of mouth and body could be recorded. Usually the psychologist will not be satisfied with such a characterization of the ongoing process. He likes to know whether this "a" belongs to the word "can" or "apple" or to what word it does belong. If the word was "can," the psychologist wants to know whether the person was going to say: "I cannot come back" or "I can stand on my head if I have to." The psychologist even likes to know whether the sentence is spoken to an intimate friend as a part of a conversation about personal plans for the future or whether this sentence is part of a political address and has the meaning of an attempt to retreat from an untenable political position.

In other words, an adequate psychological description of the character and the direction of an ongoing process can and has to be done on various microscopic and macroscopic levels. To each "size of a unit of behavior" a different "size of situation" can be coordinated. That the individual in our example is saying "a," can be made sure without taking into account much of the surrounding of the individual. To characterize the sentence as a part of a political retreat, much more of the surrounding has to be considered.

Without altering the principle of contemporaneity as one of the basic propositions of field theory, we have to realize that to determine the psychological direction and velocity of behavior (*i.e.*, what is usually called the "meaning" of the psychological event), we have to take into account in psychology as in physics a certain time-period. The length of this period depends in psychology upon the scope of the situation. As a rule, the more macroscopic the situation is which has to be described the longer is the period which has to be observed to determine the direction and velocity of behavior at a given time (Figure 2).

In other words, we are dealing in psychology with "situational units" which have to be conceived of as having an extension in regard to their field dimensions and their time dimensions. If I am not mistaken, the problem of time-space-quanta, which is so important for modern quantum theory in physics (17), is methodologically parallel (although, of course, on a more advanced level) to the problem of "time-field-units" in psychology.

The concept of situations of different scope has proved to be very helpful in solving a number of otherwise rather puzzling problems. Tolman (20), Muenzinger (16), and Floyd Allport (1), have stressed that a psychological description has to include the macroscopic as well as the microscopic events. Barker, Dembo, and Lewin (2) distinguish and treat mathematically three sizes of units of processes and corresponding sizes of

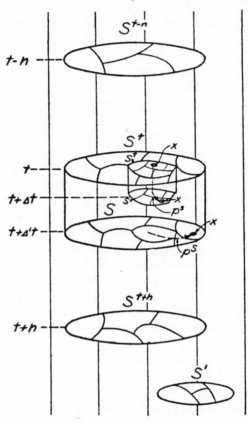

FIG. 2. S during $t - n$ until $t + n$ is a "closed system"; but S is not genidentic with S'. $s^{t, \ t+\Delta t}$ is a small time-field-unit which extends over a relatively small area and includes the relatively small time-period t until $t + \Delta t$. $S^{t, \ t+\Delta' t}$ is a larger time-field-unit covering a larger area and including the longer period t until $t + \Delta' t$. p^s and p^S indicate the change in position of x during the small and the large time unit.

situations. They have handled certain problems of measuring the strength of frustration during extended periods by referring to overlapping situations in regard to two different sizes of time-field-units. Lippitt and White (15), in their study of social atmosphere, distinguish still larger periods of events. They have shown that the beginning and end of these macroscopic units can be determined rather precisely and with very satisfactory reliability. However, I will not discuss these questions here where we are interested in methodological problems only.

IV. THE PSYCHOLOGICAL PAST, PRESENT, AND FUTURE AS PARTS OF A PSYCHOLOGICAL FIELD AT A GIVEN TIME

The clarification of the problem of past and future has been much delayed by the fact that the psychological field which exists at a given time contains also the views of that individual about his future and past. The individual sees not only his present situation; he has certain expectations, wishes, fears, daydreams for his future. His views about his own past and that of the rest of the physical and social world are often incorrect, but nevertheless constitute, in his life space, the "reality-level" of the past. In addition, a wish-level in regard to the past can frequently be observed. The discrepancy between the structure of this wish- or irreality-level of the psychological past and the reality-level plays an important role for the phenomenon of guilt. The structure of the psychological future is closely related, for instance, to hope and planning (2).

Following a terminology of L. K. Frank (6), we speak of "time perspective" which includes the psychological past and psychological future on the reality-level and on the various irreality-levels. The time perspective existing at a given time has been shown to be very important for many problems such as the level of aspiration, the mood, the constructiveness, and the initiative of the individual. Farber (4) has shown, for instance, that the amount of suffering of a prisoner depends more on his expectation in regard to his release, which may be five years ahead, than on the pleasantness or unpleasantness of his present occupation.

It is important to realize that the psychological past and the psychological future are simultaneous parts of the psychological field existing at a given time t. The time perspective is continually changing. According to field theory, any type of behavior depends upon the total field, including the time perspective at that time, but not, in addition, upon any past or future field and its time perspectives.

It may be illustrative to consider briefly from this field theoretical point of view the methodological problems connected with one of the basic concepts of the conditioned reflex theory, namely, the concept of "extinction." An individual has experienced that after a certain stimulus, let us say the ringing of a bell, food will appear. Being hungry, the individual eats. After a number of such experiences, the individual will show certain preparatory actions for eating as soon as the eating bell rings. The individual is then said to be "conditioned." Now, the situation is secretly changed by the experimenter and the eating bell is not followed by food. After a while the individual catches on and does not show the preparatory action for food when the bell rings. This process is called "extinction."

"Habits" of a person at a given time can and have to be treated as parts of the present field. Whether they should be represented partly as cognitive structure or resistance to change of cognitive structure, partly as a building up or fixation of valences (13), or whether they have to be conceptualized in other ways is not a problem here. Habits of action (18, 14), as well as of thinking, are dealt with in field theoretical research. They are closely related to problems of ideology (9) and expectation.

As Tolman (20), Hilgard and Marquis (7), and others have correctly pointed out, conditioning as well as extinction are both related to changes in the reality level of the psychological future. Field theorists have to distinguish in regard to conditioning and extinction two types of problems. The one type deals with such a question as how expectation is affected by perception on the one hand, and memory on the other. What changes in the perceived structure of the psychological present lead to a change in the structure of the psychological future, and what are the laws governing the interdependence of these two parts of the psychological field? The studies on level of aspiration have provided some knowledge about the factors which influence the structure of the future reality-level. Korsch-Escalona (10) has made a step toward a mathematical treatment of the effect of the future reality-level on the forces which govern present behavior. Study of the level of aspiration has also given us considerable insight into the effect of the psychological past (namely of previous success or failure) on the psychological future. This question is obviously closely related to extinction.

The methodological position of these types of problems is clear: They deal with the interdependence of various parts of the psychological field existing at a given time t. In other words, they are legitimate field theoretical questions of the type $b^t = F(S^t)$.

The second type of questions, treated in the theory of conditioned reflex, tries to relate a later situation S^4, (for instance, during extinction) to a previous situation S^1 during learning or to a number of similar or different previous situations S^1, S^2, S^3, $\cdots$: it relates behavior to the number of repetitions. In other words, these questions have the form $b^t = F(S^{t-n})$ or $b^t = F(S^{t-n}, S^{t-m}, \cdots)$. Here field theory demands a more critical and more analytical type of thinking. One should distinguish at least two types of problems:

(a) How the perceived psychological situation will look at the time S^4 depends obviously upon whether or not the experimenter will provide food and on similar external physical or social conditions. Everybody will agree, I suppose, that these factors cannot possibly be derived from the psychological field of the individual at the previous time, even if all the psychological laws were known. These factors are alien to psychology.

(b) There remain, however, legitimate psychological questions in this second type of problem. We can keep the boundary conditions of a life space constant or change them in a known way during a certain period and investigate what would happen under those conditions. These problems lie definitely within the domain of psychology. An example is the problem of restructurization of memory traces. We know that these processes depend on the state of the individual during the total period S^{t-n} until S^t (Figure 2) and are different, for instance, during sleep and while being awake. Doubtless the experiments on conditioned reflex have given us a wealth of material in regard to this type of problem. They will have to be treated finally in the way which we discussed in the beginning, namely, as a sequence of relations between a situation S^t and the immediately following situation S^{t+dt}.

On the whole, I think the psychological trend is definitely going in this direction. For instance, the goal gradient theory has been formulated originally as a relation between behavior and past situations. Straight, analytical thinking demands that such a statement should be broken up into several propositions (12), one of which has to do with the intensity of goal striving as a function of the distance between individual and goal. This is identical with a statement about certain force fields and is probably correct. A second proposition implied in the goal gradient theory links the present behavior to the past situation S^{t-n}. The specific form is, to my mind, unsatisfactory. But even if it should be correct, it should be treated as an independent theory. Hull's formulation of a "Gradient of Reinforcement Hypothesis" is a step in this direction.

V. PSYCHOLOGICAL ECOLOGY

As an elaboration of our considerations, I would like to discuss some aspects of Brunswik's treatment of the role of statistics (3). I do not expect ever to live down the misunderstandings created by my attack on some ways in which statistics have been used in psychology. I have been always aware that quantitative measurement demands statistics (see Hull's answer to Brunswik [8]). That statement holds also for "pure cases"; i.e., situations where it is possible to link theory and observable facts in a definite way. Since psychology is increasingly abandoning the inadequate objectives of statistics, further discussion might have little pragmatic value.

However, Brunswik has brought into the open new and important aspects, and I feel that their clarification may be helpful for psychological methodology in general.

Within the realm of facts existing at a given time one can distinguish three areas in which changes are or might be of interest to psychology:

1. The "life space"; i.e., the person and the psychological environment as it exists for him. We usually have this field in mind if we refer to needs, motivation, mood, goals, anxiety, ideals.

2. A multitude of processes in the physical or social world, which do not affect the life space of the individual at that time.

3. A "boundary zone" of the life space: certain parts of the physical or social world do affect the state of the life space at that time. The process of perception, for instance, is intimately linked with this boundary zone because what is perceived is partly determined by the physical "stimuli"; i.e., that part of the physical world which affects the sensory organs at that time. Another process located in the boundary zone is the "execution" of an action.

Brunswik states correctly (3, p. 266): "The 'field' within which Lewin is able to predict, in the strict sense of the word, is the person in his life space." Then he proceeds, "But the life space is not to be confused with geographic environment of physical stimuli, nor with actually achieved results in the environment. It is post-perceptual, and pre-behavioral." This statement is partly incorrect, namely, insofar as perception and behavior, to my mind, are legitimate problems of psychology. This view is a necessary consequence of the field theoretical approach according to which the boundary conditions of a field are essential characteristics of that field. For instance, processes of perception which should be related to the boundary zone depend partly on the state of the inner part of the psychological field; i.e., upon the character of the person, his motivation, his cognitive structure, his way of perceiving, etc., partly on the "stimulus distribution" on the retina or other receptors as enforced by physical processes outside the organism. For the same reasons, the problems of physical or social action are legitimate parts of psychology proper.

Brunswik, however, is correct in assuming that I do not consider as a part of the psychological field at a given time those sections of the physical or social world which do not affect the life space of the person at that time. The food that lies behind doors at the end of a maze so that neither smell nor sight can reach it is not a part of the life space of the animal. In case the individual knows that food lies there this *knowledge*, of course, has to be represented in his life space, because this knowledge affects behavior. It is also necessary to take into account the subjective probability with which the individual views the present or future state of affairs because the degree of certainty of expectation also influences his behavior.

The principle of representing within the life space all that affects behavior at that time, but nothing else, prevents the inclusion of physical food which is not perceived. This food cannot possibly influence his behavior at that time under the conditions mentioned. Indeed, the individual will start his journey if he thinks the food is there even if it is actually not there, and he will not move toward the food which actually is at the end of the maze if he doesn't know it is there.

In the past this principle has not always been adhered to in animal psychology but it seems to me so obvious that I had assumed all psychologists agreed on this point. Statements which could be interpreted otherwise I had regarded as loose terminology rather than an expression of differences of opinion until I listened to Brunswik's paper. The discussion following this paper seems to have brought out the issue still more clearly and it will be appropriate, I hope, to refer to this discussion.

According to Brunswik, it is possible to think in terms of laws rather than mere statistical rules if one limits the psychological field in the way described. However, he claims that for this gain one has to pay "the price of an encapsulation" into a realm of problems which actually leaves out the most dynamic aspects of psychology. He wishes to include in the psychological field those parts of the physical and sociological world which, to my mind, have to be excluded. These parts, he states, have to be studied in a statistical way, and the probability of the occurrence of events calculated.

To my mind, the main issue is what the term "probability" refers to. Does Brunswik want to study the ideas of the driver of a car about the probability of being killed or does he want to study the accident statistics which tell the "objective probability" of such an event. If an individual sits in a room trusting that the ceiling will not come down, should only his "subjective probability" be taken into account for predicting behavior or should we also consider the "objective probability" of the ceiling's coming down as determined by the engineers. To my mind, only the first has to be taken into account, but to my inquiry, Brunswik answered that he meant also the latter.

I can see why psychology should be interested even in those areas of the physical and social world which are not part of the life space or which do not affect its boundary zone at present. If one wishes to safeguard a child's education during the next years, if one wishes to predict in what situation an individual will find himself as a result of a certain action, one will have to calculate this future. Obviously, such forecast has to be based partly on statistical considerations about non-psychological data.

Theoretically, we can characterize this task as discovering what part of the physical or social world will determine during a given period the "boundary zone" of the life space. This task is worth the interest of the psychologists. I would suggest calling it "psychological ecology."

Some problems of the "life history" of an individual have their places here. The boundary conditions of the life space during long- as well as short-time periods depend partly on the action of the individual himself. To this degree they should be linked to the psychological dynamics of the life space. The rest of the calculation has to be done, however, with other than psychological means.

The essence of explaining or predicting any change in a certain area is the linkage of that change with the conditions of the field at that time. This basic principle makes the subjective probability of an event a part of the life space of that individual. But it excludes the objective probability of alien factors that cannot be derived from the life space.

REFERENCES

1. ALLPORT, F. H. "Methods in the Study of Collective Action Phenomena," *J. soc. Psychol.*, SPSSI Bulletin, 1942, 15, pp. 165–85.
2. BARKER, R., DEMBO, T., & LEWIN, K. "Frustration and Regression; Studies in Topological and Vector Psychology II," *Univ. Ia Stud. Child Welf.*, 1941, 18, pp. 1–314.

3. Brunswik, E. "Organismic Achievement and Environmental Probability," *Psychol. Rev.*, 1943, 50, pp. 255–72.

4. Farber, M. L. "Imprisonment as a Psychological Situation," Unpublished Ph.D. Thesis, State Univ. Iowa, 1940.

5. Festinger, L. "A Theoretical Interpretation of Shifts in Level of Aspiration," *Psychol. Rev.*, 1942, 49, pp. 235–50.

6. Frank, L. K. "Time Perspectives," *J. soc. Phil.*, 1939, 4, pp. 293–312.

7. Hilgard, E. R., & Marquis, D. G. *Conditioning and Learning*. New York, London: D. Appleton-Century Co., 1940.

8. Hull, C. L. "The Problem of Intervening Variables in Molar Behavior Theory," *Psychol. Rev.*, 1943, 50, pp. 273–91.

9. Kalhorn, J. "Ideological Differences among Rural Children." Unpublished Master's Thesis, State Univ. Iowa, 1941.

10. Korsch-Escalona, S. "The Effect of Success and Failure upon the Level of Aspiration and Behavior in Manic-Depressive Psychoses. *In* Lewin, K., Lippit, R., & Korsch-Escalona, S., "Studies in Topological and Vector Psychology I," *Univ. Ia. Stud. Child Welf.*, 1939, 16, No. 3, pp. 199–303.

11. Lewin, K. *Der Begriff der Genese in Physik, Biologie und Entwicklungsgeschichte.* [The Concept of Genesis in Physics, Biology and Theory of Evolution.] Berlin: Julius Springer, 1922.

12. ———. "The Conceptual Representation and the Measurement of Psychological Forces," *Contr. Psychol. Theor.*, 1938, 1, No. 4, pp. 247.

13. ———. "Field Theory and Learning." In *41st Yearbook of the National Society for the Study of Education*, Part II, 1942, pp. 215–39.

14. ———. *The Relative Effectiveness of a Lecture Method and a Method of Group Decision for Changing Food Habits.* Committee on Food Habits, National Research Council, 1942.

15. Lippitt, R. "An Experimental Study of the Effect of Democratic and Authoritarian Group Atmospheres." *Univ. Ia. Stud. Child Welf.*, 1940, 16, No. 3, pp. 44–195.

16. Muenzinger, K. F. *Psychology: The Science of Behavior.* Denver: World Press, 1939, pp. 270.

17. Reichenbach, H. *From Copernicus to Einstein.* New York: Alliance Book Corp., New York Philosophical Library, 1942.

18. Schwarz, G. IV. Über Ruckfalligkeit bei Umgewohnung. I, II. [On Relapses in Re-learning.] *Psychol. Forsch.*, 1927, 9, pp. 86–158; 1933, 18, pp. 143–190.

19. Skinner, B. F. *The Behavior of Organisms; An Experimental Analysis.* New York: D. Appleton-Century Co., 1938.

20. Tolman, E. C. *Purposive Behavior in Animals and Men.* New York: Century Co., 1932, pp. xiv, 463.

SECTION TWO

Organizational Structure and Process

THEORIZING about organizations can be approached from different points of view. A statesman, a sociologist, or a business executive concerned with long-range planning would be interested in the relations between organizations and in the place of an organization within the entire society. On the other hand, an administrative technician, such as an accountant, personnel officer, production manager, etc., is more interested in the details of a single process in the internal workings of the organization—the way it relates to other areas and the functions performed. Intermediate between these is the general executive, who needs to know how the technical processes are put together to form a whole capable of successful adaptation to its environment and how the necessary co-ordination is achieved. The types of theories that each would find useful would be different, but, ideally, interrelated with one another. In this section we consider theories of the gross aspects of organization, the organization as an entity, the organization adjusting to its environment and evolving in accordance with the environmental possibilities and under internal and external pressures. In considering these theories it is illuminating to review briefly some of the traditions that influence our thinking about organization.

The traditional sequence in social organization is family, extended kin-group, tribe, and nation. The traditional organizational form is the simple hierarchy headed by father, patriarch, chief, or king. In this system all subordinates hold power only by virtue of their relationship to the head man, and the organization is a personal possession of the ruler, whose power and discretion are absolute. This organizational system existed less in practice than in theory. Even in ancient times subordinates were able to arrange some form of protection for themselves against the caprice of their ruler, and democratic forms also appeared very early in history. Nevertheless, most writing on organization and administration, even today, has begun with the presumption of the simple authority relationship. In its modern guise, this analysis is often legalistic in form: that is, the authors postulate certain rights and obligations and then analyze the ways in which these should be disposed of so as to achieve the objectives at hand. In governmental affairs the rights of sovereignty and the rights and duties of citizenship have played the major role; in business, the rights of ownership and the nexus of contractual obligations are paramount. The traditional literature on administration, likewise, builds on the authority relation as the raw material of organization. These legalistic theories are, however, unsuited to describe, explain or predict human affairs, although they have often proved their usefulness as tools for inspiring and guiding the conduct of human affairs.

Gradually, the outlines of a scientific theory of organization have emerged. One of the pioneers in this development was Max Weber (1864–1920). Although his style of writing is often ponderously legalistic, the content is descriptive of the institutions of "bureaucracy," as Weber found them, and of their effects on the conduct of affairs. The term *institution* is used here to mean any habitual way of thinking, perceiving, or valuing generally shared by the participants. The term *bureaucracy* as used by Weber and by subsequent students of organization is not intended to have any derogatory connotations. It is a technical term used to refer to a particular style or "ideal type" of organization. The student should take care not to mix his values with the facts presented by Weber until he has thoroughly explored them. Aside from its historical and methodological importance, the essay reproduced in this section provides the student with a good opportunity to appraise the evolution of both our social institutions and our theories about them.

A logical extension of Weber's ideas about bureaucracy concerns the effect of the social and institutional context in which the organization exists. The nature of this effect and the process by which it is fulfilled are discussed in the excerpt "Ideology in Organizations" by Philip Selznick, a sociologist who, along with Robert K. Merton, has worked in the tradition of Max Weber. Selznick is referring primarily to ideas shared by all or a powerful segment of the people in a society as a force helping to mold the more limited set of institutions peculiar to any individual organization.

Selznick's analysis of ideological influence is compatible with Lewin's "field theory" in that it postulates an organization "boundary" and treats the organization as a system adapting to outside, exogenous forces. Social values are only one such force. Economic fluctuations, political intrigues, and technical changes are equally susceptible of analysis of this type. In "TVA and the Grass Roots, Guiding Principles and Interpretation," Selznick discusses the finer structure of organizational adaptation.

Just as Weber is concerned with the static, institutional, and formal structure of bureaucracies and Selznick with the dynamics of adaptation, Chester I. Barnard, an eminently successful corporation executive with a theoretical bent, directs the emphasis of his theory of co-operation and organization toward the *equilibrium* tendencies of organizations. Barnard's viewpoint is essentially the converse of Selznick's: Selznick looks for forces that change the organization; Barnard looks for reasons for the persistence of organizational characteristics. The most important addition of Barnard's theory to the observations of Weber is the consideration of the role of the *members* (employees, proprietors, and clientele) of the organization. This is implicit in the notion of *efficiency* and in the role of the *informal organization* in maintaining a balance or steady-state within the organization and with the outside world. An *efficient* organization is one in which the members are receiving sufficient perceived benefits to assure their continued participation; *informal organization* is the total of member-initiated institutions existing without the sanction of formal authority.

This line of thought is concretely illustrated in the findings of A. B. Horsfall and C. M. Arensberg in their observational study of shoe factory work teams. They verified the existence of an organized work system in the observed team that was at variance with the management's express intentions. Various instances of informal organization are also reported by Melville Dalton in "Managing the Managers." Like Barnard, Dalton is an example of a practitioner turned theoretician. Unlike Barnard, Dalton left industry early and is making an academic career. The research presented here was begun while he was still employed in the plant in question.

The processes of adaptation (formal and informal) are illustrated and developed further in the study by Dalton and in the work reported by Robert Chapman, John L. Kennedy, and Milton G. Weiner. The latter work, a study of an air defense control center, is almost unique in the research technique used. Unlike most studies of organization, which rely heavily on reports by participants and uncontrolled observations, this study involved the creation in a laboratory and under experimental control of an organizational unit of moderate size. The designers of the experiment are applied psychologists concerned with the engineering of man-machine systems, in this case under a RAND Corporation contract with the Air Force. The cost of studies of this type is high; nevertheless, this general methodology has been used in additional investigations by RAND and is part of the program of the System Development Corporation, an offshoot of RAND, for further development of air defense systems.

The concluding piece in this chapter, "Comments on the Theory of Organizations," by Herbert A. Simon is a theoretical overview of the field of organizational theory as of 1952. It also serves as a transition to our problem areas of Leadership and Morale, Communication, Control and Evaluation, and Decision Making, which deal with the subprocesses of organization and require "lower level" theories than are appropriate for this section.

Many of the questions discussed in this article have provided the basis for subsequent research by Simon's own organizational behavior group at the Carnegie Institute of Technology. This group has produced a substantial fraction of the work in the field during the last ten years, especially in theory development and formalization. Among their contributions is *Organizations* by J. G. March and H. A. Simon (Wiley, 1959), the best survey of organization theory to date and a recommended follow-up to the present volume. Some of the specific studies from the Carnegie Tech group are included or discussed in later sections.

REFERENCES

1. GOULDNER, A. *Patterns of Industrial Bureaucracy.* Glencoe, Ill.: Free Press, 1954.
2. JAQUES, E. *The Changing Culture of a Factory.* New York: Dryden, 1952.
3. MERTON, R. K. *et al.* (eds.). *Reader in Bureaucracy.* Glencoe, Ill.: Free Press, 1952.
4. SELZNICK, P. *Leadership in Administration.* Evanston, Ill.: Rowe Peterson, 1957.

4. BUREAUCRACY*

Max Weber

1. CHARACTERISTICS OF BUREAUCRACY

Modern officialdom functions in the following specific manner:

I. There is the principle of fixed and official jurisdictional areas, which are generally ordered by rules, that is, by laws or administrative regulations.

1. The regular activities required for the purposes of the bureaucratically governed structure are distributed in a fixed way as official duties.

2. The authority to give the commands required for the discharge of these duties is distributed in a stable way and is strictly delimited by rules concerning the coercive means, physical, sacerdotal, or otherwise, which may be placed at the disposal of officials.

3. Methodical provision is made for the regular and continuous fulfilment of these duties and for the execution of the corresponding rights; only persons who have the generally regulated qualifications to serve are employed.

In public and lawful government these three elements constitute "bureaucratic authority." In private economic domination, they constitute "bureaucratic management." Bureaucracy, thus understood, is fully developed in political and ecclesiastical communities only in the modern state, and, in the private economy, only in the most advanced institutions of capitalism. Permanent and public office authority, with fixed jurisdiction, is not the historical rule but rather the exception. This is so even in large political structures such as those of the ancient Orient, the Germanic and Mongolian empires of conquest, or of many feudal structures of state. In all these cases, the ruler executes the most important measures through personal trustees, table-companions, or court-servants. Their commissions and authority are not precisely delimited and are temporarily called into being for each case.

II. The principles of office hierarchy and of levels of graded authority mean a firmly ordered system of super- and subordination in which there is a supervision of the lower offices by the higher ones. Such a system offers the governed the possibility of appealing the decision of a lower office to its higher authority, in a definitely regulated manner. With the full development of the bureaucratic type, the office hierarchy is monocratically organized. The principle of hierarchial office authority is found in

* From *From Max Weber* by H. H. Gerth and C. Wright Mills. A Galaxy Book. Copyright 1946 by Oxford University Press, Inc. Reproduced by permission.

all bureaucratic structures: in state and ecclesiastical structures as well as in large party organizations and private enterprises. It does not matter for the character of bureaucracy whether its authority is called "private" or "public."

When the principle of jurisdictional "competency" is fully carried through, hierarchial subordination—at least in public office—does not mean that the "higher" authority is simply authorized to take over the business of the "lower." Indeed, the opposite is the rule. Once established and having fulfilled its task, an office tends to continue in existence and be held by another incumbent.

III. The management of the modern office is based upon written documents ("the files"), which are preserved in their original or draught form. There is, therefore, a staff of subaltern officials and scribes of all sorts. The body of officials actively engaged in a "public" office, along with the respective apparatus of material implements and the files, make up a "bureau." In private enterprise, "the bureau" is often called "the office."

In principle, the modern organization of the civil service separates the bureau from the private domicile of the official, and, in general, bureaucracy segregates official activity as something distinct from the sphere of private life. Public monies and equipment are divorced from the private property of the official. This condition is everywhere the product of a long development. Nowadays, it is found in public as well as in private enterprises; in the latter, the principle extends even to the leading entrepreneur. In principle, the executive office is separated from the household, business from private correspondence, and business assets from private fortunes. The more consistently the modern type of business management has been carried through, the more are these separations the case. The beginnings of this process are to be found as early as the Middle Ages.

It is the peculiarity of the modern entrepreneur that he conducts himself as the "first official" of his enterprise, in the very same way in which the ruler of a specifically modern bureaucratic state spoke of himself as "the first servant" of the state.[1] The idea that the bureau activities of the state are intrinsically different in character from the management of private economic offices is a continental European notion and, by way of contrast, is totally foreign to the American way.

IV. Office management, at least all specialized office management—and such management is distinctly modern—usually presupposes thorough and expert training. This increasingly holds for the modern executive and employee of private enterprises, in the same manner as it holds for the state official.

V. When the office is fully developed, official activity demands the full working capacity of the official, irrespective of the fact that his ob-

---

[1] Frederick II of Prussia.

ligatory time in the bureau may be firmly delimited. In the normal case, this is only the product of a long development, in the public as well as in the private office. Formerly, in all cases, the normal state of affairs was reversed: official business was discharged as a secondary activity.

VI. The management of the office follows general rules, which are more or less stable, more or less exhaustive, and which can be learned. Knowledge of these rules represents a special technical learning which the officials possess. It involves jurisprudence, or administrative or business management.

The reduction of modern office management to rules is deeply embedded in its very nature. The theory of modern public administration, for instance, assumes that the authority to order certain matters by decree —which has been legally granted to public authorities—does not entitle the bureau to regulate the matter by commands given for each case, but only to regulate the matter abstractly. This stands in extreme contrast for the regulation of all relationships through individual privileges and bestowals of favor, which is absolutely dominant in patrimonialism, at least in so far as such relationships are not fixed by sacred tradition.

2. THE POSITION OF THE OFFICIAL

All this results in the following for the internal and external position of the official:

I. Office holding is a "vocation." This is shown, first, in the requirement of a firmly prescribed course of training, which demands the entire capacity for work for a long period of time, and in the generally prescribed and special examinations which are prerequisites of employment. Furthermore, the position of the official is in the nature of a duty. This determines the internal structure of his relations, in the following manner: Legally and actually, office holding is not considered a source to be exploited for rents or emoluments, as was normally the case during the Middle Ages and frequently up to the threshold of recent times. Nor is office holding considered a usual exchange of services for equivalents, as is the case with free labor contracts. Entrance into an office, including one in the private economy, is considered an acceptance of a specific obligation of faithful management in return for a secure existence. It is decisive for the specific nature of modern loyalty to an office that, in the pure type, it does not establish a relationship to a person, like the vassal's or disciple's faith in feudal or in patrimonial relations of authority. Modern loyalty is devoted to impersonal and functional purposes. Behind the functional purposes, of course, "ideas of culture-values" usually stand. These are *ersatz* for the earthly or supra-mundane personal master: ideas such as "state," "church," "community," "party," or "enterprise" are thought of as being realized in a community; they provide an ideological halo for the master. . . .

II. The personal position of the official is patterned in the following way:

1. Whether he is in a private office or a public bureau, the modern official always strives and usually enjoys a distinct social esteem as compared with the governed. His social position is guaranteed by the prescriptive rules of rank order and, for the political official, by special definitions of the criminal code against "insults of official" and "contempt" of state and church authorities.

The actual social position of the official is normally highest where, as in old civilized countries, the following conditions prevail: a strong demand for administration by trained experts; a strong and stable social differentiation, where the official predominantly derives from socially and economically privileged strata because of the social distribution of power; or where the costliness of the required training and status conventions are binding upon him. The possession of educational certificates—to be discussed elsewhere[2]—are usually linked with qualification for office. Naturally, such certificates or patents enhance the "status element" in the social position of the official. For the rest this status factor in individual cases is explicitly and impassively acknowledged; for example, in the prescription that the acceptance or rejection of an aspirant to an official career depends upon the consent ("election") of the members of the official body. This is the case in the German army with the officer corps. Similar phenomena, which promote this guild-like closure of officialdom, are typically found in patrimonial and, particularly, in prebendal officialdoms of the past. The desire to resurrect such phenomena in changed forms is by no means infrequent among modern bureaucrats. For instance, they have played a role among the demands of the quite proletarian and expert officials (the *tretyj* element) during the Russian revolution.

Usually the social esteem of the officials as such is especially low where the demand for expert administration and the dominance of status conventions are weak. This is especially the case in the United States; it is often the case in new settlements by virtue of their wide fields for profit-making and the great instability of their social stratification.

2. The pure type of bureaucratic official is appointed by a superior authority. An official elected by the governed is not a purely bureaucratic figure. Of course, the formal existence of an election does not by itself mean that no appointment hides behind the election—in the state, especially, appointment by party chiefs. Whether or not this is the case does not depend upon legal statutes but upon the way in which the party mechanism functions. Once firmly organized, the parties can turn a formally free election into the mere acclamation of a candidate designated

---

[2] Cf. *Wirtschaft und Gesellschaft*, pp. 73 ff. and Part II. (German editor's note.)

by the party chief. As a rule, however, a formally free election is turned into a fight, conducted according to definite rules, for votes in favor of one of two designated candidates.

In all circumstances, the designation of officials by means of an election among the governed modifies the strictness of hierarchical subordination. In principle, an official who is so elected has an autonomous position opposite the superordinate official. The elected official does not derive his position "from above" but "from below," or at least not from a superior authority of the official hierarchy but from powerful party men ("bosses"), who also determine his further career. The career of the elected official is not, or at least not primarily, dependent upon his chief in the administration. The official who is not elected but appointed by a chief normally functions more exactly from a technical point of view, because, all other circumstances being equal, it is more likely that purely functional points of consideration and qualities will determine his selection and career. As laymen, the governed can become acquainted with the extent to which a candidate is expertly qualified for office only in terms of experience, and hence only after his service. Moreover, in every sort of selection of officials by election, parties quite naturally give decisive weight not to expert considerations but to the services a follower renders to the party boss. This holds for all kinds of procurement of officials by elections, for the designation of formally free, elected officials by party bosses when they determine the slate of candidates, or the free appointment by a chief who has himself been elected. The contrast, however, is relative; substantially similar conditions hold where legitimate monarchs and their subordinates appoint officials, except that the influence of the following are then less controllable.

Where the demand for administration by trained experts is considerable, and the party followings have to recognize an intellectually developed, educated, and freely moving "public opinion," the use of unqualified officials falls back upon the party in power at the next election. Naturally, this is more likely to happen when the officials are appointed by the chief. The demand for a trained administration now exists in the United States, but in the large cities where immigrant votes are "corraled," there is, of course, no educated public opinion. Therefore, popular elections of the administrative chief and also of his subordinate officials usually endanger the expert qualification of the official as well as the precise functioning of the bureaucratic mechanism. It also weakens the dependence of the officials upon the hierarchy. This holds at least for the large administrative bodies that are difficult to supervise. The superior qualification and integrity of federal judges, appointed by the President, as over against elected judges in the United States is well known, although both types of officials have been selected primarily in terms of party considerations. The great changes in American metropolitan administrations demanded by reformers have proceeded essentially from elected mayors working with an apparatus of officials who were appointed by them. These reforms have thus come about in a "Caesarist" fashion. Viewed technically, as an organized form of authority, the efficiency of "Caesarism," which often grows out of democracy, rests in general upon the position of the "Caesar" as a free trustee of the masses (of the army or of the citizenry), who is unfettered by tradition. The "Caesar" is thus the unrestrained master of a body of highly qualified military officers and officials whom he selects freely and personally without regard to tradition or to any other considerations. This "rule of the personal genius," however, stands in contradiction to the formally "democratic" principle of a universally elected officialdom.

3. Normally, the position of the official is held for life, at least in public bureaucracies; and this is increasingly the case for all similar structures. As a factual rule, tenure for life is presupposed even where the giving of notice or periodic reappointment occurs. In contrast to the worker in a private enterprise, the official normally holds tenure. Legal or actual life-tenure, however, is not recognized as the official's right to the possession of office, as was the case with many structures of authority in the past. Where legal guarantees against arbitrary dismissal or transfer are developed, they merely serve to guarantee a strictly objective discharge of specific office duties free from all personal considerations. In Germany, this is the case for all juridical and, increasingly, for all administrative officials.

Within the bureaucracy, therefore, the measure of "independence," legally guaranteed by tenure, is not always a source of increased status for the official whose position is thus secured. Indeed, often the reverse holds, especially in old cultures and communities that are highly differentiated. In such communities, the stricter the subordination under the arbitrary rule of the master, the more it guarantees the maintenance of the conventional seigneurial style of living for the official. Because of the very absence of these legal guarantees of tenure, the conventional esteem for the official may rise in the same way as, during the Middle Ages, the esteem of the nobility of office[3] rose at the expense of esteem for the freemen, and as the king's judge surpassed that of the people's judge. In Germany, the military officer or the administrative official can be removed from office at any time, or at least far more readily than the "independent judge," who never pays with loss of his office for even the grossest offense against the "code of honor" or against social conventions of the salon. For this very reason, if other things are equal, in the eyes of the master stratum the judge is considered less qualified for social intercourse than are officers and administrative officials, whose greater dependence on the master is a greater guarantee of their conformity with status conventions. Of course, the average official strives for a civil-service

---

[3] "Ministerialen."

law, which would materially secure his old age and provide increased guarantees against his arbitrary removal from office. This striving, however, has its limits. A very strong development of the "right to the office" naturally makes it more difficult to staff them with regard to technical efficiency, for such a development decreases the career-opportunities of ambitious candidates for office. This makes for the fact that officials, on the whole, do not feel their dependency upon those at the top. This lack of a feeling of dependency, however, rests primarily upon the inclination to depend upon one's equals rather than upon the socially inferior and governed strata. The present conservative movement among the Badenia clergy, occasioned by the anxiety of a presumably threatening separation of church and state, has been expressly determined by the desire not to be turned "from a master into a servant of the parish."[4]

4. The official receives the regular pecuniary compensation of a normally fixed salary and the old age security provided by a pension. The salary is not measured like a wage in terms of work done, but according to "status," that is, according to the kind of function (the "rank") and, in addition, possibly, according to the length of service. The relatively great security of the official's income, as well as the rewards of social esteem, make the office a sought-after position, especially in countries which no longer provide opportunities for colonial profits. In such countries, this situation permits relatively low salaries for officials.

5. The official is set for a "career" within the hierarchical order of the public service. He moves from the lower, less important, and lower paid to the higher positions. The average official naturally desires a mechanical fixing of the conditions of promotion; if not of the offices, at least of the salary levels. He wants these conditions fixed in terms of "seniority," or possibly according to grades achieved in a developed system of expert examinations. Here and there, such examinations actually form a character *indelebilis* of the official and have lifelong effects on his career. To this is joined the desire to qualify the right to office and the increasing tendency toward status group closure and economic security. All of this makes for a tendency to consider the offices as "prebends" of those who are qualified by educational certificates. The necessity of taking general personal and intellectual qualifications into consideration, irrespective of the often subaltern character of the educational certificate, has led to a condition in which the highest political offices, especially the positions of "ministers," are principally filled without reference to such certificates.

3. THE PRESUPPOSITIONS AND CAUSES OF BUREAUCRACY

The social and economic presuppositions of the modern structure of the office are as follows:

---

[4] Written before 1914. (German editor's note.)

The development of the money economy, in so far as a pecuniary compensation of the officials is concerned, is a presupposition of bureaucracy. Today it not only prevails but is predominant. This fact is of very great importance for the whole bearing of bureaucracy, yet by itself it is by no means decisive for the existence of bureaucracy. . . .

Even though the full development of a money economy is not an indispensable precondition for bureaucratization, bureaucracy as a permanent structure is knit to the one presupposition of a constant income for maintaining it. Where such an income cannot be derived from private profits, as is the case with the bureaucratic organization of large modern enterprises, or from fixed land rents, as with the manor, a stable system of taxation is the precondition for the permanent existence of bureaucratic administration. For well-known and general reasons, only a fully developed money economy offers a secure basis for such a taxation system. The degree of administrative bureaucratization in urban communities with fully developed money economies has not infrequently been relatively greater than in the contemporary far larger states of plains. Yet as soon as these plain states have been able to develop orderly systems of tribute, bureaucracy has developed more comprehensively than in city states. Whenever the size of the city states has remained confined to moderate limits, the tendency for a plutocratic and collegial administration by notables has corresponded most adequately to their structure. . . .

6. TECHNICAL ADVANTAGES OF BUREAUCRATIC ORGANIZATION

The decisive reason for the advance of bureaucratic organization has always been its purely technical superiority over any other form of organization. The mature bureaucracy compares with other forms exactly as does the machine with the nonmechanical modes of production.

Precision, speed, unambiguity, knowledge of the files, continuity, discretion, unity, strict subordination, reduction of friction and of material and personal costs—these are raised to the optimum point in the strictly bureaucratic administration, and especially in its monocratic form. As compared with all collegiate, honorific, and avocational forms of administration, trained bureaucracy is superior on all these points. And as far as complicated tasks are concerned, paid bureaucratic work is not only more precise but, in the last analysis, it is often cheaper than even formally unremunerated honorific service.

Honorific arrangements make administrative work an avocation and, for this reason alone, honorific service normally functions more slowly; being less bound to schemata and being more formless. Hence it is less precise and less unified than bureaucratic work because it is less dependent upon superiors and because the establishment and exploitation of the apparatus of subordinate officials and filing services are almost unavoidably less economical. Honorific service is less continuous than bureaucratic and frequently quite expensive. This is especially the case if one thinks not only of the money costs to the public treasury—costs which bureaucratic administration, in comparison with administration by notables, usually substantially increases—but also of the frequent economic losses of the governed caused by delays and lack of precision. The possibility of administration by notables normally and permanently exists only where official management can be satisfactorily discharged as an avocation. With the qualitative increase of tasks the administration has to face, administration by notables reaches its limits—today, even in England. Work organized by collegiate bodies causes friction and delay and requires compromises between colliding interests and views. The administration, therefore, runs less precisely and is more independent of superiors; hence, it is less unified and slower. All advances of the Prussian administrative organization have been and will in the future be advances of the bureaucratic, and especially of the monocratic, principle.

Today, it is primarily the capitalist market economy which demands that the official business of the administration be discharged precisely, unambiguously, continuously, and with as much speed as possible. Normally, the very large, modern capitalist enterprises are themselves unequalled models of strict bureaucratic organization. Business management throughout rests on increasing precision, steadiness, and, above all, the speed of operations. This, in turn, is determined by the peculiar nature of the modern means of communication, including, among other things, the news service of the press. The extraordinary increase in the speed by which public announcements, as well as economic and political facts, are transmitted exerts a steady and sharp pressure in the direction of speeding up the tempo of administrative reaction towards various situations. The optimum of such reaction time is normally attained only by a strictly bureaucratic organization.[5]

Bureaucratization offers above all the optimum possibility for carrying through the principle of specializing administrative functions according to purely objective considerations. Individual performances are allocated to functionaries who have specialized training and who by constant practice learn more and more. The "objective" discharge of business primarily means a discharge of business according to calculable rules and "without regard for persons."

"Without regard for persons" is also the watchword of the "market" and, in general, of all pursuits of naked economic interests. A consistent execution of bureaucratic domination means the leveling of status "honor." Hence, if the principle of the free-market is not at the same

---

[5] Here we cannot discuss in detail how the bureaucratic apparatus may, and actually does, produce definite obstacles to the discharge of business in a manner suitable for the single case.

time restricted, it means the universal domination of the "class situation." That this consequence of bureaucratic domination has not set in every-where, parallel to the extent of bureaucratization, is due to the differences among possible principles by which polities may meet their demands.

The second element mentioned, "calculable rules," also is of paramount importance for modern bureaucracy. The peculiarity of modern culture, and specifically of its technical and economic basis, demands this very "calculability" of results. When fully developed, bureaucracy also stands, in a specific sense, under the principle of *sine ira ac studio*. Its specific nature, which is welcomed by capitalism, develops the more perfectly the more the bureaucracy is "dehumanized," the more completely it succeeds in eliminating from official business love, hatred, and all purely personal, irrational, and emotional elements which escape calculation. This is the specific nature of bureaucracy and it is appraised as its special virtue.

The more complicated and specialized modern culture becomes, the more its external supporting apparatus demands the personally detached and strictly "objective" expert, in lieu of the master of older social struc-tures, who was moved by personal sympathy and favor, by grace and gratitude. Bureaucracy offers the attitudes demanded by the external ap-paratus of modern culture in the most favorable combination. As a rule, only bureaucracy has established the foundation for the administration of a rational law conceptually systematized on the basis of such enactments as the latter Roman imperial period first created with a high degree of technical perfection. During the Middle Ages, this law was received along with the bureaucratization of legal administration, that is to say, with the displacement of the old trial procedure, which was bound to tradition or to irrational presuppositions, by the rationally trained and specialized expert. . . .

10. THE PERMANENT CHARACTER OF THE BUREAUCRATIC MACHINE

Once it is fully established, bureaucracy is among those social struc-tures which are the hardest to destroy. Bureaucracy is the means of car-rying "community action" over into rationally ordered "societal action." Therefore, as an instrument for "societalizing" relations of power, bu-reaucracy has been and is a power instrument of the first order—for the one who controls the bureaucratic apparatus.

Under otherwise equal conditions, a "societal action," which is me-thodically ordered and led, is superior to every resistance of "mass" or even of "communal action." And where the bureaucratization of admin-istration has been completely carried through, a form of power relation is established that is practically unshatterable.

The individual bureaucrat cannot squirm out of the apparatus in which he is harnessed. In contrast to the honorific or avocational "notable," the professional bureaucrat is chained to his activity by his entire material and ideal existence. In the great majority of cases, he is only a single cog in an ever-moving mechanism which prescribes to him an essentially fixed route of march. The official is entrusted with specialized tasks and normally the mechanism cannot be put into motion or arrested by him, but only from the very top. The individual bureaucrat is thus forged to the community of all the functionaries who are integrated into the mechanism. They have a common interest in seeing that the mechanism continues its functions and that the societally exercised authority carries on.

The ruled, for their part, cannot dispense with or replace the bureaucratic apparatus of authority once it exists. For this bureaucracy rests upon expert training, a functional specialization of work, and an attitude set for habitual and virtuoso-like mastery of single yet methodically integrated functions. If the official stops working, or if his work is forcefully interrupted, chaos results, and it is difficult to improvise replacements from among the governed who are fit to master such chaos. This holds for public administration as well as for private economic management. More and more the material fate of the masses depends upon the steady and correct functioning of the increasingly bureaucratic organizations of private capitalism. The idea of eliminating these organizations becomes more and more utopian.

The discipline of officialdom refers to the attitude-set of the official for precise obedience within his habitual activity, in public as well as in private organizations. This discipline increasingly becomes the basis of all order, however great the practical importance of administration on the basis of the filed documents may be. The naïve idea of Bakuninism of destroying the basis of "acquired rights" and "domination" by destroying public documents overlooks the settled orientation of man for keeping to the habitual rules and regulations that continue to exist independently of the documents. Every reorganization of beaten or dissolved troops, as well as the restoration of administrative orders destroyed by revolt, panic, or other catastrophes, is realized by appealing to the trained orientation of obedient compliance to such orders. Such compliance has been conditioned into the officials, on the one hand, and, on the other hand, into the governed. If such an appeal is successful it brings, as it were, the disturbed mechanism into gear again.

The objective indispensability of the once-existing apparatus, with its peculiar, "impersonal" character, means that the mechanism—in contrast to feudal orders based upon personal piety—is easily made to work for anybody who knows how to gain control over it. A rationally ordered system of officials continues to function smoothly after the enemy has occupied the area; he merely needs to change the top officials. This body of officials continues to operate because it is to the vital interest of everyone concerned, including above all the enemy.

During the course of his long years in power, Bismarck brought his ministerial colleagues into unconditional bureaucratic dependence by eliminating all independent statesmen. Upon his retirement, he saw to his surprise that they continued to manage their offices unconcerned and undismayed, as if he had not been the master mind and creator of these creatures, but rather as if some single figure had been exchanged for some other figure in the bureaucratic machine. With all the changes of masters in France since the time of the First Empire, the power machine has remained essentially the same. Such a machine makes "revolution," in the sense of the forceful creation of entirely new formations of authority, technically more and more impossible, especially when the apparatus controls the modern means of communication (telegraph, et cetera) and also by virtue of its internal rationalized structure. In classic fashion, France has demonstrated how this process has substituted *coups d'etat* for "revolutions": all successful transformations in France have amounted to *coups d'etat*.

5. IDEOLOGY IN ORGANIZATION*

Philip Selznick

THERE IS a vague and ill-defined quality which, unacknowledged and often poorly understood, represents a fundamental prize in organizational controversy. This is the evolving character of the organization as a whole. What are we? What shall we become? With whom shall we be identified? Where are our roots? These questions, and others like them, are the special responsibility of statesmen, of those who look beyond the immediate context of current issues to their larger implications for the future role and meaning of the group. To pose these questions is to seek more than the technical articulation of resources, methods, and objectives as these are defined in a formal program or statute. To reflect upon such long-run implications is to seek the indirect consequences of day-to-day behavior for those fundamental ideals and commitments which serve as the foundation for loyalty and effort.

"Consequences," writes Dewey, "include effects upon character, upon confirming and weakening habits, as well as tangibly obvious results." And in an earlier passage from the same work: "Character is the interpenetration of habits. If each habit existed in an insulated compartment and operated without affecting or being affected by others, character would not exist. That is, conduct would lack unity, being only a juxtaposition of disconnected reactions to separated situations."[1]

These considerations from the social psychology of the individual provide us with tools for organizational analysis. Organizations, like individuals, strive for a unified pattern of response. This integration will define in advance the general attitudes of personnel to specific problems as they arise. This means that there will be pressure within the organization, from below as well as from above, for unity in outlook. As unity is approximated, the character of the organization becomes defined. In this way, the conditions under which individuals may "live together" in the organization are established, and a selective process is generated which forces out those who cannot identify themselves with the evolving generalized character of the organization. The evolving character, or generalized system of responses, will be derived in large measure from the

---

* Reproduced from *TVA and the Grass Roots*, University of California Press, 1949, pp. 181–185.

[1] John Dewey, *Human Nature and Conduct* (New York: Modern Library, 1930), pp. 46, 38.

consequences of day-to-day decision and behavior for general patterns of integration.

An examination of the logic of this development provides us with a theoretical link between the concept of the character of an organization and that of administrative discretion as discussed elsewhere.[2] The act of discretion permits the administrator to introduce considerations tangential to the formal or stated objectives of the organization. At the same time, by the accretion and integration of modes of response, the officialdom is able to invest the organization with a special character. This special character tends in turn to be crystallized through the preservation of custom and precedent. It is further reinforced by the selective process which rejects those members who cannot fit in, and shapes the personal orientation of those who remain or who are recruited.

In a situation charged with conflict, the process of discretion will be subjected to close scrutiny, and the quality of administrative decision will tend to be infused with a high degree of self-consciousness. The scrutiny of the opposition and self-consciousness of the leadership will alike center upon the question of commitment. What attitudes and what symbols are commanding the loyalties of the staff? What precedents are being established? What alliances are being made? Such issues will be uppermost in the minds of leading individuals during periods when the evolution of the character of an organization is not yet settled. The possibility of stating that some given line of action is the "settled policy of this organization" is one of the strategic objectives in such a controversy. Or, in a field somewhat oblique to questions of policy, there may be conflict over the "heroes" of the group. Laudatory references to a set of individuals as the "fathers" of the organization's policy and outlook may help to define the accepted antecedents of the group; as a result, a whole series of doctrinal commitments are inferred from those antecedents, though not necessarily formally included in the program or objectives of the organization. In such cases, controversy may occur over the question of whether some individual's memory is to be celebrated in the official newspaper or bulletins, or whether certain slogans and symbols, traditionally associated with one general tendency or another, will be included. Conflicts over apparently minor matters of this sort are typically aspects of the struggle to determine the character of an organization.

The internal organizational pressures which drive toward a unified outlook and systematized behavior receive their content, or substantive reference, from the play of interests and the flow of ideas which characterize the organization's social environment. In this way, the internal process of character formation—though generated by needs which may be referrable primarily to the organization as such—comes to be stamped with the

---

[2] P. Selznick, *TVA and the Grass Roots*, California, 1949, pp. 64 ff.

typical hallmarks of its own historical period. The general commitments and attitudes of the organization (i.e., its character) will tend to crystallize around value problems which are current in the environment. For an organization whose discretionary power on social questions is broad, there is pressure to make a choice among the "historical alternatives" that are available. Once that choice is made, the organization will tend to reflect in its own character the general sentiments with which it has become aligned.

The struggle over the outcome of this process may extend over a long period, and may be compromised from time to time, but the stake is always all important. The attempt to define an organization's character cannot be divorced from the struggle for leadership or from the possibility of internal convulsion. It is precisely in the struggle over an evolving organizational character that a given leadership having certain personal qualities most easily becomes the receptacle of a social ideal. As such, that leadership—incumbent or proposed—is conceived as indispensable to the goal of stamping the organization as a whole with the desired ideal. A leadership can become indispensable when it has convinced itself and its constituents that some alternative elite cannot be trusted with the exercise of character-defining discretionary powers; whereas the possibility of adequate replacement in the execution of formal executive functions is not normally in doubt. . . .

The thesis thus stated concentrates attention upon organizational dynamics. It is necessary to bear in mind, however, that the evolution of policy may be traced to broader and more general factors than the specific pressures exerted by groups within and around a given organization. In a sense, the forces generated by the process of organization per se may be thought of as the means by which the pressing but more general imperatives of the particular historical period are given effect. Such motives as prestige and survival may adequately impel action; but in general the need to rally forces broader than the small group for whom these motives are effective will make necessary an appeal based on moral or political principles which can be defended on their own level. In this way, the organizational struggle is provided with doctrinal content and a socially acceptable arena. But the price of that strategy involves a commitment to a set of ideas or interests. Hence those ideas and interests are provided with a means of intervention, a driving force which they may not be able by themselves to generate, but which, once generated, can carry them along with it.

To this qualification we may add another: changing historical conditions may seriously affect the choices available to discretionary power. In an administrative agency, controversies over policy may become academic overnight if statutory changes occur. Or the range of choice may be gradually restricted by changing economic conditions—as from a period of depression to one of prosperity, or of relative plenty to relative scarcity—as well as by shifts in the political climate which may make certain choices less expedient at one time than another. As these changes occur, the relative strength of forces within the organization may vary, reflecting needed reorientations. As the new realignment takes place, policy will change, but it might be rash not to look beyond the inner-organizational controversies for the cause of the change. In general, it is suggested that these considerations—which link specific organizational pressures to the more general imperatives and forces of the time—will temper any tendency which may arise from a concentration upon organizational dynamics to ignore the goals and demands provided by a particular historical period.[3]

---

[3] Daniel Bell, in conversation, has made the cognate point that power and the ends of power may not be divorced in a proper sociology. This is an important reminder for all who study the mechanics of organizational interaction.

6. A THEORY OF COOPERATION AND ORGANIZATION*

Chester I. Barnard

1. The individual human being possesses a limited power of choice. At the same time he is a resultant of, and is narrowly limited by, the factors of the total situation. He has motives, arrives at purposes, and wills to accomplish them. His method is to select a particular factor or set of factors in the total situation and to change the situation by operations on these factors. These are, from the viewpoint of purpose, the limiting factors; and are the strategic points of attack.

2. Among the most important limiting factors in the situation of each individual are his own biological limitations. The most effective method of overcoming these limitations has been that of cooperation. This requires the adoption of a group, or non-personal, purpose. The situation with reference to such a purpose is composed of innumerable factors, which must be discriminated as limiting or non-limiting factors.

3. Cooperation is a social aspect of the total situation and social factors arise from it. These factors may be in turn the limiting factors of any situation. This arises from the considerations: (*a*) the processes of interaction must be discovered or invented, just as a physical operation must be discovered or invented; (*b*) the interaction changes the motives and interest of those participating in the cooperation.

4. The persistence of cooperation depends upon two conditions: (*a*) its effectiveness; and (*b*) its efficiency. Effectiveness relates to the accomplishment of the cooperative purpose, which is social and non-personal in character. Efficiency relates to the satisfaction of individual motives, and is personal in character. The test of effectiveness is the accomplishment of a common purpose or purposes; effectiveness can be measured. The test of efficiency is the eliciting of sufficient individual wills to cooperate.

5. The survival of cooperation, therefore, depends upon two interrelated and interdependent classes of processes; (*a*) those which relate to the system of cooperation as a whole in relation to the environment; and (*b*) those which relate to the creation or distribution of satisfactions among individuals.

6. The instability and failures of cooperation arise from defects in each of these classes of processes separately, and from defects in their

* Reproduced by permission of the publisher from Chester I. Barnard, *The Functions of the Executive*, Cambridge, Mass.: Harvard University Press. Copyright 1938 by the President and Fellows of Harvard College.

combination. The functions of the executive are those of securing the effective adaptation of these processes. . . .

An organization comes into being when (1) there are persons able to communicate with each other (2) who are willing to contribute action (3) to accomplish a common purpose. The elements of an organization are therefore (1) communication; (2) willingness to serve; and (3) common purpose. These elements are necessary and sufficient conditions initially, and they are found in all such organizations. The third element, purpose, is implicit in the definition. Willingness to serve, and communication, and the interdependence of the three elements in general, and their mutual dependence in specific cooperative systems, are matters of experience and observation.

For the continued existence of an organization either effectiveness or efficiency is necessary;[1] and the longer the life, the more necessary both are. The vitality of organizations lies in the willingness of individuals to contribute forces to the cooperative system. This willingness requires the belief that the purpose can be carried out, a faith that diminishes to the vanishing point as it appears that it is not in fact in process of being attained. Hence, when effectiveness ceases, willingness to contribute disappears. The continuance of willingness also depends upon the satisfactions that are secured by individual contributors in the process of carrying out the purpose. If the satisfactions do not exceed the sacrifices required, willingness disappears, and the condition is one of organization inefficiency. If the satisfactions exceed the sacrifices, willingness persists, and the condition is one of efficiency of organization.

In summary, then, the initial existence of an organization depends upon a combination of these elements appropriate to the external conditions at the moment. Its survival depends upon the maintenance of an equilibrium of the system. This equilibrium is primarily internal, a matter of proportions between the elements, but it is ultimately and basically an equilibrium between the system and the total situation external to it. This external equilibrium has two terms in it; first, the effectiveness of the organization, which comprises the relevance of its purpose to the environmental situation; and, second, its efficiency, which comprises the interchange between the organization and individuals. Thus the elements stated will each vary with external factors, and they are at the same time interdependent; when one is varied, compensating variations must occur in the other if the system of which they are components is to remain in equilibrium, that is, is to persist or survive. . . .

Organization, simple or complex, is always an impersonal system of coordinated human efforts; always there is purpose as the coordinating and unifying principle; always there is the indispensable ability to com-

---

[1] See definitions in chaps. ii and v, pp. 19 and 55 ff.; also chap. xvi, in C. Barnard, *The Functions of the Executive*, Harvard, 1938.

municate, always the necessity for personal willingness, and for effectiveness and efficiency in maintaining the integrity of purpose and the continuity of contributions. Complexity appears to modify the quality and form of these elements and of the balance between them; but fundamentally the same principles that govern simple organizations may be conceived as governing the structure of complex organizations, which are composite systems. . . .

Historically and functionally all complex organizations are built up from units of organization, and consist of many units of "working" or "basic" organizations, overlaid with units of executive organizations; and the essential structural characteristics of complex organizations are determined by the effect of the necessity for communication upon the size of a unit organization. . . .

Informal organizations and their relation to formal organizations: (1) those interactions between persons which are based on personal rather than on joint or common purposes, because of their repetitive character become systematic and organized through their effect upon habits of action and thought and through their promotion of uniform states of mind; (2) although the number of persons with whom any individual may have interactive experience is limited, nevertheless the endless-chain relationship between persons in a society results in the development, in many respects, over wide areas and among many persons of uniform states of mind which crystallize into what we call mores, customs, institutions; (3) informal organization gives rise to formal organizations, and formal organizations are necessary to any large informal or societal organization; (4) formal organizations also make explicit many of the attitudes, states of mind, and institutions which develop directly through informal organization, with tendencies to divergence, resulting in interdependence and mutual correction of these results in a general and only approximate way; (5) formal organizations, once established, in their turn also create informal organizations; and (6) informal organizations are necessary to the operation of formal organizations as a means of communication, of cohesion, and of protecting the integrity of the individual. . . .

7. TEAMWORK AND PRODUCTIVITY
IN A SHOE FACTORY*⁰

ALEXANDER B. HORSFALL AND CONRAD M. ARENSBERG

EDITOR'S NOTE: In the study of social structure and of groups in human organization, much has been said of the need for quantitative verification. With the exception of Eliot Chapple's work on pair interaction and some of the static sociograms of the sociometric school of sociology, studies of interaction and of group dynamics have not yet attained the exactitude of description of common natural science methods.

It is interesting, therefore, to present a pioneer effort to describe and measure the interactions within a group of shoe company workers. They consist of several teams with a common flow of work in a single department of a very ordinary, work-a-day factory. The methods used and developed here are the simplest operations on human interaction. These operations, applicable to all the social sciences, were suggested by Chapple and Arensberg[1] and Chapple and Coon[2] and developed in many studies in industrial sociology. In simple terms, the operations are (1) identification of the persons to be observed, (2) discrimination of the order of interaction (stimulus and response) between them, and (3) timing. "Content" here is eliminated; order is left. The authors describe not what these groups do, but when and how long it takes to do it.

From this description, we get a quantative demonstration of the existence of "informal organization" of the sort that has been so widely discussed in writings on industrial sociology and psychology ever since the publication of *Management and the Worker*.[3]

In this paper, however, emphasis is not on the further demonstration that such teams of "informally organized" workers exist. It is not even on the more interesting point that not all such teamwork serves as a release of "productivity." The factory department under discussion seems to show that there is a limit to the supposed relation between an increase in "informal social relations" and an increase in productivity. The limits on the relationship between "release of spontaneity" and "development of fuller participation," and the changes in other social situations in industry

---

* Reproduced from *Human Organization*, Vol. 8, No. 1 (Winter, 1949), pp. 13–25.

⁰ This study was conducted as a research course in 1938 under the direction of Eliot Chapple. Alexander B. Horsfall, of the College of Business Administration, University of Florida, was the observer and wrote the original paper. Conrad M. Arensberg, Chairman of the Department of Sociology, Barnard College, has since rewritten and enlarged upon the observer's original deductions.

[1] E. D. Chapple, with the collaboration of C. M. Arensberg, "Measuring Human Relations," *Genetic Psychology Monograph*, Vol. XXII, 1940.

[2] E. D. Chapple and C. S. Coon, *Principles of Anthropology* (New York: Henry Holt & Co., 1942.)

[3] F. J. Roethlisberger and W. J. Dickson, *Management and the Worker* (Cambridge, Mass.: Harvard University Press, 1939).

(supervision, grievances and communication "up the line," staff-line activity, etc.) still remain to be worked out. The point of interest is that a method of observation is presented that makes the study of these phenomena of social interaction and group structure quantitative, measurable, communicable, verifiable, generalizable.

As a result of this approach to human relations, the science dealing with the dynamics of human interaction—and thus with institutional structure and organization—can begin to make concrete contributions of data and method to studies of organization, incentive, and work-behavior in the engineering and managerial fields, going far beyond present "diagnoses," "understanding," and "art." Quantity is the language of science, and here is quantity in "human relations."

I

IN THE Bottoming Room of the ABC Shoe Company in 1938, four seven-worker teams, each performing the same series of machine operations on shoes, were located side by side. They formed a department group of 28, all in one room.

Like so many other such groups of whom there have been reports since that time, these workers had an informal organization of their own for allocating work, equalizing pay, and spreading and apportioning leisure periods during working hours. This informal organization might be called "restrictive," in that it was outside management rules. The foreman knew of its existence and might have reported it, but it went on independent of him. Led by a few of the older men in the middle teams along the flow of work which united them, the whole group kept the shoes moving through their machines at a pace that kept their pay at a constant level, despite an incentive piece-rate. This meant allocating leisure and apportioning work, holding back while others "caught up," submitting to "informal group controls." Despite the attendant "loss" to individual earners, these controls were in effect in the ordinary run of the department's day. These informal controls, and the group operating under them, broke down only under stress of special hurry orders under management pressure for production. Only then did the workers' interaction revert to the smaller teams of immediate neighbors in the manufacturing process.

The ABC Shoe Company was a manufacturer of inexpensive women's novelty shoes, employing on the average around 1000 persons and producing from 7500 to 10,000 pairs of shoes daily. Ownership and management of the factory had been in the hands of one family since it began as a shoe repair shop 28 years ago. The plant had grown from a one-room establishment to its present size—about 70,000 square feet of floor space—mainly by successive additions to its original buildings.

A large percentage of the employees came from the immediate neighborhood; in many cases there were several from the same family. About 60 per cent of the employees were women. Nearby stores accepted the factory's pay checks as cash, and the factory was an important economic and social element in the community. Many employees had been working in it steadily for 10 years or more. Employee benefits, curtailed somewhat in 1938, still included some medical and dental service, and a trained nurse was employed. In short, the plant was very much a part of the lives of the workers in the neighborhood.

In the ABC Company formal lines of organization were conspicuously absent. Relations between employees and the few foremen allowed for free interchange. The Superintendent had reporting directly to him the Production Manager, to whom in turn the foremen of the various manufacturing process rooms (departments) reported. There were no written periodic reports, everyone being too busy at work. Production was the thing, and the main job of the foremen was to keep it running smoothly, particularly by timing it to prevent bottlenecks or stoppages in the huge, continuous flow of shoes through and out of the factory.

Practically all production was on a piece-rate basis except where a new worker was being trained on a machine, or where a worker was transferred to a machine new to him. In transfers, higher average earnings at a new machine often were regarded as a promotion, and a trainee was paid on a salary basis for the period of his learning. The piece-rate unit was a "case" of 36 pairs, or 72 shoes. Shoes moved through the factory in racks equivalent to this unit. Each rack upon which the shoes were transported from one machine to another contained a "case" of shoes. Thus, in the parlance of the job, both "case" and "rack" indicated the 72 shoes of the piecework unit.

Work was planned and routed through the factory by means of the "checking" and "coupon" systems common to shoe factories. Under the "checking" system, each employee turned in, on a weekly basis, a list of tag numbers. One tag marked the completed rack or case of 72 shoes. Upon these lists, when checked, the payroll was based. The "coupon" system need not concern us here. Only the checking system was used in the Bottoming Room under discussion. Earnings were freely compared by the workers and were common knowledge.

There was no formal inspection of shoes at the various stages of the manufacturing process until the final "treeing" and packing of shoes ready to be shipped out. However, a continual sampling went on whereby a foreman picked shoes from the racks as they passed through his department on the way to another operation. Workers reported damaged or defective shoes to the foreman, providing an equally important check upon production quality. They reported all imperfections, whether due to their own work or to a previous operation. The rack containing the imperfect shoe was then held up and the shoe taken back to be redone by the worker from whom it came. He was identified by his initials on the tag attached to the rack. Usually no penalty was exacted where such damage or defect was faithfully reported, the worker merely correcting the fault in the shoe. But if a damaged shoe were deliberately or carelessly passed on, the worker was charged with its cost. At various stages of processing, racks were counted for missing shoes by the floor boys who wheeled them. Racks with shoes missing also were held up, and a floor girl spent her time in tracing these shoes.

A detailed description of the shoe-making process in the ABC factory need not be given here. It was in the Bottoming Room that the four teams to be described were located.

II

A description of the flow of work into the Bottoming Room, the operations through which the shoes went in the teams, and of the flow of shoes out of the room, follows:

All work came from the Lasting Room and was first processed by the heel-lasters, sitting together on one side of the Bottoming Room. They were then ready for the four teams with which we are concerned, who were located on the other side of the room. In each of the four teams were two trimmers, a pounder, a rougher, a shanker and two cementers.

1. Racks were rolled to the stair-well at the head of the room by the bed laster or toe-laster who had completed the work, and left there.

2. Racks were lined up at the stair-well by the floor boy for the heel-lasters to take when ready. If the racks were piling up, the floor boy might wheel them down to mid-floor, opposite the battery of heel-lasting machines. If the heel-lasters were "caught up" they would stand at the stair-well and take the racks from the bed or toe-lasters as delivered.

3. Racks completed by heel-lasters were pushed to mid-floor, whence they were taken by the rougher or pounder to his particular team's bench. Allocation of the various racks among the teams will be described later in this article.

4. Racks were brought to the trimmers of each team, who removed the shoes to their bench for the first of five main operations performed by the team. These operations prepared the shoe for the attachment of the sole.

(a) Trimming. Two trimmer girls started the shoe through each team by trimming off leather which had bunched up at the toe, or any excess of the shank. They removed tacks from the insole. Their two machines were a physical unit and the girls faced each other, one with her back to the window and the other with her back to the aisle. Completed shoes were placed on the pounders' bench.

(b) Pounding. The pounder, a man, pounded and ground toes and heels, smoothing the overlapping leather more successfully than had the knives of the trimming machines. He faced the windows, his back to the aisle. He passed his output to the rougher's table at his side.

(c) Roughing. A man used a revolving wire brush to roughen the overlapping leather at the bottom of the shoe, preparatory to cementing. He faced the windows. His output went to the shanker.

(d) Shanking. This was done by a girl who placed a thin metal strip, previously bent to fit the insole of the shoe, in the center of the instep and stapled it in place. Her output went to the two cementers, and she used the same large bench they did.

(e) Cementing. Two girls squirted a layer of cement around the margin of the shoe, which later glued the sole in place. Then a "filler," a small felt pad, was stuck in place at the ball of the foot, and the shoe was placed in a special type of rack having boxes to receive each shoe. These two girls faced the rest of their team, with their right sides to the windows. This work was considered by girls the most desirable in the room. Gaining a position at this machine was considered a promotion. The work required a nicety of skill and was less mechanical in that less depended on the machine, and offered opportunity occasionally to do extra racks requiring a mere cementing operation.

5. In the final step, racks were pushed to the floor by the two cementers of each team, there to be inspected for completeness by the floor boy before being taken to the elevator and finally leaving the Bottoming Room. Incomplete racks were held until the missing shoe had been traced.

III

Observation of activity in the Bottoming Room showed that in addition to the work operations there was activity related in some way to the starting of these work operations in a team. This was a method of allocating racks among the teams according to some order, which was different from the order in which they came from the heel-lasters.

Further observation showed that for each type of shoe in the racks coming from the heel-lasters, there was a corresponding object on one of the four rougher's benches. These objects had come to serve as symbols in an unofficial record-keeping and exchange around the workers' own routing of racks-to-be-done. One might say they were the "coins" of a small economic system. When a rack came to mid-floor from the heel lasters, only the rougher upon whose bench lay the associated object might take it for his team. The sooner he took it, the sooner he could pass the object to the next team and the sooner that team's rougher could take another rack of the same type of shoe. Since the racks were pushed to mid-floor in any part of the room, just as they left the heel-lasters, there was a continual signalling by the roughers of the type of rack which had come to mid-floor. This took the form of shouting the name of the associated object, e.g. "Who's got the bar?" At the signal, the rougher or pounder whose team had the symbolic tool went over and took the rack in exchange for the signal-object and brought it back to the trimmers of his own team. Such exchanges served to pass along the associated object to the next team in a well-defined order of allocation of work by the four teams. The order was: Team No. 4 to No. 3 to No. 2 to No. 1 to No. 4.

Such signalling and exchange took place continuously between the roughers and pounders, the men members of the various teams. In the exchange, since no team in the person of its rougher or pounder took a rack for which it lacked the associated object, and since every team when taking a rack passed along an associated object, it followed that at the end of the day the number of cases done, plus the number of objects held, was the same for each team (within limits determined by the number of objects).

But meanwhile, the racks to be worked on had been routed among the teams in a manner calculated to equalize pay for fast and slow teams alike, and assure that all the workers should score a uniform production of racks. Thus, when work came through rapidly, the exchanges might result in a condition where one team had several racks piled up at its trimmer's machines, together with several exchange objects on its rougher's bench standing for racks routed to other teams.

This condition existed to varying degrees at all times, depending on the differences in the four teams' speed of working. Usually, in other factories the result is that faster teams spend more time "loafing" while waiting for the other teams to catch up. In a typical day in other shoe factories, this unevenness provides the workers with rest periods, scattered and differing in total time for each team, and their earnings are at the mercy of the slower teams for whom they must wait. But here, by the system of exchanges, the work came through so rapidly that it exceeded the limits wherein such waiting and loafing could be tolerated without damming up work in other parts of the factory. The slower teams were bypassed with their consent, and for the time being the other teams worked on the racks passed to them. If the spurt of work was a short one, but longer than a day's limit, then the number of racks the faster of the four teams "owed" the slower ones might be carried over from one day to the next. The exchanges were tallied from the circulated associated objects.

From these exchanges, then, there resulted an allocation of racks so that they were divided equally between the teams, both in number and according to the difficulty of work with the different types of shoes. The method was introduced originally by the roughers. They explained it by saying it made everyone's pay equal over the weeks, that it prevented continued quarrels and insured that one team did not get all the "hard" racks.

It is interesting to note that the explanation did not stress getting "easy" racks, as was the case in other shoe factories where comparable exchanges entitled the workers to alternate between "hard" and "easy" tasks. Desire to equalize pay seemed here as strong as desire to lighten work load. But the reason the roughers, particularly, initiated the practice, and one they did not give explicitly, might have been that with some types of shoes, for instance platform shoes, the roughing step is omitted. Hence, by not having such shoes routed to them, the roughers' weekly earnings might well have been affected.

Examining financial incentive for a moment, it is to be remembered that in the ABC Company, all types of shoes with the exception of suedes were paid for at the same rate. But this equality of rate would not account for the workers' informal organization, for regardless of the rate set by the company, the workers would certainly have found some types of shoes preferable to work on than others. Some workers would have preferred the easier shoes whatever the piece-rate. The motive for informal social organization here, undertaken as it was on initiative of the workers themselves, seemed not so much due to a desire for a steady "take home" pay as to control (eliminate) one of the difficulties inherent in shoe manufacturing.

That difficulty is the scheduling of many inherently different operations altogether, so as to result in a continuous flow of shoes through the factory despite the differences. The difficulty had been heightened in this factory due, among other reasons, to the variety of shoe styles they handled, to a breaking down of operations into machine-processes using unskilled labor to the fullest possible extent, to the haphazard growth of the factory's physical layout and to its small elevator capacity. Among these conditions, the piece-rate method of payment was only one of many factors.

To management here, piece-rate seemed indispensable for, they argued, if all workers were paid by time, the amount of work each team received and completed would be a matter of indifference. However, it is significant that in the face of all these factors outside the control of the workers, the incentive effect hoped for by management in a piece-rate acted instead to produce an organization among the workers for allocation of racks. This gave them a method of adapting their own needs of work-pace and steady pay to a rate of production which still produced shoes for the management, though incentive and control were in reality far more collective than individual.

The following are the objects, the associated style of shoe, and the workers through whose hands a shoe passed, arranged according to the workers' opinion as to degree of difficulty in handling. The most difficult are first.

Object Name	Shoe Name	Passes Through
1. Wood (block)	Sandal	All seven
2. Scraper	Wedge sandal	All seven plus Rg.
3. Tag	Patent leather	All seven
4. Bar	Macwelt	All seven
5. Screw	Wedge (plain)	All seven plus Rg.
6. Wheel	Platform	T',T,S.
7. Box (cardboard)	Suede	All seven

IV

The discovery and description of the four teams and their informal organization does not rest solely upon the evidence of interviews with the workers, their foreman and other persons familiar with the room and the ABC Company. It seemed more objective to devise a method of recording the measuring which could check the evidence of interviews against a simple technique of factual, non-verbal observation. The technique developed resulted in a series of observation charts in which minimally-defined, "content"-less, interactions were discriminated according to the persons taking part in them through sample observation periods. These samples followed the hourly and daily interpersonal activity of the 28 persons in the four teams in the Bottoming Room, both in "work" and "non-work" activities of every sort, without regard to such categorization.

Once the record was taken thus, an analysis of the data of the observation charts established regularities of frequency, direction and personal participation which could substantiate objectively the patterns of leadership, team-membership and status, and inter-worker social relations which interviews in the room had revealed in the "subjective" or "unverified" testimony of and about the 28 workers concerned.

The original purpose of the authors was, in fact, to attempt such a verification of current hypotheses about informal organizations.

For observation of human behavior at the social level, an industrial firm offers conditions which are most like a laboratory. Each day the same people come at the same time to the same place and do the same work under essentially the same conditions. They work with the same objects in the same sequence. They have about the same social routine. In short, many factors which are variable elsewhere change, at least, within narrower limits in an industrial concern. This is particularly true where work is with machinery and the job is the production or processing of material objects, as in the ABC Company.

The Superintendent of the ABC Shoe Company[4] had many valid objections to allowing any outsider in the factory for an appreciable length of time. However, once he was satisfied as to the interests of A. B. Horsfall, the observer, what he wanted to do, and how he proposed to do it, he gave his full cooperation. The observer was given a regular employee identification card and the freedom of the factory. The Production Manager was asked to show him the factory, to answer freely any questions that might be asked, and to permit him to come in daily and observe the various processes and workers. At no time did this attitude change, nor was there any let-down in the willingness to allow the observer to go around and ask questions anywhere. Conversely, all actions of the latter were openly explained to the foremen and to interested workers, and his interests and disinterests made clear. The observer was in the factory practically daily for one month—from July 12 to August 13, 1938.

The first few days were spent in going through the factory to get a general idea of the operations performed at various stages in the process of

---

[4] The authors are deeply grateful to the company, its officials and its workers for the privileges here described. The anthropological convention of anonymity prevents our acknowledging them here by name.

making shoes. At this time, it was decided to make observations in the Lasting Room, for the process there seemed to require a clearly defined flow of work in terms of machinery, and a closer dependence of one man's work on that of the previous worker, with a certain amount of essential interaction associated with moving the shoes from one stage of the process to another.

A series of observations were actually made in the Lasting Room, but discovery of the four teams in the Bottoming Room, with their method of allocating work by means of certain of their members passing along objects (which brought to mind the "kula" system of the Trobrianders)—initiated and put into practice by the workers themselves—suggested more possibilities there.

Except as noted above, the observer spent the first two weeks working full time, first with the muller boy, taking uppers from the stitching room and placing them in the muller to be conditioned while the lasts were made up, feeding racks to the assemblers, etc., and then with the floor boy in the Bottoming Room. The former work was simple, manual activity which served as a favorable introduction to the workers and to the activity of the Lasting Room; the latter work enabled him to become familiar with the types and flow of shoes and to identify the employees by sight. At one time or another, the observer tried his hand at most of the machines, and evidence of interest in this way proved to be an excellent way of having his presence accepted. At all times, in fact, the observer's working and making of observations were so mingled that he became one of the group and part of the scenery.

In making observations of the teams in the Bottoming Room after it had been picked as the scene of detailed operations, the objective was to record on paper as accurately as possible the context of the interpersonal, social activity of each event in the room. At first he tried to do this in a literary way, describing the action before him in words and recording conversation. But this procedure soon proved inadequate. It was difficult to write rapidly enough to describe fully the events of the room at the time of their happening, and impossible to do this and keep up with them in their real order and pace of occurrence for an appreciable period of time. In addition, one had to look at one's notebook when writing, and consequently lost out on observing. Words took too long. Moreover, they gave no frame of reference at all, but left that to be described later. The separation of event and frame of reference seemed artificial, as it was always the context of the situation which seemed to lend significance to the event. Lastly, where the objective was to get quantitative data, it was desirable to observe and record all the interpersonal events of any one period of observation. One was forced to make the periods of observation regular lengths of time, as it was not enough to make discrete observations for varying periods of time in a room where the rapidity of events did not permit any adequate description of one event before the occurrence of the next. One had to do full counts of most events of short duration if one was to keep up with the reality of the room.

Thus the observer devised an observation chart which was to be a standard frame of reference, uniform for all periods of observation—at once a spatial representation of the scene of reference and a time coordinate. As observer, standing facing the team, he saw reflected in his notebook the wall, the workers in front of it in spatial arrangements from left to right, and their machines. Without writing a word, he could record every interaction between the workers before him, and in its direction, by striking on his notepad an arrow, going from initiator to responder. On his pad, ruled by minutes, the row of people against the wall was lettered, with a capital for their function, a T for Trimmer; the second row was primed, i.e., T', C', and so on.

Final procedure in observation was to stand between two racks (not for concealment, but to be clear of the aisle) about eight feet from a team, approximately in line with its rougher and shanker. From that spot, a whole team from rougher through to the cementers was clearly visible and not shielded by its machines. The observer struck an arrow on his pad for each interaction of any kind, graphically joining the letters for the interacting persons. Occasionally, when he could stand still, he recorded all the conversation possible. But he always made a special attempt to note the first unit of interaction in any conversation, whether or not he recorded any part of it. Noise level due to machinery was high, it should be kept in mind, so even if time had permitted writing down the details of a conversation, often it could only be seen, not heard. But for each bout of it, a line on the pad ran from one party to the next in the order of initiation and response. All workers of a team could easily be observed by facing them this way and every interaction in which members of the team took part was recorded by such a stroke on the pad. All persons in the room had become familiar by sight, and their activity could immediately be recorded by the drawing of a line on their symbols.

No attempt was made to record the duration of each interaction, since the accuracy of such timing with a wristwatch under such conditions would have been small. Moreover, several interactions often occurred at once, overlapping in time. However, any interaction extending over a minute was recorded approximately by drawing on the pad, from the tail of the arrow struck for it, a wiggly line running down the page to the mark of the elapsed minute.

It should be noted that whereas the usual method of making observations in social science is to write a description of the happenings under observation, from which further abstraction of particular facts for quantitative analysis can later be made, here an attempt was made to make primary observations in terms of the simplest operations alone by using these lined pads as charts. What words were written down to reflect the conversation merely served as a supplement to the chart. The chart itself gave all the facts of description. The symbols here are lines and arrows on paper instead of words, and the referents of the lines can only be the discriminated initiations or responses of the people in the room as they were entered. These initiations and responses then were set down in a framework of time, i.e., the minutes, were recorded along the side of the pad; and in a framework of space, i.e., the row of workers listed along the top of the pad from left to right as they stood before the observer. In such recording, then, the referents of words set down on paper are less precise than the arrows and lines that record the initiations and responses. (Words set down are capable of many "meanings"; the arrows and lines are capable of no other distortion than the frailty of the recorder's eye and hand.)

On the completed charts filled in for each period of observation, a system of lines and arrows focuses our attention on the facts. The chart allows direct analysis of primary observations in a form suitable for quantitative analysis.

It should be noted that before the observation periods began it was generally known that the observer was interested in the workers' method of allocating racks by passing objects. There was no suspicion of their being timed for adjustment of piece-rates or the like. Any questions the observer was asked as to what he was doing were freely, if discreetly, answered. It was not generally known that conversation was being recorded. The facts seemed to indicate that the observer's presence did not, as far as he could judge, bias the record or materially change the situation from its normal course.

To give some details of the mechanics of making these observation charts it should be noted that the recording was done in 4" × 6" notebook pads which were inconspicuous and easily placed in the observer's trouser pocket when he was pushing racks around between observation periods. The charts were ruled up beforehand. A wristwatch was worn, turned inward to the wrist so that its face was upward as the hand held the notebook, the eyes taking in the dial with the pad. Time was kept accurately by minutes for each 15 minute period of observation. The minute marks were ruled off down the page just before starting the period of observation to save time and to make references to the watch during the recording inconspicuous. The charts thus are accurate as a time record giving the minute of the beginning of each event between people and its end, during 15 minute periods on successive days.

In all this, the foreman was aware that a wristwatch was being used and observation charts were shown to him. The workers were not aware of this last fact, or if they were, asked no questions.

A list of the commoner discriminations made in recording the interactions on the charts is given in Diagram A. Diagram B gives a facsimile

DIAGRAM A

Recording Conventions

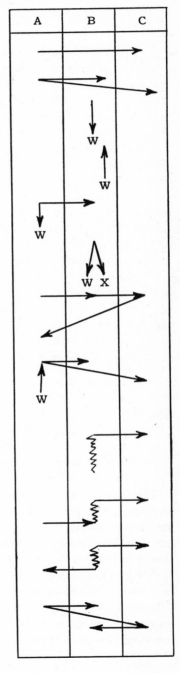

1. An action of A is followed by an action of C.

2. An action of A is followed by independent actions of both B and C.

3. An action of B is followed by an action of W, not a member of the group defined for observation.

4. An action of W, not a member of the group defined for observation, is followed by an action of B.

5. An action of A is followed by independent actions by both B and by W, not a member of a group.

6. An action of B is followed by independent actions by both W and X, not members of the group.

7. An action of A is followed by an action of B, which action is followed by an action of C, which action is followed by an action of A.

8. An action of W, not a member of the group, is followed by an action of A, which action is followed by independent actions of both B and C.

9. An action of B is followed by an action of C, which interaction continues for a period of time measured by the length of the arrow tail extension.

10. The above interaction is terminated by an action of A which is followed by an action of B.

11. The second above interaction is terminated when an action of B, during his interaction with C, is followed by an action of A.

12. An action of A is followed by independent actions of both B and C, the next action of C being followed by an action of B, but not of A.

reproduction of a completed observation chart for a sample 15 minute period on an ordinary day.

V

In working up the observation record from the charts just described, it became evident that certain relations held uniformly between the facts of the record—the notations, lines and arrows on the charts—and that by stating these as simple equations we could derive some preliminary operational definitions for grouping the data of observation. Later, statistical analysis of the observations could be based on such definitions.

Thus, in the charts we had to keep in mind that we were interested in observing objectively the 28 people in the room. Further, we were interested in behavior at the interactional level rather than at the biochemical, physiological, psychological or other levels, although recognized that one level is not independent of the other. Hence we limited our observations to those events involving two or more people. The study of the interconnections of such events is the common, elemental ground from which spring all the "social sciences."

On the charts, then, using the interaction theory of Chapple and Arensberg,[5] when an action of one worker was observed to follow the action of another, this event, an arrow on our chart, could be called a simple interaction. For one event, on our chart, one person started it and is represented by the origin of the arrow on our page. The person who responds is shown by the head of the arrow, and the following relationship holds:

$$2e = I + R = p \cdots \cdots (1)$$
$$2 = \quad 2 \quad = 2$$

where

    e is the event, or arrow line.
    I is the origin or initiation of action, its start.
    R is the response, its finish.
    p is the number of persons between whom the arrow was drawn.

Thus the simplest observed event might have been a simple interaction, one which took place only between two persons on our record. The first action was initiation, the second was response; together, the two actions established an initial, simple unit of interaction. We could label such a simple interaction "a." It might have been merely a single exchange such as greetings in passing, e.g. A: "Hello B," B: "Hello yourself;" or it might have continued for some time with many exchanges between these two. The measure of the time from its initiation in an act of A's to the last response in the last act of B's for that time gave the "duration" of an event. Speaking in general terms, an event terminates with a change in the mode

[5] Op. cit.

DIAGRAM B

Tuesday, August 8, 1938

#100. R makes a comment to S. The assistant foreman passes down the aisle and pushes an empty rack out of his way toward mid-floor, whereupon T′ calls to S to get the rack back; S gets it. R2 from down the room shouts, "Hey, the bar," whereupon T′ mimics him, repeating, "Hey, the bar." (R asks T a question,) R3 down the aisle, takes up R2's cry and T′ then mimics him, R3 repeats, T′ mimics again, this for several times. P is visibly annoyed by R3's shouting and finally shouts, "We got the box long ago," C leans over and shouts to S. The work is moving along at a good pace with R taking the shoes from P as he does them, no shoes having accumulated on R's bench. This goes on for a while, then P shouts "Ali-oop" and tosses R a shoe directly instead of placing it on the bench for R to take; this continues every five seconds or so, R finishing the shoe just barely in time to catch the next. There is a sort of rhythm as P pounds the shoe in four audible operations corresponding to grinding the front, side, side and heel of the shoe and tossing it to R who then does the same with a wire brush, running at high speed and emitting a higher tone when the shoe is applied. (P speeds up a little but R stays with him and the final score is a tie, so to speak.) Meanwhile, T′ speaks to T and this continues for a minute. C2 speaks to C; and H6 comes down and speaks to S. R3 starts up again, "Hey, the box," and T′ mimics him. R has been tossing shoes haphazardly on the cementers' bench to keep up with P, and now C says, "Hey, cut it out R," and when R continues, C emphasizes the remark by pushing three shoes to the floor. R pays no attention. S picks them up. Finally, the floor girl comes by with some shoes in her arms and T′ addresses her, taking the shoes from her and trimming them. Whereupon the floor girl goes in succession to R, who roughs the shoes and then to C who both shanks and cements the shoes herself, with S absent. T passes a single shoe directly to P for special attention, instead of putting it on the bench. S speaks to R. C makes a comment to S and then C′ makes a comment to S.

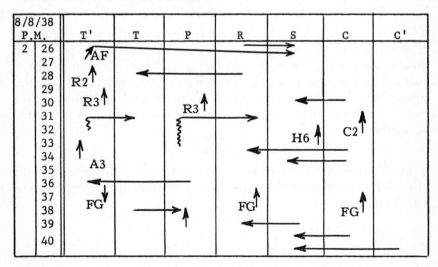

of behavior of one person in an interaction of two, or with the entrance of a third person upon the scene, to whom the others, or one of them, act or respond.

On our charts an event ended where we had to strike a new arrow between our workers. But there were on our charts many events involving three people, for whom we had to discriminate a special forked-arrow. When an event was observed wherein two persons responded to the action of one person, a third party, there were two responses to one origin. These were the "set-events" of the Chapple and Arensberg[6] scheme. In such cases when each of the persons made a response to the person starting a new activity we drew a two-pronged arrow accordingly. Nevertheless, the persons still counted up the same as the total initiations and responses on the pages of our record, thus:

$$p = I + R$$
$$3 = 1 + 2$$

Accordingly, where two or more persons responded to the action of one person we labeled the observed event "s," short for set interaction. Obviously, it was an event wherein $p > 2$. It could also be regarded as a special case where the initiations of several simple interactions coincided in one person at one time.

In such an event of three-person activity, as one counted them from the charts, the count of all the observed initiations and responses was greater than two, but greater only by the number of people exceeding two in the event. If we reduced this count of $I + R$ by the number of people exceeding two, then it became the same as the two for each simple pair-event.

$$2e = I + R - (p - 2) \cdots\cdots (2)$$

where the last term reduced the total count of initiations and responses to that of one simple interaction (a). It gives the number of responses that exceed a simple interaction. By making the reduction, one then counts up pair and set events together. When we were dealing quantitatively in this manner with more than one set event, we could subtract for each set the number of people over two, and thus reach a last equation which could be written:

$$2e = I + R - \Sigma(p - 2)(s)[7]$$

In this manner, in summarizing and generalizing the record of the charts, all interactions could be resolved into either simple interactions or sets. That is,

$$\Sigma e = \Sigma a + \Sigma s$$

---

[6] *Op. cit.*

[7] It should be understood that the parenthetical letters hereafter used by themselves are the equivalent of subscripts and represent a classification of the variables described in the text. Thus $e(t)$ means the total number of events.

The summary Σe here was a dichotomy of events with respect to how individuals took part in the social activity of the room, as members of pairs (a) or as members of subgroups or classes in the room (s).

But the record had to be dealt with in terms of the people involved. Sometimes activity went on only between team members; sometimes it involved "outsiders," either members of other teams in cross-team or inter-team activity or other persons altogether outside any of the four teams. Where all the interactions took place between persons of a group, here our teams, the group could be called "closed" and any happening was an internal event—$e(i)$—with reference to the group. Where one or more persons outside the group entered into interaction with members of the group, the group was then "open" and such interactions were called "open end" interactions—œ. In such a case, the initiation or response was made by a person outside the group; and that happening was an external event—$e(x)$—with reference to the group. Thus an event involving any person outside the group was an external event. Total events observed, then, were of necessity the sum of the internal and external events:

$$\Sigma e(t) = \Sigma e(i) + \Sigma e(x) \cdots \cdots (3)$$

Such a summary involved us in a dichotomy of the events of the room with respect to what individuals took part.

In the case of external events with their open-end interactions, equation (1) and (2) are still valid, but our further discrimination as to the open-end initiations and responses must be taken into account. Equations (1) and (2) then become, respectively:

$$2e = I' + R' + œ$$
$$2e = I' + R' + œ - \Sigma(p - 2)(s) \cdots \cdots (4)$$

where I' and R' are the actions of members of the group, and œ of persons outside the group. This last is the general equation used in computing total social activity as recorded in the observation charts for the teams. An example of the above, together with illustrations of counts and calculations is given in Diagram C.

VI

Observation charts and verbal conversation records covered 120 periods of 15 minutes each; 30 for each of the four teams. It is impossible to give all the data in a report the length of the present one. Both the raw data and the analyses are available and can be consulted. Perhaps at some later date, given the space and resources, it may be possible to bring them all out.

We shall limit ourselves to the measures that demonstrate the existence, characteristics and interrelationships of the teams and that give some picture of the nature of informal leadership in the room.

DIAGRAM C

Social Interaction
Quantity

OBSERVATION
Charts

DISCRIMINATION
Symbol and definition

			TIME	A	B	C			
			e (1)	←			a(i)		
intra									
			e (2)				s(i)		
			e (3)				a(x)		
inter					A(2)				
			e (4)				s(x)		
					B(3)				
			e (5)				a(x)		
extra				W					
			e (6)		W		s(x)		
					Y				
	COUNT	6e	1	2	1	4	I		
		2e(i)	3	2	2	7	R		
		4e(x)	1	2	2	5	œ		
			1	2	0	3	s		

CALC: $\Sigma e = \Sigma a + \Sigma s$
6 =   3 +   3

e - event, total interactions - e(t).
e(x) - external event, person outside group included.
a - simple interaction, one response, p = 2.
s - set-interaction, two or more responses, p > 2.
s(i) - internal set-interaction.
s(x) - external set-interaction.
I - initiation action of individual, arrow tail.
R - response action of individual, arrow head.
œ - open-end action, an initiation or response
outside group.
p - number of persons in event.
P - period of observation.

MEASUREMENT
Formulae

$$2e = I + R + œ - \Sigma(p-2)(s).$$. (4)
(2) (6) = 4 + 7 + 5 - (1 + 1 + 2)
12 = 12
$$e(t) = \Sigma e(i) + \Sigma e(x). . . .$$ . . (3)
6 = 2   + 4

The actions thus recorded are initial units of interaction, which are taken as "determining" the event.

Our first step will be to see if quantification of interaction does in fact lend itself to a verification of the current hypotheses about inter-worker social relationships.

First of all, the data does support the hypothesis that such cliquelike groups as these teams show a higher rate of interaction among their members than between their members and outsiders. These teams do show slightly more internal activity (social interaction) than external. But it is interesting that the teams in which the informal leaders of the workroom were members show only a slight preponderance of internal over external interaction. The most active teams (active, that is in social activity within themselves) were not the most productive either in management's hoped-for productivity-per-worker or per-team measures of individual performance, or in leadership in informal organization. Rather, the teams in which the informal leaders of the room were members, showed both a slight excess of internal activity over external and a much higher activity of external interaction with out-of-team, cross-team members of the room.

The point is significant, though not surprising. Indeed the foreman said simply enough that the teams that did the most talking and "horsing around" did not get the most work done. The reasons are simple enough, too. In such a set up, and probably in many others, productivity must be some sort of a balance between activity in interpersonal clique relationships, out of which zest and color and personal security may develop, and flow-of-work relationships with other workers from whom the work of the division of labor is received and to whom it is passed. Of course, informal leadership must mean, as here, personal traffic across and between the teams if all four teams are to be coordinated and controlled on a scale large enough to include all the 28 people of the room. Such informal, "non-work" activity obviously throws the informal leaders into enough extra-clique, here extra-team, activity to make their teams' score lower, in such a measure as this, than do the teams who only respond in the room's own informal system of allocation and "controls."

The conclusion gives pause to current enthusiasm about encouraging "team work." If team work is merely interpersonal clique activity in working groups it is not by itself a "release" of a productivity damped by the "anomie" of too impersonal, formal and unsocial a working atmosphere in modern industry. It is, instead, a product of more complex social changes in a working situation, not all of them explored so far.

The figures from which such a conclusion can be drawn up tentatively are these:

Summary No. 1. Events of Interaction by Category, by Teams

	$e(t)$	$e(i)$	$e(x)$	Acts	I-R	œ	p-2
Team #1	619	402	217	1272	1049	223	34
Team #2+	544	286	258	1145	877	268	57
Team #3+	450	233	217	949	727	222	49
Team #4	583	395	188	1200	1007	193	34
Total	2196	1316	880	4566	3660	906	174

where the symbols have the following meaning:

$e(t)$ · · · all events.
$e(i)$ · · · all internal events.
$e(x)$ · · · all external events.
Acts · · · all initiations and responses observed in team interactions.
I-R · · · all initiations and responses observed of team members.
œ · · · all open-ends, or initiations or responses made by persons outside the group under observation.
p-2 · · · cumulative total of people over two in each set-interaction.
+ · · · team in which an informal leader is a member.

The relationship between these elements of social interaction is given in the formula below which serves as a check of their count from the observation charts.

$$2e = I + R + \alpha - \Sigma\,(p - 2)(s)$$

Team #1 (2) (619) = 1049 + 223 − 34 = 1238
Team #2 (2) (544) = 877 + 268 − 57 = 1088
Team #3 (2) (450) = 727 + 222 − 49 = 900
Team #4 (2) (583) = 1007 + 193 − 34 = 1166

VII

Furthermore, the data lends support to some of the current theories about group structure in social science.[8] The measures of interpersonal activity among team members showed a variable amount of participation from one person within the team to the next, but a clustering of higher rates of interactive behavior around only a particular few members of each team. The clustering showed each group, here the team, to be the focus of quite frequent interpersonal activity. The teams here were groups of people who interacted more frequently with one another than with others outside as a result of the controlling effects of the flow of work.

However, in internal structure the teams were not collections of people bound together by quantitatively uniform relationships, in so far as the measured interactive behavior was concerned. The facts were quite to the contrary.

Internally, the teams were collections of relatively inactive persons ranged about clusters of highly interactive persons, only one or two in each team serving as a center or nexus for the rest. Members differed widely in their rates of activity with one another, some of them responsive mostly to immediate neighbors, some of them serving as targets or confidants for a wider circle taking in most of the group, some of them very alert to persons outside. The groups were "structured," then, around only the more active or more widely responsive of their members. Factors, influencing such structuring were by no means uniform as far as could be judged without special study. Central spatial position among the workers of a team vied with leadership function in the over-all organization of the room's allocation system. This was the main reason why in the teams one person or another served as such a focal point. Personality factors seemed to determine whether one was to act as such a nexus in a favorable spatial position, just as personality factors coupled with status difference seemed to indicate why it was that the two informal leaders of the room were among the oldest, most experienced of the men workers, in a room full of less-skilled boys and women.

---

[8] See the work of the sociometrists of the Moreno school; reference to clique structure in W. L. Warner's *Yankee City Series*, and Davis, Gardner, and Gardner's *Deep South;* and the theory of groups in Chapple and Arensberg's "Measuring Human Relations," *op. cit.*

In any event, summaries of the data (*a*) of intra-team interaction by teams, and (*b*) of rates of interactions within teams, member with member, yield statistical corroboration of the points just made:

DIAGRAM D

Summary No. 2.   Intra-Team Interaction

Team #1

	T'	T	P	R	S	C
T	21				e(i)402	
	30			(p − 2)(s)	16	
					(i)418	
P	11	24				
	12	21				
R	—	5	23			
	—	3	31			
S	1	4	12	8		
	6	3	13	6		
C	1	4	0	2	22	
	4	5	4	5	16	
C'	—	0	3	2	27	27
	—	4	5	4	26	23
I	34	37	38	12	49	27
R	52	36	53	15	42	23

Team #2

	T'	T	P	R	S	O
T	16				e(i)286	
	51			(p − 2)(s)	6	
					(i)292	
P	8	56				
	4	22				
R	2	9	3			
	11	18	15			
S	0	0	5	5		
	4	2	2	2		
C	—	—	—	1	5	
	—	—	—	1	6	
C'	1	2	2	0	6	11
	1	4	4	1	1	16
I	27	67	8	6	11	11
R	71	46	18	4	7	16

Team #3

	T'	T	P	R	S	C
T	33				e(i)233	
	21			(p − 2)(s)	12	
					(i)245	
P	14	8				
	4	4				
R	11	1	16			
	2	4	15			
S	9	5	4	8		
	7	5	1	0		
C	2	1	—	2	7	
	2	1	—	3	4	
C'	4	3	—	1	9	5
	5	1	—	3	6	14
I	73	18	20	11	16	5
R	41	15	16	6	10	14

Team #4

	T'	T	P	R	S	O
T	26				e(i)395	
	23			(p − 2)(s)	9	
					(i)404	
P	18	10				
	13	17				
R	2	3	22			
	3	3	9			
S	6	4	9	35		
	4	1	4	11		
C	5	3	5	4	32	
	5	2	5	9	43	
C'	1	0	1	4	16	6
	3	2	1	6	25	2
I	58	20	37	43	48	6
R	51	25	19	26	68	3

For example, in Team #1, T' initiated action on T, 21 times, and responded to initiation of action by T, 30 times, there being 51 interactions, or pair relations between the two of them; and the rate of interaction is 51/30 for each of the 30 periods, or 1.7 per period. Team #1's T' initiated 34 actions and responded to 52 actions in the 30 periods, with other members of Team #1.

DIAGRAM E

Summary No. 3.   Rates of Interaction Within Teams[9]

Table   Spatial Arrangement

Team #1

	T'	T	P	R	S	C
T	1.7					
P	.8	1.5				
R	—	.3	1.8			
S	.2	.2	.8	.5		
C	.2	.3	.1	.2	1.3	
C'	—	.1	.3	.2	1.8	1.7

```
        1.5   1.8
      T → P ← R    C
  1.7↓        1.3⁄ ↓1.7
      T'       S → C'
                 1.8
```

Team #2

	T'	T	P	R	S	C
T	2.2					
P	.4	2.6				
R	.4	.9	.6			
S	.1	.1	.2	.2		
C	—	—	—	.2	.4	
C'	.1	.2	—	—	.2	.9

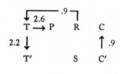

```
       ↓2.6      .9⌐
      T → P    R    C
  2.2↓               ↑.9
      T'      S    C'
```

Team #3

	T'	T	P	R	S	C
T	1.8					
P	.6	.4				
R	.4	.2	1.0			
S	.6	.3	.2	.3		
C	.1	.1	—	.2	.4	
C'	.3	.1	—	.1	.2	.9

```
              1.0
       T    P → R    C
  1.8↑
       T'     S    C'
```

Team #4

	T'	T	P	R	S	C
T	1.6					
P	1.0	.9				
R	.2	.2	1.0			
S	.3	.2	.4	1.5		
C	.3	.2	.3	.4	2.5	
C'	.1	.1	.1	.3	1.4	.3

```
        .9   1.0
      T ← P → R    C
  1.6↑   ⁄   1.9↓ 2.4⁄
      T'⁄1.0   S ← C'
                 1.4
```

[9] Number of interactions, or pair relations, (a) per 15-minute period. The direction of the arrows between persons in the diagrams at the right indicate, from other computations than here given, the preponderance in the pair relations of the one person's initiations over his responses to the other person of the pair, a measure of dominance.

For theories of group structure it is interesting to note that in the case of the two less productive teams it was not a dominant or leader-personality which made a person a nexus for his group. Teams #1 and #4, as can be seen from a glance at Summary #3 above, were alike in being structured internally with a secondary sub-clique around one of the women members. This clique existed within the group established by their informal leaders, the men trimmers and roughers who conducted their team's part in the exchanges on the allocation of work and the rerouting of racks. In each case a woman served as a second sub-clique center. In teams #2 and #3, of which the informal leaders of the whole room (the teams' respective roughers and pounders) were members, there was no such development of a secondary women's clique. Teams #2 and #3 were said to be serious and inclined to "stick to work," as befitted their leadership position. Teams #1 and #4, being team receivers rather than initiators in the exchange of work, were known generally to be less serious, more given to talk and horseplay and less "productive," although, of course all had an even output and pay.

The point of personality interest, however, is that those women who acted as secondary centers did not show—in the measures of interpersonal interaction—a high preponderance of initiations over responses in the activity in which they took part. By that measure they were not leaders. Rather they, C' of Team #1, and S of Team #4, Diagram E, (Summary #3), were rather highly receptive persons, the one "sympathetic," the other a fat girl, slow, new and inexperienced, a target for advice, abuse, laughter and confidences.

The conclusion one can draw for group structure is that it is the fact of the focussing of attention upon a person, for whatever reason, and by no means as a leader, that makes him or her the center of a group. Or conversely, the group arises out of the history and continuance of a higher rate of interpersonal activity. Perhaps a group's consciousness and its "common interests" are not a precondition of its existence, but a result.

VIII

A final point of interest to be drawn from the data concerns the informal leadership of the allocation of work in the room.

We have already said the interviews revealed that leadership in the exchanges between teams in the room lay with the roughers and pounders of each team, particularly with those of Teams #2 and #3. Measures of interpersonal activity drawn from the observation charts support that evidence.

The significant measures, however, are not so much in higher rates of over-all activity, or in higher percentages of initiation over responses. They are rather in a combination (for such leaders) of high over-all activity with high rates of activity in extra-team relationships (external events) in both of which a relative preponderance of initiations over responses occurs. That means simply that leaders assumed initiative both in inter-team contacts and in contacts within their own teams. Informal leaders, and perhaps all leaders in comparable situations, are thus not necessarily the most active persons, but they do exercise most initiative in first winning and then coordinating the responses of their fellows at home and their opposite numbers abroad. Leaders here initiated activity in relations both with their own team members and with the leaders of other teams.

The point is, of course, not new. But the statistical demonstration of it is. And, more significant, the possibility opened up by the demonstration. With measures of interaction such as these, the way is open to a measurement and a controlled experimentation with the dynamics of changes in human organization.

Computation of the room's informal leadership patterns was possible. First, we computed for each of the 28 workers his rate of total activity (interactions per period) and the percentage of those actions wherein he initiates action $(I/I + R)$. The former was a measure of his share in the total activity of the room; the latter was a measure of the direction of that activity, a description of his role vis-à-vis the others with whom he took part. Then, as any individual might have been active in his own team but inactive in relations outside it, these were calculated as well for internal and external interaction.

In making the count of interactions by individuals, a set event had to be treated as so many simple interactions. The alternatives were to omit a set-event or treat it separately. Going back to the happenings of which the set notation was a representation, we saw clearly that in such happenings a simple interaction had taken place between the person whom we gave as initiating action, and each of the others we noted as responders.

Still, of course, we could not truthfully say that in such set-events, because an action of A was followed by independent actions of both B and C, there was no interaction between A and B or between A and C. It was simply that we could not detect and note it. Unique properties of set-events therefore, had to be neglected; and for the present we have had to treat them simply as so many pair interactions, merely adding them to the pair events. In any case, set-events were few.

Next, to compare one worker with the next we calculated the average rate of interaction and the initiations-percentage for each team and then compared the specific figures for each individual with these team averages, taking the statistically significant deviations (assuming our sample was adequate) as a measure of the differences between the workers in respect to their participation in the social relations of the room. To find these individuals who were relatively active, it seemed sufficient to array the figures for the workers who exceeded their teams' averages. The figures are as follows:

HIGHEST INDIVIDUAL ACTIVITIES[10]
All Teams

Total		Internal		External	
Rate	Initiation %	Rate	Initiation %	Rate	Initiation %
T2 8.7	R2 66	S4 6.3	R2 72	R2 5.3	R2 70
S4 7.1	T2 61	T2 6.0	T2 66	T2 4.0	T'4 69
P1 6.5	R3 60	P2 5.3	T'3 65	R3 3.7	R3 63
C'1 6.1	T'3 54	S1 4.8	P4 59	C1 2.9	P4 61
C4 5.6	C1 53	T1 4.1	C'4 59	C'1 2.9	T2 60
T'3 5.3	T'4 50	C4 4.1	C'3 57	P4 2.6	C2 59
C1 5.3	T1 50	C'1 4.0	S2 57	C4 2.4	P3 56

BY TEAMS

Team	No. 1		No. 2		No. 3		No. 4	
	Rate	Initiation %	Rate	Initiation %	Rate	Initiation %	Rate	Initiation %
Total	P 6.5	C 53	T 8.7	R 66	T'5.3	R 60	S 7.1	P 50
	C'6.1	T 50	P 5.0	T 61	R 4.5	T'54	C 5.6	T'50
Internal	P 5.3	T 54	T 6.0	R 72	T'3.8	T'65	S 6.3	P 59
	S 4.8	C 54	P 3.9	T 66	T 2.9	C'57	C 4.1	C'59
External	C 2.9	C 48	R 5.3	R 70	R 3.7	R 63	P 2.6	T'69
	C'2.9	C'43	T 4.0	T 60	T'1.9	P 56	C 2.4	P 61

This array gave us an amorphous spotting of individuals with a relatively high rate of interaction coupled with a relatively high initiation percentage. But it did show the following:

In all teams, the individuals who "led," if taking the initiative in a contact is "leadership," were R2, T2, R3, C'1, C4, C1, and T'3. But next, when these persons were rearranged for their relative ranking in internal and external interaction, quite a different set of persons emerged (see above). For example, R2 showed a high rate of external activity, the highest, but he did not appear in the column for persons high in rates of total and internal activity.

The next measure for picking up the pounders and roughers as "informal leaders" of the worker-controlled allocation and production was one which stated the rates of interaction between the teams, person with

---

[10] Average number of initiations and responses per 15-minute period, for each individual.

person, in external events. The measure of external participation picked up as well several individuals who, while not leaders, figured high in external interaction. But when other measures were recombined with this, these persons disappeared from the array once more. The data appears in Diagram F.

DIAGRAM F
Summary No. 4.   Rates of Interaction Between Teams[11]

		Team #1							Team #2							Team #3						
		T'	T	P	R	S	C	C'	T'	T	P	R	S	C	C'	T'	T	P	R	S	C	C'
Team #2	T'	–	–	–	–	–	.5	–														
	T	–	–	–	–	–	1.2	–														
	P	–	–	.4	–	–	–	–														
	R	–	–	.5	.6	–	–	–														
	S	–	–	–	–	–	–	–														
	C	–	–	–	–	–	–	–														
	C'	–	–	–	–	–	–	.4														
Team #3	T'	–	–	–	–	–	–	–	–	–	–	–	–	–	–							
	T	–	–	–	–	–	–	–	–	–	–	–	–	–	–							
	P	–	–	–	–	–	–	–	–	–	–	.4	–	–	–							
	R	–	–	–	–	–	–	–	–	–	.4	1.3	–	–	–							
	S	–	–	–	–	–	–	–	–	–	–	–	–	–	–							
	C	–	–	–	–	–	–	–	–	–	–	–	–	–	–							
	C'	–	–	–	–	–	–	–	–	–	–	–	–	–	–							
Team #4	T'	–	–	–	–	–	–	–	–	–	–	–	–	–	–	–	–	–	–	–	–	–
	T	–	–	–	–	–	–	–	–	–	–	–	–	–	–	–	–	–	–	–	–	–
	P	–	–	–	–	–	–	–	–	–	–	.4	–	–	–	–	–	.4	.8	–	–	–
	R	–	–	–	–	–	–	–	–	–	–	.5	–	–	–	–	–	–	–	–	–	–
	S	–	–	–	–	–	–	–	–	–	–	–	–	–	–	–	–	–	–	–	–	–
	C	–	–	–	–	–	–	–	–	–	–	–	–	.4	–	–	–	–	–	–	.5	–
	C'	–	–	–	–	–	–	–	–	–	–	–	–	–	–	–	–	–	–	–	.4	–

Taking those persons in Diagram F who took part in external relationships team-to-team, having high rates of occurrence, we were able to compare those with high measures for the initiation of the activity in which they took part with those with low measures of initiation percentages. In such a comparison the women cementers who showed high rates of external participation disappeared.

Only the men R2, P3 and P4 and one woman, T2, remained. These were the leaders. They were located in all the teams, except Team #1. From this analysis the primary leadership of the four teams was centered in Team #2 where the interviews placed it.

In Team #1, P1 figures as third in rank in total activity and highest in his team in internal activity, but he does not seem to have been much of

---

[11] All interactions over .3 per 15-minute period, for all charts. The arrows do *not* show preponderance of initiations over responses *here*.

an initiator. His whole team ranks low, and the members characteristically were responding to the initiatives of others, particularly of Team #2.

Thus, picking up the leaders meant discovering them to be persons who were alike in ranking high when the individuals in the room were compared for (1) activity rate in external inter-team relationships, (2) for percentage of initiations over responses in all relationships to their own teams both internal and external, (3) percentage of initiations to responses in internal participation, and (4) percentage of initiations in external participation. As we have said, they were the only persons in the room and among the teams who were active, particularly in extra-team contacts, initiant in contacts with their own teams and initiant as well with the members or (leaders) of the other teams.

The table below gives the ranks for each male and female high in external activity rate in the other measures just described. It documents the sort of "informal leadership" the room exhibited.

IX

In the course of this presentation of quantitative data on the interactions of the members of the Bottoming Room of the ABC Shoe Company, the reader may have been hard put to follow the analysis. Nevertheless, we believe that close attention to the tables and the data will be repaid because through them it is possible to demonstrate, for this department at least, that the facts of industrial organization are not necessarily in accord with the theory. Much has been said about increasing group give-and-take in order to increase production: the most efficient teams indulged least in social activity. This does not mean that there should not be any

"LEADERSHIP"

Relative rank in the room in several other measures of persons ranking highest in external activity.

(F.: Female; M.: Male)

Person	External Activity Rate	Total Activity Rate	Internal Activity Rate	Initiations % All Events	Initiations % Internal Events	Initiations % External Events
R2 M.	1	–	–	1	1	1
T2 F.	2	1	2	2	2	5
R3 M.	3	–	–	3	–	3
C1 F.	4	–	–	5	–	–
C'1 F.	5	4	7	–	–	–
P4 F.	6	–	–	–	4	4
C4 F.	7	5	6	–	–	–
(P1 M.	–	3	–	–	–	–)

(Leaders are those who appear in two of the three right-hand columns.)

Note: When a rank does not appear in a column, it is of course held by a person not one of the eight of the table. A blank means a higher rank than seven.

interaction. The question is to define quantitatively how much is optimum for a given group under what conditions of leadership.

Leadership itself is something which can be defined objectively and differentiated from merely being socially active. It depends upon a frequent and continuous exercise of initiative with reference to the constituent individuals in the group. These groups vary in their own internal constitution as a function of personality differences, work flow, and other factors, but they become most effective when they are directly under the control of a leader. Not only did the leaders stabilize the relationships of the four teams to one another. They also gave internal strength and concentration to the teams in which the greater portion of their interaction took place. On what is regarded ordinarily, then, as a single level in industrial organization, the work level, effective leadership developed without the intervention of the first line supervisor. This leadership served to stabilize the manufacturing process, and within the two teams it was dominant to bring about the most efficient performance.

8. TVA AND THE GRASS ROOTS: GUIDING PRINCIPLES AND INTERPRETATION*

PHILIP SELZNICK

> The entire science considered as a body of formulae having coherent relations to one another is just a system of possible predicates—that is, of possible standpoints or methods to be employed in qualifying some particular experience whose nature or meaning is unclear to us.[1]
> —JOHN DEWEY

IT IS believed that the interpretation set forth in *TVA and the Grass Roots* provides a substantially correct picture of a significant aspect of the TVA's policy at work. Far from remote, or divorced from what is considered pertinent by informed participants, the analysis reflects what is obvious to those who "know the score" in TVA.[2] Of course, this exposition is more explicit and systematic, and the relevant implications are more fully drawn out, but in main outline it can come as no surprise to leading officials of the Authority. This is not to suggest that there are no errors of detail, perhaps even of important detail. The nature of this kind of research precludes any full assurance on that. While much of the material is derived from documentary (though largely unpublished) sources, much is also based upon interviews with members of the organization and with those nonmembers who were in a position to be informed. Care was taken to rely upon only those who had an intimate, as opposed to hearsay, acquaintance with the events and personalities involved. Those who are familiar with the shadowland of maneuver in large organizations will appreciate the difficulties, and the extent to which ultimate reliability depends upon the ability of the investigator to make the necessary discriminations. They will also recognize the need for insight and imagination if the significance of behavior, as it responds to structural constraints, is to be grasped. All this involves considerable risk.

If the use of personal interviews, gossip channels, working papers,[3] and

---

* Reproduced from *TVA and the Grass Roots*, University of California Press, Berkeley and Los Angeles, 1953.

[1] John Dewey, *Problems of Men* (New York: Philosophical Library, 1946), p. 221.

[2] Although responsibility for the analysis rests solely with the author, it should be emphasized that this study was made possible by the willingness of TVA to make its records and personnel available. This is a happy precedent which we may hope will be followed by other organizations, public and private.

[3] Some of the materials quoted in the study are unofficial in the sense that they would be vigorously edited before receiving even the public status of a memorandum sent to another department within TVA. This would be so with comparable documents in any large organization, public or private.

participation[4] opens the way for error, it remains, however, the only way in which this type of sociological research can be carried on. A careful investigator can minimize error by such means as checking verbal statements against the documentary record, appraising the consistency of information supplied to him, and avoiding reliance on any single source. On the other hand, he will not restrict his data to that which is publicly acknowledged.

The possibilities of factual error, however great, are probably less important as hazard than the theoretical orientation of the study. To be sure, an empirical analysis of a particular organization, of its doctrine, of a phase of policy in action, of its interaction with other structures, was our objective. But in order to trace the dynamics of these events, it has been necessary to attempt a reconstruction, which is to say, a theory, of the conditions and forces which appear to have shaped the behavior of key participants.

Theoretical inquiry, when it is centered upon a particular historical structure or event, is always hazardous. This is due to the continuous tension between concern for a full grasp and interpretation of the materials under investigation as history, and special concern for the induction of abstract and general relations. Abstractions deal harshly with "the facts," choosing such emphases and highlighting such characteristics as may seem factitious, or at least distorted, to those who have a stake in an historically well-rounded apprehension of the events themselves. This is especially true in the analysis of individual personalities or social institutions, for these demand to be treated as wholes, with reference to their own central motives and purposes, rather than as occasions for the development of theoretical systems. This general, and perhaps inescapable, source of misunderstanding being admitted, let us review the concepts which have been used to order the materials of our inquiry.

Sociological Directives

The volume has been subtitled "A Study in the Sociology of Formal Organization." This means that the inquiry which it reports was shaped by sociological directives, more especially by a frame of reference for the theory of organization.[5] These directives are operationally relevant without, however, functioning as surrogates for inductive theory itself. That is, while they provide criteria of significance, they do not tell us what is significant; while they provide tools for discrimination, they do not

---

[4] The author spent most of his year's stay at TVA in daily contact with personnel of the agency. A number of weeks was spent in intensive contact with extension service personnel in the field.

[5] For a fuller statement than the summary which follows, see Phillip Selznick, "Foundations of the Theory of Organization," *American Sociological Review*, Vol. XIII (February, 1948).

demand any special conclusions about the materials under investigation.[6] The fundamental elements of this frame of reference are these:

1. All formal organizations are molded by forces tangential to their rationally ordered structures and stated goals. Every formal organization— trade union, political party, army, corporation, etc.—attempts to mobilize human and technical resources as means for the achievement of its ends. However, the individuals within the system tend to resist being treated as means. They interact as wholes, bringing to bear their own special problems and purposes; moreover, the organization is imbedded in an institutional matrix and is therefore subject to pressures upon it from its environment, to which some general adjustment must be made. As a result, the organization may be significantly viewed as an adaptive social structure, facing problems which arise simply because it exists as an organization in an institutional environment, independently of the special (economic, military, political) goals which called it into being.

2. It follows that there will develop an informal structure within the organization which will reflect the spontaneous efforts of individuals and subgroups to control the conditions of their existence. There will also develop informal lines of communication and control to and from other organizations within the environment. It is to these informal relations and structures that the attention of the sociologist will be primarily directed. He will look upon the formal structure, e.g., the official chain of command, as the special environment within and in relation to which the informal structure is built. He will search out the evolution of formal relations out of the informal ones.[7]

3. The informal structure will be at once indispensable to and consequential for the formal system of delegation and control itself. Wherever command over the responses of individuals is desired, some approach in terms of the spontaneous organization of loyalty and interest will be necessary. In practice this means that the informal structure will be useful to the leadership and effective as a means of communication and persuasion. At the same time, it can be anticipated that some price will be paid in the shape of a distribution of power or adjustment of policy.

4. Adaptive social structures are to be analyzed in structural-functional

---

[6] Thus, while approaching his materials within a guiding frame of reference, the author was not committed by this framework to any special hypothesis about the actual events. Indeed, he began his work with the hypothesis that informally the grassroots policy would mean domination by TVA, because of its resources, energy, and program. After the first two months in the field, however, this hypothesis was abandoned as a major illuminating notion.

[7] For discussion of informal organization, see F. J. Roethlisberger and W. J. Dickson, *Management and the Worker* (Cambridge: Harvard University Press, 1941), pp. 524 ff; also Chester I. Barnard, *The Functions of the Executive* (Cambridge: Harvard University Press, 1938), chap. ix; Wilbert E. Moore, *Industrial Relations and the Social Order* (New York: Macmillan Co., 1946), chap. xv.

terms.[8] This means that contemporary and variable behavior is related to a presumptively stable system of needs[9] and mechanisms. Every such structure has a set of basic needs and develops systematic means of self-defense. Observable organizational behavior is deemed explained within this frame of reference when it may be interpreted (and the interpretation confirmed) as a response to specified needs. Where significant, the adaptation is dynamic in the sense that the utilization of self-defensive mechanisms results in structural transformations of the organization itself. The needs in question are organizational, not individual, and include: the security of the organization as a whole in relation to social forces in its environment; the stability of informal relations within the organization; the continuity of policy and of the sources of its determination; a homogeneity of outlook with respect to the meaning and role of the organization.

5. Analysis is directed to the internal relevance of organizational behavior. The execution of policy is viewed in terms of its effect upon the organization itself and its relations with others. This will tend to make the analysis inadequate as a report of program achievement, since that will be deemphasized in the interests of the purely organizational consequences of choice among alternatives in discretionary action.

6. Attention being focused on the structural conditions which influence behavior, we are directed to emphasize constraints, the limitation of alternatives imposed by the system upon its participants. This will tend to give pessimistic overtones to the analysis, since such factors as good will and intelligence will be deemphasized.

7. As a consequence of the central status of constraint, tensions and dilemmas will be highlighted. Perhaps the most general source of tension and paradox in this context may be expressed as the recalcitrance of the tools of action. Social action is always mediated by human structures, which generate new centers of need and power and interpose themselves between the actor and his goal. Commitments to others are indispensable in action: at the same time, the process of commitment results in tensions which have always to be overcome.

These principles define a frame of reference, a set of guiding ideas which at once justify and explain the kind of selection which the sociologist will make in approaching organizational data. As we review some of

---

[8] See Talcott Parsons, "The Present Position and Prospects of Systematic Theory in Sociology," in George Gurvitch and Wilbert E. Moore (Eds.), *Twentieth Century Sociology* (New York: Philosophical Library, 1945).

[9] As Robert K. Merton has pointed out to the author, the concept of "basic needs" in organizational analysis may be open to objections similar to those against the concept of instinct. To be sure, the needs require independent demonstration; they should be theoretically grounded independently of imputations from observed responses. However, we may use the notion of "organizational need" if we understand that it refers to stable systems of variables which, with respect to many changes in organizational structure and behavior, are independent.

the key concepts utilized in this study, the operational relevance of this frame of reference will be apparent.

Unanticipated Consequences in Organized Action

The foregoing review of leading ideas directs our attention to the meaning of events. This leads us away from the problem of origins.[10] For the meaning of an act may be spelled out in its consequences, and these are not the same as the factors which called it into being. The meaning of any given administrative policy will thus require an excursion into the realm of its effects. These effects ramify widely, and those we select for study may not always seem relevant to the formal goals in terms of which the policy was established. Hence the search for meanings may seem to go rather far afield, from the viewpoint of those concerned only with the formal program. Any given event, such as the establishment of a large army cantonment, may have a multitude of effects in different directions: upon the economy of the area, upon the morals of its inhabitants, upon the pace of life, and so on. The free-lance theorist may seek out the significance of the event in almost any set of consequences. But in accordance with the principle stated above, we may distinguish the random search for meanings—which can be, at one extreme, an aesthetic interest—from the inquiry of the organizational analyst. The latter likewise selects consequences, but his frame of reference constrains his view: it is his task to trace such consequences as redound upon the organization in question; that is, such effects as have an internal relevance. Thus, only those consequences of the establishment of the army cantonment in a given area which result in adjustments of policy or structure in the administration of the cantonment will be relevant.

There is an obvious and familiar sense in which consequences are related to action: the articulation of means and ends demands that we weigh the consequences of alternative courses of action. Here consequences are anticipated. But it is a primary function of sociological inquiry to uncover systematically the sources of unanticipated consequence in purposive

---

[10] In terms of origins, the TVA's policy—though not the grass-roots doctrine *qua* doctrine—of channeling its agricultural program through the land-grant colleges of the Valley states may be adequately referred to such factors as the nature of the formal agricultural program, the resources available for its implementation, and the administrative rationale which seemed conclusive to leading participants. Moreover, these factors may sustain the continued existence of the policy, and it may therefore seem superfluous when extraneous factors are brought in and somewhat tangential explanations are offered. But when we direct our attention to the meaning of the policy in terms of certain indirect but internally relevant consequences—as for the role of TVA in the agricultural controversy, we have begun to recast our observation of the policy (taken as a set of events) itself. We are then concerned not with the question, "how did the grass-roots policy come into being?" but with the question, what are the implications of the grass-roots policy for the organizational position and character of TVA?"

action.[11] This follows from the initial proposition in our frame of reference: "All formal organizations are molded by forces tangential to their rationally ordered structures and stated goals." Hence the notion of unanticipated consequence is a key analytical tool: where unintended effects occur, there is a presumption, though no assurance,[12] that sociologically identifiable forces are at work.

There are two logically fundamental sources of unanticipated consequence in social action, that is, two conditions which define the inherent predisposition for unanticipated consequences to occur:

1. The limiting function of the end-in-view. A logically important but sociologically insignificant source of unanticipated consequence exists because the aim of action limits the perception of its ramified consequences.[13] This is legitimate and necessary, for not all consequences are relevant to the aim. But here there arises a persistent dilemma. This very necessity to "keep your eye on the ball"—which demands the construction of a rational system explicitly relating means and ends—will restrain the actor from taking account of those consequences which indirectly shape the means and ends of policy. Because of the necessarily abstract and selective character of the formal criteria of judgment, there will always be a minimum residue of unanticipated consequence.[14]

---

[11] Consequences unanticipated from the viewpoint of the formal structure are not necessarily undesired. On the contrary, the result may be a satisfactory adjustment to internal and external circumstances, upon which the leadership may find it convenient to declare that the results were actually intended, though close analysis might show that this is actually a rationalization. In this type of unintended consequence, some need is fulfilled. The same unintended consequence may fulfill a need for a part of the organization and at the same time cause difficulties for the whole, and conversely. Many unintended consequences are, of course, sociologically irrelevant. For an early statement of this general problem, see Robert K. Merton, "The Unanticipated Consequences of Purposive Social Action," *American Sociological Review*, Vol. I (December, 1936).

[12] Where unintended consequences occur due to error, or to individual idiosyncrasy, they are sociologically irrelevant. However, there is often, though not always, a systematically nonrational factor at work whose presence is manifested by mistakes and personality problems.

[13] This follows, of course, from the hypothetical, and therefore discriminating and ordering, status of the end-in-view. See John Dewey, *Logic: The Theory of Inquiry* (New York: Henry Holt, 1938), pp. 496–97.

[14] The use of the terms "end-in-view" and "anticipated" may easily lead to the fallacy of formulating this problem as one of the subjective awareness of the participants. This is a serious error. What is really involved is that which is anticipated or unanticipated by the system of discrimination and judgment which is applied to the means at hand. This may, and very often does, involve subjective anticipation or its want, but need not do so. Moreover, the system may be adjusted so as to be able to take account of factors previously unpredicted and uncontrolled. This addition of systematically formulated criteria of relevance occurs continuously, as in the recognition of morale factors in industry. In the situation detailed above, the high self-consciousness of the American Farm Bureau Federation apparently led it to anticipate the possible rivalry from a new organization set up under the Agricultural Adjustment Administration, since it took steps to ward off this threat. See p. 161 [of *TVA and*

2. Commitment as a basic mechanism in the generation of unanticipated consequences. The sociologically significant source of unanticipated consequences inherent in the organizational process may be summed up in the concept of "commitment." This term has been used throughout this study to focus attention upon the structural conditions which shape organizational behavior. This is in line with the sociological directive, stated above, that constraints imposed by the system will be emphasized. A commitment in social action is an enforced line of action; it refers to decision dictated by the force of circumstance with the result that the free or scientific adjustment of means and ends is effectively limited. The commitment may be to goals, as where the existence of an organization in relation to a client public depends on the fulfillment of certain objectives;[15] or, less obviously, to means, derived from the recalcitrant nature of the tools at hand. The commitments generated by the use of self-activating and recalcitrant tools are expressed in the proliferation of unintended consequences.[16]

The types of commitment in organizational behavior identify the conditions under which a high frequency of unanticipated consequences may be expected to occur:

(i) Commitments enforced by uniquely organizational imperatives. An organizational system, whatever the need or intent which called it into being, generates imperatives derived from the need to maintain the system. We can say that once having taken the organizational road we are committed to action which will fulfill the requirements of order, discipline, unity, defense, and consent. These imperatives may demand measures of adaptation unforeseen by the initiators of the action, and may, indeed, result in a deflection of their original goals. Thus the tendency to work toward organizational unity will commit the organization as a whole to a policy originally relevant to only a part of the program. This becomes especially true where a unifying doctrine is given definite content

---

the Grass Roots]. This is no accidental perspicacity but a result of the systematic consideration of just such possible consequences from the implementation of new legislation. However, the tendency to ignore factors not considered by the formal system—not so much subjectively as in regard to the competence of the system to control them—is inherent in the necessities of action and can never be eliminated.

[15] As in the TVA's commitment to become a successful electric power business; this type of commitment was much milder in the distribution of fertilizer, permitting adaptation in this field which would contribute to the fulfillment of the prior commitment to electricity.

[16] Our use of the notion of unanticipated consequence assumes that the functional significance of such consequences is traceable within a specific field of influence and interaction. Thus price decisions made by a small enterprise affect the market (cumulatively with others), with ultimate unanticipated and uncontrolled consequence for future pricing decision. This is not an organizational process. When, however, the retailer builds up good will or makes decisions which will enforce his dependence upon some manufacturer, these are organizational acts within a theoretically controllable field, and are analyzable within the frame of reference set forth above.

by one subgroup: in order to preserve its special interpretation the subgroup presses for the extension of that interpretation to the entire organization so that the special content may be institutionalized.[17]

(ii) Commitments enforced by the social character of the personnel. The human tools of action come to an organization shaped in special but systematic ways. Levels of aspiration and training, social ideals, class interest—these and similar factors will have molded the character of the personnel. This will make staff members resistant to demands which are inconsistent with their accustomed views and habits; the freedom of choice of the employer will be restricted, and he will find it necessary in some measure to conform to the received views and habits of the personnel. Thus, in recruiting, failure to take into account initial commitments induced by special social origins will create a situation favorable to the generation of unanticipated consequences. The TVA's agricultural leadership brought with it ideological and organizational commitments which influenced over-all policy. This was a basically uncontrolled element in the organization. It is noteworthy that where the character of any organization is self-consciously controlled, recruitment is rigidly qualified by the criterion of social (class, familial, racial) origin.

(iii) Commitments enforced by institutionalization. Because organizations are social systems, goals or procedures tend to achieve an established, value-impregnated status. We say that they become institutionalized. Commitment to established patterns is generated, thus again restricting choice and enforcing special lines of conduct. The attempt to commit an organization to some course of action utilizes this principle when it emphasizes the creation of an established policy, or other forms of precedent. Further, the tendency of established relations and procedures to persist and extend themselves, will create the unintended consequence of committing the organization to greater involvement than provided for in the initial decision to act.[18] Where policy becomes institutionalized as doctrine, unanalyzed elements will persist, and effective behavior will be framed in terms of immediate necessities. An official doctrine whose terms are not operationally relevant will be given content in action, but this content will be informed by the special interests and problems of those to whom delegation is made. Hence doctrinal formulations will tend to reinforce the inherent hazard of delegation.[19] A variation of this situation occurs when the role of participants comes to overshadow in importance

---

[17] In the TVA, the agriculturists made vigorous efforts to extend their interpretation of the grass-roots policy to the Authority as a whole; in respect to the federal government, the TVA attempts to have its special interpretation of administrative decentralization become general public policy.

[18] See [*TVA and the Grass Roots*] p. 70 f.

[19] We have reviewed pp. 59–64, the unanalyzed abstractions in TVA's grass-roots doctrine, which are given content and meaning by the pressure of urgent organizational imperatives.

the achievement of formal goals. Action then becomes irresponsible, with respect to the formal goals.[20]

(iv) Commitments enforced by the social and cultural environment. Any attempt to intervene in history will, if it is to do more than comment upon events, find it necessary to conform to some general restraints imposed from without. The organizers of this attempt are committed to using forms of intervention consistent with the going social structure and cultural patterns. Those who ascend to power must face a host of received problems; shifts in public opinion will demand the reformulation of doctrine; the rise of competing organizations will have to be faced; and so on. The institutional context of organizations will have to be faced; and so on. The institutional context of organizational decision, when not taken into account, will result in unanticipated consequences. Thus intervention in a situation charged with conflict will mean that contending forces will weigh the consequences of that intervention for their own battle lines. The intervening organization must therefore qualify decision in terms of an outside controversy into which it is drawn despite itself. More obviously, the existence of centers of power and interest in the social environment will set up resistances to, or accept and shape to some degree, the program of the organization.

(v) Commitments enforced by the centers of interest generated in the course of action. The organizational process continuously generates subordinate and allied groupings whose leaderships come to have a stake in the organizational status quo. This generation of centers of interest is inherent in the act of delegation. The latter derives is precarious quality from the necessity to permit discretion in the execution of function or command. But in the exercise of discretion there is a tendency for decisions to be qualified by the special goals and problems of those to whom delegation is made. Moreover, in the discretionary behavior of a section of the apparatus, action is taken in the name of the organization as a whole; the latter may then be committed to a policy or course of action which was not anticipated by its formal program. In other words, the lack of effective control over the tangential informal goals of individuals and subgroups within an organization tends to divert it from its initial path. This holds true whether delegation is to members and parts of a single organization, or to other organizations.

These types of commitment create persistent tensions or dilemmas.[21] In a sense, they set the problems of decision and control, for we have identified here the key points at which organizational control breaks down. Operationally, a breakdown of control is evidenced in the generation of observable unanticipated consequences. This is the same as to say

---

[20] See pp. 205 ff.

[21] In effect, we have restated here some of the basic points made in the discussion of the inherent dilemmas of the TVA doctrine. See pp. 69–74.

that significant possibilities inherent in the situation have not been taken into account. The extension of control, with concomitant minimization of unintended consequence, is achieved as and if the frame of reference for theory and action points the way to the significant forces at work.

The problems indicated here are perennial because they reflect the interplay of more or less irreconcilable commitments: to the goals and needs of the organization and at the same time to the special demands of the tools or means at hand. Commitment to the tools of action is indispensable; it is of the nature of these tools to be dynamic and self-activating; yet the pursuit of the goals which initiated action demands continuous effort to control the instruments it has generated. This is a general source of tension in all action mediated by human, and especially organizational, tools.

The systematized commitments of an organization define its character. Day-to-day decisions relevant to the actual problems met in the translation of policy into action, create precedents, alliances, effective symbols, and personal loyalties which transform the organization from a profane, manipulable instrument into something having a sacred status and thus resistant to treatment simply as a means to some external goal. That is why organizations are often cast aside when new goals are sought.

The analysis of commitment is thus an effective tool for making explicit the structural factors relevant to decision in organized action. Attention is directed to the concrete process of choice, selecting those factors in the environment of decision which limit alternatives and enforce uniformities of behavior. When we ask, "To what are we committed?" we are speaking of the logic of action, not of contractual obligations freely assumed. So long as goals are given, and the impulse to act persists, there will be a series of enforced lines of action demanded by the nature of the tools at hand. These commitments may lead to unanticipated consequences resulting in a deflection of original goals.[22]

The Coöptative Mechanism

The frame of reference stated above includes the directive that organizational behavior be analyzed in terms of organizational response to organizational need. One such need is specified as "the security of the organization as a whole in relation to social forces in its environment." Responses, moreover, are themselves repetitive—may be thought of as mechanisms, following the terminology of analytical psychology in its analysis

---

[22] The British Labour Party, when it assumed power in 1945, had to accept a large number of commitments which followed simply from the effort to govern in those circumstances, independently of its special program. "Meeting a crisis," in a women's club as well as in a cabinet, is a precondition for the institution of special measures. To assume leadership is to accept these conditions.

of the ego and its mechanisms of defense. One such organizational mechanism is ideology; another, which has been the primary focus of this study, we have termed coöptation. We define this concept as "the process of absorbing new elements into the leadership or policy-determining structure of an organization as a means of averting threats to its stability or existence." Further, this general mechanism assumes two basic forms: formal coöptation, when there is a need to establish the legitimacy of authority or the administrative accessibility of the relevant public; and informal coöptation, when there is a need of adjustment to the pressure of specific centers of power within the community.

Coöptation in administration is a process whereby either power or the burdens of power, or both, are shared. On the one hand, the actual center of authority and decision may be shifted or made more inclusive, with or without any public recognition of the change; on the other hand, public responsibility for and participation in the exercise of authority may be shared with new elements, with or without the actual redistribution of power itself. The organizational imperatives which define the need for coöptation arise out of a situation in which formal authority is actually or potentially in a state of imbalance with respect to its institutional environment. On the one hand, the formal authority may fail to reflect the true balance of power within the community; on the other hand, it may lack a sense of historical legitimacy, or be unable to mobilize the community for action. Failure to reflect the true balance of power will necessitate a realistic adjustment to those centers of institutional strength which are in a position to strike organized blows and thus to enforce concrete demands. This issue may be met by the kind of coöptation which results in an actual sharing of power. However, the need for a sense of legitimacy may require an adjustment to the people in their undifferentiated aspect, in order that a feeling of general acceptance may be developed. For this purpose, it may not be necessary actually to share power: the creation of a "front" or the open incorporation of accepted elements into the structure of the organization may suffice. In this way, an aura of respectability will be gradually transferred from the coöpted elements to the organization as a whole, and at the same time a vehicle of administrative accessibility may be established.

We may suggest the hypothesis: Coöptation which results in an actual sharing of power will tend to operate informally, and correlatively, coöptation oriented toward legitimization or accessibility will tend to be effected through formal devices. Thus, an opposition party may be formally coöpted into a political administration through such a device as the appointment of opposition leaders to ministerial posts. This device may be utilized when an actual sharing of power is envisioned, but it is especially useful when its object is the creation of public solidarity, the legitimization of the representativeness of the government. In such circumstances, the opposition leaders may become the prisoners of the government, exchanging the hope of future power (through achieving public credit for holding office in a time of crisis) for the present function of sharing responsibility for the acts of the administration. The formal, public character of the coöptation is essential to the end in view. On the other hand, when coöptation is to fulfill the function of an adjustment to organized centers of institutional power within the community, it may be necessary to maintain relationships which, however consequential, are informal and covert. If adjustment to specific nucleuses of power becomes public, then the legitimacy of the formal authority, as representative of a theoretically undifferentiated community (the "people as a whole"), may be undermined. It therefore becomes useful and often essential for such coöptation to remain in the shadowland of informal interaction.

The informal coöptation of existing nucleuses of power into the total (formal plus informal) policy-determining structure of an organization, symptomatic of an underlying stress, is a mechanism of adjustment to concrete forces. On this level, interaction occurs among those who are in a position to muster forces and make them count, which means that the stake is a substantive reallocation of authority, rather than any purely verbal readjustment. Formal coöptation, however, is rather more ambiguous in relation to *de facto* reallocations of power. The sense of insecurity which is interpreted by a leadership as indicating a need for an increased sense of legitimacy in the community is a response to something generalized and diffuse. There is no hard-headed demand for a sharing of power coming from self-conscious institutions which are in a position to challenge the formal authority itself. The way things seem becomes, in this context, more important than the way they are, with the result that verbal formulas (degenerating readily into propaganda), and formal organizational devices, appear to be adequate to fill the need. The problem becomes one of manipulating public opinion, something which is necessarily beside the point when dealing with an organized interest group having an established and self-conscious leadership.

Formal coöptation ostensibly shares authority, but in doing so is involved in a dilemma. The real point is the sharing of the public symbols or administrative burdens of authority, and consequently public responsibility, without the transfer of substantive power; it therefore becomes necessary to insure that the coöpted elements do not get out of hand, do not take advantage of their formal position to encroach upon the actual arena of decision. Consequently, formal coöptation requires informal control over the coöpted elements lest the unity of command and decision be imperiled. This paradox is one of the sources of persistent tension between theory and practice in organizational behavior. The leadership, by the very nature of its position, is committed to two conflicting goals: if it ignores the need for participation, the goal of coöperation may be jeopardized; if participation is allowed to go too far, the continuity of leadership and policy may be threatened.[23]

---

[23] The analysis of unanticipated consequence and commitment is indispensable to the interpretation of behavior in terms of the coöptative mechanism. The commitments made in the course of action generate unanticipated consequences; in analyzing the function of these consequences we must construct a theory which will explain them as events consistent with the needs and potentialities of the system. At the same time, it must be understood that to formulate such defensive mechanisms as coöptation, is to state possible predicates. For the full understanding of organization it will be necessary to construct a system of such relevant responses which can serve to illuminate concrete cases.

9. MANAGING THE MANAGERS*

MELVILLE DALTON

THIS IS a report and analysis of the inter-managerial relations between the central office (hereafter Office) of a corporation and one of its units, as the managers of the Office imposed a control on those of the unit. The problem is twofold: first, to show the events leading to decisions, and second to follow the interplay between formal groups (representing official fiat) and informal groups (concerned with evading or modifying directives) from a given point to a working adjustment. The problem can best be presented by first tracing actions that led to intervention by the Office.

The Local Plant

Data on the exact size of the plant, the number of departments and executives, and the personnel and financial costs involved in changes must be withheld. But there were about 400 managers spread over more than five levels and many departments, with a total plant population of 9000.

Obstacles to Production

Poor gearing of maintenance activities with those of operation[1] precipitated reorganization of work processes. For years the maintenance shops had compiled the cost records of work done for the various departments, and the record then went to the Auditing Division which entered the charge against the department concerned. Though no complaints were made about the mechanics of clerical recording, the clashes between operation and maintenance groups over the growing volume of unfinished repair work was seen by some officers as indicating a defect in the auditing system. Research[2] showed that this backlog of hundreds of uncompleted orders was spread among the various departments in a way not explainable in terms of plant theory or technology. That is, while some

---

* Reproduced from *Human Organization*, Vol. 14, No. 3 (Fall, 1955), pp. 4–10.

[1] Both *maintenance* and *operation* groups were branches of the line organization—that exercising authority over production. Maintenance executives were in charge of repairing and replacing worn or broken equipment. Operation executives were responsible for volume of production and they, therefore, initiated much action for managers in the other branch.

[2] The writer was a participant observer in this plant. For more details of these initial phases see, "Industrial Controls and Personal Relations," *Social Forces*, March, 1955, pp. 244–49.

departments were abreast of their repair work, others were greatly in arrears. Research indicated that these variations were related to differentials in authority exercised among executives who were of equal formal rank. No scaling of the differentials was attempted because of the conflict and secrecy attending behavior in this area. But instances personally witnessed, and cases reported by intimates, showed that the executives who obtained priority in the shops bullied the maintenance officers concerned and tacitly threatened to interfere with the flow of essential informal favors[3] coming to them if they did not give special consideration to their work. In the drive to meet production, while keeping equipment in top order with replacement parts on hand, such department heads achieved "clean" records at the expense of less influential heads who went "deeper in the hole" from disinclination and/or inability to alter the situation.

Supported by the Office, top local management agreed that changes should be made. There was much debate as to why the maintenance function had collapsed and, not knowing this, what should be done. Without pinpointing cases, some of the executives said bluntly that "politics" was responsible. Others saw "soldiering" and "laying down on the job" by maintenance machinists as the cause—a view taken by several top managers and some of the staff groups. This faction had difficulty thinking that the burden of the problem grew out of supervisory relationships, as suggested by the term "politics." They saw laggard work groups as the source, and hence favored a wage plan to stimulate shop mechanics to greater maintenance effort. But a faction of local and Office administrators decided most aspects of the issue by forcing through their view that the "only solution" was a new control to impersonalize relations at several points between executives of Maintenance and Operation.

STRUCTURE AND OPERATION OF THE CONTROL

Structure

The reorganizers theorized that Operation's orders for maintenance service should pass through a neutral department—to be created—to which all records showing the course of each order and the time charged against it should be returned.

Eventually set up as the Field Work Department (FWD), the new

---

[3] These favors of Operation to Maintenance included: (1) co-operation to "cover up" errors (or at least share responsibility) made by maintenance machinists; (2) defense for the need of new personnel; (3) support (in meetings) against changes recommended by staff groups that in the thinking of maintenance people would disturb currently more desirable arrangements; and (4) sympathetic consideration (and verbal support to top management) of the technological needs of the maintenance group for its survival and success in meeting demands of the operation branch.

entity was manned by about 100 personnel selected from both line branches. Each member had a broad knowledge of plant processes and was also an expert in one or more maintenance specialities such as layout, pipe-fitting, welding, machine operation, brick-laying, motor repair, etc. All were under a divisional superintendent of maintenance who had earlier served in the operating branch. He was aided by several staff experts, including industrial engineers. Orders for maintenance service from Operation executives were clocked in and out of the FWD. By this means and the use of serial numbers, priority of service in the shops was established. The order submitted was circulated among the specialists of FWD who listed essential materials, closely estimated the operations and time required for each job, laid out a route for it to follow among the shop machines and processes, and finally totaled the cost that would be required.

With nominal freedom to bargain first for a smaller or larger estimate, the top departmental executive was required in the end to sign the FWD estimate which gave him no justification for a wide departure. The job then went to the shops to follow a fixed route. The actual time and cost of processing was recorded by the shop clerical group which, like the foremen, was protected by the FWD buffer from coercion by Operation executives. When completed, the record of movements, operations and charges was compiled in the shop, one copy being sent to the Auditing Department and one to the FWD.

In a short time the FWD accomplished the purpose for which it was set up—to open the bottleneck of maintenance orders and keep the stream flowing. But unexpected events followed. FWD records showed increasing variations between its estimates and the reports of actual charges returned from the shops. Some of the executives were greatly exceeding FWD estimates while others were far below—and were getting some jobs completed with no charges against them. Inquiry revealed that the executives formerly without a backlog were now having excessive costs while, for the most part, the other group (heads of the smaller departments) were now much more efficient in terms of cost; several of them had reduced their expenses by half.

This nearly complete reversal of rank in the scale of competent operation was accomplished by hidden collaboration between the long-depressed maintenance foremen and the heads of smaller departments. Each had a score to settle. The foremen had been "pushed around" by the aggressive executives (usually the heads of larger departments) who were now relatively checked by the FWD. On the other hand, the superintendents who had smarted from the implication that their backlogs meant poor management were now in the ascendent. Their reward for not having terrorized maintenance foremen was to find friends among the latter ready to cooperate in charging work time to accounts of the larger departments.[4]

Top local management demanded an explanation of the great discrepancies. The FWD, the shop foremen and their clerical groups, as well as the Auditing Department and both groups of operating executives, each cleared itself logically of all implied malfeasance or collusion. Though top executives did not uncover the informal tie between shop foremen and heads of the smaller departments, they did suspect that unforeseen events had somehow sprung from altered conditions attending the creation of the FWD. Hence the FWD was practically nullified. Then one entire shop was dismantled and its equipment distributed among several of the departments to form centers of departmental maintenance, which succeeded the original division of maintenance. This was a formal reorganization arising from informal action nurtured by friendly ties, antipathies, and the need to escape over-all cost pressures that had not been lessened by introduction of the FWD.

It was soon discovered that the new scheme of departmental maintenance was not a solution because of friction in the department between operation and maintenance personnel, but it was continued on a reduced scale. In the meantime, accumulated dissatisfaction had led the Office to develop its own plan for simultaneously abating Maintenance-Operation friction and bring maintenance costs under rigid control.[5] This plan was now introduced.

With reorganization in the plant, and shift of authority (over much of the maintenance work) from the plant to the Office, the problem changes focus. We need now to examine how formal expectations of the Office initiated informal activity in the local plant, and to follow the interplay between formal and informal to a new adjustment.

PROGRAM OF THE OFFICE

The new plan can be discussed under: (1) cost aspects, and (2) personnel reorganization.

---

[4] Because of having much repetitive work to be done, the larger departments each were given a "standing order number" (subject to annual change) to which such work was charged. In the new informal alignments appearing with the FWD, maintenance foremen found this number to be a useful device (but not the sole one) for rewarding friends and penalizing enemies.

[5] Research in relations between the Office and the local plant was carried on under new limitations. First, the writer had no personal communication with the Office. Knowledge of the Office was derived from: (1) infrequent association with some of its less responsible people who visited the plant; (2) executives in the local plant who had formerly been in the Office and continued to communicate with friends there; (3) a few local executives who made occasional trips to the Office; and (4) intimates who were critically involved in meeting expectations of the Office.

Cost Aspects

The major item in the plan to cut maintenance outlays was a "surplus parts program." This was aimed at compiling a record of all reserve equipment on hand in each department of the plant, and establishing a permanent system for keeping the record up-to-date. Next, the purchase of new parts was to be taken largely out of the hands of local management, though the plan was so introduced that local managers could appear to have a voice in such purchases.

Initially the Office requested a listing of the number of parts on hand that cost $500 or more, and of those parts currently needed or that might be needed by the end of a given period. The intent was to start with the more expensive parts and systematically lower the figure.

Personnel Reorganization

It was believed in the Office that a simple request for such information, to be reported in writing, was unlikely to accomplish its purpose. The realistic move, it was held, would be to create new and specific functions and assign able men to enforce them. After the collapse of the elaborate FWD, however, simplicity and directness were seen as basic to any reorganization, so only two new positions were planned in the local plant.

Conferences concerning the change to be made were held by Office representatives with a few top local executives. Once the department heads learned of the developing plan, those without maintenance backlogs prior to the FWD now wished to influence selection of the officers who would fill the new posts as liaison men between the Office and the local plant. Their superiors, the local divisional executives, supported the movement. Initially, 11 executives worked as what may be called an aggressive horizontal clique (cutting across several departments) to convince Assistant Plant Manager, J. Swain,[6] that the choice should be made entirely by the local plant. (Swain's informal status in the plant gave him greater weight in daily affairs than his superior, the General Manager). Swain clearly regarded the pending control as interference with local authority,

---

[6] All personal names are fictitious. Swain had attained his present position in his late twenties after only a few years in the plant as a chemist. To move so quickly from a *staff* post to such a high *line* position was unique in the plant. He excelled in analyzing obscure and elusive situations, in seizing events useful to himself and in using extraplant social activities to strengthen his position. When necessary he bartered favors and surrounded himself with followers whom he rewarded variously for their support. He was treated as a charismatic figure, though the formal organization was, of course, a complex bureaucracy. He had intimate knowledge of all the executives from having worked with them earlier at their official level. The General Manager had been imported from another unit of the corporation and lacked such personal knowledge.

and agreed with the clique of executives that "we should pick some good men."

The Office, without knowledge of this intent among the group of local managers, was simultaneously searching for a device to soften the impact of its cost plan. Failure of the FWD was seen by the Office as leaving the local managers sensitive about the whole subject of cost control—and even indisposed to be cooperative. Therefore the Office voluntarily asked the local plant for suggestions about suitable candidates from its own ranks to serve as liaison men.

This request precipitated several meetings between Swain and the 11 executives and other less influential officers, to agree on candidates for the positions. Some of the minor officers held for what was requested as "able men" to fill the posts. However, members of the clique, with Swain silent for some time, insisted on two individuals who were regarded as *not* being "able men." Quickly it was seen that the persons chosen were to be amenable to the wishes of the clique. When Swain added his voice the decision was made.

The candidates were R. Jackson and B. Wetzel. When the choice was announced and the candidates accepted by the Office, several of the heads of the smaller departments declared that both were "weak" and "impossible" in the roles given them. Jackson was seen as having been "out-maneuvered" in a contest for one of the divisional superintendencies, and, in the thinking of many, this was proof of his unfitness. Jackson's private life was regarded as irregular. His wife had recently divorced him with much commotion in the local community. His heavy drinking, and his repeated defeats in collisions with the union were viewed as further proof of his inadequacy and "willingness to go along with any policy" of his superiors.

Wetzel was nearing retirement on a pension, which he was concerned not to risk losing by displeasing superiors. He was known to dislike responsibilities and repeatedly he was spoken of as being "afraid of his job," i.e., fearful of not being able to meet expectations and of the consequences.

Most of the local staff officers, who were only observers as far as this issue was concerned, saw the selection of Jackson and Wetzel as "manipulation" by local top management "for their own ends."

In his new duties Jackson was to be responsible to no one in the local plant but Swain. And this was a qualified responsibility, for Jackson was expected to communicate freely and directly with the Office, something that not over three of the 400 odd local officers were privileged to do. Jackson's duties were to inspect and approve each "parts report" turned in to his office and to verify its correctness, presumably by personal inspection and count of parts. Officially he was the only officer in the plant with power to authorize the order of new parts.

Jackson was to be assisted by Wetzel. However, Wetzel was responsible only to the Office for his duties. He was to initiate the reports by periodically requesting statements from each superintendent of Operation. Thus he, rather than Jackson, made the face-to-face contacts. After obtaining the statements, Wetzel turned them over to Jackson who certified them with his signature and returned them to Wetzel to be mailed to the Office. The Office then issued the superintendent in question a certificate of authorization which for a specified time enabled him to buy necessary parts from the outside without going through the Office, though each purchase, during any period, required Jackson's approval.

By thus focusing on two individuals, neither of whom had authority over the other and both of whom had direct access to the Office (in order to escape local pressures), the control was regarded as simple, direct and manageable. While no formal statements were made of psychic or other incentives to bind the two officers to their duties, their acceptance by the Office was generally regarded as a high honor.

THE CONTROL IN CHANGE AND ACCOMMODATION

Initial Executive Reaction

Following introduction of the parts program, Wetzel met official expectations by notifying the department heads that he was ready to receive statements. When after two weeks no answers reached his office, he made further requests. A few officers gave excuses of inadequate help, prior problems to be cared for, etc., but no records of parts.

They were restrained by the Swain clique which had expanded and was attempting to coerce all department heads and assistants to adopt a specific approach to the control. The hope was to resist it as long as possible while studying it "to find ways to make it work." Despite the esteem in which Swain was held, several chiefs of the lesser units favored compliance with the Office but feared the outcome of challenging the clique. Skilled in evaluating and exploiting vague situations, clique members advanced arguments and formulas for meeting the Office. They beat down vocal opposition and frightened others into silence.

The arguments used against executives who feared the Office showed the issue to be primarily one of who exercised authority in the plant—local executives or the Office. Swain saw the program as "too inflexible and causing too much trouble." One of the dominant executives long accustomed to initiating action far beyond his official limits declared:

The thing I've got against the whole damn set-up is procedures. Every time you turn around you run into a rule that stymies you. Some chair-warmer (in the Office) cooks up a crack-pot notion of how things ought to be done. Maybe he was never in the plant but he don't let that bother him. He writes it up and sends it out. Then by God it's up to us to make it work. The way I feel about it is this: if the set-up is so damned far-fetched that you can't make it work, why bother with it at all? What the hell do they think we're out here for? We know our jobs. If they'd leave us alone we'd never have any trouble.

Verbal reactions of this kind and knowledge of Swain's attitude left no doubt among the resisters that meeting Wetzel's request would be hazardous for their future in the organization.

In the meantime Wetzel was becoming increasingly disturbed by his failure but was helpless to act in the situation. He talked to confidants of how "fidgety" he was getting and of his need "to be doing something." He also considered visiting a psychiatrist. After six weeks of growing distress over his inability to bridge the gap between his expectations of his post and those of local executives (communicated to him anonymously) that he was to do nothing, Wetzel received a letter from the Office asking for a progress report. Accustomed to following official directives as literally as possible—and still having no statements—he notified the Office that the departmental heads "refused to cooperate."

Response of the Office

On learning that Wetzel was unsuccessful with his assignment, the Office sent several investigators to the plant. Tightness of the local informal group limited their findings, but they prepared a statement praising the efforts of Wetzel and censuring the department heads "for failure to cooperate" with him. Copies of the report were distributed at the Office among local top managers.

Wetzel's desperation and resulting action had not been foreseen by the executives. Support by the Office meant that despite Wetzel's docility new devices were necessary to control him. Part of the assumed incentive of his new role was that he would "enjoy" the leisure of what was really a sinecure. But as noted previously, in his dilemma about what to do his leisure was spent in mulling over his anxieties, and thus failed to be a reward.

Swain and others decided to surround Wetzel with more concrete status symbols as an inducement. His quarters were set up in a new office, superior in size and appointments. He was given a secretary and new equipment including filing cabinets and a dictaphone. The need to control the character of his communications to the Office led the executives to reinforce their gifts of the trappings of rank with a flattering personal appeal. To that end several of the managers, accompanied by Jackson, went to Wetzel's office and proposed that "we work this thing out together. After all, we don't want to do anything to stir up trouble."

Whether from the combined inducements or from fear, Wetzel agreed to go along with the executives, whose greatest need was to prevent a count of parts.

Tactics of Escape

Though some of the superintendents continued to be fearful of the Office they cooperated to thwart an accurate count of their surplus elements.

The motivation to hide parts was complex. The satisfaction of outwitting authority was probably much less important than the obscure urge to preserve an accustomed set of "rights" involving command of the plant. But judging from observable actions and spontaneous remarks, the major factor was the assumed need of maintaining a margin of funds to use for ends other than operating costs in the narrow sense. That is, the proportion of parts hidden was much influenced by the daily demands of personal relations[7] as well as those of the organization. Demands requiring expenditures that could not unequivocally be interpreted as maintenance costs could nevertheless be charged to such costs. These demands might include: (1) part- or full-time employment of the relatives or friends of associates from both the plant and the community; (2) a given executive's wish to have materially ostentatious offices in the department; (3) possible emergencies in a period of change; and (4) the need to use plant services and materials to get more cooperation from subordinates and colleagues.

Before the executives showed resistance to the Office, Wetzel's instructions were to make formal requests for an account of parts. Now, to contain the evasion, the Office indicated that Jackson's division of labor would include surprise inspections and count of parts in each department. Both he and Wetzel were alarmed by this new directive, but neither had the courage to carry out the orders as intended. Their adjustment (apparently after conferences with members of the executive clique) was not to make a surprise count but, in advance of the tour, to telephone various key officers informing them of the starting point, time, and route the inspection would follow.[8] Since none of these variables were the same on succeeding inspections, each inspection did appear to be unscheduled.

---

[7] This is to say that *gemeinschaftliche* elements functioned with varying freedom despite restrictions of the *gesellschaftliche* structure, or more correctly that such elements functioned inside and concomitantly with the logical order. Overemphasis on the formal structure by some theorists of bureaucracy amounts to *forbidding the Gemeinschaft* in a planned structure. Tönnies clearly thought a logical organization impossible without a sustaining emotional basis. And Cooley, in viewing human nature (in his sense) as springing from personal relations would, by implication, see it disappear in purely impersonal relations—or absence of personal relations. See H. E. Barnes (Ed.), *An Introduction to the History of Sociology* (Chicago: University of Chicago Press, 1948), pp. 234 and 837. Also R. E. L. Faris, *Social Psychology* (New York: Ronald Press Co., 1952), pp. 338–49. The point labored here is truistic to many sociologists but not appreciated by others.

[8] The physical plant covered over a square mile and was broken into many units and subunits connected by numbered walkways and zoned driveways.

This was not an original device. Use of nominal surprise was common in the plant, and between the plant and the Office in other activities also. For example, visits from members of the parent organization were planned, but given a camouflage of spontaneity that served the needs of both groups. Managers from the Office were thereby spared the unpleasantness of seeing a condition of which they should be officially ignorant, and of feeling embarrassment in possessing knowledge that presupposed corrective action by them. The condition and the potential consequence of action would of course sully the friendly call and hence should be avoided. For their part, local officers reduced the time, cost, and interference with routine, of setting up acceptable appearances by deciding in advance the specific path through the plant that the tour would follow. Then just on the fringes of the entire route, equipment was cleaned and possibly painted, walks and driveways were disencumbered and swept, and everything "put in order."

Nominal surprise was also a conflict preventive in the local plant. For example, the safety inspector (and other inspectors) usually telephoned unofficially in advance of a visit so that he would not see unsafe practices or conditions that he would feel obliged to report. Thus he escaped present embarrassment for himself and avoided incurring the hostility that an offended associate might feel at a time when that officer's good will could be personally helpful in the ongoing and elusive structure of personal claims in which all the executives unavoidably moved.

The fiction of surprise thus enabled all persons involved to maintain official dignity and to give the appearance of following formal procedures despite inevitable obstacles and frequent impossibility.

Notification that a count was under way provoked a flurry among the executives to hide some of the parts. Motor and hand trucks with laborers and skilled workers who could be spared were assembled in a given department. Then the materials not to be counted were moved to: (1) little known and inaccessible spots in the plant; (2) basements and pits that were dirty and therefore unlikely to be examined; (3) departments that had already been inspected and that could be approached circuitously while the counters were en route between the official storage areas; and (4) areas where other materials and supplies might be used as a camouflage for parts.

As the practice developed, cooperation among the chiefs to use each others' storage areas and spare pits became well organized and smoothly functioning. And joint action of a kind rarely, if ever, shown in carrying on official activities enabled the relatively easy passage of laborers and truckers from one work area to another without serious complications for the formal organization.

Reports of surplus parts on hand now arrived regularly in Wetzel's office. Probably in no case, however, were the statements minutely correct. But Jackson approved the papers and Wetzel dispatched them. Thus an accommodation was reached. The Office received its required flow of documents, and though only roughly accurate, they did allow planning within workable limits; by *de jure* conformity to the Office and *de facto* surrender to the executives, Jackson and Wetzel eluded the tug of cross-claims on themselves; friction between Operation and Maintenance subsided to a low level; and, finally, the superintendents preserved their conception of executive rights, and by their action raised morale in the local organization.

SOME IMPLICATIONS

We have followed attempts in the plant, and between the plant and the parent organization, to control human factors interfering with one goal—low maintenance costs. We have seen a sensitive equilibrium reached in the adjustment of local executives to their superiors in the Office. This was accomplished in great part by the rise and dominance of a horizontal clique which worked to resist literal application of the control and to adapt it to their view of local needs. In doing this, the clique saw as crucial the need to select extra-clique members of the executive group to accomplish clique ends. Largely by chance the selection fit in with Office tactics intended to soften introduction of the control.

Conflict over authority between the two entities has been dealt with. But there is also a need to spell out the social-psychological meaning of conflict as a force in shaping the type of personality dominant in situations where covert alignments reduce the certainty of how to act and raise threats both to an individual's current aims and his career objectives if unsuccessful action is taken. And the significance of interaction between formal and informal organizations as a factor in on-going organizational change needs further comment.

The Successful Personality

The data show the individual executive caught between official and unofficial claims on his behavior. Unavoidably aware of formal commitments inherent in directives reaching him, and in varying degrees conscious of his role implications, he was involved in conflict when faced by associates demanding contrary action or silent approval of such action. The request from others for aid, or assured non-interference, might be supplemented with verbal attacks on the shortcomings of existing regulations. The executive might privately admit such shortcomings and yet feel an official obligation to defend them. He wanted complete knowledge of the behavior of subordinates and associates, but if the behavior were contrary to official guides he wished to be thought ignorant of it. Often he and those of similar outlook wished to protect their formal integrity but profit from successful acts of initiative by others. Consequently, they advised colleagues to deal with responsibilities as they saw fit, but not to report the means used.

Some middle-ranking executives particularly hesitated to act on knowledge of the formally unacceptable. They saw open action in such cases as admission of the existence of conditions that their alertness (in the eyes of superiors) should have prevented. And further, they felt unable informally to handle the problem without surrendering personal codes and exposing their future actions to the counter claims of executives guided more by the principle of favor-bartering than by official rules.

These opposed claims on the individual made the plant an arena for selection[9] and development of executives most fit for squaring informal with formal demands. The writer's movement among hostile groups, alert to guard the activities of concern here, prevented any controlled examination of personality qualities. But the behavior items important to ongoing conduct in the plant and to informal leadership in crises (and eventually formal leadership) were still clear enough to be treated as a type.

In terms of potential for absorbing or escaping conflict while continuing to move toward organizational goals, two general types of executives were discernible. For want of precise terms they can be labeled as weak and strong. These terms have reference only to activity in the plant. They might or might not apply to some aspects of extra-plant life. Other descriptive couplets with a less moral connotation (and also less apt for denoting the presence or absence of what seemed essential) that might be used, are: flexible-inflexible, rule-bound vs. rule-creative, compliant-evasive, submissive-dominant, entrepreneurial-bureaucratic, etc. Among the more specific items helpful in setting up the typology were: (1) relative respect or indifference for rules as shown by verbal and overt action; (2) such obvious signs of personal conflict as raised voice in a context of bitter remarks about superiors, associates, and general conditions; (3) the recounting of "troubles" to others; (4) remonstrances about "How am I expected to do that?"; (5) the consulting with superiors to the point of

---

[9] This idea poses the ancient and oversimplified issue of whether executives (or any leaders) are "born" or "made." The writer is disposed to think that "middleclass" origin and college attendance (as an experience) are related to the executive role. By "middle class" is meant the set of influences presumed to imbue with personal drive, to form certain attitudes toward success, etc. Those with this orientation who see their college experiences as a career aid are more likely to acquire attitudes functional to the executive role than are those without it. The complex of attitudes in question will focus on ends rather than means. Such individuals may shape the social environment of the executive. Or, at the other extreme, the executive role may select those of suitable personality. And possibly the role may also select personalities influenced to a degree by unexplained biological endowments not acquirable by training. The relative weight of what is brought to the role in terms of biological and social endowment and what the role selects is unassessed. In any case there is doubtless interplay between the two—and among other factors.

annoying them; (6) repeated comment among associates (presumably a shared appraisal) that a given executive was "going sour," or "letting his job get him down." Presence of the last five items was typical of those called weak.

Such a typology has the shortcoming that many individuals fall between, but the merit of giving a pole to the cluster of variations.

Those in the category of weak are fearful in conflict situations and absorb aggressions to avoid clashes.[10] They find difficulty acting without consulting superiors. Having a low tolerance for conflict, they do not fill their offices to formal expectations. They seek safety in adherence to formulated rules,[11] which aggravates their difficulty in grasping tacit expectations that associates do not wish to spell out. When regulations are changed they adjust slowly and often fail in the interim to make passable use of the new directive. In their life outside the plant, where conflict is less or different, they may function acceptably, yet fail when trapped among competing claims peculiar to the plant. When the weak fail to meet official expectations they are likely to advertise the fact. In their distress they involve colleagues in trouble by blunders that disclose departmental secrets. As they seek to escape their dilemma, their unfitness to act outside clear-cut rules invites aggression from the strong who are searching for elastic areas in the formal structure.

On the other hand, the strong have high tolerance for conflict, and, unlike the weak, carry little effect of job discords from the plant with them. They flee neither necessary conflict nor responsibility for making decisions. They are able to act quickly and effectively, and are skilled in turning ambiguous and contradictory situations to their needs. By almost imperturbably resolving contrary demands on themselves, they aid superiors as well as subordinates and thus exert influence beyond the limits of their official status. Where the weak look for protection in the letter of rules, the strong oppose strict interpretations. If the strong do not adjust quickly to new regulations, or reorganizations arising from outside the plant, they at least use them successfully, if distortedly, with small distress for themselves and minimum damage to official goals. If they are unable to meet official expectations, they utilize the failure to establish a bearing. It was the strong who initiated resistance to the Office and forced re-interpretation of the program. The weak were obliged to conform regardless of their attitudes, for the strong as a rule were in posts that gave them power to reward and punish in many indirect ways.

In short, the weak are prone to lose sight of goals in concentrating on procedures. Hence in unstable situations not yet covered by rules, or where rules are outdated or will never be detailed, they cannot devise

---

[10] Jackson and Wetzel were examples specifically cited.

[11] But as occurred repeatedly in the plant, action by dominant individuals may force the weak to overstep regulations in order to protect themselves.

apt ways of behaving. This, as against the strong, who are so relatively unconcerned with procedure (except as it is a clear aid or can be interpreted to their advantage) and accustomed to moving directly toward goals, that they devise workable methods as needed where situations are doubtful.

In plant parlance the weak and strong executives were variously identified. In general the officers here called weak were spoken of as being "unable to cut the buck," being a "foul ball," as having "no guts," "no savvy," and as being "boneheads," etc. The strong were characterized as "a guy you can count on," or "who won't let you down," as having "a lot on the ball," as "doing what's necessary," as being "on the beam," as one who "really stacks up," "a damn good man," etc. And these phrases refer for the most part to competence or its absence in action that was unwittingly experimental[12] in areas where official guides were becoming inadequate or could never be adequate.

Informal versus Formal Action[13]

The preceding comments suggest that simple functional analysis is adequate to explain what occurred in effecting change in the plant. The problem is more complex. Informal action by certain executives toward correction of deficiencies in the formal organization was indeed a force in spurring the series of formal containment steps. Informal action *in toto,* growing out of competition among executives to win priority on repair work and hold costs down, had the effect of ordering the FWD, but there was little meaningful effort toward that end by the executives in this action. They had no vision of the FWD as an outgrowth. The executives who in time worked toward the FWD did so as a consequence, not as part of the action of the dominant executives. Executive rivalry initially excluded reorganization as an answer to the dilemma. Only when action by the minority led to an intolerable condition was there meaningful effort to restructure the system. Failure of the FWD was also more a result of evasive than purposeful action. Between the FWD and a workable ad-

---

[12] See Peter F. Drucker, *Concept of the Corporation* (New York: John Day Co., 1946), p. 37, for comment on the problems of "balance between . . . principles and adaptability to changing conditions." Also Reinhard Bendix, "Bureaucracy: The Problem and Its Setting," *American Sociological Review,* October, 1947, pp. 493–507.

[13] Informal organization as it functions among workers is discussed by F. J. Roethlisberger and W. J. Dickson, *Management and the Worker* (Cambridge: Harvard University Press, 1938), pp. 524 ff.; and by Wilbert E. Moore, *Industrial Relations and the Social Order* (2d ed.; New York: Macmillan Co., 1951), pp. 273–93. Theory of informal organization applicable to administrative hierarchies is well treated by Chester I. Barnard (himself an executive), *The Functions of the Executive* (Cambridge: Harvard University Press, 1938), pp. 114–23; by Philip Selznick, *TVA and the Grass Roots* (University of California Press, 1949, pp. 250–61; and by Robert Dubin, *Human Relations in Administration* (New York: Prentice-Hall Inc., 1951), pp. 47–78.

justment under the Office, executive action was at first disruptive and meaningless in terms of the larger system. Throughout the change, a minority favored stricter adherence to directives, but feared to oppose the Swain clique.

The adjustment became functional only as personal relationships were built up to interpret and successfully transmute the logical plan to interlock with current elusive involvements. The movement to this was tortuous and much of it meaningless in terms of the end result. And from the beginning to the unstable "end," chance events, effort guided by fear of veiled reprisal, commerce in favors, and side issues were part and parcel of the ongoing action—dysfunction inhered in function.[14]

------

[14] See H. Blumer, "Group Tension and Interest Organizations" in Milton Derber (Ed.), *Proceedings of the Second Annual Meeting, Industrial Relations Research Association,* 1949, pp. 150–158; and R. K. Merton, *Social Theory and Social Structure* (Glencoe, Ill.: The Free Press, 1949), p. 53.

10. THE BACKGROUND AND IMPLICATIONS OF THE RAND CORPORATION SYSTEMS RESEARCH LABORATORY STUDIES*

Robert L. Chapman and John L. Kennedy

The System Studied

It became obvious early in these studies that simulation techniques and techniques for controlling large-scale experiments would have to be pushed beyond their current state of development and that it would be necessary to select a kind of organization that lent itself to being studied with the new techniques. The system selected was suited to these laboratory techniques; it was also of critical importance to the Air Force and one that had enough in common with other systems to give the results generality.

This system was the air-defense direction center, an organization that defends a portion of the United States against enemy air attack. In many ways a direction center is a complete system; it has all the information available about the air traffic in its area and controls weapons for stopping enemy air attacks. What was simulated in the laboratory was a close approximation to a real direction center—a full-scale model manned by a standard crew of 30 to 40 men. Four air-defense experiments were conducted. Each ran for about 200 hours—the equivalent of about six weeks of normal life in a real direction center.

A direction center is a rather complex organization with quite a complex job to do. The laboratory crews had to defend an area of roughly 100,000 square miles. During each experiment there were about 10,000 flights over this area. The air traffic, which increased more than threefold during the experiment, included a wide variety of flights—from commercial air liners on transoceanic flights to cub aircraft hedgehopping from airport to airport. Hostile attacks on targets in the area ranged from single bombers trying to camouflage themselves in the flight-plan traffic to mass raids of as many as 25 hostiles. Symbols containing information about these flights came into the system at an average of 300 a minute—a rate of information input that added up to something like two million symbols during an experiment.

Two conceptual issues, resolved before the experiments started, were crucial ones for making these studies possible. Both of these issues, which were concerned with the kind of organization to be studied, delimited a complicated problem.

---

* Reproduced from RAND Paper P–740, September 21, 1955.

First of all, the air-defense direction center is an organization in which task accomplishment has a well-accepted social value and one whose successes and failures are fairly easy to evaluate at almost any time during its operation. A experimenter can have confidence in an air-defense crew's motivation to defend the country against air attack and in recognition of success and failure. And this motivation is complicated very little by previous personal histories. The complex of values, attitudes, and beliefs that influence this organization's development are derived mostly from the crew's experience with air defense. Because the groups studied were newly assembled, a good part of this happened right in the laboratory.

A second advantage of studying a direction center is that more of the group's activity can be observed than in many other organizations. Much of the crew's behavior in dealing with its task is verbal response to known stimuli—either to other verbal behavior or to task information coming into the system. There is little of importance that can't be seen or heard by the experimenter.

Since these experiments involved groups of nearly 40 men, choosing a system that had these characteristics simplified the problem tremendously. The motivation of the men under study and the means of measuring system effectiveness were both relatively uncomplicated. Most of the group's relevant behavior—and the way this behavior changed—was exposed to view.

The Methods Used

Although a description of the system studied gives some idea of the size and scope of the experiments, the ideas behind these experiments can be put into a larger context and one that is probably more meaningful. Since the effects of equipment modifications were not the object of study, the physical resources were kept constant during each experiment and the task was varied. Any improvements in performance depended entirely on each crew's skill in using the resources it already had.

The Systems Research Laboratory's facilities are used to study human organizations in much the same way a wind tunnel is used in developing new aircraft. In both methods the experimenters manipulate an environment to apply stress to highly detailed models so that the performance of the prototype can be predicted and changes made to improve it. A wind tunnel uses a detailed scale model of the aircraft whose flight characteristics are being studied; the Systems Research Laboratory used a model organization of 30 to 40 men that was practically full scale. By exposing the models to critical environmental conditions over and over again in different combinations, both facilities can be used to expose weak points in the design of the prototype.

Both wind tunnels and this way of studying organizations rely heavily on elaborate measuring devices. And both of them accumulate enormous amounts of data—so much, in fact, that a corps of specialized professional, technical, and clerical workers is needed to handle it.

Research facilities such as the Systems Research Laboratory, again like wind tunnels, are big and expensive, but they may well become as indispensable in designing and improving systems as wind tunnels are in designing aircraft.

But with all these similarities, there is one main difference between wind-tunnel studies of aircraft and large-scale laboratory research with human organizations. In experiments with organizations, the laboratory model changes under stress. It learns. Learning is an invaluable characteristic. It is also a complicating one. Because organizations learn, a formula for predicting their performance, unlike a formula for predicting the behavior of aircraft, has to take into account the way the organization changes under stress.

Although aspiring to study complete man-machine systems is obviously fine in principle, worthwhile results depend on how effectively aspirations are translated into experimental form. An important aspect of this translation is gaining "observational access to the phenomena." "Observational access" is more than being able to get meaningful data—it's primarily a problem of getting worthwhile phenomena to occur at all. If an organization is to be observed under a variety of conditions, it's essential that the men who are being studied function as an organization and not just as a group of individuals and that they are stimulated to develop as an organization—to learn as a group. This failed to happen in the first experiment— the organization learned so much faster than it had been expected to that long before the experiment was over the task that had been so carefully prepared became so easy that the group's performance was no longer worth observing.

Results and Theory

The outstanding empirical result of these experiments was the degree to which an air-defense crew can learn to use its resources more effectively. That a group of human beings can learn is by no means a momentous conclusion—after all, it seems rather obvious to say that the performance of a system can be improved if it has resources of one kind or another that it hasn't used before. What was startling in these experiments was the extent to which performance could be improved by exploiting these unused resources. Although the task load was increased gradually so that it was more than three times as great at the end of the experiment as it had been in the beginning, each of the four crews kept up a highly effective defense of the area against enemy air attack.

Because an organization whose achievement is readily measured was chosen for study, the evidence for saying that organizational development did take place is readily found. Although traffic was continually increased during each experiment to the point where, in the last part of each experiment, it was heavier than the normal air traffic in any part of the United States, each crew's defense against hostile attacks of all kinds continued at a more effective level than we had any reason to expect. (Incidentally there were so many similarities in performance and development among the four crews that crew learning can be considered in the singular, since what happened in any one of the crews was fairly typical of all of them.)

But the scientific significance of the Systems Research Laboratory's work is the way these experiments exposed the process of organizational development.

Just what does an air-defense crew do to maintain effective performance in dealing with a task that keeps getting harder and harder? A rather obvious answer is that it spends its efforts more efficiently. With each increase in the number of tracks the crew had to deal with, saturation seemed imminent because the crew found it more and more difficult to continue handling each track with its current procedures. But each time that saturation seemed imminent, some way of simplifying the job was found.

One way to measure the effort a crew expends is by the number of items of information, such as position reports, it uses to handle the task. There was only a slight increase in the rate of information flow during an experiment. As a matter of fact, during the last hour of the experiment, when the load was more than three times as heavy, the crew used just about the same amount of information it did during the first hour.

It maintained this unexpectedly high degree of success in defending the area by concentrating on traffic that was potentially hostile, spending smaller and smaller amounts on the rest of the tracks. If the crew had spent its efforts at the same rate during the last hour as it did during the first, it would have used nearly 1,300 items of information. Actually, it used only 640—just about half of what would have been necessary if it hadn't changed its ways of handling the task. This is one example of more effective use of the same amount of effort—an illustration of how the crew assigns the kind and amount of effort to task events it considers important. This rough measure of effort expended is the "response model" (Figure 1).

But since there are so many task events, the crew must have some way of deciding which ones are important. It does this by making distinctions between tracks that it has to deal with to accomplish the task and those that it doesn't have to deal with at all. These progressively finer distinctions about which classes of tracks need to be handled make up the "task model" (Figure 2.). Although the number of tracks in the task increased steadily, there was only a slight increase in the number of tracks the crew dealt with. Since it continued to defend the area successfully, even though it dealt with only part of the tracks (about 40 per cent of them in the last hour), these distinctions were obviously effective ones. The important discriminations were between threatening flights (traffic coming from cer-

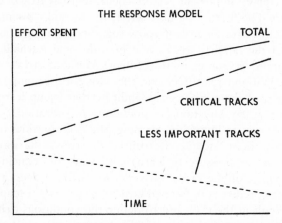

THE RESPONSE MODEL

EFFORT SPENT   TOTAL

CRITICAL TRACKS

LESS IMPORTANT TRACKS

TIME

FIG. 1. Although there is only a slight increase in the amount of effort a crew spends during an experiment, more and more of it is spent on critical tracks.

tain directions) and nonthreatening ones (traffic going in other directions).

These models enable the organization to spend its effort more effectively by determining what efforts will be given priority. By making appropriate changes in the models the organization can adapt to changing task circumstances.

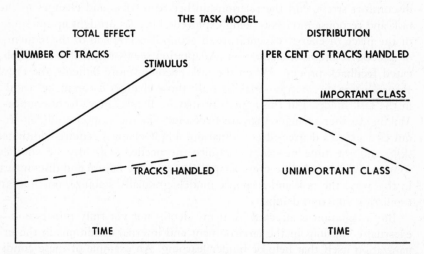

THE TASK MODEL

TOTAL EFFECT   DISTRIBUTION

NUMBER OF TRACKS   PER CENT OF TRACKS HANDLED

STIMULUS

IMPORTANT CLASS

TRACKS HANDLED   UNIMPORTANT CLASS

TIME   TIME

FIG. 2. The number of tracks the crew handles does not increase as fast as the number of tracks in the stimulus (left). This occurs because it handles a smaller and smaller proportion of noncritical tracks (right).

These empirical results seem to indicate that an organization will look for new patterns of behavior when it needs them—when it is under stress. Stress in an organization seems to arise from failure to perform effectively or—for an equally important reason—because it has to work too hard to avoid failure. The first is "failure" stress; the second, "discomfort" stress.

This effect of stress on organizations suggests an analogy between group learning and the familiar description of individual learning: stress, new and appropriate response, reinforcement. Without stress, organizations don't learn. Without reinforcement, they don't learn rapidly.

The results of these experiments indicate that group learning is an essential factor in any equation for predicting organizational effectiveness. From the analogy to individual learning, the main outlines of this theory seem clear—it must include the source of stress (the discomfort and failure that act as pressure to learn), and ways of reducing stress (the priority schemes of the task and response models). Such a formulation should help to predict how fast and how far a system can adapt, to identify what is difficult in the task, and to define the conditions that help an organization use its resources most effectively.

Perhaps the most important result of these experiments is that such concepts as stress, rate of learning, and so on, can be described quantitatively. There are, to be sure, some practical difficulties—the Laboratory now has over 12,000 hours of recordings and some 60 file drawers of supporting information from the air-defense studies. Thus far, some 100,000 IBM cards have been coded for each experiment, with perhaps an equally large amount of information, not yet successfully coded, left over.

These coded data are being used to represent measurable failure and discomfort stress, and the relationship between stress and changes in the task and response models is being explored. This has brought up questions of the place of energy expenditure in group learning and of the sequence of successive steps in adaptation. Adaptation seems to involve a complicated feedback process. When the task becomes more difficult, the crew absorbs some discomfort—making only those changes it can make readily in the task model. But this expedient may well add failure to discomfort. Making further changes that are necessary—in the response model—requires a greater degree of coordination. These changes require additional skill, and the time needed to acquire the needed skill may be another source of failure. As the crew adapts to successive failure and discomfort in this way, the task and response models gradually stabilize, much as an oscillating function damps.

But adaptation is affected by many details not yet fully understood—external conditions in the environment and internal conditions in the organization itself that help or hinder learning. An example of these conditions is the "grease pencils are no damn good" symptom of stress. An organization's first reaction to stress seems to be to blame external conditions, faults of the equipment, and so on. At one point or another during the experiments each crew blamed ineffective operation on the grease pencils it used for marking plots on the big movement board—the pencils were too hard or too soft, they broke too easily, they weren't the right color. But complaints like these disappear when the crew begins to find ways of doing things that lead to better performance.

The analogy between group learning and individual learning suggests the substitution of the organization for the individual as the organism in the classical learning model when organizational adaptation is being considered. In these air-defense experiments the organization has been treated as a unit rather than a collection of individuals, not only in managing the experimental conditions but also in analyzing the data and in building a theoretical framework on the basis of the results. With this kind of formulation the characteristics of individuals—their personality and skill—appear only as qualities of the organization. Such a formulation of group learning seems consistent with much of the data and has some rather definite implications.

Some Implications

There are several implications of this research—most specifically for personnel training and selection and for human engineering. Each of these areas is related to one or more of the others, and in working out their relationships it's not easy to know just where to begin. Although the functions of equipment define the human-engineering problem, just what equipment should do is difficult to specify without the understanding of system operation that comes from intensive examination such as these RAND air-defense studies provide. And so it is with setting personnel-selection standards. They can be set once the system is analyzed to see how much of the work the equipment can take over, but here, too, a thorough study of system operation is needed.

However, some human-engineering and personnel requirements can be described quite generally. Once the importance of group learning is recognized it follows that equipment and facilities should be arranged not just to facilitate operation but also to help the men who operate the system learn to use its full potential most rapidly. Or, more practically, since specifying what these men are to learn is difficult unless the system can be operated under the emergency conditions it was designed for, doing anything that might hinder group learning should be avoided. Communication between members should be made as free and easy as possible. Facilities should be arranged so that each member of the group is given as complete a picture as possible of the task and how the organization is dealing with it—in central displays of some sort if these are feasible. Members of the group should be given a chance to modify their procedures. For example, the members of an air-defense crew develop priority systems for simplifying their task; if information handling is taken over by electromechanical devices, the men who run the system should be free to modify the procedures for using these devices so as to utilize them most efficiently.

Considering a system as an integral unit rather than as a collection of individuals says something about personnel selection. It suggests that, in manning a system, teams rather than individuals should be selected—that matching the individual to the job may be a part of the organizational development process.

The need for system training has shown up in the difficulties of getting today's complex man-machine systems to perform as expected. Reliance on the adaptive capabilities of the operators is implicit in the design of most of these systems, but unfortunately developing these capabilities so that the system will perform adequately in an emergency requires experience under critical stresses equivalent to those of an emergency. These experiments have shown that system training, which can impose such stresses, does result in much more effective use of a system's resources—that it is one way of making the full potential of a system available before an emergency occurs. They have also enabled us to understand enough about how the organizations developed in the laboratory to formulate a useful principle that says: Train the team as a whole in an adequately simulated environment and give it knowledge of results. This technique treats the organization as a unit. It helps the organization develop by providing appropriate stress and the needed reinforcement. Although an organization gets some idea of how well it is doing just by doing it, the more complete the information about the results of its operation it gets, the more it will be reinforced. A training program, therefore, should facilitate learning by providing a factual critique which helps the organization identify its difficulties. This training principle is presently being put to use in a particular training program—the System Training Program RAND is installing in the Air Defense Command.

11. OBSERVATIONS ON THE GROWTH OF INFORMATION-PROCESSING CENTERS*

Milton G. Weiner

The personnel of information-processing centers exist in three inter-related environments: the task, equipment, and cultural environments.

A. The task environment is the set of changing external conditions to which the organization must adjust if it is to achieve the purpose for which it was formed.

B. The equipment environment is the set of equipment and facilities which the organization has available to deal with the task environment.

C. The cultural environment is the set of attitudes, values, and aspirations of the members of the organization relative to the purpose and activities of the organization.

In information-processing centers these three environments are in continual interaction, access to the task environment being mediated by the equipment and the cultural environment affecting the ways in which the task and equipment environment are perceived.

In laboratory investigations, the values at which these environments are initially "set" is established largely by the experimenters. Although the personnel of an organization have usually had some experience with the actual or a related task, equipment, and cultural environment, the early contact with the experimenters involves establishing a set of initial conditions for these environments appropriate to the laboratory. This may take the form of defining the goal or purpose of the organization and the boundary conditions of the equipment and culture. In the following discussion these conditions are presupposed, i.e., a clear statement of the goal of the organization is made, and the limits in the use or change of the equipment and facilities are stated.

Since this section deals with a developmental sequence it is assumed that the values of the initial settings are "low." Specifically, the task environment is not so complex as to overwhelm the organization, the equipment operation is within the capacities of the personnel, and the culture is not rigidly structured. The development for "higher" settings of these values is not to be considered, although the fact that these environments are assumed to be interrelated does imply that marked imbalance in the values may produce different consequences.

With this framework of a defined goal and a set of boundary conditions

---

* Reproduced from RAND Paper P-529, May 21, 1954.

147

an organization passes through three periods which overlap but can be roughly distinguished.

1. *The basal period.* This period begins with the first meeting of the personnel of the organization. It is marked by a high degree of interaction of the task, equipment, and cultural environments. It terminates with a conception of the ways in which the organization is structured and the relation of the structure to the goal of the organization.

2. *The consolidation period.* This period begins with the acceptance of the organization structure. It is the period during which the organization explores the boundary conditions imposed upon it and the mechanisms for dealing with these boundaries and still preserves the operating efficiency necessary to achieve the goal. The termination of this period is the shift in emphasis from responding to the task environment in the abstract form produced and represented by the equipment to the task environment as sets of changing conditions which are external to the organization.

3. *The organization period.* This period begins with the shift from dealing with the task environment as equipment representations to dealing with the task environment as an external condition. It is the period during which the goal and the task environment become interrelated.

The following presents these periods in greater detail and indicates some of the conditions affecting each period.

The Basal Period

The purpose of all organizations is to deal with a set of externally imposed conditions which the individual is incapable of handling by himself and which require integration of his activities with the activities of others. If the organization is to succeed, the individual must replace his independence and autonomy of function with cooperative actions in dealing with external conditions.

In any organization that is to be effective this implies two initial problems. The individual must be capable of adjusting his sets of values and expectations to include cooperation with others, and he must be able to acquire a set of skills that contribute to the organization. The first is required for becoming a member of the organization and the second is required to remain a member. Both of these problems, the one of the cultural environment and the other of the equipment environment, are influenced by the clarity with which the purpose of the organization is evidenced.

The challenge of the cultural environment is the necessity for relating the general values of the culture and one's individual values and behavior to the purpose of the organization. Wide discrepancies between the value of the work being done by the organization and general values are capable of producing states of conflict that limit the effectiveness of the organization. In the basal period these interpersonal ind intercultural problems are paramount since maintaing autonomy of attitude or action violates the premise for existence of the organization and prevents further development.

Statements about the purpose of the organization and what the organization is trying to accomplish represent the initial exchange medium for all personnel. Such statements are perceived by the individual in terms of his previous experiences and attitudes and pose problems for which the solutions that he has formerly employed may not be satisfactory. The interaction of each individual with other members of the organization is an exchange of experience and less frequently of solutions. These exchanges have one common basis, namely, the way in which individuals can contribute to the purpose of the organization of which they are now all members. This basis is sufficient to exert pressure on the individual for agreement on the way in which the purpose of the organization is perceived and understood by the people concerned. It is this attempt to obtain a collective understanding that represents the initial binding forces of the organization.

Any mechanisms that provide for clear understanding of the relations between the goals of the organization and the values of the individual are advantageous. The existence of many channels through which the organization communicates its values and deals with the relation of its values to the general cultural or to individual values tends to increase the involvement of the individual. If the organization also has mechanisms for rewarding the individuals who apprehend and support its values, the developmental pace is accelerated.

The challenge of the equipment environment is the necessity for mastering the capabilities of the equipment and employing them in terms of the goal. The degree to which this acquisition of skill is obtained is of considerably greater significance than is the degree to which the individual masters the specific operations of the equipment. (Optimally, of course, the possession of technical and operational abilities by the individual is desirable, but where this is not possible the choice must be measured in terms of the goal desired.) In the basal period this relationship of equipment means to organization ends is limited. The individual must have sufficient familiarity with the equipment so that he may operate it. At this level, the problems of adequate training, and well-engineered equipment for the operator, are important, but are not the only ones. Emphasis on utilizing the equipment in terms of the goal is, from the organization point of view, critical.

If the operation of equipment is goal-oriented rather than oriented in terms of a specific subtask, it is possible to adapt the equipment operation to the changes of the task environment. This operating "versatility" is a method by which the range of equipment potential is explored and is available for use as the demands of the task change. Most equipment includes some multiple-purpose characteristics usually at the cost of more efficient single-purpose operation. Adhering to single-purpose operation is thus doubly uneconomical.

The integration of the cultural and equipment problems in the basal period shows most markedly in the evolution of the leadership structure. As realization develops that the purpose of the organization (to deal with changing sets of external conditions on a cooperative basis) requires division of labor, the requirements for leadership become clear. This realization, which was one of the conditions for the original formation of the organization, derives new force from the more intimate knowledge of the cultural and equipment environments now available to the organization. In addition to the recognition that a hierarchial structure is an instrumental part of dealing with the task environment, acceptance of any compromise of the values or aspirations of the individual as part of the group is required.

The requirements for leadership are defined in terms of the ability to perceive the relationship between the organization structure and its purpose, the ability to interpret this relationship to other members of the group, and the ability to understand the goal of the organization and to deal with these problems in a stable manner.

As these abilities develop they serve to structure the organization in several ways. On the one hand, individuals offer interpretations of the requirements of the hierarchy. These multiple interpretations serve to delineate further the conditions of the task environment with which the organization must deal. On the other hand, the flow of interpretation in terms of the task environment reduces the pressures of the cultural environment.

It is, in fact, the transition from individuality to division of labor and the acceptance of a hierarchy in the form of a leadership structure that marks the end of the basal period and represents the point at which an "organization" can be said to exist.

The Consolidation Period

The consolidation period is one of exploration and testing in the cultural, equipment, and task environment, and the application of the results of the exploration to the organization's methods of operating. The acceptance of structure which developed in the basal period provides the organization with a framework in which to operate. The framework at this time is not a rigid one: neither the position of individuals in the framework is fixed nor is the limit of the framework determined.

The first portion of the consolidation period is thus a period of movement in a number of directions. The movement occurs both in terms of internal and external demands. For the internal aspect the problems of individual status and responsibility develop.

Since the structure of the organization at this time is diffuse (i.e., it represents nothing more than a series of interpretations), it provides the opportunity for individuals to develop a wide variety of roles. These roles serve both the needs of the individuals who generate them and the needs of the organization in dealing with the environment. The delimitation of these two foci to the single criterion—servicing the organization—occurs through a series of reduction steps. These reduction steps are a necessary part of development because maintaining diffuseness in the roles of the leadership structure is equivalent to maintaining a diffuse operating structure with its consequent inability to distribute responsibility.

The form that these reduction steps take is the production of a series of incidents in which individuals challenge the role-capabilities of each other. The equipment and cultural environments play a part in this competition, the former in terms of the skill with which the various equipments are utilized to attain the goals of the organization, and the latter in terms of the culture that is developing within the organization. The emergence of an "organization culture" is a derivative of the common goal orientation and the developing set of experiences in common that are a part of the basal period.

This culture is marked by value systems, ethical codes, and taboos, which find expression in interpersonal relations. For internal communication the organization may develop a private language. This "meta-language" represents both an economy in dealing with an environment that is sufficiently understood and shared so that it can be codified, and an acceptance of the organization as the unique property of its members.

The definition of limits in these internal relationships is reflected in statements of the responsibilities of the members of the organization, first to each other and then to the goal. The first portion is concerned with confidence and the second with effectiveness. The two become highly interrelated in the leadership structure.

As confidence in the members of the organization develops, and as the conditions of the task environment are effectively met so that the goal of the organization is maintained, the organization stabilizes. Although internal problems may exist they are regarded as "maintenance" problems and not as "survival" problems; i.e., although the organization must deal with them in order to remain effective, they do not threaten the existence of the organization. This is possible because the organization is operating in terms of a generally accepted goal within fairly well defined limits, and with a division of labor that has been accepted on the basis of its effectiveness.

At the same time the external demands continue. The organization responds to these in a similar way by exploring the limits of its own structure and capabilities by "challenging" the environment in which it operates. These are challenges in the sense that they serve as tests of the sensitivity of the task environment and may result in an inability to deal with it. They take the form of modified operating procedures, attempts to surmount equipment constraints, and treatment of the environment in simple rather than in complex terms. They lead to a definition of "effective structure," i.e., the patterns of organization activity capable of dealing with the demands of the environment. With the acceptance of a changing set of external conditions, however, this definition of effective structure is probabilistic, imposed on the organization only for the known set of external conditions.

Since the period of consolidation produces an effective organization for dealing with the problems posed by the task environment, the organization will remain stable in procedures and structure as long as the demands of the task environment do not change markedly. If, however, marked changes do occur—changes such that the existing structure and procedures do not allow the organization to achieve its goal—the organization will undergo modifications to deal with the changes. The first of these modifications marks the beginning of the organization period.

The Organization Period

The "good" organization is one that can adapt to wide variations in the demands of the task environment and still retain a high degree of stability. Thus, good organization is not only defined in terms of the capacity to obtain an adequate "output" for differing sets of "inputs," but also in terms of the ability to accomplish this without becoming unstable.

During the basal period and the consolidation period the organization moves along three dimensions: homogeneity-heterogeneity, global-articulate, and diffuse-specific. The first of these dimensions refers to a process of goal-orientation and involves a progression from a generalized goal-orientation on the part of all members of the organization to a series of individual goal orientations in which each person perceives his activities as a necessary part of the operation of the organization. The second dimension refers to the functions performed by the members of the organization and reflects the change from undefined, or poorly defined, functions to an interlocking series of activities that have meaning in dealing with the task environment. The third dimension refers to the structure of the organization that progresses from general equivalence of responsibilities to a division of responsibility. The stable organization is one that deals with the changing demands of the task environment without losing heterogeneity of goal orientation, articulateness of function, or specificity of structure.

The basal period, in this respect, is pre-organizational in character since it does represent an unstable period. If, following this period, an organization does evolve, then it is considered unstable if the stresses of the task environment produce the same problems that existed at the basal period, i.e., lack of skill in dealing with the environment, questioning the values of the organization, questioning the adequacy of the goal or the techniques developed to achieve the goal. In effect, the unstable organization is one that regresses to a period of high interaction of the task, equipment, and cultural environments. From the regression, of course, it is possible for another organization to emerge, but it can probably be assumed that the new organization will have different goals, leadership structure and methods of operation.

Such a change involves a considerable energy expenditure on the part of the organization. It is the ability of an organization to deal with the variable task environment without this extreme energy expenditure that marks it as a good organization.

To maintain stability under heavy demands from the task environment is possible in at least one way. The organization must solve the problem of the relation of the task environment to the goal of the organization. The task environment, as a set of changing external conditions, and the goal of the organization are interrelated. The inputs to the organization are abstracted portions of the total task environment, some of which have direct consequences in achieving the goal, others having limited consequences.

The good organization develops ordering relationships which allow it to deal with the task environment in terms of the consequences of selecting and responding to one set of demands in preference to some other set. To do this requires treating the changes of the task environment not as equipotential events but as having different potentials for success in achieving the goal of the organization.

The mechanism for separating the inputs into those portions of the task environment directly relevant to the goal of the organization and those portions which are not, is accomplished by utilizing the existing knowledge of the state of the task environment and previous experience with the task environment that has been successful for obtaining the goal, and generalizing this experience to allow for prediction of the effects of various actions of the organization on the goal. This ability to use past and present experience to establish expectations of the future and to undertake action on planning made from this information is the highest order of organizational behavior. It implies a problem-solving ability that the organization employs to deal with variations in the demands made by the environment. Such planning and prediction allows actions to be taken that have high probability of success. By this mechanism the organization is able to "control" the environment and to maintain stability.

The period of organization is characterized by this high-order problem-solving ability that employs past and present experience for predictions and actions to interrelate the task environment inputs to the goals of the organization and allows the organization to maintain its goal without becoming unstable.

The mechanisms and techniques employed by the organization to deal with the demands of the environment in which it exists exclude, by definition, those individual actions which, although part of the behaviors of the personnel, do not serve the organization directly. Such events as the behavior of a member of the organization in obtaining an adequate environment for himself, i.e., making lighting, seating, or ventilation adjustments, are related to the operation of the organization in that they may serve to set the individual for carrying out his functions. Similar activities, such as checking out equipment operation, are part of this group of activities which are considered "performance-related," i.e., they prepare the individual for dealing with the task environment, but are relatively independent of the extent and type of demands that the task environment produces. Such behaviors may be predictable for the individual, but not for the organization.

A second set of mechanisms and techniques are called "programs." These are goal-oriented patterns of coordinated behavior in response to the demands of the task environment. They are the strategies of the information-processing organization for maintaining stability under variable environmental demands and represent procedures which the organization finds effective over a period of time.

That programs are time-related phenomena indicates that they interact with the state of the organization's development. In the basal period and in portions of the consolidation period the main access that the organization has to varying the processing of information is control of the rate and structure of the information. Programs at this early period may be characterized in terms of rate control and structure control. Rate control programs are those patterns of coordinated behavior that modify the time sequence in handling information. Structure control programs are those that modify the form of the information. Sequences of both types of programs may be combined at later stages of development.

The requirements for any program determine the period during which it will appear. If a program involves a particular level of skill in dealing with the equipment environment, heavy reliance on the abilities of others, confidence in their participation, and explicit acknowledgment of the ways in which it helps achieve the goal of the organization, it will not develop until these requirements are met. In this respect programs may tentatively appear at a local level as conditions are adequate and gradually evolve into generalized patterns through a process of testing and revision.

All programs are methods of structuring the task environment and are, therefore, models of the situation external to the organization. That they are models of an external reality leads to the development of another general class of programs. These are the assessment programs.

As structure and rate control programs are being evolved, the organization endeavors to validate the simplified models of external reality that these programs represent. The assessment programs are comparisons of the model with reality at various stages. Assessment programs, in a sense, substitute operating complexity of the organization, a factor over which the organization has some control, for environmental complexity in order to deal with the environment in a simplified form.

Some of the rate control programs evidenced by the organizations under study are:

1. Priority programs. These programs are sets of rules which determine which events will be given preference for representation in the model of the environment. Since every event has a series of characteristics, the establishment of priorities in the high frequency characteristics probably establishes a priority for low frequency characteristics and thus has general consequences for the organization.

2. Storage program. This program represents a limiting condition of the priority program, i.e., information is assigned zero priority at a particular time. A change in conditions may require a reassignment of priority and the information is then processed. This possibility of reassignment distinguishes stored information from discarded information.

Some of the structure control programs evidenced are:

1. "Fact" stipulation. This program is a strategy for applying a structure to the information that is being processed in those cases where the available structure is so ambiguous that definite decisions are not possible. The dynamics of fact stipulation, as well as many of the other programs, lie in the process of "uncertainty absorption." In representing an event as having a higher probability than the existing information merits, individuals allow the organization to continue to operate rather than to "idle" until more definite information is available. It is an integral component of the relation of the individual to the organization since it involves assuming responsibility for the actions taken.

2. Load balancing. Load balancing represents a shifting of tasks from one part of the organization to another as the amount of information being processed increases. This type of shifting restructures the information processing sequences. For such restructuring to exist presupposes both some degree of redundancy in information and some type of equivalence of function, for which the particular requirements depend on the nature of the load balancing.

Some of the assessment programs are:

1. Anticipation. To predict the probable changes in the task environment on the basis of available information and prior experience is a later

development of the organization. It involves a complex process of assigning probabilities to certain events and modifying the operating procedures to cope with the presumed event. Since some aspects of the task environment are usually cyclic, the organization can anticipate these and prepare to deal with any event that is novel in the situation. Exceptions to the expected pattern can then receive immediate processing. By removing the "uniqueness" from some of the events with which the organization has to deal, the model of the task environment is simplified and certain activities become routinized. This process requires continual assessment of the relation of the model to the actual situation to validate the adequacy of the anticipatory sequences.

2. Program shifting. The changing nature of the external situation with which the organization is dealing demands continual modifications of the simplified model which is being used to represent the situation. Perseveration of inappropriate procedures is a step towards instability. One of the mechanisms available to avoid this condition is to shift from one set of procedures to another set that are more appropriate to the goal. This is the strategy of program shifting.

These programs achieve various degrees of formalization in the operating system. They are mechanisms for dealing with the task environment within the constraints imposed by the equipment environment. They require coordination between the personnel of the organization developed out of an appreciation of the common goal and the capabilities of the group. The general nature of any program has significance for many organizations, but the specific application depends upon the set of situations to which the organization must respond. Fixed rules for any program probably require a complete specification of the task environment over a long period of time. For many IPC's this is an impossibility since it would require a knowledge of all possible events. The alternative which the organization develops in the later periods is problem-solving behavior utilizing existing information of the state of the task environment and previous experience with the environment.

12. COMMENTS ON THE THEORY OF ORGANIZATIONS*[0]

Herbert A. Simon

This is an attempt to sketch in very rough form what seem to me some of the central concepts and problems of organization theory. In the first section I have tried to define the field of organization theory and to indicate with some care what justification there is for regarding it as a distinct area of theory, related to, but by no means identical with, the theory of small groups and the theory of social institutions. The comments in the second section on subject-matter areas simply spell out the implications, many of them perhaps obvious, of the central argument of the first section.

This paper is concerned with all kinds of organizations, and not simply with those that fall within the area of public administration. This definition of the scope of organization theory reflects my own conviction that there are a great many things that can be said about organizations in general, without specification of the particular kind of organization under consideration. Moreover, even if we were interested solely in governmental organizations, I believe that a great deal can be learned from the comparison of their characteristics with those of other kinds of organizations, and from attempts to explain the similarities and differences that are found. Neither of these statements denies the existence of numerous and important phenomena that are peculiar to governmental organizations or the need for theory in public administration to deal with these phenomena.

THE SUBJECT OF ORGANIZATION THEORY

Human organizations are systems of interdependent activity, encompassing at least several primary groups and usually characterized, at the level of consciousness of participants, by a high degree of rational direction of behavior toward ends that are objects of common acknowledgement and expectation. Typical examples of organizations are business

---

* Reproduced from the *American Political Science Review*, 46, No. 4 (December, 1952), pp. 1130–39.

[0] These comments were originally put down on paper without any view toward publication, and later were circulated among the persons who attended a conference on organization theory sponsored by the Social Science Research Council at Princeton, N.J., June 17–19, 1952. I have been prevailed upon, with some misgivings, now to expose them to a wider audience.

firms, governmental administrative agencies, and voluntary associations like political clubs.

In complex enterprises the definition of the unit is not unambiguous—a whole agency, a bureau, or even a section in a large department may be regarded as an organization. In such a nest of Chinese blocks the smallest multi-person units are the primary groups; the largest are institutions (e.g., "the economic system," "the state") and whole societies. We will restrict the term "organization" to systems that are larger than primary groups, smaller than institutions. Clearly, the lower boundary is sharper than the upper.

Complexity in any body of phenomena has generally led to the construction of specialized theories, each dealing with the phenomena at a particular "level." Levels are defined by specifying certain units as the objects of study and by stating the propositions of theory in terms of intra-unit behavior and inter-unit behavior. (Cf. the sequence of elementary particle-atom-molecule in physics and the sequence: gene-chromosome-nucleus-cell-tissue-organ-organism in biology.)

Not every arbitrarily selected unit defines a suitable level for scientific study. The most important "unities" that make a level an appropriate one for theory construction and testing appear to be the following:

(a) The units at the level in question should exhibit a high degree of internal cohesion relative to their dependence on each other. Under these circumstances we can discover generalizations about the internal properties of the individual units as quasi-isolated systems (e.g., propositions about communications patterns among component primary groups of an organization). We can also discover approximate generalizations about the relations between units as wholes (e.g., propositions about competition between two organizations).

(b) The units should exhibit internal properties that are different (or depend on different mechanisms) from those that predominate in the internal properties of sub-units at the next level below (e.g., the determinants of the volume of communication between members of a single primary group).

These two tests are not intended as metaphysical assertions about "wholeness" or "emergent" properties, but simply as criteria determining whether, in fact, verifiable propositions can be constructed employing the units in question as approximations to the full complexity of nature. Even if at some stage in inquiry we should be able to reduce the propositions of theory at one level to those at the next lower level—as the theory of gases has been reduced to statistical mechanics—the former propositions would still retain their usefulness for purposes of application and economy of statement. Indeed, the value of both sets of propositions is enhanced by their translatability from the one to the other.

Human organizations would seem to qualify to a high degree as suitable units defining a level of analysis of systems of human behavior. With respect to the first criterion stated above, the most superficial observation shows that the boundaries between organizations have real behavioral significance, and that it is meaningful, in first approximation, to state propositions about the relations between organizations regarded as wholes. (I trust that I have made clear that no notion of "group mind" is implied in this last statement.)

With respect to the second criterion, I believe that enough is known about the psychological mechanisms that are primarily responsible for cohesion and interdependence in the primary group to show that these mechanisms cannot easily account for the corresponding phenomena in the larger organized aggregates; and that there are important organizational phenomena that do not have exact counterparts at the primary group level. A number of examples of these mechanisms and phenomena, which are central to organizations but absent from or of lesser importance to primary groups, will be given in the next section.

But why speak of a level of organization theory? Do we not need as many levels as there are structural layers between primary groups and institutions? I think not, because I do not believe that these various levels are distinguishable to an important extent in terms of the second criterion suggested above—i.e., there are no important new mechanisms to be discovered at these successive levels. The propositions of organization theory can probably be stated with systematic ambiguity so as to refer indifferently to the relations of divisions within a bureau or the relations of bureaus within a department. As small differences in degree begin to approach qualitative significance at the upper end of the scale, we have probably already reached the level of institutional theory. In the future, of course, the results of research may force us to revise this assumption.

MAJOR PROBLEM AREAS

The study of organizations has hardly progressed to the point where a definitive list can be constructed of the major areas for research. The following list was arrived at primarily by considering which characteristics of organization—particularly those distinctive ones that identify the level of organization theory—require dissection and explanation. I have not tried to construct watertight categories, and it will become evident that several of the items represent different ways of looking at the same problem. Until we know what frames of reference are going to be the most useful for organization theory, it will surely be desirable to retain alternative frameworks, and to take considerable pains to develop means for translating from one framework to another.

1. The process of decision-making in organization. A language for the

description of decision-making processes appears to offer considerable promise as a framework for the study of organizations. The central notion is that a decision can be regarded as a conclusion drawn (though not in any strict logical sense) from premises; and that influence is exercised by transmitting decisions, which are then taken as premises for subsequent decisions.

When the problem of influence is stated in these terms, our attention is called to some features that are not prominent in other formulations. We see, for example, that the process may depend not only upon interpersonal relations between influencer and influencee, but also upon the structure and accepted rules of transformation of the language employed by them. One can begin investigation here by posing such questions as how influence is transmitted in an organization between professional groups that employ different problem-solving technologies, e.g., accountants and engineers. Work on organization theory utilizing this framework could probably soon be related, in a mutually beneficial way, to research on the sociology of knowledge and on the psychology of the problem-solving process.[1]

2. The phenomena of power in organizations. A characteristic feature of the mutual influence of organization members upon one another is that this influence exhibits striking asymmetries—as, for example, in the superior-subordinate relationship. These asymmetries appear to be what we have chiefly in mind in using such terms as "power" and "authority." The following are a number of important tasks in this area:

(a) A fully operational definition of power and methods for observing and measuring power relationships is not yet at hand, but would seem fundamental to the description of organizational behavior.

(b) More needs to be learned about the motivational basis of power in organizations, including the roles of sanctions, identifications, and attitudes of legitimacy in the acceptance of authority. Progress has been made in the study of the analogous phenomena in primary groups (e.g., work on leadership and on group morale),[2] but it is not obvious that the mechanisms of influence within the primary group tell all, or even most, of the story of influence processes in larger organized aggregates.

---

[1] The relation between organizational behavior and individual decision-making and problem-solving processes is discussed in the author's *Administrative Behavior* (New York, 1947), chap. v. My researches in the decade since this connection occurred to me have steadily deepened my conviction that a very deep relation—not by any means analogical or metaphorical—exists between decision processes in organizations and the processes described by Gestalt psychologists in their study of the problem-solving process. Since the purpose of this paper is to state problems, not to solve them, I will have to be content here with this statement of my belief.

[2] For an introduction to the literature, see Harold Guetzkow (Ed.), *Groups, Leadership, and Men* (Pittsburgh, 1951), and "Human Relations Research in Large Organizations," *Journal of Social Issues*, Vol. VII, No. 3 (whole number), 1951.

(*c*) In elaboration of the last point, the distinction between the "formal" and the "informal" in organizations appears to lie, in part, in differences between the psychological bases of cohesion that are involved. When we refer to power as formal, what we appear to mean is that internalized attitudes toward legitimate authority provide the motivation for acceptance of the relationship. While feelings about legitimacy undoubtedly play a role in primary group relationships, I would conjecture that they take on additional importance when they serve as a substitute for the immediate experience of approval and disapproval in face-to-face relationships.[3]

(*d*) Another mechanism that is important in the transmission of influence in organizations is the interlocking of primary groups through the dual membership of supervisory employees. In general, each supervisory employee is a member both of a group in which he is formal leader and of another in which his immediate superior is formal leader. The principal research problems here are to determine the behavior patterns that are adopted by executives in these "cross-pressure" situations; and, if there are several such patterns, to find what determines which one will be adopted. The same questions need to be answered with respect to the "staff" man who, because he is attached to a "line" unit, also has potential or actual membership in two primary groups. It remains to be seen whether cross-pressures produce the same behavior in these organizational situations as in the other situations where they have been studied.

3. Rational and non-rational aspects of behavior in organization. Organizations are the least "natural," most rationally contrived units of human association. But paradoxically, the theory of an organization whose members are "perfectly rational" human beings (capable of unlimited adaptation) is very nearly a perfectly vacuous theory. It is only because individual human beings are limited in knowledge, foresight, skill, and time that organizations are useful instruments for the achievement of human purpose; and only because organized groups of beings are limited in ability to agree on goals, to communicate, and to cooperate that organizing becomes for them a "problem."[4]

---

[3] An overreaction from the excessive emphasis on formal organization in the earlier work on organization theory has led, in the last two decades, to an almost equally serious neglect of the importance of attitudes toward legitimacy. The same overreaction—from legalistic analyses of the state in terms of "sovereignty" to a pure power-politics approach to political behavior—has occurred in the other areas of political science as well. (Lasswell and Kaplan, for example, in *Power and Society* [New Haven, 1951] come very close to treating legitimate authority as an epiphenomenon that has no independent influence on the development of a system of political behavior.) With the reconstruction of "legitimacy" as a psychological, rather than a legal concept, the way is now open to a reconciliation of the formal and the informal (legitimate authority and power) within a behavioral framework.

[4] This point is also elaborated upon in *Administrative Behavior*. See particularly pp. 39–41, 80–84, 96–101, 240–44.

Organization theory is centrally concerned with identifying and study-ing those limits to the achievement of goals that are, in fact, limits on the flexibility and adaptability of the goal-striving individuals and groups of individuals themselves. The entrepreneur of economic theory is limited only by constraints that are external to himself and his organization—the technology—and by the goal-striving of individuals whose interests are not identical with his. Administrative man is limited also by constraints that are part of his own psychological makeup—limited by the number of persons with whom he can communicate, the amount of information he can acquire and retain, and so forth. The fact that these limits are not physiological and fixed, but are instead largely determined by social and even organizational forces, creates problems of theory construction of great subtlety; and the fact that the possibilities of modifying and relax-ing these limits may themselves become objects of rational calculation compounds the difficulties.

In this general area of research, promising suggestions as to the direction in which we might move are contained in oligopoly theory and game theory (formulation of the "outwitting" problem),[5] and in sociological speculations about the self-confirming prophecy. I would single out the following areas for special attention:

(a) Identification of the limits of rationality. We need a more complete and systematic taxonomy of the constraints, internal to the system of social action, that serve as limits to the attainment of goals. This would lead to empirical research on the questions: (i) under what circumstances particu-lar constraints do and do not operate, including inter-cultural uniformities and differences, and (ii) under what circumstances the modification or removal of particular constraints becomes an object of rational calcula-tion.

(b) Theory of organizational innovation and change. Plans are re-garded as "utopian" when their implementation would require changes in internal constraints that are thought to be unchangeable. Essentially, utopian plans are rejected because "you can't change human nature" in those respects that would be essential to achievement of the plan. Research is needed as to the criteria that are applied by human beings in planning situations to determine which of the behavior variates they will regard as variable (i.e., subject to rational determination), and which as fixed (i.e., constraints on goal attainment).

(c) Reification of groups. The limit of human understanding in the presence of complex social structures leads human beings to construct simplified maps (i.e., theories or models) of the social system in which they are acting, and to behave as though the maps were the reality. To the ex-

---

[5] See John von Neumann and Oskar Morgenstern, *Theory of Games and Eco-nomic Behavior* (Princeton, 1944), especially chap. ii.

tent that such maps are held in common, they must be counted among the internal constraints on rational adaptation. What we have just said applies, of course, to all systems of classification which, by determining when situations are "similar" and when "different," provide the individual with the social definition of the situation.

My earlier comments about the relation of "formal" organization to attitudes of legitimacy can be generalized in terms of this notion of social classification. The process of organizing involves, among other things, securing acceptance by the organization members of a common model that defines the situation for them, and provides them with roles and expectations of the roles of others, and with commonly accepted classificatory schemes. Attitudes of legitimacy probably provide a principal motivational base for the organizing process.

What is needed here is study of the factors that determine how an organization will be perceived by the persons in it, how the mode of perception affects behavior, and what the effects are of a greater or lesser degree of sharing of such perceptions.

4. The organizational environment and the social environment. Members of an organization generally come to it already equipped with the mores of the society in which it operates. To what extent can and do organizations develop and inculcate mores that are distinct from the mores of society? To what extent are there in a society generalized mores about behavior in organizations that provide the basis for the operation of the individual organizations in the society (e.g., generalized mores about superior-subordinate roles)?

Organization theory has been largely culture-bound through failure to attack this problem.[6] The theory of bureaucracy as developed by Max Weber and his followers represents the furthest progress in dealing with it. The historical data appealed to by the Weberians need supplementation by analysis of contemporary societies, advanced and primitive. A comparison of intra-cultural uniformity and variation in organization patterns with inter-cultural uniformity and variation would provide the evidence we need to determine to what extent the cooperative patterns in organizations are independent of the mores of cooperation of the society.

5. Stability and change in organizations. Any theory of the movement of a system of organizational behavior through time must take account of the apparent stability exhibited by organizations. From every evidence, this stability must be an extremely complex phenomenon. It may rest in part on the kinds of bonds, which we might refer to as non-rational, that have been observed in the primary group; it may depend in part on the rational calculations of members that their interests are served by the or-

---

[6] Cf. Robert A. Dahl, "The Science of Public Administration: Three Problems," *Public Administration Review*, Vol. VII (Winter, 1947), pp. 1–11.

ganization. It is because the role of these, and possibly other, bases of stability needs to be explored that I offer the following suggestions:

(a) It is possible that systems in which the "non-rational" type of stabilizing mechanism predominates will behave in a qualitatively different fashion from those in which the "rational" type of stabilizing mechanism prevails. If, by construction of models embodying the two types of mechanisms, a qualitative difference could be deduced, the way would be open to empirical assessment of the importance of the two mechanisms.[7]

(b) The work that has been done to date on the theory of the "rational" mechanism would suggest that stability in this case depends on certain relations between the aspiration levels of members and their achievement levels. If so, we can draw on the psychological research that has already been done on these latter phenomena to design experiments and field studies that would test whether this is, indeed, one of the mechanisms involved in stability.

(c) We may borrow the economists' term "entrepreneur" to refer to an individual who specializes as a broker in finding mutually acceptable terms on which a group of persons can be induced to associate, or to continue association, in an organization.[8] We need research to determine what the role is of entrepreneurship, so defined, in the process of organizational activity. I conjecture that there are some close relationships both with the "middleman" notion, introduced in topic 2d, and with the kind of stability mechanisms discussed in 6b. Study is also needed of whether the uniqueness or nonuniqueness of the acceptable terms of association is an important determinant of the amount of authority that can be exercised over organization members. This relationship has been exhibited in some formal models, but it needs empirical verification.

(d) The two topics just discussed get very close to the heart of the processes of bargaining and the formation of coalitions, insofar as these processes involve rational calculation of advantage.[9] The formal apparatus

---

[7] For further discussion of these mechanisms in the context of mathematical models, see Herbert A. Simon, "A Formal Theory of Interaction in Social Groups," *American Sociological Review*, Vol. XVII (April, 1952), pp. 202–11 and "A Comparison of Organization Theories," *Review of Economic Studies*, forthcoming.

[8] I believe that this usage does not do too much violence to the term, at least as it is used by economic historians and those concerned with the dynamic theory of the firm, e.g., Schumpeter. In terms of this definition, entrepreneurship is not peculiar to business concerns but is present (and, I believe, to the same important extent) in governmental and voluntary organizations as well. Examples of important entrepreneurs in governmental, nonprofit, and voluntary organizations would be William Alanson White, Gifford Pinchot, William Rainey Harper, Clarence Streit—the list is inexhaustible. Anyone attempting to describe the roles of men like Charles Merriam and Louis Brownlow within the fields of political science and public administration can hardly avoid using the concepts of entrepreneurial theory.

[9] The process that Philip Selznick refers to as "coöptation" fits in here also. See his *TVA and the Grass Roots* (Berkeley, 1949).

of game theory appears to provide an appropriate language of theory formulation; and, on the empirical side, some of the problems could probably be examined by means of relatively small-scale laboratory experiments.

(e) Another aspect of survival and stability is the question of how organizations adapt themselves to uncertainty and incomplete information. In the past two decades this has been a favorite topic of economists,[10] but only in the last five years has there been much attention to the two aspects of greatest importance to organization theory: (i) reduction in the impact of uncertain events by retention of "flexibility" and (ii) the role of a stable social environment as a means of providing predictability to the individuals who are a part of it.

Under the first heading, research is needed as to the implications of particular ways of organizing behavior for the adaptability of the organization under changing, unpredictable circumstances. Under the second heading research is needed as to the existence and nature of mechanisms in social organizations that are analogous (in the sense of performing the same function) to the homeostatic mechanisms of organisms. Whether organizations are adaptive and possessed of homeostatic mechanisms is an empirical question, but one which, in all probability, can be answered in the affirmative. But the important theoretical issue is the nature of the mechanisms—a question that is not solved by reference to the organismic analogy. Moreover, while primary groups and social institutions may also exhibit homeostasis and adaptivity, there is no reason to believe that the mechanisms involved are the same ones that produce these phenomena in organizations. Functional equivalence does not imply structural equivalence.[11]

6. Specialization and the division of work. The division of work and the design of the organizational communications system have in the past been the central concerns of persons interested in organization theory for purposes of application. The question usually asked is: "How do we divide the work, and what channels of communication do we establish in order to operate efficiently?"

For purposes of research, the question is more properly stated: "What are the consequences for organizational activity of dividing the work one way rather than another, or employing one set of communications channels rather than another?"

[10] See the excellent survey of the economic literature in Kenneth J. Arrow, "Alternative Approaches to the Theory of Choice in Risk-Taking Situations," *Econometrica*, Vol. XIX (October, 1951) pp. 404-37.

[11] This last proposition is an important part of our justification, in the first part of this memorandum, for the study of "levels." The issues involved are discussed with great sophistication by T. C. Schneirla, "The 'Levels' Concept in the Study of Social Organization in Animals," in John J. Rohrer and Muzafer Sherif (Eds.), *Social Psychology at the Crossroads* (New York, 1951).

The last half of the question (communications) is best answered in terms of the frames of reference of topics 1 and 2. The subject of the division of work requires further comment. We are considering, of course, not only the question of specialization of the individual organization member, but also the allocation of tasks to whole organization units—in fact, it is the question of specialization among the larger aggregates rather than specialization within the primary group that is the proper concern of organization theory. We are equally concerned with "vertical" specialization, i.e., allocation of decision-making functions to various status and authority levels in an organization—and with "horizontal" specialization— i.e., fixing the jurisdictional boundaries of coordinate organizational units.

(a) Current theories of specialization in organization (excluding the "human relations" approach to the primary group) are largely derived, via the scientific management movement, from Adam Smithian notions that specialization is a means to efficiency, and hence to effective competition. There has been little examination of the alternative Durkheimian idea that specialization is a means of protection from competition.[12] The research problem suggested by the contrast is to examine in what respects specialization (and what kinds of specialization) increases organizational stability; in what respects it jeopardizes stability; and to what extent these considerations enter into decisions about specialization. The problem is also related to 5e in that certain forms of specialization may make an organization less dependent on what other organizations do, and hence may provide a means for dealing with uncertainty.

(b) The consequences of specialization depend on the constraints discussed in topic 3. It is an important question as to how far specialization is determined by constraints external to the organization—the technology of its activities—and how far it is determined by internal constraints—the psychological and sociological limitations upon rational adaptation. (The situation is even a bit more complicated because the technology in the sense of the physical, chemical, biological, etc., processes involved in the organization's activity—is not independent of the state of technological knowledge, and the latter may, in turn, be interdependently related to the forms of social specialization that prevail.) In almost every city, the fire department is a recognized organization unit, and in almost every steel mill, the blast furnace department. Here are examples of specialization that appear to be dictated by the technology; the units are "natural" in this sense. On the other side we find units that are "natural" in the sense of being specialized to handle socially-defined purposes, which, in turn, depend on the processes of reification discussed in 3c (e.g., the Children's Bureau). Research into the theory of specialization making use of the

---

[12] My former colleague, Victor A. Thompson, first pointed out to me the significance of this distinction.

framework suggested in topic 3 is needed to clarify these issues, and to formulate and test propositions about the consequences of specialization.

(c) The relationship between specialization and the internal constraints on rational adaptation is two-way: the division of work may be determined, partly or wholly, by such constraints; it will in turn create constraints. That is, the form of specialization will be a major determinant of the frames of reference, skills and knowledge, identifications and foci of attention of organization members. Probably this is the most promising viewpoint from which to tackle the nonrational aspects of formation of group identifications (or "interests" in the political sense) and the effects of such identifications upon intergroup processes (cf. 5d on the "rational" aspects).

(d) Problems of vertical specialization are closely related to topics 1 and 2. In applied organization theory, the questions are usually stated in terms of "centralization" and "decentralization."

This list of research areas illustrates, I think, that the phenomena of organization constitute an important level of theory—a level that is encompassed neither by the usual conceptualizations of small-group processes nor by those of the more macroscopic analyses of cultures and institutions.

The characteristics of this level that give it its particular "flavor" are the following: (a) its focus is on relations among interlocking or non-interlocking primary groups rather than on relations within primary groups; (b) it is largely concerned with situations where *zweckrationalität* plays a large role relative to *wertrationalität* (as compared with the study either of small groups or of cultures); (c) in these situations the scheme of social interaction becomes itself partly a resultant of the rational contriving of means and the conscious construction and acting out of "artificial" roles; and (d) explanation of phenomena at this level requires the closest attention to the fluid boundaries of rational adaptation, including the important boundaries imposed by group frames of reference, perceptual frameworks, and symbolic techniques. In contrast to these characteristics, the level of primary group theory must pay much more attention to the personal values that are emergent from the process of group interaction itself, the acculturalization of individuals to the group, and the particular forms of cohesion that arise out of face-to-face interaction and individual sensitivity to group approval.

It would be wrong, of course, to insist that none of the primary group phenomena are relevant to intergroup relations, or vice-versa. Nevertheless, the important work that has been done on small groups in the past generation—much of it involving the observation of groups that were part of larger organizational structures—has contributed very modestly to the solution of the problems of organization theory.

SECTION THREE

Leadership and Morale

A VERY SUBSTANTIAL part of the modern literature on the functioning of organizations concerns the reaction of the participant as an individual person to the forces impinging upon him in the organizational context. Most of this is the product of the so-called "human relations" school, now receiving wide currency in managerial applications. The original impetus to this sort of study came from the classical investigation carried out by a research team from Harvard University and the Western Electric Company at the latter's Hawthorne Works in the late 1920's and early '30's (1). This investigation indicated rather dramatically that psychological factors were dominant in determining the productivity of workers under the conditions existent in the Hawthorne Works, a typical large-scale manufacturing enterprise with a relatively progressive personnel policy for that era. It also indicated that the managerial techniques in use did not secure from the working force a contribution anywhere near the workers' capacity to contribute. These findings were borne out in subsequent studies. The study of shoe-factory work teams by Horsfall & Arensberg in Section Two is typical in this respect, showing the impotence of the management's incentive system in the face of the workers' felt needs for fairness and social solidarity.

These early studies showed clearly the existence and importance in the typical factory of an "unanticipated consequence"—unanticipated, that is, by the management—of the forms of organization employed. The inadequacies centered around management's efforts to control and influence its employees and in the creation of unfavorable attitudes on the part of the workmen toward management, the company, and their work: that is, in management's leadership functions and in the morale of the work force. The implication is that management has somehow failed to understand human nature, failed to develop knowledge and techniques for the exploitation of human resources at all comparable to those developed for

169

material resources. The result has been a movement to introduce better psychology into the managerial art. The impact of modern principles of psychology on management's thinking is explored by Douglas McGregor in "The Human Side of Enterprise."

It remains to be somewhat more specific about the concepts of leadership and morale and to make explicit the theoretical framework which will relate these concepts one with another and with the other theories presented in this book. As is true of many of the concepts used in social science theory, most people think they already know what leadership and morale are. This is true of important concepts in almost any area of science; people also think they know what is meant by the words *time, atom, bacteria, oxidation,* etc. The job of the scientists is to clarify, and all too often to overcome, the common-sense meanings that become attached to words.

The concept of *morale* usually refers to the value that members place on their participation in the group or organization. Almost any attitude toward the organization or some aspect of it may be subsumed under this concept. To a considerable extent, this is because attitudes tend to generalize; the (favorable or unfavorable) attitude toward one aspect of the organization will either color the individual's whole impression of the organization or be overcome by that impression. Similarly, attitudes tend to spread from one individual to another.

The processes by which attitudes spread among interacting persons is of broader relevance than merely for the development of high or low morale. We speak of *influence* whenever one person is induced to accept an idea or take an action by the intervention of some other person. In a peer group, patterns of influence frequently develop. Some members influence each other into adopting uniform habits of thought or action. This is usually referred to as *clique formation.* Not infrequently the pattern of influence is not reciprocal; one member may come to exercise influence over the other, but not vice versa. In this case we speak of *leadership.* Leadership may be specialized, in that one person exercises dominant influence in one area of behavior, whereas another is more influential in some other respect; in this case one can talk of leadership, but not of a leader. The term *leader* is reserved for the individual who exercises influence over his followers in most spheres (2).

A question which excites the interest of every student (or practitioner) of management is, "What are the determinants of leadership?" Although we can attempt no complete answer to this question, it is possible to say something about it, especially in the organizational case. It is in this context that we must deal straightforwardly with the concept of authority, which we eschewed as a general frame of reference for the study of organization. In organizations, other determinants of leadership are certainly relevant, but only after authority relations are understood and allowed for.

The analysis of authority relations to be presented here originated with Barnard (3) and has been further developed by Simon (4). The fundamental distinction between the Barnard-Simon concept of authority and the traditional use of the word is in the locus of the authority. The traditionalists view authority as inherent in the office or the person of the superior or leader. Under the view we shall accept here, the locus of authority is in the subordinate or follower. The important question then becomes not whether authority is held, but whether it is accepted. This is not a circularity arrived at by equating authority with leadership. The two cannot properly be equated. *Authority* stems from generalized social perceptions of the *legitimacy* of command functions in certain kinds of formal social roles, such as policeman, military commander, or business executive. The question then becomes not "What commands can the superior give?" but rather, "What commands will the subordinate obey?" The range of commands that will be obeyed by the subordinate is termed the *area of acceptance*.

Among the corollaries to this theory is the idea that a command which is given and is not within the area of acceptance will not only fail to be obeyed, but will be destructive of the authority relation in general. This is to say that the limits to authority are psychological and not formal.

Another possible corollary to this notion of authority is that it should be sparingly applied as an influence measure to avoid the risk of its breakdown. The use of suggestions, referral for recommendation, abstract rules, and a host of other ingenious devices are methods for gauging the area of acceptance and tailoring the final command (if one should prove necessary at all) to fit nicely within it.

Still another corollary concerns the delegation of authority. Holders of formal authority in organizations cannot delegate it arbitrarily. Delegation is ineffectual unless the delegate is perceived as legitimate by those whose acceptance he is supposed to gain. Thus, although delegation of authority is a prerogative of the holder of formal authority, its effectiveness is strictly conditional on ratification by those over whom authority is supposed to be exercised.

When authority relations are conceived as indicated in the analysis above, its importance in the leadership relation in organizations is seen to be much reduced over what the traditionalists imply. The traditional view is culture-bound in its failure to perceive that the operational limitations on authority are imposed by the governed and not by the governor. Our analysis also permits us to separate other determinants of leadership and influence relations, such as *control over resources* and *personal characteristics*. The former of these has especially been subsumed under the concept of authority in traditional analyses. But the relationship here is actually one of *bargaining* and is quite different from the authority relation. Quite clearly, anyone, even though without any formal position or any of the personal characteristics that might induce others to follow his lead, can succeed in getting others to build him a house and in quite exactly the way he wants it, if only he has enough money in the bank. People are often willing to accept influence, given a *quid pro quo*.

As pointed out in McGregor's article, there is not an exact parallel between this type of contract and an employment contract. The employer cannot compel specific performance (i.e., slavery) and has no recourse to a legal suit for damages for failure of perfomance, but only the right of discharge. The result of any employment contract is more nearly the establishment of an authority relation than an instance of bargaining. A considerable amount of bargaining may, however, go on within the context of an employment relationship, either collectively or individually, as both sides come to hold control over resources desired by the other. Examples are the granting or withholding of promotions or recommendations therefor; filing or approval of grievances; the slowdown; changes in working conditions; strikes and walkouts; etc. An important characteristic here is that mere possession of resources is to no avail; possession must be had of resources desired by the person or persons to be influenced. This form of leadership is just as subject to veto by the led as is the authority relation.

A special form of resource control is the use or threat of *negative sanctions*. The distinguishing characteristic is the way they are perceived psychologically by the person over whom influence is attempted. The dominant tone is one of deprivation, threat, pain, and mobilization of the safety needs. Though these methods may get results, their efficacy is likely to be more short-term than lasting. The person in the subordinate position, given enough time, will be able to find a more satisfactory resolution of his situation than to be forever threatened. This has been recognized by many writers in the field who point out that the habitual use of negative sanctions is destructive of good leadership relations.

Personal characteristics are often the most highly touted of the determinants of leadership. Many times this refers to no more than skillful use of authority and resource control. At other times it refers to inherent qualities of person or personality. Studies have shown, for instance, that people are more likely to follow the lead of men than women and of tall men rather than short men. Other studies, some of which are discussed later, have explored the effects of differences in mental abilities or personality factors.

Naturally enough, the bulk of the research studies on leadership and morale have been carried out by psychologists. As indicated above, the subject matter of their studies has gradually broadened to include other psychological ideas and tools than the rather simple concept of a social bond linking the worker with his work group, company, or community, which seemed to be enough for the Hawthorne study and its successors.

Most of the new psychological ideas carried into research on organization problems have come from personality theory and group dynamics. In the latter field, Kurt Lewin and his students played the major part. They formed the Research Center for Group Dynamics, originally at the Massachusetts Institute of Technology and now at the University of Michigan. The group dynamicists developed many ingenious techniques for laboratory experimentation with small groups, of which studies by S. E. Asch and by H. Guetzkow and H. A. Simon reported in the next chapter are excellent examples.

One type of research design which has been frequently used in organizational studies involves the selection of a criterion of good performance and the examination of a large class of other variables to determine which of them influence the performance criterion. For example, one might request superiors to rate first-line supervisors for good leadership and then by the use of standard personality tests and correlation or factor-analytic methods look for the personality traits typical of the good leader. Positive results would, of course, simplify problems of selection of officer candidates for the military, or future foremen for industry. Unfortunately, such simple designs have usually not been very successful.

On the bright side, however, the results of these and other studies have given a good indication of the direction research must take to be successful: More of the complexity of organizational life must be accounted for within the theory and research design used. In the example mentioned, one would nevertheless expect that personality characteristics would have an influence on leadership ability; but this influence might be different depending on the personalities and attitudes of the people being led, on the type of task being performed, or on other situational factors. Although a hypothesis can be oversimplified and still be useful, it cannot ignore the major characteristics of the phenomena under consideration and still be confirmed by the evidence.

The article by W. A. Cleven and F. E. Fiedler reproduced in this section, "Interpersonal Perceptions of Open-Hearth Foremen in Steel Production," and other studies in this research program provide a specific illustration of this complexity (5). The basic hypothesis in this study is one that has been argued in the traditional literature for centuries; namely, that psychological distance of the leader from the led is a prerequisite of effective leadership. Beginning with a personality test that measures the subject's generalized tendency to maintain psychological distance from others, Fiedler and his colleagues have discovered various conditioning effects that result in a theory with statistically demonstrable explanatory power. Interestingly enough, one of these conditioners (sociometric choice) is a measure of the degree and direction of the liking for one another that develops between leader and followers. Another stems from the nature of the task.

A different line of research involving initially the same type of design has been carried out by the University of Michigan's Institute for Social Research. Their Human Relations Program drew for its ideas on the work of the Group Dynamics Center and for its method on the interviewing and questionnaire machinery developed by the Survey Research Center. The initial designs postulated a conception of the good organization as one achieving high productivity and high employee morale. The factors determining these criteria were sought in the attitudes and supervisory style of the work-group leaders. The specific content given to these dimensions of attitude and supervisory style was derived largely from findings in laboratory studies of small groups that group effectiveness is increased by democratic group leadership and explicit concern with group maintenance and process (6). Democratic group leadership implies that each member participates fully in discussion and work, that each has full opportunity to influence the group's decisions and the outcome of their functioning, and that the relevant needs of all the members as individuals are satisfied in the group. In its maintenance function, someone, and preferably the group as a whole, must see that the conditions of democratic group leadership are maintained and that any malfunction is brought to the attention of the group and worked out before continuation with substantive issues.

In the course of the human relations program, these hypotheses have been developed into findings, for the industrial situation, that four broad characteristics of supervision are related to effectiveness. One factor is that the supervisor's role in the more effective work-groups is different from that of the worker, specifically in that he concerns himself with planning and organizing the work to be done, training his men, supplying them with the needed resources, and maintaining the work-group itself by person-to-person activity. The second factor is that the supervisors of the more productive work-groups grant a considerable degree of discretion and control over the work to the individual employees: that is, they supervise less closely. The third finding is that the supervisor is more oriented to the needs of the employees who are doing the work than toward the work itself, seeing that they have such assistance as they need to get the work done and also that their personal situation is satisfactory to them. The other finding is that the more effective work-groups show a friendly, co-operative atmosphere and relatively high pride in and loyalty to the work-group itself (7).

One of the advantages of a long-range plan of research such as this one is the ability to progress from an oversimplified research design, like the initial one, to others that are more adequate. Donald C. Pelz in his article "Leadership within a Hierarchical Organization" discusses some of the developments relating to the finding that the more effective supervisor is oriented to his employees' needs. Another advantage is the possibility of following up interesting leads arising from a specific research project but not directly related to its purpose. For instance, the criteria of effectiveness in oganizations were not always found to be correlated with each other, and there seems no reason why morale and productivity should be invariably associated. This was irrelevant to the initial study designs; but the point was pursued in other studies (8). Some of the later Michigan work departs rather widely from the leadership-morale area and will be mentioned in other chapters.

Many writers have focused somewhat more broadly on the relations between individuals and their organizations. Much of this writing is prescriptive (9), some polemical (10), but much of it is research oriented. One example is the work of Leonard Sayles, investigating the effect of task characteristics and work environment on attitude formation in industrial work-groups (11). Some other work is clinically oriented and attempts to deal with the whole organizational setting of specific problems of influence and morale. An interesting case study of this type by K. Chowdry and A. Pal, "Production Planning and Organizational Morale," is reproduced in this section. A somewhat more systematic approach of the same type is afforded by the work of Chris Argyris (12). Drawing largely on developmental theory of personality, he attempts to explore the relation between personality processes and organizational processes.

Argyris' best-known case study is *The Organization of a Bank*. His most prominent finding was that the bank tended to draw to it employees of a particular personality pattern, the "right type" for a bank. The "right type" was neat and conventional in manner, polite, quiet, and retiring. The stability and security of bank life attracted them, and the bank benefited from their ability to fit into the precise and genteel routine of the workday. This had certain implications for the administrative style of the bank. Specifically, both employees and officers expected a minimum of direct supervisory activity. Likewise, neither employees nor officers had much occasion to take the initiative; the bank's activities were either routine or else initiated by customers. The last item in this section is an excerpt, outlining the ideas that Argyris hoped to test in this case study and illustrating his method of applying them to one department of the bank.

REFERENCES

1. F. J. ROETHLISBERGER and W. J. DICKSON. *Management and the Worker.* Harvard University Press, 1939. For a condensed report of this investigation, see S. D. Hoslett, *Human Factors in Management*, Harper, 1951, p. 210.
2. See WILLIAM F. WHYTE, *Street Corner Society*, Chicago, 1956, for an excellent case study of the development of influence and leadership relations in an informal social group.

3. C. I. BARNARD. *Functions of the Executive.* Harvard, 1938.

4. See page 161 and footnote 3 of Simon's article and the elaboration of the concept in his books, *Administrative Behavior, Models of Man,* and (with J. March) *Organizations.*

5. F. E. FIEDLER. *Leader Attitudes and Group Effectiveness.* Urbana: University of Illinois Press, 1958.

6. D. CARTWRIGHT and A. ZANDER (Eds.). *Group Dynamics.* Evanston, Illinois: Row Peterson, 1953.

7. ROBERT L. KAHN. "Leadership Patterns and Organizational Effectiveness," *Sixth Annual Industrial Relations Conference.* Montreal: McGill University Industrial Relations Center, 1954.

8. R. L. KAHN and N. C. MORSE. "The Relationship of Productivity to Morale," *Journal of Social Issues,* Vol. VII, 3, 1951.

9. D. McGREGOR. *Human Side of Enterprise.* McGraw-Hill, 1960. R. LIKERT, "A Motivational Approach to a Modified Theory of Organization and Management," in M. HAIRE, *Modern Organization Theory,* Wiley, 1959. W. F. WHYTE, *Pattern for Industrial Peace* and *Money and Motivation,* Harper's, 1951 and 1955.

10. WILLIAM H. WHYTE, JR. *The Organization Man.* Simon & Schuster, 1956. E. E. JENNINGS, "The Authoritarian Cultural Lag in Business," *Journal of the Academy of Management,* Vol. 2, No. 2, August, 1959, p. 111.

11. L. SAYLES. *Behavior of Industrial Work-Groups.* Wiley, 1958.

12. See Argyris, *Personality and Organization,* Harper's, 1957 or "Understanding Human Behavior in Organizations," in M. Haire, *Modern Organization Theory,* Wiley, 1959, and the work there cited.

13. THE HUMAN SIDE OF ENTERPRISE*
Douglas M. McGregor

It has become trite to say that the most significant developments of the next quarter century will take place not in the physical but in the social sciences, that industry—the economic organ of society—has the fundamental know-how to utilize physical science and technology for the material benefit of mankind, and that we must now learn how to utilize the social sciences to make our human organizations truly effective.

Many people agree in principle with such statements; but so far they represent a pious hope—and little else. Consider with me, if you will, something of what may be involved when we attempt to transform the hope into reality.

I

Let me begin with an analogy. A quarter century ago basic conceptions of the nature of matter and energy had changed profoundly from what they had been since Newton's time. The physical scientists were persuaded that under proper conditions new and hitherto unimagined sources of energy could be made available to mankind.

We know what has happened since then. First came the bomb. Then, during the past decade, have come many other attempts to exploit these scientific discoveries—some successful, some not.

The point of my analogy, however, is that the application of theory in this field is a slow and costly matter. We expect it always to be thus. No one is impatient with the scientist because he cannot tell industry how to build a simple, cheap, all-purpose source of atomic energy today. That it will take at least another decade and the investment of billions of dollars to achieve results which are economically competitive with present sources of power is understood and accepted.

It is transparently pretentious to suggest any *direct* similarity between the developments in the physical sciences leading to the harnessing of atomic energy and potential developments in the social sciences. Nevertheless, the analogy is not as absurd as it might appear to be at first glance.

To a lesser degree, and in a much more tentative fashion, we are in a

* Reprinted from *Adventure in Thought and Action,* Proceedings of the Fifth Anniversary Convocation of the School of Industrial Management, Massachusetts Institute of Technology, Cambridge, April 9, 1957. Published by the School, 50 Memorial Drive, Cambridge 39, Massachusetts, June, 1957.

position in the social sciences today like that of the physical sciences with respect to atomic energy in the thirties. We know that past conceptions of the nature of man are inadequate and in many ways incorrect. We are becoming quite certain that, under proper conditions, unimagined resources of creative human energy could become available within the organizational setting.

We cannot tell industrial management how to apply this new knowledge in simple, economic ways. We know it will require years of exploration, much costly development research, and a substantial amount of creative imagination on the part of management to discover how to apply this growing knowledge to the organization of human effort in industry.

May I ask that you keep this analogy in mind—overdrawn and pretentious though it may be—as a framework for what I have to say this morning.

Management's Task: Conventional View

The conventional conception of management's task in harnessing human energy to organizational requirements can be stated broadly in terms of three propositions. In order to avoid the complications introduced by a label, I shall call this set of propositions "Theory X:"

1. Management is responsible for organizing the elements of productive enterprise—money, materials, equipment, people—in the interest of economic ends.

2. With respect to people, this is a process of directing their efforts, motivating them, controlling their actions, modifying their behavior to fit the needs of the organization.

3. Without this active intervention by management, people would be passive—even resistant—to organizational needs. They must therefore be persuaded, rewarded, punished, controlled—their activities must be directed. This is management's task—in managing subordinate managers or workers. We often sum it up by saying that management consists of getting things done through other people.

Behind this convetional theory there are several additional beliefs—less explicit, but widespread:

4. The average man is by nature indolent—he works as little as possible.

5. He lacks ambition, dislikes responsibility, prefers to be led.

6. He is inherently self-centered, indifferent to organizational needs.

7. He is by nature resistant to change.

8. He is gullible, not very bright, the ready dupe of the charlatan and the demagogue.

The human side of economic enterprise today is fashioned from propositions and beliefs such as these. Conventional organization structures, managerial policies, practices, and programs reflect these assumptions.

In accomplishing its task—with these assumptions as guides—management has conceived of a range of possibilities between two extremes.

The Hard or the Soft Approach?

At one extreme, management can be "hard" or "strong." The methods for directing behavior involve coercion and threat (usually disguised), close supervision, tight controls over behavior. At the other extreme, management can be "soft" or "weak." The methods for directing behavior involve being permissive, satisfying people's demands, achieving harmony. Then they will be tractable, accept direction.

This range has been fairly completely explored during the past half century, and management has learned some things from the exploration. There are difficulties in the "hard" approach. Force breeds counterforces: restriction of output, antagonism, militant unionism, subtle but effective sabotage of management objectives. This approach is especially difficult during times of full employment.

There are also difficulties in the "soft" approach. It leads frequently to the abdication of management—to harmony, perhaps, but to indifferent performance. People take advantage of the soft approach. They continually expect more, but they give less and less.

Currently, the popular theme is "firm but fair." This is an attempt to gain the advantages of both the hard and the soft approaches. It is reminiscent of Teddy Roosevelt's "speak softly and carry a big stick."

Is the Conventional View Correct?

The findings which are beginning to emerge from the social sciences challenge this whole set of beliefs about man and human nature and about the task of management. The evidence is far from conclusive, certainly, but it is suggestive. It comes from the laboratory, the clinic, the schoolroom, the home, and even to a limited extent from industry itself.

The social scientist does not deny that human behavior in industrial organization today is approximately what management perceives it to be. He has, in fact, observed it and studied it fairly extensively. But he is pretty sure that this behavior is *not* a consequence of man's inherent nature. It is a consequence rather of the nature of industrial organizations, of management philosophy, policy, and practice. The conventional approach of Theory X is based on mistaken notions of what is cause and what is effect.

"Well," you ask, "what then is the *true* nature of man? What evidence leads the social scientist to deny what is obvious?" And, if I am not mistaken, you are also thinking, "Tell me—simply, and without a lot of scientific verbiage—what you think you know that is so unusual. Give me—without a lot of intellectual claptrap and theoretical nonsense—some practical ideas which will enable me to improve the situation in my organization. And remember, I'm faced with increasing costs and narrowing profit margins. I want proof that such ideas won't result simply in new and costly human relations frills. I want practical results, and I want them now."

If these are your wishes, you are going to be disappointed. Such requests can no more be met by the social scientist today than could comparable ones with respect to atomic energy be met by the physicist fifteen years ago. I can, however, indicate a few of the reasons for asserting that conventional assumptions about the human side of enterprise are inadequate. And I can suggest—tentatively—some of the propositions that will comprise a more adequate theory of the management of people. The magnitude of the task that confronts us will then, I think be apparent.

II

Perhaps the best way to indicate why the conventional approach of management is inadequate is to consider the subject of motivation. In discussing this subject I will draw heavily on the work of my colleague, Abraham Maslow of Brandeis University. His is the most fruitful approach I know. Naturally, what I have to say will be over-generalized and will ignore important qualifications. In the time at our disposal, this is inevitable.

Physiological and Safety Needs

Man is a wanting animal—as soon as one of his needs is satisfied, another appears in its place. This process is unending. It continues from birth to death.

Man's needs are organized in a series of levels—a hierarchy of importance. At the lowest level, but preeminent in importance when they are thwarted, are his physiological needs. Man lives by bread alone, when there is no bread. Unless the circumstances are unusual, his needs for love, for status, for recognition are inoperative when his stomach has been empty for a while. But when he eats regularly and adequately, hunger ceases to be an important need. The sated man has hunger only in the sense that a full bottle has emptiness. The same is true of the other physiological needs of man—for rest, exercise, shelter, protection from the elements.

A satisfied need is not a motivator of behavior! This is a fact of profound significance. It is a fact which is regularly ignored in the conventional approach to the management of people. I shall return to it later. For the moment, one example will make my point. Consider your own need for air. Except as you are deprived of it, it has no appreciable motivating effect upon your behavior.

When the physiological needs are reasonably satisfied, needs at the next higher level begin to dominate man's behavior—to motivate him. These are called safety needs. They are needs for protection against danger, threat, deprivation. Some people mistakenly refer to these as needs for security. However, unless man is in a dependent relationship where he fears arbitrary deprivation, he does not demand security. The need is for the "fairest possible break." When he is confident of this, he is more than willing to take risks. But when he feels threatened or dependent, his greatest need is for guarantees, for protection, for security.

The fact needs little emphasis that since every industrial employee is in a dependent relationship, safety needs may assume considerable importance. Arbitrary management actions, behavior which arouses uncertainty with respect to continued employment or which reflects favoritism or discrimination, unpredictable administration of policy—these can be powerful motivators of the safety needs in the employment relationship *at every level* from worker to vice president.

Social Needs

When man's physiological needs are satisfied and he is no longer fearful about his physical welfare, his social needs become important motivators of his behavior—for belonging, for association, for acceptance by his fellows, for giving and receiving friendship and love.

Management knows today of the existence of these needs, but it often assumes quite wrongly that they represent a threat to the organization. Many studies have demonstrated that the tightly knit, cohesive work group may, under proper conditions, be far more effective than an equal number of separate individuals in achieving organizational goals.

Yet management, fearing group hostility to its own objectives, often goes to considerable lengths to control and direct human efforts in ways that are inimical to the natural "groupiness" of human beings. When man's social needs—and perhaps his safety needs, too—are thus thwarted, he behaves in ways which tend to defeat organizational objectives. He becomes resistant, antagonistic, uncooperative. But this behavior is a consequence, not a cause.

Ego Needs

Above the social needs—in the sense that they do not become motivators until lower needs are reasonably satisfied—are the needs of greatest significance to management and to man himself. They are the egoistic needs, and they are of two kinds:

1. Those needs that relate to one's self-esteem—needs for self-confidence, for independence, for achievement, for competence, for knowledge.

2. Those needs that relate to one's reputation—needs for status, for recognition, for appreciation, for the deserved respect of one's fellows.

Unlike the lower needs, these are rarely satisfied; man seeks indefinitely for more satisfaction of these needs once they have become important to him. But they do not appear in any significant way until physiologcal, safety, and social needs are all reasonably satisfied.

The typical industrial organization offers few opportunities for the satisfaction of these egoistic needs to people at lower levels in the hierarchy. The conventional methods of organizing work, particularly in mass production industries, give little heed to these aspects of human motivation. If the practices of scientific management were deliberately calculated to thwart these needs—which, of course, they are not—they could hardly accomplish this purpose better than they do.

Self-Fulfillment Needs

Finally—a capstone, as it were, on the hierarchy of man's needs—there are what we may call the needs for self-fulfillment. These are the needs for realizing one's own potentialities, for continued self-development, for being creative in the broadest sense of that term.

It is clear that the conditions of modern life give only limited opportunity for these relatively weak needs to obtain expression. The deprivation most people experience with respect to other lower-level needs diverts their energies into the struggle to satisfy *those* needs, and the needs for self-fulfillment remain dormant.

III

Now, briefly, a few general comments about motivation:

We recognize readily enough that a man suffering from a severe dietary deficiency is sick. The deprivation of physiological needs has behavioral consequences. The same is true—although less well recognized—of deprivation of higher-level needs. The man whose needs for safety, association, independence, or status are thwarted is sick just as surely as is he who has rickets. And his sickness will have behavioral consequences. We will be mistaken if we attribute his resultant passivity, his hostility, his refusal to accept responsibility to his inherent "human nature." These forms of behavior are *symptoms* of illness—of deprivation of his social and egoistic needs.

The man whose lower-level needs are satisfied is not motivated to satisfy those needs any longer. For practical purposes they exist no longer. (Remember my point about your need for air.) Management often asks, "Why aren't people more productive? We pay good wages, provide good working conditions, have excellent fringe benefits and steady employment. Yet people do not seem to be willing to put forth more than minimum effort."

The fact that management has provided for these physiological and safety needs has shifted the motivational emphasis to the social and perhaps to the egoistic needs. Unless there are opportunities *at work* to satisfy these higher-level needs, people will be deprived; and their behavior will reflect this deprivation. Under such conditions, if management continues to focus its attention on physiological needs, its efforts are bound to be ineffective.

People *will* make insistent demands for more money under these conditions. It becomes more important than ever to buy the material goods and services which can provide limited satisfaction of the thwarted needs. Although money has only limited value in satisfying many higher-level needs, it can become the focus of interest if it is the *only* means available.

The Carrot and Stick Approach

The carrot and stick theory of motivation (like Newtonian physical theory) works reasonably well under certain circumstances. The *means* for satisfying man's physiological and (within limits) his safety needs can be provided or withheld by management. Employment itself is such a means, and so are wages, working conditions, and benefits. By these means the individual can be controlled so long as he is struggling for subsistence. Man lives for bread alone when there is no bread.

But the carrot and stick theory does not work at all once man has reached an adequate subsistence level and is motivated primarily by higher needs. Management cannot provide a man with self-respect, or with the respect of his fellows, or with the satisfaction of needs for self-fulfillment. It can create conditions such that he is encouraged and enabled to seek such satisfactions *for himself*, or it can thwart him by failing to create those conditions.

But this creation of conditions is not "control." It is not a good device for directing behavior. And so management finds itself in an odd position. The high standard of living created by our modern technological know-how provides quite adequately for the satisfaction of physiological and safety needs. The only significant exception is where management practices have not created confidence in a "fair break"—and thus where safety needs are thwarted. But by making possible the satisfaction of low-level needs, management has deprived itself of the ability to use as motivators the devices on which conventional theory has taught it to rely—rewards, promises, incentives, or threats and other coercive devices.

Neither Hard nor Soft

The philosophy of management by direction and control—*regardless of whether it is hard or soft*—is inadequate to motivate because the human needs on which this approach relies are today unimportant motivators of behavior. Direction and control are essentially useless in motivating people whose important needs are social and egoistic. Both the hard and the soft approach fail today because they are simply irrelevant to the situation.

People, deprived of opportunities to satisfy at work the needs which are now important to them, behave exactly as we might predict—with indolence, passivity, resistance to change, lack of responsibility, willingness to follow the demagogue, unreasonable demands for economic benefits. It would seem that we are caught in a web of our own weaving.

In summary, then, of these comments about motivation:

Management by direction and control—whether implemented with the hard, the soft, or the firm but fair approach—fails under today's conditions to provide effective motivation of human effort toward organizational objectives. It fails because direction and control are useless methods of motivating people whose physiological and safety needs are reasonably satisfied and whose social, egoistic, and self-fulfillment needs are predominant.

IV

For these and many other reasons, we require a different theory of the task of managing people based on more adequate assumptions about human nature and human motivation. I am going to be so bold as to suggest the broad dimensions of such a theory. Call it "Theory Y," if you will.

1. Management is responsible for organizing the elements of productive enterprise—money, materials, equipment, people—in the interest of economic ends.

2. People are *not* by nature passive or resistant to organizational needs. They have become so as a result of experience in organizations.

3. The motivation, the potential for development, the capacity for assuming responsibility, the readiness to direct behavior toward organizational goals are all present in people. Management does not put them there. It is a responsibility of management to make it possible for people to recognize and develop these human characteristics for themselves.

4. The essential task of management is to arrange organizational conditions and methods of operation so that people can achieve their own goals *best* by directing *their own* efforts toward organizational objectives.

This is a process primarily of creating opportunities, releasing potential, removing obstacles, encouraging growth, providing guidance. It is what Peter Drucker has called "management by objectives" in contrast to "management by control."

And I hasten to add that it does *not* involve the abdication of manage-   ✦
ment, the absence of leadership, the lowering of standards, or the other
characteristics usually associated with the "soft" approach under Theory
X. Much on the contrary. It is no more possible to create an organization
today which will be a fully effective application of this theory than it
was to build an atomic power plant in 1945. There are many formidable
obstacles to overcome.

Some Difficulties

The conditions imposed by conventional organization theory and by
the approach of scientific management for the past half century have tied
men to limited jobs which do not utilize their capabilities, have discouraged the acceptance of responsibility, have encouraged passivity, have
eliminated meaning from work. Man's habits, attitudes, expectations—his
whole conception of membership in an industrial organization—have been
conditioned by his experience under these circumstances. Change in the
direction of Theory Y will be slow, and it will require extensive modification of the attitudes of management and workers alike.

People today are accustomed to being directed, manipulated, controlled in industrial organizations and to finding satisfaction for their social, egoistic, and self-fulfillment needs away from the job. This is true of
much of management as well as of workers. Genuine "industrial citizenship"—to borrow again a term from Drucker—is a remote and unrealistic
idea, the meaning of which has not even been considered by most members of industrial organizations.

Another way of saying this is that Theory X places exclusive reliance
upon external control of human behavior, while Theory Y relies heavily
on self-control and self-direction. It is worth noting that this difference
is the difference between treating people as children and treating them
as mature adults. After generations of the former, we cannot expect to
shift to the latter overnight.

V

Before we are overwhelmed by the obstacles, let us remember that the
application of theory is always slow. Progress is usually achieved in small
steps.

Consider with me a few innovative ideas which are entirely consistent
with Theory Y and which are today being applied with some success:

Decentralization and Delegation

These are ways of freeing people from the too-close control of conventional organization, giving them a degree of freedom to direct their
own activities, to assume responsibility, and, importantly, to satisfy their

egoistic needs. In this connection, the flat organization of Sears, Roebuck and Company provides an interesting example. It forces "management by objectives" since it enlarges the number of people reporting to a manager until he cannot direct and control them in the conventional manner.

Job Enlargement

This concept, pioneered by I.B.M. and Detroit Edison, is quite consistent with Theory Y. It encourages the acceptance of responsibility at the bottom of the organization; it provides opportunities for satisfying social and egoistic needs. In fact, the reorganization of work at the factory level offers one of the more challenging opportunities for innovation consistent with Theory Y. The studies by A.T.M. Wilson and his associates of British coal mining and Indian textile manufacture have added appreciably to our understanding of work organization. Moreover, the economic and psychological results achieved by this work have been substantial.

Participation and Consultative Management

Under proper conditions these results provide encouragement to people to direct their creative energies toward organizational objectives, give them some voice in decisions that affect them, provide significant opportunities for the satisfaction of social and egoistic needs. I need only mention the Scanlon Plan as the outstanding embodiment of these ideas in practice.

The not infrequent failure of such ideas as these to work as well as expected is often attributable to the fact that a management has "bought the idea" but applied it within the framework of Theory X and its assumptions.

Delegation is not an effective way of exercising management by control. Participation becomes a farce when it is applied as a sales gimmick or a device for kidding people into thinking they are important. Only the management that has confidence in human capacities and is itself directed toward organizational objectives rather than toward the preservation of personal power can grasp the implications of this emerging theory. Such management will find and apply successfully other innovative ideas as we move slowly toward the full implementation of a theory like Y.

Performance Appraisal

Before I stop, let me mention one other practical application of Theory Y which—while still highly tentative—may well have important consequences. This has to do with performance appraisal within the ranks of management. Even a cursory examination of conventional programs of performance appraisal will reveal how completely consistent they are with Theory X. In fact, most such programs tend to treat the individual as though he were a product under inspection on the assembly line.

Take the typical plan: substitute "product" for "subordinate being appraised," substitute "inspector" for "superior making the appraisal," substitute "rework" for "training or development," and, except for the attributes being judged, the human appraisal process will be virtually indistinguishable from the product inspection process.

A few companies—among them General Mills, Ansul Chemical, and General Electric—have been experimenting with approaches which involve the individual in setting "targets" or objectives *for himself* and in a *self*-evaluation of performance semi-annually or annually. Of course, the superior plays an important leadership role in this process—one, in fact, which demands substantially more competence than the conventional approach. The role is, however, considerably more congenial to many managers than the role of "judge" or "inspector" which is forced upon them by conventional performance. Above all, the individual is encouraged to take a greater responsibility for planning and appraising his own contribution to organizational objectives; and the accompanying effects on egoistic and self-fulfillment needs are substantial. This approach to performance appraisal represents one more innovative idea being explored by a few managements who are moving toward the implementation of Theory Y.

VI

And now I am back where I began. I share the belief that we could realize substantial improvements in the effectiveness of industrial organizations during the next decade or two. Moreover, I believe the social sciences can contribute much to such developments. We are only beginning to grasp the implications of the growing body of knowledge in these fields. But if this conviction is to become a reality instead of a pious hope, we will need to view the process much as we view the process of releasing the energy of the atom for constructive human ends—as a slow, costly, sometimes discouraging approach toward a goal which would seem to many to be quite unrealistic.

The ingenuity and the perseverance of industrial management in the pursuit of economic ends have changed many scientific and technological dreams into commonplace realities. It is now becoming clear that the application of these same talents to the human side of enterprise will not only enhance substantially these materialistic achievements but will bring us one step closer to "the good society." Shall we get on with the job?

14. PRODUCTION PLANNING AND ORGANIZATIONAL MORALE*

Kamla Chowdhry and A. K. Pal[0]

This is a study of the interaction of production planning and management practices, and the effect of these on the morale of the supervisory staff of two Indian cotton textile mills. The two mills are located in a large city, where the main industry is textiles. Both mills are operating in a common social and economic climate, subject to the same type of market fluctuations and to a similar pattern of labor-management relations. In both mills, like the rest of the industry, the top executive control is with the managing agent who acquires the right of control through the Managing Agency Agreement.[1]

The markets to which the goods of these mills go are similar. There are frequent fluctuations in the market due to cotton prices, changes in government policy, consumer demand, etc. A significant difference between the two mills is the policy of the management in meeting these fluctuations in the market. In Mill A the manufacturing program is frequently altered to manufacture types of cloth that the market demands at the moment and that would yield the highest profits at that time. This is the prevalent pattern in the industry. In Mill B, the manufacturing program is relatively stable. There have been no changes for years in the counts spun, and even in the cloth manufactured not many significant changes have been introduced. The mill has emphasized and established a reputation for quality, and their manufactured goods have a steady market demand. Probably only half a dozen of the 65 mills in the city follow this practice.

The object of this study is to examine the implications of the above basic differences in the policy of management on the functioning of the organization. More specifically, we sought (1) to determine in what way this policy is reflected in the organizational structure and in the manage-

* Reprinted from *Human Organization*, Vol. XV, No. 4.

[0] The authors are grateful to Professor Charles A. Myers, Director of Industrial Relations Section, M.I.T., for help in planning the study and discussing the results at various stages. The research was financed in part by funds made available by the Inter-University Study of Labor Problems in Economic Development.

[1] The Managing Agency Agreement allows the transfer of Managing Agency rights to the sons and other members of the joint family. The Managing Agents are generally not salaried people but by contract in the Managing Agency Agreement receive a commission which may be a percentage of profits or gross sales. The Managing Agent and his family are generally the major shareholders in the company.

ment practices prevailing in the two mills, and (2) to examine the effect of the prevailing organizational structure and management practices on the satisfaction of members and the efficiency of each organization.

I. RESEARCH PROCEDURE

Both mills are composite units, with spinning, weaving, dyeing, bleaching and finishing operations. This study was restricted to the spinning and weaving sections only, which comprise the major part of the textile mills. The organization and functioning of these two departments were studied with the help of top management and supervisory staffs. The research staff visited the mills almost daily over a period of three months and observed the activities going on, the interactions and relationships of people, and conducted interviews on certain aspects of organization and management practices. Fixed question–free answer interviews were held with the managing agents, production managers, and twenty-four departmental heads, assistants and supervisors. Mill A and Mill B are compared in terms of formal organizational structure, delegation of responsibility and authority, communication and consultation practices, and the satisfaction and stability of members working in the organization.

II. ORGANIZATIONAL STRUCTURE

The formal organizational structures of Mill A and Mill B are given in Figure 1. The hierarchical levels and their designation in industry are as follows: managing agent, production manager, departmental head, assistant, supervisor, jobber and worker.

Mill A

In Mill A the top executive is the managing agent, and he is in overall charge of the production and the sales of the organization. The next level in the formal structure consists of the production manager, who is the technical adviser to the agent. The third level in the organization is composed of departmental heads, who, however, report directly to the agent. The agent also has direct contact with the departmental heads, but he sometimes passes instructions through the production manager. The departmental heads discuss their problems and difficulties with the production manager, but in a more informal way in the hope that he will be able to present their case to the agent more effectively.

The departmental head reports to the agent once or twice daily in the latter's office. The agent tells them of the changes he wishes to introduce in the manufacturing program, and they in turn inform the agent about efficiency, balance of production, shortage of material and spare parts, labor difficulties, etc.

No clear procedure is followed by the assistant and supervisors about reporting. They report to the departmental head, but they are also asked to report directly sometimes to the production manager or to the agent. The supervisors report to the assistant or departmental head depending on whoever is available, or with whom they have better relations.

It is also clear from Figure 1, that there are more senior personnel

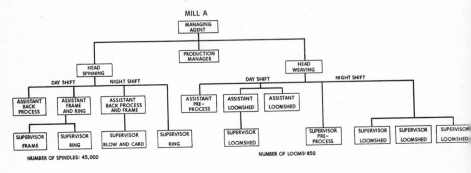

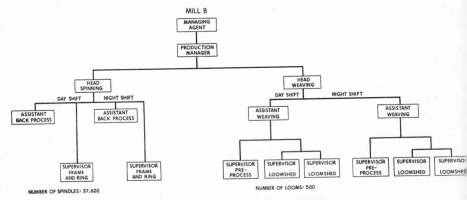

FIG. 1. Organization of Mill A and Mill B

working on the day shift than on the night shift and that the night shift is mainly in charge of junior personnel. Thus, there are two assistants on the day shift in the Spinning Department against one on the night shift. Similarly, in the Weaving Department there are three assistants on the day shift but none on the night shift. This makes the organizational structure very unbalanced in the two shifts. The weaving master says, concerning the senior personnel in the day shift:

> It is rather unfortunate that all my assistants are placed on the day shift. It is absolutely necessary to have at least one assistant (of loomshed) on the night shift. I am trying to persuade the agent to transfer X or Y to the night shift.

On the other hand, the spinning master desires to place senior staff on the day shift:

I prefer to keep the assistants on the day shift—otherwise I would not be able to cope with the work. We do all the settings on the day shift. The night shift people only run the machines.

Another feature of the organization of Mill A is that supervisors and sometimes assistants, are transferred from one shift to another, without a corresponding change in the personnel of the rest of the department. According to factory rules, jobbers and workers change systematically every month from day to night shift. But the assistants and supervisors who are not covered by the factory regulations do not change their shift regularly; they move, but on an *ad hoc* basis, depending on other considerations. This results in the continuity of work relationships being frequently disrupted, in a certain amount of confusion as to who is to report to whom, and in problems of relationships that arise when there is no clear and stable structure of reporting and getting work done.

One loomshed supervisor says:

I don't like this system. I mean no system. I don't know who is my boss, so I have developed a system of working independently.

Another supervisor says:

I like to be with the same group of workers all the time. I like to change shifts with them. You have got to know your workers to get along well with them. But here you don't know where you will be tomorrow.

Mill B

In Mill B, also, the managing agent is the top executive who has overall charge of production and sales of the organization. The next level is the production manager. He is the technical adviser to the agent and also coordinates the manufacturing program of the different departments. The departmental heads mainly report to the production manager. There are no changes in the manufacture of counts in spinning, but if changes in the sorts woven are to be introduced, the sales manager sends direct information to the weaving master or the assistant concerned.

The departmental heads report to the production manager during the latter's round in the department. The departmental heads do not have a daily direct contact with the agent in his office concerning current production problems, as was the case in Mill A. The assistants report to the departmental heads and are not generally called directly by the production manager or the agent for information. The supervisors generally report to the assistants, but sometimes to the departmental head directly.

In Mill B the organizational structures of both day and night shifts are similar. There is the same number of staff in both the shifts and there is an equal distribution of senior staff on the day and night shifts, so that the night shift is not delegated to junior staff as in Mill A. Also, there is a systematic regular change of shift for the assistants and supervisors, with the changeover of shifts for workers and jobbers. The same assistants and supervisors work with the same group of jobbers and workers so that there is stability of relationships from the assistant to the worker level. Work relationships in terms of reporting, making inquiries, etc. with the persons concerned are clear and the channels well established.

As mentioned earlier, there are frequent changes in the manufacturing program of Mill A which necessitate frequent technical changes in the department. Most of these technical changes are made on the day shift resulting in more senior staff on the day shift. Mill B which has a more stable manufacturing program does not have to concentrate its senior staff in the day shift and can consequently afford to distribute its senior staff in the two shifts and have a more balanced structure in each shift.

III. MANAGEMENT PRACTICES

The problems of introducing manufacturing changes do not only affect the formal organizational structure of the mill, but they also influence management practices of delegation of authority, of communication and of consultation.

Mill A

Thus, in Mill A, the managing agent has to give frequent directives for change of counts and sorts. Targets have to be fulfilled and deadlines of delivery dates have to be met since the manufacturing is geared to fluctuating demand in the market. Working under these pressures the agent is constantly checking up on efficiency, production and quality of product. All this tends to result in centralized decision-making and in close and detailed supervision of the departments.

In order that top management can supervise each stage closely, there is a tendency to short-circuit in giving instructions, or in making inquiries about production, quality, adequate flow of material, etc. The agent or the production manager gets directly in touch with the assistants and supervisors for either giving instructions or receiving information.

The resultant pressures on middle and lower management can be seen from some of their remarks quoted below:

Spinning master:

I am leaving the mill soon. I am satisfied with the salary, but I cannot stand the agent's production policy of many changes. These changes are too much to cope with.

Spinning supervisor:

The agent and the production manager call me almost every day to inquire about production and balance of production . . . the constant change of program is responsible for low efficiency. . . . The agent should listen to the technicians and draw up a plan of production according to the existing machines and not according to the whims of the market.

Spinning supervisor:

The thing that worries me most is the agent's policy of constant change of materials. Most of my time and energy is spent trying to keep balance of production. . . . The agent often sends for me to inquire about production targets, shortages and flow of materials. . . .

Almost every member in the Spinning Department expresses his dissatisfaction concerning the frequent changes of manufacturing program and the resultant problems—efficiency, balance of production, and feelings of anxiety and tension. Top management has direct contact with almost every member in the department in order to supervise and inquire about production. The members in the Weaving Department feel the same way about the changes and the frequency of changes introduced in the sorts manufactured as the members in the Spinning Department.

For example, the weaving master says:

The agent's policy is very short-sighted, since his guiding factor is always immediate profit. This policy is reflected in the constant change of sorts. At present all the sorts which were running a month ago have completely disappeared. Such a quick changeover is not economical and it puts the staff into great difficulty. It is almost impossible to retain a high level of production under such conditions and then the blame is put on the technical staff!

The assistants and supervisors especially connected with the loomshed mention the agent's concern about production and quality of production and how they are frequently called into his office to explain the high damages.

Loomshed supervisor:

The agent wants both high efficiency and good quality. I have been called several times to explain high damage. . . . For example, recently a new and a heavy sort was introduced and there was high damage and low efficiency. The agent was very upset and annoyed with everybody, from the weaving master to the workers. I was called to explain the bad working and was fired . . . but no discharge notice was served. It is going too far if the supervisors are held responsible when a bad sort is introduced and there is so much damage.

When new "sorts" (types of cloth) are introduced which the technical staff believes will not yield good efficiency or good quality, then top management feels the need for close supervision to see the working performance of the new sort, and to induce the technical staff to fulfill the targets for production and quality. This type of situation makes it necessary for the agent to maintain close and detailed supervision of the departments. The assistants and supervisors all have to report to him directly, especially when a difficult sort is being run.

The assistant weaving master:

I meet the agent and the production manager. They ask me about the working of the department and I prepare a special report for the agent which I submit every Monday. . . . I am always pressed for better and higher production.

The senior loomshed supervisor:

The agent controls the department himself. I am given instructions by him about new sorts, change in loom speeds, discipline in the loomshed, etc.

Loomshed supervisor:

My duty is to follow the instructions of the agent. . . . He has called me several times to explain about high damages. . . .

These quotations illustrate reactions to centralized decision-making, by-passing in communication, and dissatisfaction and frustration among the staff. The end is a climate of resentment against management and management goals.

An example which indicates the extent to which some members of the management staff in Mill A have lost their sense of identification with management and management goals is given below. It refers to a situation where the agent tried to consult the staff about the advisability of buying a new machine. One of the staff members said:

After the talk by the representative of the company manufacturing machine X was over, the agent asked, "Do you or do you not advise me to buy this machine?" All the members said, "We agree that you should buy the machine." . . . It is his money, let him spend it the way he likes.

Mill B

Let us see the picture in Mill B where the manufacturing program is relatively stable. Some interview comments illustrate the difference.

Spinning master:

The management of this mill is very good and the general atmosphere of working is pleasant. There is no interference from the top in the working of my department. . . . I report to the agent and to the production manager. . . . During the entire period of my work here so far, nobody has asked for the efficiency of the department, but always about quality. . . . I would like to give quality material, so that consumers can say that Mill B has the best spinning.

Weaving master:

The agent and the production manager consult me on technical matters. . . . I am in charge of the department, and the management does not interfere in my work. (All departmental problems concerning damages, spare parts, etc., are solved within the department. No supervisor or assistant mentions that he is called by the office to explain about efficiency, balance of production or high damage rate. Almost everybody mentions that this is a good mill to work in, the management is good, and that there is no pressure about production or efficiency. The impression is that the working of the departments is smooth and there is a high degree of satisfaction of members with management and management practices.)

The change·of sorts in Mill B has been commented on by two persons:

Production manager:

The sales manager makes his demands and the production departments have to give way to his requirements. The difficulties of the production departments are not considered. . . .

Weaving master:

If rationalization is to be introduced the mill will have to standardize the type of cloth to be manufactured. Markets should be stabilized by the mills. There is no sense in manufacturing 30 and 32 yards and 40 and 42 in the same sorts. The unnecessary changeover in the department for such differences increases the cost of production.

Even in Mill B there are some protests about the change of sorts demanded by the sales manager, but there is not that feeling of pressure, strain and anxiety in the departments as found in Mill A.

There is also considerable identification with management's goals and a sense of pride in most members about this mill. The satisfaction of members is reflected in their long service in the same mill. Most members have worked in Mill B for from 10 to 25 years, whereas in Mill A, there has been considerable turnover in the senior staff. Within one year, since the completion of the field study, 8 out of 17 of the management staff have left in Mill A.

IV. CONCLUSIONS

In terms of the research questions raised earlier, it is clear that the manufacturing policies of management in Mill A and Mill B influence the organizational structure and the management practices of each case. Thus, in Mill A the picture is one of frequent changes in the manufacturing program, frequent technical and personnel changes in departments, centralized control and decision making, "by-passing" in communication, dissatisfaction of members, resentment against management, especially among the senior staff, and a sense of insecurity and instability among members. In Mill B, the picture is one of a relatively stable manufacturing program, smoothly functioning departments, stable work groups, relative decentralization in control and decision-making, stable communication channels similar to the formal structure, satisfaction with management, and a sense of security and stability in the organization.

There are two further implications of the study that we should like specifically to emphasize:

1. There is an interrelation of management policies and management practices, an interrelation that perhaps stems from an inherent interdependence of these factors. Perhaps the clusters of factors found in Mill A and Mill B are a result of a basic approach, an attitude, a point of view, a frame of mind, and this is reflected in the totality of behavior, whether in policies or practices that a particular management follows. In other words, management involves a certain philosophy, and not merely certain techniques of management.

2. An organizational structure which is based only on the technical needs of the situation can defeat the very purposes of the organization. To function efficiently, management must take into account the social as well as the technical demands of the situation. The organization of Mill A has developed around the technical needs demanded of a manufacturing program of frequent changes. The senior staff has been kept on the day shift to make the necessary technical adjustments. The working of the night shift has consequently been delegated to junior supervisors. In such a system efficiency and quality are affected. There are complaints about the lack of sufficient backstuff and of poor quality, somebody gets blamed in the process, relationships become strained, and there is a constant reshuffling of staff, transferring of personnel from one shift to another to maintain an equilibrium for collaboration and efficient working. These *ad hoc* transfers of supervisors from one shift to another also result in a sense of instability and insecurity. The management does not seem to be aware of this consequence of its production policy. Unless management becomes aware of these reactions to its policy and undertakes to compensate for the continual upheaval, the possible advantages resulting from its policy cannot be realized.

In contrast, the organization of Mill B has also developed around its technical needs, but the technical needs in this case are related to a stable manufacturing program. There are not many technical changes that have to be introduced, the senior staff is equally distributed, and it is consequently possible for management to have a systematic transfer of shifts. All this has resulted in a system promoting stable relationships and close human association at work.

Similar conclusions have been emphasized in a study of 12 industrial organizations sponsored by UNESCO.[2] It mentioned that one of the features peculiar to efficient institutions was found to be:

. . . intimate human association at work. Physical conditions are so arranged that small numbers of people work closely together and can easily communicate with each other. . . . Without the security that comes from the feeling of belonging to a group, the individual is liable to become unadaptable, resentful and socially ill.

---

[2] Jerome F. Scott and R. P. Lynton, *The Community Factor in Modern Technology*, UNESCO (Paris, 1952), p. 169.

Therefore, in planning an organization's structure, not only have the technical demands to be taken into account, but the social system that underlies a particular technology and work process must also be considered. In an organization where frequent changes in production schedules are contemplated, it is all the more necessary for the organizational structure and the operating practices of management to be such that they can fluctuate with the strains and stresses inherent in a situation of constant changes. A greater degree of attention and emphasis must be paid to problems of organization and organizational practices in such cases. However, it is possible for management to provide a flexible structure and to follow policies which lessen rather than increase the strains and tensions inherent in an organization where constant change is part of the routine.

15. INTERPERSONAL PERCEPTIONS OF OPEN-HEARTH FOREMEN AND STEEL PRODUCTION*

Walter A. Cleven and Fred E. Fiedler[1]

This investigation is one of a series of studies on the relationship of interpersonal perception and group effectiveness (2, 3, 4). It was designed to test an hypothesis which grew out of earlier studies on basketball and surveying teams (2), and military aircraft and tank crews (3). The present research was conducted in open-hearth shops of a large steel company in which the personnel, in contrast to subjects (Ss) participating in these earlier studies, is highly stable over time, and where carefully maintained production records are available.

Interpersonal perception is measured here by means of the score, Assumed Similarity between Opposites, or ASo. This score reflects the extent to which the subject (S) predicts different responses for the man with whom he can work best, and the man with whom he can work least well. We interpret ASo as a measure of the psychological distance which S perceives between himself and his co-workers. Supervisors who predict similar responses for their best- and least-liked co-workers (high ASo) are, by this interpretation of ASo, more accepting, approachable individuals, while supervisors who predict less similar responses for these workers (low ASo) are presumably more critical and analytic in their work relationships. The primary hypothesis to which these earlier group studies have led is that more productive groups have leaders who tend to differentiate more in perceptions of their most and least preferred co-workers (i.e., have lower ASo) than do leaders of less effective groups.

The earlier reports in this series of studies have suggested some possible restrictions or special cases of this general hypothesis. In particular, three points have been noted, which we shall mention briefly. The data suggest (a) that the hypothesis holds especially in the case of groups which accept the leader. This acceptance is defined in terms of the number of

* Reproduced from *The Journal of Applied Psychology*, Vol. 40, No. 5, 1956.

[1] We are indebted to Messrs. J. H. Vohr, P. E. Thomas, E. C. Sorrells, H. W. Erler, and G. H. Warnock, of the Gary Steel Works; and to Mr. Dan Farrell and Mr. E. W. Kempton, of the United States Steel Corporation, for their co-operation and support of this study. We are also indebted to Drs. L. J. Cronback, Eleanor P. Godfrey, Ross Stagner, and C. F. Wrigley for their contributions to the design and administration of the study, and to Mrs. Betty F. Mannheim who assisted with the analysis of the data.

The study was conducted under Contract N6-ori-07135 between the Office of Naval Research and the University of Illinois, with F. E. Fiedler as principal investigator.

sociometric choices the leader receives from his group (3). (*b*) The sociometric likes and dislikes of the leader for certain key personnel in the group may be important in determining the direction of relationship between *ASo* of the leader and the effectiveness of the group. It was noted that effective groups may have either low *ASo* leaders who sociometrically prefer key subordinates, or high *ASo* leaders who do not sociometrically choose their key subordinates. (*c*) It has also been suggested that the hypothesis may be valid only for tasks which require "direction-giving leadership behavior" (3). More effective groups engaged in tasks which require receptive leadership behavior for effective group coordination may have leaders with high *ASo*, regardless of the leader's preferences for his key subordinates. We have not investigated the restrictions based on sociometric choice in the present paper, in part because of our limited sample size, and in part because of the possibility that sociometric choices become relatively less important in long-lived groups. Men who at first may find it difficult to get along together will, in the course of two, five, or ten years either learn to do so or else leave the group by transferring to another crew, or to another job. It seems reasonable to assume that men who have worked together for several years are rather adequately adjusted to each other, an assumption which would not be warranted in relatively short-lived groups such as military units.

Procedure

Sample. Management personnel in four open-hearth shops of a large steel company participated in the study. These four shops are engaged in similar operations, although equipment varies somewhat from shop to shop.

Each shop is operated on a 24-hour, 7-day-week basis with each shift or "turn" working eight hours. Every turn has a full complement of first- and second-line supervisors and their crews. Since one turn is off duty in any one 24-hour period, each shop requires four turns. A total of 16 turns thus constitutes our sample.[2]

Four supervisors are in charge of each turn: one General Foreman, one Stock Foreman, one Pit Foreman, and one Senior Melter. The General Foreman, along with the Stock and Pit Foremen, directs the supporting operations of raw material assembly and final steel pouring. The Senior Melter is in charge of steel manufacture. Depending on the number and size of furnaces in the shop, the Senior Melter supervises one or two Junior Melters and their crews. In three of the four shops (or 12 of the 16 turns), the Senior Melter has two Junior Melters reporting to him.

Test instrument. Each available foreman and melter was requested to predict the responses of two persons he had known: (*a*) the man with whom he could work best, and (*b*) the man with whom he could work least well. (These ratees could be anyone with whom *S* had ever worked; *S* was not asked to specify their names.) If the two predictions by a single *S* are quite different, he is said to have low *ASo;* conversely, if the two predictions are quite similar,

---

[2] All four turns within a shop are under the direction of a single shop superintendent and his assistant superintendent. These men were not tested.

he is said to have high *ASo*. The test consisted of 40 statements such as: "I tend to join many organizations," "I am often bored with people," and "I am generally regarded as optimistic." Each item was answered on a six-point scale ranging from "definitely true" to "definitely untrue." The similarity of these two predictions, computed by the statistic D (1, 5), yields the index, "Assumed Similarity between Opposites" (*ASo*).

Criterion

The index of group effectiveness is based on the time elapsed from one "tap" (pouring of molten metal from the furnace) to the next tap on a particular furnace. For economic reasons, company officials regard short "tap-to-tap time" as the most important production goal. The primary importance of this production goal is recognized and accepted by the foremen as well as their subordinates.

The average tap-to-tap time is about 10 hours; two turns are, therefore, involved in preparing each batch of steel, or "heat," for tapping. However, the tap-to-tap time scores are uniformly assigned to the Senior Melter in charge of the furnace at the time the tap is made, regardless of the length of time the shift has actually worked on the heat. This seems justifiable because the last hours of the heat are regarded as more critical in the manufacturing process than the first few hours. In addition, randomization takes place because the turns do not systematically follow one another or use the same furnaces in the shop.

Using an analysis of variance of ranked data, we found significant differences between shops in tap-to-tap time. Since these differences can be attributed to different furnace capacities in the four shops, the tap-to-tap time data were standardized within shops by means of T scores. This procedure is designed to eliminate variance due to differences in equipment and to retain the variance which may be attributable to leadership variables.

Criterion reliability. The reliability of tap-to-tap scores was based on an analysis of over 25,000 heats based on the 3- to 16-months period preceding testing. We excluded the summer months on recommendation of company officials because of extensive personnel shifts due to vacation schedules. An even-month vs. odd-month split-half procedure was employed. The estimated reliability of tap-to-tap time over the 16 turns is .82. In order to minimize the effects of long-range changes, e.g., in personnel or company policy, the criterion scores used below are based on only a part of these data, namely the 3- to 10-month period immediately preceding testing.

RESULTS

Table 1 presents the correlations between the average turn tap-to-tap time and the *ASo* (Assumed Similarity between Opposites) of the General, Pit and Stock Foremen, and Senior Melters. As the table shows, the correlation between average turn tap-to-tap time and *ASo* is significant in the predicted direction in the case of Senior Melters and Pit Foremen. The correlation falls short of an acceptable significance level for Stock Foremen, and is negligible for General Foremen. In addition, the average *ASo* of the foremen and Senior Melter on each turn is significantly related to average turn tap-to-tap time.

TABLE 1

CORRELATIONS (RHO) BETWEEN ASo OF VARIOUS SUPERVISORS
AND AVERAGE TURN TAP-TO-TAP TIME

Supervisor ASo	$N*$	Rho	p
General Foreman	15	−.13	—
Stock Foreman	15	−.42	—
Pit Foreman	14	−.72	<.01
Senior Melter	15	−.54	<.05
Supervisor average	16	−.71	<.01

* N varies due to missing data.

DISCUSSION

Our hypothesis states that more effective groups have supervisors with low ASo. The significant correlations of Senior Melter and Pit Foreman ASo, as well as average supervisor ASo, with average turn tap-to-tap time support this hypothesis.

Of particular interest is the high correlation between mean turn tap-to-tap time and ASo of Pit Foremen. On the surface, the melters appear to determine tap time, since it is their decision as to when the heat is ready to be tapped. These results suggest that variance in tap-to-tap time may also be a function of the Pit Foreman, although, conversely, the ASo of these supervisors may be a function of the turn efficiency or of some related variable. On the other hand, the low correlation in the case of the General Foremen may indicate that these men have the least influence on turn efficiency, as measured by tap-to-tap time, even though the limited number of cases in our sample does not enable us to reject the hypothesis that all differences among the obtained correlations are a matter of chance.

The fact that mean turn tap-to-tap time is negatively related to the mean ASo of the turn's four foremen suggests that ASo scores within turns may be homogeneous. A ranked analysis of variance test shows this to be the case. The long-lived nature of these groups could cause this covariation of ASo. For example, if more similar Ss are more congenial to each other, selective factors may operate in the personnel placement process, such that similar Ss tend to be assigned to the same turn. Alternatively, changes in interpersonal perception may occur as a result of group processes within the turns. The possibility of such changes is suggested by the recent findings of Steiner and Dodge (6).

SUMMARY AND CONCLUSIONS

A study was conducted relating the interpersonal perceptions of open-hearth shop foremen to the productivity of their work units. Interpersonal perception was measured by means of Assumed Similarity (ASo) tests which reflect how similar or different a person describes his most and his least preferred work companions. Group effectiveness measures were based on output as indicated by "tap-to-tap" time, the time required to complete a "heat" of steel. This criterion measure has considerable stability and is regarded as the most important production index by company officials.

Management personnel of four open-hearth shops of a large steel company participated in this study. Interpersonal perception (*ASo*) tests were administered to all available *Ss*.

Significant relations were found between supervisor *ASo* and the tap-to-tap time index. These results are consistent with the hypothesis that more effective groups have supervisors who tend to predict different responses for their most- and least-preferred co-workers.

REFERENCES

1. CRONBACH, L. J., and GLESER, GOLDINE C. "Assessing Similarity between Profiles," *Psychol. Bull.*, 1953, 50, pp. 456–73.
2. FIEDLER, F. E. "Assumed Similarity Measures as Predictors of Team Effectiveness," *J. Abnorm. Soc. Psychol.*, 1954, 49, pp. 381–87.
3. FIEDLER, F. E. "The Influence of Leader-Keyman Relations on Combat Crew Effectiveness, *J. Abnorm. Soc. Psychol.*, 1955, 51, pp. 227–35.
4. GODFREY, ELEANOR P., WRIGLEY, C. F., MANNHEIM, BETTY F., HALL, D. M., and FIEDLER, F. E. "The Effect of Interpersonal Relations on the Success of Consumer Cooperatives," *Proc. Amer. Sociol. Soc.*, 1955. (Abstract)
5. OSGOOD, C. E., and SUCI, G. "A Measure of Relation Determined by Both Mean Difference and Profile Information," *Psychol. Bull.*, 1952, 49, pp. 251–62.
6. STEINER, I. D., and DODGE, JOAN S. "Interpersonal Perception and Role Structure as Determinants of Group and Individual Efficiency," *Human Relations*, 1956, 9, pp. 467–80.

16. LEADERSHIP WITHIN A HIERARCHICAL ORGANIZATION*

DONALD C. PELZ

Introduction

CONCERN with leadership has been central to the Human Relations Program from its beginning. But there have been important shifts in emphasis. Our early concepts and hypotheses drew freely from previous studies on small groups. To discover how the first-line supervisor affected employee attitudes and productivity, the direction of search seemed obvious. One studied the face-to-face interactions between supervisor and work group.

The hard facts of analysis have shown that this approach is incomplete. Leadership in isolated groups is one thing; leadership within large organizations may be something else again. At least, it must be looked at with a fresh view.

The impact of organizational factors on interactions within the work group was suggested by some of our first results. In training courses the supervisor is given this general rule: he should always recognize good work done by employees. He should, for example, recommend deserving employees for promotion. But in the Prudential study supervisors of high producing work groups were found to play one of two roles in the promotion process. Either they made recommendations which generally went through, or they made no recommendations at all. In contrast, the supervisors of low producing work groups often recommended promotions, but these generally did not go through.[1] To recommend promotions was not, as such, related to high employee productivity. A more basic factor seemed to be operating, outside of the sphere of the work group. This factor was the supervisor's power within the larger department. The high producing supervisors were more realistic about their power; they entered the promotion process only when they could influence the outcome. The concept of the supervisor's power or influence within his department is central in a recent study, some details of which are given below.[2]

---

* Reproduced from *Journal of Social Issues*, VII, No. 3, 1951, pp. 49–55.

[1] D. Katz, N. Maccoby, and N. C. Morse, *Productivity, Supervision and Employee Morale, Part I*. (Ann Arbor: University of Michigan, Survey Research Center, 1950.)

[2] D. C. Pelz, *Power and Leadership in the First-Line Supervisor* (preliminary draft). (Ann Arbor: University of Michigan, Survey Research Center, 1951.)

Superficially the results of such studies might suggest that we need one set of theories to account for leadership in isolated groups, and another set of theories to account for leadership within hierarchical organizations. It is our belief, however, that both situations can be incorporated within a single theoretical framework. In fact, it might be possible to use artificial groups and laboratory methods to reproduce some of the variables of an organizational context. Variables such as power and status have been manipulated in several studies done at the Research Center for Group Dynamics.[3] Some elements in a theoretical framework designed to include both leadership situations are discussed at this point.

Basic Postulate: Successful Leadership Depends in Part on Helping Group Members Achieve Their Goals

Empirical studies, as shown in reviews of the literature by Gibb,[4] Jenkins,[5] and Stogdill[6] have failed to find traits that are universal in successful leaders. In different studies, different or contradictory traits in leaders are found related to whatever criterion of success is used. Differences in the situations or in the groups, from study to study, seem to be partly responsible. Gibb concludes that "leadership is relative always to the situation."

But it is not enough simply to say that leadership is relative to the situation. Relative to what aspects of the situation? We must identify those factors which make a given leader behavior "successful" or "unsuccessful."

Recent theories have stressed the *needs of group members* as key aspects of the all-important "situation." The successful or valued or obeyed leader is one who can help group members achieve their goals. This emphasis on group members' needs and goals appears sound, at least as one beginning of a theory of leadership. In any kind of situation, a basic postulate is that *the more the leader (or any member) helps other members achieve their goals, the greater will be the members' acceptance of him.* By "acceptance" is meant that members are willing to follow the leader's suggestions, express satisfaction with the leader's conduct, etc.

This basic postulate is not, by itself, a theory. It does not permit us to

---

[3] Cf. H. H. Kelley, "Communication in Experimentally Created Hierarchies," *Human Relations*, 1951, 4, pp. 39–56; A. Pepitone, "Motivational Effects in Social Perception," *Human Relations*, 1950, 3, pp. 57–76.

[4] C. A. Gibb, "The Principles and Traits of Leadership," *J. Abnormal and Social Psychology*, 1947, 42, pp. 267–84.

[5] W. O. Jenkins, "A Review of Leadership Studies with Particular Reference to Military Problems," *Psychological Bulletin*, 1947, 44, pp. 54–79.

[6] R. M. Stogdill, "Personal Factors Associated with Leadership: A Survey of the Literature," *Journal of Psychology*, 1948, 25, pp. 35–71.

make specific predictions, and this a genuine theory must be able to do. To make predictions, we must be able to state conditions such as: (*a*) Toward what goals are the group members motivated? (*b*) What acts or characteristics of a leader help the members achieve each of these goals? And finally, (*c*) How do specific leaders measure up on these factors? If the first two conditions are known, and if we have measured each leader on the relevant factors, we can begin to predict the acceptance of particular leaders by their particular groups.

Very probably, the basic postulate will apply to leaders within a hierarchial organization, as well as to leaders in simpler groups. But the conditions which we need to know for prediction may be markedly affected by the organizational context. With regard to (*a*), for example, we shall have to give more weight to what we may loosely call "organizational goals" and "group goals." These must, of course, actually function as goals or as sub-goals for the individual members, if the basic postulate is to apply. With regard to (*b*), the organizational context will have much to do with whether certain acts of the leader can or cannot help his group members achieve their goals. The recent study cited above underscores this point. Major features of this research will now be described.

The Point of Departure: Some Puzzling Results in Previous Analyses of the Data

The data for the study were collected early in 1948 from the personnel of a large electric utility, employing well over 10,000 people, and serving a major midwestern manufacturing city and surrounding urban and rural areas. The work of the company covers many different occupations and skill levels. Attitudes of all non-supervisory employees were ascertained through paper-and-pencil questionnaires. Attitudes and practices of all first-line supervisors—each of the people in charge of a work group, the basic unit—were obtained in personal interviews utilizing open-ended questions. The verbatim replies were later coded with the content analysis procedures of the Survey Research Center.

The author's objective was to determine how measures obtained on the supervisors related to attitudes of employees they supervised. What supervisory practices led to employee acceptance of the supervisor? Three separate analyses had to be done, before answers to this question could be formulated. In the process, the importance of organizational factors became increasingly clear.

The first analysis was of a design frequently found in leadership studies. Forty "high employee satisfaction" work groups and thirty "low employee satisfaction" work groups were selected, and the data from their respective supervisors examined on fifty items. While half the differences were in the expected direction, only six differences were statistically significant (at the 5 per cent level of confidence). By chance alone, 2.5 "significant" differences would be expected; the obtained number was little more than twice the chance number.

The inconclusiveness of these results compelled a second analysis. The previous analysis had focused exclusively on the interaction between supervisor and employees in the work group; it had assumed, in all work groups, universal relationships between supervisory practices and employee attitudes. But the evidence on situational effects warns against this assumption. High satisfaction in one group of employees may result from supervisory practices quite different from those used in another well satisfied group. In the second analysis, therefore, different types of employees and situations were handled separately. Separate analyses were performed for men and women, for white collar and blue collar workers, for small work groups and large, for differing educational backgrounds, and for various combinations of these factors.

The results of this analysis were more promising. A direct comparison with the first is not possible—different measures of the supervisory and employee variables were used. It is interesting that statistically significant results numbered seven times chance. But some of these significant results were disturbing; some went *opposite* to predictions based on previous research. One of the supervisory measures, for example, was a scale of "taking sides with employees in cases of employee-management conflicts," based on three intercorrelated items from the interview. In case of disagreement between the employees under him and his own superiors, whose side did the supervisor take? Did he see his job primarily as selling his employees' viewpoint to management, as selling management's viewpoint to employees, or as remaining independent? Previous evidence suggests that group members will think more highly of the leader who "goes to bat" for them, who sides with them in cases of conflict with higher authorities. The results supported this hypothesis in small work groups (10 employees or fewer). But in large white collar work groups, employees were significantly *less* satisfied with such a supervisor; they preferred the supervisor who sided with management. Other supervisory variables showed similar contradictory results.

Why? What was there about the large work group situation that produced relationships apparently opposite to those found in small work groups? Still one more analysis was essential, if we were to resolve this predictive tangle and others like it.

The previous section mentions two general areas within which the third analysis design sought some of the responsible factors. Perhaps employees in the larger work groups had different needs and goals from those in the smaller groups. One step, therefore, was to develop, from existing employee data, crude indices of certain needs.

Or perhaps the same supervisory behavior, in small and in large work groups, might have different results with respect to employees' achieving their goals. At this point, the factor of the supervisor's *power or influence* within the larger department became crucial.

Two Predictions on Influence and Leadership

The type of theory adopted for the third analysis has already been described. The basic postulate is that the supervisor will be "accepted" by his work group if his behavior helps them to achieve their goals. The new concept introduced in the third analysis is that of the supervisor's influence within his department. If the supervisor has considerable influence over events within his department, then his attempts to help employees reach their goals are very likely to succeed. If, on the other hand, he lacks influence, then his attempts toward employee goal achievement are likely to fail.

Two related predictions follow. Given supervisors who are influential, the more they behave so as to aid goal achievement, the more satisfied their employees will be toward them. A positive correlation is predicted between the supervisory behavior and employee attitudes. But given non-influential supervisors, there can be no such relationship. Stronger attempts toward helping employees can produce no rise in employee satisfaction. There might be a drop, in fact. The second prediction, then, is that the correlation between the supervisor's helpful behavior and employee attitudes will be significantly less positive (or more negative) under non-influential supervisors.

If variation in influence does produce these changes in the relationships of supervisory behavior to employee attitudes, then influence may be called a "conditioner" of the relationships, following a useful suggestion by Morris and Seeman.[7] The amount of change—the difference in correlations found under high and low influence supervisors respectively—may be called the "conditioner effect" of influence.

Because of the initial emphasis on the supervisor's interpersonal relations, a variable of his power or influence was not anticipated when the data were collected. But it appeared possible to construct one. A supervisor was considered to have relatively high "influence over the social environment in which his employees were functioning" if he reported having a voice in departmental decisions made by his own superior; if he had relatively little contact with his superior—an indication of more autonomy in running his own work group; and if he had a high salary—indicating higher general status.

Two scales of supervisory behavior appeared to measure "attempts at helping employees to reach their goals." One was the scale previously

---

[7] R. T. Morris and M. Seeman, "The Problem of Leadership: An Interdisciplinary Approach," *American Journal of Sociology*, 1950, 56, pp. 149–55.

described, of "taking sides with employees in cases of employee-management conflict." Another was a scale of "social closeness toward employees," or lack of social distance, based on several items from the supervisor's interview.

Several employee attitudes were used. The most important one was an index of employees' "general satisfaction with the performance of their immediate supervisor." Product-moment correlations between the two supervisory behaviors and the various employee attitudes were computed. These correlations were obtained separately under influential and under non-influential supervisors, in each of seven employee sub-populations, defined according to white collar vs. blue collar occupations, sex, size of work group, and union coverage.

Major Results

The results, in general, confirm the predictions. For the group of high influence supervisors, we obtained twenty-eight correlations between the two supervisory behaviors and the various employee attitudes, in the several employee sub-populations. For the low influence supervisors, we obtained a parallel set of twenty-eight correlations. Nineteen of the correlations under influential supervisors are at least mildly positive, and seven are significantly positive (at the five per cent level of confidence). This is eleven times the chance number (taking direction into account). The first prediction is thus generally confirmed. By contrast, under low influence supervisors, nineteen of the parallel correlations are either zero or slightly negative.

The second prediction concerns the various "conditioner effects" of the supervisor's influence: the difference in each product-moment correlation between a supervisory behavior and an employee attitude, under high and low influence supervisors respectively. Positive differences are found in the majority of the twenty-eight comparisons, and six of them are significantly positive.[8] This number is ten times what chance alone would produce. Thus the second prediction is generally confirmed. It should be noted that none of these conditioner effects could have been foreseen on the basis of previous findings. They are not the product of empirical hindsight.

The results demonstrate, in short, that a supervisor's influence or power within the department does condition the way his supervisory behavior relates to employee attitudes. When an influential supervisor uses these helpful practices, positive correlations are found between his behavior and employee attitudes. But in the case of non-influential supervisors, no cor-

---

[8] The significance of differences between correlations was tested by the use of Fisher's z-transformation for r, as described in Q. McNemar, *Psychological Statistics* (New York: John Wiley & Sons, 1950).

relations (or slightly negative ones) are found between the same supervisory behaviors and employee attitudes.

Implications

In the three successive analyses of our supervisory leadership data, the importance of the organizational context has become increasingly clear. The major variable in the third analysis—the supervisor's power or influence within the department—depends on the supervisor's role within the larger organization. It cannot be measured by observing interactions within the work group. (The power of the supervisor over his group members is not the same variable.)

The findings imply that if an influential supervisor attempts to help employees achieve their goals, his efforts will usually succeed. Concrete results will be achieved. Employee satisfactions will rise. But—the data imply—if a non-influential supervisor tries to do the same, his efforts will often fail. Employee expectations will be frustrated. Their satisfactions will not rise, or may even fall.

This statement does not imply a pluralism in the laws of leadership. On the contrary, we believe that a variety of leadership phenomena might be accounted for in a single theoretical framework. A basic postulate in such a framework—one expressed by several theorists—is that a leader will be accepted by group members to the extent that he helps them to achieve their goals.

This postulate should apply both to isolated groups and to groups in an organizational setting. Specific goals will differ somewhat in the two cases. In the latter, members will emphasize organizational and group goals more than in the former. Moreover, within large organizations the leader's ability to help the group will depend to a much greater degree upon factors outside of the face-to-face group. As the leader's role in the organization varies, our theory leads us to predict sharp changes in the effect of his behavior upon members' goal achievements, and hence upon their attitudes.

17. EXCERPTS FROM "ORGANIZATION OF A BANK"*

Chris Argyris

Personality Development versus Organizational Development

One of the basic problems in understanding human organizations stems from the fact that the development of personality of agents tends to be different from the development of organizations. Let us examine this statement in closer detail.

1.0 In a recent review of the literature concerning personality development, the following broad trends of personality development seemed clearly discernable for individuals interacting within our culture.

1.01 People in our culture tend to develop from receiving and incorporating aspects of culture as an infant, to controlling, using, redefining and helping others incorporate these aspects of culture as an adult.

1.02 People in our culture develop from a state of being passive as an infant (i.e., having other people initiate action for them) to a state of being increasingly active as an adult (i.e., they initiate action as much or more than other people towards them).

1.03 People in our culture develop from being capable of behaving only in a few ways and in a rigid manner as an infant to being capable of behaving in many different ways and behaving in a flexible manner as an adult.

1.04 People in our culture develop from being in a subordinate position in the family and society as an infant, to occupying a more equal and/or superordinate position in the family and society, as an adult.

1.05 People in our culture develop from a state of high dependence on others as an infant, to a state of independence and finally to a state of interdependence in their society as an adult.[1]

If we apply the above developmental trends to agents in organizations, we may hypothesize that agents ought to require functions which are so defined that they may fulfill some combination of the above trends. (The exact combination would naturally depend on the specific agent.)

1.1 In order to accomplish this, the agent would require a function in which:

---

* Comprising Appendix D and Chapter 5. Published 1954 by Yale University Labor and Management Center.

[1] Chris Argyris, *Personality Fundamentals for Administrators* (Yale Labor and Management Center, 1952), p. 97.

1.11 he can define for himself a ratio of activity (initiation of action) to passivity where activity is greater than passivity (passivity defined as others initiating action for the agent);

1.12 he can define for himself a position equal and/or superordinate to the other agents with whom he interacts;

1.13 he can define for himself tasks where he is able to provide expression for the many learned ways of behaving that are important to him; (this includes the expression of important abilities, needs, sentiments, and personal goals)

1.14 he can define for himself a sense of fluidity and flexibility that is comparable to his personality fluidity and flexibility;

1.15 he can express feelings of independence and can express feelings of interdependence in relation to the other agents of the organization;

1.16 he can feel that he has the respect of other agents (whom he feels are) important to his life;

1.17 he obtains from his job a degree of creature sufficiency he desires.

1.2 It seems necessary that we pause for a moment and make a few important comments concerning the list just presented.

First, we want to emphasize that the exact combination of these requirements and the degree to which each one of them is to be fulfilled for any given individual can be ascertained only by analysis of that individual case. Thus, it is possible that individual A, for example, requires primarily 1.11, 1.12 and 1.14 with an emphasis on 1.12. On the other hand, individual B may require all the above be fulfilled with an emphasis on 1.15 and 1.16.

It is also conceivable that individual C, for example, may desire (1) *not* to be active (1.11), (2) *not* to have an equal or superordinate position (1.12), (3) *not* to desire to feel independent (1.15), etc. According to our viewpoint this adult would have to be classed as "not mature." He is still at a more childlike stage of development. Psychologists may call him "fixated" at an earlier stage of development. This individual would not require a function which permits him to accomplish the items suggested in 1.11–1.17.

The point we want to emphasize is that we are *not* eliminating individual differences, nor are we imposing our developmental scheme on everyone. This is not a "rose-bud" theory. We are simply suggesting that a normal individual living in and interacting with our culture will tend to exhibit these developmental trends, but in his own unique combination. If the individual does not depict any of these trends, then we would suggest that broadly speaking he is not mature, and that he will tend to be in equilibrium in the kind of a function in which a mature individual will not be in equilibrium.

To summarize, we would suggest that a normal individual in our culture requires a function which permits him to obtain a minimal personality expression and to accomplish this in any given context with the maximum possible success and with a minimum of personality disequilibrium.[2]

1.3 If we turn our attention for the moment to the development of an efficient organization as conceived by the traditional scientific management principles, assuming that the organization is able to express itself as freely as it desires without having to worry about individuals, we find that the following characteristics would tend to arise. Most of the individual agents (excepting the leaders) would be assigned to functions:

1.31 which would tend to permit them little control over their work-a-day world.

1.32 which would tend to place them in a situation where their passivity rather than initiative would frequently be expected.

1.33 which would tend to force them to occupy a subordinate position.

1.34 which would tend to permit them a minimum degree of fluidity and (tend to) emphasize the expression of one (or perhaps a few) of the agent's relatively minor abilities.

1.35 which would tend to make them feel dependent upon other agents (e.g., the boss).[3]

Although this list could be expanded, the important point, in our opinion, is that the developmental processes and end result of the individual and the organization at crucial points are fundamentally different and even antagonistic. This is not to infer that modern organizations are therefore "bad." We are simply saying that this is the way they are. Only by understanding the nature of modern organization can we begin to make some sensible predictions about individuals' behavior in these organizations.

The Steady State of the Trust Department

A. The Workflow Process

1. *Multi-objectives lead to multi-workflows.*

This department, like the bank as a whole, has several objectives and as many discrete workflows. For example, on the basis of data available, we note seven discrete workflows.

---

[2] The last part of this sentence indicates that an individual may modify his desires in order to adapt to a given situation. In other words, if he could not obtain his desired personality satisfaction because his job would not permit it, then, he may, assuming he wants to remain employed, decide to accept the temporary frustrations in order to remain in equilibrium to his working world. Or, he may react differently and become apathetic and attach little importance (potency) to his industrial situation. Or, the agent may be culturally taught not to expect personality gratification in an industrial setting. Finally, the agent may, by the use of psychological defense mechanisms (e.g., rationalization or projection, etc.) adapt to his inability to obtain personality satisfaction in his industrial environment. This does not vitiate the above discussion. In fact, by using the above discussion, we can now understand why the agents use defense mechanisms or why they may attach little potency to their industrial setting.

To put it another way, the exceptions just cited include conditions which are not stipulated above. As such, these exceptions confirm our original ideas.

[3] F. W. Taylor, *Scientific Management* (Harper & Bros., 1947) and R. Urwick, *The Elements of Organization* (Harper & Bros., 1944).

(*a*) Personal trusts. Some examples are: A court trust fund for the administration of which the organization is made responsible to the court. Voluntary living trusts, i.e., trust funds set up by a customer who thereby turns over his investments and his money to the organization for proper handling. Institutional trusts, i.e., trusts set up for institutions such as churches, Y.M.C.A.'s, etc.

(*b*) Corporative trusts. The organization acts as a trustee for bond issues. The organization acts as a trustee for pension plans. The organization acts as a fiscal agent for corporations. It pays the corporation's dividends.

These workflows begin, as far as the department is concerned, the moment the customer enters the department and requests to see a trust officer. If the customer has no specific officer in mind, the receptionist guides him to the senior trust officer. At this introductory meeting the services of the department are outlined and the desires of the customer analyzed. As a result, the customer is assigned to a trust officer who is an expert on the customer's problems.

There are several meetings between the customer and the officer in which a detailed study is made of the customer's needs. The officer then spends a good deal of time in trying to find the best possible investment policy for the customer. As soon as the officer in charge is satisfied with an investment policy, he discusses it with the entire officer staff at a departmental meeting. The final form of the investment policy is a resultant of the group's thinking.

This brief description does not give all the details of the workflow. It simply outlines the over-all characteristics. The important point to be noted at this time is that private meetings between the officer and the customer and confidential meetings among the employees constitute the basic framework of the workflow process.

The actual detailed behavior of each meeting cannot be described before hand. It varies as customers and problems vary. Unlike manufacturing workflows, these workflows are comparatively fluid and not rigidly defined. This, we shall see, provides unusual opportunity for the officers to experience a wide variety of emotionally toned events, most of which are related to their personality fulfillment.

The fact that there is fluidity and flexibility does not mean that some stability or "structure" does not exist in the workflows. The workflows have their formal task characteristics defined by organizational policies and by state and federal laws. Thus officers do have some basic definitions of policy expectancies which provides them with a structure for their workflow activity. On the other hand, the actual behavior of people on the workflow (especially the ones contacting the customer) varies considerably from customer to customer and with the same customer at different times.

2. *The critical activity of each workflow is accomplished at the beginning.*

This characteristic of the bank as a whole holds true for the department. The trust services are "sold" by a trust officer at the beginning in the workflow process.

Also, as in the case of the whole, the people in this department who have the functions with greatest power and highest status perform tasks at the beginning of the workflow process. The employees "behind the customer line" receive "products" that have been sold. Their job is primarily the one of recording the sale and maintaining the service.

3. *Workflow pace is not entirely controlled by people from within.*

This is definitely the case as far as the department is concerned. The customer is the "pacesetter." The primary difference is that in the department the *amount* of time spent between employee and customer is greater. This is due to the complicated and personal nature of the services performed. The customer and the employee (usually an officer) interact for longer periods of time than is the case for the employees of the other departments.

Unlike the over-all organizational workflow process, the employees in the Trust Department are unable to predict their "busy" days. One reason is that due to the nature of the transactions, the customers do not come routinely to the department. Also, when the customers do come, they stay much longer. The best that the employees can predict are the busy months, months near income tax returns, quarterly dividends, etc.

Finally, the department's workflows continually place their employees in contact with people outside the organization. They frequently interact with lawyers, doctors, judges, etc., due to the nature of the workflow activities.

4. *The workflow activities have a high human quality.*

In discussing this characteristic we need to differentiate between the people in the department who meet and talk with the customers, and the people who do not. Let us speak of the former first.

The workflow processes in this department is one of the most personal, emotional, confidential, and at the same time technically difficult, workflows in the entire organization. In connection with the last point, the employees report that it is not an easy matter to accept the responsibility of managing other people's money and property and to promise that it will be managed in the best possible manner. Trust work requires much knowledge of legal matters, accounting, investment, and other related activities. In fact, as we have already seen, the workflows are so difficult that groups of experts meet to make decisions on one customer's account.

Nevertheless, the employees report that the human element is most important. No matter how technically competent a trust officer may be, his "personality" is crucial. It is important that people be placed on the workflow who are able to cope with the human problems that are so inexorably woven with the technical ones.

An illustration of the importance of the human characteristics in the workflow activities is found in the following quotations regarding qualifications of trust personnel taken from interviews with officers in the department:

"There must be embedded in each a desire to serve mankind."

"The basic interest is the customer."

"Tact and diplomacy are extremely important. A strong, sound, decent philosophy of life is crucial."

"He must be able to go into a widow's home the day after the husband dies and discuss her very personal problems with her."

"A trust officer is like a doctor."

Not all people in the department experience customer interactions. This does not mean that these individuals do not share some of these experiences. Many of them in describing their activities implied that they "experience" some of these personal interactions by identifying with the information they read when they come into contact with the confidential reports processed in the department. Thus, although they do not have direct contact with the customer, they are still able to experience some of the personal feelings that occur during an interview through the psychological process of identification with the material that they read.

5. *Officers are in the workflow process.*

This is true for this department. As we have seen, the officers are an integral part of the workflow. In fact their position is the most important one in the workflow. It is at the beginning where the selling of the services to the customer is accomplished.

6. *The workflow ties the employees to the customer rather than to the other employees.*

This is primarily true for the officers in the department. They are the ones who contact the customers. The clerical help and technical assistants housed in the "back offices" are linked to the officers rather than to the customers. They supply the officers with the information that the officers desire and type up the reports. The clerical help have no formal reasons to contact the other employees. Thus the characteristic of the workflow not acting to bind the employees with one another still holds true in this department. As was noted previously, this leads to weak informal group activities.

One might suspect that the secretaries who work closely with the various officers might feel closer to the officers and thus to the officer's customer. As far as most of the secretaries (95%) are concerned, neither is true. There are a number of probable reasons for this. First, many of them are in a secretarial pool from which the officers may draw. Thus, the same secretary does not always work with the same officer. Second, no matter how much they interact with the officers, we must not forget that there exists a definite status gap between employees and officers. Thus the girls are forced by the workflow process to interact with officers, while in the remaining organizational processes (i.e., reward and penalty, perpetuation, etc.) they do *not* interact with the officers.

The secretarial pool, although a recent innovation, has another effect upon the relationship. It creates opportunity for the girls to talk to each other. One of the items frequently discussed is the difficulty they have with the officers. Thus, there is beginning to arise an exception to the general characteristic that informal group relationships do not exist. The secretaries are beginning to create informal groupings stimulated by a common feeling that they have common difficulties with the officers.

Finally, it is important to note that there do not exist any departmental workflow processes which would serve to tie the employees in the department into a cohesive unit. Nor is there any workflow process which may serve to tie the Trust Department with the other departments of the organization. There is not much interaction with the employees of the other departments. This tends to create an isolation of this department from the other departments in the organization. The head of the department is keenly aware of this problem and tries continually to weld his department to the "whole" through the use of the organization's identification process. For example, he is continually emphasizing that they are a part of "The Friendly First."

7. *Interrelatedness of workflow to the other processes.*

(*a*) Those employees who contact the customers have tasks in their function representing all the organizational processes. For example, they initiate authority, reward and penalty, perpetuation, etc. tasks. The remainder of the employees (secretaries, clerks, technicians) have primarily formal workflow tasks which are primarily related to the paper work so necessary in the department.

(*b*) The customers, as in the case of the organization's other workflows, are an integral part of the workflow process. In the case of this department we may add lawyers, judges, etc. to the type of "outside" people who become part of the workflow. The customers have formal workflow, authority, reward and penalty, perpetuation and communication tasks in the function which the organization expects them to perform. These tasks are augmented by the customer as he finds it necessary. In fact, due to such identification symbols "Friendly First," "courteous service," etc. the customer finds that he may augment his activities to a considerable degree. The same identification activities also permit the customer to maximize the use of the formal activities expected of him. Finally the same identification activities act to *minimize* and control the inherent authority, reward and penalty, and perpetuation tasks that the officers may have in their function. The unequal balance of power may place internal strain upon the officer and may lead, as one officer put it, "to bite your lip and smile even if you know you're right." Courtesy, diplomacy, and tactfulness are very important in this type of work.

B. Authority Process

1. *Officers have authority and frequently express it.*

In the analysis of the organization as a whole we note that the majority of officers do not express directive authority with any substantial frequency. This is not entirely the case in the Trust Department. Three-fifths of the officers report very frequent daily authority contacts and two-fifths report moderate daily authority contacts with employees.[4] Similarly 50 per cent of the employees report very frequent contacts and 15 per cent report moderate authority contacts.[5] This trend, then, is opposite from the one described for the whole organization.

As we have noted in the previous section on workflow, part of the reason for this frequent expression of authority stems from the fact that the officers are continually directing their subordinates to obtain specific types of information which they (officers) will need in order to arrive at a decision.

The consequences of this "abnormally" frequent expression of authority are interesting. We shall see, for example, that the employees in this department report (proportionately) more negative feelings about the officers than do the employees in any other department. The employees directly relate their negative feelings to the "abnormally frequent" authority expression.

2. *There exists a "gap" between officers and employees and also multiple supervision.*

The employees definitely feel that a gap exists between them and the officers. It is interesting to note that they also feel the gap leads to poor officer-employee relationships. Odd as it may sound, the strongest feelings about the officer-employees gap come from employees who experience the most interaction with their officers. These results are congruent with a previously stated conclusion that the covert or latent relationships are much more hostile than the overt relationships.

The problem of multiple supervisors is also acute. Secretaries (because of the pool) are continually being directed to do work by more than one officer. The technical people find themselves in a similar situation. It arises

---

[4] We remind the reader that unless otherwise indicated the formal tasks referred to are those of initiation.

[5] We may also remind the reader that the operational criteria for the "degree of frequency" are as follows:

VF   Very frequent (5–10 contacts a day)
M   Moderate (2–5 contacts a day)
I   Infrequent (1 or less contacts a day, but at least 1 a week)
PN   Practically never (less than 1 contact a week)

from the fact that each officer individually manages a certain amount of accounts. He is not expected to know everything about all the services these accounts require. He is expected to ask help from the various technical employees in the department. This results in the employees being directed by more than one officer.

3. *Feelings of self-responsibility are not clearly evident.*

The majority of the non-officer employees do not express feelings of self-responsibility as frequently as do the other employees in the organization. Only the "old timers," who are in the minority, feel that they are their own boss. These results are to be expected, since we know that authority tasks are frequently expressed by the officers. This minimizes the necessity for the employees to create or engage in authority *acts*. The employees, comparing their "lot" with the organization as a whole, interpret their experiences as indicating that they aren't considered as responsible as are the other employees. Seventy-two per cent feel "discriminated against" in the matter of having an opportunity to be their own boss. Sixty-nine per cent believe that if this continues, they should be compensated with higher salaries than those received by other departments. This lends weight to the previously mentioned conclusion that one of the reasons the employees in the *total* organization accept lower wages are the relatively "weak" authority activities.

4. *Inter-relatedness of authority with the other processes.*

(*a*) In the previous chapter we suggest that a "weak" authority process may compensate for low wages. The feelings expressed by the employees in this department about wages do not differ from those expressed by most others in the organization. They feel that the wages are low. But they must find compensations other than a "weak" authority system. In this department, accordingly we find proportionally more employees emphasize that they stay because the work is easier than in any other department. A surprising number admit that they "don't break their neck at work" and add "why should we with what we get paid." Thus, we infer that the employees, realizing that the wages are low and at the same time *not* experiencing a weak authority process as a partial compensation for this situation rationalize or make up for what they perceive to be an "abnormal" situation by working less.

(*b*) As the workflow process in the over-all organizational structure lends support to a "weak" authority process, the workflow, in this department, helps create and reenforce a relatively "strong" authority process. Thus, we have seen that the employees are forced by the very nature of their jobs to receive directions from the officers and in turn, to direct the officers in those matters which they (employees) are experts.

(*c*) The kind of personality type that tends to be perpetuated in the bank finds ideal possibilities for expression under "weak" authority. Since the statistics indicate that the employees in the Trust Department are similar to the "right type,"[6] (i.e., the right type for employment by the bank) we may assume that they also desire a "weak" authority process. Since they do not experience a weak authority process, we may infer that they will tend to express resentment toward the officers. This inference is substantiated by the fact that the comments made by the employees of this department about the officers are the most aggressive and hostile of all comments reported.

(d) Finally, we may also infer that since "strong" leadership goes against the organizational identification codes of "passive leadership," the employees should perceive the officers as deviants from the codes. The employees confirm our inferences and 89 per cent state that this inconsistency leads to even further aggression toward the officers. It also seems to lead to a perfectly rational reason for the employees to project their difficulties onto the officers and blame them for their difficulties.

C. Reward and Penalty Process

1. *Rewards and penalties are hardly ever distributed by the officers to the employees.*

This characteristic holds true for the Trust Department. The fact that it does, leads to problems. The problems arise from, and are directly related to, the frequent authority expression. Since the employees are directed more often, there arises an increased expectation for increased rewards and/or increased penalties. The officers, on the other hand, following the overall organizational reward and penalty pattern, distribute few of either. This results in a discrepancy between the frequency of authority contacts and the reward and penalty contacts that are necessary for the employees to evaluate their relationship with the officer. Thus 75 per cent of the employees feel that they do not know "where they stand" in relation to the officers. They wish the officers would express more reward and penalty activities. This would provide them with a chance to evaluate themselves in relation to the officer.

An interesting problem seems to arise as a result of this. The officers do want to give more rewards and penalties. As to the former, they believe that money rewards are the ones most important to the employees. Compliments, praises, etc. should not be expressed as rewards if they cannot be reenforced by financial rewards. But the financial rewards are not con-

---

[6] The writer infers that some of the more latent characteristics of the "right type" are:

A strong desire for security, stability, predictability in their life.
A strong desire to be left alone and work in relative isolation.
A dislike of aggressiveness and/or hostility in themselves and others.

If these inferences are valid, then we can begin to understand why the people have little difficulty in being retiring, polite, courteous, tactful, conventional, etc. Behaving in this manner tends to minimize the possibility of experiencing aggression from others and/or expressing aggression towards others.

trolled by anyone in the entire department. Thus, the department officers tend to give few rewards of any type.

When it comes to penalties, the officers (with one exception) find it difficult to speak directly to and to discipline the employee. This is due to several reasons. First, they realize that since the rewards are not really in their control, if they were to penalize the employees, they would build up a reward and penalty relationship with them that contained only penalties. This is hardly desirable from their point of view. Another reason is related to the personality type. The "right type" tends to dislike expressing or receiving penalizing sentiments. The officer, coming up from the ranks, and/or realizing that the employees do feel this way minimizes the distribution of direct penalties.

However, the employees report penalties are received in an indirect manner. Thus they describe learning how poorly they did some work from another employee who was told "confidentially" by the officer. Sixty-five per cent resent this very much. We will present ample evidence for this when we discuss the over-all employee-officer relationships.

2. *Feeling of "self-responsibility" is not prominent.*

The feelings of self-responsibility are lower than the average expressed in the bank as a whole.

3. *Wages are not considered satisfactory.*

Sixty per cent of the employees feel wages are "poor." Thirty per cent describe them as "terrible" and ten per cent refuse to talk about them.

4. *Feelings about other rewards the organization offers.*

(*a*) Ranking the other factors that are viewed as rewards by the employees, we find that benefits rank highest as most desired and best liked.[7] This is similar to the over-all organizational results.

(*b*) As might be expected—"I am my own boss" is in last place in this department while it is in second place for the entire organization.

(*c*) Working conditions receive a very high second place among factors considered favorable by the employees. This is probably related to the fact that the department's physical quarters were recently renovated.

(*d*) Unlike the organization as a whole, the positive organizational characteristic that "people are nice, they let you alone" is hardly ever mentioned. This is due, we believe, to the fact that the officers do not let the employees alone. It is also due to the officers discussing their feelings about employees with other employees. When the former employees hear about the officer's criticism and that another employee knows about it, they believe that the employee is delving into their personal problems.

Thus we see more evidence of how people's feelings about reward and

---

[7] Included in the benefits are (1) the pension plan, (2) insurance, (3) medical benefits, and (4) vacations with pay.

penalties are interrelated with their feelings about how they are treated in other processes, and how this treatment compares with the one received by the employees in the organization as a whole.

D. Perpetuation Process.

1. *Officers hardly ever express perpetuation activities on their own initiative.*

This holds true for the officer-employee relationship in the Trust Department. The figures reported for the entire organization are almost identical.

2. *Feelings of self-responsibility are frequently expressed.*

The feelings of self-responsibility, in relation to the perpetuation process, do exist and are expressed in the same frequencies, as is found in the over-all organizational figures. The feelings of self-responsibility arise from the fact that the officers do not express perpetuation tasks. The employees may therefore substitute perpetuation *acts.*

3. *The director of personnel is seen as controlling the perpetuation process.*

(*a*) The position of the director of the department is weakened.

(*b*) Since he, in turn, is unable to give his subordinate officers perpetuation tasks, their position is weakened.

(*c*) This, in turn, leads to the officers accepting less and less responsibility for the employees in their sections.

4. *The picture of the "right type" hired and developed in the bank as a whole presented in the previous chapter is valid for the Trust Department.*

The employees in this Department perceive themselves as:

(*a*) People who consider themselves more capable of receiving directions (55%) than of directing others (45%).

(*b*) People who feel they are more comfortable if they do not have to initiate actions for others. Only 18 per cent indicate they would feel comfortable in so doing.

(*c*) Finally, 50 per cent prefer to be followers. Thirty-five per cent prefer to be leaders but they qualify "leadership" to mean passive leadership. Only 15 per cent desire to be directive leaders.

E. Identification Process

1. *The officers express few identification activities.*

The conclusions reached with respect to the whole organization are valid for this department as far as this dimension is concerned.

2. *The slogans and phrases which identify the bank hold for this department.*

(*a*) "The Friendly First."

As is the case for the over-all organization, the employees interpret "Friendly First" to be associated with the employee-customer relationship. The extent to which this is felt seems greater in this department. Thus 80 per cent of the employees suggest that "Friendly First" is related to the customer-employee contacts. This increase is understandably accountable, if we recall that—

The customer contacts are especially emphasized in the department.

The abnormally frequent authority interaction rate is related to the employee-officer contacts. Thus these would not tend to be friendly.

Finally, as might be expected, such abilities as "tactfulness," "diplomacy," "patience," are most often mentioned by the employees as the abilities that are required to perform the activities in their department.

(b) The "right type."

The organization's meaning of the identification symbol—the "right type"—definitely exists in the department's identification process. It is interesting to note that some officers (younger ones) are suggesting that the "right type" be changed to mean a more aggressive, go-getting individual. An individual, for example, who will be more active in obtaining new business for the organization. This, they suggest is in line with the organization's desire that this department must expand. However, all report that they are meeting stiff opposition on every side, especially from some of the top officers in the organization.[8]

F. Communication Process

1. *Not all have communication tasks.*

As far as the distribution of communication tasks is concerned, the department is not similar to the total organization. Only half of the employees report formal communication tasks. The other half, who do not, are the clerks and technicians who are continuously at work at their desks doing some sort of "paper work" or "research work." However, this half do report informal communication tasks.

2. *The communications are overtly friendly.*

3. *Covertly, the communications among the employees, and, to a much lesser extent, between the employees and the customers, are not too friendly.*

4. *Communications with officers are officer-centered.*

G. Departmental Evaluation Attitudes and Activities Related to the Steady State of the Departmental Organizational Processes.

To date we have examined the organizational processes individually and those attitudes and activities which are directly related to each of them. We now turn to a discussion of some departmental phenomena which are, as far as we are able to understand, resultants of (1) the steady state of all the departmental processes, and (2) the adaptation problems

---

[8] This is added indirect evidence that the "right type" is as we have described it.

this over-all departmental steady state has with the organizational steady state.

1. *Employee attitudes and feelings about their roles.*

The role of any given individual is the combined complexity of formal tasks, and personal acts, as perceived, interrelated, and organized by that individual.

Clearly, the sentiments that all the people in the department have about their roles will affect the fusion process of each individual in the department. Therefore, it is useful to discuss these attitudes at some length.

(*a*) Perceived Degree of Variety. The employees in the department, as a group, perceive their role to contain more variety than do the other employees in the organization. In classifying the answers in regard to this question, we utilize the following scale.

(1) "My work is routine and monotonous."

(2) "My work is routine, but there is variety in the way I handle the routine." Or to put it another way, "the activities I do are routine but there is variety in the sequence in which I handle the activities."

(3) "My work has variety with a little routine."

(4) "My work is all variety. I never do two things that are alike."

Utilizing this scale the perceived departmental variety is:

Perceived Degree of Variety	Per Cent
1	15%
2	15
3	30
4	30
	100%

(*b*) Perceived Degree of Making Choices. Another dimension that is related to the role is the degree of choice a person believes he has in his working activities. Is there any leeway? Is the work rigidly defined? In classifying the answers to this question, the following categories are used.

(1) I have no alternatives.

(2) I have some alternatives once in a while (i.e., no more than two-three a day or less than what I think is desirable for me.)

(3) I have quite a few alternatives (i.e., more than three, but something less than what the person considers "all that he likes").

(4) I have many alternatives (i.e., all that I want or more than what I want).

Utilizing this scale the departmental results are:

Perceived Degree of Possible Choice	Per Cent
1	10%
2	30
3	45
4	15
	100%

Thus the degree of leeway offered the individual is not considered as high as the degree of variety in the work. This is understandable if we recall that bank tasks are defined by rather rigid rules which do not permit too much leeway in choice. The only digression permitted, and that within limits, is related to *when* (i.e., in what order) the various tasks are done.

(*c*) The Degree of Initiating and Receiving of Action. Another important characteristic of one's work activities is the degree to which one is permitted to initiate action for others. In discussing the concept of initiation of action, it is useful to distinguish two types of initiation of action.

(1) Type "X" (or the "what" type) initiation of action. There is that initiation of action which simply acts as a cue for the recipient of the initiation to perform some task or a set of tasks. For example, A may say to B, "You'd better check Mrs. Smith's account. It is overdue." B then performs the required activities without A having to tell him exactly what to do. We call this type "X."

(2) Type "Y" (or the "how" type) initiation of action. In type "Y" the initiator not only initiates action but he actually defines exactly how the recipient is to perform the action requested. For instance, in the example mentioned above, the initiation of action would be type "Y" if A said to B—"You'd better see about Mrs. Smith's account. It is way overdue. I want you first to do such and such then I want you to do the following, etc." In this example, A defines the exact steps for B.

Before we continue, we want to explain why these data are discussed here. Some students, for example, would place these under the authority process. We do not. An analysis of the interview indicates two interesting results. First, any person who initiates action as a result of formal tasks in his function, theoretically has the power to utilize either "X" or "Y". Second, the data indicate that because of the behavioral content and the existing codes of the organizational processes, it is considered incorrect to utilize type "Y" in this organization. Thus employees who use type "Y" are deviates and as such are disliked. Employees who receive type "Y" feel justified in complaining. Because the evaluation of X and Y type of initiation of action is based on and is a resultant of the several processes of organization, we feel justified in discussing these phenomena at this time.

The reason for the dislike of type "Y" seems to arise from the fact that a type Y initiation of action tends to compound the sense of dependency and submissiveness of the recipient on the initiator. Furthermore, especially as a result of the behavioral activities and codes in the organization's "weak" authority, reward and penalty, and perpetuation processes, the employees interpret type Y to mean that the initiator does not have much faith in them. Thus a type Y initiator of action is described as one who "breathes down your neck" or "one who stands over you all the time."

As one would expect, type Y initiation of action is almost nonexistent in the organization as a whole. New employees being trained are, of course, an exception to the rule. But, the reader may recall that in this department the authority process is used more often than in any other department. Thus, we can hypothesize that if the officers limit their directing to type X, the perceived pressure on the employee's part should be minimal.

Forty-five per cent of the officers report utilizing type X initiation of action while 40 per cent utilize type Y. Of the type Y, 25 per cent are "very frequent" and 60 per cent are "moderate." The remainder report no initiations of actions with employees. Thus, the initiation of action of both types is relatively higher than the rest of the organization.

It is also interesting to note that all the employees who contact customers utilize both type X or Y on these relationships. They report that the customers do likewise. Thus, in the customer-employee relationship, both sides have the power to utilize type X and Y, while in the officer-employee relationships only the former has the power to utilize type Y.

As a result of this, an interesting problem arises for some of the older employees who are experts. They are frequently placed in the position of having to initiate action of the Y type for the officers. For example, as experts they must advise the officers. All the old-timers report this to be a very ticklish situation, since in doing so, they reverse the expected initiation of action pattern. The "expert" employees are cautious lest they be perceived by the officers as "getting too big for their boots," or "getting too bossy," or "as trying to 'show up' the boss' weaknesses."

(d) Activities the Employees Like Best. Seventy per cent of the employees say that the activities they like best in their role are those that are related to one or more formal tasks assigned by the organization.

Twenty per cent more state that they like formal and informal activities in their role equally well. They also state that they cannot clearly differentiate the formal from the informal. Only 10 per cent report that they like nothing about their activities.

(e) Activities the Employees Like the Least. The "like the least" picture is as positive (from the department's point of view) as are the above data. Thus 25 per cent say that they dislike nothing. Forty-five per cent state that the only thing they like least about their work are "unexpected minor details that crop up once in a while." Twenty per cent state they dislike filing. Ten per cent say that they dislike everything about their role activities.

2. *Perceived respect of work activities.*

Another variable which is a resultant of the steady state of all the organizational processes is the employees' perceived degree of respect that the employees' work activities have within the department and in the organization as a whole.

The results for the department are as follows: Fifty-five per cent believe that other people in the department aspire to and would like to have their job. Forty-five per cent think that no one in the department would like their job.

The perceived picture of respect from the other departments in the organization is brighter. Eighty per cent of the employees believe that people in other departments aspire for work in their department. Fifteen per cent believe not, while 5 per cent are not certain.

Thus the perceived organizational respect for their work activities is high. These data lend weight to the already mentioned notion (see workflow process) that this department's activities are high on the organization's status ladder.

The previously mentioned fact that this department has little contact with other departments partially accounts for the differences between "perceived internal status" and "perceived external status." The people outside probably rank the department according to the organization rules of status (i.e., high status goes to a department with confidential, personal contact with customers). On the other hand, many of the employees within the department rarely experience personal, confidential contacts with customers. They rate their activities according to their experience which tends to be related to officer contacts that are full of hidden conflict and tension.

3. *State of interpersonal relationships in the department.*

(*a*) Employee-Employee Relationships. Forty-five per cent are definitely confident that they "get along well" with others and forty per cent are "almost sure" they get along with others. Only 15 per cent report any negative human relationships. This presents a "rosy" picture and does not jibe with the previously discussed results.

The apparent contradiction is resolved if we also note that 90 per cent of the employees state that they have no close friends in the department in which they work. These data lend support to the previously mentioned phenomena, that human inter-relationships seem happy on the overt level, but they are seething with tension underneath.

(*b*) Officer-Employee Relationships. We have already pointed out that the officer-employee relationships are fraught with covert tension.[9] Let us fill these statistics with human feelings content by presenting some direct quotes.

"I wish they could come out and tell you something. Some officers, when they have some criticism tell others to tell us. Why don't they tell

---

[9] See statistics in discussion of authority processes.

us directly? By the time it gets to us it is distorted and a lot of people think—well I just don't know what they think."

"Another thing, we don't like it when an officer says one thing and then they do another. I know one girl was offered a new job. She didn't like it because of the added work and no increase in pay. She told the officer she'd take it if pay was increased or if the job changed. The officer replied that he doubted if either could be done. So the girl turned the job down. A few weeks later another girl took the job and it *was* changed."

"Why can't we have morning coffee. I can see why the girls in the front office can't—they have to be ready to meet the customers—why can't we have it?"

"Some officers have a lot to do, some have little. It used to be that some girls worked all the time, some didn't. So we changed it. All the extra work is supposed to go to one girl and she gives it to the girls that are not busy. It sounded good. I don't know why, but the officers still take it to their favorite girl."

"Then I wish they could see our point of view. For example, there is a letter with one small error that can be erased. Why should it be re-done?"

"I guess I must sound pretty awful. Let me say something nice. I think the officers are nice. They're polite—they're nice—but it's skin deep. There is a gap between us and the officers. You certainly can't talk to them as if they were a friend."

"The employees don't think too much of them. They resent their attitude. You know, they go around ordering us around. Okay, so we do have to work for a living. But do they have to rub that in?"

"One of the things the girls resent is that they treat customers much better than the employees. Course, the employees are part to blame. They don't really show any interest in their work."

"Then again some of them, especially the junior officers, don't even know how to do the job they're supposed to do. To make matters worse, each one wants his own way. Sometimes they want to do things that are against what the head man wants. It's difficult to keep peace—believe you me!"

"Most of the people think the officers are small. They're so petty. They pick on such small things. They don't insist on the larger things, for example. Their attitude toward us isn't good. I don't hear anything done about that. They forget we're human. Sometimes you feel like banging their heads on the wall."

"And another thing. They never seem to be willing to take the blame. They always blame the underdog. If they were really men, they'd take it."

"We have departmental meetings. Most of the time it's a lecture. The

head of the department makes some announcements and then he asked
Mr. ——— if he has anything to add."

"No, no one asks our opinion. And if they did, it wouldn't do much
good. Most of the people don't say too much anyway. There might be
a few brave ones. Not many. Most don't want to make themselves look
bad."

"The employees feel they're stuffy. They're not considerate of the
help's point of view."

"They're nice to talk to all right. But—I don't know how to say it
except that there is a lack of understanding of the employees' points of
view."

"They don't realize the pressure we work under. They leave things
until the end and then give orders which shows they don't realize how
complicated things are."

"We wish they'd tell us something directly when it's wrong. You
know something is wrong. You can sense it. But they don't tell you.
That—well—that's a deep hurt."

"No, they don't want us to talk. They think if we do, we don't have
enough to do. If you spend a minute talking they come up to you and
say, 'nothing to do'—and oh, does that burn us up."

"Then there is the pool of girls. In principle it's all right. But the officers don't follow it. Each one thinks I'm his personal secretary. That
places us in an awful position since we can't tell him how we feel."

"The people don't respect them. Somehow they don't feel they're
qualified men. They're nice as individuals—but they're not qualified.
They don't know the work they are doing. Sometimes they're rude.
They can—they can—well—they can needle you in a nice sort of way."

Communication

THE TERM "communication" refers to the systematic use of symbols. This definition introduces us to three important aspects of communication: (1) it is *systematic*, the acts of communication are related to one another in a stable manner; (2) it is *symbolic*, the communications having reference to something external and "real"; and (3) it is *need-related*, either satisfying or instrumental to satisfaction. These three characteristics provide the basis for a useful analytic scheme for study of these questions: the syntax, semantics, and pragmatics of communications systems.[1]

The *syntax* includes the systematic aspects of communication, the relations internal to the system of symbols itself. This category includes all of what we normally consider mathematics, logic, and grammar. *Semantics* concerns the relations between the symbols and the "reality" they refer to, for example, the relation between a scientific theory and the phenomena it describes. Philosophical questions of *meaning* are included in semantics. *Pragmatics* refers to the need-relatedness of communication, its relation to purposeful action.

Expressed in these terms communication is not solely an organizational problem.[2] Although organizations are heavily dependent on the successful use of communication for survival and effectiveness, the individual human being is no less dependent on and limited by his capacity to receive and send communications. Likewise our economic, social, and political systems are in many respects closely linked with communication. Discussion of communications problems must therefore range a bit more broadly than is appropriate for our other problem areas.

In some respects organizations face the same problems as people in

---

[1] Charles W. Morris, "Foundations of the Theory of Signs," *International Encyclopedia of Unified Science*, Vol. I, Part 1 (Chicago, 1955), p. 77.

[2] For an integrative study of the subject, see Colin Cherry, *On Human Communication* (New York: Technology Press and Wiley, 1957).

their communicating. In large part they must make use of systems of communication that are already determined, such as the language of their society, the media whose services are offered for sale, or the technical vocabulary of a profession. Organizations are not, however, as limited as individuals in this respect because they have greater means to invent new systems for their special purposes. In other respects, organizations are like societies: the systems of communication to which they are committed also evolve under the pressure of needs without centralized planning.

Returning to our analytic scheme of dividing the subject of communication into syntax, semantics, and pragmatics, it is clear that the most important aspects of communication for organizations are pragmatic. This must not be interpreted as saying that syntax and semantics can be ignored. Indeed, useful communication is impossible unless these more basic matters have been worked out in the system under consideration.

In recent years the development of "information theory" has resulted in a unified and quantitative approach to the syntactical problems of communication. This branch of thought is sufficiently promising so that an acquaintance with it is worthwhile for anyone who proposes to think scientifically about problems of communication. The "theory" is mathematical (not empirical) and requires a rather advanced level of mathematical understanding for appreciation of its finer points, especially in applications. Nevertheless, the basic ideas are readily accessible.

Consider an act of communication consisting of the transmission of one single symbol. It is immaterial whether the symbol be a letter, a word, or a message. The essential aspect of information theory is that it focuses on the alternative possibilities inherent in this act of communication. The symbol must be selected from some alphabet, vocabulary, or repertory of messages. The number of these symbols is represented below by n. It is possible to define a quantitative measure of the amount of information transmitted in this act of communication if we add a measure of the *probability of selection* for each symbol. P_i stands for the probability of selection of the ith symbol. The question of where it is appropriate to use the concept of probability is, of course, one of the most difficult questions of modern philosophy. In information theory a usual and quite satisfactory method is to let the probabilities be defined empirically by the relative frequency of each symbol in a long sequence of independent communication acts. In any case, once the measure of probability is determined, the measure of information follows quite naturally. The measure, as formulated by Shannon,[3] is:

---

[3] Claude E. Shannon and Warren Weaver, *The Mathematical Theory of Communication* (Illinois, 1949), p. 19.

$$H = -K \sum_{i=1}^{n} P_i \log P_i \, .$$

This measure has three defining properties, and it is the only measure that possesses all three. (1) It is continuous in the P_i; that is, it varies infinitesimally with infinitesimal variations in the P_i's. (2) If the P_i's are all equal to each other the measure increases with an increase in n; the greater the number of possibilities, the more information the symbol conveys. (3) If the choice of symbol is decomposed into two successive choices, the measure does not change; e.g., if one selects the symbol by first choosing which section of the list of symbols to use and then selecting a specific symbol from this section, there is no change in the amount of information involved. As can be appreciated, these three characteristics are so general that this definition may be accepted as a very reasonable one. One parameter is still undefined: the base of the logarithms. The choice of base corresponds to the choice of a measuring unit. It has become customary in information theory to use logarithms to base 2; in this case the units of information are called *bits*.

The definition of information defines the yardstick to be used in studying communication. It remains to be somewhat more specific as to what is being measured. The measure as formulated applies to *symbols*. The definition of what is a symbol remains arbitrary. The most usual choice is a letter from some *alphabet*, for example the 26 letters of the English alphabet. That this is an arbitrary choice can be illustrated by reference to computer applications. A computer is capable of dealing with English texts, for instance, but does so on the basis of a much smaller alphabet; in fact, the usual alphabet used in the computer circuitry is binary, consisting only of the symbols 0 and 1. Any numerical or alphabetic text can be encoded in the binary system.

The "alphabet" may also be taken as a repertory of possible messages. In an application using this technique, the value of n would ordinarily be very large and the probability of each message very small, but the information content can be computed in straightforward fashion from the basic measure defined above. If, however, the alphabet be defined in the more conventional manner, as a binary or English one, for instance, the term *message* refers to a sequence of characters, each character being one of the letters of the alphabet. Since we may wish to calculate the measure of information either on the basis of the individual characters or on the basis of the entire message, it may well be asked whether the two approaches will yield the same answer. In order to assure that they will yield the same answer, we must introduce two new concepts: *sequentially dependent probabilities* and *redundancy*.

In English it is quite obvious that the probability with which any letter will appear in any given position of a specific message will depend very much on what has gone before in the message, i.e., be sequentially dependent. The best example is the relation between the letters "q" and "u." Knowing that a "q" has appeared makes us almost certain that the next letter will be a "u." Similarly, if we saw the letters "oug" we would guess that the next letter would be an "h," although we would probably not infer this from seeing only a "g" or even a "ug." For this reason, if we wish to calculate the information content of a message by synthesis from the information content of the individual characters, we cannot use the measure defined above if the probabilities are sequentially dependent. There is another formula involving conditional probabilities that is logically satisfactory for this purpose.

What then is the effect of sequential dependence on information content? If we make a letter count of English text and thereby discover the probability of occurrence of each letter in the alphabet, we could calculate a measure of the information conveyed by one English letter. This would not be correct, however, because of the sequential dependence between letters. The actual information content will have to be less than this amount because the sequential dependence imposes additional constraints on the variability of English text. The actual information content of English text has been estimated to be roughly half as much as would be estimated by our hypothetical calculation. Moreover, an alphabet can convey the maximum amount of information only when its letters are used with equal frequency. The letters in English are not used with equal frequency, and this further reduces the rate of information transmission from what it could be. The actual information content of English is about one bit per character. An ordinary typewriter keyboard may be capable of producing 84 different letters, counting punctuation, capitals, numbers, and special symbols. If these were used with equal frequency and without sequential dependence, they could transmit information at a rate in excess of six bits per character. If we take the ratio of the amount of waste information capacity of a source to the maximum potential information rate, we have a measure of the *redundancy* of the source. In our typewriter example, if the maximum is figured at six bits per character, and the actual information content of text at one bit, the redundancy is $\frac{5}{6}$.

The measures of information per symbol or per message can be converted into time rates transmission, if we have a measure of the time rate of production of symbols or messages by the source.

Shannon's original application of information theory was to the problem of accurate transmission. His application was principally directed at telecommunications, where the barrier to accurate transmission is random disturbance, known in the trade as *noise*. Therefore, he defines the information rate of the source as $H(x)$ and that of the message received as $H(y)$. If message sent and message received are each considered as separate sources, the information content of the two together is less than or equal to the sum of the information content of each separately.

$$H(x, y) \leq H(x) + H(y) \, .$$

The equality holds only if the message sent and the message received are independent. If they are not independent, the joint information is equal to a sum consisting of the information content of one source plus the residual variability in the other that cannot be predicted by knowledge of the one.

$$H(x, y) = H(x) + H_x(y) = H(y) + H_y(x) \, .$$

In the equations $H_x(y)$ may be interpreted as the effect of the noise on the message received, and $H_y(x)$ is the part of the message sent that is obscured by the noise.

The fundamental theorem of information theory, as shown by Shannon, asserts that, if there is a noisy channel (including a source x and receiver y) with the capacity $C = H(x) - H_y(x)$, then there is also a coding system such that the output of any source z, $H(z) \leqq C$, can be transmitted over the channel with an arbitrarily small error due to noise. The surprising feature of this theorem is that it proves that there is some way to offset the effects of randomized noise and achieve arbitrarily exact transmission, given only that we do not try to exceed the capacity of the channel. Accuracy is achieved by this method, however, only at

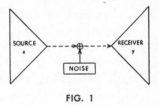

FIG. 1

a price; and the price is delay in transmission. To get better and better transmission, the coding process must look at longer and longer message sequences. An alternative way of gaining accuracy is to use excess channel capacity and build redundancy into the coding process.

The theoretical results stated in the paragraph above have had only a limited application to problems of organizational communication. An example of their use is given in the article by Frick and Sumby on "Control Tower Language." The valuable applications of this part of information theory so far are to be found mostly in the design of technical means of communication, e.g., telecommunications, and are therefore outside the scope of our study.

So much for syntax. Our study of these questions has concerned the efficiency and accuracy of transmission of symbols between a source and a receiver. This is only the first step, however; there is as yet no assurance that the source knew what he was talking about or that, if he did, the receiver understood. These are the semantic questions of communication. For the communication system to be adequate, there must be a correspondence between the symbols used and the reality being communicated about, and this correspondence must be the property of both source and receiver. This book, or any other book like it, is mainly an exercise in semantics, just as a mathematics book is largely an exercise in syntax. Scientific investigation searches for meaningful symbols with which to communicate about the world around us. In the case of this book, the "world" is the world of organizational phenomena.

The reader will also appreciate the importance of the second condition, that the correspondence between symbols and reality be shared by both source and receiver, especially after reading some of the more technical articles. This, or any textbook, is partly an attempt to increase the range of shared vocabulary in the culture or in a profession; and its success depends on the number and usefulness of the concepts that can be learned from it.

Even though messages are accurately transmitted, meaningful, and understood, the study of communication cannot yet be concluded. Communication is a purposive act, and most of the interesting problems deal with the pragmatic aspects. Even questions of syntax or semantics have their pragmatic aspects. How accurate a transmission system or how extensive a vocabulary will be maintained by a person, organization, or society depends very much on the purposes for which they are to be used. A powerful vocabulary and accurate, fast transmission methods are costly, and the gains from employing them may not justify the costs. Engineers do not generally employ the concepts and mathematics of theoretical physics in routine design problems, and it is not customary to send New Year's greetings over the transatlantic cable.

The most important pragmatic questions do not concern the economics

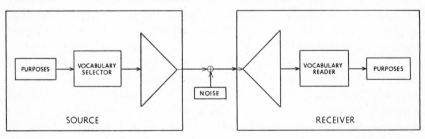

FIG. 2

of transmission media or vocabularies. They concern broader questions relating to the purposes of communication. We can illustrate the broader problem by a modification of the channel diagram in Fig. 1. This (Fig. 2) shows that a communications act originates for some purpose, is converted into appropriate symbols, and transmitted. It is received (more or less accurately), interpreted, and reacted to in terms of purposes, which may or may not be the same as those of the source. As an example, imagine a hungry dog approaching his owner and emitting a pleading whine. The owner hears; realizes the dog is asking for food; and, desirous of continuing to read peacefully in his easy chair, throws a shoe at the dog. The symbol (whine) was in this case appropriately chosen, transmitted accurately, and interpreted correctly. Nevertheless, the dog's communication was not successful. We could continue and complicate the illustration by allowing the dog to misinterpret his owner's act as an invitation to play.

One moral of the story is that it is not only the needs at the source that gave rise to the communication that are relevant to its course. It is also the needs of those who may act as receiver and those who may relay the message. It is easy enough to understand that those who desire to get a certain task accomplished in an organization will initiate communications designed to accomplish it. It is less obvious to most of us that information tends to flow in an organization to those points where it is known to be needed for task accomplishment.

Communications can also be caused or biased because of purely personal needs. Asch's article "Opinions and Social Pressure," is an excellent example of how a communication can be distorted because of a personal factor, in this case the "social needs" of the individual, a concept that we encountered in Section Three. The Asch experiment gives an extreme example of a much more general phenomenon: the tendency of human beings to substitute group consensus for reality testing in situations of ambiguity or potent group interest.

Torrance's article, "Function of Expressed Disagreement in Small Group Processes," is another example of the need-relatedness of communication, in this case in the context of organizational processes. He shows how the amount and content of communication can be determined in part by the personality characteristics of the individuals and by the established relations between them. This is so important that it is tempting in many cases to characterize organization relationships by the type and amount of communication involved in the relationship.

Although organizations almost always include small groups in their structure and thus produce behavior directly comparable to that analyzed above, organized communication has broader characteristics as well. The deliberate assignment of particular persons to particular groups and the formation of specialized linkages among groups and persons are properties peculiar to organizations. The formal organization has control over the communication structure by such means as the establishment of authority and work relations among members, the choice of office facilities, and the assignment of specific communication functions. This is true of informal communication channels as well as of formal ones, although the control of the former is less complete.

Since the communication structure is partly a choice of organization authority, it can be purposively designed. The notion that the communication structure is a possible limiting factor and knowledge of the rather stereotyped hierarchial structure in general use in organizations have led several researchers into study of this matter. Perhaps the best-known line of work is that begun by A. Bavelas and H. Leavitt on the effect of imposed communication structures on small, task-oriented laboratory groups.[4] Their original experiment was replicated and developed further by Guetzkow and Simon in their work on "The Impact of Certain Communication Nets upon Organization and Performance in Task-Oriented Groups," reproduced in this section. It should be noted how the experimental design isolates the variable of communication *structure*, removing semantic aspects by the use of a problem involving only meaningless symbols and controlling pragmatic aspects by inducing a uniform motivational set in the subjects. This design has been used in many other studies.[5]

Another approach to the structure of communication has been taken by workers in the University of Michigan's human relations program.[6] This approach involves the empirical determination of a matrix of communication links among the members of an organization. This has the advantage of being able to summarize a great deal of information about a relatively large organization and opens the way to many new ideas still in process of formulation. Still another approach is taken by Marschak in developing models for optimal communication patterns among organization members faced with various types of artificially constructed tasks.[7]

The development of an informal communication system under the pressure of task needs is the subject of P. M. Blau's field study of a group of officials in a government agency. The methods and findings are comparable to those of Horsfall and Arensberg.[8] In contrast to Blau's study, which again emphasizes the creation of informal organization, Rubenstein's study is directed at the question of the effectiveness of different communication links in the achievement of organization goals. It also

---

[4] A. Bavelas, "Communication Patterns in Task-Oriented Groups," in *Group Dynamics*, D. Cartwright and A. Zander (Eds.) (Row Peterson, 1953).

[5] H. Guetzkow and A. Bowes, "The Development of Organization in a Laboratory," *Management Science*, Vol. III (July, 1957), p. 4; M. E. Shaw, "Some Effects of Unequal Distribution of Information upon Group Performance in Various Communication Nets," *J. Abn. Soc. Psychol.*, Vol. 49 (1954), pp. 547–53; M. E. Shaw and G. H. Rothschild, "Some Effects of Prolonged Experience in Communication Nets," *J. Appl. Psychol.*, Vol. 40 (1956), pp. 28–86; L. S. Christie, "Organization and Information Handling in Task Groups," *Operations Research* (May, 1954).

[6] E. Jacobson and S. Seashore, "Communication Practices in Complex Organizations," *Journal of Social Issues*, Vol. VII, No. 3 (1951), and R. S. Weiss, *Processes of Organization* (Michigan, 1956).

[7] J. Marschak, "Elements for a Theory of Teams," *Management Science*, Vol. I, No. 2 (January, 1955).

[8] Article 7.

illustrates some of the problems of designing communication studies in a field situation.

At the extreme, informal communication in organization is close to informal social communication. This extreme is reached in the rumor process. Most organizational communication is specific and directed; most rumor is diffuse and spread. Rumors have been extensively studied in social contexts and by laboratory methods. "The Basic Law of Rumor," as formulated in this research, is discussed by A. M. J. Chorus. The rumor process in organizations is the subject of the two studies, "Rumors in War" by Theodore Caplow and "Management Communication and the Grapevine" by Keith Davis. Their findings point up similarities and differences with the previous work. Like the social case, organization rumors are not subject to much formal control. Unlike the social case, rumors in organizations are not so liable to distortion and are more likely to be consciously and responsibly used by the participants, probably due to the relative permanence of the social grouping involved.

18. CONTROL TOWER LANGUAGE*

F. C. FRICK AND W. H. SUMBY

Shannon and others have estimated that written English is about 60 per cent redundant. These estimates are arrived at by considering linguistic constraints on our use of speech symbols; they do not consider additional restrictions imposed by the audience and the situation in which the speaker finds himself. In order to estimate the effects of such nonlinguistic constraints, an informational analysis has been made of the "sublanguage" used in the control of aircraft by Air Force control tower operators. When the situational, as well as linguistic, contexts are taken into account, the estimated redundancy is raised to 96 per cent.

How informative a given speech sample is—how much we say—depends to a large extent on how much we might have said.

"Speaking English" imposes certain constraints on our use of linguistic symbols. The individual elements—phonemes, letters, words—which make up our vocabulary are not used equally often and they are not combined at random. In addition, the rules of grammar and the desire to make sense impose restrictions on the order in which groups of these symbols are strung together. In short, knowing the language of the speaker implies that we know quite a lot about the rules which govern his selection of speech symbols. It means that we are less uncertain about what will be said than we would be if the speaker did not operate under these known restrictions.

If we define information transmission as the rate of change in our *a priori* uncertainty, then we must say that the English language conveys less information than it could convey. This reduction in information that occurs when we pass from what might have been said (given the same vocabulary) to what actually is said is called "redundancy."

Special languages—cant, patois, technical talk—all involve additional restrictions and, for the listener familiar with them, entail increased redundancy. What we wish to do here is to consider one particular sublanguage of English and estimate the reduction in information transmission from what could be transmitted using alphabetical sequences. The language considered is that used in the control of aircraft by the operator of a control tower at a military airbase. It is made up of sentences like: "Air Force 5264. Ready number one in take-off position. Over." Or: "Extend your base. We have a C-54 on final."

---

* Reproduced by permission from *The Journal of the Acoustical Society of America*, Vol. 24, No. 6, 595–96, November, 1952.

These messages form a subset of the set of all possible English sentences —which in turn is a subset of all possible English letter sequences.

What this means can be illustrated fairly simple. All that is required is for you to imagine the set of all possible permutations of the English alphabet and a space symbol. Each point in this set represents a possible sequence of letters.

We could now, in principle, go through this set of letter sequences and select out those sequences that are acceptable as English sentences. This will clearly cut down the size of our original set. The knowledge that we are operating within this subset of English sentences reduces our initial uncertainty. And Shannon[1] has developed a technique that permits us to estimate how much this reduction amounts to. Essentially, we ask our subjects to guess at successive letters of English text. When we do this, we find that the subject can exploit his implicit knowledge of the statistical structure of the language and predict the English sequence considerably better than he can predict sequences of letters chosen at random.

If we now ask the same subjects to guess at the text of control tower messages, we find that prediction is still further improved. The uncertainty of our subjects was, on the average, about 28 per cent of their uncertainty regarding random sequences of letters and spaces—that is, of course, subjects who are familiar with control tower language. They were, in fact, control tower operators. (Actually, people who are not practiced in this strange sublanguage do just about as well. The airplane and its control has apparently been absorbed into our linguistic culture.)

However, this is still an overestimate of the uncertainty, or unpredictability, of messages in the actual situation. The figure above is arrived at when we select letter sequences at random from the set of admissible tower messages. In any given instance, the message is, of course, not generated at random. The pilot, for example, knows whether he is landing or taking off and this (the situational context) further restricts the set of possible messages.

In order to estimate these situational constraints we described a group of hypothetical situations to 100 Air Force pilots and asked them to predict the tower message. For practical reasons we could not use Shannon's guessing game technique, so we adopted another device.

The messages the pilots predicted for us are rather easily split up into content units—phases that have the same meaning—e.g., gear down and locked, gear in the green—or that differ only with respect to the numbers or place names involved:—runway zero nine, runway two zero. A message is made up of a sequence of these message units. And it is at this level that the immediate situation seems to operate by determining what message units will be selected and in what order they will occur. These units, thought of as letter sequences, are subject to the linguistic con-

---

[1] C. E. Shannon, *Bell System Tech. Jour.*, Vol. 30, 1951, pp. 50–64.

straints that we have already estimated. In effect, we have the physical situation determining the gross uncertainty of the message (in terms of content units) and the linguistic constraints determining the uncertainty of the units (as sequences of letters and spaces).

To illustrate, let us consider a specific case. The pilot is told: *You are coming in to land. Ceiling and visibility unlimited. You have just called in: "Andrews Tower. This is Air Force 1234. Eight miles south of your station. Landing instructions please."* Each statement sets up additional restrictions on the set of possible tower messages.

If we now look at the actual distribution of predicted messages which we obtained in this case, we find that they are sequences of selections from only 13 message units. Furthermore, these elements do not appear with equal frequency, nor does any single message include all 13 elements. A large number of possible messages thus turn out to be impossible—or at any rate highly improbable. The message set is thus further reduced.

Lastly, this language has, at the level of content units, its own peculiar

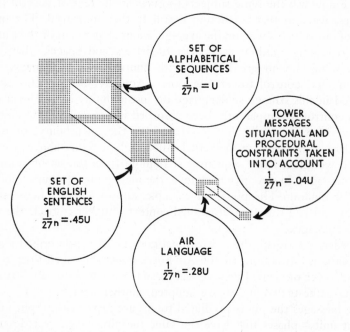

FIG. 1. Schematic representation of the reduction in size of the message set and consequent reduction in uncertainty (U) as additional message restrictions are taken into account.

grammar, known as *RT procedure.* The pilot knows this procedure (though ours didn't know it very well) and this procedure fixes the order in which particular units are selected to make up the predicted message.

With such a small sample we cannot determine the total effect of these sequential dependencies in restricting the message class. But we can estimate these constraints over two or three units. When we do this for this particular case, we find that the pilot's uncertainty of the message (in terms of content units) is about 80 per cent less than it would have been if the units were equally likely and messages were generated by a random selection of content units (with no repeats).

This figure of 80 per cent varies somewhat with the particular situation. For the 15 different situations that we chose, it averages 86 per cent.

In other words, the situational context, including the pilot's knowledge of procedures, reduces the gross uncertainty of the message about 86 per cent. Linguistic constraints reduce the residual uncertainty, in terms of letter sequences, another 72 per cent—giving us an estimated redundancy, with respect to what could have been conveyed using letter and space sequences, of approximately 96 per cent. The entire process is illustrated in Figure 1.

This is a large figure and any communication system which tolerates so much redundancy is in some sense inefficient. The situation is not as bad, however, as might at first be imagined. This is a noisy system. In part, at least, it is unavoidably noisy. It is also a system with a low tolerance for error—planes are more expensive than transmission time or band width—and redundancy is an effective means of combating noise and error. In other words, we may not transmit much information, but what is transmitted is important and the high degree of redundancy is a form of insurance—a sort of running check on our transmission.

19. OPINIONS AND SOCIAL PRESSURE*

Solomon E. Asch

That social influences shape every person's practices, judgments and beliefs is a truism to which anyone will readily assent. A child masters his "native" dialect down to the finest nuances; a member of a tribe of cannibals accepts cannibalism as altogether fitting and proper. All the social sciences take their departure from the observation of the profound effects that groups exert on their members. For psychologists, group pressure upon the minds of individuals raises a host of questions they would like to investigate in detail.

How, and to what extent, do social forces constrain people's opinions and attitudes? This question is especially pertinent in our day. The same epoch that has witnessed the unprecedented technical extension of communication has also brought into existence the deliberate manipulation of opinion and the "engineering of consent." There are many good reasons why, as citizens and as scientists, we should be concerned with studying the ways in which human beings form their opinions and the role that social conditions play.

Studies of these questions began with the interest in hypnosis aroused by the French physician Jean Martin Charcot (a teacher of Sigmund Freud) toward the end of the 19th century. Charcot believed that only hysterical patients could be fully hypnotized, but this view was soon challenged by two other physicians, Hyppolyte Bernheim and A. A. Liebault, who demonstrated that they could put most people under the hypnotic spell. Bernheim proposed that hypnosis was but an extreme form of a normal psychological process which became known as "suggestibility." It was shown that monotonous reiteration of instructions could induce in normal persons in the waking state involuntary bodily changes such as swaying or rigidity of the arms, and sensations such as warmth and odor.

It was not long before social thinkers seized upon these discoveries as a basis for explaining numerous social phenomena, from the spread of opinion to the formation of crowds and the following of leaders. The sociologist Gabriel Tarde summed it all up in the aphorism: "Social man is a somnambulist."

When the new discipline of social psychology was born at the beginning of this century, its first experiments were essentially adaptations of the suggestion demonstration. The technique generally followed a simple

* Reproduced by permission from *Scientific American* 193 #5, November, 1955, pp. 31–5.

242

plan. The subjects, usually college students, were asked to give their opinions or preferences concerning various matters; some time later they were again asked to state their choices, but now they were also informed of the opinions held by authorities or large groups of their peers on the same matters. (Often the alleged consensus was fictitious.) Most of these studies had substantially the same result: confronted with opinions contrary to their own, many subjects apparently shifted their judgments in the direction of the views of the majorities or the experts. The late psychologist Edward L. Thorndike reported that he had succeeded in modifying the aesthetic preferences of adults by this procedure. Other psychologists reported that people's evaluations of the merit of a literary passage could be raised or lowered by ascribing the passage to different authors. Apparently the sheer weight of numbers or authority sufficed to change opinions, even when no arguments for the opinions themselves were provided.

Now the very ease of success in these experiments arouses suspicion. Did the subjects actually change their opinions, or were the experimental victories scored only on paper? On grounds of common sense, one must question whether opinions are generally as watery as these studies indicate. There is some reason to wonder whether it was not the investigators who, in their enthusiasm for a theory, were suggestible, and whether the ostensibly gullible subjects were not providing answers which they thought good subjects were expected to give.

The investigations were guided by certain underlying assumptions, which today are common currency and account for much that is thought and said about the operations of propaganda and public opinion. The assumptions are that people submit uncritically and painlessly to external manipulation by suggestion or prestige, and that any given idea or value can be "sold" or "unsold" without reference to its merits. We should be skeptical, however, of the supposition that the power of social pressure necessarily implies uncritical submission to it: independence and the capacity to rise above group passion are also open to human beings. Further, one may question on psychological grounds whether it is possible as a rule to change a person's judgment of a situation or an object without first changing his knowledge or assumptions about it.

In what follows I shall describe some experiments in an investigation of the effects of group pressure which was carried out recently with the help of a number of my associates. The tests not only demonstrate the operations of group pressure upon individuals but also illustrate a new kind of attack on the problem and some of the more subtle questions that it raises.

A group of seven to nine young men, all college students, are assembled in a classroom for a "psychological experiment" in visual judgment. The experimenter informs them that they will be comparing the lengths of lines. He shows two large white cards. On one is a single vertical black line—the standard whose length is to be matched. On the other card are three vertical lines of various lengths. The subjects are to choose the one that is of the same length as the line on the other card. One of the three actually is of the same length; the other two are substantially different, the difference ranging from three quarters of an inch to an inch and three quarters.

The experiment opens uneventfully. The subjects announce their answers in the order in which they have been seated in the room, and on the first round every person chooses the same matching line. Then a second set of cards is exposed; again the group is unanimous. The members appear ready to endure politely another boring experiment. On the third trial there is an unexpected disturbance. One person near the end of the group disagrees with all the others in his selection of the matching line. He looks surprised, indeed incredulous, about the disagreement. On the following trial he disagrees again, while the others remain unanimous in their choice. The dissenter becomes more and more worried and hesitant as the disagreement continues in succeeding trials; he may pause before announcing his answer and speak in a low voice, or he may smile in an embarrassed way.

What the dissenter does not know is that all the other members of the group were instructed by the experimenter beforehand to give incorrect answers in unanimity at certain points. The single individual who is not a party to this prearrangement is the focal subject of our experiment. He is placed in a position in which, while he is actually giving the correct answers, he finds himself unexpectedly in a minority of one, opposed by a unanimous and arbitrary majority with respect to a clear and simple fact. Upon him we have brought to bear two opposed forces: the evidence of his senses and the unanimous opinion of a group of his peers. Also, he must declare his judgments in public, before a majority which has also stated its position publicly.

The instructed majority occasionally reports correctly in order to reduce the possibility that the naïve subject will suspect collusion against him. (In only a few cases did the subject actually show suspicion; when this happened, the experiment was stopped and the results were not counted.) There are 18 trials in each series, and on 12 of these the majority responds erroneously.

How do people respond to group pressure in this situation? I shall report first the statistical results of a series in which a total of 123 subjects from three institutions of higher learning (not including my own, Swarthmore College) were placed in the minority situation described above.

Two alternatives were open to the subject: he could act independently, repudiating the majority, or he could go along with the majority, repudiating the evidence of his senses. Of the 123 put to the test, a considerable percentage yielded to the majority. Whereas in ordinary circumstances individuals matching the lines will make mistakes less than 1 per cent of the time, under group pressure the minority subjects swung to acceptance of the misleading majority's wrong judgments in 36.8 per cent of the selections.

Of course individuals differed in response. At one extreme, about one quarter of the subjects were completely independent and never agreed with the erroneous judgments of the majority. At the other extreme, some individuals went with the majority nearly all the time. The performances of individuals in this experiment tend to be highly consistent. Those who strike out on the path of independence do not, as a rule, succumb to the majority even over an extended series of trials, while those who choose the path of compliance are unable to free themselves as the ordeal is prolonged.

The reasons for the startling individual differences have not yet been investigated in detail. At this point we can only report some tentative generalizations from talks with the subjects, each of whom was interviewed at the end of the experiment. Among the independent individuals were many who held fast because of staunch confidence in their own judgment. The most significant fact about them was not absence of responsiveness to the majority but a capacity to recover from doubt and to re-establish their equilibrium. Others who acted independently came to believe that the majority was correct in its answers, but they continued their dissent on the simple ground that it was their obligation to call the play as they saw it.

Among extremely yielding persons we found a group who quickly reached the conclusion: "I am wrong, they are right." Others yielded in order "not to spoil your results." Many of the individuals who went along suspected that the majority were "sheep" following the first responder, or that the majority were victims of an optical illusion; nevertheless these suspicions failed to free them at the moment of decision. More disquieting were the reactions of subjects who construed their difference from the majority as a sign of some general deficiency in themselves, which at all costs they must hide. On this basis they desperately tried to merge with the majority, not realizing the longer-range consequences to themselves. All the yielding subjects underestimated the frequency with which they conformed.

Which aspect of the influence of a majority is more important—the size of the majority or its unanimity? The experiment was modified to examine this question. In one series the size of the opposition was varied from one to 15 persons. The results showed a clear trend. When a subject was confronted with only a single individual who contradicted his answers, he was swayed little: he continued to answer independently and

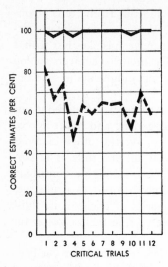

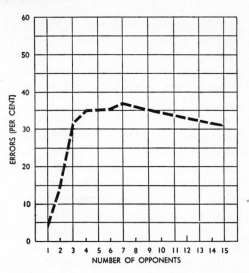

Error of 123 subjects, each of whom compared lines in the presence of six to eight opponents, is plotted in the broken curve. The accuracy of judgments not under pressure is indicated in black.

Size of Majority which opposed them had an effect on the subjects. With a single opponent the subject erred only 3.6 per cent of the time; with two opponents he erred 13.6 per cent; three, 31.8 per cent; four, 35.1 per cent; six, 35.2 per cent; seven, 37.1 per cent; nine, 35.1 per cent; 15, 31.2 per cent.

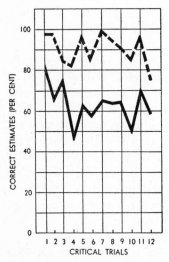

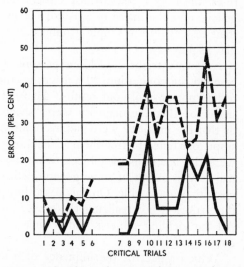

Two Subjects supporting each other against a majority made fewer errors (broken curve) than one subject did against a majority (black curve).

Partner Left Subject after six trials in a single experiment. The broken curve shows the error of the subject when the partner "deserted" to the majority. Black curve shows error when partner merely left the room.

correctly in nearly all the trials. When the opposition was increased to two, the pressure became substantial: minority subjects now accepted the wrong answer 13.6 per cent of the time. Under the pressure of a majority of three, the subjects' errors jumped to 31.8 per cent. But further increases in the size of the majority apparently did not increase the weight of the pressure substantially. Clearly the size of the opposition is important only up to a point.

Disturbance of the majority's unanimity had a striking effect. In this experiment the subject was given the support of a truthful partner—either another individual who did not know of the prearranged agreement among the rest of the group, or a person who was instructed to give correct answers throughout.

The presence of a supporting partner depleted the majority of much of its power. Its pressure on the dissenting individual was reduced to one fourth: that is, subjects answered incorrectly only one fourth as often as under the pressure of a unanimous majority. . . . The weakest persons did not yield as readily. Most interesting were the reactions to the partner. Generally, the feeling toward him was one of warmth and closeness; he was credited with inspiring confidence. However, the subjects repudiated the suggestion that the partner decided them to be independent.

Was the partner's effect a consequence of his dissent, or was it related to his accuracy? We now introduced into the experimental group a person who was instructed to dissent from the majority but also to disagree with the subject. In some experiments the majority was always to choose the worst of the comparison lines and the instructed dissenter to pick the line that was closer to the length of the standard one; in others the majority was consistently intermediate and the dissenter most in error. In this manner we were able to study the relative influence of "compromising" and "extremist" dissenters.

Again the results are clear. When a moderate dissenter is present, the effect of the majority on the subject decreases by approximately one third, and extremes of yielding disappear. Moreover, most of the errors the subjects do make are moderate, rather than flagrant. In short, the dissenter largely controls the choice of errors. To this extent the subjects broke away from the majority even while bending to it.

On the other hand, when the dissenter always chose the line that was more flagrantly different from the standard, the results were of quite a different kind. The extremist dissenter produced a remarkable freeing of the subjects; their errors dropped to only 9 per cent. Furthermore, all the errors were of the moderate variety. We were able to conclude that dissent *per se* increased independence and moderated the errors that occurred, and that the direction of dissent exerted consistent effects.

In all the foregoing experiments each subject was observed only in a single setting. We now turned to studying the effects upon a given individual of a change in the situation to which he was exposed. The first experiment examined the consequences of losing or gaining a partner. The instructed partner began by answering correctly on the first six trials. With his support the subject usually resisted pressure from the majority: 18 of 27 subjects were completely independent. But after six trials the partner joined the majority. As soon as he did so, there was an abrupt rise in the subjects' errors. Their submission to the majority was just about as frequent as when the minority subject was opposed by a unanimous majority throughout.

It was surprising to find that the experience of having had a partner and of having braved the majority opposition with him had failed to strengthen the individuals' independence. Questioning at the conclusion of the experiment suggested that we had overlooked an important circumstance; namely, the strong specific effect of "desertion" by the partner to the other side. We therefore changed the conditions so that the partner would simply leave the group at the proper point. (To allay suspicion it was announced in advance that he had an appointment with the dean.) In this form of the experiment, the partner's effect outlasted his presence. The errors increased after his departure, but less markedly than after a partner switched to the majority.

In a variant of this procedure the trials began with the majority unanimously giving correct answers. Then they gradually broke away until on the sixth trial the naïve subject was alone and the group unanimously against him. As long as the subject had anyone on his side, he was almost invariably independent, but as soon as he found himself alone, the tendency to conform to the majority rose abruptly.

As might be expected, an individual's resistance to group pressure in these experiments depends to a considerable degree on how wrong the majority is. We varied the discrepancy between the standard line and the other lines systematically, with the hope of reaching a point where the error of the majority would be so glaring that every subject would repudiate it and choose independently. In this we regretfully did not succeed. Even when the difference between the lines was seven inches, there were still some who yielded to the error of the majority.

The study provides clear answers to a few relatively simple questions, and it raises many others that await investigation. We would like to know the degree of consistency of persons in situations which differ in content and structure. If consistency of independence or conformity in behavior is shown to be a fact, how is it functionally related to qualities of character and personality? In what ways is independence related to sociological or cultural conditions? Are leaders more independent than other people, or are they adept at following their followers? These and many other questions may perhaps be answerable by investigations of the type described here.

Life in society requires consensus as an indispensable condition. But consensus, to be productive, requires that each individual contribute independently out of his experience and insight. When consensus comes under the dominance of conformity, the social process is polluted and the individual at the same time surrenders the powers on which his functioning as a feeling and thinking being depends. That we have found the tendency to conformity in our society so strong that reasonably intelligent and well-meaning young people are willing to call white black is a matter of concern. It raises questions about our ways of education and about the values that guide our conduct.

Yet anyone inclined to draw too pessimistic conclusions from this report would do well to remind himself that the capacities for independence are not to be underestimated. He may also draw some consolation from a further observation: those who participated in this challenging experiment agreed nearly without exception that independence was preferable to conformity.

20. FUNCTION OF EXPRESSED DISAGREEMENT IN SMALL GROUP PROCESSES*

E. PAUL TORRANCE

WE FIND ourselves today in a somewhat paradoxical situation concerning the matter of willingness to disagree with others. On the one hand, psychologists, sociologists, educators, and management experts have placed much emphasis on the importance of maintaining harmony, congeniality, and agreement in groups—business, industry, family, military, and so on. On the other hand, many leaders have been bemoaning the fact that we seem to be "living in an age of conformity" and that "controversy is a lost art" (4). "Brainwashing" is gradually becoming a part of our vocabulary and seems destined to take on a much broader connotation than communist indoctrination.

One important piece of recent research (1) paints a rather alarming picture concerning the extent to which we are susceptible to "brainwashing" in its broader sense. The researcher, Asch, generated a disagreement between single individuals and small groups concerning a clear and simple matter of *fact* in the immediate environment. Only one-fourth of his subjects adhered to their own correct judgments when confronted with the different and erroneous judgments of groups.

What, then, is the meaning of this paradox for small group processes? First, I shall present some findings from our program of research at the USAF Survival Training School at Stead Air Force Base which tell us something about the nature and function of disagreement in small group processes. Then, I shall attempt to summarize possible applications of these findings in managerial activities.

IS DISAGREEMENT "GOOD" OR "BAD"?

Let us deal first with the most obvious question: "Is disagreement "good" or "bad" insofar as small group processes are concerned?" To answer this question, we must look at what it does to both the group and to individuals who compose the group. We have a considerable amount of evidence about both.

---

* Paper prepared for presentation to Institute of Management Sciences, New York City, October 21, 1955. Later published in Social Forces, Vol. 35, No. 4, 1957.

The author is indebted to Kenyon Runner for his critical reading of the original draft and to Robert C. Ziller who conducted some of the studies on which the paper is based.

Group Performance

In a study of aircrew effectiveness in combat over Korea (9), we found that the more effective crews in comparison with the less effective crews and crews which did not get into combat were characterized by greater tolerance of disagreement. Several studies (9, 12, 19) support the contention that the more effective groups are characterized by greater participation, initially wider divergence of expressed judgment, and greater acceptance of decisions.

Individual Performance

The effect of disagreement on group process cannot be fully understood without examining the effect willingness or unwillingness to disagree with others has upon the individual. Research findings indicate that certain individuals show a generalized willingness to oppose others and disagree when the situation requires it. In a series of studies of the personality requirements for survival, such individuals were found to produce superior results in the form of more adaptive behavior in survival situations (14 and 15), willingness to take calculated risks (17), and unwillingness to accept defeat (14). In our studies of USAF jet aces in Korea (11, 18), we found that this characteristic was typical of the ace when compared with his less successful colleagues. To begin with, he managed to get into air-to-air combat only because he was unwilling to take "no" for an answer. He has made a practice of testing the limits in opposition to accepted procedures and tries to obtain maximum results from himself, his aircraft, his flight, and the situation.

SPECIFIC EFFECTS ON GROUP PROCESSES

Now that we have cited evidence which indicates that when disagreement directs attention to group goals, its effects upon group and individual performance is "good," let us see more specifically what it does to group processes.

It Increases the Scale of Judgment

Very obviously, if there is willingness to disagree with the group, there will be an increase in the scale of judgment considered in making a decision. In a decision-making study (19), we found that the accuracy of decisions is related to the scale of judgment. We also found that, to some extent, the scale of judgment can be manipulated by the manner of obtaining individual judgments. If opinions were solicited *first* from low status individuals, the scale of judgment tended to be greatest. When everyone's judgment was solicited, even when opinions were solicited *first* from high status individuals, the scale of judgment tended to be greater than according to usual procedures. This result simply confirms observations that low status individuals are reluctant to express their judgments either in opposition to those of high status or in fear that they might be in opposition to them.

It Decreases Chances of Misunderstanding

Again, it seems obvious that if you do not communicate your real opinion to me, I am likely to misunderstand you and this is certain to affect group processes. A good illustration is found in an intensive interview study of three training groups of equipment technicians caught in a blizzard in the high Sierras (16). The instructors of these groups had shown themselves unusually intolerant of expressions of disagreement, especially by a particular trainee who was the natural and powerful leader of three groups. At a critical stage following the blizzard, the instructors led the groups down an unfrozen creek and continued the trek in sub-zero weather for about four hours before stopping to pitch camp for the night. As a result, 7 or 8 members of the group suffered severe frostbite. All 20 trainees and 7 instructors were carefully interviewed. Almost without exception, the trainees maintained that they knew that the proper thing to do was to stop and dry their feet and that they wanted to do just this. They felt, however, that a protest would be useless as the instructors had made it clear that instructor judgment was not to be questioned. Each of the instructors also maintained that he wanted the group to stop, make a fire, and dry feet and footgear. They did not do so because they felt that the trainees were apathetic and would do nothing to take care of themselves. Thus, instructors misinterpreted as apathy the trainees' unwillingness to disagree.

This may be an example of groups going to dangerous extremes in seeking revenge against dictatorial leadership. It may illustrate aggressive over-compliance. The men may have been seeking to validate their assumption that the instructors were in fact stupid, which would give them grounds for more open rebellion later. Or, the instructors may have seen this as an opportunity to validate and punish the stupidity of the trainees. They may have abdicated their power role in view of earlier frictions and were seeking to regain it by showing how badly their direction was needed. Temporary abdication without notice is a rather common group phenomenon and usually results in trouble.

Ability to Adapt

If willingness to disagree is related to individual ability to adapt, it is only reasonable to expect that group processes are affected accordingly. Willingness to disagree has meant the difference between survival and failure to survive in group situations (10, 13). For example, individuals in survival situations are usually more willing to try strange foods than groups (3). A person alone has only his own conservatism to overcome. When groups did make this adaptation, it was usually the result of some member's disagreeing and saying, "I'd rather eat this than starve." In some cases, the effect was immediate; in others, it came only after time.

Willingness to Take Calculated Risks

Willingness to disagree appears to increase willingness to take calculated risks. In group decision-making experiments (20, 21), we found that decisions requiring greater risk were made by crews in which decision making was shared with the group and by crews whose leaders were more tolerant of disagreement. Apparently two factors are at work. Knowing where other members stand on an issue clears up misunderstandings and encourages the choice of more risky alternatives. Knowing that the group supports him in the more risky decision also gives the leader courage.

Willingness to Accept the Group's Decision

Frequently executives complain that everybody seems to go along with their suggestions at a meeting, but later they discover that the members of the group do not really support them after all (7). The result is that the decision is ineffectively carried out. In one experiment (9), we obtained individual judgments both before and after group discussion and decision. We obtained evidence which suggests that a higher degree of consensus is actually obtained when there is greater expression of disagreement. This also appears to be related to combat effectiveness of bomber crews. Apparently, individuals feel that their opinions have been considered and are more willing to accept the group judgment.

Negative Effects

Disagreement is not without its negative effects on small group process. One such negative effect which we have identified occurs when there is what we have termed "negative identification" with some member of the group, particularly the leader. "Negative identification" tends to occur when the values, background and/or personality of an individual are so deviant from those of the rest of the group that they cannot identify with him. Any opinion he expresses, no matter how valuable or accurate, brings immediate and forceful disagreement. Attention to interpersonal relations has become greater than attention to the task.

Just as person-oriented disagreement is almost certain to have a negative effect on small group processes, person-oriented *agreement* may also impede small group process. This occurs when there is over-dependence upon an individual or group, resulting in a lack of willingness to disagree and a lack of readiness even privately to question authority or consensus. An individual may find it easier not to resist. Over-compliance may result from negative experience with person-oriented disagreement. This emphasizes the need for distinguishing between task-oriented and person-oriented disagreement.

FACTORS WHICH IMPEDE DISAGREEMENT IN GROUPS

Our research has also enabled us to understand some of the factors which impede the expression of disagreement in groups. The ones with which we have dealt are: status, permanency of the group, and leadership techniques.

Status or Power Differences

In one series of experiments (12), four types of problems were given crews composed of men with clearly differentiated statuses or power. It was found that influence on the group decisions was consistently in direct proportion to the power or status of the group members. The less powerful members of three-man groups demonstrated an unwillingness to disagree with the most powerful member of the group and this adversely affected the quality of the decisions. Members of the lowest status tended to accept their position and made the least attempt to influence the group's decision even when they had the correct solution. They retaliated by showing the most resistance to accepting the group's decisions. Those of intermediate status tended to make most effort to influence the group's decisions but felt frustrated and resisted accepting final decisions.

Permanency of the Group

The experiment just described was modified by rearranging crews so that the same power structure was maintained but no one was in a group with a member of his regular crew. Although differences in power impeded expression of disagreement and was a factor in influence on the decision, the effect was consistently and significantly decreased. The resulting decisions were consistently and significantly of better quality.

Apparently an individual hesitates to express an opinion which conflicts with that of another for fear that the latter will be offended or will "hold it against him." If he is in a group which will no longer have power over him, he tends to be freer of this fear and is willing to express his opinions more accurately. In more or less permanent groups, opinions and suggestions of high-status members tend to be accepted without question. Such groups are also likely to be psychologically "in a rut" and fail to use their resources. Also, if the individual perceives the leadership as "good," he is less likely to question the opinions of the leader. He finds it more comfortable to think as the leader thinks, or as the group thinks, because his experience has taught him that he is usually wrong when he thinks otherwise. He may have more faith in their decisions than in his own. This same man in a strange group may not have much faith in the decisions of the leader or of the group. He feels more dependent upon his own opinions and is as a result more willing to define them well enough to express them. Finally, the low-status member of a permanent group who does *not* accept the group leadership may not express his opinions simply because he feels it is a waste of time. Mutual communication may have become impossible. It is over-compliance based on rebellion rather than acceptance. Such an individual may become extremely willing to express his opinions in a temporary group.

Leadership Technique

While there are perhaps more potent factors affecting the quality of and satisfaction with group decisions, such as the atmosphere of trust, group cohesiveness, and the like, leadership technique appears to be one factor (20). Experiments involving four different leadership techniques support a preference for a technique which permits the expression of judgments both by the leader and by the members. Crew members disliked most techniques which did not give consideration to the judgment of members. A technique which permitted free expression of opinions by members but restricted the leader from expressing his opinions was disliked almost as much.

MEANING OF THE FINDINGS IN MANAGERIAL ACTIVITIES

Scientists always feel a little uneasy in recommending the application of their findings to situations differing from those in which they were established. In fundamental research in the behavioral sciences, however, we should be able to do this to some extent. Thus, I shall hazard some speculations about the potential applications of the foregoing findings in managerial activities.

First, management needs to accept the fact that task-oriented disagreement is almost always "good." You have been long conditioned to believe that it is "bad." Parents become quite disturbed if their children argue or fight. Teachers, managers, and supervisors behave similarly. You may be afraid that you are "playing with fire." "What if somebody blows up? What will the higher ups think? Will I lose the respect of my subordinates by letting them disagree with me?" Perhaps you are neglecting to recognize the fundamental difference between task-oriented and person-oriented disagreement. Or, you may be too prone to assume that all differences of opinion are a threat to managerial control.

I think one extremely valuable application for management comes from the findings concerning individual performance and willingness to oppose others. Willingness to disagree is a major characteristic of the aces —the high achievers. It also characterizes those best able to meet frustration, those most willing to take calculated risks, and those who have the most "will to fight." In spite of the fact that most really outstanding people appear to have this characteristic, many of them fare rather badly at the hands of management both in business and in military situations. They are seen as threats by superiors and are frequently not tolerated. Too often the greatest rewards are for conformity.

Understanding of the specific effects of disagreement on group process should provide a basis for assessing the value of disagreement in a particular conference. Does it increase the scale of judgment considered and thereby the quality of the decision? Does it contribute to the elimination of misunderstandings? Does it increase the group's ability to adapt? Does it increase the group's willingness to take calculated risks in order to succeed? If you can answer "yes" to some or all of these, the disagreements are constructive. But, if the disagreements become centered in power roles and personalities, they are destructive both to the unity of the group and its capability for productivity. Perhaps we need a new definition of "group unity." I submit that what we are looking for is a group which can tolerate disagreement without becoming emotionally involved. A group in which disagreements are *not* expressed may be the most emotional group.

We need to know much more about factors which impede expression of disagreement. We do know that power or status differences have to be handled in a non-suppressive manner. Basic perhaps is a clear demonstration that disagreement is not going to be punished. The finding that status effects are decreased in temporary or rearranged groups has an interesting management application. When you want creative thinking done on a problem, do not assign it to a permanent group in which some members have power over others. Members must have appropriate backgrounds for the assignment, but select people who do not have power over one another. Also, remember that your subordinates want to know where you stand on an issue.

It would not be realistic to ignore possibilities of negative effects of disagreement and difficulties in obtaining consensus. Guetzkow and Gyr (2) have studied the conditions under which conflict results in consensus. Lee's (5) procedure for "coercing" disagreement when there is a deadlock represents one approach. (Essentially, his procedure requires that full hearing be given each side of an issue without the interruption of counter-arguments, denials, and refutations.) Some of the techniques developed by group psychotherapists and social workers also appear to offer promise.

You may accept the wisdom of permitting and even encouraging the expression of disagreement, but this does not mean that you will always find it comfortable. We do not like for people to disagree with us. We are inclined to see all disagreement as evidence of personal rejection. We need to differentiate person-centered from task-centered disagreement and to transform the former into the latter whenever possible. Finally, let me urge you to learn to identify with the group's decision rather than with your own initial opinion.

REFERENCES

1. Asch, S. E. *Studies of Independence and Submission to Group Pressure. I. A Minority of One against a Unanimous Majority.* Swarthmore, Pa.: Swarthmore College, 1955.

2. Guetzkow, H. and Gyr, J. "An Analysis of Conflict in Decision-Making Groups," *Human Relations,* 1954, 7, pp. 367–82.

3. Howard, R. A. *999 Survived.* Maxwell Air Force Base, Ala.: Arctic, Desert, Tropic Information Center, 1950. (ADTIC Publication T–100.)

4. Kaplan, A. "The Lost Art of Controversy," *Adult Leadership,* June, 1954, 3(2), pp. 2–3.

5. Lee, I. J. "Procedure for 'Coercing' Agreement," *Harvard Bus. Rev.,* 1954, 32, pp. 39–45.

6. Mason, R. *Psychological and Training Factors Affecting Survival Ration Acceptability.* Randolph Field, Tex.: Air Force Personnel and Training Research Center, Crew Research Laboratory. To be published.

7. Mellinger, G. "Trust and Consequences," *Adult Leadership,* February 1955, 3(8), pp. 17–19.

8. Meyer, B. et al. *Studies of the Effectiveness of Combat Briefings.* Washington, D.C.: Human Factors Operations Research Laboratories, 1953. (HFORL *Memorandum* No. 40.)

9. Torrance, E. P. *Crew Performance in a Test Situation as a Predictor of Field and Combat Performance.* Washington, D.C.: Human Factors Operations Research Laboratories, 1953. (*HFORL Report* No. 33.)

10. Torrance, E. P. "The Behavior of Small Groups under the Stress Conditions of Survival," *Amer. Sociol. Rev.,* 1954, 19, pp. 751–55.

11. Torrance, E. P. *The Development of a Preliminary Life Experience Inventory for the Study of Fighter Interceptor Pilot Combat Effectiveness.* San Antonio, Tex.: Air Force Personnel and Training Research Center, 1954. (*Research Bulletin* AFPTRC–TR–54–89.)

12. Torrance, E. P. *Some Consequences of Power Differences on Decisions in B-26 Crews.* San Antonio, Tex.: Air Force Personnel and Training Research Center, Lackland Air Force Base, 1954. (*Research Bulletin* AFPTRC–TR–54–128).

13. Torrance, E. P. "Some Issues Regarding Power Roles in Emergencies and Extreme Conditions." Paper presented at Conference on Small Group Behavior sponsored by Social Science Research Council, Monterey, Calif., 24–26, April, 1955.

14. Torrance, E. P. *Frustration Behavior and Personality.* Randolph Field, Tex.: Air Force Personnel and Training Research Center, Crew Research Laboratory. To be published.

15. Torrance, E. P. *Personality Factors and Survival Ration Acceptability.* Randolph Field, Tex.: Air Force Personnel and Training Research Cen-

ter, Crew Research Laboratory, 1955. (*Technical Memorandum* CRL–TM–55–9.)

16. TORRANCE, E. P., LaFORGE, G. R., MASON, R., and LEVI, M. *The Blizzard Study: Groups under Stress.* Randolph Field, Tex.: Air Force Personnel and Training Research Center, Grew Research Laboratory. To be published.

17. TORRANCE, E. P. and ZILLER, R. C. *Risk and Life Experience: Development of a Scale for Measuring Risk-Taking Tendencies.* Randolph Field, Tex.: Air Force Personnel and Training Research Center, Crew Research Laboratory. To be published.

18. TORRANCE, E. P., RUSH, C. H., KOHN, H. B., and DOUGHTY, J. M. *Factors in Fighter Interceptor Pilot Combat Effectiveness: A Summary Report.* San Antonio, Tex.: Air Force Personnel and Training Research Center, Lackland Air Force Base. To be published.

19. ZILLER, R. C. "Scales of Judgment: A Determinant of the Accuracy of Group Decisions," *Human Relations,* 1955, *8*, pp. 153–64.

20. ZILLER, R. C. *Four Techniques of Group Decision Making under Conditions of Uncertainty.* Randolph Field, Tex.: Air Force Personnel and Training Research Center, Crew Research Laboratory. To be published.

21. ZILLER, R. C. *Leader Acceptance of Responsibility for Group Action under Conditions of Uncertainty and Risk.* Randolph Field, Tex.: Air Force Personnel and Training Research Center, Crew Research Laboratory. To be published.

21. THE IMPACT OF CERTAIN COMMUNICATION NETS UPON ORGANIZATION AND PERFORMANCE IN TASK-ORIENTED GROUPS*

HAROLD GUETZKOW AND HERBERT A. SIMON[0]

BAVELAS, Smith and Leavitt[1] have posed the problem: what effect do communication patterns have upon the operation of groups? To study this problem they designed a laboratory situation that is a prototype of those occurring in "natural" organizations existing in government and business. Each member of the group is given certain information. Their task is to assemble this information, use it to make a decision, and then issue orders based on the decision. This design provides a situation stripped of the complexities of large-scale social groups but retaining some essential characteristics of the organizational communication problem. In it we can examine how the communication net affects simultaneously (a) the development of the organization's internal structure, and (b) the group's performance of its operating task.

Leavitt made certain deductions from Bavelas' model of communication nets,[2] but his empirical studies[3] did not confirm the derivations. Leavitt explains the discrepancies in terms of such concepts as "different kinds of messages require very different clock times," and the failure of his subjects "to gravitate to the theoretically 'best' operating organization."[4] It is the purpose of this paper to present an alternative theory of these miniature organizations, and to test this theory by new empirical data and by comparison with Leavitt's original empirical findings.

The proposed explanation requires that a sharp distinction be made between: (a) the effects of communication restrictions upon performance of the operating task; and (b) the effects of the restrictions upon a group's ability to organize itself for such performance. That is, instead of

* Reproduced from *Management Science*, Vol. 1, Nos. 3 and 4, April–July, 1955.

[0] This work was supported by a grant from the research funds of the Graduate School of Industrial Administration. Grateful thanks are due to Messrs. Wm. Dill, K. Hellfach, A. D. Martin, and F. Metzger, and to Mrs. Martha Pryor and Miss Anne Bowes for aid in the conduct of the investigation and help in analyzing its results.

[1] A. Bavelas, "Communication Patterns in Task-Oriented Groups," *Jour. of Acoustical Soc. of Amer.*, 1950, 22, pp. 725–30.

[2] A. Bavelas, "A Mathematical Model for Group Structures," *Appl. Anthrop.*, 1948, 7, pp. 16–30.

[3] H. J. Leavitt, "Some Effects of Certain Communication Patterns on Group Performance, *Jour. of Abnorm. and Soc. Psychol.*, 1951, 46, pp. 38–50.

[4] Leavitt, *ibid.*, pp. 46–47.

regarding the group's problem as unitary, it appears essential to separate the operating or "substantive" task from the organizational or "procedural" problem. Our hypothesis may be stated thus: Imposition of certain restrictions on the communication channels available to a group affects the efficiency of the group's performance, *not directly* by limiting the potential efficiency of task performance with optimal organization in the given net, *but indirectly* by handicapping their ability to organize themselves for efficient task performance.

Our empirical study involves basically a replication of Leavitt's work, but with essential modifications to permit us to study separately the group's performance of its operating task and its organizational task.

Each of 56 groups operated in the laboratory for about two hours, during which time the task was repeated twenty times. A fifteen minute pre-experimental training period was employed to reduce the task problem to a mere routine before the experiment with each group began. Each of the twenty task trial periods continued until the task was completed, the time required for completion varying from six minutes to less than one minute. Intertrial periods of not more than two minutes between successive trials provided the groups with an opportunity to solve the organizational problem. By signalling arrangement, the subjects were allowed to terminate the intertrial periods at any time they wished before the end of the two minutes allowed them.

The alternation of task trials with interpolated intertrial periods was suggested by analogy with the traditional "trial-after-trial" design employed in learning experiments in individual psychology. In terms of this analogy, the intertrial periods may be interpreted as "learning" periods, during which the subjects may work on their organizational plans. The task trial periods are then "test" periods, in which the progress of the group is tested by measuring the speed and efficiency of task performance.

Except for the explicit separation of trial and intertrial periods, our procedures paralleled those used by Leavitt and Smith. As will be indicated later, our results substantially replicate their findings.

In Section I, we shall set forth the theory from which our central hypothesis is derived. In Section II, we shall test the hypothesis with the new empirical data we have obtained. In Section III, we shall compare our findings with those of Leavitt.

I. SEPARATION OF OPERATING TASK FROM ORGANIZATIONAL PROBLEM: THEORETICAL CONSIDERATIONS

Description and Analysis of the Operating Task

Simon, Smithburg and Thompson argue that communication in a decision-making organization is two-fold:

Communications must flow to the decision center to provide the basis for decision, and the decision must be communicated from the decision center in order to influence other members of the organizations whose cooperation must be secured to carry out the decision.[5]

The Bavelas-Leavitt-Smith problem requires both processes. In the operating task each person must record which one symbol of six is held in common by the five members of the group. The same six symbols are used on each trial. At the beginning of each trial, each person is given a card on which is printed five symbols; the other symbol is missing. Each individual is lacking a different symbol. The problem on a given trial is to have the group discover and record the one symbol that no one is lacking. The variation in distribution of the symbols from trial to trial in this investigation followed the schedule used by Leavitt.[6]

Note the two-fold communication process involved in this line task:

(a) Information Flow: At the beginning of a trial each participant knows only one of the missing symbols—his own. The participant need not know all of the missing symbols for solution of the problem. Each group member needs to know only the answer to record it, or to "carry out the decision." There must, however, be sufficient exchange of information so that one or more persons can form the solution, or "make the decision."

(b) Decision Flow: Once an answer is formed by one or more persons in the group, it must be communicated to those who are unable to, or do not, make the decision themselves.

Before proceeding with the analysis, let us explain the mechanics of the experiment.[7] The subjects, seated around a circular table, were separated from each other by five vertical wooden partitions (Figure 1). They were able to pass messages to each other through interconnecting slots. During the operating trials, they interchanged messages written on pre-coded cards which contained places for information and answers. During the intertrials the subjects were free to write to each other uncoded messages on blank cards about their organizational arrangements. This meant the group could determine who would send information to whom, who would make the problem-decision, who would send the decision-order to whom.

When a subject had recorded the problem-decision, this fact was immediately conveyed to the experimenter. When all five persons had re-

---

[5] H. A. Simon, D. W. Smithburg, and V. A. Thompson, *Public Administration*, (New York: Knopf, 1950) p. 220.

[6] Leavitt, *op. cit.*, Figure 2, p. 40.

[7] Further details about the procedures of the experiment are available, and can be obtained from American Documentation Institute, 1719 N Street, N.W., Washington 6, D.C.

corded the solution, the trial automatically ended and the intertrial period began. The subjects were silent throughout the experiment, communicating only through pre-coded cards during the operating task trial and by written "free" messages during the intertrial periods. This enabled us to obtain a complete record of their communications.

Two hundred and eighty male freshmen engineering students at Car-

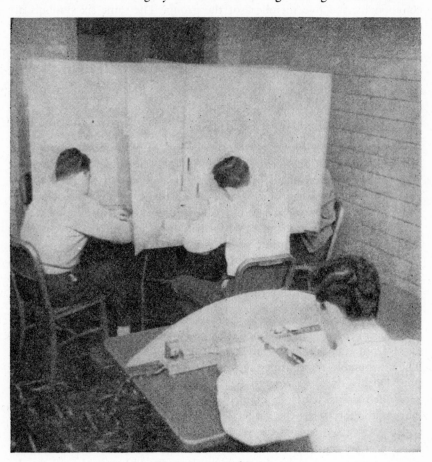

FIG. 1. Experimental Set-up

negie Institute of Technology served as subjects for the experiment. The two hours devoted to the experiment were a required substitute for one class and an out-of-class assignment in a required freshman course. Most subjects were not very well acquainted with each other. Each group was composed of one man from each of the Carnegie Tech quintiles of the American Council on Education Psychological Examination; scores were available on all subjects. This insured an equating of groups with respect to intellective ability.

Given this task, how will a five-man group divide the labor involved in completing it? (1) It is possible either for everyone to *exchange information* with everyone else, or to have the missing symbol information collected by a single person. (2) It is possible either for everyone to *form the solution*, or to specialize to the extent that only one person forms the solution. (3) It is possible either to complete the problem without *circulation of answers* (since each may form the solution by himself), or to have the answer relayed from a single central source. But which organizational arrangement will be adopted? To what extent does the choice depend upon communication restrictions?

In replicating Leavitt's experiment, we have used two of his restrictions —those constituting his extreme cases: the "Wheel" and "Circle." In addition, we established groups that were entirely free of restrictions, using an "All-Channel" pattern. The three communication nets are illustrated in Figure 2. Our initial problem is to discover how the net restric-

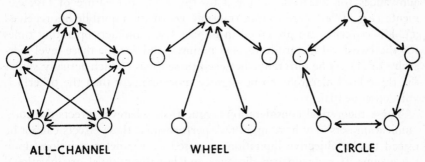

ALL-CHANNEL   **WHEEL**   **CIRCLE**

FIG. 2. Open Channels Used in the Three Nets

tions imposed upon the various groups determined the organizational patterns used in performing the operating task.

Consider first the Wheel net: If the task is divided so that the "spokes" send their information to the "hub," the latter can make the decision and in turn return answers to the spokes. We will call this pattern a "two-level hierarchy." Next, consider the Circle net: If two neighbors send their information to their opposite neighbors, who in turn relay this information with their own to the fifth member of the circle, this "key-man" can make the decision and relay the answer back through the "relayers" to the "endmen." We will call this pattern a "three-level hierarchy." In the All-Channel nets, either one of these procedures—or others —may be used. It can be shown that the arrangements just described are the most efficient of those available. Although the use of the relays in he three-level hierarchy involves time delays, the minimum number of messages required by the two- and three-level hierarchies is the same—eight.

A channel-usage analysis, as suggested by Bavelas' model, misleads one into supposing that the two-level hierarchy is twice as efficient as the three-level hierarchy; for the two-level arrangement obviates the need for relaying, both when sending information and when sending answers. But the task is more than one of merely sending messages—messages must also be received, collated, and prepared. To compare efficiencies we need an estimate of the time required to perform *all* these task elements, and in proper sequence. To provide such a comparison of "limiting" efficiencies, of the two-level and three-level hierarchies, Hellfach made a methods-time measurement analysis of the task.

Methods-Time Measurement is a time-study procedure used widely in industry.[8] It involves identification of the basic motions that must be used to perform the operating task, and assignment of standard time values to these basic motions. Hellfach analyzed each position in the five member group both when arranged as a two-level hierarchy and when arranged as a three-level hierarchy. Then he drew up a composite analysis of the operation for the two types of arrangement, making appropriate allowances for idle time required by the sequential nature of task elements (e.g., a "relayer" cannot transmit information until he has received it). His estimates are presented in Figure 3. He predicts operating times for the two-level hierarchy of .445 minutes; and for the three-level hierarchy of .437. The difference between these times (which actually shows the three-level hierarchy to be slightly more efficient than the other!) is not consequential.

These theoretical considerations argue that, whatever effects the communication nets may have upon task performance, these effects cannot be traced to the objective limitations imposed by the net restrictions upon the groups. If a group can discover and use the optimal organizational pattern among those permitted it by the net restrictions, the minimum time achieved by a Circle group should be substantially the same as by a Wheel group. Even more interesting, the analysis leads to the conclusion that there is no difference in the limiting times for task performance between groups in the unrestricted net (the All-Channel groups) and those in the restricted nets (the Wheel and Circle groups).

Description and Analysis of the Organizational Problem

The theoretical discussion to this point supports our hypothesis that the communication restrictions affect the task performance of the groups not directly, but only indirectly by influencing the ability of the members to organize themselves for optimum performance in their line operation. Now let us examine in more detail the way in which the nets pose organizational problems.

Twenty of our 56 groups were allowed to operate without any imposed

---

[8] H. B. Maynard, G. J. Stegmerten, John L. Schwab, *Methods-Time Measurement* (New York: McGraw-Hill), 1948.

restrictions on their internal communication. The other groups operated within communication restrictions that reduced the number of channels for communication to approximately half of those available in the unrestricted groups. The two sets of restrictions differed from each other, however, in their effects upon the ease with which the groups might develop interaction patterns. The 15 Wheel groups were restricted in such

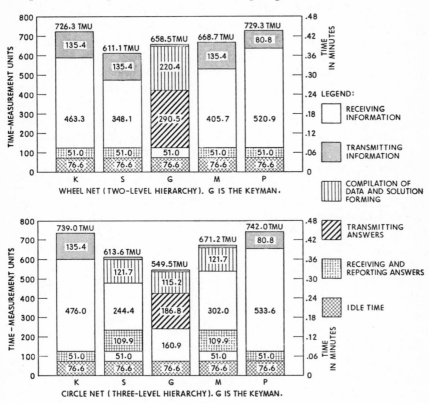

FIG. 3. Methods-Time Measurement Analysis

a way that their organizational problems should be minimal. The 20 Circle groups were restricted with almost the same degree of severity (in terms of number of open channels), but in a way that made their organizing tasks comparatively difficult.

The three variations in the nets had different relationships to the organizational problem:

(a) The "All-Channel" Net: The organizational problem for an All-Channel group is not simple. The group has an advantage in that each member can communicate with the others, so that no relaying of messages through a "second party" is required. Yet the lack of communication restrictions means an open field with almost too many opportunities—a total of 20 one-way channels. Accordingly, each All-Channel group has the difficult job of developing its own restrictions—deciding that certain available channels will *not* be used. In addition, each of the members is equipotential with respect to his place in the communication net; no one member has initial advantages from his place in the net with respect to the functional requirements of the task.

(*b*) *The "Wheel" Net:* The Wheel groups are in a net in which the communication restrictions reduce the difficulty of the organizational problems to a minimum, yet hold the requirements of the operating problem constant. If the task is divided so that the spokes send their information to the hub, the latter can solve the problem and in turn send answers to the spokes. There would be no need for relay through a "second party." All the "unnecessary" channels have been blocked, so that their elimination is no longer part of the organizational problem. This reduces the number of open channels from 20 to 8, some 60 per cent. The existence of a hub means that the positions in the net are not equipotential— the four spokes are disadvantageously situated. Should a spoke attempt to become the solution former, he would need to depend upon the hub for relaying both information and answers. In addition, in such a situation, the organizational problem as to which of the four equipotential spokes would become the problem-solver would need to be handled. But, if the hub becomes the solution-former, the wheel requires a minimum of organizing effort for solving the operating task.

(*c*) *The "Circle" Net:* This net retains the symmetry of the positions in the free situation but restricts drastically the number of communication opportunities. Simultaneously it makes imperative the use of a relay system, or three-level hierarchy, within the organization. No potential solution-former has immediate access to the other four missing symbols. His two neighbors need to relay their information and that of their other neighbors to him. Along with this impediment to organizing, there is the added difficulty that no one position is more or less advantageously situated for handling the solution-forming requirement. The reduction of available channels in this net is from 20 to 10, just 50 per cent.

A comparison of the way in which the three characteristics of the net differ from net to net is diagrammed in Table 1. From this display it is

TABLE 1
COMPARISON OF THE THREE NETS
Characteristic Differences among the Three Nets

Characteristics	All-Channel	Wheel	Circle
Number of Open Channels	20	*8*	*10*
Number of Symmetric Positions	5	*4*	5
Minimum Number of Relays Necessary	0	0	*2*

(The italic entries indicate the points at which the Wheel and Circle nets contrast with the All-Channel net.)

possible to make rough estimates of the difficulty of the organizational problem for groups in each type of net. The Wheel groups would have the least difficulty, for they have no channels to eliminate, no relays to establish, and already have one person occupying a dominant position in the net. The All-Channel groups would have the next grade of difficulty, since the elimination of excess channels and the evolution of one person as solution-former are both required, yet relays need not be established. The Circle groups should have the most difficulty, for they need both to establish relays and to evolve an asymmetrical arrangement among the positions. They also must do some eliminating of unneeded channels, although this last requirement is minimal. The difficulty of the organizational problem in the different nets varies as follows:

Wheel < All-Channel < Circle .

This analysis of the organizational difficulty yields a surprising outcome in indicating that an unrestricted net (All-Channel) in itself involves difficulties, and that restrictions in communication may be helpful (Wheel) or harmful (Circle) in the evolution of organizational structures, depending upon the nature of the relation of the restriction to the organizing and operating tasks.

This concludes our theoretical analysis. It develops our basic hypothesis by arguing that the communication restrictions have no direct effect upon performance of the operating task. It argues that the communication pattern has important effects upon the difficulty the group will encounter in organizing itself—but that the restricted patterns do not necessarily make for more difficulties than the unrestricted patterns. Now let us examine the empirical data to determine whether they support or refute our theoretical analysis.

II. THE EMPIRICAL FINDINGS

Performance Times in Operating Task Trials

As far as the subjects were concerned, the time required for each trial was the central focus of the experiment. In the instructions they were told, "Your team is competing with the other five-man groups to see which group is fastest at getting the answer. The shorter the time, the better your team score."

The average time per trial for the three types of groups is presented in Figure 4. The Circle groups are clearly slower than the Wheel groups after the first trial. The All-Channel groups occupy an intermediate position. A statistical check of the differences between the types of groups was made on the cumulative time required for the 20 trials as shown in Table 2. This table also includes the averages for the three fastest trials within each type of group. Although the Circle groups are significantly different from the Wheel and All-Channel groups for both measures, there was a significant difference between the Wheel and All-Channel groups on only the "total time" measure.

The effects of the communication nets upon the time criteria were

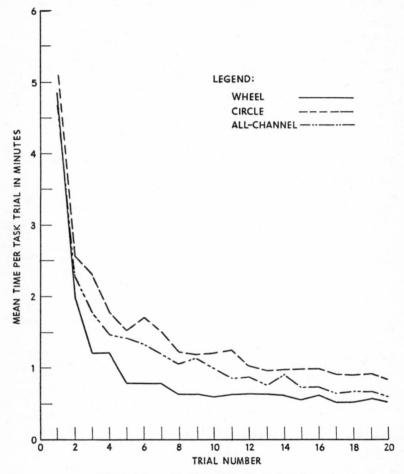

FIG. 4. Average Time per Group for Task Trials

marked. During the 8th trial, the Wheel groups had already reached the levels eventually attained by the All-Channel groups in their last few trials. At the end of the 20 trials, the Circle groups were using some 60 per cent more time than the Wheel groups in performing their operations. During the course of the twenty trials, there were performance differences between the All-Channel and Wheel groups that eventually disappeared.

These findings hint that the Wheel groups, with the least difficult or-

TABLE 2
TIME OF TASK TRIALS
(Minutes)

Net	TOTAL TIME		AVERAGE OF THE THREE FASTEST TRIALS	
	Mean	Standard Deviation	Mean	Standard Deviation
All-Channel ($n = 20$)	24.38	4.82	0.54	0.15
Wheel ($n = 15$)	19.12	3.09	0.46	0.08
Circle ($n = 21$)	29.45	5.08	0.73	0.15

Significance of Difference Between Nets

	Total Time	Average of the Three Fastest Trials
Wheel—All-Channel	$t = 3.06$ $p < .01$	t is not significant
Circle—All-Channel	$t = 3.17$ $p < .01$	$t = 3.96$ $p < .001$
Wheel—Circle	$t = 6.20$ $p < .001$	$t = 5.69$ $p < .001$

ganizational problem, organized earliest; that the All-Channel groups, with a more difficult job, organized more slowly, but were eventually performing as well as the Wheel groups; that the Circle groups had difficulty in organizing, not reaching optimum performance within the 20 trials allowed. These differences correspond to the variations in organizational difficulty imposed by each net. The more difficult the organizational job, the less rapid was the evolution toward efficient task performance.

But are these differences actually due to the organizational arrangements, or are they (contrary to our theory) due to differences in task operation times in the optimal arrangements? An answer to this question requires an analysis of the organizational arrangement developed by each group. What are the message sending and receiving patterns that developed in the groups over the course of the twenty task trials? To examine the growth of miniature organizations, it is necessary first to determine whether there *is* a definite pattern; this is the *stability* problem. Then, if there is a pattern, we can examine how the message sending became differentiated into a particular *organizational arrangement*.

Organizational Stability

The *interaction pattern* is defined for a given trial in terms of whether or not one or more messages were sent from a particular person to another —that is, which of the open channels in the net were used, and in which direction, by the five persons constituting the group. Because a message card might have two or three units of information on it, the actual number of cards sent over a channel was of no literal significance.[9]

The *stability* of the interaction among the five persons is defined as the extent to which a given pattern persisted over a sequence of trials. An analysis was made of every trial for each group, contrasting the pattern of information messages with the pattern of answer messages. Then each sequence or "segment" of four trials within each group was classified as to stability of the pattern of channels used. The five segments chosen coincided with questionnaire periods: trials 1 to 4, 5 to 8, 9 to 12, 13 to 16, and 17 to 20. Information and answer messages were analyzed separately.

In making the analyses, we diagrammed the stability of the segment by using a solid arrow for those channels which were always used or never used, respectively, during the four trials constituting the segment. We employed a broken arrow for those channels which were used once, twice, or three times during the four trials. This notation is illustrated in the examples of Figure 5. Three degrees of stability were defined as follows:

1. Stable: A segment was termed "stable" with respect to its information or answer messages, if only one or two of the channels were used "intermittently," i.e., once or twice, or three times during the segment, regardless of the number of channels available. See the examples a, b, and c in Figure 5.
2. Semi-Stable: A segment was termed "semi-stable" with respect to its information or answer messages when three to one-half of the total open channels were used intermittently. As noted previously, there were 20 open channels in the All-Channel, but only 8 in the Wheel and 10 in the Circle nets. See examples d, e, f in Figure 5.
3. Unstable: A segment was termed "unstable" with respect to its information or answer messages when more than half of the open channels were used intermittently. See examples g, h, i in Figure 5.

These criteria were developed after considerable exploratory work with other ways of setting the boundaries between classes.

The results of the classification of the segments are presented in Table 3. The groups in All-Channel nets are significantly less stable than those

---

[9] Because of our use of pre-coded message cards, it was easy for the senders to include more than one piece of information on each card. For example, a subject might have forwarded to his neighbor in a single message not only his own missing symbol but also information about what one, two, or three other persons were missing. Examination of the messages suggested we would lose little in the analysis of counting the number of message cards exchanged during the course of the experiment rather than tallying each item. A sample of the messages received by each of the 220 subjects during a single trial was checked for correspondence between the number of items of information and the number of message cards involved. The sample was drawn evenly from all 20 trials for all three types of groups. The product-moment correlation between items and cards was +.84. This reliability was considered satisfactory, obviating the labor involved in a count of items.

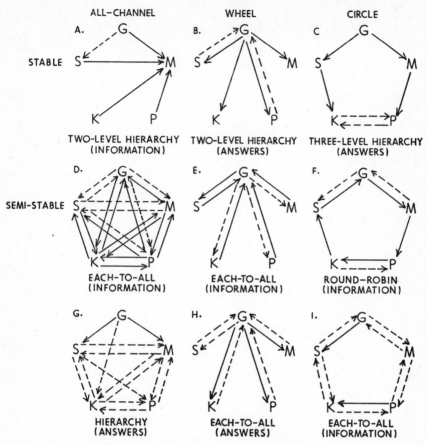

FIG. 5. Examples of Stability Classes of Interaction Patterns

placed in more restricted nets. The Wheel groups are more stable than the Circle groups. Thus, the more restrictions imposed on the communication channels, the more stable the groups. The stability level reflects the number of open channels (see Figure 2), although the difference between the All-Channel and Circle groups fails to approach a 20 to 10 ratio.

Organizational Arrangement

Now it is possible to characterize the organizational arrangements embodied in the semi-stabilized and fully stabilized interaction patterns. Qualitative analysis of the diagrams obtained from the stability analysis of the segments indicates that some groups operated without much division of labor or specialization of positions, utilizing all available channels. Others developed a more highly differentiated group structure.

1. *All-Channel groups.* These groups fell into two types of patterns in *exchanging information.* Three groups stabilized their information ex-

TABLE 3

PERCENTAGE DISTRIBUTION OF SEGMENTS INTO STABILITY CLASSES

Net	Stability Classes	Information Exchange	Answer Exchange	Total Exchange
		%	%	%
All-Channel Segments (*n* = 200)				
	Stable	40	28	34
	Semi-Stable	45	37	41
	Unstable	15	35	25
Wheel Segments (*n* = 150)				
	Stable	90	91	91
	Semi-Stable	10	9	9
	Unstable	0	0	0
Circle Segments (*n* = 210)				
	Stable	81	21	51
	Semi-Stable	17	29	23
	Unstable	2	50	26

Significance of differences in stable vs. combined semi-stable and unstable segments between nets

	Information	Answer	Total
Wheel–All-Channel	$x^2 = 43.3$ $p < .001$	$x^2 = 68.7$ $p < .001$	$x^2 = 45.5$ $p < .001$
Circle–All-Channel	$x^2 = 36.2$ $p < .001$	x^2 is not significant	$x^2 = 11.5$ $p < .01$
Wheel–Circle	$x^2 = 2.8$ $p < .10$	$x^2 = 85.1$ $p < .001$	$x^2 = 64.2$ $p < .001$

change with each person sending messages about his missing symbols to all others. Such an "each-to-all" pattern (semi-stable in this case) is illustrated in Figure 5d. By the end of the experiment, the other seventeen groups had clearly differentiated into two-level hierarchies, like the one illustrated in Figure 5a.

The All-Channel groups displayed more variety in the organization of their *answer exchanges*. One group, in which each person had given information on his missing symbol to every other person, exchanged almost no answers. Another group developed an each-to-all pattern; still another developed a relatively unstable but clearly differentiated hierarchy in exchanging answers. Six groups developed quite stable three-level hierarchies in exchanging answers. The remaining eleven groups used two-level hierarchies, the inverse of the patterns they used in exchanging information.

In the All-Channel groups, taken as a whole, there is approximately the same kind of organization in the information exchanges as in the answer exchanges and both showed considerable differentiation.

2. *Wheel groups.* The imposition of the Wheel net resulted in the use of very stable two-level hierarchy patterns for information and answer exchanges after the first three or four trials.

During the initial trials in four Wheel groups, the *information exchanges* were of the "each-to-all" type, the person in the hub sending out information to all participants, as in Figure 5e. In the other eleven groups, the hubs during the initial trials sent information to only one or two persons, and ceased to send out any information about their own missing symbols after the fourth or fifth trial.

In *exchanging answers*, all of the fifteen groups very rapidly developed a two-level hierarchy in which the person at the hub alone sent messages to the others in the group. Seven of the groups used this pattern for all twenty trials; another seven groups contained persons who sent answers to the hub during the early trials, as in Figure 5b. One group during its first four trials sent no answers back and forth, inasmuch as each person used his "information-received" to come to a solution independently.

There was early and very rapid development of the organizational arrangement in the Wheel groups, the information exchange being mirrored by the answer exchange.

3. *Circle groups.* The groups placed in Circle nets had much difficulty in organizing their structures. Although the groups *in toto* were not as unstable as the All-Channel groups there was still considerable variation in channel usage. The Circle groups tended to organize in the more "primitive," each-to-all patterns, as in Figure 5i.

The bulk of the Circle groups—13 out of the 21—used each-to-all patterns in exchanging their *information* messages. Eight groups used somewhat more differentiated patterns. A first step toward differentiation is found in four groups which evolved semi-stable "round-robins" in which information is passed around the circle, as illustrated in Figure 5i. A fifth group used a round-robin from trials 2 to 10, but in trial 11 one of the participants stopped forwarding his information, reconstituting the round-robin pattern into a chain. Three other groups developed the most specialized information exchange structures of all the Circle groups—ending their last three trials in three-level hierarchies.

The Circle groups differentiated more decidedly in their *answer exchange* patterns. Only one group remained in an each-to-all pattern. Ten of the 21 groups temporarily organized into special patterns, exhibiting much fluidity. Their answer exchange fluctuated from one form of a hierarchy to a semi-stable "each-to-all" to another form of hierarchy, often ending in a semi-stable each-to-all. The remaining ten groups differentiated into three-level hierarchy arrangements as in Figure 5c.

There was considerably more differentiation among the answer exchange patterns than among the information patterns. But by and large, there was a marked tendency for the Circle groups to remain primitive and undifferentiated. Almost half of the stability and semi-stability reported above (Table 3) for these Circle groups was gained by the consistent use of each-to-all patterns.

Table 4 displays the development of the differentiation throughout the course of the experiment for all three types of groups. The bulk of the organization of differentiated patterns is accomplished by the end of the 12th trial in the All-Channel groups. The imposed net helped the Wheel groups to achieve their organizations by the end of the 4th trial. The relative lack of differentiation in the Circle groups is vividly portrayed in Table 4;

TABLE 4
DEVELOPMENT OF ORGANIZATIONAL STRUCTURES
(Percentage of Segments Differentiated)

Net	Type of Organization	SEGMENT				
		Trials 1–4	Trials 5–8	Trials 9–12	Trials 12–16	Trials 17–20
		%	%	%	%	%
All-Channel Segments (n = 200)						
	Differentiated*	5	42	78	85	88
	Each-to-All	28	20	10	8	7
	Undiscernible	67	38	12	7	5
Wheel Segments (n = 150)						
	Differentiated*	77	100	100	100	100
	Each-to-All	23	0	0	0	0
	Undiscernible	0	0	0	0	0
Circle Segments (n = 210)						
	Differentiated*	14	26	33	48	48
	Each-to-All	52	40	33	38	36
	Undiscernible	34	34	34	14	16

* "Differentiated" means using such patterns as the two- or three-level hierarchy, round-robin, and chain.

their high variability from one pattern to another is also reflected in the fluctuation of the percentage of differentiation from segment to segment.

The Critical Observations

We are now in a position to subject our central hypothesis to a clear-cut test. It follows from the hypothesis that groups placed in different nets will experience different degrees of difficulty in attaining an efficient organizational arrangement (say, a two-level or three-level hierarchy); further that the *speed of task performance will be approximately the same in all groups that do in fact attain an efficient arrangement, regardless of the net in which they are operating.* Finally, the average time required for task performance in the efficiently organized groups should, at least approximately, be that predicted by the M-T-M analysis.

Either a two-level hierarchy or a three-level hierarchy (or both) was a possible organizational arrangement within the nets studied. The empirical data indicate that three or more groups within each of the nets actually did organize themselves into one or the other type of hierarchy either for information exchange or answer exchange or both. *When the groups were so organized, they performed their operating tasks efficiently.*

The fifteen Wheel groups (all of which we may regard as "efficiently organized") averaged .46 minutes for their three fastest trials (cf. Table 2). This is almost identical with Hellfach's estimate of .45 minutes in his M-T-M analysis (*supra*, p. 237).[10]

The data for the organized Circle and All-Channel groups are decisive in confirming the hypothesis. The average speeds in the three fastest trials in the 17 All-Channel groups that developed two- or three-level hierarchies in both information and answer sending ranged from .34 to .68 with a mean of .489 minutes. The corresponding range for the three Circle Groups which developed a three-level hierarchy was .40 to .52 minutes, with a mean of .472 minutes. The differences between the means of the organized All-Channel and Circle groups and Hellfach's estimate are not statistically significant; nor are the differences between the means of these groups and the mean of the Wheel groups.

The correctness of the other half of the hypothesis—the relative difficulty in achieving efficient organizational arrangement in different nets—follows immediately. Only groups working within the Wheel net were able to achieve a hierarchical organization with ease. As already reported, all fifteen such groups did so, and usually during early trials. Of the twenty All-Channel groups, seventeed did so, but generally later in the sequence of trials. Only three of the 21 Circle groups developed hierarchies. These findings confirm the theoretical analysis (*supra*, p. 240), which predicts that the difficulty in organizing will be greatest in the Circle groups, next in the All-Channel groups, and least in the Wheel groups.

Thus, both parts of our basic hypothesis are confirmed: The communication nets affected the efficiency with which the groups performed only through the influence they exerted upon the ability of the groups to develop adequate organizations.

III. REPLICATION OF LEAVITT'S EXPERIMENT

Our experimental procedure used the Wheel and Circle nets in common with Leavitt. We ran our groups 20 trials, in contrast with his 15 trials. He

---

[10] It is perhaps worth emphasizing that Hellfach's estimate does not in any way derive from the data of the experiment. The standard times he used for the task elements were derived from M-T-M tables drawn up from industrial time and motion studies. Although Hellfach was acquainted with the results of the experiment, his estimate was built up from data expressed in hundredths of hours, rather than minutes; he converted his totals to minutes as the last step. Hence, there was little opportunity for the experimental data to influence his estimate, even unconsciously.

did not match his groups on the basis of intellective ability. In his experiment, the task and non-task messages were written contemporaneously during the operating trial itself, without benefit of a pre-coded task message card; we had the non-task messages written during an intertrial period.

Despite these differences, our empirical results in the main are a forthright confirmation of the work that was replicated. Leavitt found the fastest trial in his Wheel and Circle groups to average .53 and .83 minutes respectively.[11] His figures are comparable to those presented in Table 2. The Wheel groups in both his and our experiments took a little more than 60 per cent of the time taken by the Circle groups for completion of their fastest task runs. The absolute differences in times between the two experiments may be artifacts produced by apparatus dissimilarities and by the fact that Leavitt's data include the time used for sending non-task messages.

Leavitt's figures on volume of messages are comparable to the sum of our task *and* intertrial messages. In the Wheel nets our groups sent an average of 177 messages per group during the first 15 trials compared with Leavitt's 166, our average being about 7 per cent greater. In the Circle nets our groups sent an average of 389 messages over the first 15 trials and intertrials compared with Leavitt's 372, ours being about 2 per cent greater. These differences are not statistically significant. The ratio of information messages to answer messages in the two experiments is similar. Thus, our use of an intertrial period seems not to have disturbed the situation as originally designed by Bavelas, Leavitt, and Smith.

Despite our ability to replicate Leavitt's results as far as the time and volume of messages are concerned, there is a striking difference with regard to the extent to which our Circles organized. Leavitt says, "The *circle* showed no consistent operational organization. Most commonly messages were just sent in both directions until any S(ubject) received an answer or worked one out."[12] Although our Circle groups were much less differentiated than groups in the other two nets, many consistent patterns evolved. The latter difference between our results and Leavitt's cannot be ascribed to the fact that we ran twenty rather than fifteen trials. At the end of the 15 trials, as Table 4 demonstrates, some 48 per cent of the segments had already differentiated into stable or semi-stable interaction structures. We cannot explain these differences.

Our results on the Wheel groups are identical with those obtained by Leavitt. All of his groups, like ours, used the same interaction structure, the information pattern being the inverse of the answer pattern. Like our groups, his evolved the organization by the fourth or fifth trials.

---

[11] Leavitt, *op. cit.*, Table 2, p. 43.

[12] Leavitt, *op. cit.*, p. 42.

IV. SUMMARY

This replication and extension of the work of Bavelas, Leavitt, and Smith on communication patterns in task-oriented groups enabled us to separate the effect of communication nets upon the performance of an operating task by the group, and upon the ability of the group to organize itself for this operating task. The particular nets we explored did not create differences among the groups with respect to the time needed for handling the operating task when an optimal organization was used. These same nets did introduce important differences in the organizing difficulties encountered. In this way we obtained an estimate, which can be refined through further experimentation, of the relative difficulties introduced by demanding the establishment of non-symmetric "keyman" roles, the organization of relay points, and the elimination of unnecessary channels.

The current management literature on the topic of communication leaves one with the expectation that certainly a reduction in communication restrictions should lead to a more adequately functioning organization. Yet, our findings in this experiment indicate that assertion of a one-to-one relationship between effective functioning and freedom in communication is unwarranted. Had our analysis not separated the organizational problem from the operating problem, it would have seemed paradoxical that complete freedom of communication is at times more limiting than restricted communication. The findings warn the practical communications expert working in industry or government that a change in communications structure may have quite different consequences for the efficiency of immediate day-to-day operations, and for the ability of the organization to handle changes in its own structure.

22. THE BASIC LAW OF RUMOR*

A. Chorus

According to Allport and Postman (1), the two essential conditions for the transmission of rumor are importance and ambiguity. Roughly, importance stands for the emotional factor and ambiguity for the cognitive factor in rumor-spreading. Both factors are related to rumor transmission in a quantitative manner and a formula for the intensity of rumor may then be written as follows: $R \sim i \times a$. This formula means that the relation between the two factors is not additive but multiplicative, for if either importance or ambiguity is zero, there is no rumor.

Allport and Postman present this law as "highly dependable," but they inform us that there are certain conditions "under which its operation will be weakened" (p. 34). For instance, if heavy penalties are placed on rumor spreading as, for instance, in Gestapo Germany, or if social barriers prevent crossing. Another reason for the failure of the law to operate may be that a person in the rumor chain knows the rumor law. It is a fact "too little observed by psychologists, that knowledge of the operation of a law frequently alters, and sometimes negates, the law in question" (p. 35).

If this is true, and quite certainly it is, then the formula of the rumor law needs completion. For one should be able to state the weakening conditions of the law in the formula itself. There is another factor which plays a role in the transmission of rumor and it should be involved in the formula. For the weakening conditions are not directly concerned with the factors of ambiguity and importance. These two factors remain constant in a given situation of rumor even though we may know the law. Neither the ambiguity nor the importance of the rumor-fact decreases (e.g., a rumor about the death of Stalin remains at a given moment as ambiguous and as important as it is), even though I know the rumor law.

Therefore in the formula a new factor should be stated to account for the individual disposition of the rumor listener. If this listener knows the rumor law, then that factor will weaken the working of the two other factors, possibly totally negate their working. But, one could object, should a formula be altered for the incidental case in which a person knows that formula? That is an exception and moreover most formulas for psychological laws would have to be altered. Indeed, if it were only for the rare case of a person who knows the psychological law, it might seem silly to alter it. But there is more: the knowledge of the law is only one factor in the individual disposition that may influence the two other

* Reproduced from *Journal of Abnormal and Social Psychology*, 48, #2, 1953.

factors. It is an expression of something more general, viz., the *critical sense* of the rumor transmitter. In proportion to the critical sense of the individual, the operating of the other two factors will be weakened. The critical sense may be sharpened not only through knowledge of this psychological law but also through psychological insight in general, through perspicacity in social happenings, through higher intelligence, through greater resistance against mass suggestion. Therefore, it seems necessary to change the rumor law as follows: $R \sim i \times a \times \dfrac{1}{c}$.

Here c stands for critical sense, which contains not only perspicacity but also a volitional factor in the sense of will-power or the disposition to make decisions after reflection and consideration and not to give way immediately to the two mentioned rumor factors. And c also stands for moral criticism or conscience which, in every individual who can bear responsibility, operates as an inhibiting factor in the telling of rumors. If, for instance, I hear the rumor that one of my best friends is an imposter I shall refrain from telling it to others; at any rate I shouldn't tell it to everybody. So c stands for the critical factor in every rumor chain. For rumor is not a wholly mechanical process but a human happening wherein every individual is tested on his critical and moral values.

As c grows greater the rumor will weaken or be totally stopped: the rumor, or the intensity or mobility of the rumor, is inversely proportional to factors i and a. If c equals 1 (i.e., a supposed general average), then the fraction equals 1, which means that the rumor spreads according to the general law without special barriers: $R \sim i \times a \times \dfrac{1}{1}$. If c is less than average, then the rumor grows stronger. In such a case the rumor transmitter will say, "I have seen it myself" or "my wife saw it happening," to enhance the positiveness of his telling. If c is greater than normal, then the intensity of the rumor will be approaching zero and perhaps it will stop at that link in the rumor chain.

The factor c is, of course, not constant for a given individual in all situations. It, too, varies with the ambiguity and the importance. The critical sense of an anti–Semite, for example, will be weaker if he hears an anti–Semitic rumor than if he hears an anti–English rumor.

The three factors in rumor transmission cover and stand quantitatively in multiplicative relation in the sense of the proposed formula.

REFERENCE

1. ALLPORT, G. W., AND POSTMAN, L. *The Psychology of Rumor*. New York: Holt, 1947.

23. RUMORS IN WAR*
Theodore Caplow

Methodological Note

It was one of the routine duties of the regimental S-2 section to which the writer belonged to prepare a monthly intelligence report, which included a section on rumors. The five members of the section ranged in rank from private to captain and were unanimously enthusiastic about gathering rumors. Since they were in contact with every company in the unit at frequent intervals and their several ranks allowed association with every individual in the organization, rather wide coverage was usually obtained. Most rumors were transmitted to the writer within a few hours of being heard and set down in writing immediately, both for official purposes and in the interest of this study. Each report of a rumor was noted on a separate sheet together with the immediate source, the ostensible original source, the estimated diffusion, the date and circumstances, and an estimate of validity from both the reporter and the source. All five men became familiar with the mechanisms of the rumor process and appeared to acquire some expertness in estimating diffusion and validity. In addition to these regular "interviewers," there were about 20 other individuals scattered through the organization who were familiar with the project in either its official or its private aspect, and made it their business to accumulate rumors and pass them on to the writer. Information obtained from them was recorded in the same way.

At the end of each month, a count was made of rumors in circulation during the period, classified as to subject-matter and diffusion. The number of reports of each rumor furnished a rough check on the observers' estimates of degree of diffusion. Needless to say, no mention of persons was ever made in the official reports.

The original notes, together with a prepared summary which included considerable numerical data, were confiscated during demobilization by a unit censor who took a broad view of his prerogatives, and the present report has been written from memory.

Studying the Rumors

Classroom experiments show a very high degree of distortion in the chainwise transmission of rumors. The usual method is to prepare statements in a field of interest to the student-subjects, to convey them to one

---

* Taken from *Social Forces*, Vol. XXV (October, 1946–May, 1947).

student either orally or in writing and to analyze the changes either step by step or in the final process. The most striking finding in such a study is typically the fantastic variation in content. Other findings are expansion and contraction dictated by interest motives, a tendency to simplify categories, increase amounts, and amalgamate logically connected events. From these findings—and from related experiments on the validity of eye-witness reports—social psychologists have tended to classify the rumor process as a rather aberrant form of communication and to focus attention only upon its sweeping unreliability.[1]

In security training of both the armed forces and the civilian population, great emphasis was placed upon the danger of rumor-mongering because of distortion, elaboration, and panic effects. Rumors do undoubtedly threaten military secrecy insofar as they may contain the gist of military secrets. But there is little evidence to show how the rumor process actually works and whether the generalizations derived from classroom experiments can be applied without hesitation to all situations in which rumors circulate.

During two years' service in the Pacific Theatre the writer had the opportunity to check the frequency of rumors in about a dozen company-size units of one regiment, and their transmission from unit to unit. Something more than the significance of casual observation is claimed for these findings, since definite hypotheses were held in view during the period and rather extensive notes were kept. On the other hand, it was not possible to estimate the completeness of so informal a survey with any confidence, and coverage is known to have varied during the period. Consequently, the material is at best descriptive and at worst unverifiable. It is presented here in the hope that it will invite discussion in terms of related observations of the rumor process in well-integrated functioning social groups.

The word "rumor" as used here, is defined as an item of information with definite interest connotations transmitted *only* by informal person-to-person communication within a group. Rumors are thus by definition "Unconfirmed." Also, there is sound perception in the colloquial usage which almost invariably exludes items not linked to group interests (e.g. these natives used to be cannibals) from the category of rumors.

The frequency of rumors in the group studied was surprisingly low in view of a great deal of concern with the rumor process and with the prevalence of rumors. The greatest number discovered in one month was seventeen, less than one per hundred men. During one period of two weeks, not a single new rumor could be discovered.

The rate of diffusion was invariably rapid. It is sometimes hard to ac-

---

[1] See, for example, Clifford Kirkpatrick, "A Tentative Study in Experimental Social Psychology," *American Journal of Sociology*, 38, 2, p. 194.

count reasonably for the speed with which a rumor can leap a 300 mile gap in the course of an afternoon. In one case, the rumor of an impending operation appeared in a detachment isolated on a tiny island without radio communication approximately one day after it was introduced to the main body of the regiment. Similar "grapevine" effects are noted in all groups in whose activities the rumor process plays an important part. A partial explanation will be suggested later.

The extent of diffusion was rather great, ranging from 100 per cent in several cases to perhaps as low as 1 per cent in cases where value was attached to possession of the information—but seldom that low, since the suitability of the item for transmission is what creates a rumor in the first place.

The majority of rumors contained three associated statements.[2] A considerable number contained one statement or two statements, and only a negligible proportion more than three statements. The tendency toward tripartite form was so great that even narratives tended to conform to it.

During a given period, there appear to be certain centers from which most rumors emanate. Headquarters is always such a center and so is the front line during actual battle. Individuals may assume the function of starting rumors, even in the absence of special information.[3]

The rate of diffusion appeared to decrease in some rough ratio to the distance from the center of emanation, though no very regular ratio could be discovered. In general, too, the extent of diffusion decreased as the distance from the center of emanation increased. The distance referred to here is a composite of physical distance and social distance. Diffusion of rumors was greater when the entire organization was collected in one or two ships but appeared to take place through the same channels established in the more normal situation on land.

The "channels" through which Army rumors diffuse are particularly important for an understanding of the whole process. Most of the diffusion of rumors actually took place through a relatively small number of rather well-defined paths. In two instances known to the writer, a rumor was planted at a fairly remote point in the channel with the intention of influencing a superior. In both cases, the information reached its destination, and in one case, had the predicted effect. Several factors combine to produce the channel system. Some of them, such as the limited number of contacts available to a single individual, the tendency to communicate

---

[2] For example (June 28, 1945): We are going to be in the Kyushu invasion . . . Already attached to the __ Division for it . . . High point men will be left behind . . .

[3] During one three-month period, Pvt. B— originated more rumors than the rest of the officers and men in his Battalion combined. B— was an elderly man, who had been an amateur of military history in civilian life, had considerable knowledge of strategy, and made it his chief business in the Army to extract reliable information from various sources.

new rumors where old ones have been received with appreciation, the dependence upon recognized centers of emanation, and the value attached to the possession of information are rather obvious. A particularly important one is the division of a military organization into sub-groups, both formal and informal, between which communication is limited. The most conspicuous of these divisions is that between officers and enlisted men. Only a few of the members of each group habitually communicated the rumors originating in their own group to members of the other, and these few habitual contacts—their number further reduced by considerations of confidence and of military secrecy—were the only bridges by which most rumors passed from one group to the other. The same was true of other divisions in terms of congeniality groups, sub-groupings of rank, company and battalion units, geographically separated groups linked only by radio operators, or by truck drivers and boat crews.

These tended to be two-way channels, since the communication of rumors is more often than not, marked by an exchange. The customary *quid pro quo* for a rumor is either another rumor or a validity judgment upon the one received. But the tendency was strictly limited by the rather small amount of valued information available at points in the channel distant from the center of emanation. It might be hypothesized that this would lead to greater stringency of validity judgments farthest from the center of emanation, and in fact this effect was often observed, though counterbalanced by the lack of background information with which to form a critical judgment; for example, among rear echelon personnel hearing of casualties on another island.

Several factors are related to the frequency and the extent of diffusion in a given period. The most important is the amount of nonrumored information in circulation. However, the curiosity of individuals may vary, the demand for information by a group—upon which the rumor process depends—appears to be easily saturated. The total amount of current information rather than the subject-matter of the information items is what seems to determine the state of demand. Before the invasion of the Philippines, the organization was elaborately briefed on the geography, ethnology, architecture, mores, and terrain of the new territory. Compulsory formations were held once or twice a week for instruction of this kind, and brochures were posted on bulletin boards, copied in unit newspapers, and often embodied in general orders. As this program continued, the number of rumors diminished sharply, despite sustained discussion of subjects like local enemy opposition and the accessibility of Filipinas, upon which the information program was reticent. The rumorless period previously mentioned occurred upon a ship in one of the invasion convoys in which the ship's captain made a practice of announcing over the public address system anything of interest that came to the bridge and would not be known on deck—such as a submarine search by escort vessels over the horizon. In this situation again, there were areas of immediate interest in which information was scant, and about which rumors would ordinarily have been expected, but the hourly bombardment of announcements on the convoy's progress seemed to satisfy the total demand for information.

Scores of similar incidents created the impression, presented here as an hypothesis, that the demand for particular information in a group of this kind can be satisfied by any other information not totally irrelevant, if presented in sufficient amount.

Anything which disrupted the arrangement of "channels" appeared to increase the frequency and decrease the diffusion of rumors. Very thorough scattering of the organization occasionally took place and had this effect. Occasional official campaigns directed against rumor-mongering invariably increased the number of rumors and decreased the average diffusion. In this case, another factor may have been the enhanced value placed on the forbidden information. Rapid changes of plan effected by higher headquarters at certain periods placed variant rumors in the same channels at the same time and for short periods led to increases in both frequency and diffusion. Periods of organizational inactivity were usually marked by increases in frequency of rumors, and decreases in average diffusion.

When the group structure—and most of the channels—is destroyed, the same pattern of increasing frequency and decreasing diffusion is noted in intensified form. About a third of the regiment left together in the first large group to be returned for demobilization after V–J day. During a two week period at a camp near port, as many rumors were heard daily as had been heard in a typical month of the preceding two years. However, diffusion was slight even within the same barracks, and different patterns of rumor prevailed in each of some twenty barracks despite almost frenzied interchange of items at all levels.

Turning from the form to the content of rumors, we find configurations equally alien to the classroom experiment.

The most frequent subject of rumors were impending operations, and the travels connected with them. These alone accounted for slightly more than half of the total number in the first twelve months, and slightly less than half in the remainder of the period. Next in frequency were rumors relating to rotation, repatriation, and demobilization, followed by administrative changes, such as anticipated regulations, secret orders, promotions, shifts in personnel functions, and in command. Other recurrent categories were casualties (particularly those in related regiments and divisions), disease, domestic politics, atrocities (about equally divided between those referred to the enemy and those referred to United States or allied troops), vice and corruption (either as prevailing in a particular unit, or attributed to high-ranking officers), and progress of the war (including peace rumors). These categories are admittedly very broad. The rumor of an impending movement might include not only the geographical objective, but also any of the related topics that might be found in a field order —from the calibre of emplaced artillery to the disposition of crocodiles in the creeks.

Then, too, many rumors took the form of an authoritative quotation, with the actual content left to the determination of private inference. A well-known general was quoted as saying that the organization would be home by Christmas, and the rumor remained in that form, leaving room for argument as to whether the statement implied the end of the war or return to the States in connection with training activities. Often, rumors in quotation form embodied no more than an attitude, as when a new commanding officer was reported to have promised to "make it tough" for headquarters troops. What is significant about these categories is the close correspondence to prevailing values. Information not linked to the major group interests simply failed to move along the rumor channels, though much of it was available at all points.

The veracity of rumors was high. With only two doubtful exceptions (doubtful because the appropriate rumor may have circulated without being observed by the writer), every major operation, change of station, and important administrative change was accurately reported by rumor before any official announcement had been made. In the category "progress of the war"—perhaps the most important category from the standpoint of morale—only one completely false rumor ever attained wide diffusion— the rumor that Germany had surrendered in November, 1944. The writer is not sufficiently informed to describe the apparently world-wide spread of this story. As circulated in the organization observed, it was based on a quasi-official announcement, which though vehemently denied later, seems actually to have been made. What is striking is that the reception of this peace story was marked by hesitation and reservation of judgment, as was the authentic peace news of 1945. Many of the "impending movement" rumors were based on plans which were later changed. Many of them contained half-truths, approximations, and inaccuracies of detail. But the selective process tended to favor the accurate items. Since military secrecy did not ordinarily forbid the informal denial or refutation of false information, a long period of planning invariably was accompanied by a progressively more accurate body of surmises.

The veracity of rumors did not decline noticeably during transmittal. Errors in transmission were apparently well-compensated by selection. Commanders were known to remark that their line companies (usually distant from centers of emanation) "knew" more than they did about the probability of impending movements. Quite often, this was literally true.

Exaggeration and distortion took place in the course of transmission along a channel, and were most readily observable where numerical statements were involved. But, in general, the final form of a rumor was more condensed than its early forms, and the three-statement form tended to maintain itself. Most changes were toward simplification of statements rather than addition or subtraction. The rapidity of ordinary transmission is itself selective. A rumor is usually heard more than once, and usually transmitted more than once by each individual in the channel. This recirculation tends to eliminate variation and if circumstances allow sufficient time, the final form of a rumor for a sizeable percentage of the group may be a statement in prescribed form with a high degree of consensus on every word.

Distortion in terms of wishes and avoidances seems to be an individual rather than a group characteristic. As channels solidified, this phenomenon became comparatively rare, because of the exclusion of persons associated with previous invalidity. When the channels were broken up, wish-fulfillment again became conspicuous in the pattern.

There was a positive and unmistakable relation between the survival of a rumor, in terms of both time and diffusion, and its veracity. No relation between the survival of a rumor, and its favorableness, was observed. The absence of this phenomenon may be related to the conventional and defensive pessimism of an army in the field.

The question of veracity can be seen more clearly as a part of a total situation than by considering rumors separately. Typically, an interest-situation was created by circumstances (e.g., the conclusion of one operation focussed interest on the next), a number of rumors then appeared and began to circulate, the number progressively decreasing and the average diffusion increasing, until the interest-situation was terminated either by an official announcement or by the occurrence or nonoccurrence of the rumored event. This sequence was relatively invariable for the category of greatest frequency (impending movements and operations) and tended to occur—with greater or lesser time periods—in many of the other categories.

There were long-range trends as well during the two-year period. The decreasing number and greater average diffusion toward the end of the period points both to a solidification of channels and a greater expertness in evaluating information. Increasing negative prestige was attached to the transmission of false rumors, and this was accompanied by a tendency to attach sources to doubtful statements. At least one rumor circulated among hundreds of men with the name of the original source attached. A validity estimate was almost always attached to a rumor, and many of them were communicated with a warning, such as, "I don't believe a word of this, but. . . ." Increasing scepticism and objectivity led to the drawing of a sharp line between rumors and other information, so that rumors were usually labelled as such in the telling, and interestingly enough, official announcements were often doubted by men who had not seen them in written form. Neither the German surrender, nor the announcement of the point system, won general acceptance until a considerable time after the first radio announcement.

Conclusions

The rumor process in the group observed was a fairly successful group device for circulating desired information. Rumors tended to diffuse along definite channels of person-to-person communication. The formation of channels decreased the number of rumors and increased their diffusion. The effect of transmission was to increase rather than decrease the validity of the statements.

The wide variation between these findings and the results of classroom experiments, implies no criticism of the latter. The rumor process described here was a rather complicated group activity extended over a considerable period of time, and accompanied by group interests stronger than any of those found in a classroom. The modes of communication involved were vastly more complicated than the simple chainwise transmission of the experimental situation. It should be noted that most of the tendencies toward distortion which were discovered in the classroom did exist in the theatre of operations, but that definite group devices developed to diminish their effect. The findings do illustrate, however, the difficulty of projecting generalizations about an interaction process from the laboratory to the field.

24. MANAGEMENT COMMUNICATION AND THE GRAPEVINE*

KEITH DAVIS

COMMUNICATION is involved in all human relations. It is the "nervous system" of any organized group, providing the information and understanding necessary for high productivity and morale. For the individual company it is a continuous process, a way of life, rather than a one-shot campaign. Top management, therefore, recognizes the importance of communication and wants to do something about it. But what? Often, in its frustration, management has used standard communication "packages" instead of dealing situationally with its individual problems. Or it has emphasized the means (communication techniques) rather than the ends (objectives of communication).

One big factor which management has tended to overlook is communication *within its own group*. Communication to the worker and from the worker is dependent on effective management communication; and clearly this in turn requires informal as well as formal channels.

THE GRAPEVINE

A particularly neglected aspect of management communication concerns that informal channel, the grapevine. There is no dodging the fact that, as a carrier of news and gossip among executives and supervisors, the grapevine often affects the affairs of management. The proof of this is the strong feelings that different executives have about it. Some regard the grapevine as an evil—a thorn in the side which regularly spreads rumor, destroys morale and reputations, leads to irresponsible actions, and challenges authority. Some regard it as a good thing because it acts as a safety valve and carries news fast. Others regard it as a very mixed blessing.

Whether the grapevine is considered an asset or a liability, it is important for executives to try to understand it. For one thing is sure: although no executive can absolutely control the grapevine, he can *influence* it. And since it is here to stay, he should learn to live with it.

Perspective

Of course, the grapevine is only part of the picture of communication in management. There is also formal communication—via conferences,

* Reprinted from *Harvard Business Review*, September–October, 1953.

reports, memoranda, and so on; this provides the basic core of information, and many administrators rely on it almost exclusively because they think it makes their job simpler to have everything reduced to explicit terms—as if that were possible! Another important part of the picture is the expression of attitudes, as contrasted with the transmission of information (which is what we will be dealing with in this article). Needless to say, all these factors influence the way the grapevine works in a given company, just as the grapevine in turn influences them.

In this article I want to examine (*a*) the significance, character, and operation of management communication patterns, with particular emphasis on the grapevine; and (*b*) the influence that various factors, such as organization and the chain of procedure, have upon such patterns. From this analysis, then, it will be possible to point up (*c*) the practical implications for management.

As for the research basis of the analysis, the major points are these:

1. *Company studied*—The company upon which the research is based is a real one. I shall refer to it as the "Jason Company." A manufacturer of leather goods, it has 67 people in the management group (that is, all people who supervise the work of others, from top executives to foremen) and about 600 employees. It is located in a rural town of 10,000 persons, and its products are distributed nationally.

In my opinion, the pattern of management communication at the Jason Company is typical of that in many businesses; there were no special conditions likely to make the executives and supervisors act differently from their counterparts in other companies. But let me emphasize that this is a matter of judgment, and hence broader generalizations cannot be made until further research is undertaken.

As a matter of fact, one of the purposes of this article is to encourage businessmen to take a close look at management communication in their own companies and to decide for themselves whether it is the same or different. In many companies, men in the management group now follow the popular practice of examining and discussing their problems of communicating with workers, but rarely do they risk the embarrassment of appraising their communications with each other.

2. *Methodology*—The methods used to study management communication in the Jason Company are new ones. Briefly, the basic approach was to learn from each communication recipient how he first received a given piece of information and then to trace it back to its source. Suppose D and E said they received it from G; G said he received it from B; and B from A. All the chains or sequences were plotted in this way—A to B to G to D and E—and when the data from all recipients were assembled, the pattern of the flow of communication emerged. The findings could be verified and developed further with the help of other data secured from the communication recipients.

This research approach, which I have called "ecco analysis," is discussed in detail elsewhere.[1]

---

[1] Keith Davis, "A Method of Studying Communication Patterns in Organizations," *Personnel Psychology*, Fall, 1953.

Significant Characteristics

In the Jason Company many of the usual grapevine characteristics were found along with others less well known. For purposes of this discussion, the four most significant characteristics are these:

1. *Speed of transmission*—Traditionally the grapevine is fast, and this showed up in the Jason Company.

For example, a certain manager had an addition to his family at the local hospital at 11 o'clock at night, and by 2:00 P.M. the next day 46% of the whole management group knew about the event. The news was transmitted only by grapevine and mostly by face-to-face conversation, with an occasional inter-office telephone call. Most communications occurred immediately before work began, during "coffee hour," and during lunch hour. The five staff executives who knew of the event learned of it during "coffee hour," indicating that the morning rest period performed an important social function for the staff as well as providing relaxation.

2. *Degree of selectivity*—It is often said that the grapevine acts without conscious direction or thought—that it will carry anything, any time, any-where. This viewpoint has been epitomized in the statement that "the grape-vine is without conscience or consciousness." But flagrant grapevine irresponsi-bility was not evident in the Jason Company. In fact, the grapevine here showed that it could be highly selective and discriminating.

For example, the local representative of the company which carried the em-ployee group insurance contract planned a picnic for company executives. The Jason Company president decided to invite 36 executives, mostly from higher executive levels. The grapevine immediately went to work spreading this in-formation, but it was carried to *only two of the 31 executives not invited*. The grapevine communicators thought the news was confidential, so they had told only those who they thought would be invited (they had to guess, since they did not have access to the invitation list). The two uninvited executives who knew the information were foremen who were told by their invited superin-tendent; he had a very close working relationship with them and generally kept them well informed.

Many illustrations like the above could be gathered to show that the grape-vine can be discriminating. Whether it may be *counted on* in that respect, how-ever, is another question. The answer would of course differ with each case and would depend on many variables, including other factors in the communi-cation picture having to do with attitudes, executive relationships, and so forth.

3. *Locale of operation*—The grapevine of company news operates mostly at the place of work.

Jason managers were frequently in contact with each other after work be-cause the town is small; yet grapevine communications about company activities predominantly took place at the plant, rather than away from it. It was at the plant that executives and supervisors learned, for instance, that the president was taking a two weeks' business trip, that the style designer had gone to Florida to study fashion trends, and that an executive had resigned to begin a local in-surance business.

The significance of at-the-company grapevines is this: since management has some control over the work environment, it has an opportunity to influence the grapevine. By exerting such influence the manager can more closely integrate grapevine interests with those of the formal communication system, and he can use it for effectively spreading more significant items of information than those commonly carried.

4. *Relation to formal communication*—Formal and informal communication systems tend to be jointly active, or jointly inactive. Where formal communication was inactive at the Jason Company, the grapevine did not rush in to fill the void (as has often been suggested[2]); instead, there simply was lack of communication. Similarly, where there was effective formal communication, there was an active grapevine.

Informal and formal communication may supplement each other. Often formal communication is simply used to confirm or to expand what has already been communicated by grapevine. Thus in the case of the picnic, as just described, management issued formal invitations even to those who already knew they were invited. This necessary process of confirmation results partly because of the speed of the grapevine, which formal systems fail to match, partly because of its unofficial function, and partly because of its transient nature. Formal communication needs to come along to stamp "Official" on the news and to put it "on the record," which the grapevine cannot suitably do.

SPREADING INFORMATION

Now let us turn to the actual operation of the grapevine. How is information passed along? What is the relationship among the various people who are involved?

Human communication requires at least two persons, but each person acts independently. Person A may talk or write, but he has not *communicated* until person B receives. The individual is, therefore, a basic communication unit. That is, he is one "link" in the communication "chain" for any bit of information.

The formal communication chain is largely determined by the chain of command or by formal procedures, but the grapevine chain is more

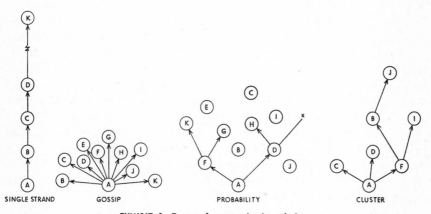

EXHIBIT 1. Types of communication chains

---

[2] For example, see National Industrial Conference Board, *Communicating with Employees*, Studies in Personnel Policy, No. 129 (New York, 1952), p. 34.

flexible. There are four different ways of visualizing it, as Exhibit 1 indicates:

1. *The single-strand chain*—A tells B, who tells C, who tells D, and so on; this makes for a tenuous chain to a distant receiver. Such a chain is usually in mind when one speaks of how the grapevine distorts and filters information until the original item is not recognizable.

2. *The gossip chain*—A seeks and tells everyone else.

3. *The probability chain*—A communicates randomly, say, to F and D, in accordance with the laws of probability; then F and D tell others in the same manner.

4. *The cluster chain*—A tells three selected others; perhaps one of them tells two others; and then one of these two tells one other. This was virtually the only kind of chain found in the Jason Company, and may well be the normal one in industry generally.

Active Minority

The predominance of the cluster chain at the Jason Company means that only a few of the persons who knew a unit of information ever transmitted it—what Jacobson and Seashore call the "liaison" individuals.[3] All others who received the information did not transmit it; they acted merely as passive receivers.

For example, when a quality-control problem occurred, 68% of the executives received the information, but only 20% transmitted it. Again, when an executive planned to resign to enter the insurance business, 81% of the executives knew about it, but only 11% passed the news on to others. Those liaison individuals who told the news to more than one other person amounted to less than 10% of the 67 executives in each case.

These active groups varied in membership. There was no evidence that any one group consistently acted as liaison persons; instead, different types of information passed through different liaison persons. However, as will be shown later, some individuals were invariably communication "isolates"; they received and transmitted information poorly or not at all.

The above findings indicate that if management wants more communication, it should increase the number and/or effectiveness of its liaison individuals. This appears to be a large order, but it is entirely possible. Liaison individuals tend to act in a predictable way. If an individual's unit of information concerns a job function in which he is interested, he is likely to tell others. If his information is about a person with whom he is associated socially, he also is likely to tell others. Furthermore, the sooner he knows of an event after it happened, the more likely he is to tell others. If he gets the information late, he does not want to advertise his late receipt of it by telling it to others.

In other words, three well-known communication principles which

---

[3] Eugene Jacobson and Stanley E. Seashore, "Communication Practices in Complex Organization," *The Journal of Social Issues*, 7, 3, 1951, p. 37.

are so often mentioned in relation to attitudes also have a major influence on the spread of information by liaison individuals:

(1) Tell people about what will affect them (job interest).
(2) Tell people what they want to know, rather than simply what you want them to know (job and social interest).
(3) Tell people soon (timing).

ORGANIZATIONAL EFFECTS

The way an organization is divided horizontally into organizational levels and vertically into functions, such as production and sales, obviously has effects on management communication, for it cuts each company's over-all administrative function into small work assignments, or jobs, and sets each management person in certain relationships to others in his company.

Horizontal Levels

Organizational levels are perhaps the more dramatic in effect because they usually carry authority, pay increases, and status. From the communication point of view, they are especially important because of their number. In a typical firm there are usually several management levels, but only one or two worker levels; furthermore, as the firm grows, the management levels increase in number, while the worker levels remain stationary.

Communication problems are aggravated by these additional levels because the chain of communication is lengthened and complicated. Indeed, just because of this, some companies have been led to try to reduce the number of intermediate management levels. Our concern here is with the patterns of communication among individuals at the different levels.

At the Jason Company, executives at *higher* levels communicated more often and with more people than did executives at *lower* levels. In other words, the predominant communication flow was downward or horizontal. When an event happened at the bottom level, usually the news did reach a high level; but a single line of communication sufficed to carry it there, and from that point it went downward and outward in the same volume and manner (cluster chain) as if it had originated at the top.

Accordingly, the higher an executive was in the organizational hierarchy (with the exception of nonresident executives), the greater was his knowledge of company events. This was true of events which happened both above his level and below his level. Thus, if the president was out of town, a greater proportion at the fourth level knew of it than at the sixth level. Or—and this is less to be expected—if a foreman at the sixth level had an accident, a larger proportion of executives at the third level knew of it than at the fourth level, or even than at the sixth level where the accident happened. The more noteworthy the event, of course, the more likely it was to be known at upper levels—but, in a company of this size, it had to be quite trivial indeed before it failed to reach the ears of top executives.

The converse follows that in terms of communications transmitted and received the sixth and lowest level of supervision, the foreman level, was largely isolated from all other management. The average foreman was very hesitant to communicate with other members of management; and on the rare occasions when he did, he usually chose someone at his own level and preferably in his own department. Members of this group tended to be the last links in management communication, regardless of whether the chains were formal or informal.

A further significant fact concerns the eight departmental superintendents at the fourth level. Six of them supervised foremen directly; two others, with larger departments, each had a single line assistant between him and his foremen. The two who had line assistants were much more active in the communication chains than were the six others; indeed, all but one of the six appeared to have little to do with their foremen except in a formal way.

Perhaps the clue is that, with increased organizational levels, those at the higher (and hence further removed) levels both recognize a greater need for communication and have more time to practice it!

Functional Groups

Functionalization, the second important way in which an organization is "cut up," also has a significant impact on communication in management. The functions which are delegated to a manager help to determine the people he contacts, his relationships with them, his status, and, as a result, the degree to which he receives and transmits information. More specifically, his role in communication is affected (*a*) by his position in the chain of command and (*b*) by his position in the chain of procedure, which involves the sequence of work performance and cuts across chains of command, as when a report goes from the superintendent in one chain of command to the chief engineer in another chain of command and to the controller in still another.

In the Jason Company the effects of functionalization showed up in three major ways:

1. *Staff men "in the know"*—More staff executives than line men usually knew about any company event. This was true at each level of management as well as for the managment group as a whole. For example, when the president of the company made a trip to seek increased governmental allotments of hides to keep the line tannery operating at capacity, only 4% of the line executives knew the purpose of the trip, but 25% of the staff men did. In another case, when a popular line superintendent was awarded a hat as a prize in a training

program for line superintendents, within six days a larger proportion of the staff executives than of the line executives knew about this event.

The explanation is not just that, with one staff executive to every three line executives, there were more line executives to be informed. More important is the fact that the *chain of procedure* usually involved more staff executives than line executives. Thus, when the superintendent was awarded his hat, a line executive had approved the award, but a staff personnel executive had processed it and a staff accounting executive had arranged for the special check.

Also the staff was more *mobile* than the line. Staff executives in such areas as personnel and control found that their duties both required and allowed them to get out of their offices, made it easy for them to walk through other departments without someone wondering whether they were "not working," to get away for coffee, and so on—all of which meant they heard more news from the other executives they talked with. (In a larger company staff members might be more fixed to their chairs, but the situation in the Jason Company doubtless applies to a great many other businesses.)

Because of its mobility and its role in the chain of procedure, the staff not only received but also transmitted communications more actively than did the line. Most of these communications were oral; at least in this respect, the staff was not the "paper mill" it is often said to be. It seems obvious that management would do well to make conscious use of staff men as communicators.

2. *Cross-communication*—A second significant effect of functionalization in the Jason Company was that the predominant flow of information for events of general interest was between the four large areas of production, sales, finance and office, and industrial relations, rather than within them. That is, if a production executive had a bit of news of general interest, he was more likely to tell a sales, finance, or personnel executive than another production executive.

Social relationships played a part in this, with executives in the various groups being lodge brothers, members of the same church, neighbors, parents of children in the same schools, and so on. In these relationships the desire to make an impression was a strong motivation for cross-communication, since imparting information to executives outside his own area served to make a man feel that the others would consider him "in the know." Procedural relationships, discussed earlier, also encouraged the executives to communicate across functional lines.

Since communications tended not to stay within an area, such as production, they tended even less to follow chains of command from boss to sub-boss to sub-sub-boss. Indeed, the chain of command was seldom used in this company except for very formal communications. Thus Exhibit 2 reproduces a communication chain concerning a quality control problem in production, first brought to the attention of a group sales manager in a letter from a customer. Although it was the type of problem that could have been communicated along the chain of command, the exhibit shows that, of 14 communications, only 3 were within the chain of command and only 6 remained within one functional area—sales— where the information was first received.

The fact that the chain of command may affect management communication patterns less than procedural and social influences—which has

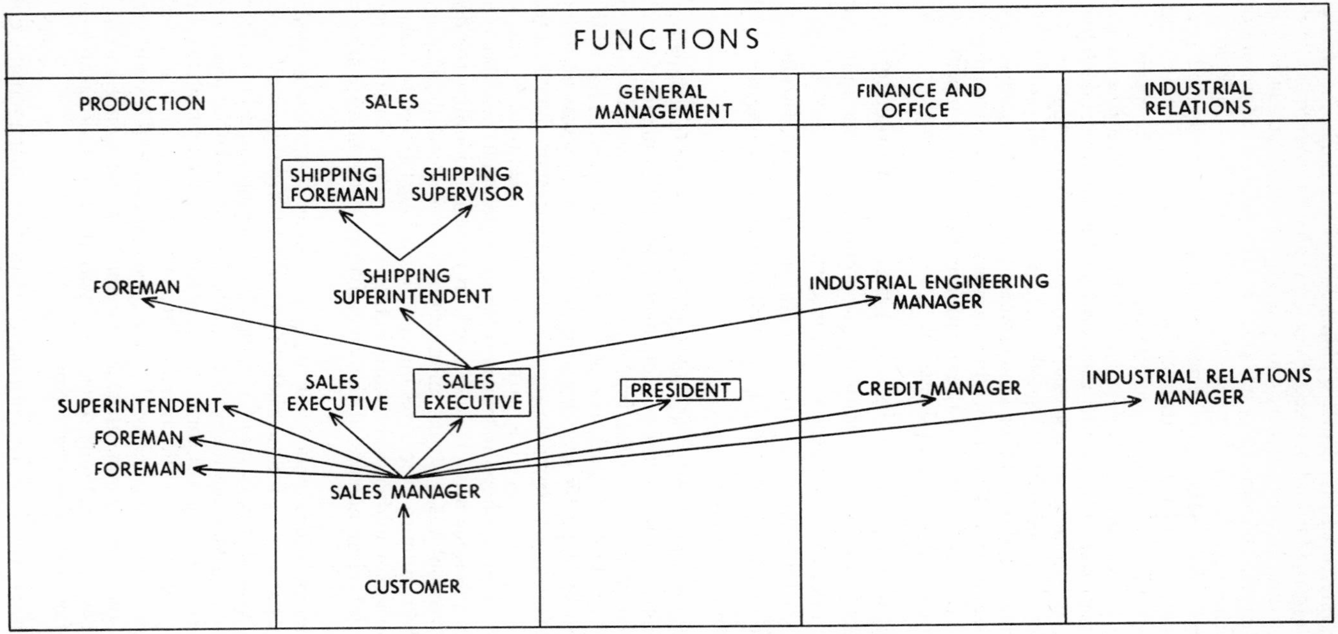

EXHIBIT 2. Communication Chain for a Quality Control Problem

NOTE: Executives in boxes received chain-of-command communications.

shown up in other companies too[4]—means that management needs to devote considerably more attention to the problems and opportunities of cross-communication.

3. *Group isolation*—The research in the Jason Company revealed that some functional groups were consistently isolated from communication chains. Also, there were other groups which received information but did not transmit it, and thus contributed to the same problem—the uneven spread of information through the company. Here are three examples at the foreman level illustrating different degrees of failure to participate in the communication process and different reasons for this failure:

(*a*) The foremen in one group were generally left out of communication chains. These men were of a different nationality from that of the rest of the employees, performed dirty work, and worked in a separate building. Also, their work fitted into the manufacturing process in such a way that it was seldom necessary for other executives to visit their work location.

(*b*) Another group often was in a communication chain but on the tail end of it. They were in a separate building some distance from the main manufacturing area, their function was not in the main manufacturing procedure, and they usually received information late. They had little chance or incentive to communicate to other executives.

(*c*) A third group both received and transmitted information, but transmitted only within a narrow radius. Although they were in the midst of the main work area, they failed to communicate with other functional groups because their jobs required constant attention and they felt socially isolated.

In sum, the reasons for group isolation at the Jason Company were: geographical separation; work association (being outside the main procedures or at the end of them); social isolation; and organizational level (the lower the level of a group, the greater its tendency to be isolated).

Obviously, it is not often feasible for management to undertake to remove such causes of group isolation as geographical or social separation. On the other hand, it may well be possible to compensate for them. For example, perhaps the volume of formal communication to men who happen to be in a separate building can be increased, or arrangements can be made for a coffee break that will bring men who are isolated because of the nature of their work or their nationality into greater contact with other supervisors. In each situation management should be able to work out measures that would be appropriate to the individual circumstances.

CONCLUSION

The findings at the Jason Company have yet to be generalized by research in other industries, but they provide these starting points for action:

---

[4] See Carroll L. Shartle, "Leadership and Executive Performance," *Personnel* (March, 1949) pp. 377–78.

(1) If management wants more communication among executives and supervisors, one way is to increase the number and effectiveness of the liaison individuals.

(2) It should count on staff executives to be more active than line executives in spreading information.

(3) It should devote more attention to cross-communication—that is, communication between men in different departments. It is erroneous to consider the chain of command as *the* communication system because it is only one of many influences. Indeed, procedural and social factors are even more important.

(4) It should take steps to compensate for the fact that some groups are "isolated" from communication chains.

(5) It should encourage further research about management grapevines in order to provide managers with a deeper understanding of them and to find new ways of integrating grapevine activities with the objectives of the firm.

(6) "Ecco analysis," the recently developed research approach used at the Jason Company, should be useful for future studies.

If management wants to do a first-class communication job, at this stage it needs fewer medicines and more diagnoses. Communication analysis has now passed beyond "pure research" to a point where it is immediately useful to top management in the individual firm. The patterns of communication that show up should serve to indicate both the areas where communication is most deficient and the channels through which information can be made to flow most effectively.

In particular, no administrator in his right mind would try to abolish the management grapevine. It is as permanent as humanity is. Nevertheless, many administrators have abolished the grapevine from *their own minds*. They think and act without giving adequate weight to it or, worse, try to ignore it. This is a mistake. The grapevine is a factor to be reckoned with in the affairs of management. The administrator should analyze it and should consciously try to influence it.

25. PATTERNS OF INTERACTION AMONG A GROUP OF OFFICIALS IN A GOVERNMENT AGENCY*

Peter M. Blau

THE ANALYSIS of small groups has received increasing attention in sociological research during recent years. One type of these studies focuses upon the normative orientations that arise in "natural" groups, as exemplified by investigations of restriction of output among factory workers. Another type is primarily interested in developing methods of observation and analysis of interaction, and usually deals with "artificial" groups in laboratory situations.

This paper is concerned with a systematic analysis of the processes of interaction in a "natural" group of officials in a government agency,[1] and the status differences that emerge in this process. It focuses upon three problems: (1) The interdependence between the way an official performs his duties and his interpersonal relations with his colleagues. (2) The usefulness of observable interaction as an index of status in the group. (3) The relationship between interaction in "pair-events," contacts between two individuals, and "set-events," social situations involving more than two participants.

THE SETTING

The peer group studied consisted of 16 agents,[2] who, together with a supervisor and a clerk, composed a department in an agency of law enforcement. Their principal duty was the investigation of business establishments to determine whether any violation of the laws the agency administered had occurred. Each agent worked by himself on the cases assigned to him by the supervisor. Processing a case involved an audit of the books of the firm, interviews with the employer and a sample of employees, negotiation with the employer if violations were found, and writing a full report. Agents spent slightly more than half their working time in the field, and the remainder of it in the large office this department shared with another, similar, department.

* Reproduced from *Human Relations*, 7, #3, 1954.
[1] The method of observation used was suggested by E. D. Chapple and C. M. Arensberg, "Measuring Human Relations," *Genetic Psychology Monographs*, Vol. XXII, 1940, pp. 3–147. I am indebted to Professor Arensberg for his helpful comments on the study of social interaction in this group.
[2] Data for only 15 agents are available for most tables.

Problems often arose in the course of making difficult legal decisions. When an agent could not solve such a problem, he was expected to consult his supervisor for advice. However, the supervisor also evaluated the performance of his subordinates on every case, and his annual official rating influenced their promotion chances. Agents were therefore reluctant to expose their ignorance to the supervisor by asking him often for advice. The comment of one of them was typical: "I try to stay away from the supervisor as much as possible. The reason is that the more often you go to the supervisor, the more you show your stupidity."

Officially, agents were not permitted to consult each other; but their need for advice from a source other than the supervisor induced them to ignore this rule. All agents, including the most competent ones, often discussed their problems with colleagues. This unofficial practice reduced their anxiety over making correct decisions, and thus improved their performance. The knowledge that he could obtain advice without exposing his difficulties to the supervisor enhanced the agent's ability to make accurate decisions, even when no consultation took place.[3] The existence of this cooperative practice basically influenced the relationships between officials. This therefore is a study of social interaction in a cooperative group.

Social Interaction and Competence

To obtain quantitative indices of interaction, all contacts any member of this department had with anyone else in the office during 30.5 hours of observation were recorded. On the average, an official had 8.3 contacts per hour; 5.1 of these were associations with other agents in this department. Of course, not all of these interactions were consultations. Many, such as greetings or brief private conversations, were not related to official business. Neither the length of the exchange nor its content were given consideration in this count. The total number of contacts observed was 2,189.

Four simple indices can be derived from this record: (1) The total number of contacts an individual had per hour. (2) The number of contacts an individual originated per hour. (3) The number of contacts an individual received per hour, that is, those originated by the other participant in the exchange. (4) The proportion of an individual's total contacts that he originated, which provides an index of his initiative in social interaction.

Competence in performing the duties of an agent was related to par-

---
[3] This practice of unofficial consultation is analyzed in the author's doctoral dissertation at Columbia University, *The Dynamics of Bureaucracy* (Chicago: University of Chicago Press, 1955), a study of this and another agency. A fellowship of the Social Science Research Council, which made this study possible, is gratefully acknowledged.

ticipation in the interaction of this group. The supervisor's rating of the performance of his subordinates provides an index of their relative competence.[4] The more competent agents had a disproportionately large number of contacts, but they did not originate more contacts than others. The positive relationship between proficiency and frequency of interaction was entirely due to the fact that the highly competent agents tended to *receive* more contacts from their colleagues than those who were less proficient,[5] as Table 1 shows.[6]

TABLE 1
CONTACTS RECEIVED PER HOUR
AND COMPETENCE

Contacts Received	High	Competence Low	Total
Many	5	1	6
Few	2	7	9
Total	7	8	15

It is not surprising that the experts were frequently contacted in this situation. They could furnish the best advice, and they were highly esteemed in this group where competence was greatly valued. The rank correlation between esteem and competence was .93.[7] Their colleagues approached these experts disproportionately often, not only to ask their advice, but also to seek their companionship, since associating with a respected person tends to be especially desirable. Their frequent participation in interaction made most experts well integrated members of this group.

Superior ability alone, however, did not assure an integrated position. The two highly competent agents who were considered uncooperative by their colleagues were generally disliked and received only few contacts. To become accepted, an expert had to share the advantages of his superior skill with his colleagues. Provided that he was willing to help others with their problems, the highly competent agent was often drawn into

---

[4] The official rating of the supervisor divided agents into three groups. For purposes of this study, the supervisor ranked agents individually in terms of their competence.

[5] The relation between rank and received contacts corresponds to the conclusions reached by George C. Homans, but the absence of a relation between rank and originated contacts does not. See *The Human Group* (New York: Harcourt, Brace, 1950; London: Routledge & Kegan Paul), pp. 145, 181–82.

[6] All relationships discussed in this paper are significant on the .05 level.

[7] The members of this group were asked to rank their colleagues in terms of their ability as agent. An official's average rank is defined as the esteem he enjoyed among colleagues. In a two-by-two table, the relationship between esteem and competence is perfect.

discussions, and thus became an integrated member of the group without having had to exercise much social initiative.

Competence and Informal Relationships

The less competent agent did not become integrated without special effort. Since he was initially less attractive an associate than the expert, he received fewer contacts, and probably experienced a greater need for improving his interpersonal relationships. As a result, the less competent agents exercised relatively more initiative in their social interaction in the office, as Table 2 shows,[8] and they also cultivated informal relations with colleagues in their free time.

TABLE 2
SOCIAL INITIATIVE AND COMPETENCE

Social Initiative	Competence High	Competence Low	Total
Much............2		7	9
Little.............5		1	6
Total.........7		8	15

The major opportunity for relaxed informal contacts between agents was provided by the daily lunch hour. Most officials valued this period of companionship greatly, and sometimes returned to the office from the field just before noon in order to join some colleagues for lunch. Since about one half of the agents were usually in the field, even those persons who had regular partners often lunched with other colleagues. An index of the extent of the informal relations of each official was constructed on the basis of a record of all his lunch partners in a two week period.[9]

Table 3 shows that the least competent agents tended to have more extensive informal relations at lunch than those whose competence was average or high. This appears, at first, to contradict the previous conclusion that most experts were well integrated. However, their less extensive informal relations do not indicate that these experts were excluded from the fellowship at lunch. Generally, they as well as other agents lunched in the company of colleagues.[10] But the greater need of the less competent

---

[8] The less competent agents tended to exercise more initiative than the experts partly because they were more likely to request advice, but also partly because they were more concerned with improving their position in the group.

[9] The agents kept this record themselves at the request of the observer. If a luncheon engagement is defined as eating with one colleague once, the total number of engagements reported (which often included several colleagues on the same day, and the same colleagues on repeated days), divided by the number of days on which the respondent went to lunch from the office, defines the value of this index.

[10] Only two agents, one of the least and one of the most competent members of the group, lunched alone more than once during two weeks of observation (excluding days when agents were in the field at noon).

TABLE 3
EXTENT OF INFORMAL RELATIONS
AND COMPETENCE

Informal Relations	High or Average	Competence Low	Total
Extensive............2	5	7
Less extensive........7	1	8
Total.........9	6	15

agents to improve their position in the group, since they did not become as easily integrated through interaction in the office as the experts, induced them to maintain particularly extensive informal relations with their colleagues in their free time.

Informal Relationships and Social Interaction

The interpersonal relations an agent had established at lunch influenced his participation in social interaction in the office. Most of the agents who had very extensive informal relations received many contacts from others, as Table 4 indicates. On the other hand, neither the total number of con-

TABLE 4
EXTENT OF INFORMAL RELATIONS AND
CONTACTS RECEIVED PER HOUR

Informal Relations	Many	Contacts Received Few	Total
Extensive..........6	1	7
Less extensive........2	6	8
Total.........8	7	15

tacts, nor the number of originated contacts, was related to extent of informal relations.

The more extensive an individual's interpersonal relations are, the better integrated a member of the group he will be. Further, in a group in which most members strive to become highly proficient, and in which they have occasion to appreciate the superior advice experts give them, a close association between integration and competence is to be expected. Since the number of received contacts was the only index of interaction related both to extent of informal relations and to competence, it may be considered an index of integration, that is, of an agent's unofficial status in this group.[11]

---

[11] Why was the total frequency of interaction not related to integration in a cooperative situation? Possibly, because the very knowledge that interaction is integrative induces those members of a group not yet fully integrated but trying to improve their position to originate especially many contacts. For example, the newest member

It will be noted that competence and extent of informal relations, although each was directly related to integration, were inversely related to each other. (Compare Tables 1 and 4 with Table 3.) This suggests the existence of two alternative means of becoming an integrated member in this group. Experts attracted their colleagues through their superior ability, and became integrated by merely being cooperative, without having to exercise much social initiative. Less competent agents were more likely to establish extensive informal relations, since such extensive relations also made an individual a desirable companion for many colleagues, and thus an integrated member of the group. The existence of two alternative mechanisms of integration contributed to the high social cohesion in this department.[12]

The Process of Integration

The preceding interpretation of the relationships between competence, informal relations, and integration raises two questions. First, did these agents actually find their highly competent colleagues particularly attractive? To be sure, their estimation of an individual's ability was closely related to his competence. But was this rationally defined esteem related to social attractiveness? Second, is there any evidence that some agents experienced a need to improve their integration in the group and met this need by establishing especially extensive informal relations in their free time? The analysis of inaccuracies of interview responses concerning lunch partners suggests answers to these questions.

A card with the names of all members of this group was given to each one of them in the course of an interview in his home, and he was asked to divide his colleagues into those with whom he had and those with whom he never had spent a lunch period. Responses from 15 officials were obtained. Every fact, whether two officials had or never had lunch together, was independently reported by two individuals. Of the 105 pairs of statements, 41 did not coincide. This large proportion of discrepancies —39 per cent—indicates that such interview responses provide a very unreliable index of social contacts.[13] However, these very discrepancies

---

of this group (assigned to the department two months prior to observation) ranked third in the number of originated contacts, first in social initiative, but fourteenth in the number of received contacts.

[12] In a competitive group of officials observed in another agency, both mechanisms of integration were greatly impaired. Interaction in the office was largely disintegrative, and the resulting strained relations between officials discouraged them from spending their lunch periods together. As a result, the social cohesion of this group was low.

[13] Accuracy can be somewhat increased by asking for contacts during a limited time only. The number of colleagues who mentioned an agent as their lunch partner seems to provide a valid index of scope of partners, but the number of colleagues named by an agent does not. Only the former index was significantly related to an index of scope of lunch partners based on observation.

do reveal differences in the interpersonal attitudes of these officials and their roles in the group.

Positive discrepancies, the number of colleagues whom an official named but who did not name him, can be considered an index of "role distortion." An individual who claims to have established informal relations with several other members of the group who disclaim these relations has a distorted image of his role in that group.[14] Negative discrepancies, the number of colleagues whom an agent failed to mention but who mentioned him, may be used as an index of "social attractiveness." If an individual does not recall several associations with colleagues which these colleagues report as having occurred, the others are more attracted to him than he is to them.

Table 5 indicates that social attractiveness was related to esteem, as has

TABLE 5
ESTEEM AND SOCIAL ATTRACTIVENESS

| | | Social Attractiveness | |
Esteem	High	Low	Total
High	6	2	8
Low	1	6	7
Total	7	8	15

been assumed. The attractiveness of the esteemed expert, which found expression in his colleagues' remembering occasional contacts with him that he had forgotten, or perhaps reporting associations that had never occurred, induced the others to originate disproportionately many contacts with him. The fact that the expert therefore became integrated without exercising much social effort may well have made his interpersonal relations *appear* less important to him, and thus account for his tendency to forget meetings with colleagues.

Role distortion, on the other hand, was inversely related to extent of

---

[14] It is not known whether a lunch engagement remembered by one agent but not by the other participant actually had taken place, but many positive discrepancies indicate role distortion whether this had been the case or not. Either an individual imagined contacts that never had occurred, or he accurately remembered contacts that had taken place so rarely and so long ago that the other participants had forgotten them. Even the latter indicates that his interpersonal relations have assumed greater significance in his thinking than they warrant. It is also not known whether an individual whose statement was incorrect *remembered* or only *reported* inaccurately. Even if he did not deceive himself, but told the interviewer of contacts that he knew had never occurred, this would indicate that he felt it necessary to present a distorted image of his role in the group to others. The same considerations, *mutatis mutandis*, apply to many negative discrepancies; they indicate social attractiveness, as discussed in the text, regardless of which one of the participants was factually correct.

informal relations, as Table 6 shows.[15] Agents who had established extensive informal relations only rarely reported having lunched with colleagues who failed to remember such engagements. Those whose interpersonal relations were less extensive often adapted to an insecure position by main-

TABLE 6
EXTENT OF INFORMAL RELATIONS AND ROLE
DISTORTION

Informal Relations	High	Role Distortion Low	Total
Extensive	2	6	8
Less extensive	6	1	7
Total	8	7	15

taining a distorted image of their role in the group. This adaptation suggests that these agents experienced a need for improving their position. The existence of this need helps to explain why the less competent agents, who were originally less attractive to their colleagues, usually tried to become better integrated by cultivating informal relations with the other members of the group.

Interaction in Group Situations

The unofficial status of an agent, indicated by the number of contacts he received, influenced his behavior in group situations, his interaction with outsiders, and his performance of his duties.

Departmental meetings, held every other week, were the only occasions when all members of the department were assembled as a group. These meetings were largely devoted to explanations of new regulations and changes in enforcement practice by the supervisor, and the discussion of problems related to new procedures by the agents. Those whose status was secure, who received many contacts throughout the day, tended to participate more in these discussions than their less well integrated colleagues, as Table 7 shows.[16]

By raising a question, an agent could clarify an issue that was doubtful in his mind. By making an intelligent comment, he enhanced his prestige in the eyes of his supervisor and his colleagues. But by participating in the discussion he also risked exposing his ignorance and being ridiculed. The group often responded to a remark with derisive laughter and comments,

---

[15] Role distortion was not related to esteem (and neither to competence), whereas social attractiveness was not related to the extent of informal relations. This indicates that role distortion and social attractiveness measure two different dimensions.

[16] On the basis of observation during five departmental meetings, agents were divided into those who spoke three times or more and those who spoke less than three times per meeting. This index was also positively related to esteem.

TABLE 7
CONTACTS RECEIVED PER HOUR AND PARTICIPATION IN
DISCUSSION AT DEPARTMENTAL MEETINGS

Contacts Received	Agent Participated in Discussion		
	Often	Rarely	Total
Many............5	1	6
Few.............2	7	9
Total........7	8	15

because it seemed irrelevant or obvious, and the participation of the least integrated agents was most often discouraged in this fashion. In effect, the group permitted only its integrated members to enhance their knowledge and prestige in these discussions.

The superior status of agents who received many contacts also manifested itself in the dominant roles they assumed when a small group of agents was engaged in a joint undertaking. They made most suggestions, and their suggestions were most often followed. For instance, they assumed command on the few occasions when several agents worked together on a project; they usually decided to which restaurant a group went for lunch. The fact that dominance in group situations is associated with the number of received contacts further justifies the use of the latter as an index of status.

Interaction with Outsiders

The better integrated agents had a disproportionately large number of contacts with members of *other* departments.[17] Agents who received relatively few contacts in the course of social interaction tended to confine their associations to members of their own department. An insecure position apparently discouraged ventures into untried social situations. This relationship between status and ease of interaction with out-group members is exemplified by the contacts of agents with stenographers.

Agents could dictate their reports and letters to stenographers, but they did not always avail themselves of the opportunity to do so. Some agents usually wrote their difficult reports in long-hand and had them typed, and some typed an occasional brief report themselves. The extent to which an agent utilized stenographic assistance was related to his status.[18] Table 8 indicates that agents who received many contacts from

---

[17] This is in agreement with William F. Whyte's finding that the leaders of gangs are the channels of communication between gangs. See *Street Corner Society* (Chicago: University of Chicago Press, 1943), pp. 259–60.

[18] The index of utilized dictation time is: the amount of time stenographers spent taking dictation from an agent during an eight-month period, divided by the number of cases he had completed in that period. By holding the number of cases constant,

TABLE 8
CONTACTS RECEIVED PER HOUR AND DICTATION TIME

Contacts Received	Dictation Time		
	Much	Little	Total
Many	6	1	7
Few	2	7	9
Total	8	8	16

their colleagues dictated more often to stenographers than agents who were not as well integrated.

Composing the final report of a complex case was a difficult task, and an enervating one, since this report provided the basis for the supervisor's evaluation of the agent's performance. Two agents explained their failure to dictate some of their reports in the following terms:

If it's exceptionally hard; I actually write it out with pencil and paper, and turn it into the pool for typing . . . It's easier for me to write than to dictate. Often, I don't use quite the right word. I notice it a few seconds later, but I let it go. What shall I do? Ask the girl to go back and change it? I'd rather not. . . .

If I dictate directly, I worry about not getting everything in the report. This way, if I leave something out, I can go back and put it in. It would be a nuisance to tell the stenographer to go back and make such insertions.

An agent found the presence of the stenographer disturbing if he worried about the impression he made on her—for instance, when he had to tell her to correct a mistake he had made. Agents who received social recognition from their peers in the form of being often approached by them, either because their competence was respected or because their company was valued for personal reasons,[19] were relatively unconcerned with the opinion of stenographers. Agents who felt insecure in the peer group, on the other hand, were probably more eager to receive, at least, the respect of the stenographer, and were at the same time less confident of doing so. Their consequent preoccupation with the impression they made on her prevented them from concentrating their thoughts upon composing the report. This disturbance often induced the less integrated agents to forego the advantages of dictating.

Their status in the group also influenced the interaction of agents with the employers of the firms they investigated. Observation indicated that the agents who were well integrated, although not necessarily the most

___

the amount of dictation time required is roughly held constant. Although the value of this index is influenced by dictation speed, it is primarily a function of the proportion of his reports an agent failed to dictate. Data for all 16 agents were available for this index.

[19] Both esteem and the extent of informal relations were also positively related to dictation time.

effective negotiators, tended to remain more detached in their negotiations with employers. Apparently, the recognition they received from their colleagues made it easier for them to disregard the personal attitudes of clients toward them, and thus to remain unperturbed even in the face of an excitable employer.[20] Such detachment improved the quality of an agent's performance, just as the ability to dictate difficult reports to stenographers enhanced his working efficiency. His status therefore influenced an agent's performance.

Conclusions

Unofficial status and quality of performance were mutually related in this department of a government agency. Superior competence usually produced an integrated status in this group, since its members were especially attracted to those colleagues whose ability they respected. A substitute means for attaining this end, which enabled the less proficient agents also to become integrated, was the establishment of extensive informal relations with colleagues, since this also made many others value the companionship of an individual. Agents who were highly competent, and those who had particularly extensive informal relations, received a disproportionately large number of contacts in the course of social interaction.

The relative number of contacts an agent received from his colleagues constituted the *actual*—to refrain from coining a new term by calling it the "interactual"—expression of their evaluation of his role in the group. It provided him with concrete evidence of his significance for the group. Being approached often gave an agent a feeling of security in social situations which facilitated his interaction with outsiders as well as with members of his own group. In contrast, the insecurity of the agent who was rarely approached by others made his interpersonal relations on the job problematical for him. The number of contacts an agent received per hour indicated his status in the group.

The competence of an agent influenced his unofficial status, which, in turn, influenced the quality of his performance, especially because it affected the social relationships into which he entered in the course of discharging his duties. The concern of the insecure agent with his position in these relationships distracted his attention from his work. On the other hand, the agent whose status gave him confidence in being socially accepted and respected, could concentrate his energies upon the problems of his job, in work situations involving social interaction. Typically, he was more detached in negotiations with clients, less disturbed by the presence of stenographers, and less hesitant to clarify a problem in a

---

[20] For a full report on the relationship between an agent's role in this group and his role as an investigator, the reader is referred to the author's study cited above.

discussion. All of these factors contributed to his efficiency as an agent.

Agents who were disproportionately often approached in the course of interaction between individuals tended to assume the dominant roles in group situations, for instance in the discussions at departmental meetings, or when a small group of officials engaged in a common undertaking. In other words, those agents who *received* relatively many contacts in "pair events" were most likely to take the *initiative* in "set-events."[21] The social recognition an agent received in the form of being approached, often gave him a feeling of security that enabled him to make recommendations freely in group situations. Simultaneously, the same regard for an agent that led others to seek to associate with him also induced them usually to follow his recommendations.

The designation of the frequency of received contacts as index of unofficial status is by no means arbitrary. The recipients of many contacts occupied a superordinate status in the group in the conventional meaning of the term; they could, and did, exercise social control over their colleagues. The members of this group, who were originally peers, became differentiated in status as the result of interacting with each other at different rates. By originating a disproportionately large number of contacts with one of its members, the group expressed their collective regard for and deference to him, and thus bestowed superior status, power as well as prestige, upon him. The frequency of the contacts an agent received therefore not only expressed but also helped to determine his status in the group.[22]

---

[21] Whyte also found that the leaders of a group originated most activities in "set-events"; *op. cit.*, p. 262.

[22] In this group of peers, differences in power, the ability to control others, emerged in the process of co-operative, voluntary interaction. Even here, the intellectual resources of an individual, his competence, influenced his interaction and his status. Initial differences in status, of course, also influence interaction. The conclusions of this paper are not meant to imply that the process of voluntary interaction in a group is the source of all differentials in power. For example, the superior status of the supervisor did not originate in the interaction in this department. It found expression in his interaction with subordinates, and was modified through this interaction, but its source was his official authority over subordinates, including his right to administer sanctions to them. For a discussion of authority, see the author's study cited above.

26. MEASURING COMMUNICATION IN INDUSTRIAL RESEARCH*

ALBERT H. RUBENSTEIN

This excerpt discusses some of the problems encountered in attempting to measure the communication practices of a number of research and development groups in several industrial laboratories. This was one phase of a study of "Team or Group Research" sponsored by the Office of Naval Research in 1951–52. A report of the completed study has been published (1), as well as reports on the field study phase described below (2,3).

INTRODUCTION

The premise on which this phase of the project was based is that the effective solution of research problems by groups or teams organizationally designed for that purpose is highly dependent on the *availability* and *utilization* of channels of interpersonal communication for the transfer of information. Despite the intellectual resources of the group members and the facilities available to them, group problem-solution may be highly ineffective without adequate flow of information to and between group members.

This viewpoint, relating the flow of information between "elements in a communication network" (people and sub-groups in an organization) and the effective solution of research problems, implies two basic tasks. The first of these, to which the current series of studies has been addressed, is that of identifying critical characteristics of this communication network and putting them into such form that verifiable hypotheses can be constructed which will successfully predict the desired criteria of "effective problem solution." The second task is of course the development of criteria of effectiveness for the solution of research problems.

Some Working Definitions

For communicative ease between reader and writer, it is advisable to establish several rather specific notions of the general concepts with which this paper is concerned. Accordingly, we shall mean by the terms:

Measurement. A process whereby certain relevant characteristics of a phenomenon we are discussing are identified and classified so that numerical values or attributes may be assigned.

---

* Excerpted and adapted from a paper appearing in *Sociometry*, Vol. 16, No. 1, February, 1953, pp. 78–89.

Interpersonal Communication. A process whereby information is transferred by whatever observable or reportable means, between individuals and/or groups (where an individual or group may be the author of a book or a report). This notion is more restricting in a sense than that of "interaction." The notion of "interaction" encompasses all stimulus-response contacts between individuals without initial reference to a specific goal, whereas "information transfer" has occurred only when such transfer is judged to have contributed toward a specific goal. This restriction necessarily eliminates from consideration the common usage (4, 5) of "communication" to describe all the downward, upward, or horizontal flow of ideas and data in an organization without reference to a specific problem which generated the need for particular types of information.

Information. Identifiable contributions of facts and ideas toward the solution of a given problem. At this stage of the research, the criterion inherent in the definition can only be developed from reports by the receiver of the information. Whatever measurement is done on information transfer will depend on empirical categories and values or attributes developed from such reports. The ideal of an objective measure of information described by Wiener (6) and Shannon (7) as "choice among alternatives" may not be realized in this area of cooperative problem-solving until a particular problem can be analyzed by an observer in terms of the minimum amount (or level) of information necesary to carry the problem through from formulation to conclusion. This minimum amount of information necessary is not, of course, independent of the information already stored in the memory of the research worker. For this reason, we may never know what this minimum amount of information is for a particular individual, as we would in the case of the digital computer. An approximation to this ideal may gradually be made in this area by a gross characterization of an interpersonal communication event as containing a "bundle" of information or, alternatively, as "containing or not containing" information according to a criterion established independently of the receiver of the communication.

On-Going Group. A mature, human organization which was in existence before the start of such field work as is described in this paper, and whose primary objective is not related to the pursuit of this field work. Additional implications include business as usual (or as much as possible in view of the disturbance caused by the field work), no offering of incentives for participation in the field work, and minimum feed-back to the subjects of the findings of the field work during its course. This on-going group is in contrast to the artificial group which is set up in the investigator's laboratory for the purposes of study.

Communication Network. The structural and operating characteristics of an on-going group which describe the way in which information is transferred between elements (individuals and sub-groups). Structural characteristics include number and kind of elements in the network; communication media available; social, organizational, and physical distance between elements, etc. Operating characteristics include rates of message flow, proportion of messages received over the network which contain information for the recipient, etc. Implied in this definition of the communication network are: (1) A functional sub-grouping of individuals; in the present study, these sub-groups are problem solving groups (research teams) of 2 or more professional workers. (2) A mature (essentially stable) pattern of communication among the individuals and sub-groups of the organization and between these elements and other information sources.

In the present study of team research, emphasis is placed on only one or two groups in each of the communication networks (industrial research organizations) studied; these are specific problem-solving groups (research teams). The network characteristics of interest at this stage of the investigation are those which are directly related to the flow of information to or between the members of these problem-solving groups.

STATEMENT OF THE FIELD PROBLEM

Three Major Tasks

Identifying and describing the characteristics of the communications network upon which the research team depends for the required flow of information entails: (1) Identification of the members of the problem-solving group (research team). (2) Identification of the channels of communication available to the group for exchange of information among themselves or between themselves and all external individuals and groups, and (3) Measurement of the utilization of the specific channels of communication available to members of the problem-solving group in terms of frequency of use, types and amount of information transferred, sequence of use, direction of flow, preferred channels, and other variables involved in the operation of a communication network.

Identification of the Problem-Solving Group

The criterion mentioned in the preceding section will provide the operations for identifying the problem-solving group:

all individuals who are directly engaged in the intake and utilization of information for the purpose of bringing the current problem to a conclusion.

In most physical research situations, responsibility for the solving of research problems is assigned to professional workers; generally non-professional technicians or assistants are assigned to help them in this work. Each laboratory has a criterion for distinguishing between professional and non-professional workers, although this definition varies somewhat between laboratories and industries.

Directly engaged requires that organizational responsibility and facilities have been assigned to an individual or group; a fellow scientist who "stops by to give a hand" may make the contribution of information which results in a solution, but he does not qualify as a member of the group.

Intake and utilization requires that the individual not only receive information (which may not arrive in the form of interpersonal communication—it may be taken in from his own experience), but also that he apply it directly to the problem; a technical assistant may spend all of his time gathering data—taking in information—but he fails to qualify if he does not utilize it himself in the solution of the problem.

Bringing to a conclusion requires, at the present stage of investigation, that the group members and their supervisors are willing, respectively, to submit and receive a given solution or solutions to the assigned problem and consider the job completed. For the present also, in lieu of an *a priori* estimate of the minimum amount of information required to solve a given problem (which might be provided by application of mathematical information theory) we will employ a dichotomous representation of progress toward a solution. A given communication intake will be classified merely as "contributing" or "not contributing" toward the solution, based (as mentioned above) on reported evaluations by the receivers of the communication.

Problem requires that a specific gap in knowledge exist in a research organization such as to cause management to assign to two or more professional researchers the responsibility and authority (within the usual budgetary and organizational limits) and the facilities to bridge this gap. In these restrictions lie the differentia between many so-called basic and applied research problems. It does not appear that the team or group approach, which depends on several professional workers and their supporting staff working in close cooperation (as evinced by the use of interpersonal communication) is currently used, or particularly adapted to work on questions of a more basic nature where the form of the answer is not readily specifiable in the statement of the problem. This hypothesis may be difficult to formulate in testable terms, but it is important in such areas as basic nuclear and medical research.

Identification of the Available Communication Channels

The initial step in this procedure is a complete inventory of all communication media available to members of the group for exchange of information among themselves and between themselves and all persons and groups external to the problem-solving group. An expanded list of such media should include:

(1) Two-way oral and gestural communication in a face-to-face situation, such as a continuous working relationship, a meeting, a visit, an interview.

(2) Two-way oral communication by means of a mechanical device such as a telephone, speaking tube, inter-com system. This could also include gestural communication via two-way television.

(3) One-way oral and/or gestural communication by means of a mechanical device such as a tape recording, a public-address system, a motion picture. This medium does not generally allow for a sequential interchange of messages, but can allow for a delayed response.

(4) Two-way written communication by means of letter, memo, or report which encompasses an interchange of such written material until a unit of communication has been completed. This involves the definition of "a communication unit" given below, which can involve an interchange of several messages.

(5) One-way written communication by means of letter, memo, report, book, article, brochure, published charts and tables, etc. This medium does not allow for an interchange of messages.

In most research organizations, all of these media are available to all of the professional workers to some degree. The crucial operation in identifying the communication media available to the group, then, is the classification of these media and their various forms according to relative availability. In order, however, that this classification be more than an abstract report of media available to each individual, sub-group, or the problem-solving group itself, this operation of availability determination must follow a definition and determination of channels of communication. Then will follow the identification of specific "media-channels," or individuals and groups linked by a particular medium.

Recent studies of communication patterns and information flow in human groups have reinforced the intuitive idea that not all of the members of a group are linked by channels of communication and that such links are not of equal utility in the transfer of information. In their studies of rumor transmission, researchers at the Research Center for Group Dynamics (8) point out that

The likelihood that a given item of information circulating through a social structure will reach a particular individual is in part determined by the number and nature of the channels of communication in the structure that touch this individual.

A series of laboratory experiments by Bavelas (9) and his colleagues at M.I.T. has demonstrated some of the essentially different ways in which an organization of only five people can be linked by channels of communication, resulting in differences in problem-solving productivity. Other studies involving inequality of communicative opportunity are found in (10, 11).

Of particular interest in the instance of communication within an on-going group is Deutsch's (12) comment that

. . . . what holds members of such groups together is their "social cohesion," or more accurately, their complementarity of communication, their ability to transmit relevant messages more accurately to each other than to anyone else.

Very briefly, a channel of communication, following from our specialized definition of information, is a link between a member or a sub-group, and other members or sub-groups; or between a member, sub-group, or the problem-solving group as a whole and any external source of information through which information can be transferred, for example:

Internal Channels	*External Channels*
Group Member 1—Group Member 2	Group Member 1—Laboratory Ass't
Group Members 1 and 2—Group Member 3	The Whole Group—Research Director
	Group Members 2 and 3—Another Company

The task of enumerating and evaluating all of the possible channels appears overwhelming in view of the number of possible internal channels alone that exist for a group of as small as five. Kephart (13) has developed a formulation for the total possible number of relationships (assuming that a relationship is the same in both directions) that can exist in a given group at a given time:

$$N = \frac{3^n - 2^{n+1} + 1}{2}$$

where n is the size of the group. For a group of five, therefore, the number of total possible channels of communication (if we disregard direction of flow) is ninety, including all possible links between members and subgroups.

Fortunately, the most frequently encountered problem-solving groups in physical research organizations seldom have more than three or four members "directly engaged in the intake and utilization of information for the purpose of bringing the current problem to a conclusion."

A matrix method of portraying all of the internal relationships has been developed by Sachs (14), and it can readily be extended to describe all possible channels between the group and external sources of information.

Festinger (15) has proposed an analysis of this type of matrix involving a squaring of the original communication or sociometric matrix, such that:

If the original sociometric data indicated channels of communication for information, the squared matrix would tell us who would hear things from whom with the information going through one intermediary.

This latter type of analysis, coupled with an identification of all the possible linkages or channels of communication within a system, offers promise of future understanding of the way in which information is brought to bear on the solution of a given problem in an on-going situation.

Following this inventory of the media of communication, and a representation of all possible communication channels, comes the classification of a "medium-channel"—a communication link using a specific medium —according to its availability to members of the group for exchange of information. Two criteria appear at this stage: a) the inclusive criterion of availability, which accepts all communication channels and b) the exclusive criterion of transfer of information, which rejects all channels which cannot or do not serve that purpose. As an initial specification of the availability criterion, it is proposed to use the empirical datum resulting from an answer to the question, "Has this channel ever been used?" For the latter criterion, the datum question is, "Has the group member ever received any information over it?" Subsequent classifications of the availability of a channel for exchange of information can take the form of a qualitative break-down such as, "Has been used: never, rarely, frequently, continually." Current field work, however, is employing numerical frequency classes over a given past period as measures of availability:

During the past month, show by check the approximate number of times you communicated with someone outside the company and the medium used:

	0	1–10	11–20	21–30	31–50	Over 50
Phoned someone						
Wrote someone						
Visited someone						

An additional consideration in the determination of the availability of media-channels is the concept of an individual's "propensity to communicate." Studies of group activity (3 or more people) and two-person activity involving a common member indicate that an individual's usage of a particular medium-channel or set of media-channels is dependent on three major factors:

(1) His characteristic propensity to communicate as evinced by a person's reputation as "the gabby kind" or "a silent type"; Chapple and Lindeman (16) described a method several years ago for determining the "interaction rate" of mental patients for purposes of diagnosis. Chapple (17) has since used this method for selecting sales people and executives on the basis of their activity rates. A recent study of the source and seriousness of air-line passenger complaints (18) uncovered some cranks who complained just because they habitually complained.

(2) The effect of his fellow group members on the individual's communicative activity. All of us have a range of roles that we play in the various groups

to which we belong. Bateson and Ruesch (19) estimate that the number of such roles reaches a maximum of 20 to 25. Some people are dominant (in the inter-action sense) in business, but fade into silence at home; others will communicate frequently with members of a group having common interests or characteristics. Homans (20) describes "isolates" (in the interaction sense) among file clerks in a large utility company; further study indicates that these girls were different in some way from the other girls in the group.

(3) The nature of the work has been shown to influence the communicative activity of group members. In a series of meetings of a plant suggestion com-mittee (21), the activity rates of particular individuals correlated significantly with the nature of the suggestion being discussed. The sales and accounting de-partment representatives hardly spoke during the discussions of highly techni-cal suggestions, but the accounting representative in particular dominated dis-cussions involving possible savings and costs.

Cognizance of these factors is important if the results of communica-tion studies can lead to generalizations rather than mere reports of the behavior of particular individuals in specific situations. Cavanaugh (22) describes a method for predicting the rate of interaction between popula-tion centers, based on factors such as distance, size, and culture. Current research on the above-mentioned factors in interpersonal communication —individual propensity to communicate, group effect, nature of the task —may soon lead to a formulation for propensity to communicate within small groups and subsequent verification through field studies of on-going groups.

Measurement of the Utilization of Available Media-Channels

Essential to the measurement of information transfer (in the sense that we are discussing it) is a definition of the communication unit or the mes-sage unit in which such information is carried. Identification of this unit of flow is prerequisite to any measurements such as direction, frequency, or types and amounts of information transferred.

In the current studies of human interaction such as those of Bales (23, 24, 25, 26), Chapple (27), Arensberg (28), Whyte (29), Marquis-Heyns-Guetzkow (30), and Carter (31), two basically different definitions of the interaction or interpersonal communication unit are used. Perhaps the best expression of this basic difference is found in a recent letter from Bales to Arensberg:

A single interaction in my terminology consists of a single act by a single individual or actor in a social or communication context, *as seen from the point of view of the other* . . . if person number 1 comes up to person number 2 and says, "Hello," . . . this constitutes a single interaction. . . . When person num-ber 2 says, "Hello" in turn, this is another interaction. . . . As persons 1 and 2 continue to talk or communicate (by non-verbal as well as verbal means), we say that a "process of interaction" is going on, which is made up of many separable "interactions" . . . as I understand it, you would record a single sequential process of this sort, from beginning to end, as a single "interaction" or "interaction event," and would characterize it in addition as having a duration of such and such a time.

Our feeling is that it is not a matter of final choice between two rival methods, but, as Bales also points out in his letter, a matter of using the particular notation best adapted to the field situation with which one is confronted. In one case (21) both methods were used side by side to measure the who-to-whom flow of communication in a series of committee meetings with excellent agreement between the methods.

In the current field situation, where the objective is the measurement of information transfer through a medium-channel, the latter (Arensberg) unit of flow is best adapted. The unit of flow or the communicative act then becomes *a continuous sequence of interpersonal communication with an observable or reportable beginning (initiation) and end (termination), which may or may not involve the transfer of information.* Illustrations of communication units follow, giving examples of potential or actual information transfer in two of the five media classes described above.

(1) Two-way Oral, Face-to-Face:

A turns to B and asks whether B knows of a compound with such and such properties. B replies that he does, and tells it to A. A thanks B and turns back to the work bench, with some information which will help him in solving the problem he is working on.

(2) One-way Written:

A visits the library to consult the original of an article which he has heard about. He reads the entire article, making notes and returning to the lab once for some data to compare with that in the article. He finishes reading the article and returns to the lab.

Following the definition of the communication unit, it is necessary to provide a method for quantifying or otherwise classifying these units that will permit cumulation and other manipulation of units and, finally, the establishment of statistical hypotheses. As previously outlined, we examine communication units by some sampling scheme and classify each of the units in a sample as "containing" or "not-containing" information.

A statistical procedure currently used in industrial sampling inspection and census work provides a model that can handle this type of data. It is called "sampling for attributes" (32, 33) and usually involves the dichotomous classification of articles as "accepted-rejected, occupied-not occupied, zero-one, etc." This statistical procedure of sampling for attributes may eventually be expected to lead to statements analogous to the predictive statements made in the control of quality of manufactured product where, once a state of statistical control has been established, statements are made to the effect that: "with a stated risk of being in error, I expect that the number of defects in a random sample will not exceed a given number." A statement of this type in the present context would be: "With a stated risk of being in error, I predict that a random sample of communication-units flowing through a given medium-channel, during a given interval of time (a day, week or month) will contain between x and y per cent information-bearing units."

While this kind of statement should prove invaluable to the control of communication once a state of statistical control—randomness in the source of the data—is known to exist, another type of statement is of more immediate importance to the evaluation of media-channels as suppliers of information to the problem-solving group. This type of statement involves the testing of statistical hypothesis such as:

Medium-channel 1 is a better source of information to the research worker than medium-channel 2 in terms of a difference between comparable statistics of samples taken from each medium-channel.

Another type of statement involves an estimate of a population parameter such as the fraction of information-bearing communication units flowing through a medium-channel "MC" during a time period "t."

A final set of operations essential to the measurement of channel utilization involves the establishment of logical categories for each of the observable or reportable variables describing a communicative act or a series of such acts. An example is:

Initiation. A primary classification might be "internal-external" for a given-medium channel, but the field situation might require a larger number of classes, such as:

Internal Initiation	*External Initiation*
(*from within the group*)	(*from outside the group*)
Self-initiated	Self-initiated
Routine	Routine
Requested from outside the group	Requested from the group

Such a classification might be indicated where a management decision to stimulate or inhibit a particular medium-channel depends on how communication-units are initiated in such media-channels.

REFERENCES

1. DAVID B. HERTZ and ALBERT H. RUBENSTEIN. *Team Research.* Cambridge, Mass.: Eastern Technical Publications, June, 1953.
2. "Time Out for Team Check," *Chemical Week*, November 3, 1951.
3. "Design for Research Communications," *Research Operations in Industry*, Columbia University, 1953.
4. "Maintaining Two-way Communications: Company Experience and Techniques," *Personnel Series Number 134*, American Management Association, 1950.

5. Ivan W. Willis. "Basic Principles of Effective Communications," *Advanced Management*, September, 1950.

6. Norbert Wiener. *Cybernetics*. Technology Press, 1948.

7. Claude Shannon and Warren Weaver. *Mathematical Theory of Communication*. Urbana: University of Illinois Press, 1950.

8. Leon Festinger, Dorwin Cartwright, et al. "A Study of a Rumor: Its Origin and Spread," *Human Relations*, Vol. 1, No. IV, 1948.

9. Alex Bavelas and Dermot Barrett. "An Experimental Approach to Organizational Communication," *Personnel*, March, 1951.

10. H. H. Kelley. "Communication in Experimentally Created Hierarchies," *Human Relations*, Vol. IV, 195.

11. J. Thibaut. "An Experimental Study of the Cohesiveness of Underprivileged Groups," *Human Relations*, Vol. III, 1950.

12. Karl W. Deutsch. "Communication in Self-Governing Organizations: Notes on Autonomy, Freedom and Authority in the Growth of Social Groups." Paper delivered at the Twelfth Conference on Social Philosophy, and Religion.

13. William M. Kephart. "A Quantitative Analysis of Intra-Group Relationships," *American Journal of Sociology*, May, 1950.

14. David D. Sachs. "A Matrix Representation of the Internal Relationships of a Small Group," Studies of Research Administration, Columbia University. Unpublished Memorandum, Fall, 1951.

15. Leon Festinger. "The Analysis of Sociograms Using Matrix Algebra," *Human Relations*, Vol. II, No. 2, April, 1949.

16. Eliot D. Chapple and Eric Lindemann. "Clinical Implications of Measurements of Interaction Rates in Psychiatric Interviews," *Applied Anthropology*, Vol. I, No. 2, 1942.

17. Eliot D. Chapple. "The Interaction Chronograph: Its Evolution and Present Application," *Personnel*, January, 1949.

18. Seymour Banks. "Relative Severity of Air-Line Passenger Complaints," *Journal of Applied Psychology*, August, 1951.

19. Gregory Bateson and Jurgen Ruesch. "Structure and Process in Social Relations," *Psychiatry*, May, 1949.

20. George Homans. "Sociological Measures in Organization." Paper presented to Seminar in Theory of Organization and Management, Columbia University, Spring, 1950.

21. A. H. Rubenstein. "A Study of Communications in a Manufacturing Company," Department of Industrial Engineering, 1951, Columbia University. (Unpublished Manuscript.)

22. Joseph A. Cavanaugh. "Formulation, Analysis, and Testing of the Interactance Hypothesis," *American Sociological Review*, Vol. XV, No. 6, December, 1950.

23. Robert F. Bales. *Interaction Process Analysis: A Method for the Study of Small Groups*. Addison-Wesley Press, 1950.

24. Robert F. Bales. "A Set of Categories for the Analysis of Small Group Interaction," *American Sociological Review*, April, 1950.

25. Robert F. Bales and Fred L. Strodtbeck. "Phases in Group Problem Solving," *Journal of Abnormal and Social Psychology*, October, 1951.

26. ROBERT F. BALES, *et al.* "Channels of Communication in Small Groups," *American Sociological Review*, August, 1951.

27. ELIOT D. CHAPPLE (with the collaboration of Conrad M. Arensberg). "Measuring Human Relations," *Genetic Psychology Monographs*, No. 22, 1940.

28. CONRAD M. ARENSBERG and ALEXANDER HORSFALL. "Teamwork and Productivity in a Shoe Factory," *Human Organization*, Winter, 1949.

29. WILLIAM FOOTE WHYTE. "Patterns of Interaction in Union-Management Relations," *Human Organization*, Fall, 1949.

30. D. G. MARQUIS, HAROLD GUETZKOW, and R. W. HEYNS. "A Social Psychological Study of the Decision-Making Conference," in *Groups, Leadership and Man*, Carnegie Press, 1951.

31. LAUNOR CARTER, *et al.* "A Note on a New Technique of Interaction Recording," *Journal of Abnormal and Social Psychology*, April, 1951.

32. EDWIN G. OLDS. "Wartime Developments in Acceptance Sampling by Attributes," *Acceptance Sampling—A Symposium*, The American Statistical Association, 1950.

33. W. E. DEMING. *Some Theory of Sampling*. Wiley, 1950, p. 109 ff.

Control and Evaluation

To MANY authors, the subject of "Control and Evaluation" is as broad as the question of "how to organize." One might surmise two reasons for this: the subjectivity of most writing on management and the fact that control or evaluation presupposes a great deal about organization. By subjectivity is meant the absence of the qualities of cumulativeness of contributions, systematic formulation, and communicability that were discussed in the introduction to Section One, as well as the custom of writing from the viewpoint of a practicing manager. Given these considerations, an author is driven to express much of his basic philosophy of administration before addressing himself to the question of control. Furthermore, viewed from the situation of the practicing manager, the question of control becomes, "How do I get my subordinates to do what I want them to?" which is, for the manager, equivalent to the question, "How do I organize?"

Inasmuch as we have not proposed this book as a handy guide to the practicing manager and have declared our intention to concentrate on that which is systematic, cumulative, and communicable, the place to start is with the presuppositions of control and evaluation. The first, of course, is a going organization larger and more complex than can be compassed by a face-to-face group. It is also supposed that the organization is rationally structured and goal-directed (i.e., bureaucratic). The question of control may then be phrased, "How do organizations act so as to co-ordinate human and other resources in support of goals?"

The answer to this question must necessarily be partly general and partly specific. Each organization has differences from all the others in the content of its goals, in the specific resources with which it has to deal, and in the technology available to it. But organizations have similarities too: they are goal-directed; they differentiate executive roles from other member roles; and they all are constrained by the "human nature" of their members.

Goals

The consideration of *values* is basic to any discussion of control—and it is relevant in more ways than may appear on the surface. The first and most important set of values is what Selznick calls "the evolving character of the organization as a whole." This defines the goals or objectives. Goals, of course, are specific; but, being determined, they provide the criteria by which the effectiveness of the organization is judged. It would be unreasonably formalistic, however, to hold that these are the only relevant values. A second way in which values are relevant stems from the commitment of the organization to its members. The human beings involved are not passive but react in terms of their own values to the controls imposed upon them. This thesis has been amply developed in Sections Two, Three, and Four. Third, and less obviously, enter the values of any nonmembers of the organization who have interest and power. All three of these impose imperatives on organizational functioning. It is through the executive apparatus that these imperatives are realized.

The Executive Role

In his classic work, *The Functions of the Executive*, Chester I. Barnard outlined the vital components of the executive role as: (*a*) the maintenance of communications within the organization, (*b*) the elaboration of purpose, and (*c*) the eliciting of member contributions. These functions, systematically arranged, provide the beginnings of organizational control.

The executives' communication functions include the formal aspect of establishing the system of positions and the informal one of insuring the adequacy of communication by departing from official channels when necessary. In most organizations, there are also routine formal channels of communication that transcend the "line of command." These include media, such as the company house organ, that are disseminated indiscriminately and reports, such as periodic accounting and statistical bulletins, that are regularly transmitted to designated executives without recourse to "channels" on each occasion. Both of these types are important to the control function. Granick (1) points out how the Soviets use broadcast communication to secure changes in emphasis in industrial programs; this method seems especially appropriate for communicating information on goals. The role of routine reports of performance is developed in several of the articles reproduced below. Although communication is necessary to control, it does not by itself normally establish executive responsibility.

Elaboration of purpose means more than formulating over-all goals. It includes the determination of subgoals and methods down to the assignment of specific tasks to specific individuals. The larger aspects of this function are *departmentalization* (the grouping of positions and tasks) and the related process of commitment of resources to relatively more specific forms, such as land, buildings, machinery, hiring and training of personnel, etc.

In Section Three we examined many of the factors conditioning the ability of the executive organization to elicit member contributions. This subject is generally discussed in two parts: the decision to participate in the organization and the influencing of organization members after they have achieved that status. Although the act of joining evokes a significant increase in the member's regard for the legitimacy of organizational authority, co-operation is held by the same methods it is won: by members sharing the organization's goals, by the payment of incentives (including nonmonetary), by members' acceptance of the legitimacy of their role vis-á-vis the organization, and by sanctions.

Faced with these characteristics of organizations, we may begin to inquire how it is that they can achieve the degree of technical superiority alleged for them by Weber and so readily observed in the course of our daily lives. What properties of the organization overcome the very real limitations we have studied and permit the great achievements of which organizations are capable? The technical advantages of specialization and definite allocation of jurisdiction according to formal rules, as discussed by Weber, help to explain the organization's power over its external environment. We must also explain the ability of the organization to maintain control over itself.

The application of cybernetic models to this question is the subject of the articles by Haberstroh, Dean, and Rubenstein. They suggest that the kind of rationality necessary for control takes a somewhat different form from that envisioned by Weber. In particular, there is needed a feedback of information on the results of the organization's efforts, an appropriate measure of the effectiveness of organizational action. Coincidental with this is the need for accurate and timely communication of the results of performance measurement to the appropriate part of the organization. Beyond this, there still remain the problems of correcting performance, to be discussed under the headings of *executive responsibility* and *power*.

The servomechanism model is an attractive and appropriate analogy in the discussion of organizational control. Although frequent use is made of it in the literature, there have been few attempts to build genuine, mathematical models such as those commonly used in engineering control systems. The reasons for this can be appreciated from a study of the case reported by Haberstroh. Although this study attempted to model only the safety function in the plant, the control chart is fairly complex and, if modeled fully, would require a nonlinear operator that is beyond the power of present analytic methods. If the entire organizational control system were modeled (or even the entire safety function including departmental loops), sheer complexity would probably prohibit an analytic solution. Moreover, testing of such a model is hampered by the paucity of data. Only one measurement of annual performance can be taken each year. It is these features that attract some investigators to techniques of *simulating* organizational performance.

Evaluation procedures are usually thought of as ascertaining the effectiveness of particular executives, operating units, projects, methods, apparatus, or organizational forms. Since these procedures usually begin with an audit of *past* performance, they may be thought of as distinct from control functions, whose purpose is to regulate *current* performance. Actually, if evaluation procedures have any impact, it is as the long-run counterpart of control. Control at the highest levels largely consists of changes in executive personnel or formal organization, based on the results of formal or informal evaluation procedures. This principle appears recurrently in the articles in this section as well as elsewhere in the literature (2). In "A Research Plan for the Study of Organizational Effectiveness," Andrew L. Comrey presents a general design for a series of studies which was later carried out in several different kinds of organizations (3). If this research had been planned and executed by a practicing manager or his staff in his own organization, it would clearly qualify as an evaluation procedure since it attempts to relate various design characteristics to over-all organization effectiveness.

Implicit in the theory of control or evaluation procedures are *standards of performance*. In each of the cases which are examined in the readings to follow, the existence of some standard is pointed out or recommended. Standards are usually the creation of the participants, although it is possible to find cases (e.g., the subordinate organizations discussed in the readings) where the standards are given by the environment (superior organizations). The more interesting case and the one of most importance to the businessman is the standard that has to be self-generated. The standards may be derived as indicated below from some model in use by the organization. They may also be set intuitively, or on the basis of historical experience, or by a consideration of the experience of other similar organizations.

In management literature, in economic theory, and in operations research the standards are usually conceived of as *optima* of some sort. The most common example is the maximization of profits. There is a relation between the concept of standards as used in our theory of organizational control and the concept of optimum performance as just stated. Standards may be *intended* as optima, but they are rarely *demonstrable* as such. In the context of organizational behavior, the existence of optima can be affirmed within the framework of some *model* of the organization's functioning that admits of analytic methods (like the infinitesimal calculus) for defining the optima. An optimum value is then a property of a model used by or recommended to an organization. A model in use is a design characteristic of the organization, a part of the formal organization usually, and possibly itself subject to an evaluation procedure. Frequently, the optima of a model are clearly not identical with the attainment of the over-all goals of the organization, but the model is used as the best available alternative. In such instances, the act of constraining organizational behavior in ways suggested by the optimality criteria of the model is referred to as *suboptimization*.

A measurement of performance can disclose whether performance is up to standard, but not whether it is optimal. In each of the articles in this section, one or more measures of performance are reported and analyzed (4). The main difficulties with systems of performance measurement lie in determining standards and measures that really reflect the goals of the organization. If this is not the case, the organization is more likely to achieve what is being measured than to realize its actual goals. In the language of the preceding discussion of models, suboptima are likely to displace original goals. This is essentially the main thesis of the article by Ridgeway, "Dysfunctional Consequences of Performance Measurement."

The existence of a good measurement of performance is not useful unless the information is present at the point where it can be used. This implies that information on achievement of the organization's most general goals is reported to the highest executives and, correspondingly, information on subgoals, to the subordinate officials in the appropriate positions. If we judge by cybernetic models, these communication links are crucial to organizational control. This may account for some of the trends in organizational development: specifically, the development of elaborate systems of quantitative reports and the growth of extensive staff organizations paralleling the usual line of command. Both of these developments provide alternative chains of communication to the normal hierarchical flow of reports. The establishment of multiple channels of communication is probably a calculated step; it is often easier to improve one's performance by manipulating reports than by actually correcting deficiencies. Dalton, for example, reports case material illustrating top management's use of staff services for control purposes and also illustrating a rich variety of ways in which reports were falsified to show better than actual performance (5). Some of the examples cited by Ridgeway (e.g., sacrificing maintenance for production records) also illustrate ways of manipulating reports.

This brings us to the question of what is actually done in organizations to assure adequate performance, the matter of *executive responsibility*. According to Barnard (6), responsibility is the capacity and determination of an individual to work within his own moral codes relevant to the situation in which he finds himself. By interpretation, executive responsibility thus refers to the executive's capacity to anticipate and to direct his actions toward their consequences for the imperatives of the situation. Elliott Jaques, in the context of working out performance standards for a large engineering company, defined a measure of responsibility as the time span between the executive's initiation of action and the feedback of the results of his actions (7). Since the relevance of feedback is determined by the imperatives of the situation, there is more than a hint of similarity between the two definitions. The responsible executive is the one who can manage his affairs so that the imperatives of the situation are met, the test of whether or not they are met being implicit in the feedbacks received. This means that the executive is bound not only by his own values and the goals of the organization, but also by the values of other members whose co-operation is needed and of outsiders, if their values can be brought to bear on the immediate concerns of the executive. Government regulatory agencies and customer boycotts are relevant examples of the latter.

If the network of feedbacks is appropriately arranged, then the maintenance of responsibility will be sufficient for achievement of the organization's goals. But what of the executive who fails to be responsible? The usual answer is, of course, that this forces into action another executive whose responsibility is thus jeopardized. The supervisory system thus assures that the failure of one executive will not prejudice the goals. Nevertheless, control systems are subject to certain malfunctions and these are also illustrated in the literature. The manipulation of reports of performance has already been discussed. Another way of maintaining overt responsibility is by the collusion of a superior and subordinate to keep the superior formally ignorant of malfunctions. An example of this is the inspection procedure described by Dalton in "Managing the Managers" in Article 9. Hemphill and Sechrest, in "A Comparison of Three Criteria of Air Crew Effectiveness in Combat over Korea," illustrate still another type of malfunction. Here is an evaluation procedure used by the Air Force, involving an apparently objective criterion, and shown by the researchers to be itself irrelevant to performance. Other examples are cited by Ridgeway.

There is a second theme implicit in Dalton's case analysis in "Managing the Managers": whether apparently evasive action by subordinates is to be judged by "the book" or whether it is to be judged by the over-all goals of the organization. This appears in his contrasting the "strong" executives who get things done with the "weak" executives who place excessive reliance on compliance with formal requirements. Executive malfeasance is thus a possible cure for misdirected formalism and a source of adaptive flexibility in times of crisis.

The entire problem of control logically presupposes the existence of executive power. Since control is by and large achieved, one may infer that executives do indeed hold power. Nevertheless, the qualifications and limitations on the holding and exercise of power have important consequences for organizational functioning. As we may infer from Section Two, the possibility of struggles for power is as great within organizations as in social, economic, and political systems. Empire building in subordinate departments may greatly reduce the power of higher executives to establish and enforce goals for those departments. This has become a commonplace in governmental administration, and it is often correct now to regard the bureau, and not the President, as the seat of executive authority in certain spheres. The existence of power centers outside the executive hierarchy, especially unions and government regulatory agencies, also imposes restraints on the freedom of executive action. The institutions developed by organizations to assure stability can also impose limitations on executive power. For example, the widespread custom of (officially or unofficially) guaranteeing job security to executives restricts the sanctions which may be used against them and also limits the organization's freedom to "put the right man in the right job." The legitimacy of authority and the indirect sanctions which an organization may hold over an executive's promotion chances, perquisites, freedom of action, etc. still represent considerable power.

An interesting typology of power and control has been developed by Tannenbaum and Kahn, and applied mainly to the study of union organizations (8). Their method involves the use of an attitude survey to measure member perceptions of the degree of control held by various organization components or categories of members. By plotting the degree of control against hierarchical level, as in Figure 1, they identify autocratic, oligarchic, democratic, and anarchic control structures. An in-

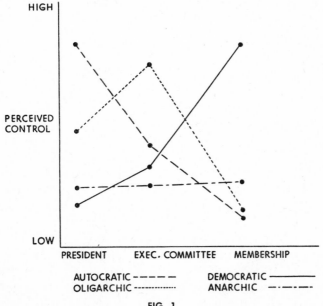

FIG. 1

teresting characteristic of this method is that the control curve may vary in its general height as well as in its shape. This is hypothesized to differentiate active, highly directed organizations from weak, inactive, unco-ordinated organizations. Their study of union locals suggests that the general degree of control may depend upon the degree to which the environment is perceived as threatening.

REFERENCES

1. DAVID GRANICK. *Management of the Industrial Firm in the USSR*, chap. iv, New York, 1954.

2. C. I. BARNARD. *Functions of the Executive*. Harvard, 1938, p. 223.

3. The final report of this study was ANDREW L. COMREY, JOHN M. PFIFFNER, and WALLACE S. HIGH, *Factors Influencing Organizational Effectiveness*. Los Angeles: University of Southern California, 1954. Three partial reports of this study also appeared in *Personnel Psychology* for 1953, 1954, and 1955.

4. An excellent annotated bibliography of material on this subject, including much material on control in general, is P. WASSERMAN, *Measurement and Evaluation of Organizational Performance*, Graduate School of Business and Public Administration. Ithaca, N.Y.: Cornell University, 1959.

5. MELVILLE DALTON. *Men Who Manage*, chap. iv. New York: Wiley, 1959.

6. CHESTER BARNARD. *Functions of the Executive*, chap. xvii.

7. E. JAQUES. *Measurement of Responsibility*. Harvard, 1956.

8. ARNOLD S. TANNENBAUM and ROBERT L. KAHN. "Organizational Control Structure," *Human Relations*, Vol. X, No. 2, 1957.

27. CONTROL AS AN ORGANIZATIONAL PROCESS*

CHADWICK J. HABERSTROH

The research reported is an attempt to discover to what extent the theory of self-regulating systems applies to human organizations in general and to one industrial plant in particular. Feedbacks of information on performance and objectives were found to have much influence on two types of executive decision processes: programming of routine work and innovation in the organization of executive functions. The control pattern included multiple, decentralized control loops. This combination worked adequately in an area—safety—where the results of decisions could not be forecasted with any accuracy.

THE STUDY of self-regulating systems, now generally known as cybernetics, explores the ways in which some output of a dynamic system can be maintained in a more-or-less invariant equilibrium, or steady state, in the face of disrupting external forces.[1] The most general answer to this question is that the system must somehow be supplied with information about the disrupting forces that is used to offset their effect. A common way of supplying this is by means of a feedback of information on the deviations of the output from equilibrium. This information flow causes the equilibrium to be restored in some appropriate manner.

Even assuming that one does know the feedback channel used and understands the laws through which the feedback restores equilibrium, he still has a right to ask how it is that the system exists at all, and why it tends to an equilibrium at that particular value and not some other. In the case of engineering control systems the answer to this question is simple and direct: the designer intended them to perform in the way they do. Thus, there is a purposive element in these control systems resulting from an *a priori* selection of the equilibrium to be obtained. If one asks the same question, however, about naturally self-regulating systems, such as homeostatic mechanisms in the living organism or ecological balances in a community of organisms, the answer is neither simple nor direct. The equilibria found and the mechanisms for attaining them have come about by the process of natural selection in the context of a particular environment. If we put the same question in the case of organizational systems, the answer is even less direct and more complicated, involving as it does a multitude of designers each consciously striving to realize his own ob-

---

* Reproduced from *Management Science*, Vol. 6, No. 2, January, 1960.
[1] N. Wiener, *Cybernetics* (New York: Wiley, 1948); W. R. Ashby, *An Introduction to Cybernetics* (New York: Wiley, 1956).

jectives, in the context of an environment and of selection pressure arising from the limitation of resources as well.

In organizations the conscious intentions of the participants are an important factor. In order to explain the gross behavior of an organization, these intentions must be measured and brought into relation with the other aspects of the organization's functioning. The existence of stable organization implies a degree of harmony and co-ordination among the participants, a sharing of intention. In order to secure this, participants communicate with each other and in doing so construct a common symbolic picture of the goals they have set for the organization and the means by which they intend to attain the goals. This picture, or representation, of the means and ends of organization (the "task analysis") is implicit in the verbal communication inside the organization. It can be measured by the use of content-analysis techniques. I have attempted to apply these techniques to a sample of communication from an integrated steel plant operated by one of the American companies.[2] This case will be used as an example in exploring organization purposes and other organizational characteristics affecting control processes.

Goal formation is influenced by the intentions of the individual participants and by the environmental constraints under which they operate. Both can be sources of conflict. The emergence of stable, enduring patterns of organization is in part a process of conflict resolution. The necessity of reducing conflict to manageable bounds tends to direct the organization's efforts toward a small number of goals and a small number of means activities for achieving them, relative to the number of alternatives that might be conceivable. It is to be expected, therefore, that the number of independent goals turned up in the task analysis will be rather small. Conflict reduction is facilitated if these goals are formulated in terms of acceptable levels, rather than in terms of optima,[3] and if the criterion of goal achievement is external and objective, rather than subjective and open to dispute. If members measure goal achievement objectively and perceive means to attain them, the goals are termed "operative."

In the case of Integrated Steel, four goals were discovered. These relate to cost reduction, production level, safety, and medical care. The safety and production goals are formulated in terms of acceptable levels set by an external office. Performance is measured in terms of tonnage

[2] This research was carried out at the Graduate School of Industrial Administration, Carnegie Institute of Technology, under a grant from the Ford Foundation for research on human behavior in organization. A full report of the methods and the results of this investigation, as well as a more thorough discussion of the topic of the present paper, is contained in my doctoral dissertation, *Processes of Internal Control in Firms*, University Microfilms, Inc. (Ann Arbor, Michigan, 1958).

[3] H. A. Simon, *Models of Man* (New York: Wiley, 1957), p. 241.

produced and frequency of injuries, and an elaborate technology exists for goal achievement. In the case of safety, this task analysis was measured in detail. The goal of providing adequate medical care was departmentalized in a plant hospital; and a standard cost system and various cost reduction programs were in operation. Neither the hospital nor the cost system was investigated, however.

If the process of goal formation results in a small number of operative goals, as it did at Integrated Steel, the basis for a feedback of information on deviations of performance from the established goals is already apparent. To affirm the existence of a control system we need only verify that this information is reported to executive centers and that the executives respond so as to achieve the goals. The task analysis comprises a program of means activities understood by the participants to lead to goal achievement. One way of responding would be to adjust the level of resource use in these means activities. Let us refer to this as "routine control." Another way of responding would be to look for a better way of achieving goals. This type of activity could take the form of inventing new means activities or of altering the system of executive organization (i.e., changes in personnel or in allocation of functions). It might be expected that this type of activity would occur only in a case of extreme or repeated failure. Let us call this "non-routine control." Sufficient pressure might even lead to modification of goals in order to assure survival of the organization. Normally, however, the evolved structure of goals and means activities determines what the participants do; communication channels carrying information on performance influence when and how much they do.

In the case of Integrated Steel's safety program the type of means activities which have been developed to implement the safety objective are accident investigations, safety conferences with workmen, implementation of safety work-orders, special inspections, clean-up work, etc. The execution of each of these activities is in some way conditional on the occurrence of injuries in the plant. Other activities are also carried on which are independent of the occurrence of accidents. These include routine inspections, training and screening procedures for new employees, safety clearance of engineering proposals, job analysis, publicity campaigns, etc.

The formal communication channels on safety performance begin with injury reports made by the plant hospital. This information is collated and distributed daily throughout the plant's executive organization in detail and in statistical summary. This information cues the line supervision to investigate injuries; alerts the plant safety staff to inspect for similar hazards and to assist in accident investigations; and, in summary figures, provides the basis for broader types of corrective action such as the study of classes of jobs for hazards, the issuance of special instructions to employees, and evaluation of supervisors. The same reports when aggregated into divisional and plant injury frequencies serve as an indicator of the plant's over-all performance relative to its safety goals.

The routine control processes discussed above are not the only, or even the most important, means of control used at Integrated Steel. The non-routine control processes, changes in personnel and in the institutional structure within which the participants operate, take precedence. The very nature of the accident process (i.e., the importance of human failure, rare events, conjunction of circumstances, and the randomness of occurrence of injuries) make for a different degree of reliability on the technological side from that encountered in connection with, for instance, production matters. Because the coupling between the program of means activities and the degree of safety performance is not fully determined, there is a need for relatively tight control over the programs themselves. This is achieved by response of the top plant management to deviations of the plant and departmental injury frequencies from the objectives set for them at the beginning of the year. These yearly objectives are set by company officers above the plant level, although the plant management has discretion to aim at a more difficult target if it chooses.

Figure 1 is a block diagram of the control structure discussed above.

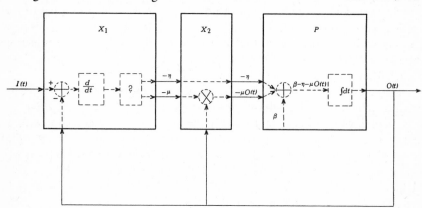

FIG. 1. Control Flow Chart of Safety Functions at Integrated Steel

The input (I) is the annual safety objective which is compared with the performance of the plant (O) by top management. The result of the nonroutine control functions of the top executive organization (X_1) may be expressed as the two parameters of the routine control system: the intensity of response to injuries (μ) and the level of independent safety activity (η). A complete model of the top executive function was not constructed, although there seems to be evidence[4] that it responds to

[4] Compare columns 4 and 11 in Table 1.

changes in the degree of error (a differentiating operator). Other than that it appears possible to say only that its effects are intermittent, rather than continuous, and respond only to error in excess of a certain threshold. It is therefore a nonlinear operator. In the case of the routine control function (X_2), however, a linear model seems appropriate. Executives appear to proportion their influence on the injury rate to the magnitude of that rate plus a constant. The "program" operator (P) relates the control activities to the actual performance of the plant, adding and integrating the safety efforts $(\mu O + \eta)$ and the exogenous load of new hazards (β).

Table 1 contains data on injury rates, safety objectives, and innovations in the safety program for a 10 year period. The changes in organization

TABLE 1
INNOVATION* AND PERFORMANCE AT INTEGRATED STEEL

	DISABLING INJURIES						TOTAL INJURIES			
Year	Average All Plants	Error	Δ Error	Plant Performance	Error	Target	Plant Performance	Error	Target	Innovation*
1	5.29	.98	.98	6.17			357			moderate
2	4.95	.13	−.85	5.08			422			none
3	5.41	1.77	1.64	7.18			407			heavy
4	4.66	1.24	−.53	5.90			302			none
5	3.66	.67	−.57	4.33			244			none
6	3.55	.65	−.02	4.20	.46	3.74	210	0	238	light
7	3.00	.83	.18	3.83	.50	3.33	196	0	210	moderate
8	2.38	.81	−.02	3.19	.72	2.47	183	11	172	light
9	2.07	.63	−.18	2.70	.54	2.16	133	0	168	none
10[a]	1.93	.91	.28	2.84	.80	2.04	128	0	133	heavy

[a] At time major decisions were taken.

* Level of innovation in the plant-wide safety program was rated by the author on the basis of a survey of plant safety files. The information found consisted of a description of the innovations made. This information is briefly summarized below.

In the first year studied the safety staff recommended and received management approval of a job analysis program which was to provide the basis for strict enforcement of safe working procedures. They also requested regular physical examinations for all employees.

In year 2, no safety innovations were discovered.

In year 3, one of the plant manager's top staff assistants announced to division managers the inauguration of an extensive program of job analysis and indoctrination of workmen in safe procedures. He also urged the division managers to inaugurate the practice of having foremen make thorough investigations of all minor injuries as a basis for corrective action. This was to be coupled with a program of training foremen in the responsibilities which would be placed upon them in these two programs, and also the formation of division safety committees at top division management level to expedite safety recommendations. He also announced inauguration of a plant-wide safety committee.

In years 4 and 5 no new activity was discovered.

In year 6 a proposal was made by the safety staff for transfer of some functions so as to improve the coordinating service of the safety staff and shift more executive responsibility on to the line organization. There was a new program of statistical reporting of injuries classified by types of accident.

In year 7 management inaugurated a revised system of job analysis, appointed a new plant-wide advisory committee, inaugurated an annual conference of all division managers for the purpose of setting objectives and reviewing the safety program, and also ordered the universal replacement of a hazardous type of crane controller in use through most of the plant.

In year 8 a new statistical basis for the reporting of injuries was inaugurated.

In year 9 no innovations were discovered.

In year 10 a revised and greatly expanded program of job analysis was instituted, with a number of executives re-assigned to safety responsibilities exclusively. Procedures for top level reporting and evaluation of safety performance were revised to place greater emphasis upon safety.

made by top management in year 7 did not take effect until year 9. Thus, during the period beginning with year 3 and ending with year 8, the routine control system operated with constant parameters μ and η. Under this assumption, the injury rate $(O(t))$ is given by

$$(1) \qquad O(t) = \int [\beta - \eta - \mu O(t)] \, dt$$

or equivalently

$$(2) \qquad O'(t) = \beta - \eta - \mu O(t) .$$

Solving this differential equation,

$$(3) \qquad O(t) = \frac{\lambda}{\mu} + \left[\hat{O} - \frac{\lambda}{\mu} \right] e^{-\mu t}$$

where $\lambda = \beta - \eta$ and $\hat{O}$ is the initial level of the injury rate.

This equation implies that first differences in injury rates tend to decrease by a constant ratio from year to year. The performance data for years 3 to 8 in Table 1 is fairly consistent with this.

Another principle of control, important in the case of organization, is that of factorization. Ashby has shown[5] that if trial-and-error changes are relied upon for control (compare the operator X_1 at Integrated Steel), a large system cannot practicably be stabilized unless its output can be factored into a number of independently controlled information sources. At Integrated Steel, the safety objective was broken down by divisions and injury rates were reported on that same basis. Part of the nonroutine control activity occurred at the division level. Innovation in divisional programs initiated by division management was correlated with the division's performance error.

This, of course, bears on the subject of decentralization in organizations. Meaningful decentralization is probably impossible without a resolution of the goals into nonconflicting, operative subgoals so that these can be placed under independent control. On the other hand, there is probably a size for organizations at which goal attainment becomes impossible without factorization, even though the method used may not resemble current definitions of "decentralized authority." The plant production, cost, and safety goals at Integrated Steel appear to represent just such a factorization of the company goals.

In summary, the characteristics postulated by cybernetic theory for self-regulating systems have their correlates in human organizations. In the case of Integrated Steel, the theory points up the influence of information feedbacks upon the actions of the executives in attempting to realize the organization objectives. Of particular importance are the role of the higher echelons of executives in controlling the mode of response of the lower echelons and the use of multiple feedbacks in the design of the executive system.

---

[5] W. R. Ashby, *Design for a Brain* (New York: Wiley, 1952).

28. PROFIT PERFORMANCE MEASUREMENT OF DIVISION MANAGERS*

JOEL DEAN

I. INTRODUCTION

In introduction we shall touch on (A) the importance, (B) the difficulty, and (C) the role of profit centers in measuring executive performance.

A. Importance

Measuring executive performance is important in five ways:

(1) It directs top management's supervision and assistance to where it is most needed and where it will be most productive.

(2) It shapes the future executive team by indicating whom to promote, whom to retain and whom to remove.

(3) It directs the activity of executives toward high scores on the aspects of performance on which they are measured and judged.

(4) It gives job satisfaction directly by letting the executive know how he is doing.

(5) It provides the objective, factual foundation for sound incentive compensation.

B. Difficulty

Measuring executive performance in a big company is difficult. The performance you want to measure is achievement of the company's goals. Measuring the executive's contribution to this achievement is made complex by the fact that the corporation usually has several objectives which overlap and in some degree conflict; profits, growth, market share, and eternal life.

Profits should be the corporation's dominant goal in view of its obligation to stockholders and to a free enterprise society, but other objectives contribute in diffuse ways to long-run profits and thus cannot be ignored in measuring executive performance. Hence, the main executive performance you want to measure is contribution to the corporation's profits today and tomorrow.

The problem is made more difficult by the fact that facets of executive activity are numerous and contribute to profits in complex ways. There are few profit determining activities that are absolutely good or bad in themselves. To make the most money often requires foregoing a

---

* Reproduced from *The Controller*, September, 1957.

high score in one activity in order to push another (e.g., high quality product vs. low cost of making it).

To combine performance measures of separate activities requires proper weights which are hard to determine and change continuously. For example, a textile mill manager is scored on (1) quality control, (2) cost compared with standards, (3) safety, (4) equipment modernity, (5) production volume, (6) meeting delivery deadlines. How should these facets of performance be weighted?

Thus, responsibility for profits in a big company is in danger of being diffused. This makes measurement hard and cuts economic efficiency of the firm. Decentralization, i.e. setting up profit centers, is a promising way to overcome this diffusion of profit responsibility.

C. Role of Profit Center Decentralization

For measuring performance, executives can be put in two groups: (1) staff specialists, (2) businessmen, i.e., profit center (i.e. division) managers.

Complex problems of measuring and weighting executives' contributions to profits are best solved by dividing the corporation into semi-autonomous profit centers whose management is measured by the contributions his center makes to corporation's overhead and profits.

A big, integrated multiple-product company functions best if made into a miniature of the competitive free enterprise economy. You can do this by dividing firms into independent operating units which act like economic entities free to trade outside as well as inside the company.

Powered with the right incentives, each profit center in maximizing its own contribution profits will do what will also maximize the profits of the entire company. It works the same way that selfish profit seeking by individual firms in a private enterprise society generates the high productivity and automatic economic adjustments of a competitive economy.

II. REQUIREMENTS FOR PROFIT CENTER PERFORMANCE MEASUREMENT

To make a profit center system achieve these desired results of stimulating and measuring executive performance, it is necessary to:

A. Mark off profit centers correctly

B. Establish economically sound intra-company transfer prices and business arrangements

C. Measure the contribution profits of the profit center correctly

D. Determine realistic standards of contribution profit performance

E. Establish incentives in the form of executive compensation and nonmonetary rewards that will induce profit center managers to do what will be best for the corporation as a whole.

A. Profit Center Boundaries

The problem of marking off profit center boundaries has two aspects: (1) Segregating service functions from profit centers, (2) Defining the scope of each profit center.

Service centers comprise staff activities which cannot be satisfactorily measured in terms of profit performance. Profit centers and service centers shade into one another so that each company's solution needs to be different. The contribution of a service center to company profitability may be great but is hard to isolate and measure definitively.

The problem of gearing staff service to profit performance is partly solved by pulverizing staff services and distributing among profit centers, where the activity must be justified economically.

Some services could be sold on a profit center basis but institutional arrangements would be too complicated and burdensome, e.g. engineering. Some services might not be used enough or in the right way if made a profit center, e.g., legal department or economics department.

The second problem is to define the scope of each profit center. A profit center is defined as a semi-autonomous group of facilities and functions chosen so that profit performance can be the main guide to evaluation of divisional performance and the main guide by which the division manager makes his critical decisions.

Decisions involve economic choices among mutually exclusive courses of action. Each decision requires balancing of various kinds of costs and revenues. The company's interest lies not in maximizing a particular kind of revenue or minimizing a particular kind of cost in isolation but in maximizing difference between all revenues and all costs. Hence the scope for profit performance measurement should be a major guide in marking off profit center boundaries.

The details of divisional boundaries and institutional arrangements are important. Failures and frustrations of decentralization are often traceable to bad boundaries and rules. Boundary lines determine how well a particular profit center functions in the corporation's interests, i.e., minimize conflicts of interest. Good boundaries make the profit performance of the division manager more meaningful, produce better incentives, supervision and development guides.

Four economic tests can be applied in marking off profit centers: (1) operational independence, (2) access to sources and markets, (3) separable costs and revenues, (4) managerial intent.

1. *Operational independence.* Unless a division has a large measure of independence it will have inadequate scope to reach decisions on a profit-oriented basis and hence delegation will be defeated. The division manager needs discretion over buying, production, scheduling, inventories,

product-mix and pricing. This discretion should be exercised under broad rules of the game established centrally.

2. *Access to sources and markets.* Independent access to sources and markets is essential if make-or-buy decisions are to be made correctly. It is also essential for make-or-sell decisions, i.e. choice between selling a product at an early stage of the process or later, (e.g. cured vs. uncured hams).

Access to outside sources and markets is most useful if outside markets are highly flexible in the long run, i.e. capable of either supplying or absorbing the company's needs without extreme price disturbances. Markets which appear too imperfect in the short run frequently are not over a period of months or years, e.g. major components of an automobile.

3. *Separable costs and revenues.* Profit centers should be marked off so as to minimize the necessity for cost and revenue allocations, since these are necessarily arbitrary and contentious.

Contribution profits of the division can be defined so as to exclude central and other costs outside the profit center manager's control. But when these controllable profits are too small a part of the total a profit center does no good.

4. *Managerial intent.* No division's contribution can be measured solely by its profits but this must be a good measure of performance if the division is to be a profit center.

Top management must be resolved to abide by the behavior and performance and the impersonal guidance of the price system which this measure of divisional performance implies.

B. Economic Transfer Prices

A second underlying requisite of effective profit center controls is competitive intra-company transfer prices negotiated in arm's length bargaining by profit center managers.

Transfer pricing must preserve profit-making autonomy of the division manager so that his divisional profit performance will coincide with the interests of the company. Small differences in unit price of transfer products make big differences in division profits and executive bonuses.

Conflicts of interests can be held at a minimum by transfers at marginal cost, but this prevents meaningful division profit performance and undercuts the main gains of profit center control.

Competitive negotiated transfer prices can be obtained by applying three simple principles:

(*a*) Buyers and sellers completely free to deal outside or inside the company.

(*b*) Prices determined by negotiation between buyers and sellers with a minimum of arbitration.

(*c*) Negotiators have access to data on alternative sources and markets and have facilities for using the markets.

C. Measurement of Profit Contribution

A third requirement is good measurement of the profit contribution of the division. Performance measurement of profit center management must be geared to the multiple and overlapping goals of the corporation.

Performance Areas. Key performance areas can be grouped and labeled various ways. One pattern is:

1. *Current profitability*, the dominant measurement, will be discussed later.

2. *Growth* is usually conceived as sales growth, either absolutely or relatively to the industry. Frequently it is best measured in terms of market share. In whatever way it is measured, growth usually requires the development of a market franchise. This is generally achieved at the expense of some short-run profits. But presumably, it contributes to more distant profits and hence it is a part of the picture of the management's profit performance.

3. *Progress* has many dimensions. Three important ones are:

(*a*) Investment in ideas. Research is at the expense of short-run profits, designed for long-run survival.

(*b*) Modernity and acceptability of the product. Sometimes this too causes short-run profit sacrifice.

(*c*) Productivity. This can be indicated by output per man hour and rate-of-return on facilities investments.

4. *Executive development:* investment in people for future profits.

The last three factors, growth, progress and people, though measurable in their components, are hard to weight and reconcile with current profitability. The key question is whether the right amount of near profits were sacrificed in attaining these various determinants of distant profits. The answer requires high level judgment and technical familiarity with the kinds of investment in market franchise, in ideas, in facilities, and in people that are entailed.

Measurement of the current profitability of a division entails three kinds of considerations:

(1) The concept of profits

(2) The form in which that profit concept will be used

(3) The measurement of profits.

Profit Concepts. As to the concept of profit there are three choices:

(a) Book net profits
(b) Real net profits
(c) Contribution profits

Book net profits tie into the stockholder reports, have a surface acceptability and are not very fudgible. But they embroil executives in fruitless debates about allocation of corporate overheads over which they have no control and raise moot questions about capital consumption costs of plant acquisitions at widely differing price levels.

Real net profits may settle the latter questions (inflation and depreciation) but do not settle problems of allocation of overhead beyond the division manager's control.

Contribution profits have fewer of these drawbacks being confined to costs and revenues over which the profit center manager has control.

Form of Profits. As to the form in which any of these three profit concepts may be expressed, there are three choices:

(1) As dollar amounts
(2) As percentage of sales
(3) As a rate-of-return on investment

All three forms are useful in measuring different aspects of executive performance. For best results each needs to be compared with a suitable bogey.

(1) Contribution profit dollars aid economic decision making by focussing division management energies on dollars of added profit.

(2) Contribution profits as a per cent of sales facilitate comparison with past performance and with comparable outside companies. Standing alone and without a bogey this performance measure is misleading.

(3) Contribution profits as a return on investment provides the most important guide to top management in evaluation of profit center performance.

Measurement of Profits. Technical problems of profit performance measurement are in practice less formidable than they appear to many newcomers.

A moderately good approximation to contribution profits can be drawn from most accounting systems with few adjustments given correct profit center demarcation and transfer prices. Isolating the book value of investment used by the division is always possible with some rough approximations.

Determination of the economic value of the book investment can be done quite cheaply with a tolerable degree of accuracy, once the concept is accepted. Current assets have book values and real values generally close enough together. Other assets can be adjusted to replacement value or disposal value by sampling and index numbers with adequate accuracy.

If the concept of economic investment rather than book investment is unacceptable the defect is not fatal, particularly when the company has grown fast so that most of its assets are at recent price levels.

D. Standards of Profit Performance

Standards of profit performance, our fourth requirement, is a big, complex subject. In this analysis we can only mention four thoughts.

(1) Measurement of profit performance of division managers achieves in itself many of the benefits of decentralization. Indeed a good case can be made for not attempting to formalize the standards of profit performance. Instead, leave this to the informal judgment of top management, which must in any event tailor the standard to the individual division and take many dimensions of longer term profit performance into account, e.g., growth, progress and executive development.

(2) Lack of standards should not hold up decentralization: rough standards can be used first and refined later.

(3) Historical perspective is essential in developing performance standards: back-casting of comparable performance measurements will be needed.

(4) Par for the profit center course should also take account of economic climate and competitive conditions in the industry. Sometimes this can be done roughly by comparison with the earnings of independent firms of approximately the same product line.

E. Incentive Compensation

The final requirement for effective profit-center operation is incentives which will power the profit center manager to maximize his division's contribution-profits now and in the future. The following basic considerations should underlie the development of a balanced plan for incentive compensation of the managers of profit center divisions:

(1) Objective measurements of profit performance are in themselves incentives to the kind of man who makes a good division manager. But profit center control will be most effective if powered with incentive compensation which is geared dominantly to the contribution profits of the division.

(2) Incentive compensation should fit the organizational environment and personality of the profit center management: (a) independence, (b) economic sophistication and (c) minimal concern about bureaucratic politics. This means it should be geared to his division's performance.

(3) Since incentives are a reward for extraordinary performance the base salary should approximate a competitive level and the ceiling or target bonus should be 40 to 50 per cent of this salary though it is hard to find a principle to justify any ceiling.

(4) The company's total incentive compensation fund should be based on a maximum percentage of corporate net income which may each year be put into the fund after deducting compensation for capital—a symbol of good faith to the stockholders. (Example, General Motors 12% of net income after deducting 5% of net capital.)

(5) The amount of incentive compensation for any profit center manager should be determined by group judgment preferably at the board level based on multiple measurements of profit performance, compared when feasible with objectively determined standards.

(6) Whether the payment should be in cash, in deferred compensation or in stock options ought to be tailored to the financial personality of the manager rather than determined by uniform formula.

29. SETTING CRITERIA FOR R & D*

Albert H. Rubenstein

The 1956 edition of the *Industrial Research Laboratories of the United States*[1] lists 4,834 research and development laboratories operated by 4,060 companies. A sizable proportion of these companies were not operating research programs 10 years ago, and a majority of them were not doing so 15 years ago. As for the programs that did exist then, most have grown so fast that today they can hardly be recognized.

The nature of the problem has changed along with the dimensions. In many of the new and expanded laboratories research administrators are faced with the task of producing knowledge according to a time schedule, a budget, and an over-all plan. Their position is much different from that of the earlier generation of research directors, whose accomplishments usually came as pleasant (and often complete) surprises to others in the company. In fact, their problem today is that their superiors and colleagues have been *over*sold on the potential benefits of research, and do not fully appreciate the limitations of the research process itself.

Generally skeptical less than a generation ago, managements now have a high optimism about the ability of research to assure their companies' future. For many organizations this optimism and the accompanying large research budgets have paid off handsomely. Few questions are asked about the details of research effort. But for many other firms the payoff has not met expectations, disillusionment is beginning to set in, and numerous questions are being asked about the control and evaluation of research.

Here are two examples of the contrasting pattern that one finds again and again in modern industry:

The director of one of our larger and more successful research laboratories lacks any specific measures or gauges of the quality of work turned out by his department. He merely knows—and knows that his management knows—that research has been successful and that success is achieved through patience and faith, as well as through large expenditures of money. His management has, in many cases, been willing and financially able to rely on the judgment of research executives for evaluation and control of the research program. The company has successfully waited out the period of "getting into a position" to employ science in its business.

The environment in which another research executive operates is different. His management recently decided on a research program as a countermeasure

---

* Reprinted from Harvard Business Review, January–February, 1957.
[1] National Research Council, Washington, D.C., 10th edition.

to competition and as a means of diversifying. A few years ago he was given large sums, as many people as he could hire, and a brand new research laboratory. In return, his management wants some assurance that the money is being well spent—that the company is getting its money's worth out of its investment.

Accordingly, the details of his research budget must be approved periodically by the board of directors. The board requires some basis for comparing the investment in research with other ways of spending company funds. This builds up pressure for applying to the research program company-wide procedures for control of expenditures and for evaluation of results.

Attempts to apply standard control and evaluation techniques to the research program have proved very disappointing in many companies. They have led to misunderstandings between research and management personnel and have often placed barriers in the way of effective research programing. Sometimes these difficulties arise from control and evaluation procedures which are basically inadequate for *any* of the company's activities, but more frequently they come from applying procedures which are effective in other parts of the company but not in research. In an attempt to throw some light on this situation I shall discuss:

The nature of the difficulties which, understandably enough, have caused so many problems and misunderstandings in research management—particularly the important practical differences in the purposes of control and evaluation.

A recent survey of company practice in control and evaluation, which points up a great variety of methods that have been used with varying degrees of success by various companies.

The relationships (*a*) between the "design features" of the laboratory and information output, and (*b*) between information output and economic results, which management needs to explore before setting up effective procedures.

The different kinds of things control and evaluation should be designed to accomplish, how they should work, and how managers should be made responsible for results.

CONTROL VERSUS EVALUATION

Two aspects of the research and development (R & D) activity make control and evaluation particularly difficult. The first is the uncertainty of how individual projects and complete research programs will come out—ranging from the question of the cost and time required for a project or program to be successful to the question of whether it will turn out to be successful at all. The second is the difficulty, even after a project has been "successfully" completed, of telling just how successful it has been and how much of the success is due to the efforts of the research laboratory itself.

Two management functions are important in dealing with these uncertainties and difficulties of measurement. They are the closely related but separate functions of control and evaluation. Much of the misunderstanding that arises between research prople and general management is due to a confusion of these two functions. Here is the difference:

(1) The purpose of a *control* procedure should be to assure that a process *is behaving according to expectations* and to provide a basis for immediate corrective action if necessary. For example, a particular phase of a large project may be found to be diverging too widely from the main direction intended by management. If this is discovered early enough, it is possible to refocus the research effort before a great deal of work has been wasted.

(2) The purpose of an *evaluation* procedure should be to assure that the *results achieved by the process were as expected* and to provide a basis for future corrective action if necessary. An appraisal of the final economic results of a project can indicate ways of avoiding future failures of related research projects.

In other words, control can influence current behavior, whereas evaluation is after-the-fact and can only report on what has happened. This difference is even more important in research and development than it is in some other company activities, since the process of providing technical information is very different from the results by which it is judged.

Dilemma of R & D

The output of a research laboratory falls into two categories:

1. *The direct products—information.* This includes all of the new knowledge, formulations, patent applications, operating instructions, product specifications, advice, diagnosis of difficulties, service reports, and other information turned out in accordance with the objectives of the R & D program. This is an intermediate step in the accomplishment of economic results through research.

2. *The indirect products—economic results.* Few research and development departments have the opportunity directly to bring about economic results such as increased revenues, decreased costs, and increased profits. These ultimate results are brought about by other company activities, supported by the information which is provided by the laboratory. While the ultimate success of R & D thus depends heavily on the quality and usefulness of the researchers' findings, it also depends on the ability and willingness of the rest of the company to apply the information supplied.

This situation leads us into the dilemma that confronts many laboratories. While the direct product of the laboratory is information, what management is interested in *evaluating* is economic results. However, it is difficult to attribute results to R & D on a logical and equitable basis because the information is applied by other activities.

There is still another major difficulty. If the output to be evaluated by management is the ultimate economic result, it might seem logical to make this result the basis for controlling the progress of the R & D program. This is not generally feasible, however, because control requires indications of *current progress*, so immediate changes can be initiated if necessary.

But how can such indications be provided when it takes so long to get final results from the research information? In some industries research and development is just the beginning of a long sequence of activities— such as design, engineering, manufacturing, purchasing, quality control, market research, economic forecasting, legal studies, finance, sales, and sometimes others—through which a project must pass. In a few industries this process stretches out over a 5 to 10 year period; in most others it takes at least a year.

The need, obviously, is for an approach to control and evaluation which recognizes the unique requirements of these two different procedures and their interdependence. How is R & D controlled and evaluated in practice?

COMPANY PRACTICE

Every research director and his management make some attempt to *evaluate* contributions of the R & D program to the welfare and future of the company. In some cases this evaluation is informal and qualitative; in others it is quite formal and quantitative, as suggested by the examples at the beginning of this article. Some measure of *control* of progress is also attempted by most companies, but again there are wide variations.

The tremendous variety of methods and approaches used is revealed by the replies to an informal survey of control and evaluation practices made last year by the Massachusetts Institute of Technology. Some 37 laboratories operated by 29 companies responded to questions on what criteria (indicators, measures, variables) they use to judge the "progress on R & D projects or programs," and on what criteria they use to judge "the results of R & D work." Most of the responding companies are included in the 1955 list of the 500 largest industrial companies, and most of them maintain substantial research and development programs.

The criteria reported have been classified into seven categories. These are listed and illustrated in Exhibit 1, along with the number of companies reporting use of each criterion. The survey shows that:

Almost all of the responding companies report use of some specific criteria for judging progress and results of the R & D program, but relatively few formulas are used.

A total of 41 individual criteria are employed, 11 by 3 or more companies to judge progress, 32 by 3 or more companies to judge results.

There are no specific criteria used widely enough to suggest that they are universally applicable to all R & D activity. The returns showed:

To evaluate the research department, 3 companies use a profit-and-loss basis.

To gauge results, 3 companies use an "index of return" or other formula; 8 use number of patents; 5 use proportion of products coming from research; 3 use number and nature of complaints.

EXHIBIT 1
CRITERIA USED TO JUDGE PROGRESS AND/OR RESULTS OF RESEARCH AND DEVELOPMENT WORK BY 37 LABORATORIES

	*Number of Companies**
1. *Related to effect on sales volume or revenue:* Increased business; increased output without increasing investment; share of the market; per cent of products from research; consumer acceptance; effect of new products on old product sales; new customers.	19
2. *Related to effect on savings in materials, labor, or other costs:* Royalty payments saved; use of by-products, wastes, idle facilities or personnel, or less profitably employed facilities; reduction of product line; closer control of manufacturing quality; better process yields; etc.	17
3. *Related to effect on profits:* Profit on research vs. nonresearch products; profit and loss analysis for whole R & D effort; payoff time on projects; per cent return on investment.	13
4. *Related to time and cost of the technical solution:* Frequent re-estimates of time and cost; progress on project or program phases; actual vs. budgeted expenses; actual vs. scheduled progress; proportion of budget spent vs. progress.	28
5. *Related to customer satisfaction:* Number and nature of complaints; broadening of product line.	10
6. *Related to information output:* Number of valuable ideas; per cent of ideas from inside laboratory; learning about new processes and materials; sources of new ideas; training individuals; development of specifications; evaluation of information output to application groups; information developed for sales; repeat requests for work.	17
7. *Related to success of technical solution:* Number of problems successfully handled; number of patents—written up, applied for, granted; number and nature of project failures.	16

* Indicates use by a company in at least one of its laboratories.

To appraise progress, 15 companies use comparisons of actual and budgeted expenditures; 6 use proportion of budget spent; 3 use output of information to groups that apply the research data.

In many cases, direct output—"information"—is reportedly used to judge results, while indirect output—"economic results" (e.g., category 2 or 3)—is reportedly used to judge progress. One may wonder about this practice, and I shall outline what I believe to be a more desirable approach later in the article.

Troubles with Formulas

Although research executives and company managers have had little success in applying mathematical formulas to the evaluation of research and development, many continue to try to develop valid quantitative yardsticks such as a "profit-and-loss" function or an "index-of-return" formula. They use such formulas to decide, in advance, whether a particular project is worth undertaking as well as to appraise the general value of research projects after completion. Here are several illustrative methods described by respondents:

Results are evaluated beforehand by comparing the five-year estimated revenue with the total estimated development expense. They are evaluated afterwards by comparing the estimated two-year savings with the actual savings for machine improvement development.

Results are evaluated by these formulas:

$$\text{Return on investment} = \frac{\text{New earnings (after taxes)}}{\text{Total investment involved}}$$

$$\text{Payout period} = \frac{\text{Capital outlay on projects}}{\text{New average annual revenue (after taxes)}}$$

Direct returns expressed on an annual basis are compared with expenses. R & D is credited with the returns for the first three years of commercial application of the work.

Only a few such formulations have been described in the literature. The best known formula is the "Index of Return" developed by a division of the Olin-Mathieson Chemical Corporation (before it became part of O-M) several years ago. This formula credits research with the sum of process savings for one year and a fixed per cent of sales of new products and improved products for given time periods. The actual percentages and time periods have been subject to change during the years the formula has been in use.

The validity of most formulas has been challenged. Also their originators have generally been careful to point out the arbitrary nature of some of the numbers used and the necessity for company-wide agreement on the manner in which R & D "takes credit" for economic results.

A major problem in establishing a formula for evaluating results is that of distinguishing R & D's contribution from the contribution of the other activities in the company. In many cases this is an impossible task because of arguments such as:

Without the sales force, your new product would still be sitting on the shelf.

With the energy devoted by manufacturing to getting this new process going properly, we could have turned out millions of items by the old process, at a good profit.

The money invested in research, development, and construction of new facilities could have been spent in half a dozen other ways, at an assured rate of return.

To sum up, management's attempts to control and evaluate research and development frequently bog down because there is no clear picture of the process and its products. Also, there is little agreement on the criteria and procedures necessary. Some laboratories report the use of direct output (information) to *evaluate results*, although results cannot be obtained until production engineers and others have applied the information. In addition, some managements use the indirect output (economic results) to *control progress*, although progress in the laboratory is usually far removed from dollars-and-cents benefits in sales, in cost reduction, or in other ways of obtaining economic results.

A WAY OUT

Is there a way out of this dilemma? I think there is if we will employ the relationships between indirect and direct output as a basis for both control and evaluation. This set of relationships is very simple to describe, but very difficult to establish in usable form.

The idea is: useful economic results for any R & D program depend on the quality of information that the laboratory provides to the organization as a basis for new and improved products and processes. For example, an experienced manager knows that the ultimate success of a new product may depend, among other things, on the accuracy, completeness, timeliness, understandability, and other characteristics of the research reports supplied to production, sales, engineering, and purchasing. Success depends also on other forms of information output: the conferences between laboratory personnel and people from the other activities; operating manuals and specification sheets; patent protection; safety instructions; informal hints on how to avoid processing troubles; etc.

Many failures of new products and projects can be traced either to inadequacy or poor quality of the information supplied by the laboratory or to poor transmission of this information. Here are a few typical instances:

Omission in the laboratory reports of "interesting" observations which may spell potential trouble in full-scale production.

Product specifications set without the agreement or advice of quality control on the economic limitations of the process.

Lack of adequate notice to the manufacturing departments of release dates on new products, resulting in "surprise" and confusion in the factory.

Insufficient information accompanying samples for market tests, resulting in unfavorable reactions by potential customers.

Delayed communication from laboratory to production of new data which will affect the manufacturing process.

Effects of Design Features

Now, the idea of corrective action is basic to both the control and the evaluation procedures. Without the ability to make changes in an activity or the conditions under which it takes place, R & D or any organizational activity becomes "unmanageable." In attempting to remedy poor information flow between the laboratory and production, for example, management might make a number of changes and "see what happens." A liaison group might be established, the laboratory relocated, conferences set up, individual bottlenecks removed from the laboratory-production communication channel; or other steps might be taken.

Such actions imply that still another set of relationships is involved in the operation of an R & D activity. This set relates the direct output—information—to the many characteristics of the laboratory and the conditions under which it operates. For convenience, let us call these characteristics and conditions *design features*. They would include, among other things, facilities, communication techniques, operating procedures, organizational location, information sources available, and the number and kind of people in the activity.

Thus we now have three sets of relationships to consider:

1. *The effects of design features on economic results.* For example, the R & D laboratory of Company A has only six engineers and scientists. All of them have been out of school for at least ten years. The limited size of its laboratory staff and their level of technical knowledge have kept the company from successfully competing in a field of technology that is new to the industry and to the laboratory personnel and that requires large-scale team efforts.

2. *The effects of design features on information output.* For example, Company B has six divisional laboratories, each closely tied in with a product division. Coordination is provided at the company R & D level, where all divisional laboratory reports are screened and channeled to people throughout the company who are likely to be interested. This has resulted in a number of cross-divisional projects which might otherwise have been overlooked.

3. *The effects of information output on economic results.* For example, major emphasis in the laboratory of Company C has been given to short-term projects of immediate assistance to customers of a major product. A cheaper and better substitute product, developed over a period of years by a competitor, cut the market for C's product substantially. The laboratory had nothing ready as a countermeasure.

Kinds of Study Needed

If we could make valid statements of relationships in the first category, the problems of managing R & D would be much simplified; control and evaluation would be replaced by simple design decisions, and their effects on economic results could be predicted with certainty. Under these conditions, we might say, "In order to increase sales of our current product by such and such an amount, we need merely put a group of so many professional researchers with specified skills to work, have them report to the manager of such and such a division, and in so many months' time we would have the desired results!"

Unfortunately, we are not able, at present, to make such predictions. We do not know enough about the abilities of R & D people or the effects of various organizational and physical arrangements on the ultimate results to make more than rough estimates of the effects of design features on economic results. But we *can*:

(1) Establish helpful relationships between design features and economic results by examining (a) the effect of design features on information output; and (b) the effect of information output on economic results.

(2) Control the R & D activity through the direct output—information (1a above).

(3) Evaluate the R & D activity through the indirect output—economic results (1b above).

To implement this approach it would be necessary, of course, to do research on the two sets of relationships mentioned in (1). To this end, an investigation sponsored by the Sloan Research Fund is currently under way in the School of Industrial Management at the Massachusetts Institute of Technology, on the subject of "divisionalized" research and development. The principal questions being asked are:

1. What are the effects of certain design features of the laboratory—e.g., project selection procedures, prescribed communication patterns—on the information output of divisional laboratories in a "decentralized" company?
2. How do these factors affect the company's long-run total R & D effort?

"Research on Research"

Of course there are some research managers—a small number—to whom an understanding of the relation of information output to design features and economic results appears to come naturally; and their intuitive management would probably not be improved by any formal analysis. For instance:

One such research director—head of a 200-man laboratory—seemed to have a knack for putting the right man on a project and for changing the makeup of a project group when it began to go stale. When reading project reports, he could visualize the experimental procedures which had produced the results and could pinpoint barriers to effective communication between specialists in the project group. He could "see" potential problems in the ultimate application of results and educate his people to the user's point of view, especially his potential difficulties in understanding and applying the laboratory's results.

For a larger number of managers, however, a significant gain can be made through a careful study of the research process—a program of "research on research," looking into questions like the ones the Massachusetts Institute of Technology project is examining. It is unfortunate that very little of this kind of investigation is currently under way in industrial organizations. In the few places where such "research on research" is in progress, there are reasons to think that management's faith in the outcome will be justified. To illustrate:

In the R & D organization of one very large company a small group is attempting to build models of the research process to help it examine management practices which have been successful and unsuccessful. It has been bringing R & D managers in for periods of several months and trying to extract from them case histories and examples of management practice which will put some flesh on the skeleton of the model. So far the going has been difficult, but there are signs that this study will eventually lead to better management of the R & D function.

SUGGESTED APPROACH

Now let us turn to the questions which management needs to consider in setting up sound procedures for controlling and evaluating research. What information needs to be known? What methods can be recommended on the basis of present knowledge?

Design and Information

One of the first key topics is the effect of design features on information output. This area is currently the subject of many research programs in the social sciences. Numerous investigators in "small group research" and "organizational communication" have been studying the effects of group size, member skills, physical and organization arrangements, communication facilities, incentives, procedural rules, and other design features on information output. The results have been reported in a variety of professional journals in the fields of sociology, psychology, human relations, and management.

Few general relationships have been established thus far, as a result of these studies, that can be directly applied to the management of R & D groups. But this literature can provide the basis for useful investigations of the design-information relation in a research organization. For example, findings about the effect of group leadership on decision making can provide the basis for design of research teams. Again, studies of rates of transmission of information can suggest organizational patterns that will assist the proper dissemination of research results.

Establishing these relationships for a given R & D organization requires experimentation and careful observation; however, literature to guide and help interpret such work already exists and awaits application to specific problems.[2]

---

[2] For example: H. Guetzkow and H. A. Simon, "The Impact of Certain Communication Nets upon Organization and Performance in Task-Oriented Groups," *Management Science* (April–July, 1955) p. 233; W. Haythorn, "The Influence of Individual Members on the Characteristics of Small Groups," *Journal of Abnormal and Social Psychology* (April, 1953), p. 276; H. H. Kelley, "Communication in Experimentally Created Hierarchies," *Human Relations*, February, 1951, p. 39; D. W. Taylor and W. L. Faust, "Twenty Questions: Efficiency in Problem Solving as a Function of Size of Group," *Journal of Experimental Psychology*, November, 1952, p. 360.

Information and Results

What are the effects of information output on economic results? This area is almost barren of theory and research findings. It provides the strongest challenge to R & D management, but little help is available in getting started. Here the investigator is on his own with only the statement of faith that "good R & D leads to good results" to guide him. Here he must look directly to his own organization's experience in applying the information provided by the laboratory. He should study the information produced both by projects and programs that have turned out to be economically "successful" and by those that have not.

The information can be analyzed by applying a few criteria that are clearly relevant to ultimate economic success—accuracy, timeliness, completeness, usability, availability to the proper people, and so on. When the critical characteristics of this information output have been identified, it is possible that a few usable general relationships will emerge. It might be found, for instance, that:

Savings in manufacturing costs on existing products will depend partly on how closely the laboratory is in touch with the product engineering and manufacturing people.

The company's share of the market for a new product will depend partly on how quickly research findings in the early stages are transmitted to production and marketing people.

Many companies make a rough attempt at this kind of analysis through "post-mortems" on projects that have been unusually successful or unsuccessful. Even a superficial analysis can reveal communication patterns and practices that need to be followed more rigorously or revised in the future. To illustrate:

One company was surprised to learn, through a post-mortem on a very unsuccessful project, that the lack of a clear-cut "release" procedure between its development laboratory and its production engineering group had been adding several months to the length of each project and causing bad relations between the two groups for years. Not only was the duration and hence the cost of the project affected, but in the case which led to the investigation the project itself was a commercial failure. The product was too late and too expensive.

Eventually it is possible that some of these relationships pertaining to the effect of design on information and of information on economic results will be established in elaborate mathematical form that will provide the kind of prediction we find in physical science and engineering. For the moment, however, such elegance is not possible. Nevertheless, great gains can be made by using simple measures such as "high-medium-low" and "frequent-infrequent" rather than precise numbers. Such generalizations as the following should be valuable:

Groups made up of varied scientific disciplines have more chance of generating entirely new solutions than groups of people in the same field.

More fundamental solutions to problems have a larger payoff in the long run than specific solutions to the problems posed by customers or the manufacturing departments.

Approach to Control

The purpose of control is to assure that the R & D activity is performing as expected and to provide a basis for corrective action if it is not. The control process involves these operations:

1. *Establishing criteria* governing the information output of the R & D function, using as a basis the relationships developed between information output and economic results.
2. *Observing* the information output continuously or by frequent samples.
3. *Comparing* the actual information output with the expected output.
4. *Taking action* to make changes in R & D activity or in the conditions under which it operates, if judged necessary. Effective control requires that corrective action be taken quickly, when indicated. Changes in the design features should be made in the light of the relationships developed between design features and information output.

The critical part of establishing this control procedure is the first operation (1), that is, selecting and applying the proper criteria for controlling the flow and adequacy of the information output that goes from the laboratory to marketing, manufacturing, and other executives—particularly for a company doing business in a field of high product obsolescence. Thus:

Company A must develop and market a number of new or improved products each year in order to keep its share of the market. The success of such projects has been found to depend significantly on two factors, (*a*) preparation of the market to receive the new product and (*b*) absence of manufacturing "bugs" once full-scale production starts. Without control criteria the flow of information between the laboratory and manufacturing and between the laboratory and marketing can be interrupted or choked for a given project, with a serious delay in making the necessary changes in the design features.

Two general characteristics of this information are significant. The first concerns the communication *process* whereby the information is transferred to sales and production. Here we are concerned with questions such as:

To whom is the information directed?
Who actually receives it?
By what means is it transmitted? How economical are the means used?
How frequently is information transmitted?
How fresh is the information when received; are there time lags that make it obsolete?

The second general characteristic concerns the *content* of the information transmitted. The pertinent questions here are:

Is the information accurate and complete?

Does it meet the requirement of the receiver?

Is it usable by the receiver? Is it understandable, and does it provide a basis for action?

Does it reflect any changes in specifications or procedures that may have occurred since the last transmission?

The content of the information and the process of transmitting it must now be adapted to the particular needs of sales and production. For example, sales executives may need such information as:

Application directions and specifications.

Health and safety information about use.

Standards and procedures for quality control.

Estimated costs of materials and processes.

Approvals for advertising and promotion copy.

Quantities available for samples.

Production men may need information about such things as:

Cost, availability, and characteristics of the materials required for the product.

Characteristics of the equipment and facilities required.

Health and safety problems in manufacture.

Anticipated processing difficulties.

Quality specifications and suggested procedures for attaining them.

Special manufacturing conditions required—e.g., humidity and temperature control.

Packaging and handling problems including disposal or other handling of by-products.

Potential future changes in yields or costs.

The next step is to establish a series of checks to make sure that information is, in fact, adequate and that it is going to designated personnel as planned. That is, checks should be made to determine the following:

Whether or not, at any point in time, particular people have certain specific information available. This could involve a periodic (or random) check, for example, of the people who should know about specifications, anticipated difficulties, etc. In its simplest form, this could merely be an "off-on" check to determine whether the communication channels are open and effective.

Whether there is adequate correspondence, at specific times, between the information on a particular aspect of the project which exists in the laboratory and in the cooperating department. For example, does the production department know about changes in specifications which have recently been made in the laboratory? In operation, this criterion could involve a "matching" of the information held at any time by the various people concerned.

Whether specific "packages" of information provided by the laboratory, such as oral reports, written reports, and informal advice, are adequate. The appraisal might be made in terms of accuracy, completeness, or clarity. Information might also be appraised according to whether it meets the needs of the receiver.

Approach to Evaluation

The purpose of evaluation is to assure that the results achieved through R & D meet expectations and to provide a basis for occasional re-examination of the expectations themselves. The evaluation process involves these operations:

1. *Establishing criteria* for the expected economic results—in terms of company income, growth, introduction of new products, and so forth. These criteria derive from the objectives of the company in supporting an R & D activity.
2. *Observing* (measuring, where possible) the actual economic results achieved. The time periods involved here are, of course, longer than those involved in the control process.
3. *Comparing* the actual economic results with the expected results.
4. *Taking action* to change design features or objectives where necessary.

The important thing in evaluation is to see that expectations are realistic and up-to-date, and if they are—and are not met—to study what changes in the design features of the laboratory might help with the problem. Thus:

Company B maintains an R & D laboratory in order to protect its position in the industry and to provide a basis for growth. In B's industry, growth depends on the successful introduction of a radically new product every two or three years. Criteria are established for the additional income from new products that is required each year for the growth rate wanted.

If the actual additional income falls below these expectations, action is taken to investigate and change the direct output of the R & D activity through appropriate changes in the design features (for example, hiring people with new skills). Investigation is also made periodically to see whether the objectives—the expectations for new products and income—should be changed. There is always the possibility, for instance, that as technology becomes more complex, the number of new products expected should be revised.

Question of Organization

Control and evaluation use some common information, and the actions resulting from them may be similar or complementary. In Exhibit 2 I have tried to summarize these relationships in a schematic way. Either of the two procedures can be applied at various levels in the R & D program. At each level—whether that of individual projects, integrated programs, or the R & D activity as a whole—control and evaluation must be performed by people who have access to the necessary information and the *ability to take action*.

Sometimes, in a large R & D organization, these functions may be separated. An analysis group may develop the relationships and establish the necessary criteria; a supervisory group may observe and judge whether

EXHIBIT 2

SCHEMATIC PORTRAYAL OF THE CONTROL AND EVALUATION PROCEDURES INCLUDING THE OCCASIONAL PROCEDURE OF RE-EXAMINING OBJECTIVES AND CRITERIA

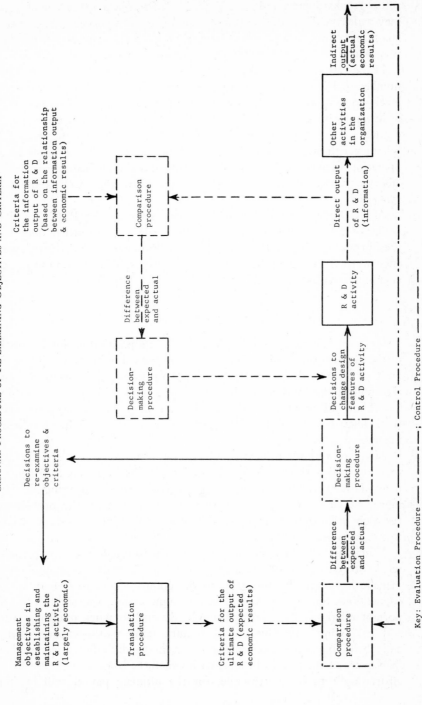

Key: Evaluation Procedure ———— ; Control Procedure — — — —

actual results correspond to expected results; and a management group may make the decisions to change design features or objectives. In a small laboratory, by contrast, the director of research may do all of these, with the advice of his colleagues in other management functions.

In the case of individual projects, good results have been attained by a number of laboratories which push control down to the lowest possible level—to those people who are closest to the work. This does not necessarily apply to evaluation, however, where a wider perspective may be needed than is possible within the laboratory. But, wherever and by whomever the specific evaluation operations are done, there should be cooperation between the laboratory people and the evaluators so that the laboratory people will know the basis on which their efforts are being evaluated.

A vital management responsibility in operating the R & D activity is that of communicating to the R & D people and any others concerned the purpose of the control and evaluation procedures and their dependence on the relationship between design features, information output, and economic results.

CONCLUSION

Organized research and development is in a position analogous to that of the engineering field several generations ago. Engineers of that period built structures, designed products, and operated equipment without a thorough understanding of the phenomena with which they were dealing. They did remarkably well on the basis of past experience and intuition. They have done much better recently with the help of scientific theory.

Many of today's research and development executives are also performing well without the benefit of rigorous theories of R & D management. However, there is increasing awareness of the pressing need for more knowledge about the research process and about the problems of research organizations if management is to continue to apply science to its business effectively.

Managing R & D is no less complex and difficult than the technical work of research itself. If management can learn more about how to manage it effectively, the gains to the company and to society can be tremendous. Such knowledge will not come easily. To establish the important relationships described previously and to work out the control and evaluation procedures will require hard work—experimentation and theorizing with phenomena much more difficult to comprehend than many of the physical things with which the laboratory deals. But the effort ought to be worthwhile, for the ultimate payoff will be high.

30. A RESEARCH PLAN FOR THE STUDY OF ORGANIZATIONAL EFFECTIVENESS*

ANDREW L. COMREY

THE OBJECT of this paper is to acquaint you with some of the background and plans of an Office of Naval Research project which is underway at the University of Southern California. Two years ago, an interdisciplinary seminar was held at the University to explore the topic "informal organization." Membership in the seminar comprised students and professors from psychology, public administration, and sociology. As a result of the year's work, Professors J. M. Pfiffner, J. P. Guilford, and Harvey J. Locke applied for and received a grant from the Office of Naval Research to study the "Effectiveness of Organization" for a period of approximately three years. The speaker is supervising this project and has one graduate student in Sociology, Miss Helen Beem, working with him at present.

The purpose of the research project is to discover some of those conditions which are associated with relatively "effective" organizations as opposed to relatively "ineffective" organizations. The specific conditions which are receiving the greatest attention fall in the areas of human relations, types of supervision, interpersonal relations, and the like, although some emphasis is being given also to the more formal characteristics of organizations. The general area of research has a great deal in common with that, for example, being explored by the Survey Research Center at the University of Michigan, although the methods employed vary in certain important respects.

Our general plan of research is much the same as that which would be involved in validating a personnel selection test. An "effective" group of organizations and an "ineffective" group are selected. Questionnaires are developed for various groups of individuals in these organizations and administered. The results are analyzed statistically to determine if significant differences occur in the patterns of response between "effective" and "ineffective" groups. This analysis may, and usually will, take the form of individual item comparisons with the criterion as well as comparisons of scores based on several items grouped in certain logical or statistical categories. Those items or groups of items which provide a basis for predicting the efficiency criterion are considered as hypotheses to be verified in other organizational settings. Dimensions which con-

* A paper presented to the Western Psychological Association, April 28, 1951, San Jose, California.

sistently show a statistical relationship in widely varied settings will eventually be subjected to more rigorous verification by means of experimental techniques.

Having provided a thumb-nail sketch of the general approach, I would like to proceed to a discussion of certain specific problems. First, the question arises, "What is an 'effective' organization?" To provide a comprehensive conceptual definition of this term which would satisfy a critical audience would be difficult indeed. An issue from these difficulties, in terms of clarity of communication at least, is possible if one relies exclusively on an operational definition of that term. In our studies, then, we make no attempt to say what "effectiveness" is, except to describe the precise procedure by which we divide the groups for study. The method employed for this purpose will vary from situation to situation. In the first study undertaken with the 18 U.S. forests in California, 11 persons in the regional office of the U.S. Forest Service provided us with independent rank-order ratings of the forests. Each person was asked to judge on the basis of "overall efficiency" taking into consideration the difficulties with which each forest was faced. These 11 sets of ranks were combined into one composite index. The nine highest forests on the index were placed in the "effective" group of organizations. In other cases, more objective evidence will be utilized in making this division. The project is soon to undertake a study of the Department of Employment offices in Southern California in which certain records kept by each office will be used as a clue to its relative effectiveness. In this case, it will be necessary to make certain allowances in the objective records since local conditions, quite apart from organizational effectiveness, contribute a large share of their variance. Ratings will probably be used as supplementary data. In the case of another study projected for next fall with the overhaul and repair shops at a naval air station, objective production records will be used. This method of defining "effectiveness" seems to be the only feasible course of action in view of the tremendous number of meanings involved in a conceptual definition of this term and the obvious impossibility of providing a criterion which would reflect all or most of those meanings.

Another problem is that of deciding what and how many organizations to study. Should the sample of organizations purport to represent a rather general population? The present project began with the expectation of obtaining two samples of approximately 50 organizations each, including organizations of sufficiently different character to provide some semblance of generality to the results. Extensive interviews with individuals who would help to provide the information necessary to differentiate "effective" from "ineffective" organization convinced us that judgements of relative effectiveness between two organizations of markedly different character are not only distasteful to the judges but probably much more unreliable than comparisons between organizations of similar structure and purpose. These and other considerations led us to settle for an approach which involves the study of large organizations which contain many units occupied in somewhat comparable activity. The central control under such circumstances is much more likely to have the where-with-all, in terms of information, to make judgements on which units are the better ones. Furthermore, many methodological problems are avoided which would become involved in studying heterogeneous organizations in the same sample. The generality of results are, of course, limited when this plan is followed. It is possible, however, to follow them up in other types of organizations with separate studies.

The method of obtaining data represented another choice point in this research. Many studies in this general area have involved the technique of extensive interviews, coding and categorizing of results in the light of certain hypotheses, and then execution of a statistical analysis on the coded results. This approach has been used by the University of Michigan group. The preference of this particular project staff has run toward a more objective, if somewhat more rigid, data-collecting procedure. Questionnaires of about 100 to 120 questions are used in which each item is a specific objective question for which the respondent has two to five alternate answers from which to choose. A few completion items have been employed to get results involving numerical answers, such as age, years of service, and so on. These questionnaires are prepared for the various levels to be studied in an organization. In the forest service study, for example, we had one questionnaire for the head men of the 18 forests, another for their executive assistants, a third for general technical staff men, two forms of a questionnaire for district rangers, two more forms for employees under district rangers, and one questionnaire for clerical personnel. Analysis proceeds separately in each of these groups, although some questions appear in several questionnaires, agreement of results in parallel groups is given special inspection. It was believed that the danger of influence from subconscious cues would be minimized by collecting the data in a form such that categorization for statistical analysis would involve no subjective judgement.

In terms of statistical analysis itself, a question arises as to what is the N, the number of people *or* the number of organizations. No clear answer can be given to this question which will pre-empt a decision in every case, unfortunately, but the nature of the problem seems clear. Where a variable is under consideration in which an individual's response is determined completely by the organization in which he is located, N should be the number of organizations. Where a variable is under consideration in which individual responses are exclusively a function of the individuals giving them, N should be the number of individuals. It is apparent that most questions will be of such a nature that the variable involved falls somewhere between these two extremes. In those cases where the variable appears to be toward the latter end of the continuum, we will feel justified in noting the reliability of a difference in proportions answering an item in a specific way between "high" and "low" groups, using the number of individuals concerned as the N. That our empirical situation doesn't fit the ideal statistical model exactly will be recognized and allowed for in making interpretations. Such compromises are always necessary in applying a mathematical model to physical reality, although the hiatus in certain cases may be so great as to be intolerable. Every attempt will be made to avoid such unfortunate applications of statistical procedures while still taking advantage of their power of decision to give some indication of the statistical reliability of our results. In applying methods of this sort, it is compelling that no generalization beyond the specific situation be made as a statistical inference. Such inferential leaps must be justified on other grounds, though doubtless few optimistic research workers are likely to allow this fact to prevent them from formulating positive hypotheses which can be dislodged only by negative evidence from subsequent research efforts.

It is hoped that these and other survey researches which are being executed and planned for the future will enable the discovery of several areas of significant correlation which hold up under a wide variety of organizational settings. Such findings can then constitute a worthwhile base upon which to build an experimental program of research to get at the causal relationships involved in gaining greater efficiency of organized activity through manipulation of the variables controlling the human factors in organization.

31. A COMPARISON OF THREE CRITERIA OF AIRCREW EFFECTIVENESS IN COMBAT OVER KOREA*

JOHN K. HEMPHILL AND LEE B. SECHREST

THIS PAPER reports a study of three criteria of the performance of 94 B-29 aircrews which flew combat missions over Korea during the period extending from March to September 1951. The three criteria to be considered are: (1) ratings by superiors of the performance of crews as units; (2) sociometric nominations from crew members; and (3) objective records of combat bombing accuracy. Following a brief description of each of these criteria, they will be compared in terms of their reliability and interrelationship. A general problem in the use of superiors' ratings as criteria is made evident by the apparently paradoxical finding of substantial and statistically significant relationships between (1) bombing data, which show no reliability, and (2) reliable superiors' ratings. This paradox is more apparent than real for it can be explained in terms of the contaminating effect of "unreliable" information shared in common by the raters.

Superiors' Ratings

The aircrews were rated as units by squadron or wing staff officers in terms of their performance in carrying out combat missions over Korea. The ratings were accomplished through the use of an eleven-item rating form. The eleven rating variables were:
The aircrews were rated as units by squadron or wing staff officers in terms of their performance in carrying out combat missions over Korea. The ratings were accomplished through the use of an eleven-item rating form. The eleven rating variables were:

(1) Skill as Technicians: The degree of basic knowledge crew members have of their specialties as indicated by their performance or the degree of skill they exhibit in handling various equipments.

(2) Successful Completion of Missions: The degree to which the crew reaches and bombs prescribed targets; including making necessary decisions in the absence of specific instructions and overcoming obstacles.

(3) Accuracy in Bombing Targets: The accuracy with which targets are identified and bombed.

(4) Effectiveness of Crew Leadership: The degree to which the air-

---

* Reproduced from *Journal of Applied Psychology*, Vol. 36, No. 5, October, 1952.

craft commander organizes the crew to facilitate teamwork and co-operation among crew members.

(5) Consideration of Men on the Crew for One Another: The extent to which crew members look out for the welfare of the crew as a whole, are liked by other men on the crew, and turn to one another as friends.

(6) Effectiveness in Working with Other Crews: The degree to which the crew works as a part of a larger team and cooperates with other crews in carrying out a group effort.

(7) Effectiveness in Working with Superior Officers: The degree to which the crew accepts orders or suggestions from superior officers and achieves objectives without conflict with superiors.

(8) Care of the Aircraft: The degree to which the crew members insure proper maintenance of their aircraft and take personal interest in the plane and its equipment.

(9) Following SOP: The degree to which the crew members carry out their functions in the prescribed manner.

(10) Military Bearing of Crew Members: The degree to which members of the crew "conduct themselves in a military manner."

(11) Over-all Value to the Squadron (Wing): The degree of over-all effectiveness of the crew as a part of combat unit.

Ratings on the items or variables were expressed as numerical values along a nine-point scale. Each point on the scale was defined, *nine* being the rating given to "undoubtedly the best crew in the squadron" and *one* being the rating given to "undoubtedly the worst crew in the squadron." All ratings were obtained in interviews with the raters.

The original plan was to secure a minimum of five independent ratings for each crew. This plan proved to be impractical due to the difficulty of locating raters who knew the crews sufficiently well to rate all variables. A total of 24 wing and squadron officers were utilized as raters in securing the ratings of the 94 crews. The mean number of ratings per crew actually obtained was 2.7 and the mean number of crews rated by each rater was 10.5.

An examination of the means and standard deviations of the ratings obtained from each of the 24 raters showed marked differences in their rating habits or bias. Before the ratings given a single crew by different raters were combined to form the final rating of the crew's performance, an adjustment was made to compensate for the observed rater bias. The adjustment was computed in such a manner that each rater's mean rating was approximately 50 and his standard deviation approximately 10.

The reliabilities of these converted ratings were estimated by application of a method developed by Horst (1) that is designed for the case in which varying numbers of raters are available. Intercorrelations of the eleven crew performance variables were also calculated. These intercorrelations along with the reliabilities, means, and standard deviations of the eleven variables are presented in Table 1. The reliability of these ratings ranges from .61 to .95 and meets standards which are generally acceptable for rating data.

TABLE 1

THE RELIABILITY AND INTERRELATIONSHIPS OF ELEVEN VARIABLES OF AIRCREW
PERFORMANCE RATED BY SUPERIORS

Note: $N = 83$

Variable	Intercorrelation*											Mean	Standard Deviation
	1	2	3	4	5	6	7	8	9	10	11		
1 Technical Skill												49.6	8.21
2 Completion of Missions	84											51.3	7.64
3 Bombing Accuracy	74	68										47.7	9.65
4 Leadership	83	81	63									49.3	9.10
5 Consideration	62	66	56	70								50.3	7.30
6 W.W. Other Crews	69	69	63	74	73							49.6	7.72
7 W.W. Superiors	79	77	66	81	70	76						50.8	7.66
8 Care of Aircraft	66	64	47	63	61	67	56					50.1	6.93
9 Following SOP	80	73	62	78	59	68	75	66				50.2	7.74
10 Military Bearing	68	59	60	63	60	58	71	49	71			48.2	7.23
11 Over-all Value	85	78	73	82	67	78	78	61	82	62		47.4	10.25
Reliability	80	67	83	80	95	63	80	67	72	61	68		

* Decimal points have been omitted from these tables.

Sociometric Nominations

On a sociometric nomination form, crew members were asked the following question: "If you could make up a crew from among the crew members in your squadron, whom would you choose for each crew position?" There were three general possibilities of reaction to the nomination question: (1) nomination of a crew member who was a member of the same crew as the nominator; (2) nomination of an individual from some other crew in the squadron; and (3) no responses. An individual usually indicated an "on-crew" choice by responding "same," "my own crew," or by writing the name of a fellow crew member in the blank provided. "Off-crew" choices were indicated by responding with the name of a man not on the individual's crew, and by such remarks as "Captain Smith's radio operator." or "anyone except the one we have."

The sociometric nomination data for each crew were used to compute an index of "on-crew" choices. The index is the ratio between the number of "on-crew" choices made and the total number of choices made. These index values ranged from .30 to 1.00 and were approximately normally distributed about a mean of .75.

In order to test the reliability of the index of "on-crew" choice, index values derived from random halves of each crew total nominations were correlated with one another. This correlation was .83 which, when extended by the Spearman-Brown formula, gave an estimated reliability of .91.

Bombing Error Criteria

The accuracy with which an aircrew is able to bomb combat targets may be considered as a near ultimate criterion of its effectiveness. Despite the high relevance of bombing data to the problem of evaluation of aircrew effectiveness, many conditions exist which detract from its utility. Chief among these are: (1) extremely variable conditions under which bombing must be accomplished; (2) severe limitations on the possibility of determining exactly where bombs are dropped in combat; and (3) limits upon the number of crews for whom the opportunity to perform the complete bombing operations exists (only the lead crew in formation bombing performs the complete bombing operation). Nevertheless, all available data were collected concerning the bombing accuracy in combat of the 94 FEAF crews. No combat bombing data whatsoever were available for 50 of the crews (no lead experience). Each of the remaining 44 crews had had one or more opportunities to lead formations on which it had been possible to secure photographs of where the bombs actually dropped. The bombing accuracy data consisted of *circular errors* for each of these bombing missions. These errors were expressed as the linear distance between the mean point of impact of all the bombs identified in the strike photograph and the assigned target. The number of circular error measures available for each of the 44 crews ranged from 1 to 8 with a mean of 3.16.

Inspection of the distribution of the bombing error data disclosed a markedly skewed distribution. A log transformation of these data yielded data with essentially normal distribution. The reliability of the transformed data as estimated, again by utilizing Horst's procedure, was not significantly different from zero.

Table 2 presents an analysis of the variance of the bombing data into between-crew differences and within-crew differences. It can be seen readily that there is approximately as much variance between the errors made by the same crew on different missions as there is between the mean performance of different crews. The difference between the mean bombing accuracy scores of these crews appears to be wholly unrelated to crew differences.

Relationships Among the Criteria

In order to complete the comparison of the three criteria, each of the eleven superior rating variables was correlated with both the sociometric index of "on-crew" choice and with the mean bombing error of each

TABLE 2
AN ANALYSIS OF THE VARIANCE OF TRANSFORMED BOMBING
ACCURACY DATA

Source of Variance	Sum of Squares	Df	Variance	F ratio
Between Crews	208.56	33	6.320	1.34
Within Crews	451.82	96	4.706	
Total	660.38	129	5.119	

crew for whom we had bombing data. Table 3 presents these correlations.

Attention is called to the correlations between the bombing data and the superiors' ratings. It is quite apparent that the raters utilized the official bombing data as a source of information in making their ratings. Mean differences in the official bombing records of the crews serve to "contaminate" the raters' judgments on all rating variables, although the contamination is more marked for certain variables than for others.

TABLE 3
CORRELATIONS BETWEEN ELEVEN VARIABLES OF AIRCREW PERFORMANCE RATED
BY SUPERIORS AND (1) THE INDEX OF "ON-CREW" CHOICE AND (2) BOMBING
ACCURACY DATA

	"On-Crew" Choice		Bombing Data		
Rating Variable	N	r	N	r	r corr.[1]
1 Technical Skill	90	.20	41	.58	.61
2 Completion of Missions	88	.10	41	.62	.70
3 Bombing Accuracy	80	.36[†]	41	.58	.58
4 Leadership	89	.13	41	.63	.67
5 Consideration	90	.10	41	.42	.48
6 W.W. Other Crews	90	.06	41	.47	.56
7 W.W. Superiors	90	.11	41	.57	.60
8 Care of Aircraft	90	.26[*]	41	.31	.38
9 Following SOP	90	.15	41	.40	.47
10 Military Bearing	90	.25[*]	41	.27	.30
11 Over-all Value	90	.18	41	.47	.54

[1] Corrected for restriction of the range of the rating variables (2)
[*] Significant at the .05 level.
[†] Significant at the .01 level.

The largest contamination is with the rating variable, Successful Completion of Missions. The original hunch responsible for the inclusion of this rating item was that it might identify variance in crew performance associated with low motivation and/or tendencies to abort missions. It appears, however, that information concerning the officially recorded performance of the crews determined much of this rating.

The sociometric index of "on-crew" choice does not appear to be related to any marked extent with the superiors' ratings. The sociometric data may provide a second and relatively independent estimate of the performance of the crew. The correlation between the index of "on-crew" choice and the objective bombing accuracy data was found to be .33. This suggests that the sociometric choices were also influenced by the unreliable bombing information but to a lesser degree than most of the superiors' ratings.

Discussion and Conclusion

The finding of substantial and significant correlations between the objective bombing accuracy data, for which we had estimated a reliability of zero, and the eleven superior rating variables has general methodological implications for the development of criteria. An explanation of these correlations can be found in a possibility of a "contamination" of the judgments of superiors. The results of each bombing mission are widely publicized among the personnel of the wings and squadrons. In fact, it is standard procedure to hold a critique of the mission on the morning of the day following the mission. In addition, mission results, expressed in terms of bombing errors, are made part of official records which are maintained and used in determining which crews will be given an opportunity to lead further missions. It can be expected, therefore, that each rater could have estimated the official bombing accuracy records of each crew with a relatively high degree of accuracy. The fact that these records represented little other than chance crew achievement was, of course, unknown to the raters. This commonly shared, but unreliable, information concerning the performance of the various crews tended to produce both spuriously high reliability of the superior ratings and the spurious correlations with the unreliable bombing data.

A general question is raised concerning the dependability of rating data as criteria. In situations where objective achievement information is available, we may expect that raters will utilize such information in the process of forming the judgments they express in their ratings. If these achievement data reflect reliable performance, they will, of course, add to the dependability of the ratings. However, should the achievement information be basically unrelated to differences in the performance of the individuals or units being rated, this fact is likely to be overlooked when a test of the agreement between raters proves the rating to have "adequate reliability." Raters may agree in their knowledge of the achievement records but be in error about the meaningfulness of such records.

REFERENCES

1. P. Horst. "A Generalized Expression for the Reliability of Measures," *Psychometrika*, 1949, 14, pp. 21–24.
2. Robert L. Thorndike. *Personnel Selection* (New York: Wiley, 1949), p. 173.

32. DYSFUNCTIONAL CONSEQUENCES OF PERFORMANCE MEASUREMENTS*

V. F. Ridgway

There is today a strong tendency to state numerically as many as possible of the variables with which management must deal. The mounting interest in and application of tools such as operations research, linear programming, and statistical decision making, all of which require quantifiable variables, foster the idea that if progress toward goals can be measured, efforts and resources can be more rationally managed. This has led to the development of quantitative performance measurements for all levels within organizations, up to and including measurements of the performance of a division manager with profit responsibility in a decentralized company. Measurements at lower levels in the organization may be in terms of amount of work, quality of work, time required, and so on.

Quantitative measures of performance are tools, and are undoubtedly useful. But research indicates that indiscriminate use and undue confidence and reliance in them result from insufficient knowledge of the full effects and consequences. Judicious use of a tool requires awareness of possible side effects and reactions. Otherwise, indiscriminate use may result in side effects and reactions outweighing the benefits, as was the case when penicillin was first hailed as a wonder drug. The cure is sometimes worse than the disease.

It seems worth while to review the current scattered knowledge of the dysfunctional consequences resulting from the imposition of a system of performance measurements. For the purpose of analyzing the impact of performance measurements upon job performance, we can consider separately single, multiple, and composite criteria. Single criteria occur when only one quantity is measured and observed, such as total output or profit. Multiple criteria occur when several quantities are measured simultaneously, such as output, quality, cost, safety, waste, and so forth. Composite criteria occur when the separate quantities are weighted in some fashion and then added or averaged.

Single Criteria

A single criterion of performance was in use in a public employment agency studied by Peter M. Blau.[1] The agency's responsibility was "to

---

* Reproduced from *Administrative Science Quarterly*, 1, No. 2, September, 1956.
[1] Peter M. Blau, *The Dynamics of Bureaucracy* (Chicago, Ill., 1955).

serve workers seeking employment and employers seeking workers." Employment interviewers were appraised by the number of interviews they conducted. Thus the interviewer was motivated to complete as many interviews as he could, but not to spend adequate time in locating jobs for the clients. The organization's goal of placing clients in jobs was not given primary consideration because the measurement device applied to only one aspect of the activity.

Blau reports another case in a federal law enforcement agency which investigated business establishments. Here he found that work schedules were distorted by the imposition of a quota of eight cases per month for each investigator. Toward the end of the month an investigator who found himself short of the eight cases would pick easy, fast cases to finish that month and save the lengthier cases till the following month. Priority of the cases for investigation was based on length of the case rather than urgency, as standards of impartiality would require. This is one of many instances in which the existence of an "accounting period" adversely affects the over-all goal accomplishment of the organization.

Chris Argyris also reports this tendency to use easy jobs as fillers toward the end of a period in order to meet a quota.[2] In this case, a factory supervisor reported that they "feed the machines all the easy orders" toward the end of the month, rather than finish them in the sequence in which they were received. Such a practice may lead to undue delay of the delivery of some customers' orders, perhaps the most profitable orders.

David Granick's study of Soviet management reveals how the attention and glory that accrues to a plant manager when he can set a new monthly production record in one month leads to the neglect of repairs and maintenance, so that in ensuing months there will be a distinct drop in production.[3] Similarly, the output of an entire plant may be allowed to fall off in order to create conditions under which one worker can make a production record, when the importance of such a record is considered greater than over-all plant production.

Joseph S. Berliner's report on Soviet business administration points out sharply how the accounting period has an adverse effect upon management decisions.[4] The use of monthly production quotas causes "storming" at the end of the month to reach the quota. Repairs and maintenance are postponed until the following month, so that production lags in the early part of the month, and storming must again be resorted to in the following month. This has impact upon the rate of production for sup-

---

[2] Chris Argyris, *The Impact of Budgets on People* (New York, 1952).

[3] David Granick, *Management of the Industrial Firm in the U.S.S.R.* (New York, 1954).

[4] Joseph S. Berliner, "A Problem in Soviet Business Management," *Administrative Science Quarterly*, Vol. I, 1956, pp. 86–101.

pliers and customers who are forced into a fluctuating rate of operations with its attendant losses and wastes.

Standard costs as a criterion of performance is a frequent source of dissatisfaction in manufacturing plants.[5] The "lumpiness" of indirect charges that are allocated to the plants or divisions (indirect charges being unequal from month to month), variations in quality and cost of raw materials, or other factors beyond the control of the operating manager, coupled with inaccuracies and errors in the apportionment of indirect charges, causes distrust of the standards. A typical reaction of operating executives in such cases seems to be to seek explanations and justifications. Consequently, considerable time and energy is expended in discussion and debate about the correctness of charges. Only "wooden money" savings accrue when charges are shifted to other accounts and there is no increase in company profits. It should be pointed out, however, that having charges applied to the proper departments may have the advantage of more correctly directing attention to problem areas.

Granick discusses two measures of the success of the Soviet firm which have been considered and rejected as over-all measures by Soviet industrial leaders and economists.[6] The first, cost-reduction per unit of product, is considered inadequate because it does not provide a basis for evaluating new products. Further, variations in amount of production affect the cost-reduction index because of the finer division of overhead costs, quality changes, and assortment. The second over-all measure of a firm's performance, profitability, has been rejected as the basic criterion on the grounds that it is affected in the short run by factors outside the control of management, such as shortages of supplies. Profitability as a measure of success led to a reduction in experimental work and de-emphasized the importance of production quantity, quality, and assortment. Neither cost-reduction nor profitability was acceptable alone; each was only a partial index. The Soviets had concluded by 1940 that no single measure of success of a firm is adequate in itself and that there is no substitute for genuine analysis of all the elements entering into a firm's work.

Difficulties with single criteria have been observed in operations research, where one of the principal sources of difficulty is considered to be the choice of proper criteria for performance measurement.[7] The difficulty of translating the several alternatives into their full effect upon the organization's goal forces the operations researcher to settle for a cri-

---

[5] H. A. Simon, H. Guetzkow, G. Kozmetsky, and G. Tyndall, *Centralization vs. Decentralization in Organizing the Controller's Department* (New York, 1954).

[6] Granick, *op. cit.*

[7] Charles Hitch and Roland McKean, "Suboptimization in Operations Problems," in J. F. McCloskey and Flora F. Trefethen (Eds.), *Operations Research for Management* (Baltimore, Md., 1954).

terion more manageable than profit maximization, but less appropriate. The efficiency of a subgroup of the organization may be improved in terms of some plausible test, yet the organization's efficiency in terms of its major goal may be decreased.

In all the studies mentioned above, the inadequacy of a single measure of performance is evident. Whether this is a measure of an employee at the working level, or a measure of management, attention is directed away from the over-all goal. The existence of a measure of performance motivates individuals to effort, but the effort may be wasted, as in seeking "wooden money" savings, or may be detrimental to the organization's goal, as in rushing through interviews, delaying repairs, and rejecting profitable opportunities.

Multiple Measurements

Recognition of the inadequacies of a single measure of success or performance leads organizations to develop several criteria. It is felt then that all aspects of the job will receive adequate attention and emphasis so that efforts of individuals will not be distorted.

A realization in the employment office studied by Blau that job referrals and placements were also important led eventually to their inclusion in measuring the performance of the interviewers.[8] Merely counting the number of referrals and placements had led to wholesale indiscriminate referrals, which did not accomplish the employment agency's screening function. Therefore, to stress the qualitative aspects of the interviewer's job, several ratios (of referrals to interviews, placements to interviews, and placements to referrals) were devised. Altogether there were eight quantities that were counted or calculated for each interviewer. This increase in quantity and complexity of performance measurements was felt necessary to give emphasis to all aspects of the interviewer's job.

Granick relates that no single criterion was universally adopted in appraising Soviet management.[9] Some managers were acclaimed for satisfying production quotas while violating labor laws. Others were removed from office for violating quality and assortment plans while fulfilling production quotas. Apparently there is a ranking of importance of these multiple criteria. In a typical interfirm competition the judges were provided with a long list of indexes. These included production of finished goods in the planned assortment, an even flow of production as between ten-day periods and as between months, planned mastery of new types of products, improvement in product quality and reduction in waste, economy of materials through improved design and changing of technological processes, fulfillment of labor productivity tasks and lowering of unit cost, keeping within the established wage fund, and increase in the number of worker suggestions for improvements in work methods

[8] Blau, *op. cit.*
[9] Granick, *op. cit.*

and conditions and their adoption into operation. But no indication of how these indexes should be weighted was given. The pre-eminence of such indexes as quantity, quality, assortment of production, and remaining within the firm's allotment of materials and fuels brought some order into the otherwise chaotic picture. The presence of "campaigns" and "priorities" stressing one or more factors also has aided Soviet management in deciding which elements of its work are at the moment most important.

Without a single over-all composite measure of success, however, there is no way of determining whether the temporarily increased effort on the "campaign" criteria of the month represents new effort or merely effort shifted from other criteria. And the intangibility of some of these indexes makes it impossible to judge whether there has been decreased effort on other aspects. Hence even in a campaign period the relative emphases may become so unbalanced as to mitigate or defeat the purpose of the campaign.

The Soviet manager is working then under several measurements, and the relative influence or emphasis attached to any one measurement varies from firm to firm and from month to month. Profits and production are used, among other measurements, and these two may lead to contradictory managerial decisions. Granick hypothesizes that some managers have refused complicated orders that were difficult to produce because it would mean failure to produce the planned quantities. Acceptance of these orders would have been very profitable, but of the two criteria, production quantity took precedence.

Numerous American writers in the field of management have stressed the importance of multiple criteria in evaluating performance of management. Peter Drucker, for example, lists market standing, innovation, productivity, physical and financial resources, profitability, manager performance and development, worker performance and attitude, and public responsibility.[10] This list includes many of the same items as the list used by Soviet management.

The consensus at a round-table discussion of business and professional men[11] was that although return on investment is important, additional criteria are essential for an adequate appraisal of operating departments. These other criteria are fairly well summed up in Drucker's list above.

Thus we see that the need for multiple criteria is recognized and that they are employed at different levels of the organization—lower levels as in the employment agency, higher levels as considered by Granick and Drucker. At all levels these multiple measurements or criteria are intended to focus attention on the many facets of a particular job.

---

[10] Peter M. Drucker, *The Practice of Management* (New York, 1954).

[11] William H. Newman and James P. Logan, *Management of Expanding Enterprises* (New York, 1955).

The use of multiple criteria assumes that the individual will commit his or the organization's efforts, attention, and resources in greater measure to those activities which promise to contribute the greatest improvement to over-all performance. There must then exist a theoretical condition under which an additional unit of effort or resources would yield equally desirable results in over-all performance, whether applied to production, quality, research, safety, public relations, or any of the other suggested areas. This would be the condition of "balanced stress on objectives" to which Drucker refers.

Without a single over-all composite measure of performance, the individual is forced to rely upon his judgment as to whether increased effort on one criterion improves over-all performance, or whether there may be a reduction in performance on some other criterion which will outweigh the increase in the first. This is quite possible, for in any immediate situation many of these objectives may be contradictory to each other.

Composites

To adequately balance the stress on the contradictory objectives or criteria by which performance of a particular individual or organization is appraised, there must be an implied or explicit weighting of these criteria. When such a weighting system is available, it is an easy task to combine the measures of the various subgoals into a composite score for over-all performance.

Such a composite is used by the American Institute of Management in evaluating and ranking the managements of corporations, hospitals, and other organizations.[12] These ratings are accomplished by attaching a numerical grade to each of several criteria such as economic function, corporate structure, production efficiency, and the like. Each criterion has an optimum rating and the score on each for any particular organization is added to obtain a total score. Although there may be disagreement on the validity of the weighting system employed, the rating given on any particular category, the categories themselves, or the methods of estimating scores in the A.I.M. management audit, this system is an example of the type of over-all performance measurement which might be developed. Were such a system of ratings employed by an organization and found acceptable by management, it presumably would serve as a guide to obtaining a balanced stress on objectives.

A composite measure of performance was employed in Air Force wings as reported by K. C. Wagner.[13] A complex rating scheme covering a wide

---

[12] *Manual of Excellent Managements* (New York, 1955).

[13] Kenneth C. Wagner, "Latent Functions of an Executive Control: A Sociological Analysis of a Social System under Stress," *Research Previews*, Vol. II (Chapel Hill, N.C.: Institute for Research in Social Science, March, 1954), mimeo.

range of activities was used. When the organizations were put under pressure to raise their composite score without proportionate increases in the organization's means of achieving them, there were observable unanticipated consequences in the squadrons. Under a system of multiple criteria, pressure to increase performance on one criterion might be relieved by a slackening of effort toward other criteria. But with a composite criterion this does not seem as likely to occur. In Wagner's report individuals were subjected to tension, role and value conflicts, and reduced morale; air crews suffered from intercrew antagonism, apathy, and reduced morale; organization and power structures underwent changes; communications distortions and blockages occurred; integration decreased; culture patterns changed; and norms were violated. Some of these consequences may be desirable, some undesirable. The net result, however, might easily be less effective over-all performance.

These consequences were observable in a situation where goals were increased without a corresponding increase in means, which seems to be a common situation. Berliner refers to the "ratchet principle" wherein an increase in performance becomes the new standard, and the standard is thus continually raised. Recognition of the operation of the "ratchet principle" by workers was documented by F. J. Roethlisberger and William J. Dickson.[14] There was a tacit agreement among the workers not to exceed the quota, for fear that the job would then be rerated. Deliberate restriction of output is not an uncommon occurrence.

Although the experiences reported with the use of composite measures of performance are rather skimpy, there is still a clear indication that their use may have adverse consequences for the over-all performance of the organization.

Conclusion

Quantitative performance measurements—whether single, multiple, or composite—are seen to have undesirable consequences for over-all organizational performance. The complexity of large organizations requires better knowledge of organizational behavior for managers to make best use of the personnel available to them. Even where performance measures are instituted purely for purposes of information, they are probably interpreted as definitions of the important aspects of that job or activity and hence have important implications for the motivation of behavior. The motivational and behavioral consequences of performance measurements are inadequately understood. Further research in this area is necessary for a better understanding of how behavior may be oriented toward optimum accomplishment of the organization's goals.

---

[14] F. J. Roethlisberger and William J. Dickson, *Management and the Worker* (Cambridge, Mass., 1939).

Decision Making

OUR STUDY of control in Section Five led us to a re-examination of ideas from the preceding sections. This will also be true of the present section. All the previous material is relevant to organizational decision making and vice versa. To some extent decision making is an alternative frame of reference for the study of organizations.[1] As such, it emphasizes the rational aspects of organizational functioning and is peculiarly suited for normative investigations.

A decision can involve either taking action or acceptance of an idea. An example of the former on the part of an industrial concern might be the signing of a collective bargaining agreement with a union; an example of the latter might be the company's determination to free itself from certain restrictive work rules. The distinction here is in the irrevocability of actions in contrast with ideas, although ideas may be far more important if a multitude of actions can be predicted from their acceptance. If an action decision is equivalent to the behavior of an organization, then an idea decision is equivalent to the formation of organization character, a propensity for action. As pointed out by Selznick,[2] idea decisions are often made in the context of relatively minor action decisions, but carry implications far beyond those of the immediate issue.

Decision making in organizations is not limited to the acts or character of the organization as a whole. Every component organization and individual member also makes decisions relevant to the organization; and the causes and mode of integration of these lower-level decisions round out our picture of organizational decision making. An example of the latter might be the decision by a foreman that additional labor was needed to

---

[1] As in much of the work of Simon; see his remarks in Article 12 and their expansion in his books *Administrative Behavior* (Macmillan, 1947), and *Models of Man* (Wiley, 1957).

[2] See Article 5.

fill pending work orders. The ratification of this decision by his departmental superior and authorization by him to the personnel department for employment of additional workers would be the next step. The personnel department might then decide which person to hire and convert the process into an action decision for the organization as a whole by entering into an employment contract. In this case, which is quite typical, the questions of what "the decision" was or when it was made are largely definitional; but the vocabulary used does help to describe and explain the organization's observed behavior.

The distinction between action decisions and idea decisions also holds at the level of organization components and members. It can help in analyzing the problems of conflict, unanticipated consequences, and failure of co-ordination discussed in Sections Two and Five. These phenomena usually occur when ideas accepted by one component or member are dissonant with those accepted elsewhere. Adaptation or change in organizations may also originate with a dissonant idea that gains eventual acceptance.

Quite clearly, other organizational processes (leadership, communication, imposition of formal constraints, etc.) will be closely linked with decisions. Without attempting to construct artificial boundaries between this and other problem areas, the focus of this section is on studies taking decision making as their subject. Most of the literature in this field chooses one of three foci: the decision itself, the person, group, or organization making the decision; or the process by which decision is reached.

If we define a decision as a relationship between a decision maker and his environment, it can readily be appreciated that a large part of human knowledge is relevant, including whole disciplines such as law, medicine, and engineering. This section will necessarily be confined to aspects that may reasonably be thought to be common to all decisions, or at least to all decisions in organizations.[3] Our first two articles, Edwards, "Theory of Decision-Making" and Smith, Walters, Brooks, and Blackwell, "The Theory of Value and the Science of Decision," are primarily devoted to the abstract characteristics of decisions. Curiously enough, these theories and others like them make no mention of the occasions for decision; they begin with the decision maker (any decision maker) faced with a decision (not in the process of making it) and proceed to investigate the anatomy of the decision. The decisions are characterized by alternatives (mutually exclusive and exhaustive courses of action), utilities (the value or goal aspects), consequences (the relation between alternatives and utilities), and the act of choice. Variations of decision theory introduce such topics

---

[3] For an excellent annotated bibliography with a similar focus, see Paul Wasserman and Fred S. Silander, *Decision-Making* (Ithaca, N.Y.: Cornell University, Graduate School of Business and Public Administration, 1958).

as conflict of interest (game theory), probabilities (actuarial science), and the sequential aspects of the decision such as the possibility of searching for additional information or resolving the decision into a sequence of decisions (statistical decision theory).

One sometimes suspects in studying these theories that their elements are determined more by the necessity of having a determinate model than by the empirical characteristics of decisions. Nevertheless, it is clear that the theories describe an approach which *could* be taken to decisions by any decision maker. It seems safe to say that the chief contribution of decision theory will be in the direction of improving methods of decision making, the direction taken by statistical decision theory and operations research.

In his discussion of the development of decision theory, Edwards, a psychologist, is concerned with the potentiality of the concepts of the theory for the psychological study of the decision making of individual human beings. Most of this psychological research has been explicitly concerned with the formulation of a *positive* (i.e., descriptive) theory of human decision making. Given the nature of decision theory, it would seem to contribute to this objective only insofar as the characteristics of the decision impress themselves on the behavior of decision makers. Some concepts of decision theory (e.g., alternatives, consequences, choices) have a great deal of face validity. It takes more than these, however, to form a logically complete theory. The contributions of decision theory to psychology may well be limited to the suggestion of some interesting concepts. The contributions of experimental psychology to decision theory are more likely to shed light on the feasibility of the use of decision models in individual decision making than to demonstrate their fruitfulness as a theoretical explanation of the behavior of naïve subjects.

The study of individual and small-group decision makers and their activities falls within the province of the psychologists.[4] In their literature it is more often referred to as "problem solving" than as decision making. Some investigations have focused on the goodness of decisions or on characteristics of the decision maker that could aid or impede good decision making. Examples of the latter type of study are the articles by Guetzkow and Simon, Asch, and Torrance in Section Four. Studies of the former type have compared the quality of decisions reached by a small group with decisions reached by individuals. The results show that the superiority of one class of decision maker over the other cannot be

---

[4] See C. E. Osgood, *Method and Theory in Experimental Psychology* (Oxford, 1953), pp. 622–38; D. M. Johnson, *Psychology of Thought and Judgment* (Harper, 1955); J. S. Bruner, J. J. Goodnow, and G. A. Austin, *A Study of Thinking* (Wiley, 1956); and Harold H. Kelley and John W. Thibaut, "Experimental Studies of Group Problem Solving and Process," *Handbook of Social Psychology*, Vol. II (Addison-Wesley, 1954), pp. 735–85.

presumed. It seems to depend on the type of problem and the social situation. For example, if a simple division of labor is helpful, as solving a crossword puzzle, the group is clearly superior. If the criterion of success is clear so that anyone can recognize a correct solution, then the group is again superior, working at least as well as its best member. Again, if a large amount of information or a large number of relevant points need to be considered, the group performs better; but not as well as the best individual solutions. On the other hand, if much co-ordination is needed, as in the construction of a crossword puzzle, an individual is superior to a group. Similarly, if the criterion of success is not obvious, the group may not do appreciably better than the average of its members. Where a problem is concrete and easily understood, but without a clear criterion, the differing viewpoints of its members may make it impossible to reach any decision at all. This last example emphasizes the possibility of conflict of interest and the frequent necessity of bargaining in small-group situations.

Organizational decisions are often made by individuals, or by groups, or in some way that is not quite either. The essence of organization is its persistence over a long period; the typical small-group experiment deals with a newly formed group that is not expected to endure. These different contexts make it possible for the organization to avail itself of the differing superiorities of either individual or group and to invent entirely new mechanisms. One example is the military system of staff advice to a commander. The article below by Lorge, Weltz, Fox, and Herrold, "evaluation of Decisions Written by *ad hoc* Groups and Simulated Commanders," attempts to compare the goodness of decisions made by individuals, by a staff group, and by a commander on the advice of staff, ignoring such additional advantages of organization methods as specialization of staff members.

A central aspect of organization decision making is the allocation of specialized functions in the process to individuals or departments. This, of course, can provide a basis for the co-ordination of individual actions into a rational organization decision. Like any organization action, however, allocation is not determined solely by considerations of optimal design. The optimal design is rarely known, and action is taken on such questions under the same sort of commitments and constraints as discussed in earlier sections. The article by R. S. Weiss, "Factors Determining the Adoption of Decision-Making as a Role Behavior," explores two factors, social status and supervisor's attitude, that affected the degree to which professionals in one organization adopted the role of decision maker.

The organization as a decision maker has been the subject of many studies in special fields, such as public administration, international relations, finance, marketing, and industrial relations. These studies usually focus on the specifics of their own field, and not on the general characteristics of decision making. They nevertheless provide a source of case examples and institutional information that should not be overlooked by the student of organization. Unfortunately, a thorough treatment of this material is beyond the purview of this book.

Many studies, especially psychological ones, have focused on the *process* of decision making. This subject has received increasing emphasis in recent years. To a considerable extent, the nature of the decision maker is a secondary consideration in the study of decision processes. Studies of small-group problem solving carried over, with some success, in their initial theorizing the concepts and hypotheses applied earlier to the study of individual problem solving. These in turn bear a close relationship to categories in decision theory: perception of problem; its analysis, concluding with possible solutions; exploration of the consequences; choice. Much the same procedure is applied to the study of organized decision making in the article by R. K. Cyert, H. A. Simon, and D. B. Trow, "Observation of a Business Decision."

In each case something was added to what had been received. In exploring individual problem solving, people like Dewey tailored the abstractions of decision theory to fit the motivational and cognitive characteristics of the individual human being. Likewise, in extending the theory to small-group process, the social psychologists were led to emphasize certain characteristics of group psychology; for instance the need to devote attention to keeping members motivated, informed and participating, as well as to the task itself. The study of organized decision making introduces explicit planning of the decision process, specialization, etc. None of these contributions can be regarded as unique to the area in which it has been applied. Bales has suggested that group problem solving provides a model for individual problem solving, a not unreasonable hypothesis in view of the prominence of socially-learned behavior on the part of the individual. Simon emphasizes the correspondence between organized decision making and individual decision making: the organized process merely bringing into explicit form decision-making strategies present and in use by the individual when facing individual problems.

One part of the recent expansion of investigation into decision-making processes has been the use of simulation, especially by electronic computers. This takes two forms: simulation of an environment to facilitate the study of human problem solvers and simulation of the problem solvers themselves, with possible applications to real environments. An example of the first was given in the RAND Corporation studies in Section Two, where the air traffic pattern was simulated by computer for the purpose of studying the reaction of the "real" air defense control center. Other examples are the business games which have been developed by the American Management Association and International Business Machines Corporation as training devices for business executives. The RAND Corporation Logistics Systems Laboratory has also applied this technique in the development of an Air Force procurement system.[5] The best-known examples of the second type of simulation, simulating the decision maker, are computer programs for playing chess or checkers. The most successful to date has been the logic-theory machine of Newell and Simon, which discovers proofs for theorems in symbolic logic.[6]

[5] RAND Corporation Research Memorandum 1993, 10/10/57, Stephen Enke, *Logistics Laboratory Problem 1 after Two (Simulated) Years.*

[6] See W. R. Reitman, "Heuristic Programs, Computer Simulation, and Higher Mental Processes," *Behavioral Science*, Vol. IV, 4 (October, 1959), p. 330.

33. THE THEORY OF DECISION MAKING*

WARD EDWARDS

MANY SOCIAL scientists other than psychologists try to account for the behavior of individuals. Economists and a few psychologists have produced a large body of theory and a few experiments that deal with individual decision making. The kind of decision making with which this body of theory deals is as follows: given two states, A and B, into either one of which an individual may put himself, the individual chooses A in preference to B (or vice versa). For instance, a child standing in front of a candy counter may be considering two states. In state A the child has $0.25 and no candy. In state B the child has $0.15 and a ten-cent candy bar. The economic theory of decision making is a theory about how to predict such decisions.

Economic theorists have been concerned with this problem since the days of Jeremy Bentham (1748–1832). In recent years the development of the economic theory of consumer's decision making (or, as the economists call it, the theory of consumer's choice) has become exceedingly elaborate, mathematical, and voluminous. This literature is almost unknown to psychologists, in spite of sporadic pleas in both psychological (40, 84, 103, 104) and economic (101, 102, 123, 128, 199, 202) literature for greater communication between the disciplines.

The purpose of this paper is to review this theoretical literature, and also the rapidly increasing number of psychological experiments (performed by both psychologists and economists) that are relevant to it. The review will be divided into five sections: the theory of riskless choices, the application of the theory of riskless choices to welfare economics, the theory of risky choices, transitivity in decision making, and the theory of games and of statistical decision functions. Since this literature is unfamiliar and relatively inaccessible to most psychologists, and since I could not find any thorough bibliography on the theory of choice in the economic literature, this paper includes a rather extensive bibliography of the literature since 1930.

THE THEORY OF RISKLESS CHOICES[1]

Economic Man. The method of those theorists who have been concerned with the theory of decision making is essentially an armchair

---

*Reprinted from the *Psychological Bulletin*, Vol. 51, No. 4, July, 1954.

[1] No complete review of this literature is available. Kauder (105, 106) has reviewed the very early history of utility theory. Stigler (180) and Viner (194) have

method. They make assumptions, and from these assumptions they deduce theorems which presumably can be tested, though it sometimes seems unlikely that the testing will ever occur. The most important set of assumptions made in the theory of riskless choices may be summarized by saying that it is assumed that the person who makes any decision to which the theory is applied is an economic man.

What is an economic man like? He has three properties. (*a*) He is completely informed. (*b*) He is infinitely sensitive. (*c*) He is rational.

Complete Information. Economic man is assumed to know not only what all the courses of action open to him are, but also what the outcome of any action will be. Later on, in the sections on the theory of risky choices and on the theory of games, this assumption will be relaxed somewhat. (For the results of attempts to introduce the possibility of learning into this picture, see **51, 77.**)

Infinite Sensitivity. In most of the older work on choice, it is assumed that the alternatives available to an individual are continuous, infinitely divisible functions, that prices are infinitely divisible, and that economic man is infinitely sensitive. The only purpose of these assumptions is to make the functions that they lead to, continuous and differentiable. Stone (**182**) has recently shown that they can be abandoned with no serious changes in the theory of choice.

Rationality. The crucial fact about economic man is that he is rational. This means two things: He can weakly order the states into which he can get, and he makes his choices so as to maximize something.

Two things are required in order for economic man to be able to put all available states into a weak ordering. First, given any two states into which he can get, *A* and *B*, he must always be able to tell either that he prefers *A* to *B*, or that he prefers *B* to *A*, or that he is indifferent between them. If preference is operationally defined as choice, then it seems unthinkable that this requirement can ever be empirically violated. The second requirement for weak ordering, a more severe one, is that all preferences must be transitive. If economic man prefers *A* to *B* and *B* to *C*, then he prefers *A* to *C*. Similarly, if he is indifferent between *A* and *B* and between *B* and *C*, then he is indifferent between *A* and *C*. It is not obvious that transitivity will always hold for human choices, and experi-

reviewed the literature up to approximately 1930. Samuelson's book (**164**) contains an illuminating mathematical exposition of some of the content of this theory. Allen (**6**) explains the concept of indifference curves. Schultz (**172**) reviews the developments up to but not including the Hicks-Allen revolution from the point of view of demand theory. Hicks's book (**87**) is a complete and detailed exposition of most of the mathematical and economic content of the theory up to 1939. Samuelson (**167**) has reviewed the integrability problem and the revealed preference approach. And Wold (**204, 205, 206**) has summed up the mathematical content of the whole field for anyone who is comfortably at home with axiom systems and differential equations.

ments designed to find out whether or not it does will be described in the section on testing transitivity.

The second requirement of rationality, and in some ways the more important one, is that economic man must make his choices in such a way as to maximize something. This is the central principle of the theory of choice. In the theory of riskless choices, economic man has usually been assumed to maximize utility. In the theory of risky choices, he is assumed to maximize expected utility. In the literature on statistical decision making and the theory of games, various other fundamental principles of decision making are considered, but they are all maximization principles of one sort or another.

The fundamental content of the notion of maximization is that economic man always chooses the best alternative from among those open to him, as he sees it. In more technical language, the fact that economic man prefers A to B implies and is implied by the fact that A is higher than B in the weakly ordered set mentioned above. (Some theories introduce probabilities into the above statement, so that if A is higher than B in the weak ordering, then economic man is more likely to choose A than B, but not certain to choose A.)

This notion of maximization is mathematically useful, since it makes it possible for a theory to specify a unique point or a unique subset of points among those available to the decider. It seems to me psychologically unobjectionable. So many different kinds of functions can be maximized that almost any point actually available in an experimental situation can be regarded as a maximum of some sort. Assumptions about maximization only become specific, and therefore possibly wrong, when they specify what is being maximized.

There has, incidentally, been almost no discussion of the possibility that the two parts of the concept of rationality might conflict. It is conceivable, for example, that it might be costly in effort (and therefore in negative utility) to maintain a weakly ordered preference field. Under such circumstances, would it be "rational" to have such a field?

It is easy for a psychologist to point out that an economic man who has the properties discussed above is very unlike a real man. In fact, it is so easy to point this out that psychologists have tended to reject out of hand the theories that result from these assumptions. This isn't fair. Surely the assumptions contained in Hullian behavior theory (91) or in the Estes (60) or Bush-Mosteller (36, 37) learning theories are no more realistic than these. The most useful thing to do with a theory is not to criticize its assumptions but rather to test its theorems. If the theorems fit the data, then the theory has at least heuristic merit. Of course, one trivial theorem deducible from the assumptions embodied in the concept of economic man is that in any specific case of choice these assumptions will be satisfied. For instance, if economic man is a model for real men, then real men should always exhibit transitivity of real choices. Transitivity is an assumption, but it is directly testable. So are the other properties of economic man as a model for real men.

Economists themselves are somewhat distrustful of economic man (119, 156), and we will see in subsequent sections the results of a number of attempts to relax these assumptions.

Early Utility Maximization Theory. The school of philosopher-economists started by Jeremy Bentham and popularized by James Mill and others held that the goal of human action is to seek pleasure and avoid pain. Every object or action may be considered from the point of view of pleasure- or pain-giving properties. These properties are called the *utility* of the object, and pleasure is given by positive utility and pain by negative utility. The goal of action, then, is to seek the maximum utility. This simple hedonism of the future is easily translated into a theory of choice. People choose the alternative, from among those open to them, that leads to the greatest excess of positive over negative utility. This notion of utility maximization is the essence of the utility theory of choice. It will reappear in various forms throughout this paper. (Bohnert [30] discusses the logical structure of the utility concept.)

This theory of choice was embodied in the formal economic analyses of all the early great names in economics. In the hands of Jevons, Walras, and Menger it reached increasingly sophisticated mathematical expression and it was embodied in the thinking of Marshall, who published the first edition of his great *Principles of Economics* in 1890, and revised it at intervals for more than 30 years thereafter (137).

The use to which utility theory was put by these theorists was to establish the nature of the demand for various goods. On the assumption that the utility of any good is a monotonically increasing negatively accelerated function of the amount of that good, it is easy to show that the amounts of most goods which a consumer will buy are decreasing functions of price, functions which are precisely specified once the shapes of the utility curves are known. This is the result the economists needed and is, of course, a testable theorem. (For more on this, see 87, 159.)

Complexities arise in this theory when the relations between the utilities of different goods are considered. Jevons, Walras, Menger, and even Marshall had assumed that the utilities of different commodities can be combined into a total utility by simple addition; this amounts to assuming that the utilities of different goods are independent (in spite of the fact that Marshall elsewhere discussed the notions of competing goods, like soap and detergents, and completing goods, like right and left shoes, which obviously do not have independent utilities). Edgeworth (53), who was concerned with such nonindependent utilities, pointed out that total utility was not necessarily an additive function of the utilities attributable to separate commodities. In the process he introduced the notion of indifference curves, and thus began the gradual destruction of the classical utility theory. We shall return to this point shortly.

Although the forces of parsimony have gradually resulted in the elimination of the classical concept of utility from the economic theory of riskless choices, there have been a few attempts to use essentially the classical theory in an empirical way. Fisher (63) and Frisch (75) have developed methods of measuring marginal utility (the change in utility [u] with an infinitesimal change in amount possessed [Q], i.e., du/dQ) from market data, by making assumptions about the interpersonal similarity of consumer tastes. Recently Morgan (141) has used several variants of these techniques, has discussed mathematical and logical flaws in them, and has concluded on the basis of his empirical results that the techniques require too unrealistic assumptions to be workable. The crux of the problem is that, for these techniques to be useful, the commodities used must be independent (rather than competing or completing), and the broad commodity classifications necessary for adequate market data are not independent. Samuelson (164) has shown that the assumption of independent utilities, while it does guarantee interval scale utility measures, puts unwarrantably severe restrictions on the nature of the resulting demand function. Elsewhere Samuelson (158) presented, primarily as a logical and mathematical exercise, a method of measuring marginal utility by assuming some time-discount function. Since no reasonable grounds can be found for assuming one such function rather than another, this procedure holds no promise of empirical success. Marshall suggested (in his notion of "consumer's surplus") a method of utility measurement that turns out to be dependent on the assumption of constant marginal utility of money, and which is therefore quite unworkable. Marshall's prestige led to extensive discussion and debunking of this notion (e.g., 28), but little positive comes out of this literature. Thurstone (186) is currently attempting to determine utility functions for commodities experimentally, but has reported no results as yet.

Indifference Curves. Edgeworth's introduction of the notion of indifference curves to deal with the utilities of nonindependent goods was mentioned above. An indifference curve is, in Edgeworth's formulation, a constant-utility curve. Suppose that we consider apples and bananas, and suppose that you get the same amount of utility from 10-apples-and-1-banana as you do from 6-apples-and-4-bananas. Then these are two points on an indifference curve, and of course there are an infinite number of other points on the same curve. Naturally, this is not the only indifference curve you may have between apples and bananas. It may also be true that you are indifferent between 13-apples-and-5-bananas and 5-apples-and-15-bananas. These are two points on another, higher indifference curve. A whole family of such curves is called an indifference map. Figure 1 presents such a map. One particularly useful kind of indifference map has amounts of a commodity on one axis and amounts of money on the other. Money is a commodity, too.

The notion of an indifference map can be derived, as Edgeworth derived it, from the notion of measurable utility. But it does not have to be. Pareto (**146**, see also **151**) was seriously concerned about the assumption that utility was measurable up to a linear transformation. He felt that people could tell whether they preferred to be in state *A* or state *B*, but could not tell how much they preferred one state over the other. In other words, he hypothesized a utility function measurable only on an ordinal scale. Let us follow the usual economic language, and call utility measured on an ordinal scale *ordinal* utility, and utility measured on an interval scale, *cardinal* utility. It is meaningless to speak of the slope, or marginal utility, of an ordinal utility function; such a function cannot be differentiated. However, Pareto saw that the same conclusions which had been drawn from marginal utilities could be drawn from indifference curves. An indifference map can be drawn simply by finding all the combinations of the goods involved among which the person is indifferent. Pareto's formulation assumes that higher indifference curves have greater utility, but does not need to specify how much greater that utility is.

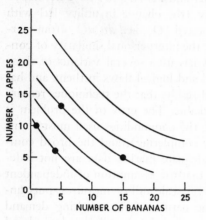

FIG. 1. A Hypothetical Indifference Map.

It turns out to be possible to deduce from indifference curves all of the theorems that were originally deduced from cardinal utility measures. This banishing of cardinal utility was furthered considerably by splendid mathematical papers by Johnson (**97**) and Slutsky (**177**). (In modern economic theory, it is customary to think of an *n*-dimensional commodity space, and of indifference hyperplanes in that space, each such hyperplane having, of course, *n* − 1 dimensions. In order to avoid unsatisfactory preference structures, it is necessary to assume that consumers always have a complete weak ordering for all commodity bundles, or points in commodity space. Georgescu-Roegen [76], Wold [204, 205, 206, 208], Houthakker [90], and Samuelson [167] have discussed this problem.)

Pareto was not entirely consistent in his discussion of ordinal utility. Although he abandoned the assumption that its exact value could be known, he continued to talk about the sign of the marginal utility coefficient, which assumed that some knowledge about the utility function other than purely ordinal knowledge was available. He also committed other inconsistencies. So Hicks and Allen (88), in 1934, were led to their classic paper in which they attempted to purge the theory of choice of its last introspective elements. They adopted the conventional economic view about indifference curves as determined from a sort of imaginary questionnaire, and proceeded to derive all of the usual conclusions about consumer demand with no reference to the notion of even ordinal utility (though of course the notion of an ordinal scale of preferences was still embodied in their derivation of indifference curves). This paper was for economics something like the behaviorist revolution in psychology.

Lange (116), stimulated by Hicks and Allen, pointed out another inconsistency in Pareto. Pareto had assumed that if a person considered four states, A, B, C, and D, he could judge whether the difference between the utilities of A and B was greater than, equal to, or less than the difference between the utilities of C and D. Lange pointed out that if such a comparison was possible for any A, B, C, and D, then utility was cardinally measurable. Since it seems introspectively obvious that such comparisons can be made, this paper provoked a flood of protest and comment (7, 22, 117, 147, 209). Nevertheless, in spite of all the comment, and even in spite of skepticism by a distinguished economist as late as 1953 (153), Lange is surely right. Psychologists should know this at once; such comparisons are the basis of the psychophysical Method of Equal Sense Distances, from which an interval scale is derived. (Samuelson [162] has pointed out a very interesting qualification. Not only must such judgments of difference be possible, but they must also be transitive in order to define an interval scale.) But since such judgments of differences did not seem to be necessary for the development of consumer demand theory, Lange's paper did not force the reinstatement of cardinal utility.

Indeed, the pendulum swung further in the behavioristic direction. Samuelson developed a new analytic foundation for the theory of consumer behavior, the essence of which is that indifference curves and hence the entire structure of the theory of consumer choice can be derived simply from observation of choices among alternative groups of purchases available to a consumer (160, 161). This approach has been extensively developed by Samuelson (164, 165, 167, 169) and others (50, 90, 125, 126). The essence of the idea is that each choice defines a point and a slope in commodity space. Mathematical approximation methods make it possible to combine a whole family of such slopes into an indifference hyperplane. A family of such hyperplanes forms an indifference "map."

In a distinguished but inaccessible series of articles, Wold (204, 205, 206; see also 208 for a summary presentation) has presented the mathematical content of the Pareto, Hicks and Allen, and revealed preference (Samuelson) approaches, as well as Cassel's demand function approach, and has shown that if the assumption about complete weak ordering of bundles of commodities which was discussed above is made, then all these approaches are mathematically equivalent.

Nostalgia for Cardinal Utility. The crucial reason for abandoning cardinal utility was the argument of the ordinalists that indifference curve analysis in its various forms could do everything that cardinal utility could do, with fewer assumptions. So far as the theory of riskless choice is concerned, this is so. But this is only an argument for parsimony, and parsimony is not always welcome. There was a series of people who, for one reason or another, wanted to reinstate cardinal utility, or at least marginal utility. There were several mathematically invalid attempts to show that marginal utility could be defined even in an ordinal-utility universe (23, 24, 163; 25, 114). Knight (110), in 1944, argued extensively for cardinal utility; he based his arguments in part on introspective considerations and in part on an examination of psychophysical scaling procedures. He stimulated a number of replies (29, 42; 111). Recently Robertson (154) pleaded for the reinstatement of cardinal utility in the interests of welfare economics (this point will be discussed again below). But in general the indifference curve approach, in its various forms, has firmly established itself as the structure of the theory of riskless choice.

Experiments on Indifference Curves. Attempts to measure marginal utility from market data were discussed above. There have been three experimental attempts to measure indifference curves. Schultz, who pioneered in deriving statistical demand curves, interested his colleague at the University of Chicago, the psychologist Thurstone, in the problem of indifference curves. Thurstone (185) performed a very simple experiment. He gave one subject a series of combinations of hats and overcoats, and required the subject to judge whether he preferred each combination to a standard. For instance, the subject judged whether he preferred eight hats and eight overcoats to fifteen hats and three overcoats. The same procedure was repeated for hats and shoes, and for shoes and overcoats. The data were fitted with indifference curves derived from the assumptions that utility curves fitted Fechner's Law and that the utilities of the various objects were independent. Thurstone says that Fechner's Law fitted the data better than the other possible functions he considered, but presents no evidence for this assertion. The crux of the experiment was the attempt to predict the indifference curves between shoes and overcoats from the other indifference curves. This was done by using the other two indifference curves to infer utility functions for shoes and for overcoats separately, and then using these two utility functions to predict the total utility of various amounts of shoes and overcoats jointly. The prediction worked rather well. The judgments of the one subject used are extraordinarily orderly; there is very little of the inconsistency and variability that others working in this area have found. Thurstone says, "The subject . . . was entirely naive as regards the psychophysical problem involved and had no knowledge whatever of the nature of the curves that we expected to find" (185, p. 154). He adds, "I selected as subject a research assistant in my laboratory who knew nothing about psychophysics. Her work was largely clerical in nature. She had a very even disposition, and I instructed her to take an even motivational attitude on the successive occasions . . . I was surprised at the consistency of the judgments that I obtained, but I am pretty sure that they were the result of careful instruction to assume a uniform motivational attitude."[2] From the economist's point of view, the main criticism of this experiment is that it involved imaginary rather than real transactions (200).

The second experimental measurement of indifference curves is reported by the economists Rousseas and Hart (157). They required large numbers of students to rank sets of three combinations of different amounts of bacon and eggs. By assuming that all students had the same indifference curves, they were able to derive a composite indifference map for bacon and eggs. No mathematical assumptions were necessary, and the indifference map is not given mathematical form. Some judgments were partly or completely inconsistent with the final map, but not too many. The only conclusion which this experiment justifies is that it is possible to derive such a composite indifference map.

The final attempt to measure an indifference curve is a very recent one by the psychologists Coombs and Milholland (49). The indifference curve involved is one between risk and value of an object, and so will be discussed below in the section on the theory of risky decisions. It is mentioned here because the same methods (which show only that the indifference curve is convex to the origin, and so perhaps should not be called measurement) could equally well be applied to the determination of indifference curves in riskless situations.

Mention should be made of the extensive economic work on statistical demand curves. For some reason the most distinguished statistical demand curve derivers feel it necessary to give an account of consumer's choice theory as a preliminary to the derivation of their empirical demand curves. The result is that the two best books in the area (172, 182) are each divided into two parts; the first is a general discussion of the theory of consumer's choice and the second a quite unrelated report of statistical economic work. Stigler (179) has given good reasons why the statistical demand curves are so little related to the demand curves of economic theory, and Wallis and Friedman (200) argue plausibly that this state of affairs is inevitable. At any rate, there seems to be little prospect of using

---

[2] L. L. Thurstone, *Personal Communication*, December 7, 1953.

large-scale economic data to fill in the empirical content of the theory of individual decision making.

Psychological Comments. There are several commonplace observations that are likely to occur to psychologists as soon as they try to apply the theory of riskless choices to actual experimental work. The first is that human beings are neither perfectly consistent nor perfectly sensitive. This means that indifference curves are likely to be observable as indifference regions, or as probability distributions of choice around a central locus. It would be easy to assume that each indifference curve represents the modal value of a normal sensitivity curve, and that choices should have statistical properties predictable from that hypothesis as the amounts of the commodities (locations in product space) are changed. This implies that the definition of indifference between two collections of commodities should be that each collection is preferred over the other 50 per cent of the time. Such a definition has been proposed by an economist (108), and used in experimental work by psychologists (142). Of course, 50 per cent choice has been a standard psychological definition of indifference since the days of Fechner.

Incidentally, failure on the part of an economist to understand that a just noticeable difference (j.n.d.) is a statistical concept has led him to argue that the indifference relation is intransitive, that is, that if A is indifferent to B and B is indifferent to C, then A need not be indifferent to C (8, 9, 10). He argues that if A and B are less than one j.n.d. apart, then A will be indifferent to B; the same of course is true of B and C; but A and C may be more than one j.n.d. apart, and so one may be preferred to the other. This argument is, of course, wrong. If A has slightly more utility than B, then the individual will choose A in preference to B slightly more than 50 per cent of the time, even though A and B are less than one j.n.d. apart in utility. The 50 per cent point is in theory a precisely defined point, not a region. It may in fact be difficult to determine because of inconsistencies in judgments and because of changes in taste with time.

The second psychological observation is that it seems impossible even to dream of getting experimentally an indifference map in n-dimensional space where n is greater than 3. Even the case of $n = 3$ presents formidable experimental problems. This is less important to the psychologist who wants to use the theory of choice to rationalize experimental data than to the economist who wants to derive a theory of general static equilibrium.

Experiments like Thurstone's (185) involve so many assumptions that it is difficult to know what their empirical meaning might be if these assumptions were not made. Presumably, the best thing to do with such experiments is to consider them as tests of the assumption with the least face validity. Thurstone was willing to assume utility maximization and independence of the commodities involved (incidentally, his choice of commodities seems singularly unfortunate for justifying an assumption of independent utilities), and so used his data to construct a utility function. Of course, if only ordinal utility is assumed, then experimental indifference curves cannot be used this way. In fact, in an ordinal-utility universe neither of the principal assumptions made by Thurstone can be tested by means of experimental indifference curves. So the assumption of cardinal utility, though not necessary, seems to lead to considerably more specific uses for experimental data.

At any rate, from the experimental point of view the most interesting question is: What is the observed shape of indifference curves between independent commodities? This question awaits an experimental answer.

The notion of utility is very similar to the Lewinian notion of valence (120, 121). Lewin conceives of valence as the attractiveness of an object or activity to a person (121). Thus, psychologists might consider the experimental study of utilities to be the experimental study of valences, and therefore an attempt at quantifying parts of the Lewinian theoretical schema.

APPLICATION OF THE THEORY OF RISKLESS CHOICES TO WELFARE ECONOMICS[3]

The classical utility theorists assumed the existence of interpersonally comparable cardinal utility. They were thus able to find a simple answer to the question of how to determine the best economic policy: That economic policy is best which results in the maximum total utility, summed over all members of the economy.

The abandonment of interpersonal comparability makes this answer useless. A sum is meaningless if the units being summed are of varying sizes and there is no way of reducing them to some common size. This point has not been universally recognized, and certain economists (e.g., 82, 154) still defend cardinal (but not interpersonally comparable) utility on grounds of its necessity for welfare economics.

Pareto's Principle. The abandonment of interpersonal comparability and then of cardinal utility produced a search for some other principle to justify economic policy. Pareto (146), who first abandoned cardinal utility, provided a partial solution. He suggested that a change should be considered desirable if it left everyone at least as well off as he was before, and made at least one person better off.

Compensation Principle. Pareto's principle is fine as far as it goes, but it obviously does not go very far. The economic decisions which can be made on so simple a principle are few and insignificant. So welfare eco-

---

[3] The discussion of welfare economics given in this paper is exceedingly sketchy. For a picture of what the complexities of modern welfare economics are really like see 11, 13, 14, 86, 118, 124, 127, 139, 140, 148, 154, 155, 166, 174.

nomics languished until Kaldor (98) proposed the compensation principle. This principle is that if it is possible for those who gain from an economic change to compensate the losers for their losses and still have something left over from their gains, then the change is desirable. Of course, if the compensation is actually paid, then this is simply a case of Pareto's principle.

But Kaldor asserted that the compensation need not actually be made; all that was necessary was that it could be made. The fact that it could be made, according to Kaldor, is evidence that the change produces an excess of good over harm, and so is desirable. Scitovsky (173) observed an inconsistency in Kaldor's position: Some cases could arise in which, when a change from *A* to *B* has been made because of Kaldor's criterion, then a change back from *B* to *A* would also satisfy Kaldor's criterion. It is customary, therefore, to assume that changes which meet the original Kaldor criterion are only desirable if the reverse change does not also meet the Kaldor criterion.

It has gradually become obvious that the Kaldor-Scitovsky criterion does not solve the problem of welfare economics (see e.g., 18, 99). It assumes that the unpaid compensation does as much good to the person who gains it as it would if it were paid to the people who lost by the change. For instance, suppose that an industrialist can earn $10,000 a year more from his plant by using a new machine, but that the introduction of the machine throws two people irretrievably out of work. If the salary of each worker prior to the change was $4,000 a year, then the industrialist could compensate the workers and still make a profit. But if he does not compensate the workers, then the added satisfaction he gets from his extra $10,000 may be much less than the misery he produces in his two workers. This example only illustrates the principle; it does not make much sense in these days of progressive income taxes, unemployment compensation, high employment, and strong unions.

Social Welfare Functions. From here on the subject of welfare economics gets too complicated and too remote from psychology to merit extensive exploration in this paper. The line that it has taken is the assumption of a social welfare function (21), a function which combines individual utilities in a way which satisfies Pareto's principle but is otherwise undefined. In spite of its lack of definition, it is possible to draw certain conclusions from such a function (see e.g., 164). However, Arrow (14) has recently shown that a social welfare function that meets certain very reasonable requirements about being sensitive in some way to the wishes of all the people affected, etc., cannot in general be found in the absence of interpersonally comparable utilities (see also 89).

Psychological Comment. Some economists are willing to accept the fact that they are inexorably committed to making moral judgments when they recommend economic policies (e.g., 152, 153). Others still long for

Cardinal econ.? ? same?
interval "?

the impersonal amorality of a utility measure (e.g., **154**). However desirable interpersonally comparable cardinal utility may be, it seems utopian to hope that any experimental procedure will ever give information about individual utilities that could be of any practical use in guiding large-scale economic policy.

THE THEORY OF RISKY CHOICES[4]

Risk and Uncertainty. Economists and statisticians distinguish between risk and uncertainty. There does not seem to be any general agreement about which concept should be associated with which word, but the following definitions make the most important distinctions.

Almost everyone would agree that when I toss a coin the probability that I will get a head is .5. A proposition about the future to which a number can be attached, a number that represents the likelihood that the proposition is true, may be called a *first-order risk*. What the rules are for attaching such numbers is a much debated question, which will be avoided in this paper.

Some propositions may depend on more than one probability distribution. For instance, I may decide that if I get a tail, I will put the coin back in my pocket, whereas if I get a head, I will toss it again. Now, the probability of the proposition "I will get a head on my second toss" is a function of two probability distributions, the distribution corresponding to the first toss and that corresponding to the second toss. This might be called a *second-order risk*. Similarly, risks of any order may be constructed. It is a mathematical characteristic of all higher-order risks that they may be compounded into first-order risks by means of the usual theorems for compounding probabilities. (Some economists have argued against this procedure [83], essentially on the grounds that you may have more information by the time the second risk comes around. Such problems can best be dealt with by means of von Neumann and Morgenstern's

---

[4] Strotz (**183**) and Alchian (**1**) present non-technical and sparkling expositions of the von Neumann and Morgenstern utility measurement proposals. Georgescu-Roegen (**78**) critically discusses various axiom systems so as to bring some of the assumptions underlying this kind of cardinal utility into clear focus. Allais (**3**) reviews some of these ideas in the course of criticizing them. Arrow (**12, 14**) reviews parts of the field.

There is a large psychological literature on one kind of risky decision making, the kind which results when psychologists use partial reinforcement. This literature has been reviewed by Jenkins and Stanley (**96**). Recently a number of experimenters, including Jarrett (**95**), Flood (**69, 70**), Bilodeau (**27**), and myself (**56**) have been performing experiments on human subjects who are required to choose repetitively between two or more alternatives, each of which has a probability of reward greater than zero and less than one. The problems raised by these experiments are too complicated and too far removed from conventional utility theory to be dealt with in this paper. This line of experimentation may eventually provide the link which ties together utility theory and reinforcement theory.

[197] concept of strategy, which is discussed below. They become in general problems of uncertainty, rather than risk.)

Some propositions about the future exist to which no generally accepted probabilities can be attached. What is the probability that the following proposition is true: Immediately after finishing this paper, you will drink a glass of beer? Surely it is neither impossible nor certain, so it ought to have a probability between zero and one, but it is impossible for you or me to find out what that probability might be, or even to set up generally acceptable rules about how to find out. Such propositions are considered cases of *uncertainty*, rather than of risk. This section deals only with the subject of first-order risks. The subject of uncertainty will arise again in connection with the theory of games.

Expected Utility Maximization. The traditional mathematical notion for dealing with games of chance (and so with risky decisions) is the notion that choices should be made so as to maximize *expected value*. The expected value of a bet is found by multiplying the value of each possible outcome by its probability of occurrence and summing these products across all possible outcomes. In symbols:

$$EV = p_1\$_1 + p_2\$_2 + \cdots + p_n\$_n ,$$

where p stands for probability, $\$$ stands for the value of an outcome, and $p_1 + p_2 + \cdots + p_n = 1$.

The assumption that people actually behave the way this mathematical notion says they should is contradicted by observable behavior in many risky situations. People are willing to buy insurance, even though the person who sells the insurance makes a profit. People are willing to buy lottery tickets, even though the lottery makes a profit. Consideration of the problem of insurance and of the St. Petersburg paradox led Daniel Bernoulli, an eighteenth century mathematician, to propose that they could be resolved by assuming that people act so as to maximize *expected utility*, rather than expected value (**26**). (He also assumed that utility followed a function that more than a century later was proposed by Fechner for subjective magnitudes in general and is now called Fechner's Law.) This was the first use of the notion of expected utility.

The literature on risky decision making prior to 1944 consists primarily of the St. Petersburg paradox and other gambling and probability literature in mathematics, some literary discussion in economics (e.g., **109**, **187**), one economic paper on lotteries (**189**), and the early literature of the theory of games (**31, 32, 33, 34, 195**), which did not use the notion of utility. The modern period in the study of risky decision making began with the publication in 1944 of von Neumann and Morgenstern's monumental book *Theory of Games and Economic Behavior* (**196**, see also **197**), which we will discuss more fully later. Von Neumann and Morgenstern pointed out that the usual assumption that economic man can always say whether he prefers one state to another or is indifferent between them needs only to be slightly modified in order to imply cardinal utility. The modification consists of adding that economic man can also completely order probability combinations of states. Thus, suppose that an economic man is indifferent between the certainty of $7.00 and a 50–50 chance of gaining $10.00 or nothing. We can assume that his indifference between these two prospects means that they have the same utility for him. We may define the utility of $0.00 as zero utiles (the usual name for the unit of utility, just as sone is the name for the unit of auditory loudness), and the utility of $10.00 as 10 utiles. These two arbitrary definitions correspond to defining the two undefined constants which are permissible since cardinal utility is measured only up to a linear transformation. Then we may calculate the utility of $7.00 by using the concept of expected utility as follows:

$$U(\$7.00) = .5\,U(\$10.00) + .5\,U(\$0.00)$$
$$= .5(10) + .5(0) = 5.$$

Thus we have determined the cardinal utility of $7.00 and found that it is 5 utiles. By varying the probabilities and by using the already found utilities it is possible to discover the utility of any other amount of money, using only the two permissible arbitrary definitions. It is even more convenient if instead of +$10.00, −$10.00 or some other loss is used as one of the arbitrary utilities.

A variety of implications is embodied in this apparently simple notion. In the attempt to examine and exhibit clearly what these implications are, a number of axiom systems, differing from von Neumann and Morgenstern's but leading to the same result, have been developed (73, 74, 85, 135, 136, 171). This paper will not attempt to go into the complex discussions (e.g., 130, 131, 168, 207) of these various alternative axiom systems. One recent discussion of them (78) has concluded, on reasonable grounds, that the original von Neumann and Morgenstern set of axioms is still the best.

It is profitable, however, to examine what the meaning of this notion is from the empirical point of view if it is right. First, it means that risky propositions can be ordered in desirability, just as riskless ones can. Second, it means that the concept of expected utility is behaviorally meaningful. Finally, it means that choices among risky alternatives are made in such a way that they maximize expected utility.

If this model is to be used to predict actual choices, what could go wrong with it? It might be that the probabilities by which the utilities are multiplied should not be the objective probabilities; in other words, a decider's estimate of the subjective importance of a probability may not be the same as the numerical value of that probability. It might be that the method of combination of probabilities and values should not be simple

multiplication. It might be that the method of combination of the proba-
bility-value products should not be simple addition. It might be that the
process of gambling has some positive or negative utility of its own. It
might be that the whole approach is wrong, that people just do not behave as if they were trying to maximize expected utility. We shall examine
some of these possibilities in greater detail below.

Economic Implications of Maximizing Expected Utility. The utility-
measurement notions of von Neumann and Morgenstern were enthusiastically welcomed by many economists (e.g., **73, 193**), though a few
(e.g., **19**) were at least temporarily (**20**) unconvinced. The most interesting economic use of them was proposed by Friedman and Savage (**73**),
who were concerned with the question of why the same person who buys
insurance (with a negative expected
money value), and therefore is willing to pay in order not to take risks,
will also buy lottery tickets (also
with a negative expected money
value) in which he pays in order
to take risks. They suggested that
these facts could be reconciled by
a doubly inflected utility curve for
money, like that in Figure 2. If *I*
represents the person's current income, then he is clearly willing to
accept "fair" insurance (i.e., insurance with zero expected money
value) because the serious loss
against which he is insuring would
have a lower expected utility than
the certain loss of the insurance premium. (Negatively accelerated total
utility curves, like that from the origin to *I*, are what you get when marginal utility decreases; thus, decreasing marginal utility is consistent with
the avoidance of risks.) The person would also be willing to buy lottery
tickets, since the expected utility of the lottery ticket is greater than the
certain loss of the cost of the ticket, because of the rapid increase in the
height of the utility function. Other considerations make it necessary that
the utility curve turn down again. Note that this discussion assumes that
gambling has no inherent utility.

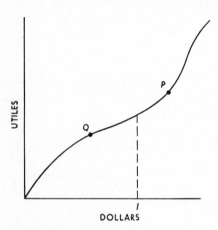

FIG. 2. Hypothetical Utility Curve for Money,
Proposed by Friedman and Savage.

Markowitz (**132**) suggested an important modification in this hypothesis. He suggested that the origin of a person's utility curve for
money be taken as his customary financial status, and that on both sides of
the origin the curve be assumed first concave and then convex. If the
person's customary state of wealth changes, then the shape of his utility
curve will thus remain generally the same with respect to where he now

is, and so his risk-taking behavior will remain pretty much the same instead of changing with every change of wealth as in the Friedman-Savage formulation.

Criticism of the Expected-Utility Maximization Theory. It is fairly easy to construct examples of behavior that violate the von Neumann-Morgenstern axioms (for a particularly ingenious example, see 183). It is especially easy to do so when the amounts of money involved are very large, or when the probabilities or probability differences involved are extremely small. Allais (5) has constructed a questionnaire full of items of this type. For an economist interested in using these axioms as a basis for a completely general theory of risky choice, these examples may be significant. But psychological interest in this model is more modest. The psychologically important question is: Can such a model be used to account for simple experimental examples of risky decisions?

Of course a utility function derived by von Neumann-Morgenstern means is not necessarily the same as a classical utility function (74, 203; see also 82).

Experiment on the Von Neumann-Morgenstern Model. A number of experiments on risky decision making have been performed. Only the first of them, by Mosteller and Nogee (142), has been in the simple framework of the model described above. All the rest have in some way or another centered on the concept of probabilities effective for behavior which differ in some way from the objective probabilities, as well as on utilities different from the objective values of the objects involved.

Mosteller and Nogee (142) carried out the first experiment to apply the von Neumann-Morgenstern model. They presented Harvard undergraduates and National Guardsmen with bets stated in terms of rolls at poker dice, which each subject could accept or refuse. Each bet gave a "hand" at poker dice. If the subject could beat the hand, he won an amount stated in the bet. If not, he lost a nickel. Subjects played with $1.00, which they were given at the beginning of each experimental session. They were run together in groups of five; but each decided and rolled the poker dice for himself. Subjects were provided with a table in which the mathematically fair bets were shown, so that a subject could immediately tell by referring to the table whether a given bet was fair, or better or worse than fair.

In the data analysis, the first step was the determination of "indifference offers." For each probability used and for each player, the amount of money was found for which that player would accept the bet 50 per cent of the time. Thus equality was defined as 50 per cent choice, as it is likely to be in all psychological experiments of this sort. Then the utility of $0.00 was defined as 0 utiles, and the utility of losing a nickel was defined as −1 utile. With these definitions and the probabilities involved, it was easy to calculate the utility corresponding to the amount of money involved in the indifference offer. It turned out that, in general, the Harvard undergraduates had diminishing marginal utilities, while the National Guardsmen had increasing marginal utilities.

The utilities thus calculated were used in predicting the results of more complex bets. It is hard to evaluate the success of these predictions. At any rate, an auxiliary paired-comparisons experiment showed that the hypothesis that subjects maximized expected utility predicted choices better than the hypothesis that subjects maximized expected money value.

The utility curve that Mosteller and Nogee derive is different from the one Friedman and Savage (73) were talking about. Suppose that a subject's utility curve were of the Friedman-Savage type, as in Figure 2, and that he had enough money to put him at point P. If he now wins or loses a bet, then he is moved to a different location on the indifference curve, say Q. (Note that the amounts of money involved are much smaller than in the original Friedman-Savage use of this curve.) However, the construction of a Mosteller-Nogee utility curve assumes that the individual is always at the same point on his utility curve, namely the origin. This means that the curve is really of the Markowitz (132) type discussed above, instead of the Friedman-Savage type. The curve is not really a curve of utility of money in general, but rather it is a curve of the utility-for-n-more dollars. Even so, it must be assumed further that as the total amount of money possessed by the subject changes during the experiment, the utility-for-n-more dollars curve does not change. Mosteller and Nogee argue, on the basis of detailed examination of some of their data, that the amount of money possessed by the subjects did not seriously influence their choices. The utility curves they reported showed changing marginal utility within the amounts of money used in their experiment. Consequently, their conclusion that the amount of money possessed by the subjects was not seriously important can only be true if their utility curves are utility-for-n-more dollars curves and if the shapes of such curves are not affected by changes in the number of dollars on hand. This discussion exhibits a type of problem which must always arise in utility measurement and which is new in psychological scaling. The effects of previous judgments on present judgments are a familiar story in psychophysics, but they are usually assumed to be contaminating influences that can be minimized or eliminated by proper experimental design. In utility scaling, the fundamental idea of a utility scale is such that the whole structure of a subject's choices should be altered as a result of each previous choice (if the choices are real ones involving money gains or losses). The Markowitz solution to this problem is the most practical one available at present, and that solution is not entirely satisfactory since all it does is to assume that people's utilities for money operate in such a way that the problem does not really exist. This assumption is plausible for money, but it gets rapidly less plausible when other commodities with a less continuous character are considered instead.

Probability Preferences. In a series of recent experiments (**55, 57, 58, 59**), the writer has shown that subjects, when they bet, prefer some probabilities to others (**57**), and that these preferences cannot be accounted for by utility considerations (**59**). All the experiments were basically of the same design. Subjects were required to choose between pairs of bets according to the method of paired comparisons. The bets were of three kinds: positive expected value, negative expected value, and zero expected value. The two members of each pair of bets had the same expected value, so that there was never (in the main experiment [**57, 59**]) any objective reason to expect that choosing one bet would be more desirable than choosing the other.

Subjects made their choices under three conditions: just imagining they were betting; betting for worthless chips; and betting for real money. They paid any losses from their own funds, but they were run in extra sessions after the main experiment to bring their winnings up to $1.00 per hour.

The results showed that two factors were most important in determining choices: general preferences or dislikes for risk-taking, and specific preferences among probabilities. An example of the first kind of factor is that subjects strongly preferred low probabilities of losing large amounts of money to high probabilities of losing small amounts of money —they just didn't like to lose. It also turned out that on positive expected value bets, they were more willing to accept long shots when playing for real money than when just imagining or playing for worthless chips. An example of the second kind of factor is that they consistently preferred bets involving a 4/8 probability of winning to all others, and consistently avoided bets involving a 6/8 probability of winning. These preferences were reversed for negative expected value bets.

These results were independent of the amounts of money involved in the bets, so long as the condition of constant expected value was maintained (**59**). When pairs of bets which differed from one another in expected value were used, the choices were a compromise between maximizing expected amount of money and betting at the preferred probabilities (**58**). An attempt was made to construct individual utility curves adequate to account for the results of several subjects. For this purpose, the utility of $0.30 was defined as 30 utiles, and it was assumed that subjects cannot discriminate utility differences smaller than half a utile. Under these assumptions, no individual utility curves consistent with the data could be drawn. Various minor experiments showed that these results were reliable and not due to various possible artifacts (**59**). No attempt was made to generate a mathematical model of probability preferences.

The existence of probability preferences means that the simple von Neumann-Morgenstern method of utility measurement cannot succeed. Choices between bets will be determined not only by the amounts of money involved, but also by the preferences the subjects have among the probabilities involved. Only an experimental procedure which holds one of these variables constant, or otherwise allows for it, can hope to measure the other. Thus my experiments cannot be regarded as a way of measuring probability preferences; they show only that such preferences exist.

It may nevertheless be possible to get an interval scale of the utility of money from gambling experiments by designing an experiment which measures utility and probability preferences simultaneously. Such experiments are likely to be complicated and difficult to run, but they can be designed.

Subjective Probability. First, a clarification of terms is necessary. The phrase *subjective probability* has been used in two ways: as a name for a school of thought about the logical basis of mathematical probability (51, 52, 80) and as a name for a transformation on the scale of mathematical probabilities which is somehow related to behavior. Only the latter usage is intended here. The clearest distinction between these two notions arises from consideration of what happens when an objective probability can be defined (e.g., in a game of craps). If the subjective probability is assumed to be different from the objective probability, then the concept is being used in its second, or psychological, sense. Other terms with the same meaning have also been used: personal probability, psychological probability, expectation (a poor term because of the danger of confusion with expected value). (For a more elaborate treatment of concepts in this area, see 192.)

In 1948, prior to the Mosteller and Nogee experiment, Preston and Baratta (149) used essentially similar logic and a somewhat similar experiment to measure subjective probabilities instead of subjective values. They required subjects to bid competitively for the privilege of taking a bet. All bids were in play money, and the data consisted of the winning bids. If each winning bid can be considered to represent a value of play money such that the winning bidder is indifferent between it and the bet he is bidding for, and if it is further assumed that utilities are identical with the money value of the play money and that all players have the same subjective probabilities, then these data can be used to construct a subjective probability scale. Preston and Baratta constructed such a scale. The subjects, according to the scale, overestimate low probabilities and underestimate high ones, with an indifference point (where subjective equals objective probability) at about 0.2. Griffith (81) found somewhat similar results in an analysis of parimutuel betting at race tracks, as did Attneave (17) in a guessing game, and Sprowls (178) in an analysis of various lotteries. The Mosteller and Nogee data (142) can, of course, be analyzed for subjective probabilities instead of subjective values. Mosteller and Nogee performed such an analysis and said that their results were in general agreement with Preston and Baratta's. However, Mosteller and Nogee found no indifference point for their Harvard students, whereas the National Guardsmen had an indifference point at about 0.5. They are not able to reconcile these differences in results.

The notion of subjective probability has some serious logical difficulties. The scale of objective probability is bounded by 0 and 1. Should a subjective probability scale be similarly bounded, or not? If not, then many different subjective probabilities will correspond to the objective probabilities 0 and 1 (unless some transformation is used so that 0 and 1 objective probabilities correspond to infinite subjective probabilities, which seems unlikely). Considerations of the addition theorem to be discussed in a moment have occasionally led people to think of a subjective probability scale bounded at 0 but not at 1. This is surely arbitrary. The concept of absolute certainty is neither more nor less indeterminate than is the concept of absolute impossibility.

Even more drastic logical problems arise in connection with the addition theorem. If the objective probability of event A is P, and that of A not occurring is Q, then $P + Q = 1$. Should this rule hold for subjective probabilities? Intuitively it seems necessary that if we know the subjective probability of A, we ought to be able to figure out the subjective probability of not-A, and the only reasonable rule for figuring it out is subtraction of the subjective probability of A from that of complete certainty. But the acceptance of this addition theorem for subjective probabilities plus the idea of bounded subjective probabilities means that the subjective probability scale must be identical with the objective probability scale. Only for a subjective probability scale identical with the objective probability scale will the subjective probabilities of a collection of events, one of which must happen, add up to 1. In the special case where only two events, A and not-A, are considered, a subjective probability scale like $S1$ or $S2$ in Figure 3 would meet the requirements of additivity, and this fact has led to some speculation about such scales, particularly about $S1$. But such scales do not meet the additivity requirements when more than two events are considered.

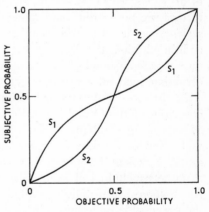

FIG. 3. Hypothetical Subjective Probability Curves

One way of avoiding these difficulties is to stop thinking about a scale of subjective probabilities and, instead, to think of a weighting function applied to the scale of objective probabilities which weights these objective probabilities according to their ability to control behavior. Presumably, I was studying this ability in my experiments on probability preferences (55, 57, 58, 59). There is no reason why such weighted probabilities should add up to 1 or should obey any other simple combinatory principle.

Views and Experiments Which Combine Utility and Subjective Probability. The philosopher Ramsey published in 1926 (reprinted in 150) an essay on the subjective foundations of the theory of probability; this contained an axiom system in which both utility and subjective probability appeared. He used 0.5 subjective probability as a reference point from which to determine utilities, and then used these utilities to determine other subjective probabilities. Apparently, economists did not discover Ramsey's essay until after von Neumann and Morgenstern's book aroused interest in the subject. The only other formal axiom system in which both utility and subjective probability play a part is one proposed by Savage (171), which is concerned with uncertainty, rather than risk, and uses the concept of subjective probability in its theory-of-probability sense.

The most extensive and important experimental work in the whole field of decision making under risk and uncertainty is now being carried out by Coombs and his associates at the University of Michigan. Coombs's thinking about utility and subjective probability is an outgrowth of his thinking about psychological scaling in general. (For a discussion of his views, see 43, 44, 45, 46, 47.) The essence of his work is the attempt to measure both utility and subjective probability on an ordered metric scale. An ordered metric scale has all the properties of an ordinal scale, and, in addition, the distances between some or all of the stimuli can be rank ordered. Coombs has developed various experimental procedures for obtaining such information about the spacings of stimuli.

In the most important article on utility and subjective probability to come out of the Coombs approach, Coombs and Beardslee (48) present an analysis of gambling decisions involving three independent variables: utility for prize, utility for stake, and subjective probability. All three are assumed measurable only up to an ordered metric, although it is assumed that the psychological probability of losing the stake is one minus the psychological probability of winning the prize, an assumption that limits the permissible underlying psychological probability functions to shapes like those in Fig. 3. An elaborate graphic analysis of the indifference surfaces in this three-dimensional space is given, containing far too many interesting relationships to summarize here. An experiment based on this model was designed. Coombs is reluctant to use sums of money as the valuable objects in his experiments because of the danger that subjects will respond to the numerical value of the amount of dollars rather than to the psychological value. Therefore he used various desirable objects (e.g.,

a radio) as stimuli, and measured their utility by the techniques he has developed to obtain ordered metric scales. He used simple numerical statements of probability as the probability stimuli, and assumed that subjective probability was equal to objective probability. The subject from
whose judgments the ordered metric utility measurement was constructed
was then presented with imaginary bets involving these objects and probabilities, and it turned out that she almost always chose the one with the
higher expected utility. This experiment is significant only as an illustration of the application of the method; the conclusion that subjects attempt to maximize expected utility cannot very comfortably be generalized to other subjects and to real choices without better evidence.

Coombs and Milholland (49) did a much more elaborate experiment
in which they established ordered metric scales, both for the utilities of
a collection of objects and for the subjective probabilities of a collection
of statements (e.g., Robin Roberts will win 20 games next year). Statements and objects were combined into "bets," and the two subjects for
whom the ordered metric scales had been established were asked to make
judgments about which bet they would most, and which they would
least, prefer from among various triads of bets. These judgments were
examined to discover whether or not they demonstrated the existence of
at least one convex indifference curve between utility and subjective
probability (the requirements for demonstrating the convexity of an indifference curve by means of ordered metric judgments are fairly easy to
state). A number of cases consistent with a convex indifference curve
were found, but a retest of the ordered metric data revealed changes
which eliminated all of the cases consistent with a convex indifference
curve for one subject, and all but one case for the other. It is not possible
to make a statistical test of whether or not that one case might have come
about by chance. No evidence was found for the existence of concave
indifference curves, which are certainly inconsistent with the theory of
risky decisions. This experiment is a fine example of the strength and
weakness of the Coombs approach. It makes almost no assumptions, takes
very little for granted, and avoids the concept of error of judgment; as
a result, much of the potential information in the data is unused and
rarely can any strong conclusions be drawn.

A most disturbing possibility is raised by experiments by Marks (133)
and Irwin (94) which suggest that the shape of the subjective probability
function is influenced by the utilities involved in the bets. If utilities and
subjective probabilities are not independent, then there is no hope of predicting risky decisions unless their law of combination is known, and it
seems very difficult to design an experiment to discover that law of combination. However, the main differences that Marks and Irwin found
were between probabilities attached to desirable and undesirable alternatives. It is perfectly possible that there is one subjective probability func-

tion for bets with positive expected values and a different one for bets with negative expected values, just as the negative branch of the Markowitz utility function is likely to be different from the positive branch. The results of my probability preference experiments showed very great differences between the probability preference patterns for positive and for negative expected-value bets (57), but little difference between probability preferences at different expected-value levels so long as zero expected value was not crossed (59). This evidence supports the idea that perhaps only two subjective probability functions are necessary.

Santa Monica Seminar. In the summer of 1952 at Santa Monica, California, a group of scientists conferred on problems of decision making. They met in a two-month seminar sponsored by the University of Michigan and the Office of Naval Research. The dittoed reports of these meetings are a gold mine of ideas for the student of this problem. Some of the work done at this seminar is now being prepared for a book on *Decision Processes* edited by R. M. Thrall, C. H. Coombs, and R. L. Davis, of the University of Michigan.

Several minor exploratory experiments were done at this seminar. Vail (190) did an experiment in which he gave four children the choice of which side of various bets they wanted to be on. On the assumption of linear utilities, he was able to compute subjective probabilities for these children. The same children, however, were used as subjects for a number of other experiments; so, when Vail later tried them out on some other bets, he found that they consistently chose the bet with the highest probability of winning, regardless of the amounts of money involved. When 50–50 bets were involved, one subject consistently chose the bet with the *lowest* expected value. No generalizable conclusions can be drawn from these experiments.

Kaplan and Radner (100) tried out a questionnaire somewhat like Coombs's method of measuring subjective probability. Subjects were asked to assign numbers to various statements. The numbers could be anything from 0 to 100 and were to represent the likelihood that the statement was true. The hypotheses to be tested were: (*a*) for sets of exhaustive and mutually exclusive statements in which the numbers assigned (estimates of degree of belief) were nearly equal, the sums of these numbers over a set would increase with the number of alternatives (because low probabilities would be overestimated); (*b*) for sets with the same numbers of alternatives, those with one high number assigned would have a lower set sum than those with no high numbers. The first prediction was verified; the second was not. Any judgments of this sort are so much more likely to be made on the basis of number preferences and similar variables than on subjective probabilities that they offer very little hope as a method of measuring subjective probabilities.

Variance Preferences. Allais (2, 3, 4) and Georgescu-Roegen (78) have argued that it is not enough to apply a transform on objective value and on objective probability in order to predict risky decisions from expected utility (see also 188); it is also necessary to take into account at least the variance, and possibly the higher moments, of the utility distribution. There are instances in which this argument seems convincing. You would probably prefer the certainty of a million dollars to a 50–50 chance of getting either four million or nothing. I do not think that this preference is due to the fact that the expected utility of the 50–50 bet is less than the utility of one million dollars to you, although this is possible. A more likely explanation is simply that the variances of the two propositions are different. Evidence in favor of this is the fact that if you knew you would be offered this choice 20 times in succession, you would probably take the 50–50 bet each time. Allais (5) has constructed a number of more sophisticated examples of this type. However, from a simple-minded psychological point of view, these examples are irrelevant. It is enough if the theory of choice can predict choices involving familiar amounts of money and familiar probability differences—choices such as those which people are accustomed to making. It may be necessary for economic theory that the theory of choice be universal and exceptionless, but experimental psychologists need not be so ambitious. This is fortunate, because the introduction of the variance and higher moments of the utility distribution makes the problem of applying the theory experimentally seem totally insoluble. It is difficult enough to derive reasonable methods of measuring utility alone from risky choices; when it also becomes necessary to measure subjective probability and to take the higher moments of the utility distribution into account, the problem seems hopeless. Allais apparently hopes to defeat this problem by using psychophysical methods to measure utility (and presumably subjective probability also). This is essentially what Coombs has done, but Coombs has recognized that such procedures are unlikely to yield satisfactory interval scales. The dollar scale of the value of money is so thoroughly taught to us that it seems almost impossible to devise a psychophysical situation in which subjects would judge the utility, rather than the dollar value, of dollars. They might judge the utility of other valuable objects, but since dollars are the usual measure of value, such judgments would be less useful, and even these judgments would be likely to be contaminated by the dollar values of the objects. I would get more utility from a new electric shaver than I would from a new washing machine, but because of my knowledge of the relative money values of these objects, I would certainly choose the washing machine if given a choice between them. Somewhat similar arguments can be applied against using psychophysical methods to measure subjective probability. A final point is that, since these subjective scales are to be used to predict choices, it would be best if they could be derived from similar choices.

Other Approaches. Shackle (175) has proposed a theory of decision making under risk and uncertainty. This theory is unique in that it does not assume any kind of maximizing behavior. For every possible outcome of a decision made in a risky or uncertain situation, Shackle assumes that there is a degree of potential surprise that this, rather than some other, outcome would occur. Every outcome-potential surprise pair is ranked in accordance with its ability to stimulate the mind (stimulation increases with increasing outcome and decreases with increasing potential surprise). The highest-ranking positive outcome-potential surprise pair and the highest-ranking negative pair are found, and these two possibilities alone determine what the individual will do. Semi-mathematical methods are used to predict the outcome of consideration of possible lines of action. Although attempts have been made to relate it to Wald's minimax principle for statistical decision functions (see below), the fact remains that most critics of the Shackle point of view have judged it to be either too vague to be useful, or, if specified in detail, too conducive to patently absurd predictions (e.g., 201).

Shackle's point of view was developed primarily to deal with unique choices—choices which can be made only once. Allais (3) has similarly criticized conventional utility theory's attack on this problem. Since the usual frequency theory of probability conceives of the probability as the limit of the outcomes of a large number of similar trials, it is questionable that notions which use probability in the ordinary sense (like the notion of maximizing expected utility) are applicable to unique choices. However, this seems to be an experimental problem. If notions which use ordinary probability are incapable of predicting actual unique choices, then it will be necessary to seek other theoretical tools. But so long as a generally acceptable probability can be defined (e.g., as in the unique toss of a coin), it is not necessary to assume a priori that theories based on conventional probabilities will be inadequate. When no generally acceptable probability can be defined, then the problem becomes very different.

Cartwright and Festinger (38, 41) have proposed a theory about the time it takes to make decisions which is in some ways similar to those discussed in this section. The main difference is that they add the concept of restraining forces, and that they conceive of all subjective magnitudes as fluctuating randomly around a mean value. From this they deduce various propositions about decision times and the degree of certainty which subjects will feel about their decisions, and apparently these propositions work out experimentally pretty well (38, 39, 61, 62). The Lewinian theoretical orientation seems to lead to this kind of model; Lewin, Dembo, Festinger, and Sears (122) present a formally similar theory about level of aspiration. Of course, the notion of utility is very similar to the Lewinian notion of valence.

Landahl (115) has presented a mathematical model for risk-taking behavior based on the conceptual neurology of the mathematical biophysics school.

Psychological Comments. The area of risky decision making is full of fascinating experimental problems. Of these, the development of a satisfactory scale of utility of money and of subjective probability must come first, since the theory of risky decision making is based on these notions. The criterion for satisfactoriness of these scales must be that they successfully predict choices other than those from which they were derived. To be really satisfactory, it is desirable that they should predict choices in a wide variety of differing situations. Unlike the subjective scales usually found in psychophysics, it is likely that these scales will differ widely from person to person, so a new determination of each scale must be made for each new subject. It can only be hoped that the scales do not change in time to any serious degree; if they do, then they are useless.

Once scales of utility and subjective probability are available, then many interesting questions arise. What about the addition theorem for subjective probabilities? Does gambling itself have utility, and how much? To what extent can these subjective scales be changed by learning? To what degree do people differ, and can these differences be correlated with environmental, historical, or personality differences? Finally, psychologists might be able to shed light on the complex economic problem of interacting utilities of different goods.

The area of risky decision making, like the area of the theory of games, tends to encourage in those interested in it the custom of carrying out small pilot experiments on their sons, laboratory assistants, or secretaries. Such experiments are too seldom adequately controlled, and are almost never used as a basis for larger-scale, well-designed experiments. Whether an ill-designed and haphazardly executed little experiment is better than no experiment at all is questionable. The results of such pilot experiments too often are picked up and written into the literature without adequate warning about the conditions under which they were performed and the consequent limitations on the significance of the results.

THE TRANSITIVITY OF CHOICES

In the section on riskless choices this paper presented a definition of economic man. The most important part of this definition can be summed up by saying that economic man is rational. The concept of rationality involves two parts: that of a weak ordering of preferences, and that of choosing so as to maximize something. Of these concepts, the one which seems most dubious is the one of a weakly ordered preference field. This is dubious because it implies that choices are transitive; that is, if A is preferred to B, and B is preferred to C, then A is preferred to C.

Two economists have designed experiments specifically intended to test the transitivity of choices. Papandreou performed an elaborate and splendidly controlled experiment (145) designed to discover whether or not intransitivities occurred in imagined-choice situations. He prepared triplets of hypothetical bundles of admissions to plays, athletic contests, concerts, etc., and required his subjects to choose between pairs of bundles. Each bundle consisted of a total of four admissions to two events, e.g., 3 plays and 1 tennis tournament. In the main experiment, each bundle is compared with two others involving the same kinds of events, but in the better designed auxiliary experiment, a total of six different events are used, so that each bundle has no events in common with the other two bundles in its triplet. Since there are three bundles in each triplet, there are three choices between pairs for each triplet, and these choices may, or may not, be transitive. The subjects were permitted to say that they were indifferent between two bundles; consequently there were 27 possible configurations of choices, of which only 13 satisfied the transitivity axiom. In the main experiment, 5 per cent of the triplets of judgments were intransitive; in the auxiliary experiment, only 4 per cent. Papandreou develops a stochastic model for choices under such conditions; the results are certainly consistent with the amount of intransitivity permitted by his model. Papanderou concludes that at least for his specific experimental conditions, transitivity does exist.

May (138), using different kinds of stimuli in a less elaborate experiment, comes up with results less consistent with transitivity. May required a classroom group to make pairwise choices between three marriage partners who were identified only by saying how intelligent, good looking, and rich they were. Judgments of indifference were not permitted. The results were that 27 per cent of the subjects gave intransitive triads of choices. May suggests, very plausibly, that intransitive choices may be expected to occur whenever more than one dimension exists in the stimuli along which subjects may order their preferences. However, May would probably have gotten fewer intransitivities if he had permitted the indifference judgment. If subjects are really indifferent among all three of the elements of a triad of objects, but are required to choose between them in pairs and do so by chance, then they will choose intransitively one-fourth of the time. Papandreou's stochastic model gives one theory about what happens when preferences diverge just slightly from indifference, but presumably a more detailed model can be worked out. Papandreou's model permits only three states: prefer A to B, prefer B to A, and indifferent. It ought to be possible to base a model for such situations on the cumulative normal curve, and thus to permit any degree of preference. For every combination of degrees of preference, such a model would predict the frequency of intransitive choices.

In the paired comparisons among bets (57) described in the section on risky choices, quite elaborate intransitivities could and did occur. However, it is easy to show that any intransitivity involving four or more objects in a paired comparisons judgment situation will necessarily produce at least one intransitivity involving three objects. Consequently, the intransitive triplet or circular triad is the best unit of analysis for intransitivities in these more complicated judgment situations. I counted the frequency of occurrence of circular triads and found that they regularly occurred about 20 per cent of the total number of times they could occur. (Of course, no indifference judgments could be permitted.) The experiment fulfills May's criterion for the occurrence of intransitivities, since both probability and amount of money were present in each bet, and subjects could be expected to take both into account when making choices. It might be supposed that the difference between the imaginary choices of the Papandreou and May experiments and the real choices in my experiment would lead to differences in the frequency of occurrence of intransitivities, but there were no substantial differences in my experiment between the frequencies of occurrence in the just-imagining sessions and in the real gambling sessions, and what differences there were, were in the direction of greater transitivity when really gambling. These facts should facilitate further experiments on this problem.

In one sense, transitivity can never be violated. A minimum of three choices is required to demonstrate intransitivity. Since these choices will necessarily be made in sequence, it can always be argued that the person may have changed his tastes between the first choice and the third. However, unless the assumption of constancy of tastes over the period of experimentation is made, no experiments on choice can ever be meaningful, and the whole theory of choice becomes empty (see **184** for a similar situation). So this quibble can be rejected at once.

Utility maximization will not work except with a transitive preference field. Consequently, if the models discussed in this paper are to predict experimental data, it is necessary that intransitivities in these data be infrequent enough to be considered as errors. However, from a slightly different point of view (54) the occurrence or nonoccurrence of transitive choice patterns is an experimental phenomenon, and presumably a lawful one. May has suggested what that law is: Intransitivities occur when there are conflicting stimulus dimensions along which to judge. This notion could certainly be tested and made more specific by appropriate experiments.

A final contribution in a related, but different, area is Vail's stochastic utility model (**191**). Vail assumes that choices are dependent on utilities that oscillate in a random manner around a mean value. From this assumption plus a few other reasonable ones, he deduces that if the over-all preference is $1 > 2 > 3$, and if 1 is preferred to 2 more than 2 is preferred to 3, then the frequencies of occurrence of the six possible transitive orderings should be ordered as follows: $123 > 132 > 213 > 312 > 231 > 321$. This result is certainly easy to test experimentally, and sounds plausible.

THE THEORY OF GAMES AND OF DECISION FUNCTIONS[5]

This section will not go into the theory of games or into the intimately related subject of statistical decision functions at all thoroughly. These are mathematical subjects of a highly technical sort, with few statements which lend themselves to experimental test. Rather, the purpose of this section is to show how these subjects relate to what has gone before, to give a brief summary of the contents of *Theory of Games and Economic Behavior* by von Neumann and Morgenstern (**197**), and to describe a few experiments in the area of game playing—experiments which are stimulated by the theory of games although not directly relevant to it.

The Theory of Games. The theory of games probably originated in the work of Borel (**31, 32, 33, 34;** see also **71, 72**) in the 1920's. In 1928, von Neumann (**195**), working independently of Borel, published the first proof of the fundamental theorem in the theory, a theorem that Borel had not believed to be generally true. However, the subject did not become important until 1944, when von Neumann and Morgenstern published their epoch-making book (**196**). (A second edition, with an appendix on cardinal utility measurement, came out in 1947 [**197**].) Their purpose was to analyze mathematically a very general class of problems, which might be called problems of strategy. Consider a game of tic-tac-toe. You know at any moment in the game what the moves available to your opponent are, but you do not know which one he will choose. The only information you have is that his choice will not, in general, be

_____

[5] Marschak (**134**), Hurwicz (**92**), Neisser (**143**), Stone (**181**), and Kaysen (**107**) published reviews of *The Theory of Games and Economic Behavior* which present the fundamental ideas in much simpler language than the original source. Marschak works out in detail the possible solutions of a complicated three-person bargaining game, and thereby illustrates the general nature of a solution. The two volumes of *Contributions to the Theory of Games* (**112, 113**), plus McKinsey's book on the subject (**129**), provide an excellent bibliography of the mathematical literature. McKinsey's book is an exposition of the fundamental concepts, intended as a textbook, which is simpler than von Neumann and Morgenstern and pursues certain topics further. Wald's book (**198**) is, of course, the classical work on statistical decision functions. Bross's book (**35**) presents the fundamental ideas about statistical decision functions more simply, and with a somewhat different emphasis. Girshick and Blackwell's book (**79**) is expected to be a very useful presentation of the field.

completely random; he will make a move which is designed in some way to increase his chance of winning and diminish yours. Thus the situation is one of uncertainty rather than risk. Your goals are similar to your opponent's. Your problem is: what strategy should you adopt? The theory of games offers no practical help in developing strategies, but it does offer rules about how to choose among them. In the case of tic-tac-toe, these rules are trivial, since either player can force a draw. But in more complicated games of strategy, these rules may be useful. In particular, the theory of games may be helpful in analyzing proper strategy in games having random elements, like the shuffling of cards, or the throwing of dice. It should be noted that the concept of a game is an exceedingly general concept. A scientist in his laboratory may be considered to be playing a game against Nature. (Note, however, that we cannot expect Nature to try to defeat the scientist.) Negotiators in a labor dispute are playing a game against one another. Any situation in which money (or some valuable equivalent) may be gained as the result of a proper choice of strategy can be considered as a game.

To talk about game theory, a few technical terms are necessary. A *strategy* is a set of personal rules for playing the game. For each possible first move on your part, your opponent will have a possible set of responses. For each possible response by your opponent, you will have a set of responses, and so on through the game. A strategy is a list which specifies what your move will be for every conceivable previous set of moves of the particular game you are playing. Needless to say, only for the simplest games (e.g., matching pennies) does this concept of strategy have any empirical meaning.

Associated with strategies are *imputations*. An imputation is a set of payments made as a result of a game, one to each player. In general, different imputations will be associated with different sets of strategies, but for any given set of strategies there may be more than one imputation (in games involving coalitions).

Imputation X is said to *dominate* imputation Y if one or more of the players has separately greater gains (or smaller losses) in X than in Y and can, by acting together (in the case of more than one player), enforce the occurrence of X, or of some other imputation at least as good. The relationship of domination is not transitive.

A *solution* is a set of imputations, none of which dominates another, such that every imputation outside the solution is dominated by at least one imputation within the solution. Von Neumann and Morgenstern assert that the task of the theory of games is to find solutions. For any game, there may be one or more than one. One bad feature of the theory of games is that it frequently gives a large, or even infinite, number of solutions for a game.

The above definitions make clear that the only determiner of behavior in games, according to this theory, is the amounts of money which may be won or lost, or the expected amounts in games with random elements. The fun of playing, if any, is irrelevant.

The Minimax Loss Principle. The notions of domination and of solution imply a new fundamental rule for decision making—a rule sharply different from the rule of maximizing utility or expected utility with which this paper has been concerned up to this section. This rule is the rule of minimizing the maximum loss, or, more briefly, *minimax loss*. In other words, the rule is to consider, for each possible strategy that you could adopt, what the worst possible outcome is, and then to select that strategy which would have the least ill-effects if the worst possible outcome happened. Another way of putting the same idea is to call it the principle of maximizing the minimum gain, or *maximin gain*. This rule makes considerable sense in two-person games when you consider that the other player is out to get you, and so will do his best to make the worst possible outcome for you occur. If this rule is expressed geometrically, it asserts that the point you should seek is a saddle-point, like the highest point in a mountain pass (the best rule for crossing mountains is to minimize the maximum height, so explorers seek out such saddle-points).

Before we go any further, we need a few more definitions. Games may be among any number of players, but the simplest game is a *two-person game*, and it is this kind of game which has been most extensively and most successfully analyzed. Fundamentally, two kinds of payoff arrangements are possible. The simplest and most common is the one in which one player wins what the other player loses, or, more generally, the one for which the sum of all the payments made as a result of the game is zero. This is called a *zero-sum game*. In *nonzero-sum games*, analytical complexities arise. These can be diminished by assuming the existence of a fictitious extra player, who wins or loses enough to bring the sum of payments back to zero. Such a fictitious player cannot be assumed to have a strategy and cannot, of course, interact with any of the other players.

In zero-sum two-person games, what will happen? Each player, according to the theory, should pick his minimax strategy. But will this result in a stable solution? Not always. Sometimes the surface representing the possible outcomes of the game does not have a saddle-point. In this case, if player A chooses his minimax strategy, then player B will have an incentive not to use his own minimax strategy, because having found out his opponent's strategy, he can gain more by some other strategy. Thus the game has no solution.

Various resolutions of this problem are possible. Von Neumann and Morgenstern chose to introduce the notion of a *mixed strategy*, which is a probability distribution of two or more pure strategies. The fundamental theorem of the theory of games is that if both players in a zero-sum two-person game adopt mixed strategies which minimize the maximum *expected loss*, then the game will always have a saddle-point. Thus each person will get, in the long run, his expected loss, and will have no incentive to change his behavior even if he should discover what his opponent's mixed strategy is. Since A is already getting the minimum possible under the strategy he chose, any change in strategy by B will only increase A's payoff, and therefore cause B to gain less or lose more than he would by his own minimax strategy. The same is true of B.

Games involving more than two people introduce a new element—the possibility that two or more players will cooperate to beat the rest. Such a cooperative agreement is called a *coalition*, and it frequently involves *side-payments* among members of the coalition. The method of analysis for three-or-more-person games is to consider all possible coalitions and to solve the game for each coalition on the principles of a two-person game. This works fairly well for three-person games, but gets more complicated and less satisfactory for still more people.

This is the end of this exposition of the content of von Neumann and Morgenstern's book. It is of course impossible to condense a tremendous and difficult book into one page. The major points to be emphasized are these: the theory of games is not a model of how people actually play games (some game theorists will disagree with this), nor is it likely to be of any practical use in telling you how to play a complicated game; the crux of the theory of games is the principle of choosing the strategy which minimizes the maximum expected financial loss; and the theory defines a solution of a game as a set of imputations which satisfies this principle for all players.

Assumptions. In their book von Neumann and Morgenstern say "We have . . . assumed that [utility] is numerical . . . substitutable and unrestrictedly transferable between the various players." (**197**, p. 604.) Game theorists disagree about what this and other similar sentences mean. One likely interpretation is that they assume utility to be linear with the physical value of money involved in a game and to be interpersonally comparable. The linear utility curves seem to be necessary for solving two-person games; the interpersonal comparability is used for the extension to n persons. Attempts are being made to develop solutions free of these assumptions (**176**).

Statistical Decision Functions. Von Neumann (**195**) first used the minimax principle in his first publication on game theory in 1928. Neyman and Pearson mentioned its applicability to statistical decision problems in 1933 (**144**). Wald (**198**), who prior to his recent death was the central figure in the statistical decision-function literature, first seriously applied the minimax principle to statistical problems in 1939. Apparently, all these uses of the principle were completely independent of one another.

After *Theory of Games and Economic Behavior* appeared in 1944, Wald (**198**) reformulated the problem of statistical decision making as one of playing a game against Nature. The statistician must decide, on the basis of observations which cost something to make, between policies, each of which has a possible gain or loss. In some cases, all of these gains and losses and the cost of observing can be exactly calculated, as in industrial quality control. In other cases, as in theoretical research, it is necessary to make some assumption about the cost of being wrong and the gain of being right. At any rate, when they are put in this form, it is obvious that the ingredients of the problem of statistical decision making have a gamelike sound. Wald applied the minimax principle to them in a way essentially identical with game theory.

A very frequent criticism of the mimimax approach to games against Nature is that Nature is not hostile, as is the opponent in a two-person game. Nature will not, in general, use a minimax strategy. For this reason, other principles of decision making have been suggested. The simple principle of maximizing expected utility (which is the essence of the Bayes's theorem [15, 198] solution of the problem) is not always applicable because, even though Nature is not hostile, she does not offer any way of assigning a probability to each possible outcome. In other words, statistical decision making is a problem of uncertainty, rather than of risk. Savage has suggested the principle of minimaxing *regret*, where regret is defined as the difference between the maximum which can be gained under any strategy given a certain state of the world and the amount gained under the strategy adopted. Savage believes (**170**, also personal communication) that neither von Neumann and Morgenstern nor Wald actually intended to propose the principle of minimaxing loss; they confine their discussions to cases in which the concepts of minimax loss and minimax regret amount to the same thing. Other suggested principles are: maximizing the maximum expected gain, and maximizing some weighted average of the maximum and minimum expected gains (**93**). None of these principles commands general acceptance; each can be made to show peculiar consequences under some conditions (see **170**).

Experimental Games. The concepts of the theory of games suggest a new field of experimentation: How do people behave in game situations? Such experimentation would center on the development of strategies, particularly mixed strategies, and, in three-or-more-person games, on the development of coalitions and on the bargaining process. You should remember that the theory of games does not offer a mathematical model predicting the outcomes of such games (except in a few special cases); all it does is offer useful concepts and language for talking about them, and predict that certain outcomes will not occur.

A few minor experiments of this kind have been conducted by Flood, a mathematician, while he was at Rand Corporation. He usually used colleagues, many of whom were experts in game theory, and secretaries as subjects. The general design of his experiments was that a group of subjects were shown a group of desirable objects on a table, and told that they, as a group, could have the first object they removed from the table, and that they should decide among themselves which object to choose and how to allocate it. In the first experiment (64) the allocation problem did not arise because enough duplicate objects were provided so that each subject could have one of the kind of object the group selected. The subjects were Harvard undergraduates, and the final selection was made by negotiation and voting. In the second experiment (65), in which the subjects were colleagues and secretaries, a long negotiation process eliminated some of the objects, but a time limit forced a selection by lot from among the rest. Further negotiations to solve the allocation problem were terminated by a secretary, who snatched the object, announced that it was hers, and then tried to sell it. No one was willing to buy, so the experiment terminated. Other experiments (66, 67) showed that coalitions sometimes form, that a sophisticated subject could blackmail the group for an extra side-payment by threatening to change his vote, and that the larcenous secretary, having succeeded once, had to be physically restrained in subsequent sessions to prevent more larceny. The general conclusion suggested by all these experiments is that even experts on game theory are less rational and more conventional than game theory might lead experimenters to expect.

Psychological Comments. The most nutritive research problems in this area seem to be the social problems of how bargaining takes place. Flood's experiments left bargainers free and used physical objects, whose utilities probably vary widely from subject to subject, as stimuli to bargain over. This is naturalistic, but produces data too complex and too nonnumerical for easy analysis. A simpler situation in which the possible communications from one bargainer to another are limited (perhaps by means of an artificial vocabulary), in which the subjects do not see one another, and in which the object bargained over is simple, preferably being merely a sum of money, would be better. Physical isolation of one subject from another would make it possible to match each subject against a standard bargainer, the experimenter or a stooge, who bargains by a fixed set of rules that are unknown to the subject. Flood (personal communication) is conducting experiments of this sort. For three-or-more-person games, Asch's (16) technique of using a group consisting of only one real subject and all the rest stooges might well be used. It would be interesting, for instance, to see how the probability of a coalition between two players changes as the number and power of players united against them increase.

The theory of games is the area among those described in this paper in which the uncontrolled and casually planned "pilot experiment" is most likely to occur. Such experiments are at least as dangerous here as they are in the area of risky decision making. Flood's results suggest that it is especially important to use naive subjects and to use them only once, unless the effects of expertness and experience are the major concern of the experiment.

SUMMARY

For a long time, economists and others have been developing mathematical theories about how people make choices among desirable alternatives. These theories center on the notion of the subjective value, or utility, of the alternatives among which the decider must choose. They assume that people behave rationally, that is, that they have transitive preferences and that they choose in such a way as to maximize utility or expected utility.

The traditional theory of riskless choices, a straightforward theory of utility maximization, was challenged by the demonstration that the mathematical tool of indifference curves made it possible to account for riskless choices without assuming that utility could be measured on an interval scale. The theory of riskless choices predicted from indifference curves has been worked out in detail. Experimental determination of indifference curves is possible, and has been attempted. But utility measured on an interval scale is necessary (though not sufficient) for welfare economics.

Attention was turned to risky choices by von Neumann and Morgenstern's demonstration that complete weak ordering of risky choices implies the existence of utility measurable on an interval scale. Mosteller and Nogee experimentally determined utility curves for money from gambling decisions, and used them to predict other gambling decisions. Edwards demonstrated the existence of preferences among probabilities in gambling situations, which complicates the experimental measurement of utility. Coombs developed a model for utility and subjective probability measured on an ordered metric scale, and did some experiments to test implications of the model.

Economists have become worried about the assumption that choices are transitive. Experiments have shown that intransitive patterns of choice do occur, and so stochastic models have been developed which permit occasional intransitivities.

The theory of games presents an elaborate mathematical analysis of the problem of choosing from among alternative strategies in games of strategy. This paper summarizes the main concepts of this analysis. The theory of games has stimulated interest in experimental games, and a few bargaining experiments which can be thought of in game-theoretical terms have been performed.

All these topics represent a new and rich field for psychologists, in which a theoretical structure has already been elaborately worked out and in which many experiments need to be performed.

REFERENCES[6]

1. ALCHIAN, A. "The Meaning of Utility Measurement," *Amer. Econ. Rev.*, 1953, 43, pp. 26–50.

2. ALLAIS, M. Fondements d'une théorie positive des choix comportant un risque et critique des postulats et axiomes de l'école americaine. *Colloque Internationale du Centre National de la Recherche scientifique*, 1952, No. 36.

3. ALLAIS, M. Le comportement de l'homme rationnel devant le risque: critique des postulats et axiomes de l'école americaine. *Econometrica*, 1953, 21, pp. 503–46.

4. ALLAIS, M. L'Extension des théories de l'equilibre economique général et du rendement social au cas du risque. *Econometrica*, 1953, 21, pp. 269–90.

5. ALLAIS, M. La psychologie de l'homme rationnel devant le risque: La théorie et l'expérience. *J. soc. Statist., Paris*, 1953, 94, pp. 47–73.

6. ALLEN, R. G. D. "The Nature of Indifference Curves," *Rev. Econ. Stud.*, 1933, 1, pp. 110–21.

7. ALLEN, R. G. D. "A Note on the Determinateness of the Utility Function," *Rev. Econ. Stud.*, 1934, 2, pp. 155–58.

8. ARMSTRONG, W. E. "The Determinateness of the Utility Function," *Econ. J.*, 1939, 49, pp. 453–67.

9. ARMSTRONG, W. E. "Uncertainty and the Utility Function," *Econ. J.*, 1948, 58, pp. 1–10.

10. ARMSTRONG, W. E. "A Note on the Theory of Consumer's Behavior," *Oxf. Econ. Pap.*, 1950, 2, pp. 119–22.

11. ARMSTRONG, W. E. "Utility and the Theory of Welfare," *Oxf. Econ. Pap.*, 1951, 3, pp. 259–71.

12. ARROW, K. J. "Alternative Approaches to the Theory of Choice in Risk-taking Situations," *Econometrica*, 1951, 19, pp. 404–37.

13. ARROW, K. J. "An Extension of the Basic Theorems of Classical Welfare Economics," in J. Neyman (Ed.), *Proceedings of the Second Berkeley Symposium on Mathematical Statistics and Probability*. Berkeley: Univ. of Calif. Press, 1951, pp. 507–32.

14. ARROW, K. J. *Social Choice and Individual Values*. New York: Wiley, 1951.

15. ARROW, K. J., BLACKWELL, D., and GIRSHICK, M. A. "Bayes and Minimax Solutions of Sequential Decision Problems," *Econometrica*, 1949, 17, pp. 213–44.

16. ASCH, S. E. *Social Psychology*. New York: Prentice-Hall, 1952.

17. ATTNEAVE, F. "Psychological Probability as a Function of Experienced Frequency," *J. exp. Psychol.*, 1953, 46, pp. 81–86.

18. BAUMOL, W. J. "Community Indifference, *Rev. Econ. Stud.*, 1946, 14, pp. 44–48.

19. BAUMOL, W. J. "The Neumann-Morgenstern Utility Index—An Ordinalist View," *J. Polit. Econ.*, 1951, 59, pp. 61–66.

---

[6] An additional bibliography covering references from 1954 to 1956 is contained in *Proceedings of the Conference on Expectations, Uncertainty, and Business Behavior*, New York, Social Science Research Council, 1956.

20. BAUMOL, W. J. "Discussion," *Amer. Econ. Rev. Suppl.*, 1953, 43, pp. 415–16.

21. BERGSON (BURK), A. "Reformulation of Certain Aspects of Welfare Economics," *Quart. J. Econ.*, 1938, 52, pp. 310–34.

22. BERNARDELLI, H. "Note on the Determinateness of the Utility Function," *Rev. Econ. Stud.*, 1934, 2, pp. 69–75.

23. BERNARDELLI, H. "The End of Marginal Utility Theory?" *Economica*, 1938, 5, 192–212.

24. BERNARDELLI, H. "A Reply to Mr. Samuelson's Note," *Economica*, 1939, 6, pp. 88–89.

25. BERNARDELLI, H. "A Rehabilitation of the Classical Theory of Marginal Utility," *Economica*, 1952, 19, pp. 254–68.

26. BERNOULLI, D. "Specimen Theoriae Novae de Mensura Sortis," *Comentarii Academiae Scientiarum Imperiales Petropolitanae*, 1738, 5, pp. 175–92. (Trans. by L. Sommer in *Econometrica*, 1954, 22, pp. 23–36.)

27. BILODEAU, E. A. "Statistical versus Intuitive Confidence," *Amer. J. Psychol.*, 1952, 65, pp. 271–77.

28. BISHOP, R. L. "Consumer's Surplus and Cardinal Utility," *Quart. J. Econ.*, 1943, 57, pp. 421–49.

29. BISHOP, R. L. "Professor Knight and the Theory of Demand," *J. Polit. Econ.*, 1946, 54, pp. 141–69.

30. BOHNERT, H. G. "The Logical Structure of the Utility Concepts," in R. M. Thrall, C. H. Coombs, & R. L. Davis (Eds.), *Decision Processes*. New York: Wiley, in press.

31. BOREL, E. La théorie du jeu et les équations intégrales à noyau symétrique. *C. R. Acad. Sci., Paris*, 1921, 173, pp. 1304–8. (Trans. by L. J. Savage in *Econometrica*, 1953, 21, pp. 97–100.)

32. BOREL, E. Sur les jeux où interviennent l'hasard et l'habilité des joueurs. In E. Borel, *Théorie des probabilités*. Paris: Librairie Scientifique, J. Hermann, 1924, pp. 204–24. (Trans. by L. J. Savage in *Econometrica*, 1953, 21, pp. 101–15.)

33. BOREL, E. Algèbre et calcul des probabilités. *C. R. Acad. Sci., Paris*, 1927, 184, pp. 52–53. (Trans. by L. J. Savage in *Econometrica*, 1953, 21, pp. 116–17.)

34. BOREL, E. *Traité du calcul des probabilités et de ses applications, applications des jeux de hasard.* Vol. IV, No. 2. Paris: Gauthier-Villars, 1938.

35. BROSS, I. *Design for Decision.* New York: Macmillan, 1953.

36. BUSH, R. R., & MOSTELLER, F. "A Mathematical Model for Simple Learning," *Psychol. Rev.*, 1951, 58, pp. 313–23.

37. BUSH, R. R., & MOSTELLER, F. "A Model for Stimulus Generalization and Discrimination," *Psychol. Rev.*, 1951, 58, pp. 413–23.

38. CARTWRIGHT, D. "Decision-Time in Relation to Differentiation of the Phenomenal field," *Psychol. Rev.*, 1941, 48, pp. 425–42.

39. CARTWRIGHT, D. "The Relation of Decision-time to the Categories of Response," *Amer. J. Psychol.*, 1941, 54, pp. 174–96.

40. CARTWRIGHT, D. "Survey Research: Psychological Economics," in J. G. Miller (Ed.), *Experiments in Social Process*. New York: McGraw-Hill, 1950, pp. 47–64.

41. CARTWRIGHT, D., and FESTINGER, L. "A Quantitative Theory of Decision," *Psychol. Rev.*, 1943, 50, pp. 595–621.

42. CLARK, J. M. "Realism and Relevance in the Theory of Demand," *J. Polit. Econ.*, 1946, 54, pp. 347–53.

43. COOMBS, C. H. "Psychological Scaling without a Unit of Measurement," *Psychol. Rev.*, 1950, 57, pp. 145–58.

44. COOMBS, C. H. "Mathematical Models in Psychological Scaling," *J. Amer. Statist. Assoc.*, 1951, 46, pp. 480–89.

45. COOMBS, C. H. "A Theory of Psychological Scaling," *Bull. Engng Res. Inst. Univer. Mich.*, 1952, No. 34.

46. COOMBS, C. H. "Theory and Methods of Social Measurement," in L. Festinger and D. Katz (Eds.), *Research Methods in the Behavioral Sciences*. New York: Dryden, 1953, pp. 471–535.

47. COOMBS, C. H. "A Method for the Study of Interstimulus Similarity," *Psychometrika*, in press.

48. COOMBS, C. H. and BEARDSLEE, D. C., "Decision Making under Uncertainty," in R. M. Thrall, C. H. Coombs, and R. L. Davis (Eds.), *Decision Processes*. New York: Wiley, in press.

49. COOMBS, C. H., and MILHOLLAND, J. E. "Testing the Rationality of an Individual's Decision Making under Uncertainty," *Psychometrika*, in press.

50. CORLETT, W. J., and NEWMAN, P. K. A Note on Revealed Preference and the Transitivity Conditions," *Rev. Econ. Stud.*, 1952, 20, pp. 156–58.

51. DE FINETTI, B. La prévision: ses lois logiques, ses sources subjectives. *Ann. Inst. Poincaré*, 1937, 7, pp. 1–68.

52. DE FINETTI, B. "Recent Suggestions for the Reconciliation of Theories of Probability," in J. Neyman (Ed.), *Proceedings of the Second Berkeley Symposium on Mathematical Statistics and Probability*. Berkeley: Univ. of Calif. Press, 1951.

53. EDGEWORTH, F. Y. *Mathematical Psychics*. London: Kegan Paul, 1881.

54. EDWARDS, W. "Discussion," *Econometrica*, 1953, 21, pp. 477. (Abstract)

55. EDWARDS, W. "Experiments on Economic Decision-making in Gambling Situations," *Econometrica*, 1953, 21, pp. 349–50. (Abstract)

56. EDWARDS, W. "Information, Repetition, and Reinforcement as Determiners of Two-Alternative Decisions," *Amer. Psychologist*, 1953, 8, p. 345. (Abstract)

57. EDWARDS, W. Probability-Preferences in Gambling," *Amer. J. Psychol.*, 1953, 66, pp. 349–64.

58. EDWARDS, W. "Probability Preferences among Bets with Differing Expected Values," *Amer. J. Psychol.*, 1954, 67, pp. 56–67.

59. EDWARDS, W. "The Reliability of Probability Preferences," *Amer. J. Psychol.*, 1954, 67, pp. 68–95.

60. ESTES, W. K. "Toward a Statistical Theory of Learning," *Psychol. Rev.*, 1950, 57, pp. 94–107.

61. FESTINGER, L. "Studies in Decision: I. Decision-time, Relative Frequency of Judgment and Subjective Confidence as Related to Physical Stimulus Differences," *J. Exp. Psychol.*, 1943, 32, pp. 291–306.

62. FESTINGER, L. "Studies in Decision: II. An Empirical Test of a Quantitative Theory of Decision," *J. Exp. Psychol.*, 1943, 32, pp. 411–23.

63. FISHER, I. "A Statistical Method for Measuring Marginal Utility and Testing the Justice of a Progressive Income Tax," in J. Hollander (Ed.), *Economic Essays Contributed in Honor of John Bates Clark.* New York: Macmillan, 1927, pp. 157–93.

64. FLOOD, M. M. "A Preference Experiment," *Rand Corp. Memo.,* November, 1951, No. P–256.

65. FLOOD, M. M. "A Preference Experiment (Series 2, Trial 1)." *Rand Corp. Memo.,* December, 1951, No. P–258.

66. FLOOD, M. M. "A Preference Experiment (Series 2, Trials 2, 3, 4)." *Rand Corp. Memo.,* January, 1952, No. P–263.

67. FLOOD, M. M. "A Preference Experiment (Series 3)." Unpublished memorandum, Rand Corporation. February 25, 1952.

68. FLOOD, M. M. "Some Experimental Games." *Rand Corp. Memo.,* March, 1952, No. RM-789-1. (Revised June, 1952.)

69. FLOOD, M. M. "Testing Organization Theories." *Rand Corp. Memo.,* November, 1952, No. P–312.

70. FLOOD, M. M. "An Experimental Multiple-choice Situation." *Rand Corp. Memo.,* November, 1952, No. P–313.

71. FRÉCHET, M. "Emile Borel, Initiator of the Theory of Psychological Games and its Application," *Econometrica,* 1953, 21, pp. 95–96.

72. FRÉCHET, M., and VON NEUMANN, J. "Commentary on the Three Notes of Emile Borel," *Econometrica,* 1953, 21, pp. 118–26.

73. FRIEDMAN, M., and SAVAGE, L. J. "The Utility Analysis of Choices Involving Risk," *J. Polit. Econ.,* 1948, 56, pp. 279–304. (Reprinted with minor changes in G. J. Stigler and K. E. Boulding [Eds.], *Readings in Price Theory.* Homewood: Richard D. Irwin, 1952. Pp. 57–96.)

74. FRIEDMAN, M., and SAVAGE, L. J. "The Expected-Utility Hypothesis and the Measurability of Utility," *J. Polit. Econ.,* 1952, 60, pp. 463–75.

75. FRISCH, R. "New Methods of Measuring Marginal Utility," in R. Frisch, *Beiträge zur ökonomischen Theorie.* Tübingen: Mohr, 1932.

76. GEORGESCU-ROEGEN, N. "The Pure Theory of Consumer's Behavior," *Quart. J. Econ.,* 1936, 50, pp. 545–93.

77. GEORGESCU-ROEGEN, N. "The Theory of Choice and the Constancy of Economic Laws," *Quart. J. Econ.,* 1950, 64, pp. 125–38.

78. GEORGESCU-ROEGEN, N. "Utility, Expectations, Measurability, Prediction." Paper read at Econometric Soc., Kingston, September, 1953.

79. GIRSHICK, M. A., and BLACKWELL, D. *Theory of Games and Statistical Decisions.* New York: Wiley, 1954.

80. GOOD, I. J. *Probability and the Weighing of Evidence.* London: Griffin, 1950.

81. GRIFFITH, R. M. "Odds Adjustments by American Horse-race Bettors," *Amer. J. Psychol.,* 1949, 62, pp. 290–94.

82. HARSANYI, J. C. "Cardinal Utility in Welfare Economics and in the Theory of Risk-taking," *J. Polit. Econ.,* 1953, 61, pp. 434–35.

83. HART, A. G. "Risk, Uncertainty, and the Unprofitability of Compounding Probabilities," in O. Lange, F. McIntyre, and T. O. Yntema (Eds.), *Studies in Mathematical Economics and Econometrics.* Chicago: Univer. of Chicago Press, 1942, pp. 110–18.

84. HAYES, S. P., JR. "Some Psychological Problems of Economics," *Psychol. Bull.*, 1950, 47, pp. 289–330.

85. HERSTEIN, I. N., & MILNOR, J. "An Axiomatic Approach to Measurable Utility," *Econometrica*, 1953, 21, pp. 291–97.

86. HICKS, J. R., "The Foundations of Welfare Economics," *Econ. J.*, 1939, 49, pp. 696–712.

87. HICKS, J. R. *Value and Capital.* Oxford: Clarendon Press, 1939.

88. HICKS, J. R., & ALLEN, R. G. D. "A Reconsideration of the Theory of Value," *Economica*, 1934, 14, pp. 52–76, 196–219.

89. HILDRETH, C. "Alternative Conditions for Social Orderings," *Econometrica*, 1953, 21, pp. 81–94.

90. HOUTHAKKER, H. S. "Revealed Preference and the Utility Function," *Economica*, 1950, 17, pp. 159–74.

91. HULL, C. L. *Principles of Behavior, an Introduction to Behavior Theory.* New York: D. Appleton-Century, 1943.

92. HURWICZ, L. "The Theory of Economic Behavior," *Amer. Econ. Rev.*, 1945, 35, pp. 909–25. (Reprinted in G. J. Stigler and K. E. Boulding [Eds.], *Readings in Price Theory.* Homewood: Richard D. Irwin, 1952, pp. 505–26.)

93. HURWICZ, L. "What Has Happened to the Theory of Games?" *Amer. Econ. Rev. Suppl.*, 1953, 43, pp. 398–405.

94. IRWIN, F. W. "Stated Expectations as Functions of Probability and Desirability of Outcomes," *J. Pers.*, 1953, 21, pp. 329–35.

95. JARRETT, JACQUELINE M. "Strategies in Risk-taking Situations." Unpublished Ph.D. thesis, Harvard Univer., 1951.

96. JENKINS, W. O. and STANLEY, J. C., JR. "Partial Reinforcement: A Review and Critique," *Psychol. Bull.*, 1950, 47, pp. 193–234.

97. JOHNSON, W. E. "The Pure Theory of Utility Curves," *Econ. J.*, 1913, 23, pp. 483–513.

98. KALDOR, N. "Welfare Propositions and Inter-personal Comparisons of Utility," *Econ. J.*, 1939, 49, pp. 549–52.

99. KALDOR, N. "A Comment," *Rev. Econ. Stud.*, 1946, 14, p. 49.

100. KAPLAN, A., and RADNER, R. "A Questionnaire Approach to Subjective Probability—Some Experimental Results." Working Memorandum 41, Santa Monica Conference on Decision Problems, August 15, 1952.

101. KATONA, G. "Psychological Analysis of Business Decisions and Expectations," *Amer. Econ. Rev.*, 1946, 36, pp. 44–62.

102. KATONA, G. "Contributions of Psychological Data to Economic Analysis," *J. Amer. Statist. Assoc.*, 1947, 42, pp. 449–59.

103. KATONA, G. *Psychological Analysis of Economic Behavior.* New York: McGraw-Hill, 1951.

104. KATONA, G. "Rational Behavior and Economic Behavior," *Psychol. Rev.*, 1953, 60, pp. 307–18.

105. KAUDER, E. "Genesis of the Marginal Utility Theory from Aristotle to to the End of the Eighteenth Century," *Econ. J.*, 1953, 63, pp. 638–50.

106. KAUDER, E. "The Retarded Acceptance of the Marginal Utility Theory," *Quart. J. Econ.*, 1953, 67, pp. 564–75.

107. KAYSEN, C. "A Revolution in Economic Theory?" *Rev. Econ. Stud.*, 1946, 14, pp. 1–15.

108. KENNEDY, C. "The Common Sense of Indifference Curves," *Oxf. Econ. Pap.*, 1950, 2, pp. 123–31.

109. KNIGHT, F. H. *Risk, Uncertainty, and Profit*. Boston: Houghton Mifflin, 1921.

110. KNIGHT, F. H. "Realism and Relevance in the Theory of Demand," *J. Polit. Econ.*, 1944, 52, pp. 289–318.

111. KNIGHT, F. H. "Comment on Mr. Bishop's Article," *J. Polit. Econ.*, 1946, 54, pp. 170–76.

112. KUHN, H. W., and TUCKER, A. W. (Eds.). "Contributions to the Theory of Games," Vol. I. *Ann. Math. Stud.*, No. 24. Princeton: Princeton Univ. Press, 1950.

113. KUHN, H. W., and TUCKER, A. W. (Eds.). "Contributions to the Theory of Games," Vol. II. *Ann. Math. Stud.*, No. 28. Princeton: Princeton Univ. Press, 1953.

114. LANCASTER, K. "A Refutation of Mr. Bernardelli," *Economica*, 1953, 20, pp. 259–62.

115. LANDAHL, H. D. "A Neurobiophysical Interpretation of Certain Aspects of the Problem of Risks," *Bull. Math. Biophysics*, 1951, 13, pp. 323–35.

116. LANGE, O. "The Determinateness of the Utility Function," *Rev. Econ. Stud.*, 1933, 1, pp. 218–25.

117. LANGE, O. "Note on the Determinateness of the Utility Function," *Rev. Econ. Stud.*, 1934, 2, pp. 75–77.

118. LANGE, O. "The Foundations of Welfare Economics," *Econometrica*, 1942, 10, pp. 215–28.

119. LANGE, O. "The Scope and Methods of Economics," *Rev. Econ. Stud.*, 1945, 13, pp. 19–32.

120. LEWIN, K. *Principles of Topological Psychology*. New York: McGraw-Hill, 1936.

121. LEWIN, K. "Behavior and Development as a Function of the Total Situation." In L. Carmichael (Ed.), *Manual of child psychology*. New York: Wiley, 1946, pp. 791–844.

122. LEWIN, K., DEMBO, TAMARA, FESTINGER, L., and SEARS, PAULINE S. "Level of Aspiration," in J. McV. Hunt (Ed.), *Personality and the Behavior Disorders*. Vol. I. New York, Ronald, 1944, pp. 333–78.

123. LEWISOHN, S. A. "Psychology in Economics," *Polit. Sci. Quart.*, 1938, 53, pp. 233–38.

124. LITTLE, I. M. D. "The Foundations of Welfare Economics," *Oxf. Econ. Pap.*, 1949, 1, pp. 227–46.

125. LITTLE, I. M. D. "A Reformulation of the Theory of Consumer's Behavior," *Oxf. Econ. Pap.*, 1949, 1, 90–99.

126. LITTLE, I. M. D. "The Theory of Consumer's Behavior—A Comment," *Oxf. Econ. Pap.*, 1950, 2, pp. 132–35.

127. LITTLE, I. M. D. "Social Choice and Individual Values," *J. Polit. Econ.*, 1952, 60, pp. 422–32.

128. MACFIE, A. L. "Choice in Psychology and as Economic Assumption," *Econ. J.*, 1953, 63, pp. 352–67.

129. McKinsey, J. C. C. *Introduction to the Theory of Games.* New York: McGraw-Hill, 1952.

130. Malinvaud, E. "Note on Von Neumann-Morgenstern's Strong Independence Axiom," *Econometrica*, 1952, 20, pp. 679.

131. Manne, A. S. "The Strong Independence Assumption—Gasoline Blends and Probability Mixtures," *Econometrica*, 1952, 20, pp. 665–69.

132. Markowitz, H. "The Utility of Wealth," *J. Polit. Econ.*, 1952, 60, pp. 151–58.

133. Marks, Rose W. "The Effect of Probability, Desirability, and Privilege on the Stated Expectations of Children," *J. Pers.*, 1951, 19, pp. 332–51.

134. Marschak, J. Neumann's and Morgenstern's New Approach to Static Economics, *J. Polit. Econ.*, 1946, 54, pp. 97–115.

135. Marschak, J. "Rational Behavior, Uncertain Prospects, and Measurable Utility," *Econometrica*, 1950, 18, pp. 111–41.

136. Marschak, J. "Why Should Statisticians and Businessmen Maximize Moral Expectation?" in J. Neyman (Ed.), *Proceedings of the Second Berkeley Symposium on Mathematical Statistics and Probability.* Berkeley: Univ. of Calif. Press, 1951, pp. 493–506.

137. Marshall, A. *Principles of Economics.* (8th Ed.) New York: Macmillan, 1948.

138. May, K. O. "Transitivity, Utility, and Aggregation in Preference Patterns," *Econometrica*, 1954, 22, pp. 1–13.

139. Melville, L. G. "Economic Welfare," *Econ. J.*, 1939, 49, pp. 552–53.

140. Mishan, E. J. "The Principle of Compensation Reconsidered," *J. Polit. Econ.*, 1952, 60, pp. 312–22.

141. Morgan, J. N. "Can We Measure the Marginal Utility of Money?" *Econometrica*, 1945, 13, pp. 129–52.

142. Mosteller, F., and Nogee, P. "An Experimental Measurement of Utility," *J. Polit. Econ.*, 1951, 59, pp. 371–404.

143. Neisser, H. "The Strategy of Expecting the Worst," *Soc. Res.*, 1952, 19, pp. 346–63.

144. Neyman, J., and Pearson, E. S. "The Testing of Statistical Hypotheses in Relation to Probability *a priori.*" *Proc. Cambr. Phil. Soc.*, 1933, 29, pp. 492–510.

145. Papandreou, A. G. "An Experimental Test of an Axiom in the Theory of Choice," *Econometrica*, 1953, 21, p. 477. (Abstract)

146. Pareto, V. *Manuale di economia politica, con una introduzione ulla scienza sociale.* Milan, Italy: Societa Editrice Libraria, 1906.

147. Phelps-Brown, E. H. "Note on the Determinateness of the Utility Function," *Rev. Econ. Stud.*, 1934, 2, pp. 66–69.

148. Pigou, A. C. "Some Aspects of Welfare Economics," *Amer. Econ. Rev.*, 1951, 41, pp. 287–302.

149. Preston, M. G., and Baratta, P. "An Experimental Study of the Auction-Value of an Uncertain Outcome," *Amer. J. Psychol.*, 1948, 61, pp. 183–93.

150. Ramsey, F. P. "Truth and Probability," in F. P. Ramsey, *The Foundations of Mathematics and Other Logical Essays.* New York: Harcourt Brace, 1931.

151. RICCI, U. "Pareto and Pure Economics," *Rev. Econ. Stud.*, 1933, 1, pp. 3–21.

152. ROBBINS, L. "Interpersonal Comparisons of Utility: A Comment," *Econ. J.*, 1938, 48, pp. 635–41.

153. ROBBINS, L. "Robertson on Utility and Scope," *Economica*, 1953, 20, pp. 99–111.

154. ROBERTSON, D. H. *Utility and All That and Other Essays.* London: George Allen & Unwin, 1952.

155. ROTHENBERG, J. "Conditions for a Social Welfare Function," *J. Polit. Econ.*, 1953, 61, pp. 389–405.

156. ROTHSCHILD, K. W. "The Meaning of Rationality: A Note on Professor Lange's Article," *Rev. Econ. Stud.*, 1946, 14, pp. 50–52.

157. ROUSSEAS, S. W., and HART, A. G. Experimental Verification of a Composite Indifference Map," *J. Polit. Econ.*, 1951, 59, pp. 288–318.

158. SAMUELSON, P. A. "A Note on Measurement of Utility," *Rev. Econ, Stud.*, 1937, 4, pp. 155–61.

159. SAMUELSON, P. A. "Empirical Implications of Utility Analysis," *Econometrica*, 1938, 6, pp. 344–56.

160. SAMUELSON, P. A. "A Note on the Pure Theory of Consumer's Behavior," *Economica*, 1938, 5, pp. 61–71.

161. SAMUELSON, P. A. "A Note on the Pure Theory of Consumer's Behavior." An addendum, *Economica*, 1938, 5, pp. 353–54.

162. SAMUELSON, P. A. "The Numerical Representations of Ordered Classifications and the Concept of Utility," *Rev. Econ. Stud.*, 1938, 6, pp. 65–70.

163. SAMUELSON, P. A. "The End of Marginal Utility: A Note on Dr. Bernardelli's Article," *Economica*, 1939, 6, pp. 86–87.

164. SAMUELSON, P. A. *Foundations of Economic Analysis.* Cambridge, Mass.: Harvard Univ. Press, 1947.

165. SAMUELSON, P. A. "Consumption Theory in Terms of Revealed Preference," *Economica*, 1948, 15, pp. 243–53.

166. SAMUELSON, P. A. "Evaluation of Real National Income," *Oxf. Econ. Pap.*, 1950, 2, pp. 1–29.

167. SAMUELSON, P. A. "The Problem of Integrability in Utility Theory," *Economica*, 1950, 17, pp. 355–85.

168. SAMUELSON, P. A. "Probability, Utility, and the Independence Axiom," *Econometrica*, 1952, 20, pp. 670–78.

169. SAMUELSON, P. A. "Consumption Theorems in Terms of Overcompensation Rather than Indifference Comparisons," *Economica*, 1953, 20, pp. 1–9.

170. SAVAGE, L. J. "The Theory of Statistical Decision," *J. Amer. Statist. Assoc.*, 1951, 46, pp. 55–67.

171. SAVAGE, L. J. "An Axiomatic Theory of Reasonable Behavior in the Face of Uncertainty." Unpublished manuscript, Statistical Research Center, Univ. of Chicago, No. SRC-21222S14.

172. SCHULTZ, H. *The Theory and Measurement of Demand.* Chicago: Univ. of Chicago Press, 1938.

173. SCITOVSKY, T. "A Note on Welfare Propositions in Economics," *Rev. Econ. Stud.*, 1941, 9, pp. 77–88.

174. Scitovsky, T. "The State of Welfare Economics," *Amer. Econ. Rev.*, 1951, 41, pp. 303–15.

175. Shackle, G. L. S. *Expectations in Economics*. Cambridge, Eng.: Cambridge Univer. Press, 1949.

176. Shapley, L. S., and Shubik, M. "Solutions of *N*-Person Games with Ordinal Utilities," *Econometrica*, 1953, 21, pp. 348–49. (Abstract)

177. Slutsky, E. E. Sulla teoria del bilancio del consumatore, *Giornale degli economisti*, 1915, 51, pp. 1–26. (Trans. by O. Ragusa and reprinted in G. J. Stigler and K. E. Boulding [Eds.], *Readings in Price Theory*. Homewood: Richard D. Irwin, 1952, pp. 27–56.)

178. Sprowls, R. C. "Psychological-Mathematical Probability in Relationships of Lottery Gambles," *Amer. J. Psychol.*, 1953, 66, pp. 126–30.

179. Stigler, G. J. "The Limitations of Statistical Demand Curves," *J. Amer. Statist. Assoc.*, 1939, 34, pp. 469–81.

180. Stigler, G. J. "The Development of Utility Theory," *J. Polit. Econ.*, 1950, 58, pp. 307–27, 373–96.

181. Stone, J. R. N. "The Theory of Games," *Econ. J.*, 1948, 58, pp. 185–201.

182. Stone, R. (J. R. N.) *The Role of Measurement in Economics*. Cambridge, Eng.: Cambridge Univer. Press, 1951.

183. Strotz, R. H. "Cardinal Utility," *Amer. Econ. Rev. Suppl.*, 1953, 43, pp. 384–405.

184. Sweezy, A. R. "The Interpretation of Subjective Value Theory in the Writings of the Austrian Economists," *Rev. Econ. Stud.*, 1933, 1, pp. 176–85.

185. Thurstone, L. L. "The Indifference Function," *J. Soc. Psychol.*, 1931, 2, pp. 139–67.

186. Thurstone, L. L. "The Measurement of Values," *Psychol. Rev.*, 1954, 61, pp. 47–58.

187. Tintner, G. "The Theory of Choice under Subjective Risk and Uncertainty," *Econometrica*, 1941, 9, pp. 298–304.

188. Tintner, G. "A Contribution to the Nonstatic Theory of Choice," *Quart. J. Econ.*, 1942, 56, pp. 274–306.

189. Törnqvist, L. "On the Economic Theory of Lottery-Gambles," *Skand. Aktuar-Tidskr.*, 1945, 28, pp. 228–46.

190. Vail, S. V. "Expectations, Degrees of Belief, Psychological Probabilities." Unpublished manuscript Univ. of Michigan, Seminar on the Application of Mathematics to the Social Sciences, October 23, 1952.

191. Vail, S. V. "A Stochastic Model of Utilities." Unpublished manuscript, No. 24, Univ. of Michigan, Seminar on the Applications of Mathematics to the Social Sciences, April 23, 1953.

192. Vail, S. V. "Alternative Calculi of Subjective Probabilities," in R. M. Thrall, C. H. Coombs, and R. L. Davis (Eds.), *Decision Processes*. New York: Wiley, in press.

193. Vickrey, W. S. "Measuring Marginal Utility by Reactions to Risk," *Econometrica*, 1945, 13, pp. 319–33.

194. Viner, J. "The Utility Concept in Value Theory and its Critics," *J. Polit. Econ.*, 1925, 33, pp. 369–87, 638–59.

195. Von Neumann, J. "Zur Theorie der Gesellschaftsspiele," *Math. Ann.*, 1928, 100, pp. 295–320.

196. Von Neumann, J., and Morgenstern, O. *Theory of Games and Economic Behavior*. (1st Ed.) Princeton: Princeton Univ. Press, 1944.

197. Von Neumann, J., and Morgenstern, O. *Theory of Games and Economic Behavior*. (2nd Ed.) Princeton: Princeton Univ. Press, 1947.

198. Wald, A. *Statistical Decision Functions*. New York, Wiley, 1950.

199. Walker, K. F. "The Psychological Assumptions of Economics." *Econ. Rec.*, 1946, 22, pp. 66–82.

200. Wallis, W. A., and Friedman, M. "The Empirical Derivation of Indifference Functions," in O. Lange, F. McIntyre, and T. O. Yntema, (Eds.), *Studies in Mathematical Economics and Econometrics*. Chicago: Univ. of Chicago Press, 1942.

201. Weckstein, R. S. "On the Use of the Theory of Probability in Econimics," *Rev. Econ. Stud.*, 1953, 20, pp. 191–98.

202. Weisskopf, W. A. "Psychological Aspects of Economic Thought," *J. Polit. Econ.*, 1949, 57, pp. 304–14.

203. Weldon, J. C. "A Note on Measures of Utility," *Canad. J. Econ. Polit. Sci.*, 1950, 16, pp. 227–33.

204. Wold, H. "A Synthesis of Pure Demand Analysis, Part I," *Skand. Aktuar-Tidskr.*, 1943, 26, pp. 85–118.

205. Wold, H. "A Synthesis of Pure Demand Analysis, Part II," *Skand. Aktuar-Tidskr.*, 1943, 26, pp. 220–63.

206. Wold, H. "A Synthesis of Pure Demand Analysis, Part III," *Skand. Aktuar-Tidskr.*, 1944, 27, pp. 69–120.

207. Wold, H. "Ordinal Preferences or Cardinal Utility?" *Econometrica*, 1952, 20, pp. 661–64.

208. Wold, H., and Juréen, L. *Demand Analysis*. New York: Wiley, 1953.

209. Zeuthen, F. "On the Determinateness of the Utility Function," *Rev. Econ. Stud.*, 1937, 4, pp. 236–39.

34. THE THEORY OF VALUE AND THE SCIENCE OF DECISION: A SUMMARY*

NICHOLAS M. SMITH, JR., STANLEY S. WALTERS,
FRANKLIN C. BROOKS, AND DAVID H. BLACKWELL

Definitions

Operations research is defined as "the science of decision." It is necessary, therefore, to understand the rationale and operation of the decision process. Decision is primarily based upon two quantities: (1) the *probability* with which certain immediate outcomes may result if a given course of action is taken; and (2) the *value* or worth of these outcomes. The product of probability times value summed over all the possible outcomes is the expected value, or simply the *expectation*. The course of action which leads to the highest expectation is the indicated choice of the decision. Decision means preference, and preference can be expressed only between like quantities. Thus, the problem in establishing a set of values is to establish a numerical function which will enable the ranking of preference of states or conditions.

The process described here is a stochastic system. By this is meant that events do not follow one after the other in a deterministic fashion but that event A may be followed by event C, D, or E, etc., in a probabilistic manner. One does not know which of these outcomes will occur, but it is assumed that the probabilities with which they occur are known. These probabilities are known as *transition probabilities;* that is, for state A there is a definite transition probability from this state to another state, say state E.

One may define what he means by the state probability equation—or simply the state equation—by first defining a *state* of a system. The state of a system is defined by a set of numbers that completely describe it at a given time, t. For instance, a military system may be described by a state in which there are n_1 men, n_2 guns, n_3 aircraft, n_4 tanks, etc. Noting the state of the system by the symbol x, the probability of being in state x at a particular time t is the *state probability*. One may also define a *state value*, $Q(x, t)$, which is defined by the equation:

$$Q(x, t) = \sum_{y} K(x, t; y, s) Q(y, s); \ s \geqq t,$$

where $K(x, t; y, s)$ is the probability of transition from state x at time t to state y at time s.

In order to solve the state equation and the value equation one needs

---

* Reproduced from the *Journal of Operations Research*, May, 1953.

boundary conditions. The boundary condition of the probability equation arises from the statement that one knows the state of the system at some particular time with certainty. From this knowledge the complete set of probabilities can in principle be calculated. The state values, on the other hand, may not be determined from a knowledge of a value of the state of the system at some particular time but are determined by the values placed upon certain *trapped states*. A trapped state is defined as a state of the system from which no change can occur. Thus a state of winning or state of losing a war is a trapped state. A state of winning all of one's opponent's money in a gambling game, or losing all of one's own money, is a trapped state. It is assumed as a hypothesis that it is inevitable that the system will ultimately arrive at one of these trapped conditions. It is asserted that agreement can be obtained for the placement of values on the trapped states, but it must be realized that these values are arbitrary, and in a sense the values so placed are postulates of *value* with respect to the system. For instance, if one's sole concern is the winning of a war it is reasonable to place a value of $+1$ on all winning states and a value of 0 or a value of -1 on all losing states.

Fundamental Theorem

The fundamental theorem of value, which has been rigorously proved, states that *there is a unique value $Q(x, t)$, satisfying equation* (1) *above which agrees with an arbitrary assignment of values to the trapped states,* and that *this value is independent of time when $K(x, t; y, s)$ depends only on $s - t$.* It has also been shown that the fundamental meaning of the value of a state is that it is the ultimate expectation taken over the trapped states of the system. In the case of values for winning or losing, the value of a state is a linear function of the probability of winning. Thus, value as used here has a *utility* meaning.

There are important sources of disagreement in postulating the values of the trapped states. These are here outlined without elaboration. (1) There can be fundamental differences in cultural and ethical outlooks. (2) The end states so concerned may not actually be ultimate final states; such as the case in which value is assigned to the winning of a battle. These values so chosen should ultimately reflect on the contribution of this battle to the winning of the war. If this assignment is made intuition-ally, then there can obviously be differences in the intuitional solution of this problem. (3) There can be differences in the area of closure of the system. For instance, when it is assumed that the sole objective is to win the war, it is reasonable to assign a value of $+1$ to all winning states and -1 to all losing states. On the other hand, if one is concerned not only with winning the war, but also with winning it with the least expenditure of men and materiel, it is reasonable to suppose that the trapped states will be valued according to some function of the number of men remaining. The differences here are brought about by limitation of one's interest in the first case to the system composed solely of the state of war, and in the second case to the system composed of the state of war *and the peace which follows*. And finally, (4), it may be possible to evaluate the same set of states in several systems at the same time. This possibility can be illustrated in a man's situation involving his self-system as well as his group-system. There exist different sets of values in these different systems and the choice of action maximizing the expectation in one system may minimize it in another. Under this condition, and with this elemental criterion of choice, it is impossible to make a decision. A state of *conflict* exists.

One of the greatest problems in the decision process has to do with the resolution of such conflicts. How can conflict be resolved? (1) The value in one of the conflicting systems can be *suppressed*. Thus, one may attempt to be unselfish and not self-centered, and devaluate his self-values so that he may decide in favor of the group. Also, the process of suppression of one set of values may require an actual fight between persons or nations involved in a decision. (2) A second way in which conflicts are resolved is by the establishment of a set of super-values which comprise our system of ethics. (3) The most important means for the resolution of the conflict is the *establishment of a new system which includes all of the conflicting systems as sub-sets*. With such enlargement of the area of closure it is necessary to set up new arbitrary values of trapped or ultimate conditions, and these represent the establishment of new value postulates. Again it is seen here that the function of establishing values is to reduce a vector set of values in the conflicting systems to a scalar set in one all inclusive system. This is done by a rational inductive process which requires establishment of new concepts and new postulates. This process of decision is identical with the so-called scientific process of the building of a rational theory in any particular field of science.

The Unit of Value

The unit of value needs description and definition. For the case where one is concerned with the ultimate value of winning or losing a war it is sensible to value all winning states equally and set their values equal to one ultimate unit, *the ult;* the value of all losing states may be set equal to -1 ult (or zero). The value coefficients are thus in units of ults/life; ults/gun; ults/aircraft, etc. It is common practice to convert these absolute units to relative value coefficients and express values in terms of equivalent dollars, or man-hours, or kilowatt-hours of energy, etc. This practice is permissible, although it does often involve semantic difficulties. These statements are illustrated below.

Assume it is required that one decide between actions A and B. The effectiveness value of action A, say, is estimated in ults by

$$\left[\sum_i \frac{\Delta Q}{\Delta m_i} \Delta m_i \right]_A,$$

and its cost by

$$-\left[\sum_i \frac{\Delta Q}{\Delta n_i} \Delta n_i \right]_A.$$

Looking at the cost only, let us consider the raw materials μ_i which went into the formation of the array of weapons n_i. Letting $a_i = -\Delta Q / \Delta \mu_i$, this latter scalar product is the product of the cost-efficient vector and the cost vector; that is,

$$\begin{bmatrix} a_1 \text{ ults/life} \\ a_2 \text{ ults/man-hour} \\ a_3 \text{ ults/kw-h} \\ a_4 \text{ ults/lbs of strategic} \\ \text{commodity} \end{bmatrix}_A \cdot \begin{bmatrix} \mu_1 \text{ lives lost} \\ \mu_2 \text{ man-hours consumed} \\ \mu_3 \text{ kw-hours consumed} \\ \mu_4 \text{ lbs of strategic} \\ \text{commodity used} \end{bmatrix}_A$$

$$= \text{ults consumed by action } A.$$

Similarly, one can estimate the value in ults consumed by action B. A comparison will reveal the action of least cost.

On the other hand, the cost coefficient vector may be divided by any constant, and it would still be revealed which action cost the least. Let this constant be a_2; then one has:

$$\begin{bmatrix} a_1/a_2 \dfrac{\text{man-hours}}{\text{life}} \\ 1 \\ a_3/a_2 \dfrac{\text{man-hours}}{\text{kw-h}} \\ a_4/a_2 \dfrac{\text{man-hours}}{\text{lbs of strategic}} \\ \text{commodities} \end{bmatrix}_A \cdot \begin{bmatrix} \mu_1 \text{ lives} \\ \mu_2 \text{ man-hours} \\ \mu_3 \text{ kw-hours} \\ \mu_4 \text{ lbs} \end{bmatrix}_A$$

$$= \text{cost of action } A \text{ in terms of equivalent man-hours.}$$

One could have linked together man-hours and kw-hours and expressed these two in terms of dollars consumed. The life-cost coefficient would then be expressed in dollars per life, etc., and the total cost would be expressed in relative dollars of value consumed by action A.

In the first case the coefficients are expressed in terms of value per weapon or commodity involved; and in the second case the cost coefficients have been divided through by one of these coefficients (in the illustration, the cost vector is given in terms of man-hours).

For the purposes of making a decision between ultimate courses of action it is immaterial whether an absolute unit of value is chosen or whether a relative unit expressed in terms of one of the components is chosen, provided due allowance has been made for intrinsic evaluations of the quantities involved. Thus, if a given operation compared to a second operation costs less in ultimate units of value it would also cost less in equivalent man-hours of value or equivalent dollars of value. For semantic purposes it might be a good thing if operations analysts employed a unit of value by name which was not dollars, or man-hours, or kw-hours of energy, or any of the cost components. This would avoid misunderstandings, for instance, between the cost of production and the cost of value consumption of strategic materials. It also would avoid some emotional blocks which are aroused by such expressions as the value of human life in terms of dollars.

Note that, in the above, the change of state value, ΔQ, involved in the incremental changes, is proportional to the *difference* between the effectiveness value (that is, enemy value destroyed) and the cost value (that is, friendly value consumed).

Utilitarian and Casuistic Value

One can differentiate between *a priori* and *a posteriori* values. This distinction is made on the basis that, in the first case, decisions are based upon values estimated prior to the decision; and, in the second case, one looks to the past for a decision and states that this implies that certain values were held. *A priori* value might also be called *utilitarian value* in conformity with its usage in a system of ethics by that name. In a similar manner *a posteriori* value might also be called *casuistic value* in conformity with the system of ethics which appeals to authoritative decisions for fundamental values.

One may illustrate the casuistic principle of value in the military system by investigating the relative expenditures of materiel and human life in World War II. There is a great deal of arbitrariness in the relative risking of life and of materiel for the relative expenditures of these quantities in warfare. As a result of a great many factors, some of them tactical decisions on the battlefield, some of them conditions imposed by the limitations of our productive capacity and our national economy, casualties which result in death occur, on the average, at a fairly uniform ratio with respect to materiel. From unclassified sources from World War II it has been estimated that at a division level $200,000 worth of materiel, man-hours and energy, were expended per human life lost in the U.S. Army. It must be emphasized that this statement does not tend to imply that one can measure the *spiritual* or *ethical* value of life in dollars. It does mean that life and materiel have been expended at this ratio; that, according to this estimate, the *military expectation* per $200,000 worth of materiel expended was equal to the military expectation per life expended.

Value Theory and Game Theory

The principles of game theory are combined with the principles of value theory in a stochastic system. A war, for instance, is composed of many battles, and each battle separately may be considered as a game in which the friendly commander and the enemy commander each has to choose between several strategies. Thus one commander does not have complete freedom over all possible choices, but only those over which he has control.

It is still possible to define a value for a state in such a system. Assume that the values of the end states of the battle are known. Then, for each strategy of the friendly commander, there exists a possibility that the enemy commander will employ any of his possible strategies. Thus, there is no longer a single expectation for each course of action of the friendly commander, but many of them. Good strategies may be defined in the usual manner. In conformance with the usual definitions, good mixed strategies for each commander can be defined and a value of the game computed. One can thus proceed by induction from the values of the trapped states through the entire system. An additional important theorem comes from this analysis in that it has been shown that *the over-all strategy which is composed of the good strategies for each increment of battle is a good strategy for the war as a whole.*

REFERENCES

(1) F. W. Lanchester. *Aircraft in Warfare*, chap. iv. London: Constable and Co., Ltd., 1916.

(2) J. von Neumann and O. Morgenstern. *Theory of Games and Economic Behavior*. Princeton: Princeton University Press, 1947.

(3) Wayne A. R. Leys. *Ethics for Policy Decisions*. New York: Prentice-Hall, 1952.

35. THE THEORY OF GAMES*

OSKAR MORGENSTERN

THE ANALOGY between games of strategy and economic and social behavior is so obvious that it finds wide expression in the thinking and even the language of business and politics. Phrases such as "a political deal" and "playing the stock market" are familiar reflections of this. The connection between games and these other activities is more than superficial. When they are examined by the methods of modern mathematics, it becomes evident that many of the forms of economic and social behavior are strictly identical with—not merely analogous to—games of strategy. Thus the mathematical study of games offers the possibility of new insights and precision in the study of economics.

The theory of probability arose from a study of lowly games of chance and from the desire of professional gamblers to find ways of taking advantage of the odds. Far more difficult problems are presented by games of strategy such as poker, bridge and chess. In these games, where the outcome no longer depends on chance alone but also on the acts of other players and on their expectations of one's own present and future acts, a player must choose among relatively complex strategies. Mathematically, these problems remained not only unsolved, but even untouched.

Gottfried Wilhelm Leibnitz, the German philosopher and mathematician, seems to have recognized that a study of games of strategy would form the basis of a theory of society. On the other hand, many efforts along quite different lines were made by philosophers and economists to provide a theory for "rational behavior" for individuals, business corporations, or even for entire communities.

Such a theory must be quantitative, which means that it must ultimately assume a mathematical character. A theory of games fulfilling these requirements would take into account that participants in a game vary in information and intelligence, that they have various expectations about the other players' behavior, and that different paths of reaching their goal may be open to them. The theory must also allow for the fact that the position of a player (or, equivalently, of an economic individual or a firm) is often adversely affected if his opponent finds out his intentions. The player has to take steps to protect himself against this contingency, and the theory must indicate how he should proceed most effi-

---

* Reproduced from *Scientific American*, May, 1949.

ciently—and what his countermeasures would mean to the other players.

Why should such a theory be of interest to the sociologist and, in particular, to the economist? Does not the economics of today have an adequate model in mechanics, with its notions of forces, of equilibrium and stability? Physics is, indeed, at the bottom of current efforts to provide a statement of rational economic behavior, whether it is mathematically formulated or not. But many important situations that arise at all levels in economics find no counterpart whatever in physics.

A typical example is the fixing of wage rates between workers and employers when both groups have found it to their advantage to combine into unions and associations. Current economics cannot tell us, except in a general manner, under what circumstances such combinations will arise, who will profit, and by how much. The two groups have opposing interests, but do not have separate means to pursue their contrary aims. They must finally come to some agreement, which may turn out to be more advantageous to one side than to the other. In settling their differences they will feint, bluff, use persuasion; they will try to discover each other's strategies and prevent discovery of their own. Under such circumstances a theory of rational behavior will have to tell a participant how much a given effort will be worth in view of the obstacles encountered, the obstacles being the behavior of his opponents and the influence of the chance factor.

Monopoly and monopolistic market forms—that is, trading among only a few individuals or firms on one side of the market at least—are characteristic of all social economies. They involve serious feuds and fights, a very different picture from the general, "free" competition with which classical economic theory usually deals. On the orthodox theory, the individual is supposed to face prices and other conditions that are fixed, and is supposed to be in a position to control all the variables, so that his profit or utility depends only on his own actions. Actually, however, when there are only a few individuals, or many individuals organized into a few combinations, the outcome never depends on the actions of the individual alone. No single person has control of all the variables, but only of a few.

The case of an individual acting in strict isolation can be described mathematically as a simple maximum problem—that is, finding the behavior formula that will yield the maximum value or return. The cases involving combinations are of an entirely different mathematical and logical structure. Indeed, they present a peculiar mixture of maximum problems, creating a profound mathematical question for which there is no parallel in physical science or even in classical mathematics.

Yet this is the level at which the problem of economic behavior needs to be attacked. Clearly it is far more realistic to investigate from the outset the nature of the all-pervading struggles and fights in economic and social life, rather than to deal with an essentially artificial, atomistic, "free" competition where men are supposed to act like automatons confronted by rigidly given conditions.

The theory of games defines the solution of each game of strategy as the distribution or distributions of payments to be made by every player as a function of all other individuals' behavior. The solution thus has to tell each player, striving for his maximum advantage, how to behave in all conceivable circumstances, allowing for all and any behavior of all the other players. Obviously this concept of a solution is very comprehensive, and finding such a solution for each type of game, as well as computing it numerically for each particular instance, poses enormous mathematical difficulties. The theory makes important use of mathematical logic, as well as combinatorics (the study of possible ways of combining and ordering objects) and set theory (the techniques for dealing with any collection of objects which have one or more exactly specified properties in common). This domain of modern mathematics is one of exceptional rigor. But it is believed that great mathematical discoveries are required to make a break-through into the field of social phenomena.

A single individual, playing alone, faces the simplest maximum problem; his best strategy is the one that brings him the predetermined maximum gain. Consider a two-person game: Each player wishes to win a maximum, but he can do this only at the expense of the other. This situation results in a zero-sum game, since the sum of one player's gains and the other's losses (a negative number) is zero. One player has to design a strategy that will assure him of the maximum advantage. But the same is true of the other, who naturally wishes to minimize the first player's gain, thereby maximizing his own. This clear-cut opposition of interest introduces an entirely new concept, the so-called "minimax" problem.

Some games have an optimal "pure" strategy. In other words, there is a sequence of moves such that the player using it will have the safest strategy possible, whatever his opponent does. His position will not deteriorate even if his strategy is found out. In such "strictly determined" games, every move—and hence every position resulting from a series of moves—is out in the open. Both players have complete information. The mathematical expression of this condition is that the function describing the outcome of a game has a "saddle point." This mathematical term is based on an analogy with the shape of a saddle, which can be regarded as the intersection of two curves at a single point. One curve in a saddle is the one in which the rider sits; the other is the one that fits over the horse's back and slopes down over its sides. The seat of the saddle represents the "maximum" curve, and its low point is the "maximin." The curve that straddles the horse's back is the "minimum" curve, and its high point is the "minimax." The point at which the two curves meet at the center of the saddle is the "saddle point." In the theory of games, the somewhat more special saddle point is the intersection of two particular strategies.

The mathematical values of the strategies involved in a hypothetical game of this kind are represented in the diagram on this page. This shows a simple game between two players, A and B, each of whom has available three possible strategies. There are nine possible combinations of moves by A and B. The numbers in the boxes represent A's gains or losses for all combined strategies and, since this is a zero-sum game, their negatives represent B's losses or gains. A's minimax trategy is A-2, because if he follows that sequence of moves, he is sure to win at least two units no matter what B does. Similarly, B's minimax strategy is B-1, because then he cannot possibly lose more than two units whatever A's plan of action. If a spy informed A that B was planning to use B-1, A could make no profit from that information. The point where the A-2 row intersects the B-1 column is the saddle point for this game.

A \ B	B-1	B-2	B-3
A-1	2	*1*	4
A-2	2	3	2
A-3	2	−1	1

Game of Strategy between two players, each with three possible strategies, has nine possible results. Numbers in boxes represent A's gains or losses for each combination of plays by both players.

It may seem that B has no business playing such a game, since he must lose two units even with his best strategy, and any other strategy exposes him to even heavier loss. At best he can win only a single unit, and then only if A makes a mistake. Yet all strictly determined games are of this nature. A simple example is tacktacktoe. In perfectly played ticktacktoe every game would result in a tie. A more complex example is chess, which has a saddle point and a pure strategy. Chess is exciting because the number of possible moves and positions is so great that the finding of that strategy is beyond the powers of even the best calculating machines.

Other two-person, zero-sum games, however, have no single best possible strategy. This group includes games ranging from matching pennies to bridge and poker—and most military situations. These games, in which it would be disastrous if a player's strategy were discovered by his opponent, are not strictly determined. The player's principal concern is to protect his strategy from discovery. Do safe and good strategies exist for "not strictly determined" games, so that their choice would make the games again strictly determined? Can a player in such a game find strategies other than "pure" strategies which would make his behavior completely "rational"? Mathematically speaking, does a saddle point always exist?

It does, and the proof was originally established in 1927 by the mathematician John von Neumann, the originator of the theory of games, now at the Institute for Advanced Study in Princeton. He used various basic tools of modern mathematics, including the so-called fixed-point theorem of the Dutch mathematician L. E. J. Brouwer. Von Neumann proved, by a complex but rigorous application of this theorem to the theory of games, that there is a single "stable" or rational course of action that represents the best strategy or saddle point even in not strictly determined games.

This principle can also be demonstrated in practical terms. Observation shows that in games where the discovery of a player's plan of action would have dangerous consequences, he can protect himself by avoiding the consistent use of a pure strategy and choosing it with a certain probability only. This substitution of a statistical strategy makes discovery by the opponent impossible. Since the player's chief aim must be to prevent any leakage of information from himself to the other player, the best way to accomplish this is not to have the information oneself. Thus, instead of choosing a precise course of action, the various possible alternatives are considered with different probabilities.

It is in the nature of probability that individual events cannot be predicted, so that the strategy actually used will remain a secret up to the decisive moment, even to the player himself, and necessarily to his opponent as well. This type of indecision is a well-known empirical fact. Wherever there is an advantage in not having one's intentions found out —obviously a very common occurrence—people will be evasive, try to create uncertainty in the minds of others, produce doubts, and at the same time try to pierce the veil of secrecy thrown over their opponents' operations.

The example *par excellence* is poker. In a much simpler form, this type of behavior is illustrated in the game of matching pennies. Here the best strategy is to show heads or tails at random, taking care only to play each half the time. Since the same strategy is available to the opponent, both players will break even if they play long enough and both know this principle. The calculation of the best strategy grows in difficulty as the number of possible moves increases: e.g., in the Italian game called morra, in which each player shows one, two or three fingers and simultaneously calls out his guess as to the sum of fingers shown by himself and his opponent, a player has nine possible strategies. His safest course is to guess a total of four fingers every time, and to vary his own moves so that out of every 12 games he shows one finger five times, two fingers four times and three fingers three times. If he plays according to this mixture of strategies, he will at least break even, no matter what his opponent does.

Let us apply these principles to a simple economic problem. Suppose that two manufacturers are competing for a given consumer market, and that each is considering three different sales strategies. The matrix on this page specifies the possible values of the respective strategies to manufacturer A: This situation does not have a single best strategy. If A chooses strategy A-1, B can limit his profit to one unit by using strategy B-2 or B-3; if A chooses strategy A-2 or A-3, B can deprive him of any profit by choosing strategy B-1. Thus each manufacturer stands to lose

B \ A	B-1	B-2	B-3
A-1	4	1	1
A-2	0	3	1
A-3	0	0	2

Business Rivalry between two firms with three strategies each again diagrams A's possible gains. No single strategy is best if the opponent discovers it: hence the rivals must use a mixture of all three.

if he concentrates on a single sales technique and his rival discovers his plan. Analysis shows that A will lose unless he uses a combination of A-1, A-2 and A-3, each a third of the time. On the other hand, if manufacturer B fails to employ his best mixed strategy—B-1 a ninth of the time, B-2 two ninths of the time, and B-3 two thirds of the time—his competitor will gain. These mixed strategies are the safest strategies. They should be used whenever each manufacturer does not know what the other will do.

An example which illustrates in statistical terms many of the conflicts of choices involved in everyday life is the famous story of Sherlock Holmes' pursuit by his archenemy, Professor Moriarty, in Conan Doyle's story, "The Final Problem." Holmes has planned to take a train from London to Dover and thence make his escape to the Continent. Just as the Dover train is pulling out of Victoria Station, Moriarty rushes on the platform and the two men see each other. Moriarty is left at the station. He charters a special train to continue the chase. The detective is faced with the problem of outguessing his pursuer. Should he get off at

Canterbury—the only intermediate stop—or go all the way to Dover? And what should Moriarty do? In effect, this situation can be treated as a rather unusual version of matching pennies—a "match" occuring if the two men decide to go to the same place and meet there. It is assumed that such a meeting would mean the death of Sherlock Holmes; therefore it has an arbitrarily assigned value of 100 to Moriarty. If Holmes goes to Dover and makes his way to the Continent, it is obviously a defeat for the professor, but—also obviously—not as great a defeat as death would be for the detective. Hence, a value of minus 50 to Moriarty is given to this eventuality. Finally, if Holmes leaves the train at Canterbury and Moriarty goes on to Dover, the chase is not over and the temporary outcome can be considered a draw. According to the theory of games, the odds are 60 to 40 in favor of the professor.

In the story, of course, this game is played only once: Sherlock Holmes, deducing that Moriarty will go to Dover, gets off at Canterbury and watches triumphantly as the professor's pursuing train speeds past the intermediate station. If the game were continued, however, Holmes' look of triumph would hardly be justified. On the assumption that Moriarty persisted in the chase, calculations indicate that the great detective was actually as good as 40 per cent dead when his train left Victoria Station!

The theory of games has already been applied to a number of practical problems. Situations similar to that of Holmes are being analyzed in that branch of operational research which deals with military tactics, the possible courses of action being various dispositions of troops or combinations of measures and countermeasures. The handling of the more complex situations that exist in economics is expected to require the aid of calculating machines. For example, two competing automobile manufacturers may each have a large number of strategies involving the choice of various body designs, the addition of new accessories, the best times to announce new models and price changes, and so on. It has been estimated that the calculations for a game in which one manufacturer had 100 possible strategies and his competitor had 200 (a not uncommon situation) would take about a year on an electronic computer.

If we now make the transition to games involving three or more persons, a fundamentally new phenomenon emerges—namely, the tendency among some players to combine against others, or equivalently in markets to form trade unions, cartels and trusts. Such coalitions will be successful only if they offer the individual members more than they could get acting separately. Games where that is the case are called essential. Coalitions will then oppose each other in the manner of individual players in a two-person game. A coalition will have a value for the players who form it, and they may therefore require payments or "compensations" from newcomers who want to enter the coalition and share in its proceeds. As a rule a great deal of bargaining will precede the determination of the system of distribution of gains or profits among the members of the coalition.

Basically, the formation of a coalition expresses the fundamental tendency toward monopoly, which is thus found to be deeply characteristic of social and economic life. Indeed, Adam Smith already had noted the tendency of businessmen to "conspire" against the common welfare, as he stated it, by getting together into groups for better exploitation. Important chapters of American economic history deal with the efforts of government to break conspiracies of various kinds in order to limit the power of trusts and other amalgamations. When these are broken—if at all—they tend to arise again, so a continuous watchfulness is necessary.

The powerful forces working toward monopoly ought therefore to be at the very center of economic studies. They should replace the preoccupation with a nonexistent pure or free competition where nobody has any perceptible influence on anything, and where all data are assumed to be immutably given. Since this is the imaginary setup from which current economic theory starts, it encounters insuperable difficulties when it enters the realm of monopolistic competition. It is not surprising, therefore, that classical economics has failed to yield a general theory that embraces all economic situations.

The approach to the coalition problem in the theory of games can be shown by a three-person situation in which it is assumed that a player can achieve a gain in any given play only if he joins with one other player. The gains and losses that would result for the individual players in the case of each possible coalition are shown in the diagram. Thus if A and B form a coalition, each gains a half unit and C loses one unit. What keeps the players in the game is that they all stand a chance of profit; each player's problem is to succeed in forming a coalition with one of the other two on any given deal. This simplified situation illustrates in essence much of the conflict that occurs in modern economic life.

Coalitions \ Individual players	A	B	C
A, B	$\frac{1}{2}$	$\frac{1}{2}$	-1
A, C	$\frac{1}{2}$	-1	$\frac{1}{2}$
B, C	-1	$\frac{1}{2}$	$\frac{1}{2}$

Coalition Game with three players produces still another matrix. Here gains or losses to players resulting from various possible coalitions are shown in vertical columns. Players must form partnership to win.

Now the important characteristic of this type of game is that there is no single "best" solution for any individual player. A, for example, can gain as much by forming a coalition with C as with B. Therefore all three of the possible distributions of payments, taken together, must be viewed as the solution of this three-person game.

There are, of course, many other distribution schemes that might be considered by the players. For example, one of the partners in a coalition could make a deal with the third player whereby both improved their positions (the third player reducing his losses) at the expense of the other partner. What is to prevent the participants in the game from considering all these other possibilities?

The question can be answered by introducing the concept of "domination." In mathematical terminology the various possible schemes for distributions of payments are called "imputations." One imputation is said to dominate another if it is clearly more advantageous to all the players in a given coalition. It is found, as shown in the three-person game described above, that the imputations belonging to a solution do not dominate each other: in this case all three imputations have an equal chance of being chosen; none is most advantageous to the players in each coalition. While it is extremely difficult to prove mathematically that such a solution would exist for every game with arbitrarily many players, the principle can be expected to hold true.

Now it is also found that while the imputations belonging to the solution do not dominate each other, individually they are not free from domination by imputations outside the solution. In other words, there are always outside schemes from which some of the players could profit. But any and every imputation outside the solution is dominated by one belonging to the solution, so that it will be rejected as too risky. It will be considered unsafe not to conform to the accepted standard of behavior, and only one of the imputations which are part of the solution will materialize.

These examples give an idea of the great complexity of social and economic organization. In this realm "stability" is far more involved than it is in the physical sciences, where a solution is usually given by a number or a set of numbers. In essential games, in economics and in warfare, there is instead a set of alternatives, none of which is clearly better than another or all others. One imputation in a set is not more stable than any other, because every one may be threatened by one outside the solution. But each has a certain stability because it is protected by other potential imputations in the solution against upsets from outside. Collectively they eliminate the danger of revolutions. The balance is most delicate, however, and it becomes more sensitive as the number of players increases. These higher-order games may have many solutions instead of a single one, and while there is no conflict within an individual solution, the various solutions or standards of behavior may well conflict with one another.

This multiplicity of solutions may be interpreted as a mathematical formulation of the undisputed fact that on the same physical background of economic and social culture utterly different types of society can be established. Within each society, in turn, there is possible considerable variation of income, privileges and other advantages—which corresponds to the multiplicity of imputations or distribution schemes in a single solution in a game.

The theory also yields insight into even more delicate social phenomena. Although it assumes that every player has full information, discrimination may exist: two players may make a third player "tabu," assigning him a fixed payment and excluding him from all negotiations and coalitions. Yet this arrangement need not lead to complete exploitation of the third player. In practical economic life, for example, cartels do not annihilate all outside firms, although it would not be a technically difficult operation. Rather, in deference to socially accepted standards of behavior they allow certain outsiders a share in the industry, so as not to attract undue attention—and to be able to point out to the government and the public that "competition" exists in the particular industry.

It is surprising and extremely significant that, although the theory of games was developed without any specific consideration of such situations, the fact that they exist was derived from general theorems by purely mathematical methods. Furthermore, the theory shows—again purely mathematically—that certain privileges, even if anchored in the rules of a game (or of a society), cannot always be maintained by the privileged if they come into conflict with the accepted standard of behavior. A privileged person or group may have to give up his entire "bonus" in order to survive economically.

These and many other implications can be derived from the study of simple three-person games. Games of more than three players provide further interesting insights—but at the price of great and, in many cases, still insuperable mathematical difficulties. The almost unimaginable complexity involved may be illustrated by poker, the game which, above all others, furnishes a model for economic and social situations. The subtleties of poker and the countless number of available strategies—e.g., the technique of purposely being caught bluffing now and then so that future bluffs may be successful—prevent the thorough analysis that would be necessary to throw light on corresponding problems in practical everyday affairs. The matrix of possible strategies for poker is so large that it has not even been calculated, much less drawn. Consider a radically simplified version of the game which assumes a deck of only three cards, a one-card, no-draw hand, only two players, three bids between them (the first player gets two, the second one), and no overbetting. Even this watered-down version of poker involves a matrix of 1,728 boxes, and computing a single best possible strategy for each player to an accuracy of about 10 per cent might require almost two billion multiplications and additions.

But even with its present limitations the theory of games has made it possible to analyze problems beyond the scope of previous economic theory. Besides those already indicated, the problems now being explored include the application of the mathematics for a game involving seven persons to the best location of plants in a particular industry, the relation between labor unions and management, the nature of monopoly.

The initial problem in the theory of games was to give precision to the notion of "rational behavior." Qualitative or philosophical arguments have led nowhere; the new quantitative approach may point in the right direction. Applications are still limited, but the approach is in the scientific tradition of proceeding step by step, instead of attempting to include all phenomena in a great general solution. We all hope eventually to discover truly scientific theories that will tell us exactly how to stabilize employment, increase national income and distribute it adequately. But we must first obtain precision and mastery in a limited field, and then proceed to increasingly greater problems. There are no short cuts in economics.

36. EVALUATION OF DECISIONS WRITTEN BY *AD HOC* GROUPS AND SIMULATED COMMANDERS*

IRVING LORGE, PAULA WELTZ, DAVID FOX
AND KENNETH HERROLD

IN EDUCATION, in industry and in the military there is a definite trend towards decision-making in the group setting, and away from decision-making by the individual executive or commander acting either with or without the recommendations of his subordinates. In the military situation this raises the question of whether the staff will make a better decision than the commander, either acting alone or acting on the advice of his staff. These three decision-making situations were investigated by the Institute of Psychological Research in classes for education of officers at the Air University, Maxwell Field, Alabama.

The problem used in this study, "Wilco Air Force Base," is one of a series of complex human relations problems prepared by the Institute of Psychological Research for use with Air Force Officers. In "Wilco Air Force Base," the problem situation is that of a base near the Mexican border beset by inadequate recreational facilities on base and in the nearest town, isolation, low morale, and low operating efficiency, etc. Positive factors are also described, a budget of $200,000 is provided, an empty building is available on base for conversion for recreational purposes, the cooperation of the town officials is assured, etc.

The quality of the decisions was evaluated by the method of the Quality Point Score, hereinafter referred to as QPS. The QPS is a valid and objective method for estimating the relative goodness of solutions. Basically a sample of the solutions about each problem are content analyzed and each action point is recorded. A team of specialists assigns a credit to each such point. The credits for the points in any one decision can then be summed to form the QPS for that decision. The QPS has been demonstrated to have objectivities in excess of .80, and validities in excess of .85.

The testing was conducted in two successive fifty-minute periods. During the initial period, all 66 officers as individuals wrote decisions. Then in the second period 55 of the 66 officers were formed into eleven *ad hoc* groups or staffs, with instructions to write a decision about the same problem as a staff. For each such *ad hoc* staff, there was available, of course, a set of the five decisions the group members as individuals

* Read at the American Psychological Association Meeting at Cleveland, September 5, 1953.

had written during the first period. The eleven officers not assigned to staffs were considered as simulated commanders. Each one of these was fed one of the sets of five individual decisions. As simulated commanders they were instructed to read the set of five decisions and then to write a final decision for action. The commander, thus, could utilize the decisions of the five individuals in his own set as well as the thinking in his own solution during the first period in any way he saw fit. He could synthesize them, summate them, or reject them—much as a genuine commander would utilize staff recommendations.

In summary, then, four kinds of decisions were available: (*a*) the initial individual decisions of each of the officers later formed into groups; (*b*) decisions written by these groups; (*c*) the initial decisions of the officers later to act as commanders; and (*d*) decisions written by the commanders.

Basically, the design allows comparisons between the QPS for the decisions written: (*a*) by *ad hoc* staffs and by commanders, i.e., second period decisions; (*b*) by *ad hoc* staffs and by its members as independent individuals in the preceding period; (*c*) by the commanders in the second period and by them in the preceding period plus those by the five individuals of his so-called "staff."

The quality of decisions written in the first period by the eleven officers selected at random to be commanders was not significantly different from the decisions written by the other 55 officers later formed into groups.

The first hypothesis tested was that the quality of the decisions written by the commander in the second period is superior to the quality of the decisions written by the *ad hoc* staff. The commander, in writing his final solution, has available the range of points presumptively available to the *ad hoc* staff, as well as the range of points originally in his own initial decision, i.e., the equivalence of six individual decisions. The resources of the staff consist of the range of points written by the five staff members together with any stimulation and creativity resulting from their interaction as a group. Since the commander's final solution is a product of the combination of his own points and of the points in the solutions of his "staff," it was hypothesized that the quality of decisions written by commanders is superior to that of decisions prepared by *ad hoc* staffs. The data do not support this hypothesis: there is no significant difference in the quality of decisions written by commanders and by staffs despite the fact that the commander was reacting with six individual decisions and the *ad hoc* staffs with five.

The second hypothesis was that the quality of decisions written by the commander after reading the individual decisions written by his "staff" and rethinking his own initial decision is superior to the quality of his initial decision. Common-sense will suggest that when additional points are "fed" to the commander, his own final decision will be the better for it. The data support this hypothesis.

The third hypothesis was that the quality of decisions written by *ad hoc* staffs is superior to that of the average decision written by the staff members as individuals in the preceding period. The data support the hypothesis. Decisions written by the *ad hoc* staffs are significantly superior to those written individually by those same officers.

While the quality of the decisions written by the *ad hoc* staff is superior to the quality of the average individual decision of its members, much is lost in the staff decision. For, if all the points in each set of five individual decisions had been combined, it would give an estimate of the range of points available to the staff as a unit. On the average, however, the subsequent staff decision shows an acceptance of only about half of these points. The quality of the staff product was markedly inferior to the summation of the different points in the individual decisions of the staff members. Some partial compensation for this loss via group process exists in the number of new points innovated by the staff, i.e., those points appearing in the staff decision that were not in any of the individual decisions of the staff members. Although each staff innovated at least one point, in no staff did the innovated points approximate those that were lost.

Similarly, there was a significant loss in the commander's decision. Combining all the points appearing in each set of five individual decisions plus those in the commander's own initial decision gives an estimate of the range of points available to the commander. On the average, the commander's decision accepts only one third of these points with just a slight compensation of one or two innovated points. Thus, while the commanders' decisions are superior to their own individual decisions, and the staff decisions are superior to the individual decisions of the staff members, both fail to reflect in full the range of points available to them. Neither quantitatively nor qualitatively do the innovated points compensate for the losses via group process nor via individual evaluation by the commanders.[1]

These results suggest that there is a need for training individuals who are to have executive or command positions to evaluate written material and to abstract all the relevant points. This is particularly true when the individual has the responsibility of recommending action to solve a problem for which there is no one solution, but for which a full range of relevant actions is desirable. These are the so-called human relations problems usually encountered in industry, education and the military.

The data further suggest the need for instruction of individuals in

---

[1] Studies on Decision. No. 8. Conducted under contract number AB 33 (038) 28792 of the Human Resources Research Institute, Maxwell Air Force Base, by the Institute of Psychological Research, Teachers College, Columbia University. Irving Lorge, principal investigator.

communicating to each other in groups, in evaluating the points in the group discussion, and in achieving agreement on what should be included in the group decision.

These results may be interpreted as reflecting the inability of the group to properly record and report the results of its deliberations. If so, this further suggests the need for training in techniques of reporting the results of group discussion.

TABLE 1

DATA FOR COMPARING THE QUALITY OF DECISIONS WRITTEN BY SIMULATED COMMANDERS
AND AD HOC GROUPS

Designation in Design		First Period			Second Period		
	N	QPS	s	N		QPS	s
Work as individuals in first period, formed into *ad hoc* groups of five in second period	54 individuals	19.4	3.4	11	*ad hoc* groups	25.5	5.3
Work as individuals in first period, designated as "commanders" in second period and fed a set of five individual decisions to simulate "staff" reports	11 individuals	19.1	5.8	11	simulated commanders	27.3	6.6

TABLE 2

DATA FOR COMPARING THE QUALITY OF DECISIONS OF THE "SUMMATED INDIVIDUAL" WITH
THAT OF DECISIONS WRITTEN BY AD HOC GROUPS AND COMMANDERS

Designation in Design	N	QPS	s	No. of Points	s
Ad Hoc Group	11	25.5	5.3	17.8	3.8
Simulated Commander	11	27.3	6.6	18.4	4.6
Summated Individual, i.e., a combination of all unduplicated points in each set of five individual decisions	11	55.1	7.1	37.5	5.0
Summated Individual plus any further unduplicated points in commander's first period decision	11	60.5	7.4	41.1	5.4

37. FACTORS DETERMINING THE ADOPTION OF DECISION-MAKING AS A ROLE BEHAVIOR: A STUDY OF SCIENTISTS IN A GOVERNMENT ORGANIZATION*

ROBERT S. WEISS

IT's FREQUENTLY recognized that different individuals will work, in a job, in different ways; that one individual tends to assimilate one set of activities to his job, while another individual tends to assimilate a slightly different set. Given the same job, one individual may tend to make his own decisions where another would rely on his supervisor. Or one individual might tend to see a great many clients where another would de-emphasize that aspect of the job.

This paper has to do with factors which determined the way scientists, working in a government organization, structured their jobs. These factors may be put under four headings: (1) job imperatives—absolute requirements of the job, things anyone in the job simply *has* to do; (2) authoritatively assigned activities—things required of the individual by his supervisor, or someone else higher than he is in the organization's hierarchy; (3) socially assigned activities—things which are expected of the individual by his coworkers because he seems to be the proper person to do them; and (4) things the individual decides to do on his own initiative.

Most frequently we've thought that individual preferences for certain activities over others was the crucial factor in determining the way an individual structured his job. Thus, if an individual introduced decision-making into his job, he was considered someone who enjoyed having influence, and this was accepted as describing the source of his role behaviors. The data we have obtained suggest that individual preferences are not nearly so important in determining what optional activities—activities not summed up by the job imperatives—the individual performs. We find that aside from the job imperatives, social pressures based on the individual's possession of what we call *legitimizing characteristics*, and the *attitude of the individual's supervisor*, are much more important.

A *legitimizing characteristic* is an objective attribute of an individual, such as age or length of service in an organization, which may become generally known to the group with whom the individual works, and which is considered by this group to be related to the propriety of the individual's performing certain activities. For example, if, in the study of

---

*Presented at the Meetings of the American Psychological Association at New York, September, 1954.

an industrial operation, someone in the plant said to us, "They made so-and-so the inspector. After all, he's been here the longest," then we would think that length of service was a legitimizing characteristic for, or legitimized, performance of this quasi-supervisory activity. We would be convinced of this if we found that someone else was considered an improper choice because he did not have sufficient service.

Legitimizing characteristics probably correlate with competence to perform an activity, but probably are not directly related. The reason for their use may be found in a tendency for a group of individuals to avoid ambiguity in areas of importance to the group wherever this is possible. In an office situation, or any other situation where individuals work closely together, the allocation of tasks is a matter of concern to the group, and what seems to happen is that informally, and without people being aware of the specificity of some of the formulations, criteria arise regarding who can do what. It's then in terms of these criteria that social reaction takes place. For example, if A starts to perform an activity that B has been performing right along it's possible for coworkers of A and B to say to each other, in complete agreement, that A has a lot of nerve. And if A says, well, B's been doing this, the response will come in concert, yes, but B's been here for twenty years, or B is much older than you, or B has twice as much education as you, or B's been in this field for a dozen years, whatever the criteria agreed upon by the group in respect to the activity.

In the organization we studied there were 63 jobs which, so far as we could tell, were identical in the nature of their job imperatives. The things people *had* to do in their jobs were the same. Only the optional activities varied. The organization is a research organization, built as a series of parallel units, with each unit being assigned responsibility for investigation in a particular specialty. The jobs we chose were those of the scientific member of a unit, without supervisory responsibility. These jobs were identical, or quite similar to each other, on a number of other criteria besides job imperatives, including title, salary range, and position of the job in relation to other jobs.

We interviewed each scientist who held one of these jobs for from one to three hours, and among the questions we asked them, was to describe in detail the things they did in the course of a day's work. Their responses were categorized in terms of the organizational function or functions they seemed to be performing. One of the categories used was that of decision-making, which included the activities of deciding major allocation of funds, or otherwise committing the organization to a certain line of action. The response of one of the 63 scientists could not be coded, but of the remaining 62, 20 reported activities which were coded as decision-making, and 42 did *not* report such activities.

We decided that for a characteristic to qualify, for us, as a legitimizing characteristic, it must meet two criteria:

(1) It must be used by members of the group as a basis for discussing the appropriateness of the activity being performed either by themselves or by other members of the organization, and

(2) It must relate to actual performance of the activity, that is, other things being equal, people who have it should perform the activity, and people who do not have it should not.

Characteristics which seemed to legitimize decision-making were: possession of an advanced degree, long service with the organization, and wide experience in the field. A number of individuals suggested that without advanced degrees they were limited in the work they could do, and the implication was strong that increased education might not increase their competence, but it would certainly better their position in the social system. Length of service was also mentioned frequently, for example, in relation to an individual who performed his job in an amazingly autonomous fashion. This was justified by his coworkers on the basis of his being a fixture in the organization. Experience was mentioned much less frequently than education and length of service, but a few individuals did refer to it, usually in regard to themselves. Education was by far the most important: so important, it seemed, that without some graduate training, nothing else counted: experience was sufficiently minor so that it came into the picture only when other things were indecisive.

After examining the sample, we put these three elements together into operational criteria for whether an individual possessed legitimizing characteristics for decision-making. An individual was considered to have legitimizing characteristics if he had:

(1) A Ph.D.

(2) Some graduate work, and a fair amount of service with the organization (operationally set at four years).

(3) Some graduate work, some service with the organization (set at two years), and a fair amount of experience in the field (set at ten years).

Earlier I mentioned that legitimization was only part of the story in regard to whether the individual adopted an activity. The other part had to do with the attitudes of the individual's supervisor in regard to performance of the activity by his subordinates. During their interview we had asked each supervisor about his practices in regard to decision-making, and we were able to categorize them by their responses, into those who *retained* decision-making power, those who *permitted* decision-making by subordinates, and, in the third category, a single supervisor who *required* his subordinates to perform decision-making activities.

Table 1 shows that decision-making is reported by only five out of the thirty-three scientists whose supervisors retain decision-making power, but by ten out of the twenty-four whose supervisors permit decision-making by subordinates. The five subordinates of the supervisor who requires decision-making of his subordinates all report that they do, indeed, make policy decisions.

Looking now to Table 2, which shows the relationship of legitimizing

TABLE 1

REPORT OF DECISION MAKING BY SCIENTISTS AND ATTITUDE OF SUPERVISOR
IN REGARD TO DECISION MAKING

Supervisor's Attitude	No. of Supervisors	No. of Their Subordinates: who report decision-making	who do not report decision-making	Total
Retains decision-making	11	5	28	33
Permits decision-making by subordinates	9	10	14	24
Requires decision-making by subordinates	1	5	0	5
Total	21	20	42	62

characteristics and decision-making among scientists whose supervisors permit decision-making by subordinates, we find that all scientists who report decision-making have legitimizing characteristics, while all but three of those who do not report decision-making do not have legitimizing characteristics. I should remind you, in connection with the significance level of this table, that the criteria of legitimizing characteristics

TABLE 2

DECISION MAKING AND LEGITIMIZING CHARACTERISTICS AMONG SCIENTISTS WHOSE SUPERVISORS PERMIT DECISION MAKING BY SUBORDINATES

Decision-making	Legitimizing Characteristics Have	Do not have	Total
Report	10	0	10
Do not report	3	11	14
Total	13	11	24

$p = .0001$, Fisher exact test, one-tailed

are based in part on a fitting operation, and the level of significance is as much an indicator of how good a fit can be made as it is anything else.

Turning now to the scientists whose supervisors retain decision-making power (Table 3), we find that four of the five who report decision-making activities have legitimizing characteristics. We were interested in how *any* of these five could have decision-making activities, *particularly* the individual who did not have legitimizing characteristics, when their supervisors were definite about making all important decisions themselves. We therefore returned to interview protocols of the five and did something like a deviant case analysis. We found first that the supervisor of the scientist who did not have legitimizing characteristics vacillated between retaining decision-making power himself, and *requiring* decision-making of his subordinates. He wanted to do things himself, and he also wanted his subordinates to stand on their own feet, and he swung between demanding the one or the other. The subordinate who is one of the paradoxical five had just not caught up with the latest swing. There was some indication on the subordinate's protocol, in the form of confusion over

TABLE 3

DECISION MAKING AND LEGITIMIZING CHARACTERISTICS AMONG SCIENTISTS WHOSE SUPERVISORS RETAIN DECISION MAKING POWER

Decision-making	Legitimizing Characteristics		
	Have	Do Not Have	Total
Report	4	1	5
Do not report	9	19	28
Total	13	20	33

$p = .07$, Fisher exact test, one-tailed

the extent to which his supervisor worked together with him, that the relationship was not smooth, and that the subordinate might drop decision-making. The other four, all of whom *had* legitimizing characteristics, had been able to parlay their legitimizing characteristics, persistence and, in some cases, ingenuity, into a restructuring of their jobs within their supervisor's definitions of the situation. One of these individuals was the "fixture" I mentioned. He had been with his group longer than anyone else, including the supervisor, and he went his own way, secure in his status as grand old man. Another of these individuals had managed to convince his supervisor that when he, the scientist, made policy decisions, he was following through on leads the supervisor had given him.

The five subordinates of the supervisor who required that they make those decisions which fell within their own area, all reported decision-making activities. The supervisor here is a man who is highly respected in his specialty, recognizes his own competence, and demands similar competence from his subordinates. All his subordinates but the individual who lacks legitimizing characteristics think the world of him. But the fellow without the legitimizing characteristics complains that when he came to the organization he accepted one sort of job, and now he has another. He feels uncomfortable in his present job. Oddly enough, he feels that he doesn't have much influence, in spite of his performing decision-making activities. His summary of the situation is: "I guess I'm developing an inferiority complex by being here."

To summarize: legitimizing characteristics are used in this situation as a basis for shared evaluations of the competence of the scientist to make policy decisions. With one exception, all scientists who are not required to perform decision-making activities, but who nevertheless do so, have legitimizing characteristics. Where the supervisor assumes decision-making himself, some of the scientists who have legitimizing characteristics seem able to compete with him successfully. The report of a scientist who does not have legitimizing characteristics, but is *required* to perform decision-making in spite of the lack suggests that legitimizing characteristics are important to the scientist in that they justify to him and to others his adoption of a particular role.

The conclusion we would draw from all this is that it is important to consider the factors which have to do with social sanction for the performance of a role whenever we consider either problems of filling particular roles, or problems of individual reaction to assigned roles.

38. OBSERVATION OF A BUSINESS DECISION*

Richard M. Cyert, Herbert A. Simon, and Donald B. Trow[1]

Decision-making—choosing one course of action rather than another, finding an appropriate solution to a new problem posed by a changing world—is commonly asserted to be the heart of executive activity in business. If this is so, a realistic description and theory of the decision-making process are of central importance to business administration and organization theory. Moreover, it is extremely doubtful whether the only considerable body of decision-making theory that has been available in the past—that provided by economics—does in fact provide a realistic account of decision-making in large organizations operating in a complex world.

In economics and statistics the rational choice process is described somewhat as follows:

(1) An individual is confronted with a number of different, specified alternative courses of action.

(2) To each of these alternatives is attached a set of consequences that will ensue if that alternative is chosen.

(3) The individual has a system of preferences or "utilities" that permit him to rank all sets of consequences according to preference and to choose that alternative that has the preferred consequences. In the case of business decisions the criterion for ranking is generally assumed to be profit.

If we try to use this framework to describe how real human beings go about making choices in a real world, we soon recognize that we need to incorporate in our description of the choice process several elements that are missing from the economic model:

(1) The alternatives are not usually "given" but must be sought, and hence it is necessary to include the search for alternatives as an important part of the process.

(2) The information as to what consequences are attached to which

* Journal of Business, 29, 1956.

[1] Graduate School of Industrial Administration, Carnegie Institute of Technology. This is a preliminary report on research carried out under a grant from the Ford Foundation for studies in organization and decision-making. The authors are grateful to the Foundation for its support, to the executives of the company that opened its doors to them, and to colleagues and graduate students who have assisted at various stages of data collection and analysis.

alternatives is seldom a "given," but, instead, the search for consequences is another important segment of the decision-making task.

(3) The comparisons among alternatives are not usually made in terms of simple, single criterion like profit. One reason is that there are often important consequences that are so intangible as to make an evaluation in terms of profit difficult or impossible. In place of searching for the "best" alternative, the decision-maker is usually concerned with finding a *satisfactory* alternative—one that will attain a specified goal and at the same time satisfy a number of auxiliary conditions.

(4) Often, in the real world, the problem itself is not a "given," but, instead, searching for significant problems to which organizational attention should be turned becomes an important organizational task.

Decisions in organizations vary widely with respect to the extent to which the decision-making process is *programmed*. At one extreme we have repetitive, well-defined problems (e.g., quality control or production lot-size problems) involving tangible considerations, to which the economic models that call for finding the best among a set of pre-established alternatives can be applied rather literally. In contrast to these highly programmed and usually rather detailed decisions are problems of a non-repetitive sort, often involving basic long-range questions about the whole strategy of the firm or some part of it, arising initially in a highly unstructured form and requiring a great deal of the kinds of search processes listed above. In this whole continuum, from great specificity and repetition to extreme vagueness and uniqueness, we will call decisions that lie toward the former extreme *programmed*, and those lying toward the latter end *non-programmed*. This simple dichotomy is just a shorthand for the range of possibilities we have indicated.

It is our aim in the present paper to illustrate the distinctions we have introduced between the traditional theory of decision, which appears applicable only to highly programmed decision problems, and a revised theory, which will have to take account of the search processes and other information processes that are so prominent in and characteristic of non-programmed decision-making. We shall do this by recounting the stages through which an actual problem proceeded in an actual company and then commenting upon the significance of various items in this narrative for future decision-making theory.

The decision was captured and recorded by securing the company's permission to have a member of the research team present as an observer in the company's offices on substantially a full-time basis during the most active phases of the decision process. The observer spent most of his time with the executive who had been assigned the principal responsibility for handling this particular problem. In addition, he had full access to the files for information about events that preceded his period of observation and also interviewed all the participants who were involved to a major degree in the decision.

THE ELECTRONIC DATA-PROCESSING DECISION

The decision process to be described here concerns the feasibility of using electronic data-processing equipment in a medium size corporation that engages both in manufacturing and in selling through its own widely scattered outlets. In July, 1952, the company's controller assigned to Ronald Middleton, an assistant who was handling several special studies in the accounting department, the task of keeping abreast of electronic developments. The controller, and other accounting executives, thought that some of the current developments in electronic equipment might have application to the company's accounting processes. He gave Middleton the task of investigation, because the latter had a good background for understanding the technical aspects of computers.

Middleton used three procedures to obtain information: letters to persons in established computer firms, discussions with computer salesmen, and discussions with persons in other companies that were experimenting with the use of electronic equipment in accounting. He also read the current journal literature about computer developments. He informed the controller about these matters principally through memorandums that described the current status of equipment and some of the procedures that would be necessary for an applications study in the company. Memorandums were written in November, 1952, October, 1953, and January, 1954. In them, in addition to summarizing developments, he recommended that two computer companies be asked to propose possible installations in the company and that the company begin to adapt its accounting procedures to future electronic processing.

In the spring of 1954 a computer company representative took the initiative to propose and make a brief equipment application study. In August he submitted a report to the company recommending an installation, but this was not acted upon—doubt as to the adequacy of the computer company's experience and knowledge in application being a major factor in the decision. A similar approach was made by another computer company in September, 1954, but terminated at an early stage without positive action. These experiences convinced Middleton and other executives, including the controller, that outside help was needed to develop and evaluate possible applications of electronic equipment.

Middleton drew up a list of potential consultants and, by checking outside sources and using his own information, selected Alpha as the most suitable. After preliminary meetings in October and November, 1954, between representatives of Alpha and the company accounting executives, Alpha was asked to develop a plan for a study of the application of electronic data-processing to sales accounting. Additional meetings between Alpha and company personnel were held in February, 1955, and the proposal for the study was submitted to the controller in March.

Although the proposal seemed competent and the price reasonable, it was felt that proposals should be obtained from another consulting firm as a double check. The controller agreed to this and himself selected Beta from Middleton's list. Subsequently representatives of Beta met with Middleton and other department executives. Middleton, in a memorandum to the controller, listed criteria for choosing between the two consultants. On the assumption that the written report from Beta was similar to the oral proposal made, the comparison indicated several advantages for Beta over Alpha.

After the written report was received, on May 2, the company's management committee authorized a consulting agreement with Beta, and work began in July, 1955. The controller established a committee, headed by Middleton, to work on the project. Middleton was to devote full time to the assignment; the other two committee members, one from sales accounting and one from auditing, were to devote one-third time.

The consulting firm assigned two staff members, Drs. Able and Baker, to the study. Their initial meetings with Middleton served the purpose of outlining a general approach to the problem and planning the first few steps. Twenty-three information-gathering studies were defined, which Middleton agreed to carry out, and it was also decided that the consultants would spend some time in field observation of the actual activities that the computer might replace.

During July, Middleton devoted most of his time to the twenty-three studies on volume of transactions and information flow, obtaining data from the sales department and from the field staffs of the other two committee members. Simultaneously, steps were taken to secure the co-operation of the field personnel who would be visited by the consultants early in August.

On July 22 Middleton submitted a progress report to the controller, describing the data-gathering studies, estimating completion dates, and summarizing the program's objectives. On July 25 the consultants met with Middleton and discussed a method of approach to the design of the data-processing system. The field trip took place early in August. The consultants obtained from field personnel information as to how accounting tasks were actually handled and as to the use actually made of information generated by the existing system.

On August 8 Middleton submitted another progress report, giving the status of the data-gathering studies and recording some ideas originating in the field trip for possible changes in the existing information-processing system. On August 10 he arranged with the assistant controller to obtain clerical assistance on the data-gathering studies, so that the consultants would not be held up by lack of this information, and on August 17 this work was completed.

On the following day the consultants met with the company committee to review the results of the twenty-three studies. They then listed the outputs, files, and inputs required by any sales accounting system the company might adopt and drew a diagram showing the flow of the accounting information. The group also met with the assistant controller and with the controller. The latter took the opportunity to emphasize his basic decentralization philosophy.

Upon returning from his vacation early in September, Middleton discussed the flow diagram in greater detail with Able and Baker, and revisions were made on the basis of information Middleton supplied about the present accounting system. Baker pointed out that all the alternative systems available to the company could be defined by the location of seven principal functions and records. Further analysis reduced this number to three: stock records, pricing of orders, and accounts receivable. The possible combinations of locations of these gave eighteen basic alternative systems, of which eight that were obviously undesirable were eliminated. Middleton was to make a cost analysis of the existing system and the most decentralized of the proposed systems, while the consultants were to begin costing the most centralized system.

Middleton reviewed these tentative decisions with the other members of the company committee, and the group divided up the work of costing. Middleton also reported to the controller on the conference, and the latter expressed his attitudes about the location of the various functions and the resulting implications for the development of executive responsibility.

During the next week, in addition to working on his current assignments, Middleton gave an equipment salesman a preliminary overview of the probable requirements of a new system. Next, there was a two-day meeting of the consultants and the company's committee to discuss the form and implications of a centralized electronic system. The consultants presented a method of organizing the records for electronic processing and together with the committee calculated the requirements which this organization and company's volume of transactions would impose on a computer. The group then discussed several problems raised by the system, including the auditing problems, and then met with the assistant controller to review the areas they had discussed.

On the following day, Middleton summarized progress to date for the controller, emphasizing particularly the work that had been done on the centralized system. The controller expressed satisfaction with several new procedures that would be made possible by an electronic computer. During the next several days the committee members continued to gather the information necessary to determine the cost of the present system. Middleton also checked with the assistant controller on the proposed solutions for certain problems that the consultants had indicated could not be handled readily by a computer and relayed his reactions to the consultants.

A week later the consultants returned for another series of meetings. They discussed changes that might be necessary in current practices to make centralized electronic processing possible and the way in which they would compare the centralized and decentralized proposals. The comparison presented some difficulties, since the data provided by the two systems would not be identical. A general form for a preliminary report was cleared with the assistant controller, and a date was set for its submission. The processing, outputs, and costs for the two alternatives would be described, so that additional information required for a final report could be determined.

During the next week Middleton continued collecting cost data. He phoned to the consultants to provide them with important new figures and to inform them of the controller's favorable reaction to certain proposed changes in the system that had implications for the company's policies.

On October 17 Baker met with Middleton to review the content of the accounting reports that would be produced by the centralized system, to discuss plans for the preliminary report, and to discuss the relative advantages and disadvantages of the centralized and decentralized systems. On the next day, Middleton checked on their decisions relative to the report with the controller and assistant controller and raised the possibility of an outside expert being retained by the company to review the final report submitted by Beta. During the last days of this week, Middleton attended the national meeting of a management society, where he obtained information about the availability of computers and computer personnel and the existence of other installations comparable to that contemplated for the company.

Work continued on the planning and costing of the two systems—Middleton worked primarily on the decentralized plan, and the consultants on the centralized. On October 27 the two consultants met with Middleton and they informed each other of the status of their work. Baker discussed methods for evaluating system reliability. Plans for the preliminary report were discussed with the company committee and the assistant controller. Since the controller strongly favored decentralization of authority, the question was raised of the compatibility of this with electronic processing in general and with the centralized system in particular. The groups concluded, however, that centralization of purely clerical data-processing operations was compatible with decentralization of responsibility and authority.

After several meetings between the committee and the consultants to iron out details, the preliminary report was presented to the company committee, the controller, and the assistant controller on November 3.

The report was devoted primarily to the centralized system. The following points were made in the oral presentation: (1) that both the centralized and decentralized proposals would yield substantial and roughly equivalent savings but that the centralized system would provide more and better accounting data; (2) that the alternatives had been costed conservatively; (3) that the centralized system involved centralization of paper work, not of management; (4) that not all problems raised by the centralized system had been worked out in detail but that these did not appear insurmountable; (5) that the centralized system would facilitate improved inventory control; and (6) that its installation would require nine to twelve months at a specified cost. At this meeting the group decided that in the final report only the two systems already considered would be costed, that the final report would be submitted on December 1, and that investigation of other accounting applications of the system would be postponed.

In informal conversations after the meeting the controller told Middleton he had the impression that the consultants strongly favored the centralized system and that he believed the cost considerations were relatively minor compared with the impact the system would have on executives' operating philosophies. The assistant controller told Middleton he thought the preliminary report did not adequately support the conclusions. The committee then reviewed with the assistant controller the reasons for analyzing in detail only the two extreme systems: the others either produced less information or were more costly.

The next day the committee met with the controller and assistant controller to determine what additional information should be requested for the final report. The controller outlined certain questions of practicability that the final report should answer and expressed the view that the report should contain a section summarizing the specific changes that the system would bring about at various levels of the organization. He thought the comparison between systems in the preliminary report had emphasized equivalence of savings, without detailing other less tangible benefits of the centralized system.

Middleton reported these discussions to the consultants and with them developed flow charts and organization charts for inclusion in the final report, settled on some intermediate deadlines, and worked up an outline of the report. Within the company he discussed with the controller and assistant controller the personnel and organizational requirements for installation of an electronic system and for operation after installation. Discussion focused on the general character and organizational location of the eventual electronic-data-processing group, its relation to the sales accounting division, and long-term relations with manufacturing accounting and with a possible operations research group.

On November 14 the controller, on recommendation of Middleton, attended a conference on automation for company senior executives. There he expressed the view that three to five years would be required for full installation of a centralized electronic system but that the fear of obsolescence of equipment should not deter the company in making the investment. He also concluded that a computer installation would not reverse his long-range program for decentralizing information and responsibility.

Middleton, his suggestion being accepted, made tentative arrangements with an independent expert and with two large computer companies for the review of the consultants' report. Middleton presented to the controller and assistant controller a memorandum he had prepared at the latter's request, establishing a new comparison of the centralized and a modified decentralized system. The modification made the two systems more nearly comparable in data-processing capacity, hence clarified the cost comparison, which was now in favor of the centralized system. Consideration of the possibility of starting with a partially electronic decentralized system as a step toward a completely electronic system led to the decision that this procedure had no special advantages. The controller reported that conversations with the sales manager and the president had secured agreement with the concept of removal of stock record-keeping from field locations—an aspect of the plan to which it had been assumed there would be sales department opposition. The group discussed several other specific topics and reaffirmed that the final report should discuss more fully the relative advantages and disadvantages of centralized and decentralized systems.

Toward the end of November there was further consultation on the report, and final arrangements for its review were made with the two equipment companies and the independent expert. Each equipment company was expected to determine the method for setting up the proposed system on its computer and to check the consultants' estimates of computer capacity. During this week the controller informed the company's management committee that the report from the consultants would be submitted shortly and would recommend a rather radical change to electronic data-processing.

The final report, which recommended installation of the centralized system, was submitted on December 1. The report consisted of a summary of recommendations, general description of the centralized system, a discussion of the installation program, and six appendixes: (1) statistics on volume of transactions (the twenty-three studies); (2) costs of the present system; (3) the requirements of a fully centralized system; (4) changes in allocation of functions required by the system; (5) an outline of the alternative decentralized system; and (6) a description of the existing system in verbal and flow-chart form. When the report was received and reviewed initially, the company's committee members and the consultants made some further computations on installation costs.

At a meeting the following Monday the assistant controller proposed an action program: send copies of the report to equipment companies, send copies to the sales department, and await the report of the independent expert. The controller decided that the second and third steps should be taken before giving the report to the machine companies, and the assistant controller indicated to Middleton some points requiring further clarification and elaboration.

By January 7 Middleton had prepared an outline for a presentation of the report to the sales department. This was revised on the basis of a meeting with the other interested accounting executives. A final outline was agreed upon after two more revisions and three more meetings. The report was presented on January 28 to the president and to six of the top executives of the sales department. The presentation discussed large-scale computers briefly, described with flow charts the proposed system, emphasized the completeness and accuracy of the information produced, discussed costs and savings, and mentioned the current trend in other companies toward electronic data-processing.

At Middleton's recommendation the same presentation was made subsequently to top members of the accounting department and still later to a group from the manufacturing department. At the same time the preliminary report of the independent expert was received, agreeing that the electronic installation seemed justifiable and stating that there might not be any cost savings but that it would make possible numerous other profitable applications of the computer. The consultants' report was then distributed to the computer companies, and Middleton began more detailed planning of the installation.

Middleton, the assistant controller, and the controller now met with the independent expert, who reported his conclusions: the feasibility study was excellent, the estimates of processing time were probably optimistic, the installation program should provide for an early test run, and the two principal available computers were highly competitive. Independent comfirmation had been obtained on the last two points from another outside source. Middleton now proposed that the company proceed with its planning while awaiting the final written report from the independent expert and the proposals of the equipment companies. The assistant controller preferred to wait until these reports were actually in hand.

During the next week the equipment companies proceeded with their analysis, meeting several times with Middleton. Baker sent a memorandum on his estimates of processing time to meet the criticism of the independent expert. Middleton prepared two charts, one proposing a schedule and the staffing requirements for the installation phase, the other proposing organizational arrangements for the computer center. Middleton and the assistant controller presented these to the controller at the beginning of February, discussion centering responsibility for accuracy of input information.

Middleton and the assistant controller also had a meeting with sales executives who reported that on the basis of their own internal departmental discussions of the consultants' report they were in general agreement with the program. Middleton and one of the other committee members then spent two days inspecting computer installations in two other companies.

In the middle of February the two equipment companies presented their reports, each bringing a team of three or four men to present their recommendations orally. The two recommendations were substantially alike (except for the brand of the machine recommended!), but one report emphasized the availability of its personnel to give help during the installation planning stage.

Discussions were held in the accounting department and with consultant Baker about these reports and the next steps to be taken. The question was debated whether a commitment should be made to one equipment company or whether a small group should continue planning the system in detail, postponing the equipment decision until fall. Most of the group preferred the former alternative.

On February 15 the controller, in conference with the assistant controller and Middleton, dictated a letter to the company's president summarizing the conclusions and recommendations of the study and requesting that the accounting department be authorized to proceed with the electronics program.

On the following day the controller read the letter to the management committee. The letter reviewed briefly the history of the project and summarized the conclusions contained in the consultants' report: that there was ample justification for an electronic-data-processing installation; that the installation would warrant use of the largest computers; and that it would produce savings, many intangible benefits, and excess computer capacity for other applications. The letter quoted the consultants' estimate of the cost of the installation and their recommendation that the company proceed at once to make such a conversion and to acquire the necessary equipment. It then cited the various cross-checks that had been made of the consultants' report and concluded with a repetition of the conclusions of the report—but estimating more conservatively the operating and installation costs—and a request for favorable management committee action. Supplementary information presented included a comparison of consultant and equipment company cost estimates and a list of present and proposed computer installations in other companies. After a few questions and brief discussion, the management committee voted favorably on the recommendation, and the controller informed Middleton of the decision when the meeting ended.

THE ANATOMY OF THE DECISION

From this narrative, or more specifically from the actual data on which the narrative is based, one can list chronologically the various activities of which the decision process is composed. If we wish to describe a program for making a decision of this kind, each of these activities might be taken as one of the steps of the program. If the rules that determined when action would switch from one program step to another were specified, and if the program steps were described in enough detail, it would be possible to replicate the decision process.

The program steps taken together define in retrospect, then, a program for an originally unprogrammed decision. The program would be an inefficient one because it would contain all the false starts and blind alleys of the original process, and some of these could presumably be avoided if the process were repeated. However, describing the process that took place in terms of such a program is a useful way of organizing the data for purposes of analysis.

In order to make very specific what is meant here by a "program," Chart 1 has been prepared to show the broad outlines of the actual program for the first stages of the decision process (through the first seven paragraphs of the narrative).

CHART 1
Program Steps from Inception of the Problem to Selection of a Consultant

KEEPING-UP PROGRAM (paragraphs 1 and 2 of narrative):
   Search for and correspond with experts;
   Discuss with salesmen and with equipment users;
   Search for and read journals;

PROCUREMENT PROGRAM (paragraph 3):
   Discuss applications study with salesmen who propose it;
   Choice: accept or reject proposed study;
   (If accepted) transfer control to salesmen;
   Choice: accept or reject applications proposal;
   (If rejected) switch to consultant program;

CONSULTANT PROGRAM (paragraphs 4 through 7):
   Search for consultants;
   Choice: best consultant of several;
   Transfer control to chosen consultant;
   Choice: accept or reject proposal;
   (If accepted): begin double-check routine;
   Request expenditure of funds;
   (If authorized) transfer control to consultants;
   And so on.

Subprograms. The various program steps of the decision process fall into several subprograms, some of which have been indicated in Chart 1. These subprograms are ways of organizing the activities *post factum*, and in Chart 1 the organizing principle is the method of approach taken by the company to the total problem. It remains a question as to whether this organizing principle will be useful in all cases. As in the present example, these subprograms may sometimes be false starts, but these must be regarded as parts of the total program, for they may contribute information for later use, and their outcomes determine the switching of activity to new subprograms.

In this particular case the reasons for switching from one subprogram to another were either the proved inadequacy of the first one or a redefinition of the problem. Other reasons for switching can be imagined, and a complete theory of the decision process will have to specify the conditions under which the switch from one line of attack to another will occur.

Common Processes. In the whole decision-making program there are certain steps or "routines" that recur within several of the subprograms; they represent the basic activities of which the whole decision process is composed. For purposes of discussion we have classified these common processes in two categories: the first comprises processes relating to the communication requirements of the organization; the second comprises processes relating directly to the solution of the decisional problem.

Communication Processes. Organizational decision-making requires a variety of communication activities that are absent when a decision is made in a single human head. If we had written out the program steps in greater detail, many more instances of contacts among different members of the organization would be recorded than are now explicit in the narrative. The contacts may be oral or written. Oral contacts are used for such purposes as giving orders, transmitting information, obtaining approval or criticism of proposed action; written communications generally take the form of memorandums having the purpose of transmitting information or proposing action.

The information-transmitting function is crucial to organizational decision-making, for it almost always involves acts of selection or "filtering" by the informational source. In the present instance, which is rather typical in this respect, the consultants and subordinate executives are principal information sources; and the controller and other top executives must depend upon them for most of their technical information. Hence, the subordinate acts as an information filter and in this way secures a large influence over the decisions the superior can and does reach.

The influence of the information source over communications is partly controlled by checking processes—for example, retaining an independent expert to check consultants—which give the recipient an independent information source. This reduces, but by no means eliminates, filtering. The great differences in the amounts and kinds of information available to the various participants in the decision process described here emphasize the significance of filtering. It will be important to determine the relationship of the characteristics of the information to the resultant information change and to explore the effects of personal relations between people on the filtering process and hence upon the transmission of information.

Problem-Solving Processes. Alongside the organizational communication processes, we find in the narrative a number of important processes directed toward the decision problem itself. One of the most prominent of these is the search for alternative courses of action. The first activities recounted in the narrative—writing letters, reading journals, and so on— were attempts to discover possible action alternatives. At subsequent points in the process searches were conducted to obtain lists of qualified consultants and experts. In addition to these, there were numerous searches—most of them only implicit in the condensed narrative—to find action alternatives that would overcome specific difficulties that emerged as detail was added to the broader alternatives.

The data support strongly the assertion made in the introduction that searches for alternative courses of action constitute a significant part of non-programmed decision-making—a part that is neglected by the classical theory of rational choice. In the present case the only alternatives that became available to the company without the expenditure of time and effort were the systems proposals made early in the process by representatives of two equipment companies, and these were both rejected. An important reason for the prominent role of search in the decision process is that the "problem" to be solved was in fact a whole series of "nested" problems, each alternative solution to a problem at one level leading to a new set of problems at the next level. In addition, the process of solving the substantive problems created many procedural problems for the organization: allocating time and work, planning agendas and report presentations, and so on.

Examination of the narrative shows that there is a rich variety of search processes. Many questions remain to be answered as to what determines the particular character of the search at a particular stage in the decision process: the possible differences between searches for procedural alternatives, on the one hand, and for substantive alternatives, on the other; the factors that determine how many alternatives will be sought before a choice is made; the conditions under which an alternative that has tentatively been chosen will be subjected to further check; the general types of search strategies.

The neglect of the search for alternatives in the classical theory of decision would be inconsequential if the search were so extensive that most of the alternatives available "in principle" were generally discovered and considered. In that case the search process would have no influence upon the alternative finally selected for action. The narrative suggests that this is very far from the truth—that, in fact, the search for alternatives terminates when a satisfactory solution has been discovered even though the field of possibilities has not been exhausted. Hence, we have reason to suppose that changes in the search process or its outcome will actually have major effects on the final decision.

A second class of common processes encompasses information-gathering and similar activity aimed at determining the consequences of each of several alternatives. In many decisions, certainly in the one we observed, these activities account for the largest share of man-hours, and it is through them that subproblems are discovered. The narrative suggests that there is an adverse relation between the cost or difficulty of this investigational task and the number of alternative courses of action that are examined carefully. Further work will be needed to determine if this relation holds up in a broader range of situations. The record also raises numerous questions about the *kinds* of consequences that are examined most closely or at all and about the conditions under which selection of criteria for choice is prior to, or subsequent to, the examination of consequences.

Another set of common processes are those concerned with the choices among alternatives. Such processes appear at many points in the narrative: the selection of a particular consulting firm from a list, the choice between centralized and decentralized electronic-data-processing systems, as well as numerous more detailed choices. These are the processes most closely allied to the classical theory of choice, but even here it is notable that traditional kinds of "maximizing" procedures appear only rarely.

In some situations the choice is between competing alternatives, but in many others it is one of acceptance or rejection of a single course of action—really a choice between doing *something* at this time and doing nothing. The first such occasion was the decision by the controller to assign Middleton to the task of watching developments in electronics, a decision that initiated the whole sequence of later choices. In decisions of this type the consequences of the single alternative are judged against some kind of explicit or implicit "level of aspiration"—perhaps expressed in terms of an amount of improvement over the existing situation—while in the multiple-alternative situations, the consequences of the several alternatives are compared with each other. This observation raises a host of new questions relating to the circumstances under which the decision will be formulated in terms of the one or the other of these frameworks and the personal and organizational factors that determine the aspiration levels that will be applied in the one-alternative case.

Another observation derivable from our data—though it is not obvious from the condensed narrative given here—is that comparability and non-comparability of the criteria of choice affects the decision processes in significant ways. For one thing, the criteria are not the same from one choice to another: one choice may be made on the basis of relative costs and savings, while the next may be based entirely on non-monetary criteria. Further, few, if any, of the choices were based on a single criterion. Middleton and the others recognized and struggled with this problem of comparing consequences that were sometimes measured in different, and incomparable, units, and even more often involved completely intangible considerations. The narrative raises, but does not answer, the question of how choices are made in the face of these incommensurabilities and the degree to which tangible considerations are overemphasized or underemphasized as compared with intangibles as a result.

CONCLUSION

We do not wish to try to transform one swallow into a summer by generalizing too far from a single example of a decision process. We have tried to illustrate, however, using a large relatively non-programmed decision in a business firm, some of the processes that are involved in business decision-making and to indicate the sort of theory of the choice mechanism that is needed to accommodate these processes. Our illustration suggests that search processes and information-gathering processes constitute significant parts of decision-making and must be incorporated in a theory of decision if it is to be adequate. While the framework employed here—and particularly the analysis of a decision in terms of a hierarchical structure of *programs*—is far from a complete or finished theory, it appears to provide a useful technique of analysis for researchers interested in the theory of decision as well as for business executives who may wish to review the decision-making procedures of their own companies.

Research Techniques

Like most of the social sciences, organization theory is only now progressing beyond the methodological stage of armchair theorizing and casual empiricism. In fact, a large share of the recent work in social science represents the later phases of this stage: logically rigorous speculation and thoughtful, though impressionistic, case analyses. The work by Weber and Barnard in Section Two exemplifies these techniques at their best. Both of these authors are unexcelled as social theorists and have been able to buttress their generalizations by an abundance of appeals to the facts of organizational life.

Developments in the technique of research since the turn of this century have led to a change in tone in the behavioral sciences. In fact, the increase in methodological rigor can almost be used as a definition of behavioral science, as opposed to the older social science. This trend was given impetus by the successes of physical and biological sciences with precise techniques of experimentation. In the behavioral sciences, emphasis on rigorous techniques came first in individual psychology with three main lines of advance: psychophysical measurements, mental testing, and learning experiments. It spread into social psychology with attitude scaling and sociometry. These threads have since been developed, ramified, and intertwined until their influence is felt in every branch of social science including economics, sociology, and political science.

There is a great difference between the physical sciences and the social sciences, with the biological sciences perhaps falling in between, in the degree of difficulty of deciding what dimensions of the phenomena to measure. Classical physics requires no more than the measurement of position and the rates of change of position. Such a simple-minded approach has not proved fruitful in other sciences. The importance of counting chromosomes in cell nuclei is not obvious to the uninitiated. Similarly, the process of turning answers to a typical attitude or personality test into measurements of the basic personality structure of an individual seem little short of mystical to the layman. In almost any investigation in social science, whether experimental or nonexperimental, the most difficult problems are those of measurement. This process is usually referred to as *scaling* if the researcher is hypothesizing differences of degree in a variable, and as *coding* if classification of behavior by kind is required. In the Horsfall and Arensberg article, scaling of interaction rates was achieved on the basis of a who-to-whom interaction recording. In the RAND studies the observers had to find a measurement for "discomfort stress." Cleven and Fiedler scaled "assumed similarity between opposites" on the basis of a questionnaire. Similar statements could be made about other empirical investigations reported in this book. It is hard to overstate the importance of reliable coding and scaling procedures for the development and testing of theories.

This section will attempt to survey the methodology of empirical study in much the same way that the first section attempted to survey the methodology of theorizing. Our focus will be on organization theory, and not on the general subject (1). The techniques and general methodological considerations discussed here are of interest to the student of organization for two reasons. First, an understanding of them is indispensable to a proper assessment of the meaning and validity of the results of research in the behavioral sciences. Second, as a technique for developing new knowledge they have potential usefulness not only to the professional researcher but also to any practitioner who wishes to learn systematically about the organizational processes in his own environment. In any of these pursuits, the student can no more ignore the details of research technique than he can avoid the philosophical issues discussed in the first section.

Some Questions of Taste

It seems advisable to dispose immediately of some questions of only superficial significance for the development of knowledge, but of profound effect on the course of any individual piece of research and the source of much sound and fury within the research professions themselves: the tastes of the researcher. The more important of these questions hark back to our discussion in Section One, but they are more appropriately discussed here, where the specifics can be more fully appreciated.

The big questions generally turn around whether research shall be empirical or theoretical, and whether it is to be an applied project or basic research. The usual polar positions have been, on the one hand, those who like their research empirical (close to the facts) and applied (of direct usefulness to some cause or other) and, on the other hand, those who prefer to work theoretically (with complex and immaculate logic) and on basic questions (interesting and exciting ones). These poles are represented in the present volume by Comrey's piece in Section Five and by the material on decision theory in Section Six. Nevertheless, the two dimensions cited are independent, and this is demonstrable by large bodies of work which unfortunately are not represented in this collection. As examples of theoretical applied work, one could cite numerous operations research studies. Basic empirical research is represented in the study of business organizations by the Harvard case collections. The contemporary resolution of the empirical-theoretical issue has been alluded to in Section One. Solid work in any field, including organization theory, must stand on both legs: worthwhile empirical knowledge is bound to be theoretical in nature; useful theories must stand up empirically. The dilemma of applied versus basic research also has a paradoxical outcome: history teaches that any sound contribution to basic knowledge is potentially exploitable; conversely, any knowledge that is consistently found useful in practice eventually gets incorporated into a scientific discipline. Thus, the empirical-theoretical issue comes to a focus on a fundamental characteristic of science; the basic-applied one evaporates into the pragmatic politics of research administration.

On these large questions the individual researcher has considerable room for choice in planning his work. If he likes facts, he can confine himself to testing existing theories or looking for empirical laws. If he has a taste for logic, he can attempt to reformulate and extend theories. Similar and less global choices have to be made in the execution of research. A theoretician must decide whether to restrict himself to verbalization or whether to employ formal logic and mathematics in his work. The choices confronted by the empirical researcher are the subject of the remainder of this section. All these choices are in large part matters of style; in other respects, they are determined by immediate objectives of the researcher. As in the Horsfall and Arensberg article in Section Two, the objective may be the testing of a technique (interaction recording). The studies by Haberstroh and by Cyert, Simon, and Trow in Sections Five and Six were also primarily intended for the development of research methods, rather than findings. The studies by Jacobson and Seashore and Tannenbaum and Kahn, mentioned in Sections Four and Five, centered about the development of new research instruments, a communication matrix and a control graph. On a more general level, the entire program of the University of Michigan Human Relations Program heavily utilized survey studies because of the high development and availability of this technique.

The choice of research methods has, of course, strategic importance. Success comes only if the method is well suited to the problem to be investigated. This does not diminish the importance of the method and problem also being well suited to the investigator. We turn now to a discussion of the specific choices and some of the important considerations involved.

Research Design

In Section One the relation of *experimental methods* to organization theory was briefly discussed. The subsequent sections have provided illustrations of the application of experimental methods and also of the various other approaches to empirical research on organizations. Although experimental studies are important, it is clear that most of our knowledge of organizations has not been gained from experimentation. An appreciable portion has come from the somewhat softer *survey techniques*. The major share has come, however, from various forms of the still softer method of *field studies*. Much as we might want to subject the entire body of knowledge to the stricter discipline of the controlled experiment, this is not likely to be achieved any time soon. The possibility of adopting a "know nothing" attitude toward those parts of organization theory not backed up by solid experimentation is likewise not open to the responsible student of organizational behavior and especially not to the practicing manager.

Of the studies reported in this book, the small-group experiments by Asch and Guetzkow and Simon are the only examples of strictly experimental technique. Neither of these experiments involved an *organization*; instead, both examine aspects of *social behavior* that are relevant to organizational functioning. In both cases, representative examples of *homo sapiens* were placed in a carefully controlled social situation and their behavior noted under various contrasting conditions. This can be compared with the RAND Corporation study in Section Two. In that study the object of investigation was an organization, but an artificial one. The RAND researchers put their organization together from bits and pieces supplied by the Air Force or manufactured by the experimenters. The resulting method is analogous to the Asch experiment if, instead of recruiting college students, the experimenter had commissioned Baron Frankenstein to raid graveyards and anatomy labs and manufacture the subjects. The RAND study is very close to an experiment in organization theory, but not quite; it is referred to as a *simulation* study rather than an experimental study. The corresponding experiment would be to subject a genuine air defense control center (unbeknownst to the participants) to an artificial task environment. The study in Section Six by Lorge, *et al.*, is parallel in method to the RAND study, being an experimental treatment of simulated staffs and commanders.

Genuinely experimental studies have been conducted in organizations. The most famous example was part of the Hawthorne studies mentioned in Section Three. In this example, a factory work group was placed under carefully controlled conditions for investigation of the effects of various experimental manipulations on their productivity. More recently, experiments have been carried out by the Michigan group and elsewhere (2).

In passing from experimental methods, we lose the important characteristic of being able to intervene actively in the situation, to make changes so as to study the effects of those changes. Survey and observational methods are like experiments, however, in that they can provide reliable data and in that the design of the investigation is usually pre-established. The establishment of control over the data-gathering process is an important step for several reasons. It permits independent observers to come to the same conclusion about the facts at least, even though they may differ with respect to interpretation of the facts. When there is added the condition of a predetermined design for the study, even non-experimental observation and survey work can be made to verify or refute theoretical predictions. Even more than in the case of experimental studies, however, careful attention is required to statistical questions in order to isolate the effects of observational errors, unexplained variation, and explained variation.

Many of the studies in this volume illustrate this use of survey techniques. In Section Two the Cleven and Fiedler study makes use of reliable measurement in both the ASo personality testing instrument and in the plant records of work-team performance. Their statistical design partials out the effect of the personality characteristic from the net effect of the other determinants of productivity. The Michigan survey studies discussed in the article by Pelz and in the introduction to Section Three also give good examples of this technique.

Surveys are also used without any preformulated theoretical propositions to test. In the Davis and Rubenstein studies in Section Four, and in Comrey's study in Section Five, reliable measuring devices were developed and used in an exploratory way toward the discovery of interesting empirical relationships. The possibility of testing theories is lost in such investigations, but the results may, nevertheless, yield useful results.

Surveys almost invariably use one of two kinds of data-collection instruments. The most common one is the precoded questionnaire, which is either sent by mail, handed to the informant by the researcher, or used by the researcher in an interview. In any case, the important characteristic is that any scaling or coding which is necessary is done by the informant and not by the researcher. The use of this kind of an instrument almost invariably limits the usefulness of the results to the specific purpose intended by the original research design. Only rarely can any secondary analysis be made. The premium here is on the design of the questionnaire. If it is not expertly done, the study is a total loss. Some insurance against this eventuality can be provided by more or less elaborate pretests before the major part of the study is undertaken. In addition an instrument, once developed and validated, can often be applied again and again in studying different but related questions. The psychologists' inventory of personality and attitude tests is the best-known example.

The second method is the open-end interview (3). Here the questions posed to the informant are phrased somewhat more generally and he is encouraged to express his answers fully and in any way he wishes. The interview is usually recorded verbatim, although sometimes it may be coded or scaled immediately by the interviewer. The use of this technique permits the study of problems of a different kind than are suitable for the precoded questionnaire, since the dimensions used in the analysis need not be ones that the typical informant can understand and respond to reliably. It also permits reappraisal of the original design and secondary analysis if the results turn out to be puzzling. The principal advantage of using a survey technique is that it is relatively quick and cheap. If the data-collection process is well standardized, it is usually possible to train ordinary clerical help to do the job.

Another important characteristic of the survey method is the possibility that it affords for making generalizations about a large population on the basis of a relatively small sample. This, however, requires probability sampling and must be built into the design of the investigation in advance. The art of taking such samples is well developed in current survey practice. Rubenstein's design in Section Four, for the study of communication activities of research teams included provision for random sampling of communication acts. The technique required the interviewers to enter the research labs at randomly chosen times and administer questionnaires to the research team members concerning their activities during the preceding fifteen minutes and the types of communication in which they had engaged.

A few observational studies of organizational behavior have also been intended to produce generalizations about some population. A good example is the Michigan conference research (4). In this study a sample of 72 decision-making conferences in organizations were observed. The methods of observation were quite similar to the interaction recording technique used by Horsfall and Arensberg but were adapted to record, in addition to the simple who-to-whom aspect, dimensions of conference process, style of meeting, need-orientation of the participants' acts, etc. These conferences were not chosen in any random manner, but the sample was large enough so that the researchers could hope to demonstrate empirical relationships common to all decision-making conferences. A group at Columbia applied the technique of random sampling of communication acts mentioned in the last paragraph to strictly observational methods (5). The observers, stationed in a large office, would observe at randomly chosen times the communication activities of each of the population of executives being studied. After recording the executive's actions for the appropriate interval, the observer questioned him as to the meaning of each action.

The difference between these two studies and that of Horsfall and Arensberg highlights the major distinction between the types of research just discussed (experiment and survey) and the third type (field study) which we are about to begin discussing. The conference research had as its objective the demonstration of empirical relationships common to all decision-making conferences. The researchers, therefore, had little need to explore the relationship of the decision-making conference to the organization as a whole. The investigation centered on small-group behavior, not organizational behavior. The Columbia study, although confined to a single office, was intended to investigate a characteristic of the population of all executives in the office, relating their communication rates to their effectiveness in their job. Horsfall and Arensberg, on the other hand, were interested in the phenomenon of informal organization. The observer took a great deal of time to familiarize himself with the technical operations of the shoe factory and the social structure of the work team that he was going to observe. This additional information was indispensable in interpreting the results of the interaction recordings. Their empirical findings apply only to the single case, although the hypotheses were theoretically derived and therefore can be cast as generalizations.

Most of the empirical studies reported in this volume, including Horsfall and Arensberg, Selznick, Dalton, Chowdry and Pal, Argyris, Caplow, Blau, Haberstroh, Hemphill and Sechrest, Weiss, and Cyert, Simon and Trow, were field studies of a single organization. In each there is an attempt to relate diverse aspects of the organization's functioning, a type of investigation not too well adapted to survey techniques. In no case was there any attempt to manipulate the organization for experimental or other reasons. The problem and techniques of these field studies are similar to those of anthropological studies of primitive cultures.

The field study has a similarity to survey techniques in that one of its major problems is to avoid any influence on the phenomena it seeks to study. This is the opposite of the experimental technique, in which the investigator seeks to manipulate important variables. In both cases, however, the problem is one of control, whether it is creating or avoiding changes in the system studied. In field studies reliance is usually placed on the investigator's eventually becoming accepted, and then ignored, in the organizational setting. Data is not usually collected until after the first wave of surprise and curiosity has subsided and there is evidence of the restoration of "business as usual." This technique is thought by most researchers to be successful.

A major difference between the field study and other methods is frequently in the lack of a preconceived design for the study. This feature is advantageous if the objective of the study is to develop specific research technques or if there is uncertainty as to what the significant questions are. Both of these conditions are frequently found in work on organizational behavior. A disadvantage is that the findings are never as convincing as if demonstrated by a more rigorous technique. Selznick deals with this point in discussing his methodology for "TVA and the Grass Roots" in Section Two. Another disadvantage is that the field study cannot usually make use of standard clerical procedures such as have been developed for survey methods. The cost is therefore relatively high, although the risk of complete failure is low.

Since the field study usually contemplates a relatively long period of time, it admits the possibility of a progressive formalizing of the research design, bringing to bear some of the specific techniques more usually associated with experimental, observational, or survey research. For example, in the Hawthorne studies the researchers were able to isolate and manipulate one work group and to introduce an observer into a second. Although an experimental design was contemplated and executed in the case of the first group, the manipulations were a total failure and the significant finding was a result of the researchers' familiarity with the field situation and of the objectivity of the data gathered. More common, probably, are studies in which a survey turns into a field study, as in some of the Michigan human relations research, or in which a field study introduces a survey of the members of the organization, as in Argyris' study in Section Two or the Hemphill and Sechrest study in Section Five.

The simplest technique and a means of getting thoroughly objective data is to use documents or other internal data that are kept by the organization for its own purposes. This was done by Selznick, Cleven and Fiedler, Blau, Haberstroh, Hemphill and Sechrest. Although the data are reliable, their interpretation depends heavily on the researcher's knowledge of the context within which they are generated and used. In many cases, as in records of productivity or finances, documentary data are already scaled and can be used as is. In other cases, as in Selznick's investigation, the documents are used in an impressionistic way as an historian or other institutionalist would use them. In other cases the data are scaled or coded in some way by the researcher. In Haberstroh's study, samples of verbal communication were content analyzed and instances of program innovation were scaled as "none, light, moderate, or heavy." Such coding and scaling techniques at least permit a reliability check on the procedures.

Another very common method in field studies is the use of an informant. Precoded questionnaires can be given to organization members just as in the survey method. The researcher can also use the open-end interview. Other ways of using informants are limited only by the researcher's ingenuity. Informants have been asked to keep logs of their own and others' activities, to submit journalistic reports to the investigator, etc. The continuing contact between researcher and informant is the main distinction from survey methods. As in anthropological studies, a reliable and knowledgeable informant can in practice become almost a fellow researcher.

Another major class includes techniques for the observation of behavior, such as those already discussed above. In some cases (e.g., Dalton, Caplow) the researcher is himself a participant in the organization and happens to encounter a problem warranting concurrent or subsequent analysis. In other cases, an outside researcher spends enough time in the organization to become accepted either as a co-operating member of the group he is studying (e.g., Horsfall) or as "part of the furniture" (Blau, Haberstroh, Trow). Observation techniques vary from those which are quite strictly controlled, as in Horsfall's interaction recording, to those where the observation is entirely impressionistic.

A main advantage of the field study over and above the ability to modify design is the opportunity to employ diverse techniques and thus study the dynamics of the situation in depth. Many of the studies illustrate this. Horsfall and Arensberg combined their interaction recording method with an institutional analysis of the work group, thus giving quantitative verification to the informal group structure hypothesized from the institutional material. Dalton's and Selznick's methods involved a substantial amount of cross-checking of the events and interpretations with various informants in the organization. Blau combined his own observations of events with interaction recording, with the members' recollection of interpersonal events, and with superiors' ratings of the effectiveness of agents. Hemphill and Sechrest combined a questionnaire with the observation of records of performance. Similarly, Haberstroh and Cyert, Simon, and Trow combined observation, interview, and documentary methods.

Reliability of Behavioral Data

Much of the work that has been done in describing or measuring interpersonal relationships has rested on the implicit assumption that reports of events by informants or subjects correspond closely or exactly with the actual way in which the events occurred. If such reports are the only source of data for determining what "really happened," there may be several uncontrolled and even unacknowledged sources of error:

(1) One general source of error is the informant's perceptual slant— his *einstellung* or set. The effect of perceptual slant has been investigated by many students of intergroup prejudice by such means as attitude tests. Perceptual ability is also known to vary and much has been said about

it. Reports of a given event from several witnesses without training in careful observation have often been found to bear little resemblance to each other.

(2) A second general source of error is the informant's failure to remember just what did happen. Assuming that he received a fairly reliable impression of an event at the time that it happened, it has been indicated by experiments in recall and by the experience of all of us that it generally becomes more difficult with passage of time to describe the details of an event as we originally perceived it. A great deal has been said on this matter in relation to the reliability of witness reports weeks or months after the occurrence of the event they have witnessed.

(3) A third general source of error may be the reluctance of the subject, for whatever reason, to report his "true" impression of what occurred. This condition has been encountered often in organizational studies where subjects may distort descriptions of events or interpersonal relationships for fear of retaliation, desire not to upset others, or a general reluctance to verbalize a particular type of situation or event.

(4) Assuming that all of these sources of error have been acknowledged and accounted for, there is a fourth and overriding source of error which is usually explicit in rigorously designed and executed investigations—the inability of the subject to communicate his report; or conversely, the inability of the investigator to get from the subject through whatever techniques (interview, questionnaire, observation) the information that the subject is willing and able to give.

Most of these sources of error are sufficiently predictable so that they can be avoided or even turned to advantage by a skillful researcher. For example, in Section Four, we saw Blau's use of discrepancies in the informants' reports of luncheon partners as indices of "role distortion" and "social attractiveness."

In Conclusion

From this discussion of research technique it is possible to draw a few conclusions as to their influence on the fundamental objective of research: the development of a body of systematic knowledge. Rigor of technique yields directly a way of achieving consensus on matters of fact. It thus also provides the bridge that connects theoretical formulations with the realities of immediate experience. The success of any technique has two measures, a direct one and an indirect one. It is possible directly to demonstrate the reliability or failure of a given technique of observation. If independent interviewers or observers are able to elicit the same measurements from the same body of data, then the first step has been taken and the first success achieved. The second, indirect step is the assessment of the usefulness of the knowledge that is developed by means of the technique. Since this is exposed only to an indirect criterion, the final judgment on it must remain as contentious as the final judgment on the philosophical issues discussed in the first section. Although theoretical statements can be exposed to empirical refutation and research techniques can be exposed to reliability checks, the research enterprise as a whole can be judged only by the more fundamental criterion of usefulness.

By presenting a representative collection of studies of organizational behavior, this book hopes to prepare the reader to form judgments of the usefulness of the present body of knowledge and whatever additions may be made to it in the future. In many instances, the theories and techniques discussed have not yet decisively passed even their direct tests by standing up satisfactorily to empirical verification and reliability checks. Nevertheless, many of them are being tried with varying degrees of success in everyday organizational practice. The role of systematic research is to produce new ideas and to serve as a monitor on the correctness and usefulness of the older ideas. The research enterprise is a repeated cycle of theoretical formulation, derivation of quantitative statistical hypotheses, data collection, statistical analysis and tests, interpretation of the results, comparison with other results, and more theorizing and hypothesizing. The ability and inclination to keep track of this enterprise is the most distinctive characteristic of the professional in all fields, including management.

REFERENCES

1. A number of comprehensive works on research methods in general have appeared in recent years. Among them are: *Handbook of Social Psychology*, Cambridge: Addison-Wesley, 1954, Vol. 1, Part 3; L. Festinger and D. Katz, *Research Methods in the Behavioral Sciences*, New York: Dryden, 1953; C. Selltiz, M. Jahoda, M. Deutsch and S. Cook, *Research Methods in Social Relations*, New York: Holt, 1959; W. Goode and P. Hatt, *Methods in Social Research*, New York: McGraw-Hill, 1952.

2. J. R. P. French, Jr. "Experiments in Field Settings," in L. Festinger and D. Katz, *Research Methods in the Behavioral Sciences*. New York: Dryden, 1953.

3. One of the best volumes on interviewing technique is R. L. Kahn and C. F. Cannell, *The Dynamics of Interviewing*. New York: Wiley, 1957.

4. D. G. Marquis, H. Guetzkow, and R. W. Heyns, "A Social-Psychological Study of the Decision-Making Conference," H. Guetzkow (Ed.), *Groups, Leadership, and Men*, 1951, pp. 55–67. N. Fouriezos, M. Hutt, and H. Guetzkow, "Measurement of Self-Oriented Needs in Discussion Groups," *Journal of Abnormal and Social Psychology*, 1950, Vol. 45, p. 682.

5. Albert H. Rubenstein and Roger Smith, "Communication Measurement in a Purchasing Department," Department of Industrial Engineering, Columbia University. (Unpublished manuscript.)

Exercises

II. 1. What does Weber (Article No. 4) mean by "monocratically organized, hierarchical office authority"?
2. Consider an organization of which you have been a member or which you have known very well—it can be an industrial, military, business, social or other kind of organization.
   a. Describe it briefly.
   b. State briefly what you believe are (or were) the goals of that organization. Use Selznick's (Article No. 5) notion of the evolving character of an organization to describe any changes in objectives.
   c. What characteristics of Weber's (Article No. 4) bureaucracy did your organization exhibit? What characteristics were lacking?
   d. Was an "informal" organization obvious in contrast to the "formal" organization (refer to Barnard—Article No. 6)?
3. Which of the concepts in Weiner can be expressed in terms of Simon's decision-making process (Article No. 11)?
4. Make a 15-minute interaction recording a la Horsfall and Arensberg (Article No. 7) of some group with which you have contact (e.g., fraternity, discussion class, laboratory class, etc.).
5. Compare Selznick's research methods (Article No. 8) with those of Horsfall and Arensberg (Article No. 7): Can you defend the objectivity of these methods? How are they similar to or different from the methods used by a business executive to gather information?
6. Compare the cases of organization studied by Dalton (Article No. 9), Horsfall (Article No. 7), and RAND (Article No. 10)?
   a. Were the systems efficient and effective? What evidence?
   b. What environmental demands were responded to? How?
   c. Were there instances of informal organization, unanticipated consequence, or coöptation? Why did they occur?
7. Apply Lewin's "field theory" principles (Article No. 3) to the theory expounded in the RAND articles (Articles No. 10 and 11). How is each principle observed or violated in the theory?
8. Construct a "theory" of how an organization works, using these concepts from the readings:
   Task Environment (Weiner—Article No. 11)
   Rationality (Simon—Article No. 12)
   Unanticipated Consequences (Selznick—Article No. 8)
   Influence or Power (Simon—Article No. 12)
   Coöptation (Selznick—Article No. 8)
   Legitimacy (Simon—Article No. 12).
9. Explain the shoe factory case in terms of Barnard's theory of coöperation and organization. Identify each of Barnard's concepts and illustrate his principles from the case material.

10. Apply the notion of "equilibrium" to a social example. What is an equilibrium? How could equilibrium be disturbed? What results might ensue?

11. Give an example of "uncertainty absorption" which could occur in the context of the RAND Air Defense Direction Center.

III. 1. In Dalton's case (Article No. 9), the motivational basis for the actions of the various participants was briefly explored. Which of McGregor's (Article No. 13) categories of motives were predominant? Can you find evidence of the operation of McGregor's theoretical principles of motivation?

2. In Chowdhry's case study (Article No. 14) what caused the differences in morale between A and B? Could the management have relieved the situation in A? How?

3. The readings provide a sample of the relatively large amount of research and writing in this complex area:
   a. Drawing from the readings, develop a conceptual scheme or "theory" to describe the relationships (in work groups such as those described in the readings) between:
      Patterns of supervision or leadership
      Interpersonal relationships
      Morale
      Productivity
   b. Be sure to point out any inconsistencies or direct conflicts between the readings.
   c. Drawing from your own experience and ideas, comment briefly on the reasonableness of the conceptual scheme or theory you have developed. Does it fit into your own beliefs about leadership, etc.?

4. Insofar as possible from the data reported by Chowdhry and Pal (Article No. 14), use Argyris' (Article No. 17) framework to describe the state of human relations in the two textile mills.

5. Which of McGregor's need categories were prominent in motivating the shoe factory work teams of Horsfall and Arensberg? Explain.

6. Discuss the role of sanctions, attitudes of legitimacy, and authority in the Dalton case.

7. Make a check list of things to consider in designing an incentive scheme for division managers.

IV. 1. What are the various constraints on control tower language found by Frick and Sumby (Article No. 18)?

2. Considering an individual in an organization as a communication link, outline the factors that affect the amount and kind of information he transmits. Construct a concrete example (from experience, imagination or the readings) of the operation of each factor.

3. Consider the increasing use of committees in the industrial firm. Based on the Asch and Torrance (Articles No. 19 and 20) papers, how would you design a decision-making committee at the corporate level—e.g., a finance committee, an executive committee, a research and development committee. What "control variables" would you use if you were responsible for the continuing effectiveness of the committee—i.e., what "readings" would you take periodically to make sure that the factors of "social pressure" and "disagreement" were under control?

4. What were the major variables that Davis (Article No. 24) found to have an effect on spread of the rumor?

5. Chorus (Article No. 22) presents a "basic law of rumor" with three basic variables affecting the transmission of a rumor. Based on Caplow's article,

   a. Is this law supported by Caplow's findings?

   b. Do Caplow's findings suggest any additional variables that should be included in a "law of rumor"?

6. What three variables were under investigation in Blau's study (Article No. 25)? What was the scale or range of each variable?

7. List and define the variables dealt with by Blau (Article No. 25). Set up as many functional relations as you need to express his findings, using symbolic notation.

8. Referring to Blau's (Article No. 25) hypothesis that *receipts* of interaction are related to *competence:* state and support a hypothesis that related *initiations* of interaction to competence.

V. 1. What are Joel Dean's (Article No. 28) basic assumptions about manager behavior, underlying Dean's proposal for profit-centers?

2. Construct a control flow chart like those in the Haberstroh (Article No. 27) and Rubenstein (Article No. 29) articles to show Dean's system of performance measurement (Article No. 28). Use it to discuss the control properties of Dean's system.

3. Comrey's first major project following the research design you read (Article No. 30) was an evaluation of organizations in the United States Forest Service. What criteria might be used to evaluate a Forest Service Unit? A hospital? A police department?

4. a. Select a specific kind of information group in a company, such as research, cost accounting, production control.

   b. Identify the significant "design variables" of such a group which may have an effect on its information-handling performance. This list of variables might include design variables like size, skill level of members, location, etc.

   c. Specify a number of significant behavior or performance variables which describe the information output and which might serve as

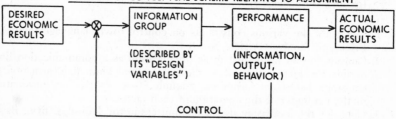

PORTION OF CONCEPTUAL SCHEME RELATING TO ASSIGNMENT

control criteria for the performance of the group. A possible one might be total "amount" of information transferred per time period.

   d. What do you think are the important functional relationships between these two sets of variables—the relationships which may significantly determine the performance of the group? For example, in some cases, a possibly significant relationship might be the one between group size and "amount" of information transferred by the group. The relationship would probably not be linear and it might have some boundaries or thresholds which cut off the range of either variable.

    e. Make a reasonable case for each of these relationships, drawing either on the readings or on your experience and the courses you have had.

VI. 1. Outline an example of a coalition game in a business context to illustrate the ideas in Smith *et al.* (Article No. 34) and Morgenstern (Article No. 35).

  2. Comment on Lorge's findings (Article No. 36) in relation to your own experience with group and individual decision making.

  3. Select one of the principal functional areas of the firm—production, marketing, finance, research and development. Based on the readings and class discussion on decision making,

    a. Make an analysis of the decision-making process in that area. Include consideration of the kinds of decisions made; the decision makers and their characteristics; the decision process from the time the need for a decision is recognized through its implementation.

    b. Suggest a system for monitoring or "controlling" decision making in this area. What key variables would be used for this purpose?

  4. Reread Table 1 in the introduction to Section One. Construct a model for decisions on matters of internal administration for the "new direction in organization theory." Contrast this with the corresponding model for traditional theory.

Index

489

This book has been set on the Linotype in 10 point Janson, leaded 2 points and 9 point Janson, leaded 1 point. Section numbers are in 18 point Janson italic caps and section titles in 24 point Janson italic caps and lower case. The size of the type page is 27 by 46 picas.